How We Reason

How We Reason

Philip N. Johnson-Laird

OXFORD
UNIVERSITY PRESS

Great Clarendon Street, Oxford ox2 6DP

Oxford University Press is a department of the University of Oxford.
It furthers the University's objective of excellence in research, scholarship,
and education by publishing worldwide in

Oxford New York

Auckland Cape Town Dar es Salaam Hong Kong Karachi
Kuala Lumpur Madrid Melbourne Mexico City Nairobi
New Delhi Shanghai Taipei Toronto

With offices in

Argentina Austria Brazil Chile Czech Republic France Greece
Guatemala Hungary Italy Japan Poland Portugal Singapore
South Korea Switzerland Thailand Turkey Ukraine Vietnam

Oxford is a registered trade mark of Oxford University Press
in the UK and in certain other countries

Published in the United States
by Oxford University Press Inc., New York

© Oxford University Press 2008

British Library Cataloguing in Publication Data
Data available

Library of Congress Cataloging in Publication Data
Data available

Typeset by SPI Publisher Services, Pondicherry, India
Printed in Great Britain
on acid-free paper by
CPI Antony Rowe, Chippenham, Wiltshire

ISBN 978–0–19–955133–0 (Pbk.)

10 9 8 7 6 5 4 3 2 1

Preface

Why are some of us expert reasoners and others of us duffers? What causes mistakes in our reasoning that can lead to disasters such as Chernobyl? How can we improve our reasoning? How is it possible for us to have inconsistent views? How do conjurors work out illusions that will fool us? Why do we revise some beliefs but hold on to others at almost any cost? Why do some of us develop irrational fears? Why do terrorists develop "crazy" ideologies? Why do people believe that there are witches, that the earth is flat, and that it has existed for only four thousand years (and that's just here in the USA)? Why do paradoxes akin to Catch-22 occur in real legal systems? Aren't we rational? And, if we are, how is that possible as we were never taught logic?

This book tackles each of these questions, because they all depend on how we reason—on how our minds use information to reach novel conclusions. That's what the book is about. Our skill underlies our intelligence. Our mistakes underlie our stupidity. Good reasoning can lead to success and to a longer life, and bad reasoning can lead to catastrophe. Yet, how we reason and why we make mistakes aren't obvious, because so much of mental life goes on outside our awareness. Despite these unconscious foundations, a scientific understanding of reasoning has grown over recent decades, but it has yet to reach those outside a narrow band of professional researchers in cognitive science. This book aims to make the new science accessible to anyone.

We reason in many ways, and the book deals with most of them.

We reason when we have an intuition. We look at photographs of two candidates in an election, and we can see that one looks more competent than the other. The process goes beyond simple perception. It is inferential, but we cannot tell what creates this judgment. We can even reason without becoming aware of our conclusion—an unconscious process that psychologists detect only in our later behavior.

We reason when we have an emotional reaction. We see the Twin Towers collapse and an emotion wells up in us. The transition to the emotion is unconscious, and sometimes its strength surprises us. A New York taxi driver witnessed the events of September the 11, 2001, and became so terrified of tunnels that he could no longer drive passengers into them. Some clinicians believe that faulty reasoning is the cause of this sort of neurotic reaction. The idea led to a revolution in psychotherapy. But, when my colleagues and I tested the reasoning of individuals with neurotic tendencies, the result was shocking. They reasoned *better* than the rest of us, though only about topics related to their symptoms. The book describes how this clue led to a new theory of psychological illnesses and the role of reasoning in them.

We reason when we deduce the logical consequences of premises. Sudoku puzzles, which have spread all over the world from Japan, are solved by logical deductions. From East to West, we all have the ability to make them. Those of us who are good reasoners do better in schools and universities than those of us who are less good. That is good news for academia—study and research ought to demand an ability to reason. And it is good news for mental tests—they ought to measure something useful. But, it is bad news for the handful of scholars who believe that deduction is beyond us—that we use other methods based on guesswork, and that at best it is a skill that we acquire only if we study logic. Tell that to the Sudoku puzzler! We can all make deductions from our childhood onwards. But, we don't rely on the laws of logic. Instead, the book argues, we reason by thinking about what's possible, and seeing what is common to the possibilities. This theory predicts that we should go wrong with certain sorts of deduction, and we do. These mistakes are so seductive that nearly everyone makes them. They are cognitive illusions in which we fail to think of the right possibilities just as we do when stage illusionists bamboozle us with their tricks.

We reason when we go beyond the information given to us. We make an *induction*—a generalization, say, that leads us from one or two events to a conclusion about all events of the same kind. One experience with a wheel clamp is enough for us to infer that we shouldn't park on double yellow lines in London. We use our knowledge to draw this conclusion. We also use our knowledge when we infer an explanation of an event. As you'll see, the doctor who was the real-life model for Sherlock Holmes was a master of this sort of reasoning. But, we are all capable of it.

We reason about our own reasoning. This ability is necessary if we are to create logic as an intellectual discipline. It helps us to develop strategies for reasoning about problems that are new to us. We use it when we tackle our first problem in reverse engineering—to figure out, for example, how to wire up an electrical circuit to control the lights in our hall. And the book describes how we can use it to make a striking improvement in our reasoning.

We reason about cause and effect, we reason about obligation and permission, we reason about conflicts between our beliefs and the world. Above all, we reason when we do research in logic, science, and technology, and the book considers three test cases: the Wright brothers' use of analogies in inventing their flyer, the cryptanalysts' deductive and probabilistic reasoning in breaking the German's Enigma code in World War II, and Dr. John Snow's inductive and explanatory reasoning in discovering the mode of communication of cholera, before anyone knew of the existence of bacteria.

The book outlines a theory of the mental processes for each of the different sorts of reasoning. The components of the theory have been simulated in computer programs, and its predictions have been tested in psychological experiments. The experiments have examined how we make deductions, solve problems, detect and reconcile inconsistencies, create counterexamples, infer probabilities, and carry out reverse engineering. And with brain scans, they have begun to identify which regions of the brain are active during reasoning.

I have tried to write a book that provides its own intellectual life-support system. The main text lays out the argument for everyone, the glossary is for those new to the subject, and the notes at the end of the book contain technical and scholarly matters for specialists. My goal above all is to explain how we reason, and to do so in a way that will satisfy any readers who are interested in scientific answers to my opening questions. They include, I hope, colleagues in the cognitive sciences, experts in other fields, students, addicts of logical puzzles, and, as Virginia Woolf once dubbed anyone who reads for fun, the common reader.

Contents

Chapter 1

Introduction

Do you want your mind to be immortal? Your mind is who you are. It governs what you think and what you do. In the past, when people died they left behind them only a few mementos: letters, photographs, a handful of tape recordings and videos. But, today we have the technology to preserve your mind after your death, and so your descendants—even those who never met you—can interact with you forever. They can talk to you, and they can learn what you believe and what you think. They can even learn your *new* thoughts about things that did not exist during your lifetime. They can continue to educate you.

How is this miracle accomplished? Each week you interact with a computer for twenty minutes, answering simple questions. The computer builds up a representation of your knowledge and beliefs, and it creates a program that thinks in the same way as you do. Twenty minutes a week is a tiny fragment of your life, but after three years, your mind has been captured in a computer. Now it can continue to exist forever. Before the sun explodes, human beings will leave the solar system. They will take with them a vast data bank of human minds. Your mind could be among them.

The preceding advertisement is science fiction. Yet, the barriers to the construction of this program are not obvious. That may merely show how ignorant we are. Programs can access vast amounts of information, and the amount of information on the World Wide Web is much greater than the amount that each of us acquires in a lifetime. Our net gain of information is equivalent to about a thousand novels verbatim (see the notes at the end of the book for references to the relevant research*). Cognitive scientists, however, have yet to write a computer program that can think in the same way as we do. Psychological theories are rudimentary, and too simple to explain the thinking that went into their own construction. Robots perceive the world using crude imitations of our perceptual abilities. Human cleverness (and stupidity) are so hard to understand that many theorists have given up the task in favor of "artificial intelligence". They write programs that at least solve problems, albeit in ways remote from human thinking.

You might suppose that the brain works in a way that cannot be modeled in a computer program. But, any clear description of a process from the weather to the economy can be simulated in a computer program. This conjecture

* This is the only footnote in the book.

was made seventy years ago and named after its two originators as the Church–Turing thesis. The thesis can't be proved, because no test exists for what counts as a clear description. But, the thesis would be refuted by a proof that a set of comprehensible instructions cannot be implemented in a program. If the instructions for implementing your theory of the mind were clear and you could prove that they could not be simulated in a computer program, then you would have refuted the Church–Turing thesis. The refutation would be more important than your theory. The difficulty in modeling the mind has nothing to do with computers and everything to do with the lack of a theory of how it works.

Many philosophers have doubted whether it is possible to have a scientific theory of thinking—a skepticism that goes back at least to Descartes. He thought that free will doomed the enterprise. Dostoyevsky echoed him. And, more recently, the novelist Arthur Koestler bet a psychologist that he couldn't make one accurate prediction about Koestler's behavior during the coming month. The psychologist, Stuart Sutherland, should have offered a bet of a hundred pounds that Koestler wouldn't give him a thousand pounds. But, Sutherland rejected this idea as unfair.

The nub of this controversy is simple: psychologists cannot predict what you will think on Friday morning or indeed what you will think next, but this inability does not doom a science of the mind. Nor does it doom the project of simulating your mind, because *you* cannot predict what you will think next. You can make a self-fulfilling prophecy: "I predict that I'll think about green", and then you can try to form a visual image of a green leaf. But, it can be hard to fulfill your own predictions, e.g.: "I'm *not* going to think about George W. Bush". Sometimes our thoughts take us by surprise. Mostly we just have thoughts. Psychology is like evolutionary biology. Biologists cannot predict what species will evolve next, but that doesn't make a scientific biology impossible. Science depends on the observable consequences of theories, and biology yields testable predictions. Psychology too leads to testable predictions.

* * *

Thinking seems seamless, but only its surface is reflected in the stream of consciousness. Hence, to model thinking, psychologists need to consider its varieties. Some simple contrasts, which I shall frame as questions, yield a broad taxonomy suitable for our purposes.

Has a process of thought an immediate goal? If it hasn't, then psychologists say that it is "associative". That is, one idea leads to another in the absence of any design, plan, or purpose. The thinker is in a daydream or reverie. Associations have a long history in philosophy and psychology, and you might suppose that they are simple to understand. In fact, no theory explains how we make associations between ideas. It is easy enough to explain how one *word* can lead to another by an association. You say, "bread", and I say, "butter", because words are stored in our minds with links between them. In associative thinking, however, one idea can lead to another, and the chain can yield novel ideas that we've never had before. I say, "man cannot live by bread alone", and you say, "no, but it is better than butter alone", never having had the thought before. There can't be a link in your memory leading to this idea, because it's new to you. No one understands how associations yield novel ideas. Fortunately, my concern is reasoning, not association.

Given that thinking has a goal, is the process deterministic? It is when each step in the process is determined by the current state of the system. Computers are deterministic (appearances to the contrary). Likewise, when we carry out mental arithmetic, barring interruptions, we think in a deterministic way. In contrast, logicians have imagined machines that are not deterministic. The current state of a machine of this sort doesn't determine what happens next. It may constrain the possibilities, but not determine a unique one. Thinking seems much the same. Our thoughts do not seem to unwind like clockwork with no choice at any point. If we could step back in time and start over with no memory of our first thoughts, then we might proceed in a different way the second time around. A lack of determinism is of practical value. It allows us to approach problems in different ways, and it prevents us from becoming stuck in a loop of obsessional thoughts. No one knows whether human thinking is *nondeterministic*, but it is a useful assumption. It allows for psychologists' ignorance—they cannot predict what our next thought will be. In theory, the assumption costs nothing, because a deterministic computer can simulate one that it is not deterministic.

Thinking that has a goal and that is not deterministic falls into two categories: creating and reasoning. I will have something to say about creativity, but my main concern is reasoning or inference—I use the two terms as synonyms—and my working definition of reasoning is:

> A set of processes that construct and evaluate implications among sets of propositions.

This definition needs some unpacking, so please bear with me. Implications are of two sorts corresponding to the two principal sorts of reasoning: deduction and induction. A deduction—or *valid* inference—is one yielding a conclusion that must be true given that its premises are true. If the premises are not true then the conclusion could be true, but no guarantee exists. Any other sort of implication is an induction. Textbooks often define induction as "reasoning from the particular to the general", as opposed to deduction, which they define as "reasoning from the general to the particular". Neither definition is quite right. As you'll see, deductions can be drawn from particular propositions to particular propositions, and inductions can be drawn from general propositions to general propositions.

An accurate way to distinguish between deduction and induction is by their effects on information. The more possibilities that a proposition eliminates, the more information it contains. For example, the proposition:

> It is sunny and it is hot

conveys more information than:

> It is sunny

which leaves open whether or not it is hot. Valid inferences yield conclusions that do not convey more information than their premises. You might wonder why in that case we bother to make deductions. The reason is that a deductive conclusion can make explicit a proposition that was only implicit in the premises. Here, for instance, is a valid deduction from particular premises to a particular conclusion:

> The patient has chicken pox or she has measles.
>
> She doesn't have chicken pox.
>
> Therefore, she has measles.

The conclusion adds no information to the premises, but makes explicit a proposition that holds in the one possibility consistent with them.

Inductions, in contrast, no matter how plausible they are, go beyond the information in the premises. Their conclusions convey more information than their premises: they rule out possibilities compatible with their premises. Yet, they can yield true conclusions, even though they are not guaranteed to do so even if their premises are true. The pioneer aviators, for instance, made all sorts of inductions. "Give us a motor," said Sir Hiram Maxim, the inventor of the eponymous machine gun, "and we will very soon give you a successful flying machine". Equipped with two such steam engines, however, his own behemoth fluttered from its track in 1894, and crashed. In contrast, Wilbur Wright put no priority on motors, but inferred instead that what was crucial was the control of aircraft. I will return to how he reasoned later when I examine why the Wright brothers were more successful than their rivals. But, it is conceivable that Wilbur Wright's induction—from general propositions to a general proposition—could have been wrong, and that light and powerful engines would have conquered the problem of flight.

* * *

To be intelligent is to be able to think, and to be able to think is to be able to reason. Reasoning is the core of human thinking, because without it we would be irrational. But, are we rational? Philosophers are always arguing about this question. I refer here, not to the view that our unconscious seethes with irrational excogitations, which it may do, but to whether we are able to reason in a rational way. Every conceivable answer to this question has its defenders. The most optimistic view is that we never make mistakes in reasoning: we are as impeccable as angels. A middling view is that we can cope, sometimes right, sometimes wrong. An insidious view is that we only seem to reason, but in fact carry out quite a different process. Human evolution has adapted us, say, to coping with our environment in a probabilistic way, and we apply the same methods even to deductive reasoning. A more insidious doctrine is that we don't reason at all, but make guesses constrained by the surface character of the premises. Perhaps the bleakest view of all is that we don't reason at all unless we've been trained in logic. Yet, logic itself couldn't have been invented if no one was able to reason prior to its invention. It is safe to conclude that some of us reason some of the time.

We do differ in our ability. As experiments have shown, the differences from one individual to another couldn't be any greater. Some of us are correct on almost all the inferential problems—a result that is inexplicable on the view that no one can reason. Others of us do little better than guessing—a result that is inexplicable on the view that we are logically impeccable. Inferences themselves also differ in difficulty. Some are child's play. Indeed, even little children can make them. Others are beyond all but the most gifted of us. And still others are beyond all but superhuman aliens.

These findings eliminate the extremes from the gamut of views. We are neither angels nor insects. We are rational, according to the theory that I shall defend, because we grasp the force of counterexamples. Even without training in logic, we realize that an inference is no good if we can think of a counterexample to it. From childhood onwards, all of us but those with severe brain damage are capable of some rational thought. But, we all make mistakes. We all are unable to make certain inferences. We all can improve our abilities—and I will have something to say later about how we can do so. But none of us is among the angelic orders. We are rational—to some degree, as Aristotle knew—but reasoning is a dizzying business.

* * *

Psychologists haven't pinned down what intelligence is, but a plausible conjecture is that a major part of it is the ability to reason. Those who reason well in experiments in the psychological laboratory do well in intelligence tests. If you live in the United States and want to go to graduate school, you take a national test known as the Graduate Record Examination (GRE). And if you want to go to law school, you take an exam known as the Law School Admission Test (LSAT). These two exams have in common tests of your ability to reason. A typical item from the LSAT is shown in Box 1.1.

What is the point of the test? The Law School Admission Council, which administers the LSAT, says: "Logical reasoning questions evaluate your ability to understand, analyze, criticize, and complete a variety of arguments." And why should law schools select candidates in part on their ability to reason in these ways? The answer in the short term is that the tests predict performance in the first year of law school. The answer in the long term is that lawyers need to reason well. Those who can't get themselves embroiled in the following sort of mess, which comes from an actual deposition of an expert witness about the plagiarism of a computer program (the "source code"):

Lawyer: So although you say our expert's findings are fatally flawed because she did not look at the source code, you didn't look at the source code either, did you?

Witness: No.

L: You mean that is incorrect?

W: Yes.

L: So you did look at the source code?

W: Yes.

L: So show me in your report where you looked at the source code?

W: Where I described that I looked at the matching hits "in the context in which they occur."

L: But you say that in order to learn the truth about what a program does you have to look at all the source code, and you were trying to learn the truth about the program, correct?

W: No.

L: So are you saying that you do not have to look at the source code to understand the truth?

W: No.

L: So what are you saying?

W: That in order to understand the truth of what a program does, you need to look at the source code.

L: So why did you answer no, previously?

W: Because what you said was false.

L: What did I ask you that was false?

W: Each question to which I answered "no."

Box 1.1 A typical LSAT logical reasoning question

Most regular coffee is made from arabica coffee beans because the great majority of consumers prefer its generally richer flavor to that of coffee made from robusta beans. Coffee drinkers who switch to decaffeinated coffee, however, overwhelmingly prefer coffee made from robusta beans, which are unlike arabica beans in that their flavor is not as greatly affected by decaffeination. Depending on the type of bean involved, decaffeination reduces or removes various substances, most of which are flavor-neutral but one of which contributes to the richness of the coffee's flavor.

The statements above provide the most support for which one of the following conclusions?

(A) The annual world crop of arabica beans is not large enough to satisfy completely the world demand for regular coffee.

(B) Arabica beans contain more caffeine per unit of weight than do robusta beans.

(C) Coffee drinkers who drink decaffeinated coffee almost exclusively are the ones who prefer regular coffee made from robusta beans to regular coffee made from arabica beans.

(D) Decaffeination of arabica beans extracts more of the substance that enhances a coffee's flavor than does decaffeination of robusta beans.

(E) There are coffee drinkers who switch from drinking regular coffee made from arabica beans to drinking decaffeinated coffee made from arabica beans because coffee made from regular beans is less costly.

Analysis

As you read each of the options, you are likely to think that the text seems irrelevant to (A), (B), and (E), that it doesn't imply (C), but it probably implies (D). A closer analysis shows that the text boils down to the following propositions pertinent to the inference:

> Arabica beans have a richer flavor than robusta beans. The flavor of robusta beans is less affected by decaffeination.

Hence, option (D) does follow from the text, and is the correct choice.

What trips the lawyer up is a single word that is often critical in reasoning, "all". The witness looked at the source code but denies that it is necessary to examine *all* the source code to understand a program.

* * *

Some individuals are expert reasoners who are capable of astonishing feats. As an example of expertise in inductive reasoning, here is a sequence of inferences made by one of Wilfred Thesiger's Bedouin fellow travelers in the deserts of Southern Arabia in the 1940s. Thesiger writes:

> A few days later we passed some tracks. I was not even certain that they were made by camels, for they were much blurred by the wind. Sultan turned to a grey-bearded man who was noted as a tracker and asked him whose tracks they were, and the man turned aside and followed them for a short distance. He then jumped off his camel, looked at the tracks where they crossed some hard ground, broke some camel-droppings between his fingers and rode back to join us. Sultan asked, "Who were they?" and the man answered, "They were Awamir. There are six of them. They have raided the Januba on the southern coast and taken three of their camels. They have come from Sahma and watered at Mughshin. They passed here ten days ago". We had seen no Arabs for seventeen days and we saw none for a further twenty-seven. On our return we met some Bait Kathir near Jabal Qarra and, when we exchanged our news, they told us that six Awamir had raided the Januba, killed three of them, and taken three of their camels. The only thing that we did not already know was that they had killed anyone.

Yet another form of expertise, a somewhat perverse one, is illustrated in a sequence of inferences that a patient made when she was asked why she thought that she might have contracted AIDS from touching a newspaper photograph of the movie star Rock Hudson, who had died of the disease. She argued:

> The photographer must have been close to Hudson, because the photograph was a "close up".
>
> So, the photographer might have been contaminated.
>
> So, when he developed the negative, he could have contaminated it.
>
> The negative was in contact with the print of the photograph and so could have contaminated it.
>
> The man who made the newspaper photograph used the photograph in the newspaper's printer, and so it could have passed its contamination to the newspaper's printer. The printer could have passed the contamination on to the picture in every newspaper.
>
> So, when I touched the newspaper, I too might have been contaminated.

The patient was suffering from an "obsessive-compulsive" disorder. Like most expert reasoners, she can think of more than just the obvious possibilities. She realizes that her conclusion is improbable, yet she cannot reject it, and so she obsesses about the possibility.

As these examples illustrate, psychologists tend to think of reasoning as the business of drawing conclusions or of evaluating them. But, there are other sorts of inferential task. When we detect that our beliefs are inconsistent, we are reasoning. Likewise, to quote the Law School Admission Council again, the ability "to understand, analyze, criticize, and complete a variety of arguments", all call for reasoning. If we think of a possibility that undermines an argument for a particular conclusion, we have reasoned—at the very least, we had to determine that, given the possibility that we imagined, the conclusion is no longer supported by the premises. Problems of this sort have seldom been studied in the psychological laboratory, but they occur in life.

* * *

Many cognitive scientists suppose that logic plays a central role in reasoning, and so I need to say a few words about it. A valid inference, as I pointed out earlier, yields a conclusion that must be true if its premises are true. If the premises are not true, then the conclusion may or may not be true. Hence, an argument is guaranteed to yield a true conclusion granted two conditions: true premises and valid inference. That these two conditions are independent of one another was the foundation of logic as an intellectual discipline, which in the West goes back to Aristotle. He invented logic—at least he says he did—and it concerns valid inferences.

Modern logic distinguishes between form and content. To illustrate the contrast consider again the inference based on a disjunction (a premise containing "or"):

The patient has chicken pox or she has measles.

She doesn't have chicken pox.

Therefore, she has measles.

On the one hand, the inference can be proved in a logic that has formal rules of inference, including a rule that matches its logical form:

A or B.

Not A.

Therefore, B.

These rules operate on the forms of premises—on symbols rather than on their content—and they make up a logic for proofs. On the other hand, the logic has an interpretation. If a disjunction *A or B* is true, then at least one of its two constituent propositions, *A* and *B*, is true. Logicians lay out the possibilities in a table, a so-called "truth table". Given that the premise *not A* is true, then *A* is false, and so the only way in which the disjunctive premise can be true is if *B* is true. Hence, the truth of both premises implies that *B* must be true: the inference is valid. Truth tables concern the ultimate content of propositions, their truth or falsity, and they make up a system of interpretations.

Logicians have proved various relations between the two systems of inference—proofs and interpretations. For the logic of "or", "and", and "if" (so-called "propositional" or "Boolean" logic), they have shown that every inference that is valid using truth tables can also be proved using formal rules of inference, and vice versa. But, their most startling discovery is that equivalences of this sort break down for more powerful logics: interpretations yield valid inferences that cannot be proved in any consistent system of formal rules. This discovery drives home an irremovable wedge between form and content.

Logic is different from natural language. Logic is timeless: the interpretation of its sentences does not depend on their context. But, in life, a speaker uses a sentence to assert a proposition with a significance that almost always depends on the context in which the speaker utters the sentence. The sentence, "I can hear you now" (all too frequent in public places these days) signifies different propositions depending on its context. You understood the *meaning* of the sentence when you read it a moment ago, because you understand English. When someone uses it in reality, your knowledge of the context enables you to understand its *significance*—the particular proposition that it expresses, which may be true or false, depending on whom "I" refers to, whom "you" refers to, and the time of the utterance. If "I" refers to me and "you" refers to my wife, and I assert it as I write this sentence, then the proposition is true, because I can hear my wife right now. But, if "I" refers to me and "you" refers to *you,* the reader, then the proposition is false, because right now I can't hear you. Hence, a sentence with a single meaning can express many different propositions referring to many different situations. I will ignore this distinction between meaning and significance as far as possible.

In the past, many logicians have thought that the formal rules of logic were the laws of thought. Hilbert, one of the greatest mathematicians of the twentieth century, wrote: "The fundamental idea of my proof theory is none other than to describe the activity of our understanding, to make a protocol of the rules according to which our thinking actually proceeds." In fact, even if human reasoning were impeccable, logic could never be a complete psycholog-ical theory, because it allows valid conclusions that we never draw. To see why, I need to answer an initial question about reasoning: what does the process do—or, to speak by analogy with a computer program, what does the process compute?

* * *

When we reason, we can aim to draw conclusions that are valid. But, there are many valid conclusions that we would never draw. When psychologists claim, as they sometimes do, that reasoning is nothing more than logic, they overlook this point. To see why, ask yourself what follows from these two propositions:

> Ali was the greatest boxer.
>
> Today is Wednesday.

Most of us say: "nothing", because the two premises are unrelated to one another. We couldn't be more wrong, because an infinite number of differ-ent valid conclusions follow from any premises. For example, the preceding propositions yield this series of conclusions:

> Ali was the greatest boxer and today is Wednesday.
>
> Ali was the greatest boxer and today is Wednesday and Ali was the greatest boxer.
>
> Ali was the greatest boxer and today is Wednesday and Ali was the greatest boxer and today is Wednesday.
>
> And so on, ad infinitum.

You may say: These conclusions are silly: they may be valid, but they don't tell us anything that we don't already know, and they keep repeating the same propositions over and over. That is the point. The conclusions *are* silly; yet they are valid. No sane person (other than a logician) would make these inferences. Hence, when we draw valid conclusions, we don't draw just any valid conclusions. Given the premises:

> If the patient has pimple-shaped spots then she has chicken pox.
>
> The patient has pimple-shaped spots.

we infer:

> She has chicken pox.

This conclusion takes into account the information in both premises, it is parsimonious, and it makes explicit a proposition that was only implicit in the premises. When a set of premises yields no such conclusion, as in the example about Ali and Wednesday, we say that nothing follows from them. And it is true that nothing of any interest or use follows from them.

The conclusion that the patient has chicken pox doesn't express all the information in the premises. It doesn't state that the patient has pimple-shaped spots. But, there's no need to repeat a premise. The maintenance of information implies that we do not make inferences, such as:

> The patient has chicken pox.
>
> Therefore, the patient has chicken pox or measles, or both.

The inference is valid, but its conclusion throws information away: the premise is consistent with one possibility in which the patient has chicken pox, whereas the conclusion is consistent with three possibilities. We therefore know more when we know the premise than when we know the conclusion.

When we make inductions, we are still further from throwing information away. We increase it. Our aim is to reach new and parsimonious conclusions that are plausible given the premises and our knowledge. Our reasoning in everyday life doesn't occur in a vacuum. (Matters may be different in the psychological laboratory.) We reason because we have a goal beyond that of drawing a conclusion. We have a problem to solve, a decision to make, a plan to devise. The goal constrains the sorts of conclusion that we draw. Depending on our interest in, say, a particular patient or in a particular disease, we will draw different conclusions from the same premises about patients and diseases. Reasoning, however, is not just a matter of drawing conclusions. We also reject some conclusions. We may reject them because we know that they are false or improbable. But, we may also reject them because they are based on false premises or on invalid inferences. That, in outline, is what we do when we reason.

* * *

What we do is not *how* we do it. The difference between the two is the difference between the boss who orders a computer program to do the company's pay roll and the programmer who writes the code for the program. The first stipulates what the program should do; the second works out how the program will do it. Many psychologists theorize only about what the mind does when we reason. Nothing is wrong with that. But, when they say, for instance, that one sort of reasoning depends on automatic, implicit, and associative processes, you should know that no mechanisms are attached to these labels. It would be more accurate to say that the reasoning is done by processes unknown.

How we reason is a mystery that desk-bound detection alone cannot solve. It calls for experimental investigations too. The difficulty of the mystery will be easier to grasp if I consider the range of possible solutions. Consider again this inferential problem:

If the patient has pimple-shaped spots then she has chicken pox.

The patient has pimple-shaped spots.

What follows?

It is easy to infer that the patient has chicken pox—so easy that we aren't aware of how we do it. One possibility is that we have already encountered the inference or one similar to it, and so we recall our previous conclusion. Theorists refer to this procedure as "case-based" reasoning. It depends on a memory for inferences, a way to match new inferences to those in our memory—allowing for some discrepancies in content—and the use of the conclusion in memory to generate a conclusion to the current inference. The camel tracker might be using case-based reasoning.

Yet, there has to be a first time. We have to make an inference in order to store it in memory. By definition, this virgin occurrence cannot be solved by a memory for a previous case. Could our memory be equipped with a large set of innate inferences, much as our bodies are equipped with a large set of innate antibodies? Perhaps; but this hypothesis passes the explanatory puzzle back to a theory of innate knowledge. What is more likely is that we can reason without relying on memories of previous inferences.

One theory of how we reason is that we follow the "laws of thought". These laws are made explicit in formal logic. No doubt people can acquire these laws, and even use them to solve difficult problems. The question at issue is whether those of us with no training in formal logic follow the laws of thought. We are not aware of doing so. We cannot describe them. But, here's a sketch of how they would work.

A formal system of reasoning is akin to a set of rules in logic that operate on the forms of premises. One rule, for example, applies to sentences with the logical form:

If A then B.

A.

and it yields the conclusion:

B.

The premises for the chicken pox inference above have the required form, where A stands for "the patient has pimple-shaped spots", and B stands for "the patient has chicken pox". The rule spits out the conclusion: B, which translates back into the conclusion: The patient has chicken pox.

For well over a century, theorists have argued that the laws of thought are formal rules of inference. The logician George Boole had suggested it in the mid-nineteenth century, but its most influential godfather was Jean Piaget, a pioneer Swiss investigator of children's psychology. He argued that the mental construction of formal logic was the last great step in their intellectual development, and that it occurred at about the age of twelve. Other theorists have postulated formal rules for inductive reasoning. Yet, several observations suggest that reasoning is not a formal affair.

One observation is the occurrence of systematic errors in reasoning. Here's an example. We have to select evidence to find out whether a general claim about four cards is true or false:

> If a card has an "A" on one side then it has a "2" on its other side.

The four cards are laid out in front of us: A, B, 2, and 3, and we know that each of them has a letter on one side and a number on the other side. Given this task, we tend to select the A card and perhaps the 2 card. We fail to see the relevance of the 3 card. But, if this card has an A on its other side, the general claim is false. The late Peter Wason, who founded the modern experimental study of reasoning, invented this so-called "selection" task. To anyone who has studied logic, the error of omission in the selection task is puzzling. The conjunction of an A and 3 shows that the claim above is false. The failure to select the 3 card is also contrary to Piaget's claim that we master logic in childhood. Hence, over thirty-five years ago, Wason and I started some research to try to understand why people went wrong. We investigated several plausible sources of confusion, but we were unable to make the error of omission go away. Wason then suggested changing the *content* of the general claim. Perhaps because my head was stuffed with formal logic, I thought that this manipulation was crazy (though I didn't say so), because formal rules work the same regardless of content.

Wason went ahead with his experiment. He used a general claim about journeys:

> Every time I go to Manchester I travel by train.

Sentences don't always wear their logical form on their sleeves, and, despite its different grammar, this claim has the same logical form as the earlier claim about letters and numbers. Just to be sure, however, Wason included the following claim in the experiment: *Every card with an "A" on one side has a "2" on its other side.* The participants went wrong with it, but they realized that a journey by *car* was pertinent to the truth or falsity of the claim about journeys. If the destination of the trip by car was Manchester, then the claim was false. A change in content alone had a striking effect on reasoning, even though the two sorts of contents had the same logical form.

These findings were embarrassing for the formal theory. On the one hand, the systematic error of omission with the letters and numbers was contrary to the laws of thought embodied in formal rules. On the other hand, a change in content alone should have no effect on performance, because by definition formal rules are blind to content. One possibility, however, is that the selection test fails to tap into our deductive ability. Some psychologists take this view. I don't; but the matter has not been settled to everyone's satisfaction.

An alternative theory of reasoning, which was first developed in the field of artificial intelligence, moves the formal approach towards a more sensitive handling of content. Formal rules concern logical terms, such as "not", and "if". But, formal rules can be couched so that they match other sorts of words too, including particular nouns and verbs. For example, a dedicated system for reasoning about patients and diseases could maintain records, such as:

Patient: Mary Smith   Symptoms: pimple-shaped spots.

It could contain rules for making inferences, such as:

If the goal is to show that patient x has chicken pox

and patient x has pimple-shaped spots

then the goal is satisfied.

Rules of this sort are *content-specific*, because they are sensitive to certain contents, such as patients, spots, and chicken pox. They are used in computer programs that embody human expertise and that give advice on such matters as medical diagnosis. The rules can contain detailed contents, e.g.:

If the site of the culture is blood, the gram of the organism is neg, the morphology of the organism is rod, the burn of the patient is serious, then there is some evidence (0.4) that the identity of the organism is pseudomonas.

Despite their name, content-specific rules work in a formal way. The procedure is still to match the form of premises to rules, but the notion of form has been expanded to include words that are not logical terms. A program using the preceding rule knows nothing about the meaning of the word "blood", or the significance of propositions about patients, but it can make formal inferences.

No current programs grasp the significance of a sentence that we type on a computer's keyboard. They no more deal with real significance than programs simulating hurricanes deal with real winds. Until computational systems— robots, perhaps—can perceive the world, access their own internal states, and act on the world, they can only *simulate* a grasp of significance. We human beings are the only known entities that can grasp the significance of propositions, and imagine the situations that they describe.

Consider one more time these premises:

> If the patient has pimple-shaped spots then she has chicken pox.
>
> The patient has pimple-shaped spots.

When we understand the first premise, we realize that is compatible with at least two possibilities. One possibility is that the patient has pimple-shaped spots and chicken pox, and the other possibility is that the patient doesn't have pimple-shaped spots. But, we also grasp that the second premise rules out this latter possibility. Only the first possibility remains, and so it follows that the patient has chicken pox. An inference is valid if its conclusion holds in all the possibilities in which the premises hold, and so it guarantees that its conclusion is true given that its premises are true. It is invalid if there is a counterexample—a possibility consistent with the premises but not with the conclusion. No counterexample to the preceding conclusion exists, and so the inference is valid. We have made a deduction, not using the logical form of the premises, but using their contents to imagine possibilities.

In the preceding example, I described the possibilities, but how is the significance of sentences represented in our minds? Here are the inklings of a solution:

> It is possible that from the meanings of sentences in connected discourse, the listener implicitly sets up a much abbreviated and not especially linguistic model of the narrative ... Where the model is incomplete, material may even be unwittingly invented to render the memory more meaningful or more plausible—a process that has its parallel in the initial construction of the model. A good writer or raconteur perhaps has the power to initiate a process very similar to the one that occurs when we are actually perceiving (or imagining) events instead of merely reading or hearing about them.

Subsequent research has supported this conjecture. We construct *mental models* of situations, and we use these models to represent possibilities.

Over the last decade, research on mental models and reasoning has burgeoned beyond the point where any one person can keep track of it all. And the theory itself has undergone a metamorphosis. The distinction between logic and reasoning, which was presaged in Wason's findings, has now proceeded to a far greater degree than anyone could have imagined. Logic is an essential tool for all sciences, but it is not a psychological theory of reasoning. The scope of the model theory has also widened to include all the main sorts of reasoning, and to give a comprehensive account of them—from low-level unconscious processes to the development of inferential strategies.

* * *

Memory, formal rules, content-specific rules, and models of possibilities. Are there any other ways in which we could reason? Perhaps, but it is unlikely. Colleagues sometimes ask: What about systems that mimic the operations of a network of idealized neurons as they learn to carry out a task? These so-called "connectionist" networks can make crude inferences. But, to make inferences of the modest degree of complexity within our competence, these networks may have to implement one of the theories that I have already described.

How do real neurons in the brain implement our processes of reasoning, and in what regions of the brain are they located? These questions have begun to be investigated, and I will have something to say about them. But, little is known about their answers. The brain may not be a computational device at all, though that wouldn't imply that it could not be modeled in a computer program. It may not use mental representations at all, as the German philosopher Heidegger and his intellectual heirs have argued. It may not use unconscious mental mechanisms, as other philosophers have argued. But, these views cannot account for our ability to reason. To reason is to carry out a mental process. Introspection doesn't reveal to us how that process works. (If it did, then psychologists would have understood how it worked long ago.) Hence, the process is unconscious. When we reason about some event that we have remembered, that event must be represented in our mind. That much seems self-evident, though not to these skeptics. To argue with them is a strange experience—as I imagine arguing with aliens from Alpha Centauri—but they have no theory of how we reason. Granted that our reasoning depends on at least one of the four sorts of procedure that I have described, which of them is the most plausible candidate? And what are the details of its implementation? That's what the rest of this book is about.

Part I

The World in Our Conscious Minds

A sentence uttered makes a world appear

Where all things happen as it says they do;

We doubt the speaker, not the tongue we hear:

Words have no word for words that are not true.

Auden

Chapter 2

Icons and Images

Are you sitting comfortably? If so, please answer this question:

> In what direction are you facing: North, South, East, or West?

If you're like me, you don't know the precise answer. All I know is that I am facing roughly westwards. I am not oriented in relation to the compass points, but there's no need for me to be. The Guugu Yimithirr, an Australian tribe, are always oriented in relation to their analogues of the compass points. Steve Levinson, a linguist and anthropologist, made a movie of a group of men chatting, and what was striking was how often they pointed in this direction and that. He took a group of them on a zigzagging bus ride through the outback, and stopped the bus from time to time. He then asked them to point in the direction of various well-known landmarks, such as their home. They could do this task much better than we could, perhaps because their ancestors couldn't afford to be lost in the outback. A notable failure occurred once, and they still laugh about it. One of their fellows went up in an airplane, and during the flight he lost his orientation—an anxiety-provoking incident until he was able to re-orient himself back on the ground.

Even if you failed to know your compass orientation, you should be able to answer this question:

> In what direction are you facing in relation to the front door of the building in which you are sitting?

If you're not in a building right now, then imagine that you're in a familiar one. The question is easy unless you are lost in some vast edifice.

One more question. Imagine that you're lying on your bed at home, what is the path from it to the front door? You should trace out the path in the air with your finger.

This task should have been quite easy. You used your dominant hand. And you moved your index finger through the path from the bed to the bedroom door, down the stairs if there are any, and through the house to the front door. You may have had visual images of parts of the route, or even some kinesthetic imagery as you went down the stairs. (Kinesthetic imagery represents movements of your limbs and other parts of your body.) If you're like me, however, you weren't aware of any images, but just moved your finger along an appropriate three-dimensional path.

How are we able to do these tasks? The broad answer is that we rely on a mental representation of the world whose contents are available to consciousness. I knew, for example, that I was facing roughly westwards, because I knew that I was facing roughly at right angles to Nassau Street, the main thoroughfare of Princeton, which runs roughly—very roughly—north–south. So, even though I had no visual images—I knew at once that I was at right angles to Nassau Street. I had an internal representation of this relation. Its contents enabled me to infer my orientation.

One of the greatest feats of mental orientation is the navigational ability of certain inhabitants of the Caroline Islands in the Pacific Ocean. These navigators can sail their outrigger canoes distances of several hundred miles across the open sea and make a successful landfall on another tiny island. They do so without a compass or any other navigational instruments. They have little margin for error: a degree or two off course and they will miss their island destination and as a result die. Navigators learn the positions of all the islands, and the prevailing winds and ocean currents. But, most important of all, they learn the rising and setting positions of all the main stars. They imagine the boat as stationary with the islands drifting past them, and the stars wheeling overhead as the earth turns. As a reference point, they keep in mind an island off to the side of their track and well below the horizon. This marvelous representation enables them to navigate by dead reckoning, where "dead" abbreviates "deduced".

* * *

When psychologists first showed that animals appeared to construct cognitive "maps" of the mazes in which they ran, skeptics argued that perhaps the animals laid down a record of their sequence of responses as they ran through a maze. These "behaviorists" called each component in this sequence a "fractional anticipatory goal response", which was about as far as they would concede that any animals, including us, have a mental life. On this account, my mind doesn't contain a representation of the spatial relations between my chair and Nassau Street. All it contains is a sequence of "fractional" responses: turn left, proceed forwards for ten feet, go through the sitting room door, turn left, go out the front door, and so on. It was easy to show to the contrary that rats do construct internal maps. They learned a dog-legged route to a box containing food. When the experimenter blocked this route, they were able to choose a direct path to the food box. They couldn't have made this switch if all they had

Fig. 2.2 A view of Professor Higgins's study. (See p. 25).

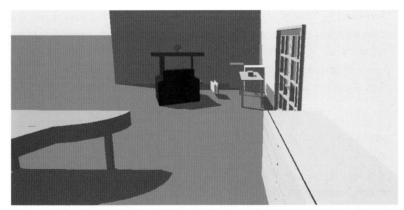

Fig. 2.3 Another view of Professor Higgins's study. (See p. 25).

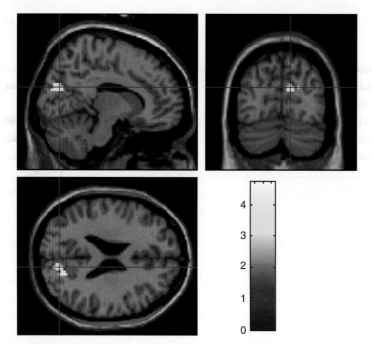

Fig. 2.6 Three "slices" through the brain showing a region (secondary visual cortex) towards the back of the brain that was active in reasoning about visual relations but not other relations. The cross-hairs locate the peak area of activation. The scale represents the chance probability of differences, with white in the figures equal to a chance probability of less than 1 in 20. (See p. 34).

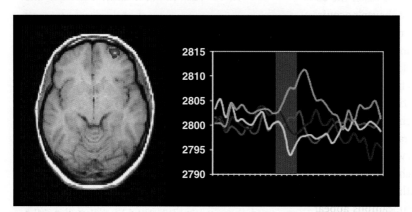

Fig. 16.2 On the left is an image of a horizontal slice through the brain with the front of the brain at the top of the page. The region in red is a part of the right frontal lobe known as the "frontal pole". The graph on the right shows the amount of activation in this region in four different conditions of an experiment: pink shows the activation for reasoning problems in which the participants searched for counterexamples, red shows the activation for reasoning problems in which the participants did not search for counterexamples, light blue shows the activation for easy arithmetical problems, and dark blue shows the activation for difficult arithmetical problems. The horizontal axis is time, and the gray vertical band is the eight seconds for which the problem was displayed. (See p. 226).

was a record of responses. Studies of foraging animals also refute the skeptics: chimpanzees and birds can recover food from various caches in an order that differs from the one in which they were shown the caches.

Spatial orientation is not unique to mammals. Worker bees that find nectar do a dance on the vertical honeycomb when they return to the hive. The main maneuver in this dance is to waggle their abdomens as they go up and down the honeycomb at a particular angle to the vertical. The angle indicates the angle that other bees must fly in relation to the sun to get to the source of the nectar. The rate of waggles indicates its distance. Bees communicate a simple message, and their system of "dead" reckoning gets them to the nectar. It also enables them to make spatial inferences: after they have flown a dog-legged route to nectar, their dance signals the direct route.

The proponents of fractional responses are in some difficulty to explain the birds and the bees. The Guugu Yimithirr strain this account still further, because they haven't learned a sequence of responses that would enable them to point in the direction of a distant city. They must have an internal representation of the geometry of their environment, which they update with every twist and turn of the road. You and I can also embarrass the hypothesis of fractional responses. We can draw a route in the air of how we would fly like Peter Pan from our beds, out of the window, down to the ground floor, and through solid walls to reach the cooker in the kitchen. We have never taken this route, and so we haven't acquired its sequence of responses. What enables us to imagine the route is that we have an internal representation of the spatial layout of our homes. Even individuals who are blind construct these representations from walking around their homes.

The hippocampus is the organ in the brain that appears to be crucial to spatial orientation. It lies deep in the temporal lobes with many connections to the cortex on the surface. It is also crucial for laying down new memories. A tragic case concerned a patient who had parts of his hippocampus removed. He was unable to remember anything new that happened after the operation. Each day was the start of the rest of his life, because he could remember nothing of what had happened the day before. These diverse functions of the hippocampus appear to have in common the processing of spatial and other relations.

* * *

Suppose that instead of looking at a room, we read a description of it, such as:

> It is a room on the first floor, looking on the street, and was meant for the drawing room. The double doors are in the middle of the back wall; and persons entering find

in the corner on their right two tall file cabinets at right angles to one another against the walls. In this corner stands a flat writing-table, on which there is a phonograph, a laryngoscope... [and here the author lists other paraphernalia].

Further down the room, on the same side, is a fireplace, with a comfortable leather-covered easy-chair at the side of the hearth nearest the door, and a coal-scuttle. There is a clock on the mantelpiece. Between the fireplace and the phonograph table is a stand for newspapers.

On the other side of the central door, to the left of the visitor, is a cabinet of shallow drawers. ... The corner beyond, and most of the side wall, is occupied by a grand piano, with the keyboard at the end furthest from the door, and a bench for the player extending the full length of the keyboard. ...

The description is from Bernard Shaw's stage directions for the layout of Professor Higgins's study in his play *Pygmalion* (also known as *My Fair Lady* in its transmogrification into a musical by Lerner and Loewe). The description is clear enough for us to draw a rough plan of the room. Figure 2.1 shows wire frames of the objects in the room using a computer program (Design-Workshop_Lite) to construct a three-dimensional model of it. The program allows the user to view the room from any point of view, and even to walk through it. Figure 2.2 shows a view of the room with the objects rendered in colour, and Figure 2.3 shows another view. We, too, if we listened to someone read the description, could imagine the room, and even view it from different angles. But, our representation is not as complete as the computer's model. As the description proceeds, we cannot hold in mind all the details. But, our mental representation is similar to the program's in that it depicts the spatial relations between the main objects in the scene, and some rough "metric" information about the distances between them. This claim is borne out by

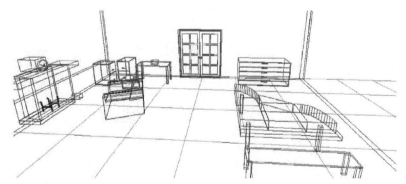

Fig. 2.1 Professor Higgins's study (as described in Bernard Shaw's *Pygmalion*) as a wire-frame of the objects in the program DesignWorkshop_Lite. The description is ambiguous, and so the table might be located between the two filing cabinets.

Fig. 2.2 A view of Professor Higgins's study. Please see plate section for a colour version of this figure.

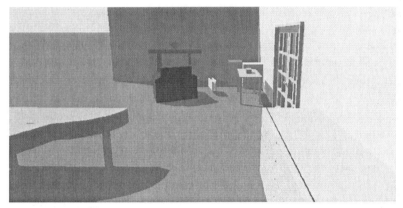

Fig. 2.3 Another view of Professor Higgins's study. Please see plate section for a colour version of this figure.

psychological evidence. We can make inferences from the description, e.g., the following three objects line up along one wall in this order: the clock on the mantelpiece over the fire, the newspaper stand, and the filing cabinets. Later, I will come back to how we make these spatial inferences.

With no more ado, I shall assume that human beings can construct internal representations of spatial layouts, and I shall refer to these representations as *mental models* of spatial layouts. A mental model is *iconic*, that is, its parts and the relations among them correspond to the parts of the layout and the relations among them. In contrast, the logical form of a sentence is not iconic, because its structure is remote from the structure of the situation it describes. A spatial model, however, is an icon of what it represents.

* * *

Could a mental model be nothing more than a visual image? For the Renaissance man, Leonardo da Vinci, to visualize was to think: the two processes were one and the same. The eye was the instrument of thought, and the artist's ability to make pictures was a medium in which to carry out imaginary experiments. In the late nineteenth century, the physicist, Ludwig Boltzmann, wrote: "All our ideas and concepts are only internal pictures". He also wrote, "The task of theory consists in constructing an image of the external world that exists purely internally and must be our guiding star in thought and experiment; that is in completing, as it were, the thinking process and carrying out globally what on a small scale occurs within us whenever we form an idea."

Many commentators have remarked that visual imagery is fundamental in the arts, sciences, and technology. Anecdotes bolster its reputation. Friedrich August von Kekulé, for example, described how in 1865 he discovered the ring-like chemical structure of benzene from a daydream. He wrote:

> I turned my chair to the fire and dozed. Again the atoms were gamboling before my eyes. This time the smaller groups kept modestly in the background. My mental eye, rendered more acute by repeated visions of this kind, could now distinguish larger structures, of manifold conformation; long rows, sometimes more closely fitted together; all twining and twisting in snakelike motion. But look! What was that? One of the snakes had seized hold of its own tail, and the form whirled mockingly before my eyes. As if by a flash of lightening I awoke.

The snake biting its tale, he claimed, was the crucial clue to the circular structure of benzene.

In one of the first investigations of visual images, Francis Galton, Darwin's cousin, carried out a questionnaire study among his fellow scientists. It revealed—to his consternation—that many of them claimed to think without using images. Yet many other scientists emphasized the role of imagery in their thinking. Darwin himself wrote to Galton: "I remember the faces of persons formerly well-known vividly, and can make them do anything I like." Perhaps the best testimonial occurs much later in a letter that Einstein wrote to the great French mathematician Hadamard:

> The words of the language, as they are written or spoken, do not seem to play any role in my mechanism of thought. The psychical entities which seem to serve as elements in thought are certain signs and more or less clear images which can be "voluntarily" reproduced and combined.
>
> There is, of course, a certain connection between those elements and relevant logical concepts. It is also clear that the desire to arrive finally at logically connected concepts is the emotional basis of this rather vague play with the above-mentioned elements. But taken from a psychological viewpoint, this combinatory play seems to be the essential feature in productive thought—before there is any connection with

logical construction in words or other kinds of signs which can be communicated to others.

To base a psychological theory on introspections, no matter how distinguished their provenance, is to build without foundations. It is impossible to establish the veridicality of subjective reports. At worst, they may be fraudulent, as some have claimed about Kekulé's dream; at best, they may be misleading, because none of us has access to the wellsprings of thought.

* * *

To find out how good your imagery is try this problem:

> I have a thousands and thousands of very thin needles, which I hold in a bundle in my hands. I throw them up into the air, imparting a random force to each of them. They fall to the ground, but, before any of them hits the ground, I stop them by magic in mid-air. Many of the needles are horizontal or nearly so, and many of them are vertical or nearly so. Are there likely to be more needles in the first category, more needles in the second category, or do the two categories have roughly equal numbers?

Most people to whom I've given this puzzle say that the two categories have roughly equal numbers. They're wrong. Think of it this way: a needle is horizontal if it points north, south, east, or west, or in any intermediate compass direction. There's no equivalent for a vertical needle: it must point more or less upwards at a 90° angle to the horizontal. Hence, the correct answer is that there are likely to be more horizontal needles.

Here's another similar problem:

> I have thousands and thousands of very thin circular disks, which I hold in a bundle in my hands. I throw them up into the air, imparting a random force to each of them. They fall to the ground, but, before any of them hits the ground, I stop them by magic in mid-air. Many of the disks are horizontal or nearly so, and many of them are vertical or nearly so. Are there likely to be more disks in the first category, more disks in the second category, or do the two categories have roughly equal numbers?

Now that you know the answer to the first problem, you may get this one right. But, people who haven't heard the first problem tend to opt for roughly equal numbers of the two sorts of disks. They're wrong. A disk that is vertical can be aligned north-to-south, east-to-west, or in any intermediate compass direction. But, there's no equivalent for a horizontal disk. You might imagine a notch on the edge of a disk, and think that the disk could be turned in the horizontal plane so that this notch is aligned north, south, east, west, or in any intermediate compass position. But, if the disk is vertical, the disk can be similarly rotated so that the notch is aligned to 12 o'clock, 1 o'clock, 2 o'clock, and so on, all around the clock. In addition, it can be aligned in any compass direction, regardless of the position of the notch. Hence, the vertical disk does have more possible positions. These two problems are difficult because we are poor at envisaging objects in three dimensions independently from our point of view. Like our attempts to visualize Higgins's study, we're swamped by the amount of information that we have to hold in mind.

Not everything can be visualized. You may think of quantum mechanics as an example. A nice irony is that one of its major practitioners, the late Richard Feynman, had a remarkable ability to visualize. When people complain that it is impossible to visualize how quantum events occur, they forget that many everyday concepts are also impossible to visualize. How could we draw a picture of "habit", Auden asked. We cannot reduce it, or other abstract concepts such as *possibility* and *ownership*, to perceptible characteristics. We can perceive various documents or events that serve as evidence for the proposition that I own a car, but we cannot perceive the relation of ownership itself.

Perhaps we have two separate systems for reasoning. One system works with images of concrete entities, and the other system works with abstract representations. We are not aware of any wrenching of intellectual gears when we reason about a mixture of concrete and abstract contents. Another possibility is that we have a single system for reasoning based on imagery of various sorts—visual, auditory, kinesthetic—and we somehow represent abstractions in images. It seems feasible, but a third possibility seems most probable: the brain represents everything in models.

Mental models should not be confused with visual images. A visual image represents how something looks from a particular point of view. It is an *egocentric* representation. In contrast, a mental model is an abstract structure akin to the three-dimensional spatial arrays used in the computer program that modeled Professor Higgins's study. It is not egocentric, but independent of point of view. The program uses this three-dimensional array to project a two-dimensional picture of the object on to the computer's screen. Likewise, our brains could use an underlying three-dimensional mental model of an object to construct a two-dimensional image of its appearance from a particular point of view. You may wonder what evidence exists to support this claim. I will describe three experiments to corroborate it, but first I want so say something about psychological experiments.

* * *

Experiments with human participants are social interactions in a microcosm, and so they are sensitive to many unforeseen factors. The participants may construe the task in ways quite different from what the experimenter has in mind. The experimenter may use inappropriate materials or procedures, or fail to control the experiment in a proper way. The instructions explain the task, but the participants think for themselves. This point became vivid to me when I read a participant the instructions to an experiment, and he said, "Yes, but what do you *really* want me to do?" So, the first potential pitfall is that an experiment doesn't assess what the experimenter designed it to do.

A second pitfall can be illustrated by an example from the days when the English made tea from loose leaves in a tea pot. Should you pour the milk into the cup before or after you've poured the tea in? The controversy was endless. It didn't seem to matter any more than whether you should eat a boiled egg from the big end or the little end. But, Sir Ronald Fisher, the mathematician and biologist, met a woman who claimed that it mattered to her because she could taste whether the milk had gone in first or second. Fisher was skeptical, and so he carried out an experiment. He made ten cups of tea, poured the milk in first for five of them, and the tea in first for the other five. Without knowing which was which, the woman took a sip from each of them in a random order and made her judgment. She was right nine times out of ten. Was she able to tell the difference or was she lucky? This dilemma faces all experimenters who have results that appear to corroborate their predictions. Is the difference real or are they lucky? To check on this possibility, psychologists carry out a statistical test of "significance". They assume that no real difference exists between the experimental conditions, and calculate the probability that the observed difference occurred by chance. For example, how often by chance would a person make nine out of ten correct guesses between two alternatives? Fisher deduced the answer from the probability calculus: about once in a hundred experiments. He made the induction that the woman could taste the difference, because her results would occur so rarely by chance if she had been guessing. Psychologists settle for a less striking difference. They infer that a result is significant if it would have occurred by chance in less than one in twenty experiments, i.e., it has a chance probability of less than 5 percent. This level of significance is arbitrary, but customary. It is an induction, and so nothing guarantees that the conclusion is true. Indeed, on average, for every twenty experiments at this level of significance, one yields findings that *are* a result of chance. Fisher had some sound advice to experimenters, which they neglect at their risk. A significance test tells them only what to ignore— experiments that fail to yield significant results. They have established a result as real when they can replicate it. Different schools of thought exist in statistics, but this criterion is the one that I follow. The experimental results that I'll report are significant and replicable.

* * *

Images derive from models. Evidence for this claim comes from a famous study devised by the psychologist Roger Shepard. The idea came to him in a dream. The participants saw two drawings of a "nonsense" figure made out

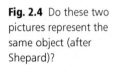

Fig. 2.4 Do these two pictures represent the same object (after Shepard)?

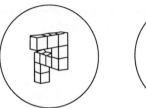 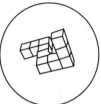

of blocks glued together to form a rigid object with right-angled joints. An example is shown in Figure 2.4. Their task was to decide whether the pictures depicted one and the same object. They carried out the task by a mental rotation of the object in the first picture so that they could superimpose it on the object in the second picture. The greater the angle that they had to rotate the object, the longer the task took. It took them on average about one second to make a mental rotation of 60°. They took about the same time whether the rotation was in the plane of the picture or in depth. To rotate an object in the picture plane is as though we are rotating the picture itself as it rests on top of the table. But, as the figure shows, to rotate the object in depth is as though we are turning the object away from us or towards us. The task cannot be done with a two-dimensional image, but only with a three-dimensional internal model of the object. Our visual system constructs a mental model of the object in the first picture, finds its major axis, and rotates the object by this axis to try to bring the model into alignment with a model of the object in the second picture.

Consider the simple mechanical system illustrated in Figure 2.5. If the handle on the left is turned in the direction shown by the arrow, then in which direction does the axle on the right move, *A* or *B*? The psychologist Mary Hegarty

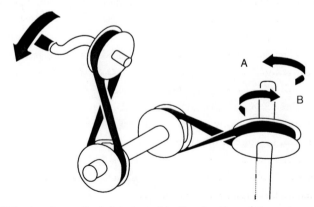

Fig. 2.5 If the handle on the left is turned in the direction of the arrow, which way does the axle on the right rotate (after Hegarty)?

has shown that when we have to solve problems of this sort, we first animate one part (the handle), work out the consequences for the next part (the pulley on the same shaft as the handle), work out the further consequences for the next part, and so on, until we either lose track of the rotation or else arrive at the solution—the axle on the right rotates in direction *A*. The underlying three-dimensional model of the system is animated in a kinematic way, but only part by part. A superhuman being would animate the entire device at once. The great electrical engineer Nikola Tesla was said to have this ability and to use it to imagine which bearing on one of his dynamos would wear out first. Some of us are more skilled than others in mental animation. Most of us can move our mental models only piecemeal.

In a third well-known study, Stephen Kosslyn asked participants to scan from one landmark to another in an image of a simple map that they had committed to memory. The time it took them depended on the distance that they had to scan. Many investigators took this sort of study to imply that imagery is a distinct medium of representation, and Kosslyn suggested that all high-level cognition, including reasoning, depends on images. He argued that images are views of objects, and he modeled them as two-dimensional arrays in a computer program. A similar vein of theorizing is current in psychology: the mind eschews abstract representations in favor of representations rooted in perception, such as visual or kinesthetic images.

Some skeptics, such as the cognitive scientist Zenon Pylyshyn, argue that images are "epiphenomenal"—Thomas Huxley's word for something that plays no causal role in a system, like the whistle on a steam engine. We may have intense visual images, but for Pylyshyn they play no causal role in our thinking. What does play a causal role are the *formal* computations that our mind carries out on a single medium of representation, so-called "propositional representations", which are expressions in a mental language. This claim dovetails with the view that reasoning depends on formal rules of inference.

So, are images central to reasoning or mere epiphenomena? The resolution of the controversy is subtle. On the one hand, all mental representations reduce to nerve impulses and events in brain cells, just as the execution of any computer program reduces to the shifting of electrical "bits" from one memory register to another. In this sense, Pylyshyn is right: imagery must be reducible to a lower-level representation based on neuronal events in the brain. On the other hand, imagery *is* a distinct form of mental representation, and, as we'll see presently, it can play a causal role in thinking, though not perhaps the role that the defenders of imagery had in mind.

* * *

Visual images are icons. Their appearance corresponds to the structure of the object or scene that they represent. Some theorists, as I mentioned, doubt whether any mental representations exist that are not rooted in sensory experience. This hypothesis has much to recommend it. It is easy to underestimate the power of perceptual representations. Certainly, we can have a visual image of, say, part of the scene described in Bernard Shaw's stage directions. And, according to the model theory, this image is a projection from an underlying three-dimensional model. Yet, not everything can be represented in an icon, whether it is an image or a model.

No image alone can capture the content of a negation, such as:

The cabinet is *not* behind the piano.

We could superimpose an image of a large red cross on our image of the cabinet behind the piano. But, we would have to know that the large red cross signifies negation, and nothing in the image itself tells us that. Likewise, we would have to know the meaning of negation: if a proposition is true then its negation is false, and vice versa. Again, nothing in the image captures this meaning. We could represent the negation in images of all the affirmative possibilities. The cabinet is *not* behind the piano, and so we form images of the cabinet in front of the piano, to the left of the piano, to the right of the piano, below the piano, and so on. We do sometimes think of these various possibilities, and we realize that only one of them holds in reality. To capture their equivalence to negation, we need to think of a disjunction of all the different possibilities. But, nothing in the sequence of images tells us that they represent a disjunction of the form: *A or B or C or*.....

Suppose we have in mind two different representations. What does their co-occurrence mean? One interpretation is that the two are in a conjunction: they are both true, just as a conjunctive proposition (one formed with "and") conveys that both its propositions are true. Another interpretation is that the two are in a disjunction: one of them is true, just as a disjunctive proposition (one formed with "or") conveys that one of its propositions is true. The great nineteenth century American logician Charles S. Peirce devised two separate diagrammatic systems for reasoning, and one system used the conjunctive interpretation, whereas the other system used the disjunctive interpretation. As he realized, mere inspection of a representation can never tell us what it means. We cannot *see* which system of interpretation we are looking at. Likewise, what a mental model represents depends both on the model and on the system that interprets it. The same model can have different interpretations depending on the system of interpretation.

The moral is that representations are iconic because of the way in which the interpretative system uses them. A representation in itself does not convey its interpretation. Concepts such as negation, conjunction, and disjunction, go beyond an iconic system. They call for symbols that refer to their meanings. They are abstract: they cannot be represented just in visual images. Yet, they are essential for reasoning, and so models must contain symbols to represent them.

* * *

Does reasoning depend on images or models? One way to answer this question is to vary how easy it is to form images of the premises in a reasoning problem. If we rely on images, then we should reason better from premises that are easy to visualize, whereas if we rely on models, then we should reason no better, or perhaps worse, from these premises. Psychologists have carried out a number of experiments of this sort, and at first sight the results look chaotic. Sometimes reasoning is enhanced by materials that are easy to visualize; sometimes it is unaffected; sometimes it is impaired. What seems to have happened is that experimenters have confused visual images with spatial models. Relations such as *above* and *below* are easy to visualize and easy to represent in a spatial model. However, not everything that is easy to visualize evokes a spatial model. Relations such as *lighter* and *darker* evoke visual images, but not spatial models. If we re-examine the literature through this lens, then it comes into focus. When experimenters used spatial relations in premises, reasoning was better. But, when they used visual relations in premises, reasoning was either unaffected or impaired.

An experiment tested this hypothesis by comparing spatial relations with visual relations. A separate panel of judges rated a large number of relations. They rated spatial relations, such as *above* and *below,* as evoking both visual images and spatial representations. But, they rated visual relations, such as *cleaner* and *dirtier,* as evoking visual images rather than spatial representations. The experiment tested a new group of participants, who had to evaluate inferences, such as:

> The dog is cleaner than the cat.
>
> The ape is dirtier than the cat.
>
> Does it follow: The dog is cleaner than the ape?

These visual relations slowed down the participants' inferences by about half a second in comparison with spatial relations. The difference may seem small, but a statistical analysis showed it was most unlikely to occur by chance, and it was a substantial proportion of the total time to make an inference, which was on the order of two seconds. Further experiments replicated the finding, and one study showed, as you would expect, that congenitally blind individuals are not impeded in reasoning about visual relations, though they do take longer to reason in general.

A subsequent experiment used the technique of *functional magnetic resonance imaging* (fMRI) to determine which regions of the brain were active during reasoning with these materials. In this procedure, the participants are tested with their heads in a large magnet, and observations yield an indirect measure of the relative amounts of oxygen taken up by the various regions of the brain. Those regions that are more active require more oxygen. The participants listened to the premises through acoustic headphones so that their visual imagery would not be inhibited by having to read them. Not surprisingly, reasoning activated many regions of the brain. Figure 2.6, however, shows a region of the brain that was activated only by reasoning about visual relations.

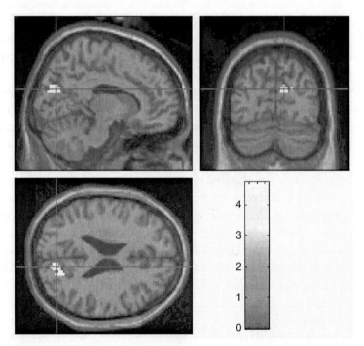

Fig. 2.6 Three "slices" through the brain showing a region (secondary visual cortex) towards the back of the brain that was active in reasoning about visual relations but not other relations. The cross-hairs locate the peak area of activation. The scale represents the chance probability of differences, with white in the figures equal to a chance probability of less than 1 in 20. Please see plate section for a colour version of this figure.

It is a region that is known to underlie vision. Visual relations may slow down reasoning because they evoke a representation in this area of the brain, and this representation is irrelevant to reasoning.

* * *

Images play a causal role in thinking because they can impede reasoning. But, how are we to make sense of all the claims that scientists have made about the role of imagery in their thinking? In the psychological laboratory, Ronald Finke and his colleagues have shown that the manipulation of images can be creative. Their participants had in front of them an array of fifteen shapes: circle, square, triangle, rectangle, horizontal line, D, I, L, T, C, J, 8, X, V, P. On each trial, the experimenter named three of the shapes, and the participants had to close their eyes and to imagine assembling these shapes into a recognizable figure. They then drew the figure. The participants were free to combine the parts in any way—rotating, translating, superimposing, or juxtaposing them. They could change the sizes of the shapes, but they were not allowed to distort them. An independent panel of judges rated about 15 percent of the drawings of their efforts as creative. The task seems to depend on a visual play with images, and the participants were unable to predict in advance what the resulting shape would be.

The visual play with images in these studies is reminiscent of scientists' reports of their own use of imagery in solving problems. Visualization alone, however, cannot solve problems. Images need to be backed up by an independent representation of the problem if they are to be used to solve it. As an example, consider again Kekulé's problem. His goal was to specify the molecular structure of benzene in the light of the chemical theory of valencies—of which he was one of the founders. The theory specifies the propensities of atoms to combine with other atoms. Kekulé knew that each molecule of benzene contained six carbon atoms and six hydrogen atoms, and that the valency of carbon was four, i.e., each carbon atom has to combine with four other atoms. The only known molecular structures at that time were strings of atoms, but a string of six carbon atoms would require three hydrogen atoms at each of its ends, and two hydrogen atoms to combine with each of the four atoms in the middle of the string. That's a total of fourteen hydrogen atoms, but there are only six in the molecule: not enough to do the job. The puzzle stumped him until in mental play with a string-like structure, he formed an image of a circle. A circular arrangement of the atoms still doesn't solve the problem, because each carbon atom bonds with two other carbon atoms in the circle and two hydrogen atoms. Once again, there weren't enough hydrogen atoms to do the job—only six instead of twelve. Kekulé had to make the further assumption that alternate links between the carbon atoms had a double valency, and so each carbon atom in the ring had a single link to one carbon atom and a double link to another. There remained one valency on each carbon atom unaccounted for, and it was a bond to a single hydrogen atom. Because carbon atoms are identical, the single and double bonds oscillated from moment to moment. Kekulé's image of the atoms "all twisting and twining in snake-like motion" may have suggested this oscillation, but no one knows whether the solution did come to him in a daydream.

The manipulation of images is a method for solving visual problems. It changes the appearances of objects. In solving a problem, such as the structure of benzene, the use of images is part of the process. The image must relate to an independent representation of the problem. Otherwise, nothing represents the number of atoms and their valencies apart from what is in the current image. Visualization can yield deep conceptual innovations but only within a system that can represent more abstract information.

If you can, please form a visual image of this proposition:

> The bench for the piano player extends the full length of the piano's keyboard.

Now, ask yourself these questions:

> Where is the bench in relation to the piano?
>
> How far apart are they?
>
> What is the shape of the bench?

If you had a vivid image, you should be able to answer these questions. That is to say, it is hard to have a visual image of the bench and the piano without representing their salient visual properties and relations. Of course, many people find it difficult to form images, or to hold them in mind while they retrieve information from them. Nevertheless, an image of a scene makes manifest the visual characteristics of the objects in the scene from a particular point of view.

Mental models are different. Their content is available to consciousness, but we cannot inspect them as we can inspect images. If we mentally rotate an object, we're rotating a three-dimensional model, but all that we're aware of is a moving two-dimensional image. The evidence for models is therefore indirect. They are often abstract and represent a small amount of information. But, their power lies in their abstraction. A mental model can represent what is common to all the different ways in which a possibility might occur. Each model therefore corresponds to a *set* of possibilities—the set defined by what is in the model. A model can represent the length of the bench as equal to the length of the piano, but the model can be stripped of the "accidents" of color, absolute size, substance, detail. It can be updated to include information about these characteristics. Yet, no matter how many details are added to a description of a scene, the description is always consistent with a swarm of possibilities. A single model can represent them all by leaving out the accidents that distinguish them.

* * *

Like the birds and the bees, we construct representations of the world. These representations are iconic, that is, the relations and entities in them mirror those in the world. One source of iconic representations is perception, but part of the power of language is that it too can lead us to construct iconic representations of the world. One sort of icon is a visual image. It represents a scene from a particular point of view. Another sort of icon is a mental model, which is a three-dimensional representation akin to an actual model of the scene. We can also think about matters that we cannot visualize, such as the concepts of *negation*, *possibility*, and *ownership*. Models are iconic as far as they can be, but they also contain symbols to represent these abstract concepts. They can be used to create conscious visual images of scenes from a particular point of view. Reasoning, however, is based on models rather than images. We use images to think about changes in the appearance of objects, but our visual play with them to solve problems depends on an independent representation of the problem. Images are therefore neither central to reasoning nor epiphenomenal. They are real, but they are not to be confused with mental models, because images get in the way of reasoning. William Golding in his wonderful novel *The Inheritors* described a Neanderthal woman impeded by an image as she tried to think:

> "I am by the sea and I have a picture. This is a picture of a picture. I am—" She screwed up her face and scowled—"thinking." ... She paused, frustrated by the vivid detail of her picture, not knowing how to extract from it the significance she felt was there.

Chapter 3

Models of Possibilities: From Conjuring Tricks to Disasters

Not long ago, I lost a small notebook in an airport hotel. I had just eaten dinner in the hotel's restaurant and returned to my room when I discovered that the notebook was missing. The first thing we ought to do when we've lost something is, *not* to look, but to think. We have to recall the last time for certain that we had the missing object, and then to retrace our steps from that point to the present to locate all the places it might be. The last time I had used the notebook was in my hotel room: I had made a note in it before I went down to the restaurant. So, there were several possibilities: it could be somewhere in my room, it could have fallen from my pocket on the way to or from the restaurant, or it could be in the restaurant. After thought, action. I checked the room. I rang the hotel restaurant: they had found no notebook. But, just to be sure, I went down and checked around my table. I also checked the stairs and the whole of my route to and from my room. I asked at the reception desk. No notebook. It was unlikely to have fallen from my jacket pocket, and my waiter was certain that I hadn't left it on the table. When you've eliminated the impossible, Sherlock Holmes remarked, then whatever remains, how improbable, must be the case. I had eliminated all but one possibility: despite my cursory search, the notebook must be somewhere in my room. The next lesson in the "science" of finding is: think again. Where had I been when I was writing the notes in the book? I had been lying on the bed. I looked under the bed. I looked under the pillows. And then I looked down the side of the bed next to the wall. Eureka! It had fallen there after I had finished writing and dozed off.

This example illustrates an important point: when we think, we think about what's possible. There were three main possibilities for the whereabouts of the notebook: my room, the restaurant, or on the route between them. To be able to think about possibilities is an enviable ability, because it means that we're not stuck with what's in front of our noses.

A model can represent a real possibility, or one that we know to be imaginary or fictitious. Our minds keep track of the status of the models that they construct. We have, as philosophers say, "propositional attitudes". That is, we know that some propositions are true and some are false; we believe some propositions and disbelieve others; and we are prepared to entertain some propositions as hypotheses or assumptions for the sake of argument. Our mental models of these propositions have symbolic labels so that we can try to keep track of their status. From time to time, I will use a label on a diagram of a model to indicate the status of the model. You should remember, however, that all mental models must have these labels. We don't just think about possibilities: we represent the fact that they are possibilities.

* * *

If a person tosses a fair coin, how many possible outcomes are there? We are likely to think of two: heads or tails. Perhaps you thought of a third possibility in which the coin remains balanced on its edge. Two possibilities is the norm, of course, provided the person tossing the coin isn't the well-known statistician and magician Persi Diaconnis, who can make a coin come down whichever way he wants. Yet, there is another way of thinking about a coin toss. An infinite number of possibilities could occur. The coin might go up in the air for a short distance, say six inches, or for a considerable distance, say five feet; it might go up vertically or off at an angle; it might spin in the air twice or a dozen times, it might fall flat on the floor or spin like a top before it settles down on one side; and so on. But, when we toss a coin, we are interested in two sets of possibilities: those that have in common that the coin comes up heads and those that have in common that it comes up tails. Hence, when we refer to a possibility almost always we refer to a set of possibilities that have in common a particular state of affairs that is relevant to us. It's tedious to have to keep writing "a set of possibilities with a particular state of affairs in common", and I won't do so again. But, you should remember that when I refer to a possibility it is in fact a set of possibilities.

No one would deny that thinking *can* concern possibilities. A much more controversial claim is that when we reason, our reasoning is always founded on possibilities. An obvious alternative is that it is based on necessary states of affairs—those that are bound to occur—rather then mere possibilities, or it is based sometimes on possible states and sometimes on necessary states. Still another alternative, which I discussed in Chapter 1, is that it is based on logical forms that are empty of content. But, if reasoning is based on mental models, then possibilities take center stage, because models represent possibilities. One corollary is that reasoning should be straightforward when we follow up the consequences of a single possibility, but it should be harder when we have to follow up the consequences of more than one possibility. And when reasoning is harder, it will take us longer and we will be more likely to err. That, in a nutshell, is the argument of the present chapter. It aims to show that reasoning *is* based on possibilities.

* * *

Suppose someone tells us the whereabouts of two famous cricketers who are captains of their national teams:

> Sachin is in India or Inzamam is in Pakistan, or both.

What are the possibilities? When we are asked to enumerate them, we tend to write down three possibilities in this order: Sachin is in India, Inzamam is in Pakistan, Sachin is in India *and* Inzamam in Pakistan. The disjunction is known as "inclusive" because it includes the possibility in which both propositions are true (the third possibility). An "exclusive" disjunction excludes this case, and is often expressed in a legalistic way as follows:

> Sachin is in India or else Inzamam is in Pakistan, but not both.

It rules out the third possibility, and so we list just the other two possibilities.

In life, we don't fuss much about disjunctions. We say, for example, "the book is in the bedroom or it's in the restaurant," and general knowledge reminds us that the book can't be in both places. Linguists have argued that the basic meaning of "or" allows that both possibilities can co-occur. This meaning can be made explicit with the addition of, "or both", or by the ugly usage "and/or". In contrast, the use of "or else", "or otherwise", or the tag "but not both", makes clear that both possibilities cannot occur. The difference between the two sorts of disjunction is illustrated in a story about the logician Abraham Fraenkel, who was born in Germany but went to live in Israel. He got on a bus there that was scheduled to leave the bus station at 9 a.m. At five past nine, it still hadn't left, and Fraenkel asked the driver why it hadn't left, waving the schedule at him. "What are you," the driver asked, "a German or a professor?" He replied: "Is your "or" inclusive or exclusive? If inclusive, my answer is *yes*; but if exclusive, it's *no, I'm both*".

If you understood my account of the lost notebook, you thought of three possible places for its whereabouts. You didn't have to think about all of them at the same time, but just one at a time. It isn't easy to have more than one possibility in mind at the same time. It's unsettling and it imposes a load on the memory system known as "working memory", which is where we hold things in mind while we think about them. Working memory doesn't hold very much at any one time. It is a bottleneck in intelligence. Indeed, the heart of computational power is the capacity to hold the results of intermediate computations in memory. Given a tiny number of basic operations, the power of a computational system to make complicated computations depends solely on the capacity of its working memory. For instance, we cannot do long multiplication without working memory or an external substitute, such as a pen and paper.

To experience the state of "memory overload" for yourself, try this problem:

> June is in Wales or Charles is in Scotland, but not both.
>
> Charles is in Scotland or Kate is in Ireland, but not both.
>
> What, if anything, follows?

You might be tempted to give a quick intuitive answer based on the surface form of the sentences:

> June is in Wales or Charles is in Scotland or Kate is in Ireland.

But this conclusion is a valid inference only if "or" allows for all the possibilities to hold, and it throws a way of lot of information, because it is compatible with seven possibilities. So, please do think for a moment about what follows from the premises.

Each premise is consistent with just two possibilities. The problem, of course, is to combine the possibilities. One strategy is to realize that one possibility is common to both sets of possibilities:

> Charles is in Scotland

But, what happens if Charles isn't in Scotland? The one possibility according to the first premise is:

> June is in Wales

And the one possibility according to the second premise is:

> Kate is in Ireland

Both premises have to hold, and so these two possibilities have to co-occur. Hence, the premises together yield two possibilities, which I've listed on separate lines:

> Charles is in Scotland
>
> June is in Wales   Kate is in Ireland

They correspond to the conclusion:

> Either Charles is in Scotland or else June is in Wales and Kate is in Ireland.

In an experiment testing a sample of the general population with this problem, twenty-one percent of them drew this valid conclusion or one equivalent to it, but the rest of them were wrong.

The participants in the experiment also tackled problems based on *inclusive* disjunctions such as:

> June is in Wales or Charles is in Scotland, or both.

> Charles is in Scotland or Kate is in Ireland, or both.

There are now five possibilities compatible with the two premises, and I have spelt them out in the notes to the chapter. They support the valid conclusion:

> Charles is in Scotland or June is in Wales and Kate is in Ireland, or all three.

This inference should be harder because it depends on five possibilities rather than the two possibilities needed for the inference based on exclusive disjunctions. Indeed, only six percent of the participants drew a valid conclusion. If they had used formal rules to make these inferences, then, contrary to these results, the second inference should have been easier than the first. The predicted difficulty switches because psychological theories based on formal rules have no rules for dealing at once with exclusive disjunctions, and so they need to take extra steps with them. We could add a formal rule for them, but there's still no reason to suppose that its use should be easier than the rule for inclusive disjunctions.

Most people go wrong with both inferences, and you might wonder what conclusions they draw. If they are trying to construct models of possibilities, then there are two obvious predictions. The first is that if people grasp that there's more than one possibility but are unable to discern what holds over all of them, then they should respond that there's no valid conclusion. About a third of responses were of this sort. The second prediction is that if people overlook one or more possibilities, then their conclusion should correspond to just *some* of the possibilities compatible with the premises. When the participants did draw a conclusion, most of their conclusions were of this sort. Indeed, the most frequent errors were conclusions based on just a single possibility compatible with the premises. These errors cannot be attributed to blind guessing, because of the improbability of guessing so many conclusions compatible with the premises. The nature of the erroneous conclusions is so hard to explain if reasoners are relying on formal rules that no one has devised such an explanation.

A simple way in which to prevent reasoners from being swamped by possibilities is to give them an extra premise, which establishes the definite whereabouts of one of the individuals, e.g.:

> June is in England.
>
> June is in Wales or Charles is in Scotland, but not both.
>
> Charles is in Scotland or Kate is in Ireland, but not both.

The interpretation of the first two premises yields a single possibility:

> June is in England   Charles is in Scotland

The combination of this possibility with those for the third premise yields:

> June is in England   Charles is in Scotland   Kate is *not* in Ireland

In this way, the number of possibilities that have to be kept in mind at any one time is reduced to one. The experiment included some problems of this sort, and they were easy.

Lance Rips reported a rare experimental result that failed to corroborate the model theory. He compared two sorts of inference, which were each based on three premises, including two conditionals, i.e., propositions based on "if". One sort had an initial premise that was a conjunction, such as:

> Anna is in Granada and Pablo is in Barcelona.
>
> If Anna is in Granada then Teresa is in Toledo.
>
> If Pablo is in Barcelona then Teresa is in Toledo.
>
> Is Teresa in Toledo?

The other sort of inference had a disjunctive premise instead of the initial conjunction: *Anna is in Granada or Pablo is in Barcelona.* The correct answer for both inferences is, "yes". But, because a conjunction has only one model, and a disjunction has multiple models, the conjunctive inference should be easier than the disjunctive inference. Yet, there was no reliable difference between them. Juan García-Madruga and his colleagues also failed to detect a difference using the materials above translated into Spanish. But, these investigators carried out some further studies that showed what had happened. When the participants in an experiment drew their own conclusions from the premises instead of answering a question about a given conclusion, the conjunctive problems (ninety-five percent correct) were easier than the disjunctive problems (seventy-two percent correct). It is harder to generate a conclusion than to evaluate a given one. Likewise, when the conjunctive and disjunctive premises followed the two conditional premises, the conjunctive inferences were also easier than the disjunctive inferences even in the evaluation of given conclusions. The task is more demanding because the participants' working memory is already preoccupied by the models of the conditionals when they encounter the final disjunction. And when the premises were presented one at a time, the participants spent longer perusing the disjunctive premise than the conjunctive premise. No reliable difference in the accuracy of inferences occurred in this case, but the participants took longer to evaluate the disjunctive inferences than the conjunctive inferences. Hence, when the premises and conclusion are presented together, as in Rips's experiment, the evaluation task appears not to be sensitive enough to detect the difference between the two sorts of initial premise.

* * *

Suppose that a cure for all diseases was found. What would be a *possible* consequence?

You might try to answer this question. A common response is that there might be fewer doctors, or that many doctors might go bankrupt—unless they were required to administer the cure.

Suppose that there was a nuclear war. What would be a *necessary* consequence—something that was bound to occur? Again, you should try to answer this question for yourself. The most frequent response is: many people would die. Questions about possible consequences, as an experiment showed, are easier to answer than questions about necessary consequences. When we create a possible consequence, we have to think of a scenario in which the consequence occurs, and it doesn't matter if there are other scenarios in which it doesn't occur. But, when we create a necessary consequence, we have to think of one that occurs in all the scenarios we can imagine. It therefore took the participants a few seconds longer to think of necessary consequences, and they were less confident in their answers.

For premises that have several models, a single model consistent with them—an example—establishes a conclusion about what is possible; but all the models must be examples to establish a conclusion about what is necessary. The opposite is the case for refutations: a single counterexample refutes a conclusion about what is necessary, whereas all models must be counterexamples to refute a conclusion about what is possible. And so we should draw a conclusion about what's possible faster than a conclusion about what's necessary, but we should draw a conclusion about what's *not* necessary faster than a conclusion about what's *not* possible. This prediction is crucial for a theory that takes possibilities as fundamental, and several experiments have corroborated it. One caveat, learned the hard way, is that it's no use asking adults whether something is possible if it's necessity is obvious. They baulk at saying, "yes", in these circumstances; and so inferences have to be hard enough that when an event is possible its necessity isn't obvious too. Here is a typical trial from an experiment. The premises are about a game of one-on-one basketball in which two players take part:

> If Allan is in [the game] then Betsy is in.
>
> If Carla is in then David is out.

The participants were more accurate and faster to infer that Betsy could be in the game than to infer that she must be in the game. If you list the possible games compatible with the premises, you'll discover that there are three games and that Betsy is in all of them: Allan versus Betsy, Betsy versus Carla, Betsy versus David.

A way to create a problem to which the answer is, "no", to both a question about what's possible and a question about what's necessary is to change "in" to "out" in the premises, and vice versa. The premises above are thereby transformed into:

> If Allan is out then Betsy is out.
>
> If Carla is out then David is in.

The participants were now more accurate and faster to infer that Betsy need not be in the game than to infer that Betsy cannot be in the game. The only possible games are: Allan versus Carla, Allan versus David, and Carla versus David.

Critics might argue that we are biased to respond "yes" to questions about possibility and "no" to questions about necessity, and that this bias yields the crucial result. However, in the first study that I described, the participants created possible consequences faster than they created necessary consequences. Because they imagined the content of these propositions, the result cannot be explained by a bias to respond "yes" to questions about possibilities.

* * *

We think about possibilities when we reason. That's why it is so hard to reason from pairs of disjunctive propositions. That's why it is easier to reason from an exclusive disjunction that allows two possibilities than to reason from an inclusive disjunction that allows three possibilities. And that's why our erroneous conclusions tend to be compatible with just some possibilities: we overlook the others. The problem in reasoning is to keep track of possibilities, and I will show later in the book that diagrams that help us to do so improve our reasoning.

You might suppose that for some other unknown reason exclusive disjunctions are simpler than inclusive disjunctions. In fact, no such difference exists. If we are trying to learn a new concept, then exclusive disjunctions are harder than inclusive disjunctions. They are also harder if we are trying to create a wiring diagram for switches and a bulb so that the bulb comes on with a disjunction of switches. I will explain why later. It is only when we're reasoning from premises that exclusive disjunctions are easier than inclusive disjunctions. The number of possibilities that we have to represent explains the difference.

Pairs of disjunctions do not seem typical of most reasoning problems in daily life. But, complex documents that lawyers have prepared often lead to a multiplication of possibilities beyond our ability to keep track of them. Here, for example, is an extract from a UK government leaflet describing who was eligible for a so-called "death grant", which helped to defray the cost of a spouse's funeral:

> Death grant is payable where either of the following conditions is satisfied by the person on whose [National Health] contributions the grant is claimed:
>
> The contributor must have paid or been credited with at least 25 contributions of any class at any time between 5 July 1948 or the date of entry into insurance, if later, and 5 April 1985, or the date on which he reached 65 (60 for a woman), or died under that age, whichever is the earliest; or
>
> Since 6 April 1985 the contributor must have actually paid contributions in any one tax year before the relevant year, on earnings of at least 25 times the lower earning limit for that year. The relevant year is usually the income tax year in which the death occurred, but if immediately before the date of death, the person on whose contributions the grant is claimed was himself dead or over 65 (60 for a woman), it is either the year in which he reached that age, or the year in which he died, whichever is earlier.

There are so many possibilities that we begin to lose track of quite who has died. Nevertheless, pairs of disjunctive premises are atypical, and so I will present more evidence in subsequent chapters that we reason about possibilities. Much of this evidence comes from studies of inferences closer to those in daily life.

* * *

Whenever there are alternative possibilities, cognition becomes harder whether in reasoning, planning, solving a problem, or in making a decision. The tendency to overlook possibilities has many repercussions, both benign and malign. Stage magicians anticipate how we will reason and rely on our inability to think of possibilities. David Devant, one of the best twentieth century magicians, invented a striking stage illusion called the "Mascot Moth" that defies our ability to think of a possibility. An actress costumed as a beautiful moth arrives on stage. The magician goes to embrace her, but she folds her wings over her face and as he puts his arms around her, she withers and disappears in an instant, like the snuffing out of a candle. The idea for the illusion, Devant wrote, came to him in a dream. You might like to think how it is possible to create this effect. One clue: the illusion does not depend on mirrors. You will find the solution at the end of the chapter.

The inability to think of possibilities occurs in many disasters in everyday life. I will give you just one example, but there are plenty of others. The operators of the nuclear power station at Three Mile Island on March 28, 1979 inferred that the high temperature at a relief valve was caused by a leak. For over an hour, they overlooked the possibility that the valve was stuck open. They did well to think of this possibility, because soon after the problem developed over a hundred alarms were ringing, and the needles on many instruments had gone off their scales.

The model theory, unlike other accounts of reasoning, takes the representation of possibilities as fundamental. Each mental model represents a possibility in as an iconic way as possible, but it is hard to hold multiple models in working memory. More models call for more work, which leads to longer times to reason and to a greater tendency for error. I have presented some evidence supporting this prediction, and I will return to the topic later, but next I need to consider the unconscious processes of reasoning.

The solution to the magic of the Mascot moth is that the actress playing the moth wore a dress that looked the same whether she was in it or not. A vertical black tube about four inches in diameter slid up behind her on stage, and a plug at the back of the dress slipped into the tube. The dress hung from its collar, which contained a steel spring to act as a yoke. The dress also had a reel of strong cord attached to it, which Devant in one of his movements to the moth dropped down the tube. The actress stepped to a precise mark on the stage over a trapdoor. She folded her wings across her face and locked them together. She tapped on the trap door with her foot, which slipped beneath the stage. The dress was now an empty shell supported by the tube. Devant stepped to the side of the empty dress with his left foot behind it in front of the tube. He went to embrace the moth, and on his cue, a stagehand beneath the stage pulled the strong cord, the spring wires in the dress collapsed, and the dress was pulled through the end of the upright tube. Devant masked the tube from the audience until it was withdrawn. He then stepped away to show that the stage was empty. The illusion was brilliant because it didn't seem to depend on any apparatus. One moment the moth was in plain view, the next moment she had vanished.

Part II

The World in Our Unconscious Minds

The centre that I cannot find

Is known to my unconscious mind
                                        Auden

Chapter 4

Mental Architecture and the Unconscious

You're going to make a quick intuitive judgment about two men from pictures of them. Just look at their pictures in Figure 4.1, and decide which man looks more competent.

Like most people, you probably judged that the man on the left looks more competent. We are able to make rapid intuitive inferences of this sort. My colleague Alex Todorov and his co-workers collected judgments about pictures of pairs of competing candidates in six hundred elections to the US Senate and House of Representatives. What is remarkable is that those whom the participants judged to look more competent tended to win their elections. (Yes, the man on the left won his election.) In a subsequent study, the participants looked at the pictures for just one second, and their judgments of competence predicted two-thirds of the election results, whereas their judgments of honesty or charisma did not. Of course, individuals who *look* competent may *be* competent, but counterexamples do occur. Warren Harding seems to have been elected the President of the USA on the strength of his good looks alone, but he was incompetent in office.

Fig. 4.1 Which person looks more competent?

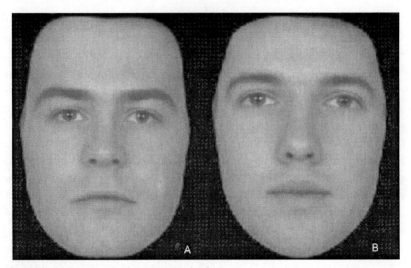

Fig. 4.2 Which person looks a stronger leader?

Now, please take a look at the next pair of pictures in Figure 4.2. Which man looks like the stronger leader? In an unpublished experiment by Tony Little and his colleagues (at the University of Liverpool), the participants tended to choose the man on the left. They also judged that he'd be a better leader during times of war, whereas they judged that the man on the right was more likeable, more intelligent, and a better leader in peace times. The two pictures derive from the same person. A computer program morphed this man's picture either in the direction of a picture of Bush (the left-hand man) or in the direction of Kerry (the right-hand man).

That elections can be decided on "face" validity is a startling possibility. But, my concern is the nature of the intuitive inferences that enable us to assess competence from a snapshot of a face. We're not aware of the mechanisms underlying it. They are so deeply unconscious that lying on a psychoanalyst's couch and "free associating" won't reveal them to us (or to the analyst). Freud proposed the unconscious as the locus of irrational thought processes distinct from the rational processes of conscious reasoning. But, the unconscious inferences to which I am referring go back to the nineteenth century German polymath Hermann von Helmholtz. He argued that vision must depend on unconscious inferences, which, for instance, give rise to our perception of depth. Helmholtzian unconscious mechanisms cannot enter consciousness, because they construct its contents. We cannot pick up our introspections by their own bootstraps.

The notion of two distinct sorts of reasoning goes back at least to Pascal, who distinguished between intuitive and mathematical reasoning. Many modern psychologists have also defended "dual process" theories of reasoning. In broad terms, they distinguish between rapid intuitive inferences and slower deliberate inferences. The evidence bears out this distinction. What is less clear is whether there are other sorts of reasoning, and whether they depend on separate processes or merely a single process that operates at different levels of efficiency. My immediate aim is to clarify the distinction between processes and representations, and then in the next chapter to provide a theory of the processes of unconscious inference. This theory in turn has ramifications for human emotions and for the role of reasoning in mental illnesses.

* * *

We carry out mental processes on mental representations, and so I need to be clear about the distinction between them. Consider, as an example, how we reason about spatial relations. We're given, say, this problem:

> The cup is to the right of the plate.
>
> The spoon is to the left of the plate.
>
> What's the relation between the cup and the spoon?

Our brains contain a hierarchy of processors, and they can deal with this problem. At the topmost level, we make a decision to try to solve the problem (or, if we're lazy, we decide not to bother). If we do go ahead, we read the premises and we understand them. This ability depends on processes that identify words, that recover the grammatical relations among them, that use these relations to compose meanings, and that establish the references of expressions. We are oblivious of how these processes work, but according to the model theory, we use the resulting significance of the premises to construct an iconic model of the layout. The process of construction is unconscious, but it yields a representation, and this mental model enables us to draw a conclusion, by another unconscious process, that the cup is to the right of the spoon. The model also enables us to make a sketch from memory of the layout of the objects. In general, the world in our conscious minds is a sequence of representations that result from a set of processes, and the world in our unconscious minds is the set of processes themselves. It also contains some representations of which we are not aware, such as the two slightly disparate images of the world that our eyes form, and that enable us to see the world in depth. In other words, all mental processes are unconscious. We are aware at best only of some of their results. When we have an intuition, such as that one man looks more competent than another, we are not even aware of its premises—those aspects of his face and expression that lead us to this conclusion. But, when we make a conscious deduction, we are aware at least of the significance of its premises and its conclusion.

* * *

A computer program that I wrote simulates the use of models in spatial reasoning, and it depends on over a hundred separate processes. They range from those that start the construction of a model to those that find the particular relation in a spatial model that holds between a given pair of entities. Figure 4.3 is a simplified diagram of the program's structure. As you can see, the program is organized in a hierarchy. It has two main modules: one parses sentences and composes their meanings out of those of their parts, and the other constructs models and interprets them. In both modules, however, the processes at the top of the hierarchy interact just with those near to them, whereas those lower in the hierarchy are often used by several higher processes. The result, as the figure shows, is a "tangled hierarchy" rather than a neat classification. I did not design this hierarchy and implement a program to embody it, but instead wrote the code that would parse a sentence, then wrote the code for using its results to update models, and so on. The writing of a computer program to simulate cognition is a dialectical process: the programmer aims for parsimony by allowing high-level processes to call on lower level ones. My program could have ended up with many other designs, but all of the efficient ones would be tangled hierarchies.

My laptop computer has a single central processor, which carries out each step in the program from the one at the top of the hierarchy that initiates an inference down to those that carry out trivial operations. Hence, the hierarchy in Figure 4.3 represents how one process that the central processor is executing

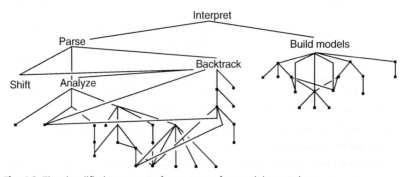

Fig. 4.3 The simplified structure of a program for spatial reasoning.

calls another, which calls another, and so on and on. In contrast, the brain contains billions of tiny processors—nerve cells—that operate together in parallel. Each of these individual nerve cells is slow to carry out a process in comparison with my computer's central processor. But, their parallelism allows them to allocate complex tasks to separate modules working simultaneously, so that the brain's overall response is fast. A similar architecture is advantageous for the control of any complicated system, such as an automated assembly line, in which a number of processes need to be carried out in parallel.

The most general design for parallel computation is a network of processors wired up to each other so that they can exchange instructions and data. One processor cannot observe, or influence directly, the inner workings of another. No central clock exists to synchronize the processors. Instead, each processor springs to life as soon as it receives data on which to carry out its computations. Many variations on this design exist. The channels of communication may allow for complex symbolic messages to be interchanged among processors, or they may allow only a tiny repertoire of possible signals. There may be a large array of processors that all carry out the same computation but on different data—a so-called "grid" computation. Whatever the design, parallel processing cannot compute anything that cannot, in principle, be computed by a single serial processor. That is why it is possible for my computer to simulate the behavior of a parallel processing system.

Parallel computation can speed up computations vastly. Separate processors can specialize in particular computations, and reliability can be checked in parallel by other processors. The system is robust and resistant to damage. Yet, inferences that yield many possibilities, such as those in the previous chapter, are *intractable*. This technical term means that with a large enough number of premises, any system of reasoning is liable to run out of time and memory before it can represent all the possibilities. Machines as vast as the universe working at the speed of light still take billions of years to make an inference based on thousands of premises. And, alas, parallel processing doesn't convert these inferences into tractable ones. It merely postpones the crunch. Intractability is to computation as Malthus's doctrine of population growth is to civilization. The rate of human reproduction goes up in an exponential way, whereas the rate of food production goes up only in an additive way. Result: famine. The time required for computing a conclusion to an inference goes up in an exponential way with the number of premises, whereas the time available to wait for an answer does not. Result: intractability.

Parallelism has advantages, but it also has dangers. If one processor is waiting for information from a second processor, which in turn is waiting for information from the first processor, the two will become locked up together in a "deadly embrace". Similarly, if one processor says *advance,* and another processor says *retreat,* what is the poor organism to do—tear itself in half? A remedy for these dangers is to promote one processor to oversee others—to adjudicate conflicts, and to override deadly embraces. The replication of this design on a large scale leads to a hierarchy of processors.

An advantage of a hierarchical organization is that the overall controller sees the "big picture". It sends out general commands, which percolate down the hierarchy, becoming refined into precise instructions. Nineteenth century neurologists postulated this sort of architecture for the brain in order to explain how it governs skilled performance. The decision, say, to ride a bicycle is passed to the brain centers that govern the separate modules of the skill, such as pedaling and steering, which in turn pass on instructions to the lower centers that control the movements of limbs, and so on ... all the way down to the nerves that control the contraction of muscles. Each center is computing in parallel with the others, and so they control the events that occur at the same time when we are riding a bicycle, admiring the scenery, and whistling the opening theme from Beethoven's Pastoral Symphony. Other centers enable us to make inferences from propositions. Like my computer program, they recognize words, parse sentences, compose their meanings, and manipulate models. Each of these activities calls for exquisite interactions among processors. They must operate in parallel like workers on a factory production line that takes sentences as its raw material and transforms them into the finished product of an inference. We are aware of understanding the meaning of the premises, perhaps of an image or two, and of the conclusion that we draw. Our awareness corresponds to the outputs of high-level processors, and these mental representations are held in working memory.

* * *

Consciousness may owe its origins to the emergence of a high-level controller from the hierarchy of processors. It sets goals for lower level processors, uses them to formulate plans, receives information from them, and monitors their performance. Its instructions are formulated as messages, equivalent to, say, *I am going to ride my bicycle,* rather than to detailed instructions about which muscles to contract. These instructions are formulated much lower down in the hierarchy. Conversely, the information that the high-level controller receives is complex, such as a model of the world based on vision. Our experience of visual reality is a consequence of the architecture of the mind. If we could introspect on the processes that construct it, then the vividness of contact with the world would be shattered. We might doubt the veridicality of the process, which could be fatal in the case of danger. When we start to cross the road, we want to be aware of a motorbike bearing down on us, not of the inner processes of visual perception. Suppose we duplicate this architecture in an autonomous robot. It, too, would have a high-level controller that sees the big picture, and makes the big decisions. Its controller would be a functional equivalent to our consciousness. Would the robot be conscious? It's hard to say, and what's worse is that there's no obvious way to find out.

Some mental processes construct the contents of consciousness; others are deep in the unconscious. What is the biggest difference between them? The hypothesis that I propose is that working memory is available only for those processes that yield conscious representations. Working memory sometimes contains a goal, sometimes a model of the world, sometimes a signal from the internal milieu of the body, such as hunger or thirst, and sometimes a long-term memory. These contents are what we are aware of at any moment as we go about our business in life. They are a result of what we refer to as "conscious" thinking, though it depends on processes outside our awareness.

We have knowledge of ourselves. We know what sort of persons we are. We know, to some degree, our tastes and preferences, our abilities and disabilities, our past and our likely future. We have a sense of "self", a sense of our own integrity, continuity, and individuality. We have access, not to our mind's inner workings, but to its high-level outcomes. And we can reflect on all these matters when we try to make a decision. To make an intentional decision depends in part on our awareness that we *can* make intentional decisions. These self-reflections are our way of understanding ourselves.

What would it mean to say that a computational system understood itself? One answer would be that it had access to a complete description of itself, and that it could use this description in, say, formulating plans for what it should do. In this case, the description would not be complete unless it also included this use for itself. Inklings of a vicious circle lurk here. We, however, do not have access to complete descriptions of ourselves. The nature of mental architecture precludes this possibility. We have instead access to *mental models* of ourselves. We developed these models from childhood onwards, and certain people played a privileged role in their development—our parents, our mentors, our peers. We listened to what they had to say, and we observed their actions. We observed our own actions too, we thought about ourselves, and we assessed ourselves. And from all of this information we *inferred* a model of our self. But, it is a model, which means that it is incomplete and liable to be erroneous. It is also unfinished. We continue day by day to refine our models of our selves. They may not change much once we have reached maturity, but every now and again we surprise ourselves for better or worse, and in consequence revise our models. Sometimes they get so out of line with reality that we need help to restore them.

* * *

The theory of mental architecture that I have described implies a split between conscious and unconscious behavior. And there is such a split. For instance, if a photographer asks us to smile, we can decide to smile. Our decision is conscious, and our expression is the result of a voluntary action. But, if something amusing happens we may smile involuntarily. This smile is a result of unconscious processes controlling our facial muscles. The two sorts of smile differ in a subtle way, and an expert can tell whether our smile is deliberate or spontaneous. If we are at a cocktail party we can shift our attention voluntarily away from a speaker to a nearby conversation. We keep nodding at the speaker but in reality we are listening, not to him, but to another person. In contrast, our attention will switch involuntarily if someone else in a nearby conversation utters our name. A low-level processor lies dormant until the right sequence of speech sounds—corresponding to our name—wakes it up, and switches our attention to the other speaker.

On most occasions we can direct our behavior. Yet sometimes, much as we would like to, we are unable to control ourselves. We may intend to be polite to someone we dislike—that is part of our model of our self, but he says something very irritating and we snap back at him. We may intend to do our physical exercises in the morning, but when we get up we just don't feel like doing them. We comfort ourselves with a rationalization—"I did them yesterday, and I'll do them tomorrow"—and so we don't do them. But, in contrast to our actions, we have no more control over our emotional feelings than over our bodily feelings, such as hunger or thirst.

A single serial processor, such as the one in my computer, cannot be in a conflict. But, a parallel system can be in conflict, and so the controller at the top of the hierarchy in the brain can be in a conflict with other processors. It says, in effect: *don't laugh, it's rude.* But other processors lower down in the hierarchy say *that's funny, laugh.* The conflict is not resolved by a conscious act of the controller, but by the architecture of the system, that is, by interactions among its processors. They can excite one another, recruiting "like-minded" processors; and they can inhibit opposing processors. A set of processors can be interconnected with both excitatory and inhibitory links, and the whole system may take several iterations of signaling before it settles down, one way or another, in a stable way. Which way it goes depends on several factors. Our age matters: infants and children do not suppress behaviors for the sake of social decorum. But we also differ from one another. And we ourselves differ from one occasion to another. As the great French poet Paul Valéry remarked, cognition reigns but it does not rule. The controller is not in complete control, and thus the road to hell is paved with good intentions.

* * *

The brain contains a hierarchy of processors that operate in parallel. An advantage of parallelism is that it allows slow processors to deliver fast responses by sharing out the work to be done among them. This design doesn't eliminate the intractability of certain problems, but it allows the brain to deal with vastly more information than our working memory can hold. But, working memory allows powerful computations to be carried out on the limited information that it holds. An advantage of a hierarchical organization is that the overall controller copes with the "big picture". In order to do so, however, it needs access to a model of the system as a whole. Like all models, it is incomplete and likely to be erroneous. Yet, it enables us to act in intentional ways—in the light of our knowledge that we can act intentionally.

The hierarchical architecture implies the existence of a split between conscious and unconscious behavior. We cannot be aware of the operations of low-level processes. There are behaviors, such as smiling or the switching of attention, which can be conscious or unconscious. Some aspects of mental life, notably emotions, are outside conscious control. As a result, conflicts can occur between voluntary and involuntary behaviors. Unconscious processes cannot use working memory, and so they have limited computational abilities to process their vast amounts of information. Quite what they are able to do is the topic of the next chapter.

Chapter 5

Intuitions and Unconscious Reasoning

And all our intuitions mock

The formal logic of the clock.

Auden

The camel-tracker I described in Chapter 1 made a series of extraordinary inferences. From an examination of the tracks of the camels, he inferred the number of camels that had passed by, the tribe of their riders, that three camels had been stolen from another tribe, the starting point of the journey, and where the camels had been watered. These were conscious inferences from signs in the tracks, and they led to conscious conclusions. For simplicity, I'll call them "conscious" inferences, and just to be certain that I'm not confusing you with terminology, I use "inference" and "reasoning" as partners to one another: reasoning yields inferences, and inferences depend on reasoning.

When *we* make more commonplace inferences, such as:

The notebook is in my room or it is in the restaurant.

In fact, it isn't in the restaurant.

Therefore, it is in my room.

We too make a conscious inference that yields a conscious conclusion. What the camel tracker's and our inferences have in common is that they depend on unconscious processes. All conscious thinking does. The process that leads the tracker to infer the identity of the tribesman is unconscious. He looks at the tracks and identifies them. He is aware of his premises, which include his knowledge of the different sorts of tracks that camels make, but how he combines them to infer that the riders were Awamir is outside his conscious awareness. We also are not aware of how we made a conscious inference about the notebook. We don't know how we built a mental representation of the premises, or of how we used it to formulate a conclusion. What we are aware of is our attempt to reason, the significance of the sentences, the conclusion that seems to follow, a visual image if we relied on one, and perhaps the relative difficulty of the task. In terms of the architecture in the brain, our awareness corresponds to the *outputs* of a few processors at the top of the hierarchy. We can explain why our conclusion follows from the premises. We can draw a diagram of the two possible locations of the notebook, and explain why, given the premise that rules out one of them, it follows that it must be in the other one. Even the construction of this explanation relies on unconscious processes, and sometimes an explanation may be a rationalization rather than a reflection of our real reasoning. Yet, when we think aloud while we reason, our awareness appears to be a genuine description of the sequence of thoughts that unconscious processes construct.

A corollary of the theory of mental architecture is that all inferences depend on unconscious processes. Hence, in principle, there are four sorts of inference, because inferences can begin consciously or unconsciously, and their conclusions can be conscious or unconscious. But, could an inference be initiated consciously, and yet have only an unconscious conclusion? Perhaps. The best example is a case of emotional "leakage" in which we are aware, say, that we are angry and suppressing its overt signs, but unaware that for a brief moment our facial expression has betrayed our true feelings. The other three sorts of inference do also occur. The camel tracker's inference and our inference about the notebook are instances of conscious inferences. But what about inferences that are wholly unconscious and inferences that are initiated unconsciously but that yield conscious conclusions? I will present examples of each of them as a precursor to an analysis of unconscious reasoning.

* * *

Some inferences are wholly unconscious. They are initiated unconsciously, carried out unconsciously, and yield unconscious conclusions. You might wonder how psychologists have detected their occurrence. The answer is that these inferences affect our behavior without our realizing it. A number of studies have demonstrated their effects, and I will describe two striking ones.

John Bargh and his colleagues carried out a marvelous experiment of this sort. The participants had a test of their language proficiency in which they had to make up sentences from lists of words. For example, they had to use four of these words to make a sentence:

be will sweat lonely they

Hence, they might respond:

> They will be lonely.

The participants made up a series of thirty sentences in this way. And that, for them, was the end of the experiment. The lists of words, however, contained many words that suggest the stereotype of elderly individuals, e.g., "lonely" in the list above, and other words such as, "old" and "gray". As psychologists say, these words *prime* the stereotype, that is, make it more active even if the participants are not aware of its activity. After the experiment was over, the participants walked down the corridor to the elevator. Those who had received the primes to old age walked at a slower pace than those who had carried out a similar sentence-making test that did not prime old age. Yet, the slow walkers were neither aware of the primes to old age, which contained no words referring to slowness, nor of the effects of these primes on their behavior. And, as a subsequent study showed, the primes did not affect their emotions, at least not in a conscious way. You might say that they haven't made a proper inference, but an unconscious association. I won't argue with you; but in a moment I will try to pin down the nature of the underlying mental process.

Another brilliant illustration of wholly unconscious inferences occurs in Claude Steele's studies of stereotypes. The mere act of identifying our own membership in a group can influence our performance in a test. If we have to identify ourselves as members of a minority, such as African Americans, who have a stereotype of poor performance on the Graduate Record Examination, then we tend to score less well on this exam than if we have not had to identify ourselves. Women likewise do less well on a test of mathematical ability when their gender is primed. When we face a challenge, the mere threat of conforming to a negative stereotype impairs our performance. The effect, which is robust and reliable, is not one of which we are aware.

Could an unconscious inference yield a different conclusion from one that we are conscious of? The question arises because we take longer when we have to classify something that goes against a stereotype, e.g., it takes us a fifth of a second longer to associate "female" with "entrepreneur" than to associate "male" with "entrepreneur". These differences are malleable, but with certain contents they develop at a young age. For some individuals, the results are in line with their conscious attitudes; for other individuals, they come as a shock. They show, for example, that those of us who are white tend to associate "blacks" with words denoting bad qualities to a greater degree than we associate "whites" with such words. And the effect may occur even though, as far as we know, we don't have racial prejudices. Do we have an unconscious prejudice? Perhaps. But, "prejudice" may be too strong a word. We show comparable effects when we associate "birds" with good words to a greater degree than "trees". The phenomenon seems to concern broad evaluative categories rather than our *moral* attitudes to individuals.

* * *

Inferences can occur at so low a level in the hierarchy that the premises for the conclusion may be inaccessible to us. As in the judgments of the pairs of photographs in the previous chapter, the conclusions don't even seem to be the result of inferences. Unconscious reasoning of this sort yields conscious judgments, but we cannot explain our reasons for them, or else we have to try to reconstruct reasons, with the danger that we'll rationalize. These unconscious inferences underlie hunches, intuitions, gut reactions, guesses, and insights. As we'll see, they often yield emotional reactions, but they also occur when we have to control complex systems containing more variables than we can handle consciously, such as a computer simulation of a town. I'll use *intuition* to refer to inferences of this sort in which we are aware of a conclusion or judgment but not of its premises.

Many intuitive inferences occur in everyday life. Peirce, the logician, had his overcoat and an expensive watch stolen from his cabin on a ship. He quizzed the likely suspects among the crew, and identified the thief, but he couldn't explain the reasons for his identification. Yet, he was right, and later he recovered his stolen property. Of course, not all of our hunches are correct, but, as Peirce pointed out, we are right more often than chance warrants.

You yourself may have the intuition from reading this chapter so far that unconscious reasoning is about people. Indeed, some psychologists have argued that personality traits are the hinge on which these inferences swing. But, they haven't always tested whether comparable inferences occur in other domains. In fact, we also reason unconsciously about inanimate entities. If we are experts in some domain, say, fire-fighting or the attribution of paintings, we form immediate impressions of fires or pictures. We decide how to tackle the fire, or who painted the picture, almost without having to think about it.

A classic experiment demonstrating the growth of intuitions is due to Clark L. Hull. The participants saw a series of Chinese ideograms, and their task was to learn a nonsense name for each of them. They carried out the task for several sets of ideograms. Each set was different and presented in a different random order, but the same names applied from one set to the next. The participants learned to anticipate the correct name for each ideogram, and yet they were unable to explain why the names were correct. In fact, an underlying shape—a "radical"—was common to all the ideograms with the same name, but masked by other elements in them.

Norman Maier carried out another classic study of intuition in which unconscious reasoning led to a conscious conclusion. The participants' task was to tie together two ropes hanging from the ceiling of a room. There was just one snag. When they held one rope and walked towards the other, they were unable to reach it. It is easy enough to think of some solutions, e.g., tie one rope to a chair and then bring the other rope to it. One particular solution, however, calls for an insight that eluded most participants. The trick was to set one rope swinging, and to catch it while holding the other rope. Some of the participants saw the experimenter walk across the room and accidentally (on purpose) brush against one of the ropes to set it swinging. These participants tended to have the crucial insight. After the experiment was over, only one of them could remember the clue that the experimenter had given them. The others came up with all sorts of rationalizations for their discovery of the solution without mentioning the clue. They had made an unconscious inference from its occurrence without realizing it. When we have to think aloud as we try to solve problems that depend on such an insight, we are less likely to succeed. It's like thinking about how to tie our shoelaces as we tie them. We get ourselves in knots.

Here is an easy inference for you to make:

> If he put the sculpture on the flimsy table next to the door then it will have collapsed.
>
> He did put it on the table.
>
> What happened?

You inferred, I expect, that the table collapsed. But, did you make any other inferences? You may think that you didn't; but you're wrong. You were aware of their results, but not that you had inferred them. You inferred that "it" in the first sentence referred to the table, not the sculpture or the door. You inferred that "it" in the second sentence referred to the sculpture, not the door. These unconscious inferences prepared the way for your conscious inference that it was the table, not the sculpture, that collapsed.

Just as there are experts such as the camel tracker, who can describe the premises of their inferences, so there are other experts who have no access to the basis of their expertise. Here is one example. Avid listeners to music can recognize the composer of a piece of music even if they have never heard the particular composition before. That's Mozart, they say, or that's Gershwin. They recognize the sequences of notes in a melody as characteristic of a particular musician. Like the participants in Hull's ideogram experiment, they have learned to recognize a musician's style without a conscious access to the principles underlying their ability.

In summary, unconscious reasoning occurs in at least three ways. It can be unconscious as a whole and influence our behavior outside our awareness. It can yield intuitions that we are aware of, though we are unaware of inferring them. And it underpins even the simplest of our conscious inferences.

* * *

The theory of mental architecture constrains the power of unconscious reasoning. It cannot use working memory. Working memory, you may recall, is where we hold things in mind while we work on them. It is the heart of computational power, because it holds the results of intermediate computations. So, what can the unconscious inferential system do?

Here is a way to think about it, which I have borrowed from Michael Frayn's satirical novel, *The Tin Men*. The novelist's protagonist, Goldwasser, is an English journalist who imagines that hackneyed articles might as well be written by computers. If he has to write yet another story about a Royal Occasion, then the whole piece will be a cliché from one end to the other. He imagines a way in which it could be done using a series of file cards. Suppose he has to write a story about a Royal wedding. He takes out the first card, and it says: "Traditionally". He selects next a card appropriate for weddings, and it says, "weddings are occasions for rejoicing". The alternatives are sequences of cards covering stories on *coronations, engagements, funerals, comings of age, births, deaths,* and *the churching of women*. If he had been writing about a funeral, then he might have chosen instead a card bearing, "are occasions for mourning". The next card for weddings says, "The wedding of X and Y". It leads to a choice between, "is no exception", and "is a case in point". At this point, there is no choice, the next card says: "indeed." Whatever the story is about it always reaches this particular juncture. And so in this way, choosing at random among alternative cards, Goldwasser can string together the rest of the story:

> It is a particularly happy occasion. Rarely can there have been a more popular couple. X has won himself a special place in the nation's affections, and the British people have taken Y to their hearts already. It is especially fitting that … etc. etc. etc.

You will notice that the system depends on the contents of a long-term memory—the phrases on the file cards. It could be organized so that it didn't even have to remember whether a male or female personage was the topic of the current sentence. There could be separate sequences of cards, one for males, one for females, and one for couples. So, if a sentence began, "Charles has won himself", there would be a sequence in which the pronouns were "he";

if it began "Camilla", there would be a sequence in which the pronouns were "she"; and if it began, "The happy couple," there would be a sequence in which the pronouns were "they". This system avoids the need for working memory to keep track of gender and number.

Without working memory, our unconscious system for intuitive inferences has an analogous organization. At each choice point, the system is in a particular state in which it can carry out one of a set of alternative operations, which each produce a single output. Each state of the system allows a choice akin to one among alternative phrases in a Royal story, but our unconscious system can remain in the same state to carry out one of the same set of operations, or shift to another state. Unlike Goldwasser's system, it can even cycle back to an earlier state in the sequence. It comes to a halt—perhaps with some output to another system—when there is no state to which it can make a transition. It then remains in a hiatus until it is jolted into a new state by an input from elsewhere in the hierarchy of processors.

Our unconscious system can make a transition to one of a number of possible new states, and the choice may not be fixed by the current state, just as Goldwasser made random choices among alternatives. Some transitions, however, may be more likely than others. Indeed, the probabilities may depend on the recent history of states through which the system has passed. Mathematicians refer to systems of this sort as "k-limited Markov finite-state automata", which is a bit of a mouthful. (Andrei Markov, a Russian mathematician, studied these systems.) For simplicity, I'll just refer to a process of *transitions* from one state to another.

The biggest difference between Goldwasser's file cards and our unconscious system is that in our system the transitions are likely to be constrained by content rather than words or phrases. If the system is prompted by the proposition, say, *they will be lonely*, its content can match many other representations in long-term memory, and in this way prime the concept of *elderly persons*. If a transition yields a conclusion, then a further transition can yield another conclusion, and so on in a stream of conclusions that are simple ascriptions of properties or instructions for behavior. The content of each conclusion can instantiate other concepts or principles in long-term memory.

If the system has no access to working memory, then unconscious inferences will lack the computational power of conscious reasoning. They won't cope with the alternative possibilities of a disjunction, with comparisons between possibilities—such as alternative future events, or sequential possibilities in a temporal order, or comparisons between the facts of the matter and an alternative history in which other events occurred. They won't cope with propositions that concern only some members of a set, e.g., "Some frightening things are dangerous". They won't cope with relations that hold among multiple entities. They won't count beyond a small number. They won't carry out a specified sequence of operations in a reverse order. They won't embed one sequence of operations within another sequence, and so on in an indefinite way. Hence, they won't establish long-range dependencies within long-range dependencies. The system of file cards can make sure that the right pronouns are used in a story about Charles, but they cannot create a story that includes embedded within it another story about Camilla, which in turn includes one about Prince Harry, and so on. Our unconscious inferences will be similarly constrained, because such "embeddings" call for a working memory. Unconscious reasoning will concern one possibility at a time, typically one that is here and now. It will lead from one possibility to another, and rely on access to certain general concepts and principles in long-term memory, which I'll come to in a moment. Only if intermediate conclusions become conscious will our reasoning overcome the limitations that I have listed here. But, working memory has its limitations too, and so our conscious reasoning is human, not superhuman.

When we recognize a musical style, we appear to rely on transitions. I wrote a computer program that *learned* the transitions of pitches and durations—one pair jointly to the next pair—from a corpus of musical improvizations. It then used these transitions to generate new improvizations. They were identifiable simulations of an individual musician's style. The improvization of melodies does not seem to need working memory, though it is needed to cope with the large-scale structure of composed music. Musical notation, however, can function as a substitute for working memory.

We also appear to rely on transitions to identify who painted a particular picture. Connoisseurs can identify a picture as a Picasso or a Monet even if they have never seen it before, and they can do so without being able to articulate the cues they use. That such a skill does not depend on the computational power of working memory is corroborated by the ability of pigeons as art connoisseurs. They learned to distinguish between paintings by Monet and by Picasso. Their skill also extended to paintings that they had never seen before. And, when they saw pictures by new painters they made sensible attributions. Given a Renoir or a Cezanne, they judged it to be a Monet. Given a Matisse or Braque, however, they judged it to be a Picasso. They therefore showed some appreciation of the lineages of Impressionism and early twentieth century art.

Another clue to reasoning without working memory comes from studies of infants, who have very limited working memories. As Gary Marcus has shown in a brilliant study of seven-month-old infants, they can generalize to all instances of an abstract category. The infants heard a series of utterances, such as: "ga na ga," and: "li ti li". The utterances all conformed to the abstract structure ABA, where each letter denotes a syllable. Other infants in the experiment heard utterances that all had the structure, ABB, e.g., "wo fe fe". After listening to two minutes' worth of these utterances, the infants heard utterances made up from novel syllables that were not used in the training session. Half of the utterances were consistent with the structure of the earlier sentences, and half were not. For example, the utterance: "wo fe fe," would be inconsistent with the ABA structure. The children paid more attention to the novel utterances that were inconsistent with the abstract structure that they had acquired during the training phase. Hence, the infants generalized that structure to all possible syllables including those that they had not heard before in the experiment. This result challenges theories of learning that represent relations only between particular syllables, and that lack the power to generalize to all syllables of any sort.

Some transitions yield emotions. For example, the unconscious system evaluates a situation as dangerous, and then makes a transition to an emotion. You see something dangerous, such as a car spinning out of control in front of you. And you feel frightened and take evasive action. In effect, the system has made this inference:

> That is dangerous.
>
> Therefore, that is frightening.

But, instead of a conclusion, you have an emotion, and carry out an action. One corollary is that we can be aware of the cause of the emotion, the spinning car, and of the fear itself. But, we cannot be aware of the transition from one to the other. I will come back to this point when I deal with emotions in the next chapter.

* * *

Our system of unconscious inferences depends on long-term memories. They are likely to be principles of general knowledge that we've acquired from induction. But the principles themselves may be unconscious—like the transitions that the music critic has acquired for Mozartian melodies. Other aspects of our general knowledge may be in the form of mental models of how the world works. And as you will see later in the book, we can stitch together a causal account of an event from these elementary links in our general knowledge. We can use them to make a series of elementary inferences, e.g.:

> Viv insulted Pat.
>
> So, Pat got angry.

So, Pat lost her temper.

So, Pat was rude.

Our intuitions based on unconscious inferences can conflict with conscious inferences. For instance, consider this problem:

We're all prejudiced against prejudiced people.

Anne is prejudiced against Beth.

So, does it follow that Chuck is prejudiced against Di?

Our intuition is: no, of course not, because nothing has been said about Chuck or Di. But, our conscious ability allows us to follow this argument: Granted that Anne is prejudiced against Beth, Anne is a prejudiced person and so we're all prejudiced against her. But, if so, then Di is prejudiced against her, and so Di is a prejudiced person. So, we're all prejudiced against Di and that implies that Chuck is prejudiced against her too. The inference depends on a loop of repeated operations to keep updating our model of the situation, and such loops depend on working memory. Back in the 1960s, advertisers experimented with subliminal advertising, flashing brief pictures in movies to encourage spectators to buy sodas. It didn't work. The inferences we need to make to decide to buy a Coke go beyond the power of our unconscious reasoning. They call for planning a sequence of interdependent actions, and plans of this sort depend on working memory.

* * *

Transitions rely in part on general principles in long-term knowledge. These principles tend to be *heuristics*—simple rules of thumb that are easy for transitions to use. Their content is revealed in those inferences that are rapid, automatic, and involuntary. Here are three different examples:

We hear a loud explosion. We infer that something caused it.

We grasp someone by the shoulders and they cry out. We infer that we have hurt them.

One object collides with another, which starts to move. We infer that the first object caused the movement of the second object. We make this inference if the timing of the events is appropriate, even when we know that we're watching a computer display.

These inferences depend on a set of causal principles embodied in the unconscious system:

- ◆ Every event has a cause.
- ◆ Moving objects are causes.

- ◆ Humans and other animals can initiate causes.
- ◆ Causes are in physical contact with their effects.
- ◆ Similar causes have similar effects.

These principles may seem reasonable, but when we examine them close up, some of them are quite suspect. So, why do we have them? And why do we have other analogous principles that enable us to make inferences about intentional actions and social interactions? The answer may be that we are equipped with them, because we often have to induce causal relations, and induction calls for us to go beyond the information given to us. The induction of correct causal relations is intractable: the number of possible inductive hypotheses grows at an exponential rate with the number of concepts that may be relevant. But, we don't know which concepts *are* relevant, and so it is easy to invoke erroneous ones. Hence, constraints on the search for possible causes help us, and the causal heuristics above are often useful.

One manifestation of the heuristic constraints is in what anthropologists refer to as "magical" thinking. It yields erroneous conceptions of cause and effect. *Contagious* magic ascribes causation to physical contact. For example, fishes' tails shake, so if we eat fish, we will shake. The woodcarvers on the Pacific island of Kitawa therefore do not eat fish, because they don't want their hands to shake when they carve. That similar things behave in similar ways lies at the root of another species of magical thinking, so-called *homeopathic* magic. People who live in slums are bad—at the very least they are poor and that is bad, and so their behavior is bad—they are immoral. Hence, God punishes their wickedness with diseases such as cholera. Similarity as a basis for inference leads to a conception of "action at a distance"—no matter that this principle is inconsistent with causation by contact. I want to harm my enemy, and so I make an effigy of him and stick pins in it. The result is that my enemy feels pain. When George Orwell was a schoolboy, he and a friend made a wax model of another boy whom they hated. They broke the arm off the model. A few weeks later, the boy broke his arm, and not long afterwards he died from a fatal disease. Orwell and his friend were overcome with guilt. A recent biographer suggests that part of the reason that Orwell wrote under a pseudonym (his real name was Eric Blair) was because he feared that people who knew his real name could work magic on him too.

Contagious and homeopathic magic can work in concert. An African tribe, the Azande, observed a striking behavior of the red bush monkey. When it wakes up, it stretches itself as though it were having an epileptic seizure, but then recovers. The Azande reasoned that a cure for epilepsy should work in the same way. Those suffering from the disease should eat the ashes of a monkey's skull. Causation by contact would give them the monkey's powers. Similar causes have similar effects, and so now they too would recover.

Magical thinking constrains induction, and so it occurs in all cultures including our own. Alien people's magical thinking is conspicuous, but our own is harder to perceive, because we have used it to induce our beliefs. Nevertheless, we don't have to look far to find examples of magical thinking in our own culture. The tendency to ascribe causation to physical contact can be overwhelming. We press a key on our computer and the screen goes dark. We infer that the cause was pressing the key. Perhaps it was. But, we may discover later that the battery in the computer was dying, and as a result the computer shut itself down.

An excellent example of Western magical thinking is the use of electro-convulsive therapy (ECT) to cure depression. Doctors observed that epileptics seldom suffer from schizophrenia. They reasoned that schizophrenia might be alleviated if they induced epileptic fits in patients—a step that parallels the Azande's thinking. They therefore induced epilepsy in their patients by using ECT. The treatment didn't work. But, the physicians noticed that it did alleviate depression, and so it became a standard method of treatment for severe cases. It even worked when, unknown to the doctors in a London hospital, the ECT machine was broken and malfunctioned.

* * *

The theory of mental architecture allows that inferences can be initiated either consciously or unconsciously. Conscious inferences, of course, are never *wholly* conscious. We cannot introspect on the processes leading from the premises to the conclusion: if we could, then these processes would not be mysterious. Conscious inferences, however, do have access to working memory to hold the results of intermediate computations. In contrast, guesses, hunches, and intuitions emerge from unconscious inferences, which are crude, because they are made without access to working memory. The unconscious system makes transitions based on simplistic principles. It enables us to make intuitive judgments about danger, attraction, and character. These judgments are rapid and compelling. Some theorists have therefore supposed that we are equipped with an innate toolbox of "fast and frugal heuristics". And some have even supposed that we have no other way to reason. Yet, we shouldn't be too impressed by unconscious reasoning. It is also the source of magical thinking.

Unconscious reasoning enables us to infer causal relations based on constraints, such as: similar causes have similar effects. We see something threatening, and almost before we have become aware of it, low-level processors are preparing us for defense. What differs from one unconscious inference to another is not the process, but its contents. The generalizations on which the system relies can be a result of experience. We can acquire them without knowing what they are. To revert to my earlier example, we can learn to recognize a musician's style without ever having been aware of the principles we use.

Unconscious inferences can bias our behavior without our being aware of them. Likewise, we may make an inference without knowing its grounds. It was a quick intuitive guess. Intuitions are useful, and they are intriguing because they seem to come from nowhere and yet be helpful. Imagine that you're trying to make a choice among, say, a set of four cars. You have access to descriptions of various aspects of them, such as their gas mileage, age, and other such attributes. Conscious reasoning is fine as long as there aren't too many attributes to take into account. But, if you have information about a dozen attributes of each car, it will take you a long time to make a sensible choice. Indeed, a study has shown that you tend to make a wiser choice if you are prevented from thinking—at least in contrast to having only a few minutes to think. Subsequent surveys of shoppers showed that they rated themselves as happier with their choices if they had thought with care about buying goods, such as oven mitts, with only a few pertinent attributes. But, for those purchases with many pertinent attributes, such as computers, they were happier the less they had thought about them.

Such studies are open to misinterpretation. Experts can make intuitive decisions in a blink—to use the title of Malcolm Gladwell's provocative book on the topic. Unconscious processes can take into account a vast amount of information because they are carried out in parallel. But, as I've argued, the procedures that they carry out are computationally trivial because they have no access to working memory. Conscious reasoning can carry out more powerful processes, but it cannot take into account vast amounts of information. It is easily swamped. You may want to switch off your conscious deliberations in such a case. If the task is one in which there is no single right answer and an approximation suffices, it may not harm to let your mind go blank—to use the title of Noah Tall's parody of *Blink*, and in his words to exploit the power of not actually thinking at all. But, beware. Unconscious inferences are quite inadequate for many tasks. They are not enough for running a nuclear power station or for solving the sorts of problems that I discuss later in the book, such as the breaking of the Nazi's Enigma code in World War II. These problems call for conscious reasoning, and so expert reasoners learn to treat their intuitions with some skepticism.

Chapter 6

Emotions as Inferences

signals of interrogation, friendship, threat and
appeasement, instantly taken in, seldom, if ever,
misread.

Auden

Human reasoning is of limited power. This claim may seem extraordinary in
the light of what it has achieved—from a deep understanding of the physical
world to the potential solution of many of humanity's problems. Yet, it is
limited in comparison with the superhuman intelligence that I have invoked
from time to time. Indeed, we confront inferential problems that would defeat
even this powerful being in their computational demands. Reasoning with
multiple premises containing *if*'s, *and*'s and *or*'s, as I have remarked before,
is intractable. Another source of intractability is our need to juggle multiple
goals and beliefs, which are not always compatible with each other. And still
another source is our need to coordinate our actions with one another. I email
you to invite you to lunch next Tuesday; you email me accepting. I email you
back so that you know that I've received your acceptance; otherwise, you might
think that it got lost in cyberspace, and that I won't expect you for lunch. You
email me back so that I know that you know that I've received your acceptance.
Perhaps, I should email you so that you know that I know that you know
that I've received your acceptance. In fact, only those of us punctilious to
the point of paranoia proceed to this interminable round of emails. But the
task of co-ordination gets even worse if several of us are trying to schedule an
appointment in this way. These problems can all grow to a size that defeats any
computational system. Our reasoning *is* limited in power.

The vital problems that we must solve boil down to those created in our
internal environment, such as fatigue and pain, those created in our physical
environment, such as the need for food and shelter, and those created in our
social environment, such as the desire for a mate and for offspring. We cope,
and yet we make appalling reasoning errors in the psychological laboratory.

We sometimes make them in real life too, though it is not polite to mention this fact in the company of psychologists who believe that we are rational in daily life. This discrepancy between our knowledge and our performance is the fundamental paradox of rationality. On the one hand, we can understand the principles of rationality—the canons of logic and the calculus of probabilities. On the other hand, we fail to live up to them. The resolution of the paradox is straightforward: the process of understanding principles is tractable, whereas the work of following them is not.

* * *

If someone insults us, then, as Aristotle remarked, we may have an emotional reaction. We understand the insult and that it threatens our self-respect (a cognitive evaluation), various changes occur in our brain (neurophysiological processes) and, as a result, hormones released into our bloodstream prepare us for action and our heart pumps faster (somatic changes), we feel anger mounting within us (a subjective feeling); we grimace in anger (a facial expression), and we say something rude in reply (an action). A typical emotional experience therefore brings together thoughts, feelings, bodily changes, and behaviors. Just which elements of this experience are an "emotion" is a matter about which theorists squabble. They also squabble about the causal relations among the various components. William James, for instance, argued that we don't run away because we're frightened: we're frightened because we run away. Emotions, he thought, arise as a consequence of bodily responses. This back-to-front view, however, is contrary to common sense and to the psychological evidence. Individuals in a total paralysis still experience emotions.

Emotions are a meeting place of mind, body, and behavior. In a complete emotion, we have a subjective feeling, we're aware of its cause, we experience bodily changes as a consequence of our *autonomic* nervous system, and we may make various expressions, gestures, and actions. The autonomic nervous system controls various organs, such as the glands that release hormones into our bloodstream, and the central nervous system controls our behavior.

Emotions are puzzling. For instance, what function do they serve? Some authors regard them as useless, as an irrelevant mental organ that gets inflamed for no good reason just as the appendix does. For many philosophies and religions, emotions are to be avoided—Plato, the Stoics, the Russian mystic Gurdjieff, have all inveighed against them as disruptions of rationality. Tibetan Buddhists don't have a concept of emotions equivalent to ours, but they argue that hatred is destructive, whereas true enlightenment yields a profound happiness and a loving kindness. Jean-Paul Sartre, the existentialist philosopher, argued that when we experience an emotion, we are engaging in nothing more than wishful thinking. Yet, the fact that all social mammals appear to have emotions suggests that they do have a function.

Another puzzle is why we are conscious of our feelings. We are not aware of the release of hormones or of other somatic changes. We are not always aware of our facial expressions, and we cannot reproduce voluntarily a proper smile, at least one that would fool an expert. Yet, we are aware that we are happy, sad, angry, or frightened. We may even be aware of these feelings without knowing what caused them.

I want to propose a solution to these puzzles, and to show how emotions and reasoning affect one another. My plan is to follow the course of emotions in our minds. They are created by cognitive evaluations, which can be rudimentary and unconscious or complex and conscious. We can reason ourselves into an emotion. We can even reason ourselves into an emotion about imaginary events. Once we feel an emotion, however, it affects our thinking. In this way, we are open to what engineers refer to as "positive feedback". A certain thought yields an emotion, the emotion makes us think some more, the thinking increases the emotion, and so we think still more, and so on, to the point that the circle may turn into a vicious spiral. The emotion takes over our mental life and governs what we do. More on this topic in the next chapter.

* * *

Charles Darwin wrote in his classic book, *The Expression of the Emotions in Man and Animals*:

> The power of communication between the members of the same tribe by means of language has been of paramount importance in the development of man; and the force of language is much aided by the expressive movements of the face and body.

A "communicative" theory, which Keith Oatley and I formulated, takes this remark as its starting point, and postulates that emotions are communications among members of the same species, in which one of a small set of mutually exclusive signals conveys an individual's emotional state. Other species may also be sensitive to these signals. Dogs, for example, appear to pick up some of their owners' emotions. The signals that communicate emotions are innate, and hence universal to all human cultures: facial expressions of emotion are the same the world over. Their interpretation is very different from the interpretation of language. The meaning of a sentence is composed from the meanings of its parts according to the grammatical relations among them. That is why the interpretation of sentences calls for working memory. The meaning of a facial expression is not composed from the separate meanings of what the lips, eyebrows, cheeks, signify. These elements all contribute to a distinctive signal

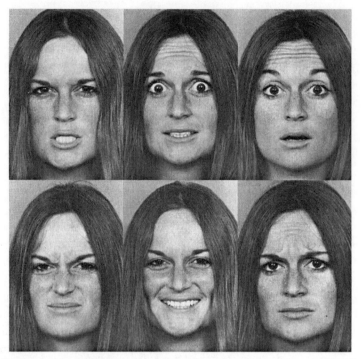

Fig. 6.1 Six facial expressions of emotions (Copyright P. Ekman and W.V. Friesen, Consulting Psychologists Press, Palo Alto, CA).

of an emotion, akin to the various signals of alarm, threat, and submission that other social mammals make. Their interpretation is carried out unconsciously in specialized regions of the brain. If photographs of different emotions are jumbled up so that, say, the eyes are from an expression of happiness, but the lips are from an expression of anger, and so on, the end result is a chimera—an odd and unreadable expression. I found some photographs of facial expressions of emotion on the website of Paul Ekman, who is the world's leading researcher of the subject, and Figure 6.1 presents them. I edited them to produce chimeras. Figure 6.2 presents two examples and, as you'll see, the expressions are weird.

To understand the next assumption of the communicative theory, you need to recall the overall architecture of the mind, which I described at the start of this part of the book. The brain has a modular structure that is hierarchical in form, and consciousness is akin to an operating system that has some control of the modules, but that may conflict with them. Certain modules can communicate meaningful propositions or models of them. The communicative theory, however, postulates an alternative, evolutionarily older, and cruder form of internal communication: a small set of mutually exclusive signals

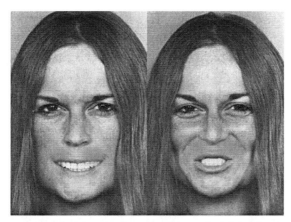

Fig. 6.2 Two anomalous facial expressions. The face on the left has lips from the happy expression in the previous figure imposed on the angry face in the figure, and the face on the right has lips from the angry expression in the previous figure on the happy face from the previous figure.

propagate from one module to another. These signals are simple. Like facial expressions, they do not require working memory for their interpretation, because their meanings are not composed from the meanings of their parts. They are instinctive and distinctive. One set of these signals are bodily feelings such as hunger and thirst. They reflect the monitoring of the internal environment. Another set of these signals are *basic* emotions. They speed through the brain to direct attention, to mobilize innate bodily resources, and to prepare an appropriate suite of behaviors. The signal begins with a cognitive evaluation, which may or may not yield a conscious message, and a key link in the chain is an unconscious *transition* to the emotional signal. (The transition is a Markov transition of the sort that I described in the previous chapter.) Hence, our emotions are a primitive sort of unconscious reasoning that issues, not in conclusions, but signals.

Emotional signals help us to co-ordinate our multiple goals and plans, given the constraints of time pressure and of our limited intellectual resources. They can arise at junctures in the execution of plans. They are a more flexible control system than innate reflexes, such as eye blinks. But, they are more rapid than conscious reasoning, because they make no demands on working memory.

The experience of emotion depends on whether the emotional signal and the cognitive message become conscious. If the signal becomes conscious, it creates a distinctive emotional feeling. This feeling is common to any sort of situation that gives rise to the emotion. If we're dangling from a rope on the side of a mountain, about to make a speech in public for the first time, or

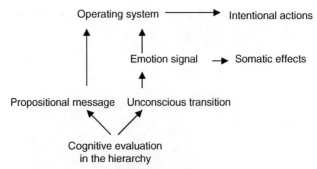

Fig. 6.3 A schematic diagram of the two channels of communication in emotion.

dealing with a violent person, we feel fear—and the feeling, if we divorce it from the cognitive evaluation, is much the same in these cases, differing only in its intensity. If the message becomes conscious, we know the cause of our emotion. Typically, we are aware of both the signal and of the message. But, what we cannot be aware of is the transition creating the emotion. Hence, introspection can tell us, say, that we're angry because someone insulted us, but it cannot reveal the transition from the evaluation to the emotion. That is why our emotional reactions to music without words are so mysterious. We know that music caused the emotion, but we don't understand why. Figure 6.3 is a diagram summarizing the organization of the emotional system in terms of the two channels of communication.

The communicative theory allows for dissociations between the emotional signal and the cognitive message. The emotion may be unconscious even though the cognitive message impinges on consciousness. Hence, we may be unaware of our full emotional state, and may even experience an emotional "numbness" or an almost pathological lack of feeling. You might suppose that this doctrine is Freudian, but it isn't. Freud went out of his way to deny that emotions could be unconscious. In the other case, we are unaware of the cognitive evaluation, and so we feel an emotion, but we don't know its cause. We say, for example:

I feel happy but I don't know why.

Different emotions *feel* different even when we don't know their causes.

The communicative theory distinguishes between *basic* emotions and *complex* emotions. Basic emotions are innate and have their own distinctive signals in the brain and in universal facial expressions. They include *happiness, sadness, anger, fear,* and *disgust.* The amygdala, two small organs on either side of the brain beneath the cortices, to which they are connected, are critical for basic emotions. They activate the release of hormones, the suppression of pain, and various responses in the autonomic nervous system that prepare the body for emergencies. Damage to the amygdala impairs basic emotions in rats, in monkeys, and in us. It also impairs our ability to recognize facial expressions of emotions.

The prediction of two separate channels of communication—a rapid signal of an emotion, and a slower cognitive message—has been corroborated in the case of the basic emotion of fear. Joseph LeDoux, a distinguished neuroscientist, has shown that there are two separate pathways for perceptual information to reach the amygdala. One route is rapid. It goes from the sensory thalamus—a way-station for perceptual information—straight to the amygdala. It bypasses the cortex, and so it depends on a crude cognitive analysis that can elicit the signal. The other route is slower. It goes from the sensory thalamus to the cortex and then to the amygdala. It is the route that the message about the cognitive evaluation takes. The relative independence of the signals and messages is borne out by clinical observations. A condition known as "encephalitis lethargica" leads patients to know what emotions they ought to be experiencing, but not to feel them. The message system works but not the signal system. A condition known as "alexithymia" leads patients to have feelings, but not to be able to articulate them. The signal system works but not the message system.

If emotions have a communicative function, then basic emotions must map a diversity of possible situations into a few distinct signals, which relate to significant entities in the life of the species. The theory postulates that the set of basic emotions, their somatic consequences, and their expressive correlates, are innate and universal. They relate to the goals of human beings, which I summarize in Box 6.1 together with examples of the feelings and emotions that they elicit. The emotions are universal, but culture influences the cognitive evaluations giving rise to them.

Some basic emotions can be experienced for no known reason, e.g., happiness and sadness, and anger and fear. Other basic emotions have a known object. They include sexual love, disgust, hatred, the emotion of children's attachment to their care-givers, and the reciprocal emotion of parental care. The emotional signal that propagates in the brain depends on linking the emotion to the representation of an object. We cannot experience, say, disgust without an object for the emotion.

Unconscious inferences that underlie magical thinking, which I discussed earlier, make transitions to emotions. Paul Rozin, the doyen of disgust, has demonstrated their effects. Suppose I offer you a drink in a new and unused bottle for urine samples. Would you drink it? Probably not; most people wouldn't. The function of the bottle is "contagious" and contaminates it. How would you fancy a pleasant mixture of peanut butter and cheese? Just

Box 6.1 The goals of human beings and examples of the bodily feelings and emotions that they create

- Eating, drinking, breathing, and the elimination of their waste products: hunger, thirst, breathlessness, and feelings arising from the need to urinate, defecate, and exhale.
- The maintenance of health: feelings of bodily well-being or weakness.
- The avoidance of noxious substances: emotion of disgust.
- The maintenance of life and meeting goals: emotion of happiness or frustration.
- The avoidance of dangerous situations: emotion of fear.
- The maintenance of relations between caregivers and children: emotion of attachment.
- Sexual relations: feeling of sexual desire or frustration. Emotion of love or loss.
- Social relations with peers, including superiors, peers, and inferiors: emotion of amity or hatred. Emotion of anger or fear.

one snag: it is in the shape of a dog turd. Toddlers, to the horror of their parents, are happy to eat the mixture. The parents refuse to eat it, and you might too. Disgust is rooted in an aversion to the unpleasant taste of toxic substances, but its causes are cognitive. One man's meat *is* another man's poison, as Darwin discovered during his circumnavigation of the globe. He was sitting at a portable table eating his lunch in Tierra del Fuego surrounded by a group of fascinated locals. They had never seen preserved meat, which he was eating. One of them pushed his thumb into the meat, and recoiled, disgusted by its moist sponginess. Darwin recoiled too, disgusted by a strange thumb in his lunch. Diet is a mine of evidence confirming the cognitive causes of disgust. Buddhists don't eat meat; Hindus don't eat beef; Jews and Muslims don't eat pork. What believers in one religion eat, believers in another religion shun. And only the English love marmite. Conscious evaluations of a moral or religious nature can lead to emotional reactions based on unconscious transitions. It is wrong to eat dogs, I think; and so if I saw someone eating dog, I would be disgusted.

* * *

Basic emotions are the biological foundation of the complex emotions that appear to be unique to us. Complex emotions depend on conscious inferences that relate to our models of ourselves and often to comparisons between alternative possibilities or between actual events and possibilities that we imagine in alternative histories. They therefore can be experienced only for known reasons. They include the emotions of remorse, indignation, pride, and embarrassment. We feel remorse, which is sadness about an action or inaction, because we judge ourselves to have violated the moral code embodied in our idealized model of our selves. Thus, complex emotions integrate a basic emotional signal and a conscious cognitive evaluation. The Western conception of romantic love is also a complex emotion. Its innate components are sexual desire and happiness. Its cognitive components include altruism, and idealized models of our selves and those whom we love. These components exist in many societies, but their integration into a recognizable and namable complex was a cultural accomplishment.

Complex emotions appear to depend on a region in the prefrontal lobes of the brain. If this region is damaged, we no longer experience these emotions, and we cease to be able to plan our lives or to make sensible decisions. The classic case concerns a patient called Phineas Gage, who in the late nineteenth century worked on the construction of the railways in the USA. He was tamping an explosive charge with a metal bar when the charge exploded and sent the bar flying through his head. He survived, but he suffered massive damage to his prefrontal lobes. He was quite changed as a result and unable to cope with life. The neuroscientist Antonio Damasio has described a similar modern patient, who was successful in business and a good family man until he developed a brain tumor. Its surgical removal led to the excision of some tissue from his prefrontal lobes. After his recovery from the operation, he seemed normal in most respects. He remained very intelligent. He experienced basic emotions, such as fear. Tests of his memory showed that it was better than expected for someone with prefrontal damage. However, he was unable to plan even for a few hours ahead. He couldn't manage social relations. He was fired from jobs; he had several marriages and divorces. He went bankrupt. The role of prefrontal cortex in managing emotions and social relations has also been demonstrated in monkeys. Their social life is organized around "dominance hierarchies" in which lower status monkeys kowtow to higher status monkeys. Every monkey knows its place in the hierarchy, just as every Englishman knew his place in Victorian society. But, monkeys with damage to their prefrontal lobes can no longer function in the hierarchy.

Emotional shocks make us sweat—a reaction mediated by the autonomic nervous system. The increase in the sweat on our palms reduces the electrical resistance of our skin. Hence, a measure of the skin resistance on our palms detects this change when we see a shocking scene. This reaction is known as the "galvanic skin response", or GSR for short. Patients with damage to the prefrontal lobes lack this reaction. They also fail to make sensible decisions in an experimental gambling game that Damasio designed to mimic decisions in everyday life. They had to choose cards from various packs, and depending on what was on the card, they either won or lost a certain amount of dummy money. Two packs yielded small rewards consistently. Two other packs yielded rather larger rewards but an occasional massive loss. Participants with no brain damage soon developed a GSR in anticipation of these losses, and they learned to shun these packs—even before they could explain why. But, the patients with prefrontal damage never learned to avoid them. As in life, so in the game: they went bankrupt.

The communicative theory postulates that emotions ensure that we make decisions rather than get lost in a maze of reasoning. The transition to an emotion provides a signal either of good outcomes to encourage us to persevere or of bad outcomes to warn us of impending danger. These gut reactions, or "somatic markers" as Damasio refers to them, enable us to respond with a minimum of thought.

* * *

The cognitive evaluation that leads to an emotion can be conscious or unconscious, but the transition to the emotion is always unconscious. We can't switch it on, or off. As Aristotle said, we can't choose to feel anger or fear. Our feelings are involuntary. For St. Augustine, one of the consequences of Adam's fall was that our disobedient flesh became ascendant over our will. Before the fall, man could summon erections at will; thereafter, erections could be involuntary, importunate, inopportune. Contrary to the lawyers, Auden said, there was no problem in identifying pornography—just ask a jury to vote, and see how many male members rise. We cannot control our emotions, either. We see a child weeping because she has been orphaned, and we feel deep sympathy for her. We witness a piece of barbaric cruelty, and we feel outrage. No matter how much effort we make we cannot exert a direct control on our feelings. At best, we can distract ourselves by trying to think of something else, or we can try to re-appraise the events causing the emotions. We can't feel happy (or sad) as a result of a simple voluntary intention. The one way in which we can summon up an emotion is by thinking of some episode that we know is liable to evoke it. We may be able to control our expression of our feelings. But, even with ironclad willpower, our true feelings may seep out into brief facial expressions. As I mentioned, a movie of our face viewed in slow motion may reveal an involuntary "seepage". We may be smiling to mask our anger, but a momentary frown, barely visible, flashes across our face.

Our emotions often impel us to act. But, we can still reason, and sometimes our reasoning conflicts with our emotion. We may infer that an action would be immoral or imprudent. The resolution of the conflict is an open question: we cannot predict it. An irreducible element of nondeterminism exists in our behavior. Some circumstances precipitate strong feelings that are inappropriate. Some of us, for instance, are terrified of spiders. Others of us are overcome with panic on getting into an elevator. These emotions are abnormal, and I consider them by and by.

Novels, plays, and movies, can all stir up real emotions about unreal events. We laugh or weep about what we know are fictions. Music is still more puzzling, as it can move us even though it refers to nothing at all. We feel happy as result of listening to a piece of music, but the music isn't the object of our emotion, but its cause. We cannot say why this piece of music makes us happy whereas that piece makes us sad. The reason, as I have argued elsewhere, is that music imitates emotional behaviors, and that the cognitive evaluations yielding basic emotions are rudimentary. They do not check for the reality of events, but depend on unconscious transitions. This propensity to experience real emotions to unreal events seems to be universal to all cultures.

* * *

The traffic between reasoning and emotions moves in both directions. Inferences evoke emotions: emotions evoke inferences. Even though the main link in the evocation of an emotion is an unconscious transition from an evaluation, the first event in the causal chain may be a conscious inference. We draw a conclusion of which we are aware, and it leads to an unconscious transition to an emotion. I left my office one day years ago, went to where I had parked my car, and saw that it was missing. Someone had stolen it (I inferred), and so I was shocked and angry. I went back to my office and telephoned the police to report the theft. I left again, and turned down a different road to catch a bus home. As I walked along the road, I saw my car parked nearby. I had parked it there in the morning, because my regular parking lot had been full. My anger was at once replaced by relief, but also by embarrassment at my fallible memory and my stupidity in inferring that the car had been stolen. That inference had made me angry, and perhaps my emotion had clouded my memory.

Inferences that create emotions can concern imaginary or hypothetical events. We read in the newspaper that a fire has occurred in an apartment near to where we live. We imagine that it could have happened in our building, and we experience a whiff of anxiety. Our ability to imagine ourselves in others' shoes, and even to imagine what they are thinking, is the mainstay of empathy. Hence, the full range of inferences from unconscious intuitions to conscious deductions can create emotions.

When we reason about our anticipated emotions, we're often wrong. Imagine that you inherit a vast amount of money, will you be happy ever after? You may think so. Imagine instead that you're in a crippling accident that leaves you a quadriplegic. Life will not be worth living, right? Wrong. Neither prediction is accurate. After a few years, big lottery winners are on average no happier than the rest of us, and quadriplegics no less happier than the rest of us. That is how they rate themselves on a scale of happiness. You may say: perhaps they are mistaken. But, how else can we assess their feelings? If you remain skeptical, think about the consequences of a change—for better or worse—in your life, and compare how you feel about it now with how you anticipated you would feel. Emotions, like radio-active substances, have a half life. They decay with time.

* * *

Our emotions affect our choices among options. For classical economists, it's rational to choose whichever option yields the greatest "expected utility". *Utility* refers to the value of an outcome. A gift of $100 has a certain utility and so does a poke in the eye with a burnt stick—a rather negative utility. All options, economists assume, can be put onto a single scale of utilities. *Expected* refers to the likelihood of an outcome, and so to compute expected utility, we multiply our estimate of the probability of an outcome by its utility to us, e.g., an outright gift of $95 has the same expected utility as a 95 percent chance of $100.

My former Princeton colleague Danny Kahneman and the late Amos Tversky showed that we violate the principles of rationality based on expected utilities. For a long time, many economists refused to believe their results, but the evidence will out, and Kahneman won a Nobel prize for economics in 2002. Here is an illustration of a typical observation that you can check for yourself. Which of these two options would you choose:

A sure gain of $900 or a 90 percent chance of $1000?

Like most of us, you would probably settle for the sure gain. Why risk getting nothing for a chance of an extra measly hundred dollars? Now, in contrast, suppose that you have to undergo a loss. Which of these two options you would prefer:

A sure loss of $900 or a 90 percent chance of a loss of $1000?

Like most of us, you would probably prefer the second option. You may lose $1000, but there is a chance that will get off without losing a penny. It's worth risking the extra hundred dollars for the chance of losing nothing. If we had a series of gains of those in the first pair, then the amount that we would expect to gain would be the same for both options: if we win $1000 on 90 percent of occasions, our average overall gains are about $900. So, both options have the same positive expected utility. Similarly, a series of losses like those in the second pair have the same negative expected utility (a loss of $900). So, with gains of the same expected utility, we shun the gamble in favor of the sure thing; but with losses of the same expected utility, we shun the sure thing in favor of the gamble. Why?

Expected utility cannot explain the difference, but our emotions can. Kahneman and Tversky's "prospect" theory reflects an asymmetry in the value we place on gains and losses, and it postulates that we assess these values in relation to the *status quo* or some other relevant reference point. The pain of a loss is greater in proportion than the pleasure of an equivalent gain, and so we tend to take risks to avoid losses, but not to achieve gains.

For the classical theory, only expected utility matters when we make a choice. Yet, we reason rather than calculate utilities when we make choices. We infer how we'll feel as a consequence of the possible outcomes. Would you, for example, have your child vaccinated against whooping cough when there is minute chance that the vaccination has a fatal side-effect? Many people refuse. They anticipate how terrible they'd feel if their child died, even though the child is more at risk from dying from whooping cough. The assessment of risk isn't easy, and our dread of fatal outcomes weighs on us.

* * *

Our emotions preoccupy us. As a result, we may err in reasoning. Stress and anxiety are well-established causes of cognitive failures, from pilots who switch off the wrong engine when one engine is on fire, to the engineers at Chernobyl, who refused to believe that the reactor had been destroyed. Emotions appear to inhibit us from thinking of alternative possibilities. Similar effects occur in the psychological laboratory. If we watch a movie that inculcates an emotion of happiness or sadness, then we are less likely to make the correct choices in Wason's selection task. You may recall that in this task, we have to select evidence to determine the truth or falsity of a general claim. We do better if the film is not emotional or if we watch no film at all.

You might suspect that when we are happy we reason better than when we are sad. Dozens of experiments support this conjecture. One set of studies called for the participants to solve problems that depended on a key insight.

An example of such a problem, well-known to psychologists, is the "candle" problem. The task is to fix a candle to a door given just the candle and a box of tacks. We can try pushing a tack through the candle, but it isn't long enough to do the job. The key insight is that the box holding the tacks can also serve as the candle holder. We use the tacks to pin it to the door, and then it supports the candle. To realize that an object serving one function can serve another sounds easy, but it isn't. Indeed, it is so difficult that psychologists have some jargon for the problem: they call it "functional fixity". Participants who were feeling happy because they'd seen a clip from a humorous movie were more likely to have the key insight. They suffered less from functional fixity than those who had seen a sad or neutral movie, or no movie at all. Happiness aids insight.

An emotion may preoccupy us like a man hitting us on the head with a rubber mallet, or it may chivvy us up or retard us depending on whether we're feeling up or down. But, an emotion may be pertinent to the task that we're doing. Psychological experiments have established a swathe of these results: Anxiety leads us to think about future risks, and we assess ourselves as more at risk than we do when we're not anxious. Anxiety also makes us more vigilant when various events compete for our attention. In contrast, depression does not, but focuses us on the past: it is an emotion of loss, and we ruminate about past events. It enhances our memory for sad events, whereas anxiety doesn't affect our recall of threatening events. Likewise, mild depression makes us more accurate in estimating our control over outcomes in which we won or lost small sums of money. We're sadder but wiser.

You now have ten seconds to answer this question:

> I am worse than my boss.
>
> My boss is worse than my colleagues.
>
> Who is worst?

This sort of problem is harder for most of us than one that isn't depressing. We don't often think about negative aspects of our own performance. But, if we're depressed, we are used to ruminating about our shortcomings—too used to it, perhaps—and so the preceding problem is no harder for us than one about our happiness.

Keith Oatley and his colleagues have demonstrated similar effects in the inferences that participants made about stories. For instance, in Russell Banks's short story, *Sarah Cole: a type of love story*, a heartless man breaks off a love affair with great cruelty. Its effect on the participants in an experiment was to make them either sad or else angry. Those who were sad tended to reason about earlier events in the story. Those who were angry tended to reason about future events. As Aristotle wrote, anger leads us to reason about ways of exacting revenge.

Emotions set us reasoning about their causes. To take an example inspired by Kahneman and Tversky, suppose that you drive to an airport to catch a plane, and that on the way you stop to have a drink. You arrive at the airport a few minutes late, and just miss your flight. You are disappointed, and your emotion is liable to lead you to think to yourself:

If only I hadn't stopped to have a drink, then I wouldn't have missed my flight.

The thought is "counterfactual" in that it concerns an imaginary alternative to the facts. It concerns two states of affairs: what happened and what might have happened in the alternative, but counterfactual, possibility in which you didn't stop for a drink. In a brilliant book, *The Rational Imagination*, Ruth Byrne has shown that it takes imagination to think about counterfactual possibilities. We entertain them to learn from our mistakes, to correct plans that failed, and sometimes to rejoice in our luck. But, when things go badly, we often think about counterfactual possibilities. Many complex emotions, such as regret, guilt, and shame, are elicited in this way. They in turn predispose us to think in a counterfactual vein.

When we compare what happened with what might have happened, we can imagine better outcomes. And sometimes we count ourselves as blessed when we think of a worse outcome. Here is a true story leading to my favorite counterfactual conditional. I once drove nonstop from Italy to the north coast of France in order to get home to England as fast as possible. As I pulled into Dieppe harbor in the late afternoon, I saw the car ferry sailing away from the quay. I had missed it by five minutes. I asked when the next boat would be, and was told 10 p.m. To console myself, I went off to eat a magnificent French dinner. After dinner, I returned to the harbor. I noticed that a gale was beginning to blow, and the man at the harbor gate told me that the 10 p.m. ferry was cancelled because of the weather. There'd be no more ferries until the next day. With redoubled disappointment, I telephoned my wife and checked into a hotel for the night. The next morning, down on the quayside, a ferry arrived at last. The passengers on deck looked forlorn, a bit "green about the gills", and still stranger they did not disembark. It was the same ferry that I had just missed the day before. The seas had been so rough that it had been unable to get into Newhaven harbor in England, and the passengers had spent the whole night tossed around in the ship during one of the worst storms on record in the English channel. *If I hadn't missed the boat, I would have been with them too.*

* * *

Emotions are so vital to us that a surprising number of people think that they are unique to human beings. A computer may be able to beat the world chess champion, they say, but it doesn't have feelings. In fact, the evidence implies that emotions antedate *Homo sapiens* by at least two hundred million years. All social mammals, including rats, have the brain organs for basic emotions, and all of them appear to experience these emotions.

The function of emotions is to prepare us for various courses of action or inaction. They are faster than conscious reasoning in getting us to react. They make us smart in an emergency, but they can make us dumb when they swamp our conscious reasoning. They communicate our state of mind to others. We are usually aware of the cause of an emotion. We are never aware of the transition to the emotion. We are usually aware of the emotion, and it can influence our intentional actions. But, when our intellect pulls us one way, and our emotion pulls us another way, we are powerless to switch off the emotion. Sometimes we cannot even control our behavior. Here is Darwin describing the outcome of one of these conflicts:

> I put my face close to the thick glass-plate in front of a puff-adder in the Zoological Gardens, with the firm determination of not starting back if the snake struck at me; but, as soon as the blow was struck, my resolution went for nothing, and I jumped a yard or two backwards with astonishing rapidity. My will and reason were powerless against the imagination of a danger which had never been experienced.

Chapter 7

Reasoning in Psychological Illnesses

Here's a person reasoning about a stomach ache:

> I'm afraid of the little pain I feel in my abdomen on the same side as my liver. It could be a symptom of cancer, a liver cancer. I remember an uncle of mine who died from liver cancer after suffering a lot. But he was in his eighties and I'm thirty, and a liver cancer at my age is rare. On the other hand, it's not impossible. Moreover, it seems to me that I look unhealthy; my tongue is dirty; sometimes my mouth tastes bitter. I seem to be pale, and I could have anaemia. Of course these are common symptoms and they can be trivial. I have had them many other times. But they are there, and they are not incompatible with cancer. Moreover, they don't exclude it. My doctor prescribed several tests for me, and the results were all negative. But, the results could be those for another person—sometimes laboratories mix up test tubes, or the secretary makes a mistake in writing the patient's name, or she puts the results for one person in the folder for another patient. A mistake can always occur. The laboratory may be very professional, but there cannot be a hundred percent guarantee that it didn't make a mistake. Moreover, I am the main person responsible for my own health. You can imagine how I would feel if I really had cancer and had left it too late. The best I can do is to go back to my doctor.

Now, here's a different person reasoning on the same topic:

> I'm afraid of the little pain I feel in my abdomen on the same side as my liver. It could be a symptom of cancer, a liver cancer. I remember an uncle of mine who died from liver cancer after suffering a lot. In the beginning, his symptoms were the same as mine: he had a similar stomach ache. He didn't care, and the doctors told him that he wasn't ill. But, meanwhile the cancer was spreading. Now, in the same way the cancer may be spreading in my abdomen. Indeed my symptoms seem to have become worse during the last few weeks. Nobody believes me, and nobody takes me seriously. When they do start to treat me, it will be too late! Moreover, it seems to me that I look unhealthy; my tongue is dirty; sometimes my mouth tastes bitter. I seem to be pale, and I could have anaemia. What a trauma it will be for me and my family when the cancer is correctly diagnosed, and it will be too late! Afterwards my life will be one of suffering, drugs, medical tests, checks and surgical operations. The best I can do is to go back to my doctor.

The first vignette is characteristic of a person who is suffering from "obsessive compulsive" disorder. She ruminates about a possible illness, and reasons in a dialectal way, alternating between a case for and a case against the worst scenario, and is never quite able to dismiss the latter. The second vignette is characteristic of a patient suffering from hypochondria. His reasoning starts with bodily symptoms, focuses on them, and amplifies the dire consequences of neglecting them.

This chapter is about psychological illnesses and our reasoning when we are afflicted with them. However, I need first to consider a crucial question: Are there illnesses that have a psychological origin rather than a cause in the pathology of the brain? Some psychiatrists doubt it. But, many others do believe in the occurrence of "neuroses", as these illnesses used to be known until the American Psychiatric Association removed the word from its diagnostic manual in 1980. These illnesses, if they exist, must have their origins in experiences that affect subsequent thoughts and feelings, and that lead us to suffer, often to the point that we seek professional help. An organism that cannot modify its behavior as a result of experience—an amoeba, perhaps—cannot become mentally ill. It might show symptoms of derangement, but the cause must be damage to its nervous system.

The distinction between mental disorders and those that originate in damage to the brain sounds dualistic: the mind exists, the brain exists, and the two interact from time to time, perhaps by way of the pineal gland (as Descartes imagined). Yet, the brain could be the material foundation of the mind. Imagine a robot controlled by a complex piece of software that modifies itself as a result of experience. It learns, say, that the robot should not try to pass through openings that are too narrow. But, it may acquire a pathological behavior, such as not to pass through any openings: no program for learning can be foolproof, because of the intractability of induction. The robot might also suffer damage to the hardware that runs its program. We can therefore draw a sensible distinction between malfunctions that result from experience, yielding bugs in the program, and malfunctions that result from damage to its processing unit, yielding bats in the belfry. We make an analogous distinction when we decide that a computer has crashed because of a bug in its word processor, or because of a problem with its hard disk.

Granted the distinction between mind and brain, we can pose the question: what causes mental illness? Our knowledge about the answer is worse than medical knowledge about, say, cholera a hundred and fifty years ago. Physicians then at least realized that there was an epidemic disease that came from Asia, and that killed about a third of those infected with it. What they disagreed about was the cause of the disease. With mental illnesses, however, there's no consensus about either existence or cause. The human propensity to treat diseases is in no way constrained by lack of knowledge. There are several hundred varieties of psychotherapy from Active analytical therapy to Zaraleya psychoenergetic technique.

Those psychiatrists who reject mental illness attribute the pathology to a faulty brain. The development of appropriate brain-altering drugs, or gene therapy, they say, is the best approach to a cure. A major puzzle for this view is that psychotherapy can cure mental illness. Indeed, some sufferers recover without treatment, though psychotherapy leads to a more rapid recovery. If experience can heal an illness, then perhaps experience can cause the illness.

Behaviorists argued that mental illnesses are bad habits. Patients learned maladaptive responses to certain stimuli. Hence, the treatment is to teach them more appropriate responses to these stimuli. Behavior therapy can eliminate maladaptive responses. Whether it is an effective cure, however, is a matter of dispute.

Of those who admit a mental cause of illness, Freud and his followers and rivals suppose that unconscious conflicts emerge into consciousness in a distorted way that yields neuroses. Freud aimed to set up a scientific psychology, but it has been hard to test his theory. Psychologists can test bits and pieces of it, but not Freud's fundamental hypothesis, which he held to the end of his life: infants have sexual feelings, and their repression—an unconscious process itself—causes neuroses. Psychoanalysts support this hypothesis with their intuitions gained from treating patients. These intuitions may be correct, but they are no more secure than the intuitions of early nineteenth century doctors about cholera. What we can be sure of, however, is that unconscious processes concern more than unacceptable sexual desires and destructive wishes. A vast set of processes of which we are not aware makes consciousness possible.

Psychotherapeutic theory underwent a revolution thirty years ago with the development of "cognitive therapy". Aaron Beck and its other proponents argued that the cause of neuroses is faulty reasoning, either invalid inferences or inferences from false beliefs. The sources of false beliefs are the testimony of others, inaccurate perceptions, and invalid reasoning. But, the testimony of others is unlikely to be a factor in creating false beliefs that cause psychological illnesses. Likewise, those of us with psychological illnesses, as opposed to more serious psychoses such as schizophrenia, seldom suffer from faults in perception. Hence, on Beck's account, the prime source of false beliefs is faulty reasoning itself. Indeed, the idea is pervasive. Even Auden, whom I have often quoted in this book, wrote, "The neurotic is someone who draws a false general conclusion from a particular instance".

Cognitive therapy has been used to treat various psychological illnesses including anxiety and depression. Yet, the theory's fundamental tenet about faulty reasoning has no robust support. My aim is therefore to re-examine the role of reasoning in psychopathology, and, in the light of recent evidence, to propose a new theory of psychological illnesses developed with my Italian colleagues Francesco Mancini and Amelia Gangemi. This theory, which we refer to as the "hyper-emotion" theory of psychological illnesses, rests on the account of unconscious reasoning and emotions earlier in this part of the book.

* * *

What happens in a mental illness according to this theory is that we make a cognitive evaluation of a situation. It leads by an unconscious transition to a *basic* emotion that is appropriate to this evaluation, but that is out of proportion in its intensity. It's a *hyper-emotion*. We are aware of the aberrant nature of our response, and so we reason about it. This reasoning, in turn, can amplify our problems. As an example, consider the case of the woman, whom I mentioned in the Introduction, who looked at a photograph of Rock Hudson in a newspaper. She had a basic emotion of inappropriate intensity: she worried about having contracted HIV from handling the newspaper. She reasoned about her worries, and the effect was to amplify her problems.

What is the origin of inappropriate unconscious transitions? These transitions occur in all of us, and so we may be susceptible to inappropriate emotions and to mental ailments. In their mildest form, they are not debilitating. They lead to thoughts and sometimes to actions that are irrational. But, we can be happy and successful even if we have, say, an irrational phobia throughout our lives. The environment plays a part. Prolonged stress, as the soldiers in the trenches experienced in World War I, makes us susceptible to psychological illnesses. We also differ in our innate susceptibility to them. Identical twins come from the same egg and have identical genes, and if one twin tends to be neurotic so does the other, and the correlation is greater than between twins who are not identical. Hence, a genetic predisposition to mental illness does exist, and studies are beginning to pinpoint the relevant genes.

* * *

The original transition to an aberrant emotion occurs as a result of an event that we can recall unless it happened in childhood. The event may be innocuous to others, but it is traumatic to us because of its consequent emo-tion. But, it may be a real trauma. For example, a patient was too frightened to fly after the intense fear she had in a plane that was struck by lightning. Traumatic events may predispose individuals to these reactions. A New York taxi driver told me—while we were stuck in a short tunnel in Manhattan—that after he saw the collapse of the World Trade Center towers on September 11, 2001, he was about to drive into the Holland tunnel under the Hudson river, when he was overcome with intense anxiety. He was terrified that he might get stuck there and have a panic attack. It had taken him several years to recover and to be able to drive through tunnels again. Only a few patients are unable to recall the origins of their mental illnesses—a claim borne out by a study that I report later. The new theory allows, however, that an unconscious transition to a hyper-emotion can occur in anyone as a result of arbitrary fluc-tuations. Subsequent events and our mental constitution determine whether it is just a momentary aberration or becomes more deep-seated.

The hyper-emotion theory implies a taxonomy of mental illnesses. They can arise from any of the bodily feelings or basic emotions in the lives of social mammals (see Box 6.1 in the previous chapter). At first glance, a potential exception is breathing. But, a search yielded some corroboratory evidence: psychological illnesses can arise from breathlessness in asthma and bronchitis. Box 7.1 shows how each of the roots of emotions can also give rise to a corresponding mental illness.

Box 7.1 Examples of common symptoms and their roots in bodily feelings and emotions (see Box 6.1 for the underlying ontology)

- disorders of eating, drinking, and breathing, e.g., anorexia nervosa
- disorders concerning health, e.g., hypochondria
- the avoidance of noxious substances, e.g., obsessive-compulsive disorder
- the maintenance of life and meeting goals, e.g., hypomania
- the avoidance of dangerous situations, e.g., phobia
- the maintenance of relations between caregivers and children, e.g., depression
- sexual relations, e.g., psychological impotence
- relations with peers, e.g., social anxiety

When we feel an intense emotion about an event, it concentrates our minds. We reason about the event to try to make sense of the emotion, and to decide what, if anything, to do about it. The effect of this conscious reasoning, which will become well practiced, can be to maintain our mental illness. It focuses us on the situation leading to the aberrant emotion. It enables us to elaborate our original cognitive evaluation, and so it can enlarge the circumstances that trigger the unconscious transition. The practice we get in making these inferences predicts that our reasoning on matters pertaining to our emotion should be better than both the reasoning of others on the same topics and our own reasoning on other topics. This prediction is crucial because it distinguishes the theory from the view that faulty reasoning causes mental illness. I turn now to some examples of mental illness to illustrate the theory.

* * *

Those of us with obsessive-compulsive disorder often go through life compelled to carry out ritual cleansing behaviors. One patient, known as "Ruth", devoted hours of each day to washing herself. After she used the lavatory, she scrubbed each finger, then the sides of her hands, and then her arms. She carried out this procedure first with soap, and then with disinfectant. She then cleaned the toilet and sink. And then she repeated the hand-washing ritual. If she still felt contaminated, she took a shower. She washed her hands after cooking and cleaning her house, but only to the degree that these jobs made her feel dirty. She washed her hands three or four times an hour, and showered six or seven times a day. Not all dirt was "bad", however. Ruth enjoyed painting pictures, and she did not object if she got spots of paint on herself. They were "good" dirt. Ruth had no social life, and became anxious in social interactions. She was frightened that she would lose control of herself. The origin of Ruth's compulsions went back to her childhood. She was carrying out her hand washing rituals by the age of five. She first went to a therapist at the age of ten.

According to the hyper-emotion theory, the immediate cause of the cleansing rituals is the evaluation of certain events—household dirt, defecation, and the like, as disgusting. They elicit feelings of disgust in most people. In Ruth, however, they elicit an unconscious transition to a hyper-anxiety about the danger of contamination. This inference corresponds to causation by physical contact, and it is an instance of contagious magic. Ruth would be remiss not to take precautions against contamination. And, like many people with this problem, she makes the conscious inference that she is at fault in putting herself at risk of contamination, and so she feels guilty. She makes the sensible induction that the danger is not overwhelming, and she even reasons that no mechanism for harm exists. But, these inferences increase her thoughts about the probability of contamination. As long as there is the slightest risk, she would be derelict in her duty if she did not wash herself. If the washing is not complete, then the risk of contamination remains. Her mother had inculcated a regimen of hyper-cleanliness and neatness during her childhood. The acquisition of the unconscious transition was, I assume, a consequence of this regimen.

If we suffer from obsessive compulsions, our ruminations have a characteristic pattern illustrated in the vignette at the start of the chapter. But, like any thinking, our reasoning is not deterministic. We may omit a step or stick with a particular worry for some time. Our reasoning starts with a thought about potential danger, and it appears to come from nowhere, just as many thoughts do in daily life. It contains a kernel of rational anxiety, but leads to an unconscious transition to extreme anxiety. We then *focus* on the improbable danger as a result of this emotion. Our hyper-anxiety may lead us to overestimate the severity and the likelihood of the danger. In a characteristic pattern of reasoning, we search for counterexamples to the worst-case scenario and then for examples of it. This dialectical form of reasoning usually leads us to accept the danger as real. And so we go into an indefinite loop of thoughts and feelings, oscillating between a case for the worse outcome and a case against it.

Some psychologists have proposed that individuals with obsessive-compulsive disorder reason in an abnormal way in which they somehow fuse thoughts with actions or events. In contrast, the present theory postulates that patients reason normally, and that their many inferences about the sources of their anxiety should make them expert reasoners on the topic. As the AIDS example illustrates, they are able to construct extended sequences of inferences. Likewise, they rely on normal mechanisms to judge probabilities. Whenever we think about any event in detail, we are liable to recruit more evidence that raises its probability. Patients' ruminations about examples and counterexamples to a danger should flesh it out in more detail, and thereby raise its subjective probability. Over a series of episodes, which could last a lifetime in the absence of treatment, the risk of contamination becomes more plausible and more general. That is why Ruth came to devote so many hours of the day and night to her ritual washing.

* * *

Those of us with hypochondria go through life worried that we are ill, perhaps mortally ill. Thomas Carlyle, the nineteenth century author of *The French*

Revolution, was a famous hypochondriac. He seems to have had some insight into his illness, and I imagine that he had this dialogue with his doctor:

Carlyle: Doctor, I'm worried that I may be a hypochondriac.
Doctor: Don't worry, you're only imagining it.

A more typical case of an episode of hypochondria happened to a young executive who was about to go abroad with his family to take up a fellowship. Shortly before he left, he woke up with blurred vision, and had a sudden and overwhelming fear that he had developed multiple sclerosis. He was so worried that he made an emergency appointment with his doctor. The doctor gave him a thorough physical check up, including an ophthalmoscopic eye examination. After the patient's initial skepticism, the doctor was able to explain the relation between the patient's symptoms and his worries about spending time abroad. The patient, much relieved, accepted the doctor's diagnosis. Many patients, however, are resistant to the idea that they have a mental malady, and their hypochondria, like Carlyle's, lasts for a lifetime.

Hypochondria begins with certain bodily feelings. These feelings—stomach aches, slight dizziness, queasiness, and so forth—can be interpreted as signs of illness, and this evaluation initiates an unconscious transition to an aberrant degree of anxiety. Anyone can experience a bout of hypochondria. We feel a pain in the chest, and we think: perhaps I am having a heart attack. But, those of us who are robust tend to think: it may just be indigestion, let me wait and see. The pain dissipates, and we resume life as normal. The environment can contribute to the incidence of hypochondria. Medical students are well-known as a group who often have signs of hypochondria. Similarly, if we consult a medical encyclopedia, a vivid description of a disease can elicit the inference that we too are suffering from it. And some of us focus on bodily feelings to such a degree that we develop an anxiety about mortal illness. We ruminate about the possibility, and our bodily feelings keep us focused on the worst case, and so, as the opening vignette illustrates, we do not oscillate between the case for the worst outcome and the case against it. Instead, we make inferences to justify our fears, and these inferences exacerbate our problems.

One consequence of hypochondria is that we focus so much on our bodily feelings that small sensations make us anxious. Another consequence is that we have frequent encounters with physicians—to the point that we become experts about the illness that we imagine we have. We may spend the whole day thinking about it. Our predicament is analogous to Pascal's wager about the existence of God—it is rational to believe in God, he argued, because nothing of consequence happens if the belief is erroneous, but skepticism has disastrous consequences if it is erroneous. Likewise, we believe that we are ill.

Hence, it is rational for us to consult a doctor because nothing of consequence happens if our belief is erroneous, but a failure to consult a doctor is disastrous if skepticism about the illness is erroneous. We go to the doctor, who fails to find anything wrong with us. We still have our bodily symptoms, and so we may reject the doctor's diagnosis.

* * *

The hyper-emotion theory postulates that psychological illnesses are caused by unconscious transitions yielding aberrant basic emotions, and that they are maintained by characteristic patterns of conscious reasoning. I have already presented evidence demonstrating unconscious reasoning, and so the crucial question is whether psychological illnesses result from transitions to *basic* emotions. It is hard, but not impossible, to obtain evidence on this point.

Earlier, I reviewed the findings that the amygdala mediate basic emotions. It follows from the theory that the amygdala should be active whenever events elicit the signs and symptoms of a psychological illness. This prediction has been confirmed in several brain-imaging studies, using functional magnetic resonance imaging (the fMRI procedure that I described in Chapter 2). They have shown a high degree of activity in the amygdala when relevant stimuli are presented to individuals suffering from obsessive-compulsive disorder, hypochondria, phobia, and post-traumatic stress disorder. Likewise, activity in the amygdala correlates with depression of various sorts and with its severity.

A small-scale epidemiological study also corroborated the role of basic emotions in the onset of psychological illnesses. Twenty-four psychiatrists who practice in Rome or Verona filled out a 15-item questionnaire about their most recent patients whom they had diagnosed as obsessive, agoraphobic, hypochondriac, or depressed. The questionnaire included items about the diagnosis, the sex and other details of the patient, and whether the patient had any other morbid symptoms. It also queried whether the patients remembered the onset of their illness, and if so, what emotion had occurred then. This question included a checklist with five words referring to basic emotions (anxiety, disgust, fear, anger, and sadness) and five words referring to complex emotions (guilt, shame, pride, embarrassment, envy). The words were in a random order, and the psychiatrists could write in other emotion words, if necessary. None of them knew the purpose of the study, the hyper-emotion theory, or even that these were the critical questions. The psychiatrists all filled in the questionnaire, and provided data from forty-nine male and fifty-seven female patients. Of those patients who recalled the onset of their illness (all but five of them), the majority reported a basic emotion at its onset (over eighty percent of them), and the one exception was the experience of guilt in cases of obsessive-compulsive disorder or depression (twelve percent of cases). Guilt may have occurred later in the illness, and the patients' memories may have misled them. Even so, the results corroborated the prediction that basic emotions are by far the most frequent at the start of a mental illness.

* * *

Those with a tendency towards a mental illness should focus on matters pertinent to their illness, and, as a result, reason *more* accurately about them than control participants do. With neutral materials, however, the difference should disappear. It would have been unethical to submit patients to a regimen likely to bring on their signs and symptoms, and so instead we tested university students with tendencies towards psychological illnesses, who had neither sought treatment nor been diagnosed as ill. The crucial prediction was that these participants should reason better than control participants, but only with materials relating to their potential illnesses; with neutral contents, the difference between the two groups should disappear. This prediction is contrary to those accounts of psychological illnesses that locate their causes in faulty reasoning.

We carried out two experiments to test the prediction. Our epidemiological survey suggested that two telling comparisons should be, first, between those with a tendency towards obsessive compulsions and a control group, and, second, between those with a tendency towards depression and a control group. Because the participants with tendencies towards obsessions or towards depression were also likely to be prone to anxiety, the two experiments examined reasoning about guilt in those participants with a tendency towards obsessive-compulsive disorder, and reasoning about sadness in those participants with a tendency to depression.

On each trial, the participants' task was to read a short vignette that led to a particular proposition, and then to list what was possible and what was impossible according to this proposition. Given a sentence, such as:

The alarm rings or I feel tired, or both.

the participants were told to imagine that the sentence was true, and to list what was possible in terms of the possible combinations or whether or not the alarm rings and whether or not they feel tired. The correct performance would be to list the following *complete* possibilities, which make clear the status of both clauses in the disjunction in each possibility:

> Alarm rings. I don't feel tired.
>
> Alarm doesn't ring. I feel tired.
>
> Alarm rings. I feel tired.

The participants then had to list what was impossible in the same way:

> Alarm doesn't ring. I don't feel tired.

In the first study, 290 students were given a test of obsessive-compulsive tendencies, and those with the top five percent of scores and those with the lowest five percent of scores took part in the experiment. These two groups were further subdivided into two. In the first case, the participants had to list possibilities for propositions with contents designed to elicit an emotion of guilt. The story preceding the proposition concerned the culpability of the protagonist, e.g.:

> Suppose I am at my house with some friends. We decide to join some other friends in a bar. We leave the house joking among ourselves, but I forget to close the bathroom window.

The sentence for which possibilities had to be listed was:

> The burglar alarm rings and I feel guilty.

In the second case, the participants had to list possibilities either with sentences concerning depression, e.g.:

> The burglar alarm rings and I feel depressed.

or the with neutral propositions. The participants in each group carried out the task four times in a different random order: two of the stories had a test proposition based on "and" and two of the stories had a test proposition based on "or".

The obsessive participants listed as true possibilities more correct complete possibilities for the sentence about guilt (sixty-three percent) than the participants who were not obsessives (twenty-three percent). But, when the story and proposition had either a content concerning depression or a neutral content, there was no reliable difference between the obsessive (seven percent) and nonobsessive groups (nineteen percent) in the correct listing of complete possibilities. A similar pattern occurred in the listing of what was impossible. Both patterns held up when we examined possibilities that the participants described in an incomplete way. A predisposition to obsessive-compulsive disorder can enhance reasoning about contents relevant to the disorder.

A second study showed that participants with a tendency to depression, as shown by a questionnaire test of depression, also had a comparable increase in their ability to reason about materials concerning depressing matters. That is, they reasoned more accurately than control participants with no depressive tendencies. The difference, however, disappeared with neutral materials or with materials concerning guilt. The moral of the studies is that the reasoning of individuals with a propensity towards mental illness is better about matters pertinent to their illness than either the reasoning of others or their own reasoning about other matters.

* * *

Those of us suffering from mental illness make unconscious transitions to basic emotions. We may know the cause of our emotions, but we do not know the reasons for their aberrant intensity. When a Manhattan electrician who did some work for me gets into an elevator, he is overcome with anxiety. Why? He says: he is frightened that he will lose control of himself if the doors close and the elevator begins to move. Why? He has no ready account. In the past, this sort of vacuum has been filled by various theories. Psychoanalysts have filled it with appeals to repressed desires remote from the immediate object of the emotion. Cognitive therapists doubt the role of these unconscious factors. They stress that a closer questioning of patients yields thoughts revealing that the source of illnesses is in faulty inferences. But, according to the present theory, the patients' remarks do not elucidate the cause of the hyper-intensity of their emotions, but merely their thoughts about the precipitating object or situation yielding the emotion. Their reasoning is not the cause of their illness, but its consequence. Indeed, those of us with a propensity to mental illness reason better than control participants, though only on matters concerning the illness. Unfortunately, our conclusions tend to exacerbate our condition rather than to remediate it. The pattern of reasoning depends on the emotion—whether it is fear of contamination, a mortal illness, or a panic attack. Its results strengthen the focus on the precipitating situation, and may lead to a generalization of the symptoms.

And the therapeutic moral? If we have a mental illness, the system of transitions to basic emotions needs to be re-educated. Various procedures already exist among the many forms of therapy that can help to re-educate the system. In order to reduce an unconscious transition to anxiety, "exposure" therapy seems to be the most effective. After an initial training, the patients are exposed to events that elicit their aberrant emotion. Throughout the entire treatment, they have to refrain from the actions that they carry out to reduce their anxiety—avoidance or escape in the case of agoraphobia or panic disorder, compulsive actions in the case of obsessive-compulsive disorder, and self-reassurances in the case of hypochondria. Their anxiety abates within an hour, and it is less intense on their next encounter with the relevant situation. The therapy works. Once we have faced our worst fears and mastered them, we are likely to revise our models of ourselves and to regain our former confidence.

Part III

How We Make Deductions

Could one not almost say that the

Cold serpent on the poisonous tree

Was l'esprit de géométrie,

That Eve and Adam till the Fall

Were totally illogical

But as they tasted of the fruit

The syllogistic sin took root?

Auden

Chapter 8

Only Connections

In Agatha Christie's detective story, *Murder on the Orient Express*, Mr. Ratchett (alias Cassetti, a notorious kidnapper) is stabbed to death on the train from Stamboul to Calais. Hercule Poirot, a superhuman intelligence if ever there was one, infers that more than one person had a hand in the murder, and he has to find out who amongst the thirteen suspects in the Stamboul-Calais car stabbed Ratchett. Box 8.1 presents one way to describe the situation, albeit not Poirot's, who relies on a certain amount of guesswork. Because there are thirteen suspects, who each may or may not have taken part in the murder, there are over eight thousand distinct possibilities in which more than one person stabbed Ratchett. Now you should understand why reasoning is intractable: if there were a hundred suspects, the number of possibilities is astronomical. A logician can lay out the possibilities for the stabbing of Ratchett in a vast truth table, and then use the meaning of each premise to eliminate possibilities from the table. The first premise, for instance rules out all the possibilities in which the Countess helped in the murder but Cyrus didn't. When all the premises have been used to eliminate possibilities, whatever remains must be the case. The logician's truth table is impossible to use without benefit of pencil and paper, and we'd have to be quite ingenious to think of the method.

In Part I of this book, I argued that we grasp the meanings of propositions, and then use these meanings and our knowledge to construct mental models of the significance of the propositions, i.e., the possibilities to which they refer. What I am going to describe in this part of the book is how we make deductions from conscious premises to conscious conclusions—conscious deductions, for short. As I argued in Part II, all thought processes are unconscious, and so these conscious deductions depend on unconscious processes. The inference about the stabbing of Ratchett depends only on the connections that the premises assert between various simple propositions, such as *the Countess helped* and *Cyrus helped*. We have no need to delve into the innards of these propositions in order to infer who took part in the murder. From a logical standpoint, inferences of this sort are the simplest that can be made, and the branch of logic that is most relevant to them is known as the "propositional" or "sentential" calculus. We also make deductions that do hinge on the innards of propositions.

Box 8.1 Who stabbed Ratchett on the Orient Express?

Ratchett was stabbed twelve times, and here's a description of who helped to stab him:

If the Countess helped then Cyrus helped too.

Edward helped or the Countess helped.

If Pierre helped if Hubbard did then Greta also helped.

Greta didn't help or Hubbard did.

If not both Hildegarde and Hector helped then Hubbard didn't help.

Edward helped or the Princess, Mary, and the Colonel helped.

If Hector or Mary helped then, Pierre helped or the Colonel didn't.

The Countess helped or else both Hildegarde and Hector helped.

If the Countess didn't help then Pierre, Greta, and Edward helped.

If the Count didn't help then not both Hubbard and Hector helped.

Cyrus and the Princess helped or else the Count and the Countess helped.

If not both Mary and the Colonel helped then the Countess helped.

These premises show that all but one individual took part in the stabbings. So, who dunnit, or rather who didn't dunnit? You'll find the answer at the end of the chapter.

* * *

These deductions are more complicated logically, and the subsequent chapters are about them, but this chapter is going to describe how we make deductions that depend only on logical connections between propositions. It's a puzzle that psychologists have been investigating for forty years, and the chapter presents the solution based on mental models and the solution to who murdered Mr. Ratchett. You will understand these solutions better if I begin with a little light logic.

* * *

You may recall from Chapter 1 that a sentence, such as, "I can hear you now", has a *meaning* that we understand from our knowledge of English, but that its *significance*—the particular proposition that it asserts—depends on who the speaker is, who the listener is, and the time of the utterance. Logic, however, treats sentences as though they expressed unique propositions regardless of context. And so I am going to consider sentences that have a significance close to their meanings, that is, they are as independent as possible from their context. We can now ask what it means to say that that a connective such as "if" has a *logical* meaning.

A major step to answering the question was taken by the nineteenth century logician George Boole. He invented "Boolean algebra", which is the algebra of *not*, *and*, and *or*; and it pops up everywhere from the design of computers to the propositional calculus. (Mary Boole, his wife, wrote that Macbeth's problem was that he hadn't mastered Boolean algebra.) Logical connectives are those words that can be decomposed into *not*, *and*, and *or*, in their logical meanings. We're getting there, except that now I have to define the logical meanings of *not*, *and*, and *or*.

To return from Boole to Stamboul:

> Poirot put his ticket in his pocket and he boarded the Orient Express.

We understand that the two events occurred in a temporal order: first Poirot put the ticket in his pocket, and then he got on the train. We know that there's a temporal order, because a sentence with the two clauses in opposite order says something different:

> Poirot boarded the Orient Express and he put his ticket in his pocket.

A good test for the logical meaning of *and* is that the order of the two clauses that it connects has *no* effect on the significance of the sentence, e.g.:

> Poirot had a ticket and he was traveling on the Orient express.

This sentence is true provided that both of the two propositions that it expresses are true; and its truth value, whether it is true or false, depends on nothing else. Hence, granted that it's true that Poirot had a ticket, and that it's true that he was traveling on the Orient express, the conjunction of the two propositions is also true. That is the heart of what is meant by a logical connective: the truth value of the proposition based on the connective depends only on the meaning of the connective and the truth values of the individual propositions that it connects. Logicians have a piece of jargon to express this idea. They say that the connective is "truth functional". A logical connective is truth-functional.

Now, we're there. A logical connective between propositions yields a proposition whose truth depends on the truth of its constituent propositions. The nature of the dependence varies from one connective to another. The logical meaning of *and* is that the conjunction it forms is true provided that all the propositions in the conjunction are true; if any of them is false, then the conjunction is false too. The logical meaning of *or* is that the disjunction it forms is true provided that at least one of the propositions in the disjunction is true; if all of them are false, then the disjunction is false too. What about *not*? It isn't a connective, but its logical meaning is simple: a negative sentence is true provided that the proposition that is negated is false, and vice versa. For example, the proposition that *Poirot does not have a ticket* is true, if the proposition that *Poirot has a ticket* is false. When a character in one of Agatha Christie's plays says, "We can't *not* phone for the police", her double negatives are logical, and cancel out to yield an affirmative: we must phone for the police. The Oxford philosopher J.L. Austin once commented in a lecture that, unlike negations, double affirmatives don't cancel out to yield a negative. "Yeah yeah," said another philosopher, the late Sydney Morgenbesser, from the back of the lecture hall.

We don't need to treat Boole's three connectives as primitives. For example, we can define any connective in terms of the two connectives, *not* and *and*. Indeed, with ingenuity we can define everything with a single connective, *nand*, which is short for *not both ___ and ___*. We can also define new connectives using our set of three. You may have noticed, for instance, that my definition above of "or" was for its inclusive meaning that allows the disjunction to be true if each proposition in the disjunction is true. We can use the three connectives to define the *exclusive* meaning of "or". An exclusive disjunction, such as:

> Either Edward helped or else the Countess helped, but not both

is equivalent to the proposition:

> Edward helped or the Countess helped, and not both Edward helped and the Countess helped.

Hence, exclusive disjunction also has a logical meaning.

In an analogous way we can define a logical meaning of "if". The sentence:

> If the Countess didn't help then Pierre did

means:

> The countess helped or Pierre did, or both.

In its logical meaning, the conditional is compatible with three possibilities: the Countess didn't help and Pierre did, the Countess helped and Pierre didn't, the Countess helped and Pierre helped. The only possibility that the conditional rules out is that neither the Countess nor Pierre helped. The three possibilities that the conditional allows are the same as those for the inclusive disjunction.

This equivalence, as we'll see, doesn't hold for all conditionals, but just for those with a logical meaning.

Logicians can use truth tables to determine whether or not an inference is valid: it is valid if its conclusion must be true given that its premises are true. But, they can also define a logic with formal rules of inference that allow them to prove that the conclusion follows from the premises. As I mentioned, one of the glories of twentieth century logic was the discovery that there are logics in which not all valid inferences can be proved using a consistent set of formal rules of inference. However, the logic of the three connectives— the propositional calculus—has the happy property that all inferences that are valid on the basis of meanings are also provable in a system of consistent formal rules of inference, and vice versa.

* * *

The search for a proof using formal rules of inference for the propositional calculus can take a very long time, because the domain is intractable. The use of truth tables is also problematic because the size of the truth table doubles with each elementary proposition in the inference. That is why there are over eight thousand possibilities in the truth table for the murder on the Orient express. The first step towards a psychological theory of propositional reasoning is to consider a more efficient version of truth tables, which I have implemented in a computer program.

I have mentioned computer programs several times already, but before I describe this particular program, it is time to say a word about the role of programs in cognitive psychology. When psychologists theorize about processes, one danger is that they take too much for granted, and so their accounts are vague or hard to understand. Another danger is that they invoke a homunculus to provide the explanation. They risk positing a little man inside the brain who does all of the work, and so by magic a cog in the machine turns out to have all the powers of the complete machine itself. A safeguard against vagueness and homunculi is to implement the key components of a theory in a working computer program. As Lord Kelvin, the nineteenth century physicist, wrote:

> I never satisfy myself until I can make a mechanical model of a thing. If I can make a mechanical model I can understand it. As long as I cannot make a mechanical model all the way through I cannot understand . . .

A computer program is a mechanical model. However, it embodies too many tiny assumptions for the coarse blunderbuss of an experiment to delineate. We could make alternative tiny assumptions and reach a different program that still simulates the same theory. Hence, experiments test theories, not programs.

Computer programming is not a spectator sport. To read a description of a computer program is like reading the description of a knitting pattern. Nothing is more impenetrable and less fun—unless you want to knit the actual sweater, or write the actual program. So, you may want to move rapidly on, grasping just the general idea of how the program works.

The input to the program is a set of premises, such as those for Ratchett's murder, and its output is the set of possibilities compatible with them, followed by a parsimonious description of the possibilities. In the case of Ratchett's stabbing, the program reveals the identity of the one person who didn't participate in the murder. It represents in a complete and fully explicit way the set of possibilities. It constructs these *complete* models of the possibilities for the first premise, and then updates them by forming a logical conjunction of each of them with each of the complete models for the second premise, and so on, until it has taken into account all the premises. The mechanism for conjunction is simple. If two models contain contradictory propositions, then the result is *nil*, which is the null or empty model that the program uses to represent self-contradictions. If two models are free from contradiction, then the result is a model representing all the propositions in both models. And, if one of the models in a conjunction is the null model, then the result is the null model. Box 8.2 describes these rules and illustrates them for the first two premises in the puzzle about Ratchett's murder. The result is four models, which is less burdensome than the truth table of the premises. In general, the program represents only models of the possibilities consistent with the premises and so it is more efficient than the use of truth tables, which also represent the possibilities that the premises rule out. It solves the murder mystery without ever having to construct more than seventy-five possibilities at any one time in comparison with the truth table representing over eight thousand possibilities.

Box 8.2 The mechanism for making a conjunction of complete models

The premises:

> If the Countess helped then Cyrus helped.
> Edward helped or the Countess helped.

have the following complete models respectively:

Countess helped	Cyrus helped
Countess did not help	Cyrus helped
Countess did not help	Cyrus did not help

Box 8.2 *(continued)*

and:

Edward helped	Countess did not help
Edward did not help	Countess helped
Edward helped	Countess helped

The mechanism updates the models of the first premise by forming a logical conjunction of each of them with each of the models of the second premise. Three procedures form conjunctions in general:

1. The conjunction of a pair of models containing respectively a proposition and its negation yields *nil*, the empty model that represents contradictions, e.g.:

   Countess helped   Cyrus helped

   and

   Edward helped   Countess did not help

   yield nil.

2. The conjunction of a pair of models that do not contain a contradiction yields a model representing all the propositions in both models, e.g.:

   Countess helped   Cyrus helped

   and

   Edward helped   Countess helped

   yield Countess helped Cyrus helped Edward helped.

3. The conjunction of a pair of models in which at least one of them is the null model yields the null model, e.g.:

   Countess helped

   and

   nil

   yield nil
   The result of conjoining the models of the first premise above with those of the second premise is therefore:

Countess helped	Cyrus helped	Edward did not help
Countess did not help	Cyrus did not help	Edward helped
Countess helped	Cyrus helped	Edward helped
Countess did not help	Cyrus helped	Edward helped

Like us, the program can evaluate given conclusions or draw conclusions for itself. It draws parsimonious conclusions, that is, those that use the smallest number of connectives. Logicians and engineers have developed various procedures for this problem, which is known as the "Boolean minimization" problem. It is important because the components of many electronic circuits are Boolean. Hence, the fewer of them there are in a circuit, the cheaper the cost of its manufacture. I have implemented a procedure that works by decomposing sets of models into subsets, until it can assemble an appropriate description. It is guaranteed to yield a minimal description. However, the problem is also intractable. No matter how efficient a procedure is sooner or later the number of models becomes too great for a solution to be computed in a reasonable time.

* * *

Our model-building system constructs one model at a time, and, as far as possible, seeks not to construct more than one model. The structure and content of a model capture what is common to the different ways in which the possibility could occur. When we are forced to try to hold in mind several possibilities, the task is hard, because our working memory has a limited capacity. A superhuman intelligence wouldn't be limited in this way. Its memory would not be a bottleneck, and so it could solve the murder on the Orient Express without benefit of paper and pencil using the same mechanism as the computer program. We don't realize our limitations because our social world is no more complicated than our ability to think about it, and our reasoning about the physical world is good enough for us to survive and to reproduce.

In general, a conclusion is valid if it holds in all the models of the premises. A conclusion is invalid if at least one model of the premises is a counterexample to it. As I said at the start of the book, the foundation of human rationality appears to reside in nothing more than this principle: an inference is valid if its conclusion holds in all possibilities compatible with the premises, and it is invalid if there is a possibility compatible with the premises but not with the conclusion. Human reasoners appear to grasp this principle and to realize that an inference is fallible if they can think of a counterexample.

A fundamental assumption of the model theory is the so-called principle of "truth": unlike *complete* models, which I described above, *mental* models represent a simple proposition in the premises only when the proposition is true in the possibility. The mind seems to work this way in order to reduce the load on working memory. Hence, the principle of truth applies unless something exceptional occurs to overrule it. It seems innocuous enough, but when I've explained it, we will come to its most striking and unexpected consequence.

As an example of the principle of truth, consider the first premise in the stabbing problem:

If the Countess helped then Cyrus helped.

In its logical meaning, the conditional is compatible with the three possibilities illustrated in Box 8.2. However, because it's difficult to hold three possibilities in mind, when we reason from a conditional, we focus on the case in which both the propositions in the conditional hold. And so we construct the mental model of the salient possibility:

Countess helped   Cyrus helped

If we were to construct this model alone, then we would have represented a conjunction: the Countess helped *and* Cyrus helped. But, we realize that the "if" clause needn't hold: the Countess may not have helped. In effect, we defer the construction of an explicit model of this possibility. We add to the previous mental model one that has no explicit content. This implicit model acts as a "place holder" to remind us that there are other possibilities, and, for a while at least, we bear in mind that in these possibilities it is false that the Countess helped. The *mental* models of the conditional are accordingly:

Countess helped   Cyrus helped

. . .

where the ellipsis denotes the implicit model. If we remember what is false in models, then we can flesh out our mental models into the three complete models in Box 8.2.

The task of judging truth and falsity is rather different from the task of listing possibilities. We have to relate models of a conditional to models of the world in order to determine whether the conditional is true or false. We rely on mental models to carry out this task. Hence, we tend to think that a conditional is *true* just in the case that both its clauses are true, corresponding to the single explicit mental model of the conditional. To list possibilities, however, we need only to understand a sentence, and so we can flesh out our mental models into complete models.

The second premise in the stabbing problem is an inclusive disjunction:

Edward helped or the Countess helped.

Its mental models according to the principle of truth are:

Edward helped

              Countess helped

Edward helped   Countess helped

The proposition that the Countess helped is false in the first possibility, and so it is not represented in the first mental model. Likewise, the proposition that Edward helped is false in the second possibility, and so it is not represented in the second mental model. You shouldn't confuse falsity with negation: a negative sentence can be true or false. It is false propositions, whether affirmative or negative, that are not represented in mental models.

In these simple diagrams of mental models, each horizontal row denotes a model of a separate possibility. Real mental models, unlike diagrams of them, are not made from English sentences, which I use for convenience. Mental models represent possibilities in as iconic a way as possible, though not everything can be iconic. As I showed earlier, neither negation nor the status of a model as representing a possibility can be represented in an icon. They both have to be represented as symbols. Our mental models are therefore much richer than the diagrams above.

* * *

We have a natural tendency to think of possibilities. Hence, when we draw a conclusion from a set of premises, we think of the possibilities compatible with the premises. We build the mental models of one premise, and then update them according to the next premise, and so on. The computer program that I described also builds mental models of the premises as well as complete models. One additional process is necessary to cope with the incomplete nature of mental models. When a proposition, such as: *Edward helped*, is missing from one model of a premise, but occurs in another model of the same premise, the program interprets its absence as its negation. But, if it doesn't occur in any other model of the premises either, then its absence is treated as consistent with its affirmation.

As an illustrative example, let's consider again the first two premises from our stabbing problem:

If the Countess helped then Cyrus helped.
Edward helped or the Countess helped.

You might like to think for a moment what possibilities are compatible with them. Most people think that there are three:

Countess helped	Cyrus helped	
		Edward helped
Countess helped	Cyrus helped	Edward helped

Box 8.3 Mental models and complete models for propositions based on connectives

Each row in the diagrams below represents a possibility compatible with a proposition.

Propositions	Mental models		Complete models	
A and B	A	B	A	B
If A then B	A	B	A	B
	...		not-A	B
			not-A	not-B
A or B, or both	A		A	not-B
		B	not-A	B
	A	B	A	B
A or else B, not both	A		A	not-B
		B	not-A	B

What they overlook is the fourth possibility shown in Box 8.2 in which only Cyrus and Edward helped. Reasoners who rely on mental models won't think of this possibility. This prediction is typical of the model theory.

The contrast between mental models and complete models is summarized for the main connectives in Box 8.3. These differences and the principles for conjoining them can lead to radical differences between mental models and complete models. As a result, we are liable to err in reasoning about connections because we rely on mental models.

* * *

Two contrasting inferences illuminate the theory. The first inference is:

> Either Jane is kneeling by the fire and she is looking at the TV or else Mark is standing at the window and he is peering into the garden.
>
> Jane is kneeling by the fire.
>
> Does it follow that she is looking at the TV?

Most people say: "yes".

The second inference has the same initial premise, but it is followed instead by the categorical proposition:

Jane is not kneeling by the fire.

and the question is:

Does it follow that Mark is standing by the window?

Again, most participants say: "yes". Let's see what the theory predicts.

The first premise in both inferences is an exclusive disjunction of two conjunctions. The theory predicts that we should rely on mental models. Hence, we should build a model representing the first conjunction, *Jane is kneeling by the fire and she is looking at TV*. I abbreviate this model as follows:

Jane: kneeling looking

We should build an analogous model of the second conjunction:

Mark: standing peering

We must combine these two models according to the exclusive disjunction in the premise. An exclusive disjunction has two mental models, which represent its clauses in the possibilities in which they are true. Hence, the exclusive disjunction has two models:

Jane: kneeling looking

Mark: standing peering

In the first inference, the categorical premise has a single mental model:

Jane: kneeling

Its conjunction with the models of the disjunction yields:

Jane: kneeling looking

And so the participants should respond: yes, Jane is looking at the TV. This analysis may strike you as obvious.

In fact, the inference is a fallacy. The principle of truth postulates that we represent what is true, not what is false. When I first wrote a program to simulate the theory, I inspected its output and thought that there was an error in the program. I searched for this bug for half a day, before I realized that the program was correct, and that the error was in my thinking. What the program revealed is the discrepancy between mental models, which don't represent what's false, and complete models, which do. The theory therefore predicts that we should commit systematic fallacies for certain inferences. Indeed, the fallacies turned out to be so compelling in many cases that they resembled cognitive illusions, and so my colleagues and I refer to them as "illusory" inferences.

The first of the two inferences is illusory, and the complete models of the premises reveal the correct conclusion. There are six complete models of the exclusive disjunction, because when one conjunction is true, the other conjunction is false, and there are three ways in which a conjunction can be false. Its first proposition can be false, its second proposition can be false, and both of these propositions can be false. So, if Jane is kneeling by the fire, it doesn't follow that she's looking at the TV—the conjunction can be false provided that the other conjunction is true, that is, Mark is standing at the window and peering into the garden. That's why the illusory inference is invalid.

The second problem above has the categorical premise that Jane is not kneeling by the fire, and poses the question of whether it follows that Mark is standing by the window. Most people respond, "yes", which is a conclusion supported by the mental models shown above. This inference *is* valid. An experiment examined a series of illusory inferences and control problems of this sort. The participants were correct much more often for the control problems (seventy-eight percent correct) than for the illusory problems (ten percent correct), and all but one of the participants showed this difference. To rely on truth is a sensible way to cope with a limited working memory. In some cases, however, it leads reasoners into the dangerous illusion that they grasp possibilities that are in fact beyond them.

* * *

Possibilities are at the heart of the model theory, because models represent possibilities. The principle of truth, however, specifies that mental models represent the possibilities consistent with the premises, and within each possibility they represent just those simple propositions in the premises that are true. Complete models, however, also represent what is false in possibilities. The advantage of mental models is that they contain less information. They take up less room in working memory; but they can lead us astray. We are susceptible to illusions because we do not represent the set of complete possibilities consistent with the premises. For example, we think about the truth of each proposition in an exclusive disjunction, but when we do so, we fail to take into account the concurrent falsity of the other proposition. It is as though this other proposition has ceased to exist. Rules sensitive to the logical form of propositions cannot predict the occurrence of the illusions. These rules need to deliver valid conclusions on pain of contradiction, and so they have no way in which to predict systematic fallacies.

If the connectives *and*, *or*, and *if*, had only logical meanings, the present chapter would have given a full account of their interpretation. But, later, we will see how knowledge modulates their interpretations—to the point that they no longer have logical meanings. We will also see that people develop a variety of strategies for reasoning, including the use of counterexamples to refute invalid inferences. Finally, the solution to the Murder on the Orient Express is that everyone except the Countess stabbed the wicked Mr. Ratchett. The problem is trivial for the computer program when it uses complete models.

Chapter 9

I'm my own Grandpa: Reasoning About Identities and Other Relations

A fellow of a Cambridge college, Ernest Harrison, became a naval officer during World War I, and while on active duty he shaved off his mustache. He came back for a visit to Cambridge, and the Master of his old college, not recognizing him, asked him at dinner whether he was related to "our dear Ernest Harrison". Adopting a certain philosophical view of relations, he replied: No.

The philosophical view that Harrison held was that a relation cannot hold between anything and itself. Modern logic is more sensible and allows that *identity* is a relation that holds between anything and itself. Logic concurs with the old song: "I'm my own grandpa." Indeed, we make many inferences about relations from day to day, and the logical notion of a relation embraces, not just kinfolk, but everything from *taller than* to *the employer of the husband of the student of*. For example, we can infer the spatial relation between the cabinet and the table from this description of Professor Higgins's study (see Chapter 2):

> The cabinet is to the right of the door.
>
> The table is to the left of the door.

We have no difficult in concluding:

> The cabinet is to the right of the table.

The inference seems so trivial as not to need any explanation. Yet, psychologists disagree about how we make it. Everyone, however, accepts one point. To draw this conclusion, unlike the inferences described in the previous chapter, we have to examine the innards of the propositions in the premises in order to establish a relation between a piece from one proposition and a piece from another. Relations can hold between individual entities, as in the preceding example, or between sets of entities, as in the proposition, "Not all the cabinets are on the right of all the tables". As you can imagine, relations among individuals are much simpler than those among sets, and so I am going to postpone until later an account of reasoning about sets.

* * *

What is a relation? Logicians have given us a precise answer to this question, which I will use. Let's start with the relation, *taller than*. It holds between a vast number of pairs of entities. It holds, for instance, between this pair in the order stated: Michael Jordan and George W. Bush, and it also holds between this pair in the order stated: Mount Everest and Mont Blanc. To use a piece of logical terminology, I shall say that the relation takes two "arguments," which are entities such as Jordan and Everest. Logic pins down a relation as all the pairs of arguments for which the relation holds. In everyday life, the *meaning* of the relation determines whether or not it holds for a given pair of arguments. Meaning is a slippery business, but later in the chapter I will describe how we can analyze the meanings of spatial relations. An adjective such as "happy", as in "Pat is happy" takes one argument, such as Pat, and it denotes a *property* rather than a relation. The logic of properties is simple, and was first outlined by Aristotle. The logic of relations is not simple, and was not fully pinned down until over two thousand years later.

Psychologists are always tempted to reduce relations to properties, because properties are simpler. Language helps us to make these reductions. For example, the proposition: "Dumbo is small," seems to ascribe a property to Dumbo. But, in fact, it asserts that Dumbo is small *in relation to* the typical size of elephants. That is why there is no contradiction in asserting: "A small elephant is large". It means that an elephant that is small for an elephant is large for a typical animal. We make similar reductions in life. We look at the speedometer on our car, and see that we're traveling at sixty miles per hour. The position of the needle on the dial displays the car's instantaneous velocity as though it were a property. But, the velocity of a car depends on a relation between distance and time.

Psychologists often treat relations in perception as though they are "features"—just another word for properties. It's doomed as a general account of cognition, because relations are reduced to properties at a cost. To see why, suppose that we wanted to analyze the relation, *father of*, as a set of properties. We might propose this set:

human, adult, male, has-a-child

The last of these properties looks like a relation in disguise, but no matter. Relations can be combined with other relations to make more complicated relations. Here, for example, is such a relation:

the wife of the grandpa of.

If we treat it as a set of properties then we cannot distinguish it from the very different relation:

the grandpa of the wife of.

Dorothy is the wife of the grandpa of Ben, but she is nobody's grandpa, and Ben is nobody's grandpa, either. Relations are relations: we reduce them at our peril.

An object can enter into many relations. Perhaps, for example, *you* are reading this book, sitting in a chair, sipping a gin and tonic, eating foie gras, listening to the sound of trumpets, and hoping for astonishment. All these relations hold between just two entities, or, to use the terminology I introduced earlier, two arguments: you and something else. Some relations hold among three arguments, and on a rare occasion among four, e.g., *Ben swapped his stamp collection with Carl for a penknife*. In theory, they can hold among any number of arguments. The greater the number of arguments that a relation has the harder it is for us to understand, and the psychologist Graeme Halford refers to this factor as "relational complexity".

Relations yield many sorts of inferences, and logicians have identified several systematic patterns in them. Relations are *transitive*, they say, if they yield this sort of inference:

A is related to B.

B is related to C.

Therefore, A is related to C.

Other relations are intransitive. For example, if Alan is next in line to Bill, and Bill is next in line to Chuck, then Alan is *not* next in line to Chuck. And many relations are inert on this score because they are neither transitive nor intransitive. For example, if Ann is next to Beth, and Beth is next to Cath, it follows neither that Ann is next to Cath nor that she is not. They could be standing in a line or else in a small huddle.

Consider the spatial relation in this proposition:

Alan is behind Bill.

What follows? The answer depends on our frame of reference. We can use an egocentric frame of reference based on our point of view. We can say: As I view the world, Alan is behind Bill. It then follows that Bill is in front of Alan.

In contrast, we can use an objective frame of reference independent of our point of view. Alan and Bill are standing back to back, and so Alan is behind Bill. It no longer follows that Bill is in front of Alan. When we say that we are facing westwards, we are using an objective frame of reference that is also independent of point of view. The Guugu Yimithirr, the Australian group that I described in Chapter 2, have only an objective point of view about spatial relations.

The ambiguity about frame of reference runs through the English terms for spatial relations. We think of many objects as having intrinsic tops and bottoms, intrinsic fronts and backs, and even intrinsic right-hand sides and left-hand sides. A square wooden box without a lid has an intrinsic top and bottom, but no intrinsic front and back, and no intrinsic right-hand side and left-hand side. Put a hinged lid on top of the box, and by magic it acquires all these parts. Its front is the side on which the lid opens, and its right-hand side is on the right if we face its front. Intrinsic parts depend on how we orient ourselves to objects—in this case to open the lid of the box. Intrinsic sides contrast with the sides of objects that we describe from our point of view. The intrinsic right-hand side of the box can be the left-hand side as we see it. No wonder that sailors use a special jargon to refer to the intrinsic parts of ships. "Full steam backwards and turn left", would be confusing.

* * *

In relational reasoning, we aim to infer a novel relation that holds between arguments in the premises. We can make these inferences without relying on a memory for a similar inference, and without using rules of inference with a particular content. So, once again, the question is whether we use form or content. Consider this inference, and from now on I'll assume an egocentric frame of reference:

> The triangle is to the right of the circle.
>
> The circle is to the right of the diamond.
>
> Therefore, the triangle is to the right of the diamond.

Is it valid? In the sense that its conclusion must be true given that its premises are true, it is indeed valid. From a formal standpoint, however, it is missing a premise. This premise stipulates that "to the right of" is a transitive relation:

> If a first entity is to the right of a second entity, and the second entity is to the right of a third entity, then the first entity is to the right of the third entity.

This principle holds for any entities in an egocentric framework. It is axiomatic. Logicians refer to these axioms as "meaning postulates" because they are postulates about the meanings of terms. They may look like rules of inference with a specific content, but premises—and axioms are premises—should not be confused with rules of inference. We use rules of inference to draw conclusions from premises, not vice versa. Premises are data, from which rules of inference enable us to derive conclusions.

Once we have the meaning postulate for "to the right of", we can prove that the conclusion above follows from the premises using formal rules of inference. The proof calls for the substitution of particular entities into the meaning postulate and then a simple inference based on a formal rule for conditional propositions. The details of the proof are logical book-keeping, and I have relegated them to Box 9.1. Theories of reasoning that rely on

---

Box 9.1 A formal proof of a transitive spatial inference

The premises are:

1. The triangle is to the right of the circle.

2. The circle is to the right of the diamond.

3. If a first entity is to the right of a second entity, and the second entity is to the right of a third entity, then the first entity is to the right of the third entity. (A meaning postulate.)

The proof proceeds as follows.

4. Substitute particular entities in the meaning postulate to yield:

   If the triangle is to the right of the circle and the circle is to the right of the diamond then the triangle is to the right of the diamond.

5. Use a formal rule to form a conjunction of the premises 1 and 2:

   The triangle is to the right of the circle and the circle is to the right of the diamond.

6. Use a formal rule (*If A then B*; *A*; therefore, *B*) on 4 and 5 to yield the conclusion:

   Therefore, the triangle is to the right of the diamond.

formal rules are clear and precise. They can deal with any aspect of relational reasoning that can be captured in meaning postulates. And, at first sight, it does seem that any aspect of relational reasoning can be explained in this way. A major logician in the twentieth century, Yehoshua Bar-Hillel, suggested a useful way to simplify the book-keeping: just have one all-purpose axiom for transitivity, and label those relations, such as "to the right of", to which it is applicable.

* * *

A mental model of spatial relations is iconic and it integrates the information in the premises, and so it embodies novel relations that do not correspond to any of the propositions used in its construction. When we make relational inferences, we can use these novel relations to formulate conclusions. Unlike an approach based on form, a system using mental models does not need axioms to capture the logical properties of relations. The transitivity of a relation is an emergent property from the construction of models based on the meanings of sentences. To illustrate this point, I'll describe a computer program that simulates the model theory, but you should skim this account if you are not interested in the workings of programs.

The input to the program is a spatial description with, or without a given conclusion, e.g.:

> The triangle is to the right of the circle.
>
> The circle is to the right of the diamond.
>
> Therefore, the triangle is to the right of the diamond.

The program constructs a model of the first premise. It uses the meaning of *the circle* to insert a token representing the circle into a three-dimensional spatial model:

○

The meaning of *to the right of* specifies that the system scans in a rightwards direction from the circle, and so the program increments the left-to-right axis from the circle while holding constant the values on the other two axes (up-and-down and front-and-back). It then uses the meaning of *the triangle* to insert a representation of it into the first empty location in the model:

○   △

The left-to-right axis in this diagram corresponds to the left-to-right spatial axis of the model.

The program can search for referents in its spatial models. Hence, given the second premise:

The circle is to the right of the diamond

it discovers that the circle is already represented in its current model of the premises. It uses the meaning of the sentence to update this model. It therefore inserts a representation of the diamond into an appropriate position in the model:

With the first premise, we can scan from the circle in the direction that the relation specifies in order to find a location for the triangle. But, with the second premise, this natural procedure is not feasible. Like the program, we have to scan in the opposite direction to the one that the relation specifies— from the circle to a location for the diamond. This task ought to be a little bit harder, and the evidence shows that it is.

If a premise refers to nothing in the current model, then the program constructs a new model. Later, given an appropriate premise, it can integrate the two separate models into a single model. This case also adds to the difficulty of our reasoning.

Given the putative conclusion in the example:

The triangle is to the right of the diamond

the program discovers that both referents are already represented in its current model. It checks whether the appropriate relation holds between them. It scans in a rightwards direction from the diamond until it finds the triangle. The relation holds. Next, it checks whether any other model of the premises is a counterexample to the conclusion. It finds none, and so it declares that the inference is valid. In case a conclusion doesn't hold in the current model, the program checks whether any other model of the previous premises allows the relation to hold. If not, the proposition is inconsistent with what has gone before.

I have now described the main procedures that the program uses, and Box 9.2 summarizes them. If our inferential system uses models, it needs them too. These procedures can make valid inferences, they work without a homunculus, and they do not use meaning postulates. Such axioms are not needed, because the validity of inferences emerges from the meanings of relations, which specify the direction in which to scan models. The model theory postulates that we make relational inferences in the same sort of way.

Box 9.2 Seven procedures for reasoning using models

1. Start a new model. The procedure inserts a new referent into the model according to a premise.
2. Update a model with a new referent in relation to an existing referent.
3. Update a model with a new property or relation.
4. Join two separate models into one according to a relation between referents in them.
5. Verify whether a proposition is true or false in models.
6. Search for a counterexample to refute a proposition. If the search fails, then the proposition follows validly from the previous propositions in the description.
7. Search for an example to make a proposition true. If the search fails, then the proposition is inconsistent with the previous propositions.

One point is easy to overlook. The program's search for counterexamples works because it has access to the representations of the *meanings* of the premises. Without these representations, if the program were to change a model, it would have no way to check whether the result was still a model of the premises. Any inferential system that constructs alternative models therefore needs an independent record of the premises. It must either have a memory for their meanings, or be able to return to each premise and to reinterpret it.

The strategy embodied in the spatial reasoning program is to construct a single model at a time. When a description is consistent with more than one layout, the program builds whichever model requires the least work. An alternative strategy, which I have implemented in a program for reasoning about temporal relations, is to try to build all the different possible models. Still another strategy is to represent the alternative possibilities within a single model using a way to indicate the uncertain positions of entities in the model. We can probably develop any of these strategies depending on the particulars of the problems that we tackle. This notion of *strategy*, as you should have inferred, concerns the sequence of steps in making inferences that cannot be carried out in a single mental operation, and later in the book I return to the question of how we develop inferential strategies.

$* * *$

Identities are a special sort of relation, but they can also be inferred from models. The inferences fall into two main classes, those that establish an identity, and those that that establish a nonidentity. Here is an inference establishing an identity:

> Ernest is Mr. Harrison.
>
> Mr. Harrison is the Bass drinker.
>
> Therefore, Ernest is the Bass drinker.

And here is an example of an inference establishing a nonidentity:

> Ernest is Mr. Harrison.
>
> Mr. Harrison isn't the Guinness drinker.
>
> Therefore, Ernest isn't the Guinness drinker.

Both these inferences are valid, and they show that we can refer to individuals both by a name and by a definite description that picks out a unique individual, at least in the context of its use.

Because mental models are as iconic as possible, each individual entity is represented just once in a model. The proposition that Ernest is Mr. Harrison is represented as follows:

> Ernest   Mr. Harrison
>
>   . . .

where each row in the diagram represents a separate individual. The ellipsis allows for the existence of other individuals, and a mental footnote represents that none of them is either Ernest or Mr. Harrison. The proposition that Mr. Harrison is the Bass drinker updates the model:

> Ernest   Mr. Harrison   Bass drinker
>
>   . . .

And this model yields the conclusion:

> Ernest is the Bass drinker.

In contrast, the negative proposition that Mr. Harrison isn't the Guinness drinker updates the initial model in this way:

> Ernest   Mr. Harrison
>
>   Guinness drinker
>
>   . . .

and the footnote on the implicit model is updated to indicate that none of the individuals that it represents is a Guinness drinker. The model represents two individuals: Ernest Harrison and the Guinness drinker. It yields the conclusion:

> Ernest is not the Guinness drinker.

Logical puzzles in magazines and in mental tests are often based on descriptions of individuals and their unique properties (see Box 9.3). The two central inferences in these puzzles once again concern identity and nonidentity. If an individual is not identical with anyone except one member of a set, then the

---

Box 9.3 The solution to a puzzle of identity

Ernest, Mr. Littlewood, and two other men each prefer a particular one of four different sorts of beer, including Guinness. The four men are uniquely identified as the Bass drinker, Mr. Hardy, and two who don't drink Adnams: John and Mr. Russell.

Neither Bertie nor Mr. Harrison who is Godfrey's friend drink Harp.

Bertie who is Mr Hardy's neighbor doesn't drink Bass.

To solve the problem, fill in the four unique individuals in an array:

	1	2	3	4
First name			John	
Second name		Hardy		Russell
Preferred beer	Bass			

Given that neither John nor Russell drink Adnams, and person 1 drinks Bass, it follows that Hardy drinks Adnams. Bertie is Hardy's neighbor, and so he cannot be Hardy. Hence, Bertie also is not John or the Bass drinker, and so he must be Russell. As Bertie doesn't drink Harp, John must drink it. Hence, Bertie must drink Guinness. Harrison doesn't drink Harp, and so he must be the Bass drinker. Hence, Littlewood is John. Harrison is Godfrey's friend, and so Godfrey is Hardy, and Harrison is Ernest. The solution is accordingly:

First name	Ernest	Godfrey	John	Bertie
Second name	Harrison	Hardy	Littlewood	Russell
Preferred beer	Bass	Adnams	Harp	Guinness

individual is identical to this odd one out. Likewise, if an individual is one of a set of unique relations, e.g., he is the Guinness drinker, then it follows that Guinness is not the beer for any other individual. One way to determine that two expressions refer to different individuals is from a relation that cannot hold between an entity and itself, e.g., given that Bertie is Hardy's neighbor, it follows that Bertie isn't Hardy. You cannot be your own neighbor. Box 9.3 presents a puzzle of identity, and it gives its solution based on my computer program implementing these principles.

* * *

The limits of iconicity may be greater than I described earlier in the book. To understand why, consider this model and ask yourself what it represents:

Earlier I used it to represent the spatial relations among the three shapes. But, you have no way to know that from the model alone. It could represent that the three shapes are present, or that they appeared one after another in the order: diamond, circle, triangle. In a spatial model, the axes represent spatial dimensions; in the model of the mere presence of the shapes, the axes represent nothing; in a temporal model, the principal axis represents time. Our brains could maintain separate dedicated systems for these various sorts of model. But, a sequence of spatial events may unfold over time, and so the spatial system would have to be embedded within the temporal system. Sometimes a temporal sequence may concern the presence of objects, so these sorts of models would also have to be embedded within the temporal system. To make matters worse, we may sometimes represent a temporal sequence in a static spatial model such as a graph.

Perhaps a more plausible possibility is akin to what happens when a retired colonel explains the battle of El Alamein to us over the dinner table. He uses the salt and pepper pots and assorted pieces of cutlery to represent the dispositions of Montgomery's and Rommel's armies. The problem is: how do we know that the salt pot represents Montgomery's 1st Armoured Division? The answer is that the colonel told us, and we and he can bear it in mind. Likewise, when the reasoning system constructs a model of a spatial arrangement, it can represent that the axes have a spatial interpretation. As you already know, the reasoning system needs an independent representation of the meanings of sentences so that when it modifies a model in searching for a counterexample, it can check that the resulting model still represents the premises. Hence, the meanings of the sentences could stipulate how the model is to be interpreted. In this case, what a model represents depends on both the model and the meanings of the sentences used to construct it.

* * *

The evidence corroborates the use of models in reasoning. Participants in experiments report that they imagine spatial layouts. They often make gestures with their hands that suggest they have a spatial model in mind. Likewise, if they have paper and pencil, they draw diagrams. Yet, the evidence does not rule out the possibility that deep down the unconscious inferential processes are guided by form rather than content. Is there perhaps a crucial experiment that would show us that people rely on one method rather than the other? I will describe three.

The first experiment used descriptions of two-dimensional spatial layouts of household objects that we might find on a table. One sort of problem was, for example:

> The cup is on the right of the plate.
>
> The spoon is on the left of the plate.
>
> The knife is in front of the spoon.
>
> The saucer is in front of the cup.
>
> What is the relation between the knife and the saucer?

If we use formal rules to derive the answer, then we have to proceed in two main steps. We have to use meaning postulates and the first two premises to infer the relation between the spoon and cup:

> The spoon is on the left of the cup.

And then we have to use a "two-dimensional" meaning postulate to derive from this conclusion and the remaining two premises the answer to the question:

> The knife is on the left of the saucer.

Hence, we first draw a transitive conclusion and then we use it to draw a conclusion about the entities in the question.

A second sort of problem was, for example:

> The plate is on the right of the cup.
>
> The spoon is on the left of the plate.

The knife is in front of the spoon.

The saucer is in front of the plate.

What is the relation between the knife and the saucer?

In this case there is no need for the initial transitive inference. The second premise asserts that the spoon is on the left of the plate, and the "two-dimensional" postulate and this conclusion yields the answer that the knife is on the left of the saucer. This problem should therefore be easier than the first one.

The model theory makes the opposite prediction. The premises of the first problem yield a two-dimensional model of the spatial layout of the objects, shown in this diagram as if from above:

spoon   plate   cup

knife   saucer

This model yields the conclusion that knife is on the left of the saucer. The premises of second problem, however, are consistent with two distinct layouts, because they don't fix the relation between the spoon and cup:

spoon cup plate   cup spoon plate

knife   saucer   knife   saucer

Both layouts, however, support the conclusion that the knife is on the left of the saucer, but two models—or a single model representing the alternative positions of the cup—should be harder to hold in mind, and so this problem should be more difficult than the first one.

You may have noticed that the first premise in the second problem is irrelevant to the inference. The premise may disrupt reasoning, and thereby lead to a greater difficulty for this problem. To check for this possibility, the experiment also used problems that yield a single model, but that have an irrelevant first premise. If the occurrence of an irrelevant premise is critical, then these problems should be harder than first sort, even though they both call for just one model. But, if the model theory is correct, the irrelevant premise should make no difference. The participants had no difficulty with irrelevant premises, and they made seventy percent correct responses to the problems with a single layout but only forty-six percent correct responses to the problems with more than one layout. The correct conclusions were also faster for single layouts (a mean of 3.1 seconds) than for multiple layouts (3.6 seconds). Other studies have replicated these results. They have also shown the same effect of number of possibilities for temporal relations such as *before* and *after*, and for more abstract relations such as *studying more than* and *copying from*, which should tend to evoke abstract models. Even when all the problems have one irrelevant premise, problems yielding a single model are easier than those yielding multiple models.

A second experiment examined reasoning about temporal relations, but it depended on verbs and their tenses to convey the order of events. Here's a typical problem from the experiment:

> John has cleaned the house.
>
> John is taking a shower.
>
> John is going to read the paper.
>
> Mary always does the dishes when John cleans the house.
>
> Mary always drinks her coffee when John reads the paper.
>
> What is the relation between Mary doing the dishes and drinking coffee?

The tense of the verbs and the various auxiliaries, such as "has", establish the order of John's three actions: he cleans the house, takes a shower, and then reads the paper. The fourth and fifth premises tie Mary's two actions to John's, and so we can construct a temporal model of the entire description. The following diagram depicts the model, where time is the left-to-right axis, and each line shows the sequence of actions of one of the protagonists:

> John: cleans the house   takes a shower   reads the paper
>
> Mary: does the dishes   drinks her coffee

It follows that Mary does the dishes before she drinks her coffee. A problem consistent with two different temporal orders has a different second premise:

> John has taken a shower.

In this case, there are two possible orders for John's first two actions, because he can't do them both at the same time. The experiment showed that correct answers occurred more often for problems yielding one mental model than for problems yielding multiple models. The difficulty for a formal account is to frame meaning postulates that make these inferences possible. It is difficult, because the inferences depend on auxiliary verbs, tense, and aspect. The postulates would have to jumble up all these matters, e.g.:

> If a sentence contains "has" followed by a verb in the past tense and describes an event, and if a second sentence contains "going" prior to an infinitive and describes an event, then the event described in the first sentences happens before the event described in the second sentence.

This postulate violates the principle that meaning postulates concern the logical properties of words.

A third experiment demonstrated a still greater difficulty for meaning postulates. It examined such inferences as:

> Alice is a blood relative of Brian.
>
> Brian is a blood relative of Charlie.
>
> What follows?

You may be tempted to infer that Alice is a blood relative of Charlie. Perhaps you thought of a set of siblings or a line of descendants. Yet, there are counterexamples to the conclusion. Suppose, for instance, that Alice is Brian's mother, and Charlie is his father. Alice is related to Brian, and he is related to Charlie, but his mother and father are probably not blood relatives. These "pseudo-transitive" inferences depend on relations that are neither transitive nor intransitive, but that yield models of typical situations in which a transitive conclusion holds.

We use our knowledge when we reason. Given these premises:

> Armstrong overtook Hamilton.
>
> Ullrich overtook Armstrong.

we are likely to infer that Ullrich overtook Hamilton. But, there is a counterexample. Suppose, for example, that the premises refer to a time trial in the Tour de France. The riders set out one at a time at two-minute intervals. Armstrong catches up with Hamilton, and overtakes him. Hamilton drops out of the race at this point. And then Ullrich, who set out behind Armstrong, catches up with him and overtakes him. Both premises are true, but because of these extraordinary events, the transitive conclusion is false. Ullrich never overtook Hamilton, because Hamilton was no longer in the race. Indeed, he could have been waiting at the finish for Ullrich to arrive.

We make pseudo-transitive inferences because the premises elicit a model of a typical situation in which the transitive conclusion happens to hold. The model theory therefore predicts that the way to block these inferences is to get the participants to search harder for counterexamples. Another experiment tested participants in two different conditions. In one condition, they carried out the original pseudo-transitive problems. In the other condition, each pseudo-transitive problem was presented with a verbal clue designed to help the participants to think of an atypical case. For example, the problem about "blood relatives" was prefaced with the clue: people can be related either by blood or by marriage. Each participant encountered a particular problem once, in one or other of the two conditions. The clues had a robust effect on reasoning. Without them, the participants drew pseudo-transitive conclusions on sixty-two percent of occasions, but with them, this percentage fell to forty-one percent.

If we use formal rules to reason, then we depend on a meaning postulate that captures the transitivity of a relation. In Bar-Hillel's scheme, each relation that takes two arguments is tagged as transitive, intransitive, or neither. So, what sorts of relations should be tagged as transitive? You might suppose that good candidates would include relations such as, "taller than". But, consider this problem:

> Cate is taller than Belle.
>
> Belle *was* taller than Alice (until Alice drank the magic potion).
>
> Who is tallest?

The change in tense and the magic potion no longer guarantee transitivity. The burden of this example is that no relational terms, not even "taller than" can be classified as transitive in all cases. Transitivity depends on the significance of the proposition as a whole, which in turn depends on its context. Hence, the logical properties of relational terms in natural language cannot be captured in meaning postulates. Fortunately, we don't need meaning postulates if we reason using models. We consider the meanings of the premises, we take context and our knowledge into account, and then we imagine all the possibilities compatible with this information. If a transitive conclusion holds in all these possibilities, then the inference is valid.

The French poet Paul Valéry once suggested that the following question might be a good test for mathematical giftedness:

> If Peter resembles Paul, and Paul resembles James, does James resemble Peter?

Those who say "yes" at once are the gifted ones. His hopes for his test were dashed when one of the best mathematicians he knew began to cogitate at length. No wonder, for it is a moot point whether the relation is transitive. I'd say that Marx resembles Lenin, and that Lenin resembles Stalin, but not that Marx resembles Stalin. Perhaps a better test would be to ask prospective mathematicians to solve this problem:

> I was married to a widow who had a grown-up daughter. My father fell in love with her, and soon they too were wed. This made my dad my son-in-law and now my daughter was my mother, because she was my father's wife. To complicate the matter, I soon became the father of a bouncing baby boy. My little baby then became a brother-in-law

to Dad, and so became my uncle. If he was my uncle, then that also made him brother of the widow's grown-up daughter, who, of course, was my stepmother. Father's wife then had a son who became my grandchild, for he was my daughter's son. My wife is now my mother's mother, and although she is my wife, she's my grandmother, too. Now if my wife is my grandmother, then I'm her grandchild, and I have become the strangest case you ever saw. What am I?

* * *

The model theory postulates that our reasoning depends on the significance of propositions. The transitivity of relations is an emergent property of building iconic models. These models represent many relations that were not asserted in the discourse, and so our task is to find a useful relation and to formulate a conclusion embodying it. Experimental evidence corroborates this account. The computer programs are working models showing that everything can be done by simple processes. No magic required; no homunculi required; no meaning postulates required.

Chapter 10

Syllogisms and Reasoning about Properties

Suppose I have just returned from an art exhibition, and you ask me: "What sort of artists are they?" I reply:

Most of them are painters and sculptors.

And you say:

So, most of them are sculptors and painters.

You have made an inference about two *properties*—the property of being a painter, and the property of being a sculptor. And the inference is trivial because it does no more than re-order these two properties. Yet, it is also remarkable, because none of the current psychological theories of reasoning based on formal rules can explain how you did it. The problem for them is the quantifier, "most". It lies outside the scope of their formal rules, which concern only standard quantifiers such as "every" and "some". Logicians realized long ago that "most" and other quantifiers, such as "more than half", are different from the standard quantifiers, and that they call for a more powerful logic. This high-powered logic provides a uniform way to handle all quantifiers. In essence, it treats a proposition such as:

Most of the artists are painters and sculptors

as meaning that the set of artists who are painters and sculptors is larger than the set of artists who are not both painters and sculptors. Psychological theories based on formal rules have yet to be formulated in this way.

Let me try to meet the formal theories half way. Suppose I had replied to your question about the artists:

Everyone is a painter and a sculptor.

And you inferred:

So, everyone is a sculptor and a painter.

The formal theories can explain how you make this inference. You use a rule to drop the quantifier and to replace it with an arbitrary individual in the relevant set, e.g.: *Fred is a painter and Fred is a sculptor*. You use another rule to detach first one clause from this conjunction, and then the other, and another rule to join them up in the opposite order. Finally, you use still another rule to replace the arbitrary individual with the quantifier:

Everyone is a sculptor and a painter.

Hence, you have to make a sequence of five separate inferences to draw your conclusion. Even those devoted to formal rules may be skeptical that it takes so many steps to make such a trivial inference.

An obvious remedy is to postulate a formal rule that carries out the inference in a single step. This remedy exacts a cost: it is *ad hoc*, and, worse still, it increases the number of rules in the theory, and so the search for a proof has more rules to try out at any stage in a proof. But, there is another more general problem. The first step in using formal rules is to extract the logical forms of the premises so as to match them with appropriate rules. The recovery of this representation is akin to a translation of a sentence into a logical formula. But, this problem is so difficult that no computer program exists to translate English sentences into their logical forms. And so no automatic method exists to use logic to assess arguments couched in the vernacular. Leibniz dreamt of such a method over three hundred years ago. His dream is still unfulfilled and that, as another logician Bar-Hillel has said, is a scandal of human existence.

* * *

One way in which you could make the two previous inferences is to hire a group of actors to play the various roles. They could form a tableau to represent the proposition, *most of the artists are painters and sculptors*. They could hold brushes and palettes to represent that they are painters and they could hold mallets and chisels to represent that they are sculptors. This analogy reveals a central assumption of the model theory. A mental model represents a set of entities as an iconic set of referents. It is the abstract representation that lies behind any image of the actors that you mind form in your mind's eye. Hence, the mental model of the proposition is like the actors' tableau, but it doesn't represent the details of their appearance or how they look from a particular point of view. It uses an arbitrary number of referents to represent the set of individuals:

artist	painter	sculptor
artist	painter	sculptor
artist	painter	sculptor
artist		

Each row in the diagram corresponds to a single individual, and so the first row represents a person who is an artist, painter, and sculptor. As you can see, the model represents the proposition that most of the artists are painters and sculptors, because three out of four of them are. This model can also be described as:

> Most of the artists are sculptors and painters.

Hence, the conclusion that you drew is an immediate outcome of the model, and no need exists for the complicated sequence of formal inferences that I described earlier.

A similar model represents the proposition that everyone is a painter and a sculptor:

artist	painter	sculptor
artist	painter	sculptor
artist	painter	sculptor
artist	painter	sculptor

It, too, yields the immediate conclusion with the two properties in the opposite order:

> Everyone is a sculptor and a painter.

However, I am getting a little ahead of myself, because how do we know that the model above, or indeed the group of actors, represents everyone in the relevant set, as opposed, say, to just four of the individuals in the set? In other words, how do we know that the model represents an *entire* set?

No iconic model can show that it represents an entire set. This information is in the meaning of the sentence that the model represents, and earlier I argued that reasoning based on models also depends on a representation of this meaning. It's needed so that any modification to a model can be checked to ensure that the result is still a model of the premises. We have now encountered another reason to have access to the meaning of premises.

In computer programs simulating the theory, I have sometimes used a special footnote to denote the representation of an entire set. For example, a proposition such as:

> Every painter is a sculptor

has the model:

painter	sculptor
painter	sculptor
painter	sculptor

...

The ellipsis represents other possible individuals in the situation under description, but it has a footnote that no painters occur among them. The model therefore represents the entire set of painters.

How do we know that the model doesn't mean that there are only three painters in the set? The problem is to distinguish between accidental properties of a representation, such as the number of painters in the preceding model, and essential properties, such as the fact that they represent an entire set. Philosophers struggled with this sort of problem for a long time. How, for example, can a single diagram of triangle in a geometric proof stand for any triangle? Its particular angles are accidental, but the fact that it is a triangle is essential. Kant thought the task was impossible, and so concepts had to be represented as abstract schemas. Wittgenstein argued to the contrary that a single object, such as a leaf, could represent any leaf, provided that it was used in the right way. What the right way was, he didn't stop to explain. However, David Hume, the great philosopher of the Scottish Enlightenment, had anticipated the solution:

> ... after the mind has produced an individual idea, upon which we reason, the attendant custom, revived by the general or abstract term, readily suggests any other individual, if by chance we form any reasoning that agrees not with it. Thus, should we mention the word triangle, and form the idea of a particular equilateral one to correspond to it, and should we afterwards assert, *that the three angles of a triangle are equal to each other*, the other individuals of a scalenum and isosceles, which we overlooked at first, immediately crowd in upon us, and make us perceive the falsehood of the proposition...

In sum, geometers know that the diagram is intended to represent an arbitrary triangle, and so they can think of another sort of triangle to refute an erroneous conclusion holding just for their initial diagram. Likewise, we know that the choice of three painters in the model above was arbitrary and so we can alter the number.

* * *

The underlying processes for reasoning about sets are straightforward and echo those for reasoning about identities and non-identities. Two sorts of inference are fundamental. We infer that entities are in a set or we infer that they are not in a set. Box 10.1 illustrates both sorts of inference. They both

Box 10.1 The two fundamental inferences about sets

1. The first sort of inference establishes that an individual is in a set, e.g.:

> Stella is a sculptor.
>
> Every sculptor is a painter.
>
> Therefore, Stella is a painter.

The premises yield the mental model:

Stella	sculptor	painter
	sculptor	painter
	sculptor	painter

. . .

No matter which sculptor Stella is identified with, it follows that Stella is a painter, because the model represents the complete set of sculptors. Hence, when entities are in a set, they inherit any properties that hold over the complete set.

2. The second sort of inference establishes that an individual is *not* in a set, e.g.:

> Cristo isn't a painter.
>
> Every sculptor is a painter.
>
> Therefore, Cristo isn't a sculptor.

The premises yield the model:

Cristo

sculptor	painter
sculptor	painter
sculptor	painter

. . .

It follows that Cristo is not a sculptor. Hence, when entities do not have a property that holds over a complete set, they are not in the set.

hinge on a property, or its lack, that holds for an entire set. Given a premise asserting such a property, another premise can be based on a standard quantifier, such as "some" or "all", or on quantifiers that are not standard, such as "most" or "more than half". For example, this inference is valid:

> Most of the artists are sculptors.
>
> Every sculptor is a painter.
>
> Therefore, most of the artists are painters.

I fancy that Aristotle was aware of the principle. Certainly, his Scholastic followers in Medieval times were—they referred to terms denoting an entire set as "distributed".

Once we can infer that individuals are in or out of a set, we can cope with all inferences about properties, because properties define sets. The processes enabling us to combine the information from separate premises into single models are those that I have already described for relational and propositional reasoning, but geared up for dealing with individuals in sets. They form models, update them, formulate conclusions or verify them, and search for alternative models.

* * *

If some of the painters are sculptors, then it follows that some of the sculptors are painters. But, if more than half of the painters are sculptors, does it follow that more than half of the sculptors are painters? A general principle in building models is parsimony. We aim to represent as few distinct sorts of individual as possible. Hence, we are likely to represent the latter premise as follows:

painter	sculptor
painter	sculptor
painter	

…

The footnote on the implicit model states that the individuals it represents are not painters. If we assume in error that the model also represents the entire set of sculptors, then we will infer that the conclusion follows. But, of course, there could be other sculptors, e.g.:

painter	sculptor
painter	sculptor
painter	
	sculptor
	sculptor

…

This model is a counterexample to the conclusion. Experiments suggest that individuals do draw invalid conclusions of this sort.

* * *

Suppose I tell you more about the art exhibition that I visited:

> Some of the artists are designers, and all the designers are minimalists.

You can infer that some of the artists are minimalists. The inference is an example of a *syllogism*. Aristotle devised a logic for syllogisms, which are inferences about properties based on two quantified premises. He restricted the quantifiers to "all", "some", and their negations. Box 10.2 describes syllogisms. They are part of the logic of properties, which in turn is part of modern logic. But, much of traditional logic was based on Aristotelian syllogisms. Every self-respecting Medieval theologian was skilled in their use. The BBC once broadcast a monastic debate couched only in syllogisms, and the debaters showed great skill in casting arguments into their unwieldy form.

Bertrand Russell, one of the founders of modern logic, had no time for syllogisms, and once argued that the one use that he'd ever heard for them, was by a German philosopher who was puzzled by the advertisements in a spoof issue of the journal, *Mind*. At last the philosopher argued to himself: Everything in this book is a joke; the advertisements are in this book; therefore, the advertisements are a joke. Syllogisms are the object of many other jokes. Woody Allen in his movie *Love and Death* argued: "All men are mortal. Socrates was mortal. Therefore, all men are Socrates. Which means that all men are homosexuals." No joke like an old joke. Plato had a sophist argue: That dog is a father; that dog is yours; therefore, that dog is your father.

We do make inferences about properties, but usually about the properties of individuals, as in the inferences about Stella and Cristo. And syllogisms do occur in life outside monasteries, but they tend to be hidden in informal language, and often take for granted an unstated premise, e.g., all the electrical devices are British, and so they won't work in the USA. Once, after I had given a talk about syllogisms, a distinguished animal psychologist said to me: the trouble with syllogisms is that they are artificial. I said: I suppose you think that psychologists shouldn't study artificial problems. Yes, he said. I said, so you infer that psychologists shouldn't study syllogisms. Yes, he said. And then he laughed. I didn't need to explain to him that the two of us had just constructed a syllogism together, though not one in its full formal dress.

Box 10.2 Syllogisms

A categorical syllogism, or syllogism for short, is an argument consisting of two premises and a conclusion. Each of these three sentences is in one of the following "moods":

All ___ are ___

Some ___ are ___

No ___ is a ___

Some ___ are not ___

For example, the following premises yield a syllogistic conclusion: Some artists are designers; all designers are minimalists. The terms in premises, e.g., *artists*, *designers*, and *minimalists*, can be arranged in four different "figures":

| A–B | B–A | A–B | B–A |
| B–C | C–B | C–B | B–C |

There are therefore sixty-four possible sorts of syllogistic premises (4 moods × 4 moods × 4 figures). Medieval logicians allowed conclusions only of the form: C–A. Psychologists realized that they could also be of the form: A–C. Hence, there are 512 possible forms of complete syllogism (sixty-four sorts of premises ×4 moods of conclusion ×2 figures of conclusion).

Medieval logicians identified valid syllogisms using such rules as:

1. The term that is in both premises must be "distributed" in at least one of them (i.e., refer to an entire set) for the premises to yield a valid conclusion.
2. No term can be distributed in the conclusion unless it is distributed in the premises.
3. If both premises contain "some", then no categorical conclusion follows.
4. If both premises are affirmative, the conclusion is affirmative; otherwise, it is negative.

In modern logic, a sentence such as, "Any deserters are shot", does not imply that there are deserters. In contrast, Aristotle and his Medieval followers assumed that each term in a syllogism refers to existing entities. Psychologists tell their experimental participants that individuals of each sort do exist. In this case, twenty-seven of the sixty-four possible forms of premises yield valid categorical conclusions.

* * *

Most psychological studies of reasoning about properties have examined syllogisms. The reason, I suspect, is the baleful influence of traditional logic. Early studies almost always presented conclusions to be evaluated, either singly or in a multiple-choice test. The results led some investigators to argue that we often do not reason but instead select a response that matches the "atmosphere" of the premises. For example, if both premises contain the quantifier "all", then we are supposed to be more likely to accept a conclusion containing "all" on these grounds alone. Variants of this view have many adherents to the present day. Of course it is impossible to show that none of the participants in an experiment are ever affected by atmosphere. The same sort of effect leads to careless grammatical mistakes, e.g., in the previous sentence "is" should occur in place of "are". But, I suspect that the atmosphere effect has been exaggerated because of an unfortunate coincidence: most valid conclusions do match the atmosphere of the premises. When we draw conclusions in our own words, we often respond, "Nothing follows". The atmosphere hypothesis cannot explain this response, because there is always a putative conclusion fitting the atmosphere of the premises. Moreover, we even make this response when there *is* a valid conclusion, and indeed one that matches the atmosphere of the premises.

An experiment on syllogisms used premises such as, "Only the lonely are brave". Even when both premises contained the quantifier "only", the participants were about three times more likely to draw a conclusion containing "all" than one containing "only". What convinces me that those of us who are untutored in logic make deductions in syllogisms is the world-wide popularity of Sudoku puzzles, which hinge on more complex quantified relations, and which cannot be solved in any way other than by deduction. I will come back to them later in the book. Belief in the atmosphere hypothesis could be the best instance of the phenomenon that it purports to explain—a failure to reason.

Studies of syllogisms yield two robust results. The first is that individuals differ in ability. In a university with stringent selection criteria for admitting undergraduates, a study showed that the participants varied in accuracy from fifty-five percent correct to eighty-five percent correct. A similar study in a university with open admissions showed that the participants varied in accuracy from thirty-seven percent correct to fifty-six percent correct. You may wonder, as I do, what causes these differences. The processing capacity of working memory accounts for some of the variability in performance, but other unknown factors must be at work. If you say, it's a matter of intelligence, then you are right, because mental tests of intelligence correlate with reasoning ability. Unfortunately, no one knows what underlies intelligence, and many of its measures depend on tests of reasoning. So, there's a degree of circularity in your claim. A major intellectual challenge for psychologists is to pin down what underlies differences in the ability to make deductions.

The second robust result is that syllogisms differ in difficulty. Some are child's play, such as this example:

> Some of the authors are bakers.
>
> All the bakers are cricketers.
>
> What, if anything, follows?

Nearly everyone, from seven-year old children to adults, draws the valid conclusion:

> Some of the authors are cricketers.

A few participants draw the valid converse conclusion:

> Some of the cricketers are authors.

But, few draw any other conclusion or respond that nothing follows from the premises. In contrast, other syllogisms are so difficult that hardly anyone makes a correct response to them. If you want to test yourself, try this problem:

> None of the artists is a beekeeper.
>
> All the beekeepers are chemists.
>
> What, if anything, follows?

I'll give you a moment to think about this problem, but don't be dismayed if you go wrong. Most of us do. Some people draw the conclusion:

> None of the artists is a chemist

or its converse:

> None of the chemists is an artist.

Some people say that nothing definite follows about the artists and chemists. Some people draw the conclusion:

> Some of the artists are not chemists.

But, only a handful draw the valid conclusion:

> Some of the chemists are not artists.

As you'll see, the model theory explains this difference in difficulty between the two sorts of inference.

The theory postulates that a premise, such as:

Some of the authors are bakers

has a single mental model representing a small, but arbitrary, number of individuals:

author	baker
author	baker
author	

...

When participants used a set of cut-out figures to reason, this model was the most frequent one that they constructed for the premise. In logic, the premise is treated as meaning that *at least* some of the authors are bakers, and so it is compatible with all the authors being bakers. The mental model can be fleshed out to represent this possibility by adding further referents.

A second premise:

All the bakers are cricketers

can be used to update the previous model. Each baker is represented as a cricketer too:

author	baker	cricketer
author	baker	cricketer
author		

...

This model yields the conclusion that *some of the authors are cricketers*. No other model of the premises refutes the conclusion, and so it is valid.

A program that simulates this account uses procedures similar to those for forming conjunctions of possibilities (see Chapter 8), because each individual is akin to a possible model. Box 10.3 illustrates how the procedures work for the difficult inference above. A key principle is that given a premise interrelating, say, bakers and cricketers, where authors and bakers are already represented in a model, individuals update their representation of bakers. Hence, they tend not to consider at first whether any authors are cricketers unless the relation is established by way of bakers. The models in the box yield a single valid conclusion, and the box shows why it is difficult to infer. As the program reveals, syllogisms yielding valid conclusions are of two sorts: those that depend on a single mental model like the example above, and those that depend on

Box 10.3 An illustration of the procedures for syllogistic reasoning

The first premise: *None of the artists is a beekeeper*, has the mental model:

artist

artist

        beekeeper

        beekeeper

   ...

with a footnote that individuals represented by the ellipsis are neither artists nor beekeepers.

The second premise: *All the beekeepers are chemists*, is used to update this model:

artist

artist

      beekeeper   chemist

      beekeeper   chemist

    ...

This model yields the conclusion: *None of the artists is a chemist*, and its converse. **The procedure for searching for alternative models can add new properties to an individual, break an individual into two, and join two individuals into one. But, it is constrained by the footnotes about the possible sorts of entity. The procedure constructs the model:**

artist   chemist

artist

      beekeeper   chemist

      beekeeper   chemist

     ...

This model refutes the two previous conclusions, but supports the conclusions: *Some of the artists are not chemists*, and its converse. The procedure constructs a third model:

artist   chemist

artist   chemist

      beekeeper   chemist

      beekeeper   chemist

    ...

Only one conclusion holds in all three models: *Some of the chemists are not artists*.

multiple models like the example in the box. Experiments have shown that reasoners are faster and make fewer errors with inferences that depend on one model than with those that depend on multiple models. This result has been replicated in many studies, and no study so far has failed to corroborate it.

The very first experiment in which the participants drew their own conclusions from syllogistic premises revealed a new phenomenon. Given, for instance, the premises:

> Some of the authors are bakers.　　(A–B)
>
> All the bakers are cricketers.　　(B–C)

the participants were more likely to draw the valid conclusion:

> Some of the authors are cricketers.　　(A–C)

than its valid converse:

> Some of the cricketers are authors.　　(C–A)

In general, the disposition or "figure" of the terms, such as *authors*, *bakers*, and *cricketers*, which I've symbolized, *A*, *B*, and *C*, biased the conclusions that the participants drew (see Box 10.2). Several competing explanations have been advanced to explain this bias. The definitive explanation is due to Klaus Oberauer. When we construct a model of a quantified proposition, such as: *Some of the authors are bakers*, we first represent a set of authors and then update them to ensure that some of them are bowlers. It is harder to proceed in the reverse order. Hence, the meaning of a quantified sentence leads us to represent its grammatical subject first. As you may recall from the previous chapter, the opposite holds for the meaning of a premise about spatial relations, such as: *the triangle is to the right of the circle*. In this case, we prefer to represent the object first, and to scan to the right in the direction corresponding to the meaning of the relation.

* * *

When naïve participants think aloud as they tackle syllogisms, they have little to say. But, many of them draw diagrams known as *Euler* circles. As a mnemonic, you may care to remember that the circles are called "Euler" circles because Leibniz (!) invented them. Euler got the credit, because he popularized the method in his letters to a Swedish princess instructing her in logic. Euler circles are like complete models as opposed to mental models. Hence, a premise of the form, *All A are B*, calls for two separate diagrams,

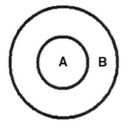 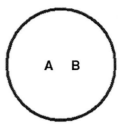

Fig. 10.1 The two Euler circle diagrams representing a proposition of the form, *All A are B*.

which are shown in Figure 10.1. The diagram on the left represents the possibility that although all *A* are *B*, some *B* are not *A*. The diagram on the right, however, represents that all *B* are *A*. The traditional use of Euler circles calls for diagrams of all the different possibilities for syllogistic premises. This demand leads to a large number of diagrams—sixteen, for instance, for the easy inference above. We do not appear to use Euler circles in this way, because when we draw them we almost always draw just a single diagram. Psychologists who defend Euler circles as *mental* representations have therefore devised more efficient ways to use them. Because the circles are the invention of a great mathematician, I suspect that naive individuals don't create the method for themselves, but remember it from their schooldays. Euler circles, however, are a legitimate hypothesis about the nature of complete models. Psychologists don't know whether those of us who draw Euler circles use mental representations of them to reason when we have no paper and pencil.

In the nineteenth century, the Reverent John Venn invented a superior sort of diagram for reasoning about properties. Figure 10.2 presents an example. Venn diagrams are often confused with Euler circles, but a single Venn diagram of three overlapping circles suffices for any syllogism, and it uses a special notation to represent alternative possibilities. Naïve individuals do not draw Venn diagrams, though a psychological theory has been based on them.

Valid syllogistic reasoning can be explained in terms of mental models, formal rules, Scholastic rules such as those in Box 10.2, Euler circles, Venn diagrams, and still other principles. You might suppose that it is impossible to find out which system we use when we make syllogistic inferences. In fact, the theories differ in their predictions about the process of inference and about the relative difficulty of different syllogisms. A long-standing tradition in psychology distinguishes between those of us who use Euler circles and those of us who use some other method. But, the evidence isn't decisive. The results

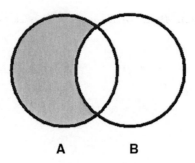

Fig. 10.2 The single Venn diagram representing a proposition of the form, *All A are B*. The part of the circle representing *A* that is not *B* is shaded out to show that it is empty.

A   **B**

could be explained by the model theory together with the assumption that some of us encountered Euler circles at school. No consensus exists, and some psychologists don't even believe that we reason when we tackle syllogisms. One way out of the impasse is to ask whether a theory generalizes to other domains, and whether other findings might provide crucial evidence. The next chapter considers a generalization of the model theory to inferences beyond the scope of Euler circles or Venn diagrams.

Other evidence supports the model theory and runs counter to the alternative accounts. If we use mental models, then we should succumb to illusory inferences about properties. These illusions do occur. Suppose we're told:

> Only one of the following statements is true:
>
> At least some of the plastic beads are not red, or
>
> None of the plastic beads is red.
>
> Is it possible that none of the red beads is plastic?

The statement of the problem made clear, as did the instructions, that one proposition is true and the other proposition is false. According to the principle of truth, which I outlined earlier, we consider the truth of each proposition on its own, and we don't represent the falsity of the other proposition. The model of the first premise is consistent with the possibility that none of the red beads is plastic, and so is the model of the second premise. Hence, we should respond, "Yes". Yet, the response is an illusion. If the first premise is true, then the second premise is false. And, if the second premise is false, at least some of the plastic beads are red, and so some of the red beads *are* plastic. Conversely, if the second premise is true, then the first premise is false, and so all of the plastic beads are red. In either case, the conclusion is impossible. If you have difficulty in understanding this explanation, that's the main point.

It *is* hard to think about what's true and what's false at one and the same time.

Control problems should elicit the correct response even if reasoners fail to consider falsity. An example based on the same premises as those above poses a different question:

> Is it possible that at least some of the red beads are plastic?

It should elicit the answer, "Yes", because the mental model of the first premise supports it. This response is correct. The study examined various sorts of illusory problems and control problems. It also examined illusions of impossibility for which mental models support the erroneous answer, "No", and control problems for which this response is correct. The chance of guessing the correct answer is fifty percent, and the participants performed little better than chance with the illusory problems (fifty-four percent correct). They were very much better with the control problems (ninety percent correct). All twenty of the participants showed this difference.

A subsequent study tested an antidote to the illusions. The participants were told to work out the case in which the first premise was true and the second premise was false, and then to work out the case in which the second premise was true and the first premise was false. In effect, they were told to construct complete models representing both what's true and what's false. The antidote improved performance with the illusions (from thirty-nine percent to seventy-one percent correct). But, the procedure was taxing and exacted a cost on performance with the control problems, for which it was unnecessary. Performance with them declined (from eighty-seven percent correct to seventy-two percent correct). The effects of the antidote corroborate the principle of truth. They seem inexplicable if we don't reason from what is true in possibilities.

* * *

Quantified propositions can be represented in models, whether the quantifier is a standard one, such as "all" and "some", or one that is not standard, such as "most" and "at least half". The theory treats these propositions about properties as relations between sets of entities. If we could hold any number of models in mind at the same time, we wouldn't err. The brutal fact is that we have a strong inclination to reason on the basis of a single model.

The mere ability to draw a correct conclusion does not discriminate among theories of reasoning—though some reasoners are so competent that the atmosphere of the premises cannot explain their performance. A computer program implementing the model theory has a striking emergent property: it yields an initial conclusion for each syllogism that matches the quantifier in at least one of the premises. This coincidence shows that those who are reasoning without the hindrance of atmosphere may nevertheless draw conclusions that appear to support its effects. On balance, most of us may be reasoning when we tackle syllogisms.

Chapter 11

Isn't Everyone an Optimist? The Case of Complex Reasoning

Once upon a time, there was a space station orbiting the moon, and on that space station there were four people: Anne, Beth, Charles, and Diana. Diana loved Charles, and one general principle was true: everyone loved anyone who loved someone. Indeed, everyone does love a lover. Did everyone love Diana? Of course. She loved Charles, and everyone loved anyone who loved someone. Did Beth love Anne? We have no idea, I would say, and so I imagine would you. We'll see.

Inferences of this sort depend on individuals, such as Diana and Charles, and on relations, such as "loved". But, they also depend on a relation among the members of various sets of individuals: *everyone loved anyone who loved someone. Every, any,* and *some* are all quantifiers. When each argument in a relation is a phrase containing a quantifier, the logic is much more complicated than the logic of properties. It's known as the "quantificational" or "predicate" calculus. It includes the logic of properties and connectives too. It is powerful enough to prove most of mathematics. If the quantifiers, such as *every*, concern individual entities, as in "everyone loves some movies", then a valid inference can always be proved in a finite number of steps, but it may be impossible to prove that an inference is invalid. Hence, as we grind away trying to prove an inference, we have no way of knowing whether we will ever reach a decision about whether it is valid or invalid.

Perhaps because of this complexity, psychologists have rarely studied relations among sets of individuals. Those psychologists who think that our reasoning is formal have suggested that our minds contain a version of quantificational logic. We saw in the previous chapter that their account copes only with standard quantifiers, and makes it difficult to prove some trivial inferences, whereas they are easy to make from models that represent sets. My goal now is to explain how we can use models to make inferences about relations among sets.

* * *

The task for reasoners is to make a parsimonious representation of multiple possibilities. Suppose, for instance, I claim:

All the boys are in the same place as some of the girls.

Do I mean that the boys are all together in one place with some of the girls, or that all the boys are scattered in several places that they share with girls? Probably I don't much care, and neither do you. We will both settle for the interpretation in which each boy is with some girls, and there may not be a single place where all of them are together. In contrast, the sentence:

Some of the girls are in the same place as all the boys

seems to have the stronger interpretation in which some of the girls are in one place with all the boys. You might suppose that I—or at least logicians—are fussing about how many angels it takes to split a logical hair. Perhaps. But, the differences do have logical consequences. For example, if the preceding sentences have their most salient interpretations, then this inference is valid:

Some of the girls are in the same place as all the boys.

Therefore, all the boys are in the same place as some of the girls.

If the first proposition is true then so is the second one, but the converse is not necessarily the case.

We can construct mental models of these propositions, and a computer program that I wrote uses them to make inferences too. Each quantifier calls for a loop of repeated operations to construct a model, and one loop is embedded within another. Box 11.1 illustrates how the program works. The program can also build a model of the salient meaning of the sentence:

All the boys are in the same place as some of the girls.

The program runs the two loops, but in the opposite order. For the sentence in the box, the loop for girls includes the loop for boys. For this sentence, the loop for boys includes the loop for girls, and the result is a model, such as:

| boy girl girl girl | boy girl girl | boy boy girl girl |

Logicians have a highfalutin term for loops of operations; they call them "recursive" operations. They lie at the heart of computation, and they demand

Box 11.1 An illustration of the procedures for constructing models of quantified relations between sets

The program constructs a model of the salient meaning of the sentence:

> Some of the girls are in the same place as all the boys

It starts with the phrase, "some of the girls". It constructs a representation of a girl, and it interprets "are in the same place as" by constructing a representation of a place as a cell in a spatial array, and it inserts the referent into that place:

| girl | the first use of the loop for girls

It interprets "all the boys" by looping round repeating a set of instructions that add another boy to the place in which the girl is. So, the effect is to update the existing model in a series of loops:

| girl boy | the first use of the loop for boys

| girl boy boy | the second use of this loop

| girl boy boy boy | the third use of this loop

The number of iterations of the loop is small but arbitrary, and the loop could end at this point. The quantifier refers to the entire set of boys, and so the process adds a footnote that the model represents the entire set of boys. The phrase, "some of the girls" is plural, and so the program repeats the loop for girls. It adds a representation of another girl in the same place:

| girl girl boy boy boy | the second use of the loop for girls

At this point, the loop for the boys is run again. But, on each occasion it just checks that the entire set of boys is represented in the model, and so it does not add any further referents. Each loop for a quantified phrase always verifies first whether the corresponding referents are already represented in a model. It adds new referents only if necessary. The loop for girls may end at this point, or it may add a further referent. It also constructs a small but arbitrary number of them.

a working memory to keep track of the process so that it can switch from one loop to another.

As the box shows, the model of the salient interpretation of the sentence:

Some of the girls are in the same place as all the boys

is as follows:

| girl girl boy boy boy |

with a footnote that the model represents the entire set of boys. The same procedures allow a model to be updated according to another premise, such as:

None of the boys is in the same place as any of the teachers.

The program runs a loop for "none of the boys", which verifies that the entire set of boys is represented in the model, and for each verification, it runs a loop for "any of the teachers" adding a referent in a different place. The result is this model of both premises:

| girl girl boy boy boy | teacher teacher teacher |

The model has a footnote to the effect that it represents the entire sets of boys and teachers. The program uses this model to draw a conclusion that relates those entities that did not occur in the same premise:

None of the girls is in the same place as any of the teachers.

A search for an alternative model of the premises constructs a new model, by adding entities from the set that isn't represented in its entirety, e.g.:

| girl girl boy boy boy | teacher teacher teacher girl |

This model refutes the conclusion, but this model and the previous one support a new conclusion:

Some of the girls are not in the same place as any of the teachers.

No model of the premises refutes this conclusion, and so it is valid.

The procedure for constructing models uses arbitrary numbers of entities, and in this way one model can represent many possibilities of the same sort. It uses loops of repeated operations to construct interpretations for each quantifier, and one loop is embedded within another in order to deal with multiple quantifiers. In principle, this procedure extends to relations among any number of sets. It also accommodates unorthodox quantifiers such as "more than half". Hence, premises such as:

More than half the girls are in the same place as all the boys.

All the boys are in the same place as more than half the teachers.

elicit this sort of model:

| girl girl boy boy boy boy teacher teacher | girl | teacher |

The model yields the valid conclusion:

More than half the girls are in the same place as more than half the teachers.

One complication is that there are many sorts of premise, and many sorts of model for pairs of sentences that each contain two quantifiers. Hence, I won't go any further into the details of the procedure. The important point to grasp is that the construction of models of these premises calls for loops within loops, where each loop is responsible for a quantified phrase, and the order of the loops is crucial.

The theory yields testable predictions, which experiments have corroborated. As in other domains, it is easier for us to draw conclusions from premises that need one model than from those that need multiple models. These premises, for example, which were used in an experiment:

All the Avon letters are in the same place as all the Bury letters.

None of the Bury letters is in the same place as any of the Caton letters.

yield just one model:

| Avon Avon Avon Bury Bury Bury | Caton Caton Caton |

We also tend to draw erroneous conclusions from multiple-model premises that are consistent with just one of the possible models. Once, on television, the distinguished physiologist Colin Blakemore, asked me to give him an inference to draw. I gave him one that started with the premise:

None of the Avon letters is in the same place as all the Bury letters.

As he repeated the premise to himself, he made a gesture with his hands as if he were dividing letters into two separate piles. That gesture, which is visible on the film, is a vivid sign of a reasoner building a mental model.

* * *

We left the four inhabitants of the space station knowing only that Diana loves Charles, and that everyone loves Diana, because this inference follows at once from the general premise that everyone loves anyone who loves someone. But, does Beth love Anne? Your intuition is likely to be that this conclusion doesn't follow from the premises. Intuitions are unconscious inferences based on simple principles—in this case, that there's no relation between Beth and Anne, because no relation was asserted about them (see Chapter 5). Likewise, the participants in an experiment inferred that everyone loved Diana (ninety-eight percent), but very few of them (six percent) inferred that Beth loved Anne. The happy few who did infer a relation, however, were right. Here's why. We already know that everyone loves Diana (the immediate inference). Hence, Anne loves Diana, and so Anne loves someone. We can now use the general premise again to infer that everyone loves Anne, and so it follows in turn that Beth loves Anne. The general premise has the subtle but striking property that as soon as we establish that one person loves another, it follows that everyone loves everyone.

The model theory predicts that the inferences that depend on a repeated use of a premise—a recursion—should be harder than immediate inferences. The first model of the two premises, including the fact that Diana loves Charles (and herself), is:

As this model shows, everyone loves Diana. It also yields the conclusion that Anne loves Diana. The general premise can be used again to update the model:

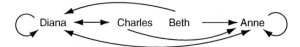

And so it follows that Beth loves Anne. A third use of the general premise yields the conclusion that everyone loves everyone (including themselves), and at this point the model cannot be expanded any further.

Expunge from your memory the previous example, and consider a new case that concerns Alan, Bessie, Carol, and David. You know that Alan doesn't hate Bessie, and that this general premise holds in this new world:

Everyone hates anyone who hates someone.

Given this information, does it follow that Carol doesn't hate David? Our intuition is that there's no information either way: she might, or she might not. Once again, however, our intuition conflicts with a conscious deduction. Suppose Carol did hate David, then everyone would hate Carol, including Bessie. Hence, everyone would hate Bessie, and so Alan would hate Bessie. But, we know that Alan doesn't hate Bessie, and so it follows that Carol doesn't hate David.

Inferences that depend on a repeated use of a premise are more difficult than immediate inferences. One reason may be that we assume that once a premise has been used in an inference, we have no need to use it again. Indeed, we tend not to expand models when we have already constructed a model that yields a conclusion. The repeated step also depends on the use of an initial model, and the representation of this model preoccupies working memory. This load may impede any further process of inference. In one experiment, however, the participants were given conclusions to evaluate. They wrote down their arguments and thoughts as they tried to understand why the conclusions followed from the premises. On three-quarters of occasions, they gave a correct explanation of the validity of the repeated step, though the negative inference I illustrated above was harder than the affirmative one. Box 11.2 presents a typical protocol in which the participant, not without difficulty, at last understands that the affirmative conclusion does follow.

In theory, we could have reasoned about these problems in quite a different way. We could have considered the recursive consequences of the quantified premise alone, before we considered the premise about the individuals, such as Charles and Diana. Given the general premise:

> Everyone loves anyone who loves someone.

we could argue:

> Suppose that a person loves someone.
>
> Therefore, everyone loves that person.
>
> Therefore, everyone loves someone.
>
> Therefore, everyone loves everyone.
>
> Therefore, if a person loves someone then everyone loves everyone.

We could then combine this conclusion with the premise:

> Anne loves Beth

to conclude that everyone loves everyone. It follows at once that Charles loves Diana. Hence, a possible strategy is to keep updating the model of the quantified premise over and over in a recursion *before* the model is combined with the premise about particular individuals. None of the written justifications ever reported this strategy. Perhaps we don't reason in this way, because we don't like reasoning in an abstract way. That is, we prefer to think about particular individuals, and so our first step is to interpret the premise about Charles and Diana. In contrast, a superhuman alien would grasp the recursive consequences of the general premise. It would see at once that as soon as one person loves another, everyone loves everyone.

* * *

Box 11.2 A protocol of a participant making a recursive inference (translated from the Italian)

The problem was:

Everyone esteems anyone who esteems someone.

Anna esteems Berta.

Does it follow that Diana esteems Carla?

The participant wrote and drew everything that follows apart from the parenthetic remarks in italics:

The conclusion does not follow necessarily, because if I assume premise 1, I know for sure that a person is esteemed if she esteems someone. Hence, if I knew that Carla esteemed someone I could definitely accept the conclusion, but given that the premises say nothing explicit about the fact that Carla esteems or does not esteem someone the conclusion *could* follow but does not follow necessarily. From premise 2, I reckon that:

(Everybody: Berta, Carla, Diana, esteems Anna.)

But I do not find any direct relation between Diana and Carla. I understood the solution after solving [another] problem. It is:

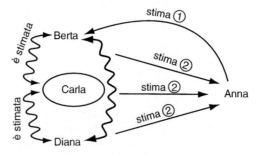

But then Carla esteems Anna, and hence she is esteemed by everybody and also by Diana; so Diana does esteem Carla

("stima" = esteems; "è stimata" = is esteemed. The upper arrow represents the first premise; the three arrows below represent the immediate inference; and the wavy arrows include the recursive inference.)

We reason about relations among members of sets in a similar way to our reasoning about relations among particular individuals. We build models, and we represent sets of entities using sets of referents. We keep the numbers small but arbitrary, and we prefer to work with one simple model, otherwise inferences get too complicated for us to make. The evidence corroborates this account. One advantage of an iconic representation of sets of individuals is that we can reason from quantifiers such as, "more than half" as well as from quantifiers, such as "all" and "none".

Do the inferences in this chapter occur anywhere outside the psychological laboratory? In fact, they do crop up from time to time. I was sitting at the exit of a chain store, and a young man was sitting next to me filling in a form, which I knew was to apply for a job in the store. (I'd seen it lying on the next chair when I had first sat down.) At one point, the young man got stuck, and turned to me and asked: "what's an optimist?" I said: "Someone who always expects good things to happen." I almost added my favorite definition of an optimist, "An optimist is anyone who believes that optimists exist," but his accent betrayed that he was not a native speaker of English. My unspoken coda, however, has an interesting property.

Is it true that optimists believe that optimists exist? Everyone to whom I have put this question, thinks for a moment, and then assents to the proposition. As one person said, "If you didn't think there were any optimists, you wouldn't be very optimistic." I asked a class of some fifty students whether they accepted my definition. They all did. Yet, it can't be true, and our inability to grasp its defect illustrates the problem we have in making inferences that depend on recursion—the repeated use of a general premise. Ask yourself: do you think that optimists exist? Of course, you do. I believe that there are optimists, and so do you. So, it follows from my definition that we are both optimists too. If others realize that we're optimists (because we believe optimists exist), they are in the same position as us: they think that optimists exist—namely, us—and so they are also optimists. The definition is a mental infection. It spreads optimism among the population like a happy plague. You pass on the definition, and others succumb at once to it and become optimists. This consequence of the definition is not obvious. Unlike superhuman reasoners, we do not grasp at once the consequences of repeated uses of general propositions. We prefer to think about particular individuals, and then perhaps to use general propositions to update our models. This bias is in keeping with the fundamental principle of the model theory: models represent individuals.

Why is the definition of optimists false? Optimists do think that optimists exist, but so do many pessimists. Hence, the definition doesn't apply only to optimists. The proper definition of an optimist is: a person who expects good things to happen. And not everyone is an optimist.

* * *

Many sentences contain more than just two quantifiers, and the grammar of English allows for an indefinite growth in complexity, e.g.:

> None of the teachers...

> None of the teachers of all the children...

> None of the teachers of all the children of some of the employees...

> and so on, ad infinitum.

Our language runs away with us. As soon as three quantified sets occur in a single relation, where each set has infinitely many possibilities, no guarantee exists that we can prove that an inference is invalid. And we can soon construct sentences that we can neither understand nor reason about correctly. Psychologists have barely peeped into this abyss.

Part IV

How We Make Inductions

An abstract model of events

Derived from past experiments.

Auden

Chapter 12

Modulation: A Step Towards Induction

We use the meaning of premises and our knowledge to construct mental models of what's possible, and we sometimes flesh them out into complete models. If we draw deductions from complete models without making mistakes, then our reasoning is valid. Our capacity to hold things in mind is limited, and so we tend to reason with mental models. Unfortunately, they can lead us astray because they follow what I referred to earlier as the principle of truth: they represent only what is true. Nevertheless, our method of deduction strives to be logical, and so you might picture logic as the basis for the psychology of reasoning.

If this picture were right, then I could end this book right now. As you may have noticed, the book doesn't end so abruptly, and so you can draw your own conclusion. In fact, much of our reasoning is inductive and outside the scope of logic. Our conclusions may be true, but even with true premises no guarantee can exist for their truth, because induction is fallible. I mentioned in the opening chapter that textbooks often define induction as reasoning from the particular to the general. But, as I remarked there, the definition isn't quite right. We can make inductions that yield particular conclusions. And so I defended this working definition: inductions go beyond the information given, and rule out more possibilities than their premises do. That is their hallmark.

Induction is the theme of this part of the book, and I shall argue that it always depends on knowledge. In this chapter, we'll take a step towards induction, because we'll consider how knowledge modulates the interpretation of sentences. One result is that connectives such as "or" and "if" cease to have their logical interpretations, and so our inferences go beyond the literal information given to us.

Psychologists sometimes give the impression that logical form is just a matter of grammar. That, for example, any sentence in which "or" connects two clauses is a disjunction of some sort. Theorists of a formal persuasion often have this point of view, and the late John Macnamara once epitomized it as follows:

> By a formal logical rule, I take it, we mean a rule that applies to a string in virtue of its form. That is, the rule can apply whenever a string is described as having a certain form.... The question of whether there is a psychological version of this rule in the minds of normal people (not trained in logic) turns on whether they have a secure intuition, applying equally to any content, that [the rule applies]. I take it that they have. And for me, that's an end of it.

This view of form as "applying to any content" is too close to grammar. In contrast, *logical* form is supposed to capture the significance of propositions—the conditions in which they would be true. And philosophers have argued for over a hundred years that the logical form of many sentences is quite remote from their grammar. My immediate aim is therefore to show why a grammatical view of form is not a good model of our reasoning. The reasons are instructive, and lead to a more accurate picture of our thinking.

* * *

This proposition is true:

> At school, Mo learned Latin or she learned Greek.

If we discover that she didn't learn Greek, then we can infer that she learned Latin. The processes described earlier in the book yield this inference. It is valid in logic, and formal theories include a rule to make the inference: *A or B*; *Not B*; therefore, *A*. But, consider this premise:

> At school, Mo learned Latin or she learned some language.

And now suppose that we discover that Mo didn't learn any language at school. If we apply the preceding formal rule to these premises, we infer: Mo learned Latin. Yet, the conclusion is absurd. No one in her right mind (apart from a logician) would draw it. The reason is obvious. We know that Latin is a language: it's part of the meaning of the word. So, if Mo didn't learn any language, she can't have learned Latin. At the very least, we no longer have the secure intuition that the formal rule applies to any content. This sort of case occurs so often that it casts doubt on the idea that the logical form of disjunction is just a matter of the occurrence of "or" connecting two clauses.

A sensible reaction to this example is to argue that the real logical form of the apparent disjunction is:

> At school, Mo learned some language (either Latin or another language).

This reaction defends a formal approach to reasoning, but how do we recover this logical form? We would have to work out the *possibilities* consistent with the significance of the proposition. And once we have done that, we might as well rely on them to reason. We have arrived back at the model theory.

How do we work out the possibilities consistent with the proposition? The model theory introduces a simple principle to explain how it's done. Our knowledge of the meaning of the word, "Latin," *modulates* our interpretation of the connective. It blocks the construction of a model of a possibility in which Mo learned Latin but didn't learn a language, because we know that Latin is a language. As a result, we construct models of just two possibilities. In one of them, Mo learned Latin; and in the other, she learned another language. Either way, she learned a language. The second premise asserts that she didn't learn a language, and so it eliminates both possibilities. Contrary to the formal rule of inference, most of us infer: Mo didn't learn Latin. This result shows that the meaning of a word can modulate the interpretation of a propositional connective, and can block a possibility that the logical meaning of the connective otherwise allows.

Here's another inferential problem:

Either Welles didn't enter the elevator or Hearst got out one floor up.

Welles entered the elevator on the second floor.

What happened?

We imagine a possibility in which Welles entered the elevator on the second floor, Hearst was already in it, the two of them traveled up together up to the third floor, whereupon Hearst got out. We infer this sequence of events from the premises and from our knowledge of elevators. Our knowledge modulates the interpretation of the first premise, adding information about both the temporal and spatial relations between the events. In one possibility, Welles entered the elevator before Hearst got out. Another possibility is that Welles didn't enter the elevator. In this case, it isn't clear what it would mean for Hearst to get out one floor up—one floor up from where?

Still another effect of knowledge is to lead us to flesh out mental models into complete models. Given the sentence:

Either the roulette wheel comes up red or else Viv goes bankrupt

modulation should lead us to think of two complete possibilities. In one, the roulette does come up red, Viv wins and so doesn't go bankrupt; in the other, the roulette wheel doesn't come up red, Viv loses and goes bankrupt. We should represent both possibilities in a complete way, unlike our interpretation of disjunctions that do not engage our knowledge, such as: "Either there is a triangle or else there is a circle". Our knowledge overrides the principle of truth, which I described in Chapter 8, and so we think about both what is true and what is false in the two possibilities.

* * *

Both meaning and general knowledge can modulate the interpretation of propositional connectives. They can block the construction of a model of a possibility. They can add information to a model, such as a temporal relation. And they can help to elicit complete models. The first two effects add information: models contain more information than the meaning of the premises, and this information comes from our knowledge. Hence, if we draw a conclusion from the resulting models, then we are going beyond the information in the literal premises: we are making an induction rather than a deduction. The third effect enables inferences to take into account information that is present in the premises, but that is often neglected. So, what are the processes underlying the modulation of premises? My answer has been implemented in a computer program that simulates modulation.

Our long-term knowledge can be represented as models of possibilities. For example, we know that coffee tastes sweet if it has sugar or artificial sweetener added to it. This knowledge can be represented in complete models of these possibilities: with sugar added, coffee tastes sweet; with sweetener added, coffee tastes sweet; and with neither sugar nor sweetener added, coffee does not taste sweet. We take a sip from our morning coffee and it tastes sweet, and so we infer that there's sugar or sweetener in it. The process here is that an event matches models in our knowledge, and they yield our disjunctive conclusion.

On most occasions, long-standing knowledge takes precedence over what people tell us. We know, say, that Viv doesn't like sweet coffee, and so: *Either coffee isn't sweet or else Viv won't drink it.* Pat tells us: Viv's cup of coffee isn't sweet. But, we see someone add sugar to the coffee. This perception triggers our knowledge of the consequences of this possibility: the coffee is now sweet. This proposition contradicts Pat's remark, but takes precedence over it, and yields the inference: *Viv won't drink the coffee.*

The process that fleshes out mental models into complete models functions in an analogous way. The mental models of *either the coffee contains sugar or else sweetener* represent two possibilities. These possibilities trigger those in knowledge and so each model is fleshed out into a complete model representing that in both possibilities the coffee is sweet.

The process that adds information, such as a temporal relation, to models is easy to understand in principle. For instance, we have a model of elevators that unfolds in a kinematic sequence. We know that they move people from one floor to another in buildings. We know the protocol. Passengers press a button to summon the elevator to their floor. It arrives and the doors open. They enter, and press the button of the floor that they want to go to unless someone has already pushed it. The doors close and the elevator takes them there, perhaps stopping at other floors on the way. We also know that on a rare occasion, like all machines, things can go wrong. Someone tells us:

> Hearst entered the elevator and he got out one floor up.

Our knowledge of the meaning of "elevator" triggers our model of how elevators work. We make a mental simulation, piece by piece, of the sequence of events: Hearst enters the elevator on one floor, the door closes, the elevator travels up one floor, the doors open, and Hearst gets out. We infer this kinematic sequence from our knowledge, but it is an induction. We have gone beyond the information in the proposition to make a fallible sequence of inferences. It may be, for instance, that Hearst levered open the doors on one floor, got out into the elevator shaft, climbed up the cables into the elevator through a door in its floor. It was stuck between two floors with its doors open. He stood on someone's shoulders and got out of the elevator one floor up. Every event in our simulation turned out to be false. Not impossible, but very unlikely. That is why it pays us to use our knowledge: it is almost always correct. But, without recourse to a mental model of elevators, it is hard to see how we could make these inferences.

* * *

Modulation affects quantifiers too. A common sign in England at the entrance to a country estate is:

> Trespassers will be prosecuted.

We know that it leaves open the question of whether or not there will be any trespassers. In contrast, a university's course catalogue states:

> Graduate students will be funded on fellowships for their first year.

We have no doubt that there are graduate students at the university.

Knowledge can also determine the relations between sets of individuals. In logic, a sentence such as, *at least some phykods are entalics*, leaves open two questions: it may be that *all* phykods are entalics. And it may also be that all entalics are phykods or that only some of them are. Given that we know nothing of phykods or entalics—a safe assumption, because I made up these terms, we have no way of knowing the precise relation between the two sets. But, in the case of the sentence: *some animals are dogs*, we know both that some animals are not dogs, and that *all* dogs are animals. In contrast, with the sentence: *some conservatives are businessmen*, we know that not all businessmen are conservatives. Experiments have confirmed these sorts of difference in the interpretation of quantified propositions. Analogous effects occur with "many" and "a few". Our knowledge of the size of a set tends to affect our estimates of the number of individuals that are referred to in propositions such as:

Many Frenchmen like wine. (We're talking millions.)

Many Senators accept gifts from lobbyists. (We're talking tens.)

In logic, "every" ranges over everything in the domain under discussion. Hence, a proposition such as:

Grandma hates everyone in her family

means that Grandma also hates herself because she is in her family. Yet, knowledge often blocks these interpretations. Participants in experiments often overlook them—to the extent that if a study needs them to be taken into account, the experimenter has to explain their existence to the participants. The moral is that knowledge modulates the interpretation of quantifiers. They too have logical meanings, but knowledge can block a particular possibility or, alternatively, make it more salient.

* * *

Modulation has been demonstrated in studies in which the participants list what is possible for a variety of sentences. These studies showed that sentences of the same grammatical form but different contents do yield the predicted effects of modulation. Sentences such as: *Pat is in Rio or she is in Norway*, elicit knowledge that one person cannot be in two places at the same time, and so the truth of one clause implies the falsity of the other clause. Participants are therefore faster and draw more valid conclusions of the form:

Pat is in Rio or she is in Norway.

Therefore, If Pat is not in Norway then she is in Rio.

But, they baulk at inferences, such as:

Pat is in Rio or she is in Brazil.

Therefore, If Pat is not in Brazil then she is in Rio.

Contrary to the disjunctive form of the premise, the truth of its first clause implies the truth of its second clause.

* * *

Why isn't logic psychology? To answer this question, I want to pull together arguments that you have already encountered in this book and then deal with the findings presented in this chapter. The quantificational calculus, which I introduced in the previous chapter, captures the implications among sentences (in a formal language), whereas reasoning is a *process* of drawing conclusions from premises. The calculus tells us little more about reasoning than arithmetic tells us about book-keeping. It allows an infinite number of valid conclusions from any set of premises, including many silly conclusions, such as a mere conjunction of the premises. It has nothing to say about the particular conclusions that human reasoners tend to draw or their tendency to say that nothing follows from certain premises. Psychologists who suppose that our minds contain a tacit version of the calculus therefore provide an inferential "engine" that uses rules of the calculus to derive conclusions. They must also contrive ways to avoid derivations yielding valid but trivial inferences of the sort we would never make.

When we create an argument in life, its logical analysis is difficult. Many inferences are beyond the scope of the classical quantificational calculus, because they concern conclusions about possibilities. And we take for granted the meanings of words, their context, and our background knowledge. For instance, we know what, "taller than", means and so we can use it to construct a model from which a transitive conclusion may, or may not, emerge. Transitivity cannot be captured in a meaning postulate for "taller than", because it depends on the proposition as a whole. For example, a change in tense from one premise to another may violate transitivity, as with these premises (from Chapter 9):

Cate is taller than Belle.

Belle *was* taller than Alice (until Alice drank the magic potion).

We assume a common background of knowledge and beliefs. For instance, I once asked someone to make a case for local government to subsidize opera. He replied that art is good for cultural life and commerce. Logically, the argument has several missing links, which I can try to spell out:

Art is good for cultural life and commerce.

Anything that is good for cultural life and commerce should be subsidized.

Opera is an art.

Therefore, opera is good for cultural life and commerce.

Therefore, opera should be subsidized.

To lay out an argument in this way, like a formal proof, is a little ridiculous, but logic demands it. The first premise is what the speaker asserted. The second premise is perhaps one of his general beliefs, which he takes for granted. The third premise is based on knowledge of the meaning of the word, "opera". Hence, everyday arguments depend on the meanings of words, general knowledge, and beliefs. The consequent difficulty of making logical analyses is borne out by the fact that no computer program exists for carrying out this job.

The examples in this chapter are more life-like than the artificial sentences of experiments. What makes them more natural is that their contents are sensible propositions about everyday matters. A corollary, however, is that the meaning of their individual clauses and general knowledge about the situations to which they refer may modulate the interpretation of connectives. Some usages correspond to the meanings of terms in logic and some do not. The potential modulation of connectives and quantifiers means that our system for interpreting sentences must always be on the lookout for these effects. It must always examine the contents of sentences to check whether they and the knowledge that they elicit modulate interpretation. This step occurs even for sentences that turn out to have a logical interpretation. The system for interpreting propositional connectives cannot work in the way that logic works, taking into account just truth and falsity. The system works with models of possibilities, not truth values; and it must take content and knowledge into account. That is why the process of interpretation is never pure logic. The fact that modulation can add spatial and temporal relations between the events described in a sentence means that propositional connectives have an indefinite number of different interpretations.

One reaction of some theorists to the discrepancies between logic and reasoning is to argue that logic has no bearing on inferences in life. These theorists are cutting off their heads to cure a headache. Validity is important in everyday life, and it is a logical concept. Another reaction is to go outside classical logic and to invoke other sorts of logic, including logics that allow conclusions to be retracted, which I will discuss later in the book.

You might suppose that logic does at least underlie the mental abilities of mathematicians and logicians. Some of them have thought so too, but the disciplines demand more than just deduction. The Indian genius Srinivasa Ramanujan, who died in 1920, left behind a body of work that continues to occupy mathematicians, but proof was not crucial to his many conjectures. As another great mathematician, G.H. Hardy wrote about him, "[he] combined a power of generalization, a feeling for form, and a capacity for rapid modification of his hypotheses, that were often really startling, and made him, in his own peculiar field, without a rival in his day."

We all of us have some power of generalization. And a final reason for rejecting logic as a model of our reasoning is that so many of our inferences are not deductive, but inductive. For example, when we detect a clash between the facts and our beliefs, we try to reason our way back to consistency. We try to modify our beliefs to make them consistent with the facts, and to create a plausible diagnosis of what has gone wrong. Logic cannot tell us which belief to give up, or how to resolve the conflict. The way we do so is a matter to which I return later, and it illustrates the importance of reasoning that is not deductive.

* * *

Modulation is the bridge from deduction to induction. In life, we cross the bridge without effort or awareness. What is harder for us is to refrain from bringing our knowledge to bear in reasoning, and to try to make strict deductions. Normally, the meanings of words, the entities they refer to, and our knowledge of the world all modulate our interpretation of connectives and quantifiers. One consequence is that the process of interpretation can never proceed in an idealized logical way. Another consequence is that modulation affects the process of inference: implicit possibilities that we seldom bother to envisage may become salient as a result of our knowledge. Induction depends on knowledge, and the ubiquity of the introduction of knowledge into models means that many, if not most, inferences in life are inductive.

Chapter 13

Knowledge and Inductions

On my first trip to Italy, I did something that I had never done before. I went into an Italian coffee bar to get a coffee. I stood in the crush at the bar until I attracted the attention of one of the men making the coffees, and uttered in an approximation to Italian: "un cappuccino per favore". He waved me away. I tried again: he waved me away again. And then he turned to the customer standing next to me and served him. I was doing something wrong. But, what? I noticed that the man after me handed over a small piece of paper. Indeed, the people waiting to be served had these pieces of paper, which they were waving at the barmen. They seemed to be receipts from a cash register, and I inferred that they all had them. Yet, no one was paying the barmen. It followed that they must have paid someone else. I looked around, and there in the direction that the barista had waved me was a woman sitting at a cash register, and a line of people waiting to pay her. That was it. One paid first, and took the receipt to the bar to make one's order. This system is still in operation in many coffee bars in Italy, but until that moment it had been quite unknown to me.

My thoughts in the coffee bar took me less time than you took to read my description of them, yet they illustrate what I want to discuss. At their heart are a number of inductions. You remember that if the premises are true, a deduction yields a conclusion that must be true, whereas an induction does not—the conclusion may be true, but no guarantee exists. Inductions solved my problem of how to get a coffee. In England, if a barman had refused to serve me a pint of bitter in a pub, then I would have walked out in a huff. But, by the time I went to the Italian bar, I had already formed the impression that Italians were friendly and helpful to foreigners. This impression was also an induction. I had experienced various acts of kindness in which individuals had been friendly and helpful, and so I had inferred from this small sample that Italians in general were of the same disposition. I might not have assented to the proposition that *all* Italians are friendly and helpful. But, it was an assumption that I would take for granted until proved wrong, and so I didn't infer that the barman was being hostile towards an obvious foreigner.

I made the induction that in Italian coffee bars one should pay first and order afterwards. And this generalization was a result of a single experience. It was a generalization because it applied to an indefinite number of Italian coffee bars. It was an induction, because it could have been false, that is, my conclusion was not a deduction from the premises. The premises—that is, the coffee bar—might have been exceptional, and everywhere else might have operated on the same lines as coffee bars in England, where payment comes last, if you survive the coffee. One reason why I doubted that the Italian bar was exceptional was that if it had been, then other customers would have been as flummoxed as I was, and would have had to make the same detour—to the bar, to the cash register, and back to the bar. That didn't happen. The clientele proceeded in a correct way—they entered, paid at the cash register, and went to the bar with their receipts to order their coffees. So, I made a deduction from a plausible premise: If the coffee bar was exceptional then other people would be flummoxed. But, as I could see, others were not flummoxed; hence, the coffee bar was not exceptional. And this deduction supported my induction.

Another supporting reason was that I inferred an explanation for the coffee bar's modus operandi. The place was very busy, and just two men were working at the bar. They were operating espresso machines without pause and had no time to be making bills or change at a cash register. An efficient solution was therefore for the customers to present receipts, showing what they had paid for, and for the barmen to prepare the corresponding drinks.

When our reasoning goes beyond the premises to increase the amount of information, we are making an induction. My generalization that coffee bars in Italy required customers to pay first was an induction. My inference of an explanation for this regimen is also an induction, and some theorists refer to inductions of explanations as *abductions*. And when we have made an abduction to explain an induction, as I did, our belief in the induction tends to increase. We have not just made a generalization, but we have explained it too. And that's a good reason to believe it. Some philosophers have argued that we should always make minimal changes to our beliefs. I doubt whether we always follow this advice or even that we should. Our propensity to make inductions and to explain them often leads us to make quite grand changes to our beliefs.

One psychological observation in the case of the coffee bar is striking and, I think, universal. When we reason, we are not aware of jumping from inductions to deductions to abductions, and back again. In contrast, we are aware of a shift when we switch, say, from reading a sonnet to trying to write one, or from following a mathematical proof to trying to create one. Reasoning seems seamless. I want to explain how induction works. And so I will describe what counts as an induction, and make the case that abduction is a special case of induction. I then focus on those "pure" inductions that yield generalizations, and propose a theory of how we make them. I explain abductions in the next chapter.

* * *

When we make inductions our aim is to reach new and parsimonious conclusions that are at least plausible given our premises and our knowledge. But, our reasoning in life doesn't occur in an intellectual vacuum. We reason in service of our goals. We want a cappuccino and we reason in order to get one. Our goals constrain the sorts of conclusions that we try to infer. The same premises but different goals may lead us to different conclusions.

A common sort of induction in life yields a conclusion about a particular event. For example, when the car ferry, *The Herald of Free Enterprise*, sailed from the Belgian port of Zeebrugge on March 6, 1987, the master of the vessel made the plausible induction that the bow doors had been closed. They had always been closed in the past, and there was no evidence to the contrary. The chief officer made the same induction, as did the bosun. But, the assistant bosun, whose job it was to close the doors, was fast asleep in his bunk. And he had not closed the doors. Soon after the ferry left the harbor, the sea rushed in through its open doors. It capsized and sank, and 188 people drowned. Induction can be a terrible risk.

Another sort of induction leads to a generalization, such as my inference that we pay before we order in Italian coffee bars. Scientific laws are also inductive generalizations. Kepler's first law of planetary motion, for instance, states that a planet moves in an elliptical orbit around the sun with the sun at one focus. Scientific theories go beyond these regularities in order to explain them in more fundamental terms: Einstein's theory of gravitation explains planetary orbits in terms of the effects of a star's mass on the curvature of space–time. The late Sir Karl Popper, a philosopher of science, argued that induction plays no role in scientific thinking. Science, he argued, is based on conjectures that are open to falsification, and the origins of these conjectures are not the philosophers' concern. In fact, Popper to the contrary, the history of science contains many cases in which scientists made systematic observations, and looked for parsimonious generalizations of their results (also known as scientific laws). For example, Marbe's law in psychology—in case you wondered whether there were any psychological laws—states that the more common an association is to a given word, the faster it tends to be made. For example, "white" is the most frequent, and the fastest, of responses to the word, "black". Marbe induced the law from observations of associative responses.

The abduction of an explanation also increases information, and so abduction is a sort of induction. How, you might wonder, can one tell the difference between abductions that yield explanations and inductions that do not? The clue is the end product. My induction from the bar to bars in general did not introduce any new concepts over and above those that concerned my getting a coffee. It re-ordered the temporal sequence of ordering, consuming, and paying. My explanation, however, concerned the workload of the barmen and their lack of time to handle cash. These were new concepts beyond those that concerned how to get a coffee and to pay for it.

The relation between a successful explanation and the generalization that it explains is much more problematic. One view is that the generalization is a logical consequence of the explanation: we can deduce the generalization from the explanation. Several philosophers have disputed this view, and it may be too strong. It misses the heart of the psychology. We can describe an event without understanding it, but we cannot explain an event unless we have some putative understanding of it. Descriptions at best allow one to mimic an event mentally, whereas explanations allow one to build a mental model of its underlying mechanism. We can take the event to pieces: we know what causes it, what results from it, how to influence, control, initiate, or prevent it, how it relates to other events or how it resembles them, how to predict its onset and course, what its internal or underlying structure is, how to diagnose unusual events, and, in science, how to relate the domain as a whole to others. Scientific explanations may make use of theoretical notions that are unobservable, or that are at a lower physical level than descriptions of the events. An explanation accounts for what we do not understand in terms of what we do understand: we cannot construct an explanatory model if the key concepts are not available to us.

The induction of a generalization is often just as well described as the induction of a concept. In the earlier example, I (and you too, perhaps) acquired knowledge about the concept:

Italian coffee bars with cashiers.

These *ad hoc* concepts are put together in an inductive way out of more basic components, such as the concepts of coffee, bars, and cashiers. We continue to acquire such concepts throughout our lives. We learn some from direct experience and some from descriptions. We cannot acquire the full concept of a color, a piece of music, or an emotion, without a direct acquaintance with them. But, we can learn about quarks, genes, and the unconscious, from descriptions of them.

In summary, inductions can be about a particular event or about matters in general. They can be descriptions or explanations. They include the acquisition of *ad hoc* concepts and the formulation of conjectures to explain sets of observations, even perhaps a set containing just a single datum, such as my inductions about Italian cafés, or Sir Alexander Fleming's more striking observation of the destruction of bacteria on a culture plate—an observation that led him to the discovery of penicillin. All these inferences are fallible, but we can be aware of their fallibility.

* * *

The theory that I'll outline has as its fundamental assumption that induction depends on knowledge. To establish its centrality for yourself, you should try to make an induction without relying on knowledge. For example, suppose that a strange purple blob appears on your computer screen. You have no idea what it is. It undulates towards you and all at once explodes, leaving no remains. Another purple blob appears, undulates towards you, and explodes. A third blob appears, and does the same thing. And now a fourth blob appears. What do you expect to happen? I imagine that you'll think: it too should explode. You have this thought because you *know* that the previous blobs exploded. Hence, although you started with no prior knowledge about the blobs, you soon acquired enough to lead you to expect certain events. If each of the three blobs had done something different, you would have had little idea about what the next blob would do, except that perhaps it would do something different from the previous ones. Similarly, if you observed that purple blobs explode, green blobs shrink to nothing, and yellow blobs spin larger and larger until they fill the screen, your prediction about a blob should depend on its color. You are sensitive to the frequency with which different events occur, and you can use your knowledge of these frequencies to make inductions about what should happen.

The induction that a purple blob will explode is a case of what theorists sometimes refer to as induction by "enumeration". As we encounter more and more instances of the same sort of entity, such as purple blobs that explode, so we are liable to infer that perhaps *all* purple blobs explode. These inductions are at one end of the scale of homogeneity. Often, inductions are about the frequencies of events. For instance, when an English cryptanalyst was working on breaking the German's Enigma code in World War II—a problem that I'll come back to later in the book, his observations led him to infer that the

Germans were transmitting at least a hundred messages a day with a given key for the code.

Many inductions in life depend on *prior* knowledge. It reduces our need for multiple observations, and enables us to make inductions from single events. If we learn that Dovis made the lowest bid on the contract to build the apartment block, then we may infer that they got the contract. If we learn that a man was arrested at the exit to a store with clothes that he hadn't paid for stuffed into secret pockets in his overcoat, then we may infer that he's a thief. If we discover that the starter on our car won't turn over the engine, we may infer that the battery is dead. We know that lowest bids tend to get the job, that thieves steal clothes from stores by hiding them on their person, and that car engines often fail to start because their batteries are dead. Experiments have corroborated our propensity to make these inferences.

We also know that we could be wrong. The bid from Dovis may have been rejected because it was too low to be feasible. The man with clothes stuffed in his pockets may have been hired to test the store's security. The starter may not have turned the engine because there was a break in the circuit. We need more knowledge to eliminate these possibilities: we need to test our inductions. But, tests are demanding and may not be necessary for our current goals. Particular inductions crop up so often in everyday life because we seldom have enough information to make useful deductions. We need to go beyond the information that we have.

* * *

No comprehensive computer program exists for making inductions, though programs simulate various sorts of learning from examples. To simulate inductions, it is necessary to represent knowledge and to use it to construct models of the world. I can illustrate what a program needs to do, and the interaction between induction and deduction, with a reconstruction of my initial inferences in the coffee bar. My first inference was an "enumerative" induction:

All the people waiting to be served have receipts.

The process could depend on a rule of the form:

Individual a has an object g.

Individual b has an object g.

Individual c has an object g.

...

Therefore, all individuals have an object g.

After some number of observations that members of a set have a property or relation in common, the rule kicks in and allows us to infer that all of them have the property or relation in common. The problem with this rule is that it yields spurious generalizations that none of us would make. I am waiting for my wife at the airport. The first person off the plane is a man, and so is the next person, and the next. Suppose the first ten people are all males. The rule above leads to the generalization that all the people coming off the plane will be men. Ergo, my wife wasn't on the flight. The conclusion is absurd, and so is the unfettered rule.

What is missing is knowledge. The basis for my generalization about the people at the coffee bar was my knowledge of an abstract principle: institutions such as restaurants, bars, and cafés have a "script" that their clientele follow. Its main components are ordering, consuming, paying. The first two of these components call for a certain routine of actions and interactions with the staff. The routine may allow exceptions or deviations. It specifies what we should do by default. But, the bigger and busier the institution is, the more likely it is to be a standard routine, which we violate at our risk. Hence, if at least some people waiting to be served their coffee have receipts, then it is likely that all of them have receipts.

Our knowledge could be in a system that uses formal rules. It would be a mental equivalent to the premise:

> Institutions such as coffee bars have a standard sequence in which customers order drinks, pay, and get receipts.

It follows that this coffee bar has a standard sequence. Whatever the sequence is, it applies to everyone. My observation was that some customers waiting for their orders at the bar had receipts. And so I can use formal rules to draw the conclusion: Everyone waiting to order at the bar has receipts. Many theoretical proposals about induction rest on this idea, and Box 13.1 summarizes some typical formal rules that these systems use.

One drawback of rules is that no obvious way exists to determine which rule to use, or which sequence of rules, in order to make an induction.

Any inference in which the conclusion holds in at least all the possibilities consistent with the premises is a valid deduction; conversely, any inference in which the conclusion holds in less than all the possibilities consistent with the premises is an induction. The first rule in Box 13.1 eliminates possible individuals—those that don't have the relevant property. The effect of each of the remaining rules is achieved by a single operation on models, namely, the elimination of a model of a possibility. For example, the proposition:

Box 13.1 Formal rules of inference for inductive generalizations

Many theorists have advocated formal rules for inductive generalization. Such rules include the following ones:

1. Item 1 has property P; so do items 2, 3, 4, etc.
   Therefore, all items have property P.
2. If A and B then C.
   Therefore, If A then C.
3. If A then (B or C).
   Therefore, If A then C.
4. If A and B then C; and if A and D then C.
   Therefore, If A then C.
5. If A then C.
   Therefore, If A or B then C.
6. If A then C.
   Therefore, If A then (B and C).

An example of the use of rule 2 would be to argue: If you have paid and have a receipt then you will be served; therefore, if you have paid then you will be served. The effect of all these rules is to eliminate possibilities.

> If you have paid and have a receipt then you will be served

is compatible with a set of models that includes the possibility:

> paid   no receipt   not served

If this model is eliminated, the remaining set of models is equivalent to the conclusion:

> If you have paid then you will be served.

So, the induction is equivalent to rule 2 in the box. The operation of adding information to a model may also enrich the model by introducing a novel relation.

Another drawback of formal rules is that the premises may use different terms than those in the mental representation of knowledge, and so the premises cannot trigger the knowledge. One solution is to introduce further principles in knowledge that allow the premises to map on to knowledge. These meaning postulates would include the axioms:

> *Pays* means *hands over money to someone for something.*
>
> *An order* means *a request for goods or services.*
>
> *A customer* means *a person who pays for goods or services.*

Perhaps the system could be made to work, but meaning postulates have some severe difficulties, which I described earlier in the book. An alternative is to use models to represent knowledge. They have the advantage that visual perception—the basis of my observations in the coffee bar—can be matched to them without the intermediary of language. In deduction, we concentrate on what is explicit in our models, and so we may fail to make certain deductions. In induction, we also focus on what is explicit in our models, and so we seek evidence that corroborates our inductive hypotheses. We don't look for negative instances of our hypotheses, and encounter them only by chance.

The most mysterious step in the whole process of my thinking was my recognition that the small piece of paper that the man next to me held was a receipt. It too is an induction. But, how we recognize objects is not well understood, despite investigations into the process for over a century.

* * *

David Hume set philosophers worrying about the rational justification of induction. In truth, as he argued, it has none (that does not in turn depend on induction). But, deduction cannot be justified without deduction, either. Induction is just something that animals, including human beings, do to make life possible. More recently, philosophers have worried about which properties of objects warrant inductive inferences. The answer rests on knowledge: we don't infer that all the passengers on a plane are male because the first ten off the plane are men. We know that this observation doesn't rule out the possibility of a woman passenger. In contrast, one experience was sufficient for me to infer the order of paying and ordering in Italian bars with a cashier.

The number of possible inductions that we can make about a finite set of data is too vast to be tractable. Knowledge constrains us, however. Its relative availability is in itself a constraint. Information about one sort of event is more accessible than information about another sort of event, and so we infer that the first sort of event is more probable than the second sort. There may be other general constraints too. One is to frame the most *informative* hypothesis consistent with the evidence, that is, the hypothesis that admits the fewest possibilities. This constraint is crucial when we can observe only positive instances of a concept, and have no teacher to point out negative instances in a helpful way. For example, if we encounter patients suffering from diarrhea, vomiting, low blood pressure, and muscle spasms, then the most specific hypothesis is that they are suffering from a single disease with these signs. If we now encounter several similar patients, who have all of these signs except muscle spasms, our initial hypothesis was probably too specific. But, if we had started with the hypothesis that the first patient was suffering from several simultaneous diseases, then we would have no reason to change our minds in the light of the subsequent patients.

Another general constraint is *similarity*. If a blob is similar to one that exploded, then it too may explode. As Hume remarked, similar causes have similar effects, and this principle does seem to lie behind many of our inductions. That is, we infer that one event is similar to another, and expect it to have similar consequences. What is problematic is the basis of our judgments of similarity. Some cases are simple enough: the two events are hard to tell apart. But, no general computer program exists that assesses the similarity among things. Part of the problem is that we can almost always find some similarity between any two entities chosen at random. How is a piano similar to a banana? Well, they're both physical objects; they both have characteristic shapes; they both have an inside and an outside; people are fond of both of them; both owe their existence to trees; and so on. The moral is that we use similarity as a basis for inductions, but it is not a transparent notion, and often depends on our knowledge of entities. A bat looks like a bird, but a bat is a mammal and a bird isn't. A German shepard doesn't look like a chihuahua, but they are both dogs.

* * *

Here is a fact that you may not know:

> Women of exceptional intelligence tend to marry less intelligent men.

Why? If you mention this fact in conversation, people will create all sorts of impromptu explanations for it—perhaps smart women don't like smart men, perhaps they feel threatened by them, perhaps they like to dominate their husbands, and so on. There's a bundle of similar puzzles. Brilliant parents tend to have less brilliant children. Athletes who have an outstanding season tend to follow it up with a less than stellar season. A terrific meal at a restaurant tends to be followed by a less terrific meal the next time you eat there. Again, mention one of these facts in conversation, and your friends will astonish you with their ingenious explanations. But, don't let their ideas run away with you. A statistical fact, "regression to the mean," can explain all of these phenomena. Observations at the extreme end of a distribution are rare. There are only a few individuals of exceptional intelligence. Many more are closer to the average, i.e., the mean. Hence, the chances are that an exceptional individual meets and marries someone closer to the mean or average. Athletes who have an exceptional year are likely to do so as a result of both talent and chance. The next year their performance tends to fall back towards their average over the years. The concept of regression to the mean is tricky. It is a piece of technical knowledge from statistics. We can understand it when it is explained to us. But, its instances aren't so easy for us to identify. Instead, our propensity to create explanations leads us to violate the norms of probability.

* * *

How do we make inductions? The theory outlined in this chapter does not treat induction and deduction as so different as they appear in logic. When we make deductions, we often step over the boundary into induction because we rely on knowledge that goes beyond the premises. Knowledge is fallible: the price of induction is invalidity. We usually focus on the triumphs of induction and the minor imperfections that yield clues to its nature. And we overlook its catastrophes—the fads of pseudo-science, the superstitions of daily life, and the disastrous inductions that lead to events such as the sinking of *The Herald of Free Enterprise*. The origin of these errors is in human induction. As I mentioned earlier in the book, its heuristics, or rules of thumb, are what students of other cultures refer to as "magical" thinking.

Chapter 14

Sherlock Holmes's Method: Abduction

A Scottish doctor interviewing a patient makes a series of successful inferences:

Well, my man, you've served in the army.

Aye, sir.

Not long discharged.

No, sir.

A highland regiment?

Aye, sir.

A non-com. officer?

Aye, sir.

Stationed at Barbados?

Aye, sir.

These inferences may remind you of Conan Doyle's great fictional detective Sherlock Holmes. In the story *The Red-Headed League*, Holmes astounds his friend Dr Watson. A visitor has come to consult them, and Holmes remarks: "Beyond the obvious facts that he has at some time done manual labour, that he takes snuff, that he is a Freemason, that he has been in China, and that he has done a considerable amount of writing lately, I can deduce nothing else". The similarity between Holmes and the Scottish doctor is no accident. When Conan Doyle was a medical student in Edinburgh, he had worked as the clerk for the doctor in the dialogue, Joseph Bell. And he later described how Bell made his uncanny chain of inferences:

"You see, gentlemen," he would explain, "the man was a respectful man, but did not remove his hat. They do not in the army, but he would have learned civilian ways had he been long discharged. He has an air of authority and he is obviously Scottish. As to Barbados, his complaint is elephantiasis, which is West Indian and not British."

> To his audience of Watsons it all seemed quite miraculous until it was explained, and then it became simple enough. It is no wonder that after the study of such a character I used and amplified his methods when in later life I tried to build up a scientific detective who solved cases on his own merits and not through the folly of the criminal.

Indeed, when Holmes explained the basis of *his* inferences, the visitor remarks, "I thought at first that you had done something clever, but I see that there was nothing in it, after all."

Holmes claimed that his method was deductive, and that his deductions were as infallible as Euclid's proofs. He was wrong. For instance, he inferred that the visitor was a Freemason because he was wearing an arc-and-compass breast-pin. Does it follow of necessity that a man wearing this pin is a Freemason? Of course, not. He could wear it with the intention to deceive, or without even realizing its significance. I sometimes long for an anti-Holmes who announces his brilliant "deductions" with the same insouciance as the great detective, but who is wrong in every instance.

Yet, Sherlock Holmes and his model, Joseph Bell, *are* reasoning. So, what is their method? In another story, *The Adventure of the Cardboard Box*, Holmes gives a more accurate account of his thinking: "The case is one where … we have been compelled to reason backward from effects to causes". This sort of reasoning yields explanations. Why is the man wearing an arc-and-compass breastpin? Answer: because he is a Freemason. Why didn't he remove his hat? Answer: because he is recently discharged from the army. Why has he contracted elephantiasis? Answer: because he was stationed in Barbados where it was rampant. Of course, Holmes and Bell have to notice these clues before they can explain them. But, their method is *abductive* and fallible.

In the previous chapter, I described the interplay between induction and abduction. I solved the problem of how to get a cappuccino in an Italian coffee bar: one pays first and then gives the receipt to the barman. This induction seemed to apply to Italian bars in general because I was able to make an abduction that explained it: the barmen were too busy making coffees to operate a cash register. An explanation strengthens our belief in an induction. Peirce coined the term "abduction" to refer to the inferential process that yields causal explanations, because, like Sherlock Holmes, we reason backwards from an effect to a cause that explains it. However, I have appropriated the term to refer to inferences that yield any sort of explanation, and my aim is to try to characterize the mental processes underlying them.

* * *

Philosophers have argued that abduction should yield the *best* explanation of events. That seems laudable. The problem is to characterize what counts as best. Several factors appear at stake. A good explanation should be truthful. One that claims that bars have cashiers because the barmen are too busy to cope with payments is wrong if, say, the barmen have plenty of time but don't want to handle money.

A second factor in a good explanation is parsimony. Unfortunately, it is not easy to assess. If we count the number of words in a description, then it depends on the particular words in our vocabulary. It will also differ from one language to another. We might think of defining parsimony in terms of the shortest computer program that outputs the explanation (in some universal programming language). But, this idea leads to even worse problems, which I have relegated to the notes for the chapter. Perhaps the best way is to think of parsimony as a medieval philosopher William of Ockham did. He is supposed to have declared: "Entia non sunt multiplicanda praeter necessitatem". That is, "Entities are not to be multiplied without necessity". The principle is known as Ockham's razor, and it often guides scientific explanations. We examine the number of distinct sorts of entity in an explanation, and perhaps the number and complexity of relations among them.

A third factor in a good explanation is the number of observations that it covers. My abduction didn't explain much beyond the order of business in Italian bars. In contrast, a scientific explanation of observations often goes beyond them to explain, and even to predict, other observations. Ptolemy explained the motions of the planets but Newton explained both them and local events on earth, such as the fall of an apple. Newton's explanation is better than Ptolemy's, because it is closer to the truth, more parsimonious, and has a wider purview. The upshot is that a good explanation is desirable, impossible to prove, and a matter of informal judgment.

* * *

Do you understand how sewing machines work? Of course, you do. But, let's see how well you understand them. You know that the machine has a needle and thread and that it pushes them through the pieces of cloth to be stitched together. But, what happens then? A loop of thread comes through the cloth, and somehow another thread passes through the loop, and is pulled up tight against the underside of the cloth. But how can a thread pass through the loop? Perhaps you (and I) have now realized that we overestimated our understanding of sewing machines. It's a state of mind that happens so often that psychologists refer to it as the illusion of depth of understanding. We don't make the analogous mistake about our knowledge of facts. However, we do often think we understand something only to discover, when we try to explain it, that we have at best a superficial grasp of it. For a profound understanding of anything, describe it, teach it, and then research it.

When we explain how a device works, as studies have shown, we first describe how it functions at one level, and then outline the underlying mechanism. We may progress to a deeper level, and describe the functioning of each component in the mechanism, and then its mechanisms, and so on. In the case of a sewing machine, there's a bobbin of thread rotating beneath the plate on which the garment rests, and when the needle's eye pushes the loop of thread through the garment, the thread on the bobbin is made to pass through the loop. But how? That's the whole trick of it. The bobbin has a long thread wound round it, one end of this thread has already been stitched into the garment, but the other end of the thread is wound round the bobbin. It's this free end that we want to poke through the loop of the upper thread. The machine can't push the bobbin through the loop. So, instead it pulls the loop round the bobbin, which is rotating vertically. The loop then draws the thread from the bobbin up tight against the underside of the garment. And how does the machine do all this? The answer is that as the loop comes through the garment, it is snagged on a notch on the bobbin. As the bobbin rotates, the notch pulls the loop of thread around the bobbin. By this time, the needle is moving upwards and so the loop is pulled taut with the bobbin's thread within it, up against the garment. The whole cycle is ready to repeat. As you can see, my account has followed the general recipe of explaining matters at an ever deeper level. In case you had difficulty in following it, Figure 14.1 gives you six "snapshots" of the sequence to help you to understand how the mechanism works.

* * *

The preceding account of a sewing machine is causal. It explains how the machine causes one event in the process, which brings about another, and so on. If we weren't familiar with the operations of a sewing machine, then it would be difficult for us to create this sequence—we would have to re-invent the sewing machine. Many simple explanations in life, however, can be constructed from our general knowledge of causes and their effects. The ability to imagine possible causes is at the heart of explanations. We use our general knowledge to retrieve or to construct causal chains. Every culture appears to use causal explanations, and many cultures including our own put a high value on them. Westerners, however, tend to explain people's actions in terms of their intentions and abilities, whereas Asians tend to explain them in terms of the social context.

A plausible explanation of a physical event should be a causal one, and, given a choice between a deduction and a causal explanation, Westerners and Asians alike are biased towards the latter. Here's a simple illustration of this contrast.

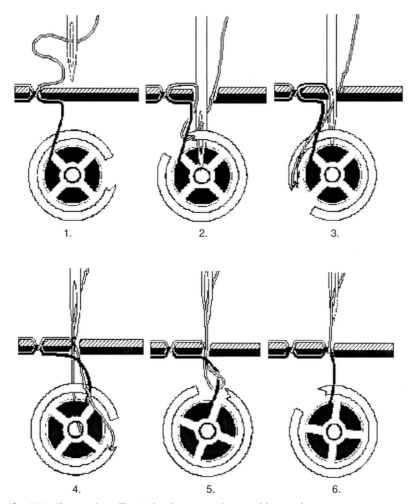

Fig. 14.1 Six snapshots illustrating how a sewing machine works.

Suppose I tell you: if a pilot falls from a plane without a parachute then the pilot dies. Yet, *this* pilot did not die. And I ask you: Why not? Most participants in an experiment responded with these sorts of explanation:

> The plane was on the ground and so he (sic) didn't fall far.
>
> He fell into a deep snowdrift and so his fall was broken.
>
> The pilot was already dead and so his fall didn't kill him.

Just a few responded with a deduction:

> The pilot didn't fall from a plane without a parachute.

You may have inferred that he *did* fall without a parachute. The way I couched the question may have led you to make this inference. Yet, if I tell you that he did in fact fall without a parachute, you have no difficulty in coming up with causal explanations of why he didn't die, now that I have blocked you from offering the deductive account.

The best sort of explanation of events is causal. But, how long is the optimal chain? Suppose you learn that an acquaintance of mine was in a car crash, and you ask me for an explanation. I could tell you, he lost control of the car. But, this explanation seems *ad hoc* and unmotivated: it stands in need of an explanation. A more plausible explanation provides a motivation in terms of a cause: He was driving too fast on an icy road and he lost control of the car. Of course, you might also ask for an explanation of this cause, but as a causal chain grows, it becomes more improbable. Indeed, the preceding explanation is already more improbable than the minimal explanation that the driver lost control of the car. But, a cause and an effect seem optimal. The cause provides motivation for the effect; the effect explains the event in question; and the explanation is not long enough to seem improbable.

How do we create causal explanations? Some are in our long-standing memories, waiting for us to use them. Others are not, and we have to create them. We know many elementary causal relations, which could be represented in knowledge as explicit models of sets of possibilities, and we could stitch these links together to make a novel chain of events.

Suppose we have to explain why a man jumped into a swimming pool fully clothed. We may not know any reason for this action. But, we know it's stupid, and we can retrieve a cause for stupid actions, such as drunkenness. And so we can infer: perhaps the man was drunk. This possibility in turn can trigger a further cause in our general knowledge: perhaps he was drunk because his girlfriend had jilted him. We could continue to grow the causal chain in this way. We are making up a story:

> Perhaps his girlfriend had jilted him because she thought that he had been unfaithful to her, even though he hadn't, and so in despair he drank too much and as a result jumped into a swimming pool fully clothed.

These chains may be original in the sense that we have never thought of them before. We retrieve the links from memory, but at each point several possibilities may come to mind, and we select those that seem appropriate in order to construct the chain. Our unconscious reasoning is making a sequence of Markov transitions of the sort that I described in Chapter 5.

I have written a computer program that constructs chains of causal relations in this way. It is based on the assumption that our knowledge of possibilities is represented in models of causes and their effects—some psychological evidence corroborates this ordering. The input to the program is a model of an event. The program uses the content of this model to search its knowledge base, and, if possible, to trigger a possibility relevant to explaining it. If the search is successful, the program uses this possibility in turn to search its knowledge base again, and, if possible, to trigger a possibility that causes the new effect. In this way, the program constructs a causal chain working backwards from the event to its causal explanation. Its plan is analogous to Conan Doyle's way of writing many of his stories. He thought of a crime, and then constructed a chain leading backwards from it to a singular and perplexing event that called for Sherlock Holmes to unravel. Why, for instance, would someone advertise for red-headed men to apply to join a league entitling them to paid a large amount for nominal services? The reader is hooked just as Holmes was.

People are imaginative in constructing explanations. An experiment showed that their ability went beyond any existing computer program. They could explain arbitrary conjunctions of events. They were given pairs of sentences taken at random from different stories, e.g.:

John made his way to a shop that sold TV sets.

Celia had just had her ears pierced.

In another condition of the experiment, the sentences were modified to ensure that the same individual was referred to in both sentences in the pair:

Celia made her way to a shop that sold TV sets.

She had just had her ears pierced.

The participants encountered a given content only once, and they had to explain what was going on in each vignette. They went beyond the information given to them in order to account for what was happening. They proposed, for example, that Celia was getting reception in her ear-rings and wanted the TV shop to investigate, that she was wearing new earrings and wanted to see herself on closed circuit TV, that she had won a bet by having her ears pierced and was going to spend the money on a new TV set, and so on. The participants were almost as ingenious with the sentences that did not refer to an individual in common. But, sometimes they were stumped for an explanation. This failure is what I refer to as the "Mary Celeste" effect. The eponymous example is based on an historical case: we believe that if we board a ship at sea, the crew will be there. We board the Mary Celeste. We discover that the crew is not aboard. And, like the original sailors who boarded her, we are unable to infer what has happened to them. This Mary Celeste effect shows that our everyday reasoning doesn't always succeed.

* * *

Some psychologists argue that our everyday reasoning depends on a tractable procedure, because we dream up explanatory hypotheses so readily. The argument seems plausible, but it is impossible to assess the efficiency of a procedure unless one knows what it is supposed to compute. To infer that Celia wanted to see her ear-rings on TV seems like a satisfactory explanation to the problem above, but consider this response:

Celia wanted to buy a TV set.

Is it satisfactory? It doesn't say anything about the ear-piercing, and so perhaps it isn't an adequate explanation. And what about the Mary Celeste response:

I can't explain what's going on.

Does that count as satisfactory? If it does, then the process is efficient in a trivial sense: we know when we can't explain a certain event. If it doesn't, then perhaps our everyday reasoning is not so efficient after all, because it doesn't always yield an explanation.

* * *

Abduction relies on another source of explanations: analogy. As an example, consider this problem:

Tom's enemy Jerry was stabbed to death in a cinema during the afternoon showing of *Bambi*. Tom was on a train to Philadelphia when the murder took place. What follows?

A plausible induction is that Tom is innocent. We represent the premises in a mental model of the cinema in one place and the train in another place. Jerry is in the cinema; Tom is on the train. So, Tom couldn't have stabbed Jerry. In an experiment with a series of these sorts of problem, all the participants inferred that Tom was innocent. The experimenter then told them, "No, that's not so". He then asked them, "Can you think of any other possibility?" So, can *you* think of any other possibility?

Your task is to make an abduction that explains how, despite the facts of the matter, Tom could be guilty of Jerry's murder. A salient opening maneuver is a spatial modification of the model in order to satisfy the constraints that Tom stabs Jerry. You can relocate the cinema so that it is on the train. Nothing in the premises precludes this possibility. So, you suggest: the cinema was on the train. No, the experimenter says, that's not so. A similar spatial maneuver allows the train to run past the cinema—it's an open-air cinema. Tom leans out of the window, and is armed with a very long knife. No, the experimenter says once more, that's not so. (By now, you may have induced that he's going to make this response to all your ideas.) In the experiment, the participants varied in their ability to think of possible scenarios. But, those that they did create tended to occur in roughly the same order from one participant to another. For instance, after they had inferred that Tom was innocent, they tended to make spatial manipulations of the sort I've just described.

What to do next? Your initial model of Tom and Jerry was correct: they *were* in different places. So, how could Tom nevertheless be guilty of murder? At this point, you need an insight. Here, an analogy can help. You may think of one that yields the insight. But, in case you're stuck, let me suggest one. I have a small garden attached to my house, but I don't have enough time to look after it and so I employ a gardener to tend it for me. Does that suggest any possibilities?

With luck, you should have had the thought that perhaps Tom paid an accomplice to commit the murder (just as I pay my gardener to mow my lawn). No, the experimenter says, that's not so, can you think of any other possibilities? Many people are disposed to give up at about this point. But, you should push on, because there are other possibilities.

An accomplice allows a criminal to act at a distance, and you need to pursue this thought. Participants who persevere dream up new possibilities for action at a distance:

> Tom fixed a spring-loaded knife into the seat of the cinema.
>
> He suspended a knife in a block of ice over Jerry's seat.
>
> He used a radio-controlled robot. (Engineers tend to think of this idea.)
>
> He used psychokinesis. (No, the experimenter says, that is not so.)

During the years that the late John Frankenheimer, the movie director, refused to allow his masterpiece, *The Manchurian Candidate*, to be shown in cinemas, only one person in several hundred to whom I give this puzzle suggested that Tom might have given Jerry a post-hypnotic suggestion to stab himself. (It happened in Sweden, and the person who thought of this idea, as I found out later, was a Swedish princess.) *The Manchurian Candidate* features the most sinister psychologist in all moviedom, a man from the "Pavlov institute", who uses post-hypnotic suggestion as an assassination technique. After Franken-heimer allowed the movie to be shown again in cinemas, this response to the problem became more frequent, at least one person in every audience to whom

I gave the problem would think of it. The movie was perhaps more available as a source of an analogy.

At what point can you infer that no other possibilities exist and that Tom is innocent? Alas for Tom, you can never reach this conclusion. It is not deducible: you can never be sure that you have eliminated all the possibilities in which Tom is guilty. Indeed, abductive problems seem closer to those in life than those in logic textbooks. The sole limits to possible scenarios are the limits of your imagination. I have heard most of the possibilities. But, who knows? The next person to whom I give the problem may create an original solution based on a novel analogy. Come to think of it, no one has suggested time travel!

* * *

Various psychological theories of analogy exist, and in broad terms they agree that once we have found an analogy, we carry over certain components from it to the problem that we're trying to solve. Your problem was to show that Tom is guilty of Jerry's murder, and my analogy was that I employ a gardener to mow my lawn. So, we can begin with these mappings from the analogy to the problem:

Phil——Tom
|
employs
|
gardener
|
to mow
|
lawn——Jerry

We should be able to complete the mappings to come up with a new idea that makes Tom guilty:

Phil —— Tom
| |
employs   employs
| |
gardener   accomplice
| |
to mow   to murder
| |
lawn —— Jerry

Once we have thought of a fruitful analogy, we shouldn't have too much difficulty in making the right mappings. The difficult problem both in theory and in practice is to find the analogy.

We seem to differ in our ability to come up with apposite analogies. Some of us have a genius at it. Wilbur Wright, whom I discuss later in the book, drew several deep analogies between the bicycle and a heavier-than-air flying machine. Indeed, it is extraordinary how apt his analogies were, at least for early aircraft. Another source of Wilbur's analogies was bird flight. He argued that for a plane to turn, it needed to do what some birds do, namely, to twist its wings in opposite directions. But, how could the twist be done without compromising the structural stability of the wings? As he was talking to a customer in his bicycle shop, he had an insight that is illuminating. He was holding a long thin box for a cycle inner tube in his hands and happened to twist one end of the box in one direction and the other end in the opposite direction. He saw at once the analogy to a biplane. It depended on visualizing the upper and lower sides of the twisted box as the wings of a biplane. But, he also *felt* the consequences: the twisted box retained its lateral rigidity.

The computer programs that draw analogies represent knowledge in linguistic terms. To represent the idea that twisting a wing causes it to turn, they use representations of this sort, which I have simplified a little:

(causes (twists wing)(turns wing))

The only meaning that these words have for the programs is that they match the same words in other data. So, the use of English, as opposed to Latin or numerals, is for the convenience of the computer programmer. Verbal representations are plausible if thinking were just talking to oneself—a view once popular among behaviorists. The late Richard Feynman was disabused of this error as a schoolboy when a skeptical friend asked him what word he used to describe the shape of a crankshaft. Visual imagination is not verbal manipulation. But, also it is not a manipulation of two-dimensional images. As I argued in Part I of the book, mental representations of the world are often models, and Wilbur Wright's analogy depended on the manipulation of a three-dimensional model. The visual system constructs a mental model of the box. This model serves as the analogy, and the upper and lower surfaces of the box are mapped on to a mental model of a biplane. We "see" the upper and lower surfaces of the box as wings. To twist the box is analogous to twisting the wings. And the kinesthetic sense of torsion and its lack of effect on the box's lateral stability can be mapped on to the model of the wings. No current computer program using analogies can carry out this process of forming analogies between dynamic three-dimensional models, but it was one of the

Wright brothers' fundamental abilities. Analogies are often between models of the world rather than between propositions. Feynman himself reports an all-purpose method of building analogies from models:

> I had a scheme, which I still use to-day when somebody is explaining something that I'm trying to understand: I keep making up examples. For instance, the mathematicians would come in with a terrific theorem ... As they're telling me the conditions of the theorem, I construct something that fits all the conditions. You know, you have a set (one ball)—disjoint (two balls). Then the balls turn colors, grow hairs, or whatever, in my head as they put more conditions on. Finally, they state the theorem, which is some dumb thing about the ball which isn't true for my hairy green ball thing, so I say, 'False'!

* * *

Not all explanations are causal. We explain proofs by outlining their general principles. We explain our actions by giving our reasons for them. Tom might say, for example, "I killed Jerry because he ran off with my wife". That's his reason. But, we might say that the cause for the murder was Tom's insane jealousy and his inability to control it. Most explanations in life do seem to depend on causal relations. We stitch chains together from elementary links. We carry chains over from analogous models. When we explain an event, whether we offer a full-dressed scientific theory or an informal everyday abduction, the result is a powerful constraint on induction. It cuts down the number of possible inductions; it also makes it easy to generalize on the strength of just a single observation of an event. The constraints of a theory often override the pure inductive process: we ignore counterexamples to the theory. The eighteenth century German scientist and aphorist, Georg Lichtenberg once remarked: "One should not take note of contradictory experiences until there are enough of them to make constructing a new system worthwhile". The molecular biologist James Watson has also observed that no good scientific model ever accounts for all the data because some of the data are bound to be wrong. Most of us appear to follow this methodological prescription. Even children who are trying to solve a problem ignore counterexamples to their current hypotheses. This neglect of evidence implies that pure induction has a limited role in the development of explanations. An explanation doesn't just increase the information in the observations: it can eliminate observations as erroneous.

Chapter 15

The Balance of Probabilities

You go to your doctor to have an annual check up, and the doctor gives you various tests. Later, she tells you that you tested positive for Pel Ebstein disease, and that individuals with this disease test positive 99 times out of 100. The disease is serious, but you'll be fine as long as you're treated without delay. It's natural to be worried when you get this news, but if you inferred that you probably have the disease, you succumbed to a subtle fallacy. I will explain the fallacy in due course. It is typical of what can go wrong in our reasoning about probabilities. This reasoning is difficult, not least because the probability calculus is an intellectual invention, and not native to us. Aristotle, who invented logic, told us nothing about how we ought to reason about probabilities. He had little to say about them beyond the fact that probable events occur often. The probability calculus, as every infant poker-player knows, was not invented until 1654 when the Chevalier de Méré wrote to Pascal about a gambling game, and Pascal in turn consulted with Fermat. Of course, people reasoned about probabilities before the 1650s, but no one knew how they *ought* to reason about them. That is to say, the probability calculus enables us to deduce the right answers about certain probabilities. It provides, as psychologists say, a "normative" theory. Strangely, however, the calculus doesn't tell us what probabilities mean. We can interpret them as frequencies of events, measures of subjective belief, or objective propensities of physical devices such as roulette wheels. Theorists debate without end which interpretation is proper.

Few of us either master the probability calculus or form a settled opinion on how to interpret it, but that doesn't stop us from reasoning about probabilities. One way is inductive, much as I imagine that Aristotle reasoned. We know that if Paolo went to get the car then he'll be back in five minutes. We also know that he went to get the car. Yet, he hasn't come back after a quarter of an hour. So which of these events is more likely to have happened?

He ran into a system of one-way streets and had to drive out of town.

He had to drive out of town.

Most people choose the first option (when they occur among a set of other choices). It is an induction, because the choice is fallible. Indeed, the first option is just a special case of the second one, and so it cannot be the more probable of the two. Of course, the juxtaposition of the two options suggests that in the second case Paolo had to drive out of town for some other reason. But, why should that make the case less likely? In these sorts of judgment, we use evidence and general knowledge to make inferences about the likelihood of an event. If pressed—perhaps by an importunate psychologist—we are even prepared to put numbers to our estimates: we induce from our knowledge of Italian towns that the probability that Paolo ran into a system of one-way streets is about one in three. Psychologists make similar inductions about their experiments when they infer that they have a real effect because its chance probability is so small.

Kahneman and Tversky carried out a masterly series of experiments examining intuitive inductions of probabilities. The results overturned the classical conception of human rationality—the view that the probability calculus was just common sense. Their studies showed, for example, that if knowledge makes a possibility available to us, then we tend to think that it has a higher probability than events that are less available. Someone asks us:

> In the US which is the most probable: death in an automobile accident, by stroke, or by stomach cancer?

We tend to say, "automobile accident". In fact, the most frequent cause of death is stroke, followed by stomach cancer, followed by automobile accident. Deaths in automobile accidents are more available to us: they are a common topic in the media, whereas the deaths of most people go unrecorded, and they tend to die from diseases. Availability is a heuristic that we tend to use in unconscious intuitive judgments about probabilities.

When we are asked the probability that an individual is a member of a particular set or category, we often use how representative of the category he or she seems to be. This heuristic is sensible, but it can lead us into error if we fail to test our intuitions. A famous example from Tversky and Kahneman's studies concerns a woman called Linda:

> Linda is 31 years old, single, outspoken, and very bright. She majored in philosophy. As a student she was deeply concerned with issues of discrimination and social justice and also participated in antinuclear demonstrations.

From this description, participants in many experiments gave a higher ranking to the probability that Linda is a feminist bank teller than to the probability that Linda is a bank teller. Her description is more representative of the former than the latter (as independent ratings showed). But, the set of bank tellers includes the set of feminist bank tellers, and so the rankings of their probabilities violate a basic principle of probability. Our intuitions are answering the wrong question, and our deductive powers are overlooking the error.

We do make deductions about probabilities. The prize is behind one of three doors. You guess it's behind the left-hand door. I know its true location, and I open the right-hand door to show you that it isn't there. Should you switch your choice to the middle door or rest content? You deduce that the prize is either behind the left-hand door or behind the middle door, and so the odds are even. And so you stick with your choice. Most people do. But they're wrong, and later you'll see why. In this sort of deductive reasoning, there are several mutually exclusive possibilities, and you use them to deduce probabilities.

Psychologists want to understand how naïve individuals make these inferences. By *naive*, I mean those of us who have not mastered the relevant piece of intellectual technology, the probability calculus. They include judges on the British Court of Appeals, who rejected its use in evidence, to your friend in the saloon bar who opts not to switch doors in the puzzle above.

A few psychologists reject Kahneman and Tversky's results and argue that much of our reasoning is based on mental processes, which unbeknownst to us, embody principles from the probability calculus. These principles lie dormant unless information is presented in the form of natural occurring frequencies. On this account, everyone from Aristotle to people in cultures that count only "one", "two", "many," *is* equipped with an unconscious embodiment of parts of the probability calculus. Yet, the abilities of naïve individuals may be better described in terms of simple principles governing the inference of probabilities from mental models. This hypothesis does not deny the normative status of the calculus for inferences about probabilities. We are rational in inferring probabilities to the extent that we abide by its principles, though, from time to time, life or psychologists lure us into irrational inferences.

My plan is to explain how models underlie deductions about probabilities, and to say something about the calculus. I will jack up the complexity of the inferences until they reach those that are on the outer edges of our competence, and I will explain why they are so difficult for us. Some people suffer from existential nausea as soon as they see numbers, and so if you're one such individual, please avert your gaze (and don't even look at the two boxes).

* * *

In earlier chapters, I argued that reasoning is based on mental models of possibilities, and that each mental model represents a different possibility. Hence, granted a representation of the likelihood of these possibilities, models provide a way of reasoning about probabilities. If we know, say, that the prize is behind one of three doors, then barring information to the contrary, we assume that it has an equal chance of being behind each door. This notion that alternative possibilities have equal probabilities has a long history in the development of the probability calculus, and it is sometimes known as the principle of "indifference". Good evidence exists that we follow this principle, though we assign equal probabilities to *models* of possibilities. Given a proposition, such as: *There is a red marble or a green marble, or both, in the box*, the participants in an experiment estimated the probability that both marbles were in the box as roughly a third. That estimate follows from the assumption that they thought of the three possibilities as equally likely: red marble in the box, green marble in the box, red and green marble in the box. They then worked out the proportion of possibilities in which the critical case occurred. The experiment examined a variety of different sorts of problem and corroborated the assumption of *equiprobability*.

These results might be open to other explanations, so how can psychologists show that we use mental models? The answer is that the theory predicts the occurrence of systematic biases, because mental models represent what is true, but not what is false. This principle of truth, which I discussed earlier (in Chapter 8), applies at two levels: we construct models of true possibilities, and each model represents just those propositions that are true within it. As an example, consider this problem:

> There is a box in which there is at least a red marble, or else there is a green marble and there is a blue marble, but not all three marbles. What is the probability that there is a red marble and a blue marble in the box?

As the mental models of the proposition predict, we tend to think of two possibilities. In one possibility there's a red marble, and in the other there's a green and a blue marble. So, it is impossible for the marbles in the question—the red and the blue—to occur together. The probability that both of them are in the box is therefore zero. Our imperfect reasoning is a perfect illustration of the use of mental models. Let's retrace the inferential steps, but this time let's get the right answer.

The premise means that when it is true that there is a red marble in the box, it is false that there is a green and a blue marble in the box, and vice versa—that's the force of the "or else". The falsity of the conjunction of a green and a blue marble can occur in three ways: green without blue, blue without green, and neither green nor blue. Each of these possibilities can occur with the red marble. The premise also means that when it is true that there is a green and blue marble in the box, it is false that there is a red marble in the box. And so there are four distinct possibilities for what's in the box:

Red	Green	
Red		Blue
Red		
	Green	Blue

If each of these possibilities is equiprobable, then the probability of a red and a blue marble in the box is, not zero, but a quarter.

An experiment examined various inferences of this sort, which the theory predicts should give rise to illusions, and it compared them with inferences from matching control problems in which mental models yield the correct answers. Here is an example of a control problem:

> There is a box in which there is a red marble or else a green marble, and there is a blue marble in the box, but not all three marbles. What is the probability that there is a red marble and a green marble in the box?

The premise suggests again that there are two possibilities, depending on whether the red or green marble is in the box, but in both possibilities there is a blue marble. So, the theory predicts that it is impossible for both the red and green marble to be in the box. And this time the predicted response is correct. There are just these two possibilities. The participants succumbed to the illusions, and did very much better with the control problems. Three-quarters of the participants estimated a probability of zero, or thereabouts, for the proposition in the illusory example above, and only a couple of the participants made the unbiased estimate. In contrast, most of the participants made a correct response to the control problem. These results were typical of the experiment as a whole.

In general, we can infer the probability of an event by representing each of the mutually exclusive possibilities in a separate model. We assume unless we have evidence to the contrary that each possibility is equiprobable. We compute the probability of a proposition by working out the proportion of possibilities in which it occurs. But, we make errors, because we tend not to represent what is false.

* * *

Phil has two children. One of them is a boy. What's the probability that the other is a boy? Most of us reason like this: there are two possibilities for Phil's second child: a boy or a girl. Ergo, the probability is one-half that the second child is a boy. Plausible, but wrong. The right way to proceed is to enumerate all the possibilities:

First-born child	Second-born child
Girl	Girl
Girl	Boy
Boy	Girl
Boy	Boy

The fact that Phil has one boy rules out the first of these possibilities. There remain three possibilities, and in just one of them both children are boys. The correct answer is therefore one third. If I had said that Phil's *first-born* was a boy, then the probability that his second-born child was a boy would indeed be a half. But I framed the question so that there was no way to identify which of Phil's children was known to be a boy.

The preceding problem hinges on a *conditional* probability. We can cope with some conditional probabilities. For example, there are two bags, and one of them has a coin in it and the other is empty. I choose one of the bags at random. If it contains the coin, I spin the coin, and if it comes down heads, you win. But, in any other case, you lose. Granted that all's fair, what's the probability that you win? You should think to yourself:

> It's 50:50 whether Phil chooses the bag with the coin, and then it's 50:50 whether it comes down heads. So the probability of the bag with the coin is a half, and given that bag, the probability that the coin comes down heads is a half, and so the probability that I win is a half of a half, which is a quarter.

You multiply the two probabilities and you get the right answer. To prove it, here is the full set of possibilities with the chances of their occurrence, which I have expressed as idealized frequencies out of a hundred repetitions of the game:

Phil gets the bag with the coin:	50.	It lands heads:	25.
		It lands tails:	25.
Phil gets the empty bag:	50.		

So, the chances that you win are indeed twenty-five times out of 100, or a quarter. A correct analysis depends on your knowledge that when two events that are independent of one another do both occur, their joint probability is the product of their individual probabilities. Most of us retain at least this much knowledge from our schooldays, or else we can imagine the appropriate models—akin to those above—tagged with the appropriate numerical probabilities.

Yet, conditional probabilities are at the edge of our competence. What goes wrong with the problem about Phil's children is that we misunderstand it. We don't realize that it is a question of a conditional probability: *given that one child is a boy, what is the probability that the other child is a boy.* The phrase "given that..." is a clue that passes us by. As a consequence, we fail to think about the full set of possibilities, and instead take the question to concern a simple absolute probability: what's the probability that a child is a boy?

We are no more likely to imagine a set of four different possibilities in order to infer a probability than to do so in making a regular deduction. They are too many for us to hold in mind at once, and so we tend to think about them one at a time. As a case in point, let's go back to the problem at the start of the chapter:

> If individuals have Pel Ebstein disease then they test positive 99 times out of 100. You test positive. What's the probability that you have the disease?

Most participants in an experiment responded with a high probability to questions of this sort. An expert on the probability calculus would be reluctant to answer. To see why, you can consult Box 15.1, which lays out the possibilities and their frequencies. The moral of the box is that a conditional probability, such as:

> If you have the disease then you test positive 99 times out of 100

does not imply the converse conditional probability:

> If you test positive then you have the disease 99 times out of 100.

One conditional probability tells you next to nothing about the other conditional probability unless you have additional information (see Box 15.2). Yet, the participants in the experiment baulked not once about making a whole series of these inferences about both high and low probabilities. Why? They didn't assume as a matter of course that the two conditional probabilities were the same. But, the medical example is one for which they didn't know any alternative causes for testing positive. The experiment also included problems in which there were obvious alternatives, such as:

> If an object is put in boiling water, then the chances that it becomes hot are 99 out of 100. An object is hot. What is the probability that it was put into boiling water?

The participants could think of many other possibilities that would make the object hot, e.g., it was standing in the sun, it was put in a furnace, it was subjected to intense friction. They didn't baulk about inferring a probability, but it was lower than the probability stated in the problem. After the

Box 15.1 The risk that you have Pel Ebstein disease

Here are the possibilities and their frequencies for the conditional probability that a person with Pel Ebstein disease tests positive 99 times out of 100:

		Frequencies
Has Pel Ebstein disease	Tests positive	99
Has Pel Ebstein disease	Does not test positive	1
Does not have Pel Ebstein disease	Tests positive	Not known
Does not have Pel Ebstein disease	Does not test positive	Not known

You want to know the conditional probability that you have the disease given that you test positive. You therefore need to know the frequencies of the cases in the first and third rows above in which you test positive, and then the proportion of them in which you have the disease (the first row). You have no information about the frequency with which individuals test positive and don't have the disease (the third row). Suppose the complete frequencies are as follows:

		Frequencies
Has Pel Ebstein disease	Tests positive	99
Has Pel Ebstein disease	Does not test positive	1
Does not have Pel Ebstein disease	Tests positive	1,000,000
Does not have Pel Ebstein disease	Does not test positive	2,000,000

In this case, even though you tested positive your risk of having the disease is small: 99/1,000,099, i.e., roughly one chance in ten thousand.

This way of inferring the conditional probability of A given B is known as the *subset* method, because it depends on the ratio:

$$\frac{\text{The probability of the conjunction of A and B}}{\text{The probability of B}} \quad \begin{array}{l}\text{(the subset)}\\\text{(the set)}\end{array}$$

Once you know the probability of each conjunction of events, as in the preceding table, you can work out any conditional probability using the subset method. You know everything that is to be known about the probabilities in the domain.

experiment, they said that they had thought about the alternative ways in which an object could be heated and took them into account in making their inference. Yet, they also inferred converse conditional probabilities when they had no pertinent knowledge in examples akin to the case of Pel Ebstein disease.

The model theory explains their performance. It postulates that we tend to think about one possibility at a time. Given a conditional probability, such as, *if a person has Pel Ebstein fever then they test positive 99 times out of a 100*, we tend to build one at a time the following two mental models:

Has Pel Ebstein disease	Tests positive 99
. . .	1

The ellipsis represents an alternative possibility that we do not make explicit. When we are told that a person tested positive, and are asked for the conditional probability that the person has the disease, we assume that the same models apply, and infer the same value: 99 out of 100. Likewise, if we were told instead that the person did not test positive, we assume that the possibility corresponds to the implicit model. And so now we infer a low probability that the person has the disease. When we think about other possibilities, as in the example about boiling water, we also build models of these possibilities. We then estimate a lower probability for the converse conditional probability.

Consider, again, the problem about Phil's two children. Given that one child is a boy, we need to assess the conditional probability that the other child is a boy. To calculate the right answer, we need to think of the three possibilities in which at least one child is a boy:

Girl	Boy
Boy	Girl
Boy	Boy

We then find the *subset* of possibilities in which the other child is a boy. There is just one such possibility. We calculate the proportion of the subset to the set as a whole: 1/3. And that result is the required conditional probability. This subset method of assessing a conditional probability from explicit models is within the competence of most of us. Several studies have shown that naïve participants are able to infer conditional probabilities in this way provided that they can carry out the process step by step and the arithmetic is easy.

* * *

There are two events, and each of them has a probability of a half of occurring. What's the probability that both of them occur? Those of us unfamiliar with the probability calculus tend to say: one-quarter. We multiply two probabilities together to infer the probability of a conjunction of two events. In the earlier example of the bag and the coin, this procedure is right. But, in this example, it is wrong. We can see our mistake at once if we learn that one event was the toss of a coin coming down heads and the other event was the same toss of the coin coming down tails. The two events cannot both occur, and so the probability of their conjunction is zero. The description was vague in order to entice us into error. It didn't tell us anything about the relation between the two events. They could be dependent on one another as in heads versus tails. But, they could also be independent as in tosses of two separate coins.

Let me make a digression into this business of dependence. The degree of dependence between two events, such as my remembering to take an umbrella and it raining later in the day, is reflected in the conditional probability that given one event, the other event occurs. Suppose that the "base rate" of rain on any day, i.e., the probability that it rains, is one in ten. And suppose that the conditional probability that it rains given that I remember to take an umbrella is also one in ten. It follows that whether or not it rains is not affected by my remembering to take an umbrella: the two events are independent. This case contrasts with a weather forecast. The probability is, say, nine out of ten that it rains given that the forecast is for rain, whereas the base rate for rain is only one in ten. This difference shows that rain and a forecast of rain are not independent events. Indeed, the forecast is useful, because when it predicts rain, the probability of rain is higher than the base rate. In general, two events are independent if the probability of one event is the same as its conditional probability given the occurrence of the other event.

If we are playing roulette and we observe a sequence of twelve reds one after another, we might think that the next spin of the wheel must be more likely to yield black in order to ensure that the split between the two colors is roughly 50:50. This way of thinking is known as "gambler's fallacy". Given a fair roulette wheel, each outcome is independent of the others, and the chances of red and black are equal on every spin. So, a prior sequence of reds has no effect on the probability of red on the next outcome. The real implication of a sequence of 12 reds is illustrated in what happened when casinos first became legal in the UK in the 1960s. An American statistician told me that on a visit then to the UK he observed that casinos did not pair up the rotors of the roulette wheels—the parts that spin—with different bases from one session to another. He therefore made small bets for a long time and kept a record of the frequencies with which the different numbers came up. After a day or two of play, he sometimes discovered that a wheel was biased in that some numbers came up more often than one would expect by chance. He carried out a statistical test to discover whether the bias was significant. If it was significant, thereafter he would bet on these numbers, and win a large amount of money. He continued to use this method for some days until the manager of the casino realized what was going on, and introduced the policy of pairing up different rotors and bases from one day to the next. When a long sequence of improbable events does occur, gambler's fallacy is the wrong inference to make. We should continue to observe the sequence, because the data may show that the process is biased.

Now, we can understand how to work out the probability of a conjunction of two events. When the two events are independent—as in my bag and coin example, we multiply their probabilities to get the probability of their conjunction. But, a safe way to assess the probability of the conjunction of two events, even when they are dependent, is to multiply the base rate of one event by the conditional probability that given this event the other event occurs. A description of this principle is in the first sentence of Box 15.2.

Box 15.2 Bayes's theorem and the Pel Ebstein example

1. In general, the probability of A *and* B = (probability of A)(probability B *given* A). It is also the product of the probability of B and the probability of A *given* B.

2. The subset ratio from Box 15.1 is:

$$\text{The probability } A \text{ given } B = \frac{\text{probability}(A \text{ and } B)}{\text{probability}(B)}$$

3. For the probability of A *and* B here, we can substitute its equivalent from 1 above:

$$\text{Probability of } A \text{ given } B = \frac{(\text{probability of } A)(\text{probability of } B \text{ given } A)}{\text{probability of } B}$$

This is Bayes's theorem, which interrelates one conditional probability to its converse.

4. As an example, consider the following three probabilities from Box 15.1, where "≈" means "equals approximately":

   A: The probability that a person has the disease is 100/3,000,100 ≈ 1/30,000

   B: The probability that a person tests positive is 1,000,099/3,000,100 ≈ 1/3

   B given A: The probability of a positive test given the disease is 99/100.

   Bayes's theorem stipulates: the probability of the disease given a positive

   $$\text{test} = \frac{(1/30\,000)(99/100)}{1/3} \approx 1/10\,000$$

Hence, given that a person tests positive, the probability that the person has Pel Ebstein disease is low, roughly one in ten thousand.

A conditional probability by itself tells us next to nothing about the converse conditional probability. So, what information *do* we need in order to infer this converse probability? The probability calculus provides alternative ways to compute its value. If we know the full set of probabilities for each conjunction of events, we know everything that is to be known about the probabilities at issue. In this case, Box 15.1 above shows you how to use the subset method. But, an alternative method depends on a famous theorem in the probability calculus, which is named for the English nonconformist minister, the Reverend Thomas Bayes, whose discovery of it was in a posthumous publication in 1764. Instead of knowledge of the full distribution of probabilities for each conjunction of events (as in Box 15.1), we need to know three probabilities: the conditional probability that is our starting point, e.g., if a person has Pel Ebstein disease then the probability that the person tests positive is 99 out of a 100; the probability that a person has Pel Ebstein disease; and the probability that a person tests positive. Armed with these three possibilities, Bayes's theorem, which I explain in Box 15.2, allows us to compute the converse conditional probability. If the theorem looks like mumbo-jumbo to you, don't worry. It looks that way to most of us. We don't know the theorem; we find it hard to understand; and, as the evidence shows, we don't use it to infer conditional probabilities.

As I explained at the start of the chapter, we sometimes make intuitive inductions about probabilities, relying on simple heuristics, such as the availability of relevant knowledge. But, we also deduce probabilities from our knowledge of the alternative possibilities and their likelihoods. In life, the two methods are often intermingled. But, when one method is pitted against the other, relevant knowledge is more vivid and makes a bigger impression. In a well-known study, Tversky and Kahneman compared the two, and discovered that intuitive descriptions trumped numerical probabilities. The participants were told, for instance, that a panel of psychologists had given personality tests to thirty lawyers and seventy engineers. The participants were then given descriptions of five of these individuals selected at random, and asked to rate the probability that each individual was an engineer. They were also told that they would be paid extra if their estimates came close to those of a panel of experts. If the participants are sensitive to these frequencies, then their ratings should take into account the respective numbers of lawyers and engineers. But, their estimates did so only when they were given no information whatsoever about an individual. With a neutral description of an individual, they tended to rate the probability that the individual was an engineer as 50:50. And with a vivid description of a person who sounded like an engineer, they would rate him as such, even if they had been told that there were 30 engineers but 70 lawyers.

* * *

Our education and cultural background affect our views about probability. The biggest difference is whether our culture is one with any knowledge of the probability calculus. As a philosopher once remarked, "anyone who played dice in Roman times armed with the probability calculus would soon have won the whole of Gaul". One happy consequence of our naïve grasp of probabilities, however, is that it suffices for us to acquire expert knowledge. This expertise, however, depends on knowledge of various sorts. One sort is knowledge of combinations and permutations. For example, if Phil has four children, it's most likely that he has two girls and two boys, isn't it? No, it isn't. It seems plausible, because the chances of a boy or girl are equal. Experts know that it is necessary to take all the possibilities into account, and that it's most likely that Phil has three children of one sex and one of the other sex. Whether expertise of this sort is a result of observation or of the development of conceptual knowledge is a moot point. Another element of expertise is the ability to do arithmetic—a factor that is easy to overlook in studies of probabilistic reasoning. We can do arithmetic with frequencies more easily than with fractions or percentages. These elements enable us to learn the calculus of probabilities, and the ability to acquire this expertise rests on the simple principles of reasoning that I have explained in this chapter.

* * *

When we make inductions about probabilities, we base our judgments on various heuristics, such as the availability of relevant knowledge. When we make deductions about probabilities, we represent the different possibilities in mental models, though we don't as a rule represent what is false. Unless we have knowledge to the contrary, we assume that each model represents an equiprobable alternative. We infer the probability of an event from the proportion of models in which it occurs, sometimes using numerical tags on models to represent probabilities. We infer conditional probabilities in the same way, by considering subsets of models. Any probability that we cannot infer in these ways may be beyond us. We all make mistakes. We fail to realize that a conditional probability tells us next to nothing about the converse conditional probability. None of us appears to have an unconscious knowledge of the laws of probability. If the doctor tells you that those with Pel Ebstein disease test positive 99 times out of a 100, and that you tested positive, no need for alarm.

You need to work out the relative frequencies of all the possibilities. If you can't fill in the numbers completely, then beware of propositions about conditional probabilities.

I have one item of unfinished business—the problem of the three doors. You'll remember that a prize was behind one of three doors, and that you chose the left-hand door. The chances that the prize is behind this door are one in three, and the chances that it is behind one or other of the remaining two doors are two in three. I know the true location of the prize, and I open the right-hand door to show you that the prize isn't behind it. My action doesn't change the location of the prize or the probability that your choice was correct. So, the chances that the prize is behind the left-hand door remain one in three, and the chances that it is behind the middle door are two in three, because I've eliminated the possibility that it is behind the right-hand door. I offer you the opportunity to switch your choice to the middle door. Most people refuse, but you should switch to the middle door, because the chances that the prize is behind it are two in three. Of course, you could use Bayes's theorem to work out the answer, but it would be the same. If you erred then do not be alarmed. You are in excellent company.

Part V

What Makes us Rational

Our last to do by is an anti-model,

Some untruth anyone can give the lie to

A nothing no one need believe is there.

Auden

Chapter 16

Counterexamples

What is a counterexample? Well, suppose I tell you:

> Everyone who smokes marijuana goes on to take hard drugs.

You counter with a counterexample:

> That's not true. Bill smoked marijuana, but he didn't go on to take hard drugs.

And I say:

> But, he didn't really smoke marijuana, because he didn't *inhale*.

You say:

> Well, I know several people who smoked marijuana and they didn't go on to take hard drugs.

At this point, I am forced to make a concession:

> Well, maybe not everyone, but it's true for most people.

This rejoinder is difficult for you to rebut, but it's also difficult for me to sustain. One way for us to proceed is to do a complete count of marijuana smokers, or else to survey a random sample of them and to compute some statistics and a margin of error. We would have to agree beforehand what counts as "most marijuana smokers".

If instead of my last claim, I asserted:

> Some marijuana smokers go on to take hard drugs

then your only possible rebuttal is:

> No marijuana smokers go on to take hard drugs.

And now you must check every marijuana smoker, whereas I need only to find an example or two. This to-and-fro quality is like a game, and some philosophers have analyzed the meanings of quantifiers, such as "all" and "some", in terms of these games. But, what the game shows is that you and I both understand the notion of a counterexample, at least to claims about sets of individuals.

Counterexamples are also crucial for reasoning. A valid inference has a conclusion that must be true if its premises are true. An *anti-model* of a proposition represents a possibility in which the proposition is false. And so a counterexample is a model of the premises that is an anti-model of the conclusion. It establishes that the conclusion is false in at least one possibility consistent with the premises, and so the conclusion is not a valid inference from the premises. I suggested at the start of the book that a cornerstone of human rationality—insofar as humans are rational—is that they grasp the force of counterexamples. It is time to make good on this claim.

A counterexample to a general proposition shows that the proposition is false. Yet, we often fail to search for counterexamples. In Chapter 1, I described a well-known experimental paradigm, Wason's selection task, in which the participants have to select evidence that would show whether a general claim is true or false. You may remember that the experimenter presents a claim, such as, "If a card has an 'A' on one side then it has a '2' on the other side", and invites the participants to select those cards from a set of four (A, B, 2, and 3) that it is necessary to turn over in order to find out whether the claim is true or false about the four cards. The participants know that each card has a letter on one side and a number on the other side. They often fail to select the card bearing a "3" on one side, but it is a potential counterexample, because an "A" on its other side would show that the general claim is false. The principle of truth leads them to focus on a true possibility: cards bearing an *A* and a 2. However, any experimental manipulation that makes it easier for them to think of counterexamples appears to improve their performance in the task. Hence, we are capable of grasping the force of counterexamples if the conditions of an experiment enable us to overcome the principle of truth. Alas, no consensus exists about the selection task. Some psychologists argue that it fails to test reasoning, and one psychological journal has refused to publish any more papers about it, because of its controversial status.

Another task that Wason devised also suggests that we tend not to search for counterexamples. The experimenter shows us a sequence of numbers, "2 4 6", and he says that they are an instance of a general rule that he has in mind. Our task is to discover what this general rule is, and we proceed as follows. We make up a sequence of three numbers, and the experimenter tells us whether or not it is an instance of his rule. We write down, say, "6 8 10", and he says, "yes, that's an instance of my rule". We make up another three numbers, and the experimenter responds to them. And we continue in this way until we have identified the rule. The task isn't easy. When we think of a hypothesis about the rule, such as "numbers increasing by two", we tend to make up a sequence that is an instance of it, such as: 3 5 7. But, it is hard to solve the problem in this way, because we don't realize that the experimenter's rule is very general. It is, in fact: *any three numbers of increasing magnitude*. Most of our hypotheses are likely to be less general. Positive tests of our hypotheses are therefore of no use, because every instance of them is also an instance of the experimenter's rule. And so we can never learn that our hypotheses are wrong. Some participants accordingly fail to solve the problem even after working on it for an hour. If our hypothesis is, "numbers increasing by two", then a better way to proceed is to make up a sequence that is a counterexample to it, such as: 1 2 3. The experimenter tells us that this sequence *is* an instance of his rule, and so we know that our hypothesis is wrong: its counterexample is an instance of his rule.

Why do we test positive instances of our hypotheses? Perhaps we have a bias to confirm our hypotheses, but a simpler and more plausible explanation is the principle of truth. We focus on true instances of our hypotheses, which are easier to think of than false instances.

In its original formulation, the model theory postulated that reasoners construct models of premises, draw a conclusion, and then, given a modicum of competence, search for counterexamples to the conclusion. But, do they? In fact, they often construct a model, draw a conclusion from it, and that's that. It takes work to overcome the principle of truth, and some of us seem unwilling or unable to search for counterexamples. This chapter therefore needs to answer three questions: Do we recognize the force of counterexamples? In what circumstances, if any, do we search for them? And does the model theory explain our performance?

* * *

One problem in the use of counterexamples is to realize the need for them. We don't always grasp their relevance when we test the truth of general propositions. Likewise, when we draw our own conclusions from premises, we tend to focus on a single model of the premises. To construct such a model, and to formulate a conclusion, is so preoccupying that we may fail to search for counterexamples. We have no capacity left over to think about them. One way to reduce the load on our mental capacity, and our working memory, is to give us a conclusion to evaluate rather than to ask us to formulate one. This procedure may also create a more critical attitude, because we have to deal with someone else's conclusion rather than our own.

Another problem with counterexamples is to determine what counts as one. Suppose we draw a conclusion that is an exclusive disjunction:

Either Pat is here and Viv is here, or else Eve is here.

What is a counterexample to this conclusion? It is any anti-model in which the conclusion is false but the premises are true, but we don't have an immediate access to these models. We have to construct them. Suppose that Pat isn't here. That would refute the initial conjunction in the conclusion, but if Eve is here, the conclusion is still true. Let's add the further assumption that Eve isn't here. So, Pat isn't here and Eve isn't here. That would be a counterexample. Are there any others? We can imagine the possibility in which Viv isn't here and Eve isn't here. We may even imagine the possibility in which none of the women is here. But, we may not think of one final possibility in which both clauses of the disjunction are *true*: all three women are here. Yet, it is a counterexample too, if the disjunction is exclusive.

Experiments in which participants have to list the anti-models of propositions show that they use various ways to do so. But, their performance is still constrained by the principle of truth, because they think first about what's true, and then try to refute it. Hence, they can cope with propositions that contain just a single connective, though they may fail to list all the possibilities in which a conjunction is false. However, as the use of mental models predicts, their performance with propositions containing two or three connectives is often dire. When participants have to make separate lists of what is possible and what is impossible given a proposition, i.e., its models and anti-models, they seldom construct two lists that together exhaust all the relevant possibilities. The one sure way to construct counterexamples is described in Box 16.1, but only those of us with a training in logic are likely to use it. Hence, when we think of counterexamples, we are at risk of error.

Another way to construct counterexamples is to think of the negation of a sentence, and then to try to imagine the possibilities compatible with it. But, it isn't easy to think of the correct negation of many sentences. Consider a proposition, such as:

All the women are here.

The proposition is false if just one of the women isn't here, and so its proper negation is:

Not all the women are here.

As this example shows, a proper negation *contradicts* the proposition that it negates. That is, one of the two propositions must be true and one of them must be false. Many of us, however, suppose that any introduction of a negation into the original proposition negates it. So, we may think that the negation of the proposition is: *none of the women is here*. But, this proposition

Box 16.1 How to create a counterexample to an assertion

Example: Either Pat is here and Viv is here, or else Eve is here.

1. Construct the complete possibilities in which the assertion as a whole is true. The main connective is "or else", which we can treat as an exclusive disjunction, and so combine the true possibilities for one clause with the false ones for the other clause:

Pat	Viv	not Eve	[True first clause and false second clause]
Pat	not Viv	Eve	[False first clause and true second clause]
not Pat	Viv	Eve	[False first clause and true second clause]
not Pat	not Viv	Eve	[False first clause and true second clause]

where "Pat" stands for "Pat is here", and "not" negates this proposition.

2. Remove this set from the set of all eight possible combinations of *Pat is here, Viv is here, Eve is here*, and their negations. The remainder is the set of anti-models of the original assertion, i.e., the set of possibilities in which the assertion is false:

Pat	Viv	Eve
Pat	not Viv	not Eve
not Pat	Viv	not Eve
not Pat	not Viv	not Eve

These are the possible counterexamples to the original assertion. In words, all three individuals are here, only Pat is here, only Viv is here, or none of the women is here.

doesn't contradict the original proposition, because both it and the original proposition could be false—as when some but not all of the women are here.

So, what is the correct way to negate a proposition? The one secure method is to make a negation that contradicts it. This method, however, leads us back to the procedure in Box 16.1. And so we often make an improper negation. We intend to find a counterexample to a conclusion, but we search for the wrong case.

* * *

The use of counterexamples in syllogisms has been examined in experiments. You will recall that a syllogism is an argument about sets of individuals, e.g.:

All the artists are beekeepers.

All the chemists are beekeepers.

Therefore, all the artists are chemists.

This inference is invalid, and one way to demonstrate its invalidity is to think of a counterexample. For instance, there are two sorts of beekeeper, those who are artists and those who are chemists. In this case, all the artists are beekeepers and all the chemists are beekeepers, but contrary to the conclusion no artist is a chemist.

How else could we establish that an inference is invalid if we don't use a counterexample? Current psychological theories based on formal rules make no use of counterexamples, and invalidity is established either by proving that the premises imply the negation of the conclusion, or, where a conclusion is at least consistent with the premises, by the failure to find a formal proof that the conclusion follows from the premises. One drawback to this procedure is that we should take a long time to search for all possible proofs. Another drawback, as logicians have pointed out, is that if we fail to find a proof, we'll always have a nagging doubt about whether our search was complete. In contrast, a counterexample is an "in your face" anti-model that demonstrates invalidity.

Some poor reasoners almost always draw a conclusion to any syllogistic premises. They have failed to search for alternative models of the premises. Other poor reasoners almost always respond that nothing follows from syllogistic premises that have multiple models. They haven't been able to grasp that the models support a conclusion in common (see Box 10.3).

Not only do theories based on formal rules of inference ignore the role of counterexamples, but at least one account based on mental models does so too. Thad Polk and the late Allen Newell proposed this theory, which uses alternative models, but not counterexamples. Their theory gives a good account of differences in syllogistic performance from one individual to another. But, I suspect that some other process in the theory carries out the work of counterexamples. One reason for my suspicion is a finding from a more recent study. An experiment externalized the process of searching for counterexamples. The participants were given syllogisms with putative conclusions, e.g.:

Some of the chefs are musicians.

None of the musicians is a painter.

Therefore, none of the chefs is a painter.

All the syllogisms referred to chefs, musicians, and painters, and the participants were given simple cut-out paper shapes to depict them—chef's hats to represent the chefs, guitars to represent the musicians, and palettes to represent the painters. Simple "stick" figures represented individuals, and the participants could add hats, guitars, and palettes, in order to represent the premises. Their task was to construct an external model with the cut-outs in order to refute the conclusion, or else to say that the task was impossible if they thought the conclusion followed from the premises. The experiment examined twenty syllogisms, four with valid conclusions, and sixteen with invalid conclusions.

The participants were able to construct correct counterexamples for fifty-nine percent of the invalid inferences—a result that was much better than chance performance, because most models of the premises are not counterexamples. Every participant was able to construct correct counterexamples, but the range in performance was from ninety-five percent correct for the best participant down to only twenty-five percent correct for the worst participant. This range in ability is characteristic of syllogistic reasoning in the population at large.

As the model theory predicts, a major cause of error was that the participants often did not grasp what was a counterexample to certain sorts of proposition. For instance, with conclusions of the form: *some of the chefs are not painters*, they sometimes constructed a model in which some of the chefs are painters, and sometimes a model in which none of the chefs is a painter. The correct counterexample is one in which *all* the chefs are painters. The participants were assessed in a strict way, and so these errors did not count as the construction of counterexamples.

A striking aspect of the results was the great variety of different procedures that the participants developed. Critics had argued that a major flaw in the model theory was its failure to specify how we search for counterexamples. The problem was not a conceptual one, because a computer program implementing the theory contained a procedure that created counterexamples. The difficulty was instead to find out how *we* carry out the search. The experiment with cut-out shapes showed that we can construct counterexamples. In fact, we use the same procedures as the program for constructing new sorts of individual, but a major discrepancy occurred between program and person. The program followed a single fixed procedure for finding counterexamples; the participants did not. They usually used the operation of adding new individuals to models in order to search for alternative models. But, it was impossible to predict whether they would add one or two new individuals or the order in which they would add them.

Those of us without training in logic can construct counterexamples to refute invalid conclusions given to us to evaluate. But, do we think of counterexamples in drawing our own conclusions? A second experiment compared reasoning with and without the use of cut-out shapes. No difference in accuracy occurred between these two conditions. You may recall that some syllogisms yield a valid conclusion from just a single model, whereas others yield one only from multiple models. Those that called for only one model were easier than those that called for multiple models. For those that require one model, the majority of the participants' conclusions were based on a single external model using the cut-outs. But, all the participants constructed multiple external models for some syllogisms, ranging from two participants who built them on three-quarters of the problems, down to one participant who built them on less than a tenth of the problems. A crucial result was that the participants were all more likely to do so for those syllogisms that called for multiple models. But, the experiment didn't show that they were searching for counterexamples. They may just have been exploring different possibilities: one problem with syllogisms is indeed that their premises are open to many interpretations. I now turn to some studies of reasoning with propositional connectives that corroborate the use of counterexamples.

* * *

The conclusion of an invalid inference need not be true even if the premises are true, and so there are two sorts of invalid inference. In one sort, the conclusion is inconsistent with the premises. That is to say, it does not hold in any of the possibilities compatible with them, e.g.:

> Either Dan is in Madrid or else Bill is in Seoul, but not both.
>
> Therefore, Dan is in Madrid and Bill is in Seoul.

With these simple sentences about different people in different cities, neither meaning nor general knowledge modulates the logical interpretation of the connective. And so the premise is consistent with two possibilities, but they are both inconsistent with the conclusion, and so it cannot follow from the premises.

A second sort of invalid inference is subtler. The conclusion is consistent with the premises, but doesn't follow from them. That is, it holds in at least one possibility consistent with the premises, but not for all such possibilities, e.g.:

> Dan is in Madrid or Bill is in Seoul, or both.
>
> Therefore, Dan is in Madrid and Bill is in Seoul.

The premise yields three possibilities, and the conclusion holds in one of them—the one in which both individuals are in their respective cities. But, the conclusion isn't a valid inference, because two possibilities compatible with the premise are its anti-models: Dan is in Madrid and Bill isn't in Seoul, and Dan isn't in Madrid and Bill is in Seoul. Reasoners who can build a model of one of these possibilities and recognize it as a counterexample know that the inference is invalid: the premises can be true, but the conclusion false.

In summary, a conclusion that is inconsistent with the premises does not hold in any of the models of the premises. But, another sort of invalid conclusion holds in at least one model of the premises, but not all of them. Hence, we should be more likely to use counterexamples for these inferences. The theory also predicts that it should be easier to infer that a conclusion is invalid when it is inconsistent with the premises than when it is consistent with them. Any model of the premises is an anti-model of a conclusion inconsistent with them, but not any model of the premises is an anti-model of a conclusion consistent with them. If, as often happens, we fail to consider all the models of the premises, we should still be correct in evaluating an inconsistent inference, because its conclusion conflicts with any model of the premises. But, we are at risk of erring with a consistent conclusion, because we may overlook a model that is a counterexample to it. It follows that inconsistent conclusions should yield a greater number of correct evaluations than consistent but invalid conclusions.

Several experiments have corroborated these predictions, and their results provide the best evidence for the use of counterexamples in reasoning. The participants evaluated given inferences, and to discover whether they grasped the force of counterexamples, they had to write down justifications for their judgments. Two separate judges assessed the written justifications, and they agreed about almost all of them. They categorized a justification as using a counterexample only if the participant described an anti-model—a possibility in which the premises were true but the conclusion was false. The studies showed that participants used a variety of methods, including counterexamples and contradictions. The results corroborated the model theory's predictions. The participants used counterexamples more often to refute conclusions consistent with the premises (fifty-one percent of problems) than to refute conclusions inconsistent with them (twenty-nine percent of problems)—in this case, they tended instead to point out the contradiction. The participants were more accurate in recognizing invalid conclusions that were inconsistent with the premises than those that were consistent with the premises. In general, the use of counterexamples correlated with correct evaluations.

The task of writing justifications for evaluations might have affected the participants' judgments. Another experiment therefore compared participants who wrote justifications with those who did not. There was no difference in the accuracy of their evaluations. Those who wrote justifications tended, as before, to use counterexamples to refute conclusions consistent with the premises, and to detect the contradiction with conclusions inconsistent with the premises. The similarity in accuracy and speed of response suggests that the participants in the two groups were using similar procedures. They were able to use counterexamples to refute invalid conclusions whether or not they had to justify their evaluations.

* * *

More than half of the people in the room speak French.

More than half of the people in the room speak English.

Does it follow that more than half of the people in the room speak both French and English?

We reject the inference as invalid. But, do we imagine a counterexample? An experiment answered this question. The participants evaluated a series of inferences from one, two, or three premises, which were each claims about "more than half" of a given set. The conclusions were based either on "at least one" or "more than half" of them. An example of a difficult three-premise inference is:

More than half of the patients have shnupfosis.

More than half of the patients have hustosis.

More than half of the patients have frognosis.

Does it follow that more than half of the patients have at least two of the three diseases?

The participants had pencil and paper, and could write down notes or draw diagrams, and they also had to think aloud as they tackled the inferences. As in the previous experiments, they developed various methods, but for

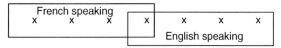

Fig. 16.1 A diagram of a counterexample based on a drawing made by a participant in an experiment. Each "x" represents a person. The premises were that more than half of the people in the room speak French, and that more than half of them speak English. The diagram is a counterexample to the conclusion that more than half of them speak both languages.

over three-quarters of the problems, they drew diagrams of the premises. In typical diagrams, they represented the set referred to in the subject of each premise with a number of tokens, such as X's. They then represented the other sets with tokens that were just a little larger in number than half the size of the subject set, and they tried to minimize the overlap between the sets. In short, they searched for a counterexample. Every participant produced at least one counterexample. Figure 16.1 shows a typical counterexample to the first inference above with the conclusion that more than half of the people in the room speak both French and English. It is based on a diagram that a participant drew. This participant aimed to minimize the overlap of the two sets, and the diagram refutes the conclusion. However, it does not refute the conclusion:

> At least some person speaks both English and French.

No correct diagram does, and so this conclusion is valid.

The protocols revealed how participants tackled the problems and showed that they constructed counterexamples on sixty percent of the trials with invalid conclusions. Their typical error was to fail to find a counterexample where, in fact, one existed. These errors were often a result of the participants adopting the wrong search procedure. Once they adopted a procedure for the problems, they tended not to change it. The three inferences in Box 16.2 illustrate this point. The diagram to refute the first conclusion does not require the chemists to be split into two groups, whereas this split is necessary for an anti-model of the second conclusion. The possible counterexamples to the first conclusion include those that refute the second conclusion, and so the first conclusion should be easier to refute than the second conclusion. The tendency to minimize overlaps, which is the most frequent procedure, fails to yield a counterexample to the third conclusion. That is why this problem is so difficult. We have to *maximize* the overlap of the three sets, provided that the overlap is less than half of the set of people (see diagram 3 in the box). Hence, the difficulty of the problem comes from a dogged, but incorrect, application of an otherwise successful method.

Box 16.2 Three invalid inferences based on "more than half"

The premises:

More than half the persons are artists.

More than half the persons are beekeepers.

More than half the persons are chemists.

1. Does it follow that more than half the persons are artists, beekeepers, and chemists? (all twenty of the participants said: no.)

2. Does it follow that at least one person is an artist, a beekeeper, and a chemist? (only eight of the participants said: no)

3. Does it follow that more than half the persons are at least two of the three occupations: artist, beekeeper, chemist? (Only one participant said: no).

Three sorts of diagrams are anti-models that refute the preceding inferences:

1. This diagram refutes the first conclusion: More than half the persons are artists, beekeepers, and chemists:

Artist	Beekeeper	
Artist	Beekeeper	
Artist	Beekeeper	Chemist
		Chemist
		Chemist

2. This diagram refutes the first conclusion and the second conclusion: At least one person is an artist, a beekeeper, and a chemist:

Artist		Chemist
Artist		Chemist
Artist	Beekeeper	
	Beekeeper	
	Beekeeper	Chemist

Box 16.2 *(continued)*

3. This diagram refutes the first conclusion and the third conclusion: more than half the persons are at least two of the three occupations: artist, beekeeper, chemist:

Artist	Beekeeper	Chemist
Artist	Beekeeper	Chemist
Artist		
	Beekeeper	
		Chemist

* * *

One of the nuisances for experimenters studying counterexamples is that they have to use a special procedure in order to detect them. They have to ask the participants to think aloud, or to write justifications for their evaluations, or to construct external models out of cut-out shapes. A potential way round this nuisance is to find a region in the brain that becomes active when people are reasoning, but only if they are trying to find a counterexample. An unpublished study using functional magnetic resonance imaging (fMRI)—a procedure that I described earlier (in Chapter 2)—addressed this question.

The fMRI procedure calls for repeated observations and so the experiment couldn't use inferences based on, "more than half", because the answers would soon become familiar. Instead, it used problems with numbers and contents that varied from one trial to another, such as:

There are five students in a room.

Three or more of these students are joggers.

Three or more of these students are writers.

Three or more of these students are dancers.

Does it follow that at least one of the writers in the room is a student?

This particular conclusion follows at once from the third premise, and so there is no need to search for counterexamples. But, consider this alternative conclusion:

Does it follow that at least one of the students in the room is all three: a jogger, a writer, and a dancer?

The conclusion is consistent with the premises, but it doesn't follow from them, and so its correct evaluation, granted the use of models, calls for a search for counterexamples. In a preliminary to the fMRI study, the participants had to evaluate the inferences, and to carry out mental arithmetic tests based on a separate presentation of the same premises. A typical example of an arithmetical test based on the premises above was:

X is the number of students. Does $(X + 24) + (X - 1) = 29$?

The premises above state that there are five students, i.e., $X = 5$, and so a simple calculation shows that the answer to this question is: No. The preliminary study made it possible to match the relative difficulty of the two sorts of inference—easy ones that didn't call for a search for counterexamples and hard ones that did—with the relative difficulty of two sorts of mental arithmetic problem. The preceding example was an easy arithmetical problem.

The fMRI study showed that once the participants had understood the premises, the regions of the brain active during reasoning and during arithmetic were separate from one another. Reasoning recruited regions in the

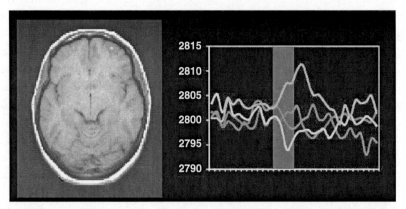

Fig. 16.2 On the left is an image of a horizontal slice through the brain with the front of the brain at the top of the page. The region in red is a part of the right frontal lobe known as the "frontal pole". The graph on the right shows the amount of activation in this region in four different conditions of an experiment: pink shows the activation for reasoning problems in which the participants searched for counterexamples, red shows the activation for reasoning problems in which the participants did not search for counterexamples, light blue shows the activation for easy arithmetical problems, and dark blue shows the activation for difficult arithmetical problems. The horizontal axis is time, and the gray vertical band is the eight seconds for which the problem was displayed. Please see plate section for a colour version of this figure.

right hemisphere of the brain—in the frontal lobes, whereas mental arithmetic recruited regions in the left hemisphere. Figure 16.2 shows the most striking result. A region known to the experts as the "right frontal pole" was active only when a reasoning problem called for a search for counterexamples. The other fluctuations in the levels of activation in the figure did not yield any significant results. One study is not decisive, but it does suggest that activation in the right frontal pole may underlie a search for counterexamples. If so, experimenters can test conjectures about counterexamples without requiring the participants to speak their thoughts aloud, to write justifications, or to draw diagrams.

* * *

We grasp the force of counterexamples, but we may have difficulty in grasping their relevance when we formulate our own conclusions. We may have difficulty in framing the correct counterexample to a conclusion. For instance, we may think that a counterexample to the conclusion, *some of the artists are chemists*, is an anti-model of a possibility in which some of the artists are *not* chemists. Both these propositions could be true, however, and so they are not inconsistent with one another. Yet, even if we have no training in logic, we can construct counterexamples in reasoning with propositional connectives and in reasoning with quantifiers, such as "more than half" and "at least three".

The propensity to use counterexamples varies from one person to another, and some of us seldom use counterexamples. Several factors appear to give rise to this variation. One factor is intellectual ability: a mark of intelligence is the accurate use of counterexamples. It correlated with *correct* evaluations of conclusions. Another factor is whether or not an invalid conclusion is consistent with the premises. We tend to refute inconsistent conclusions by detecting the contradiction between them and the premises. But, consistent conclusions cannot be refuted in this way, and so we tend to imagine counterexamples. Our experience is also likely to affect our use of counterexamples. We may have acquired an expertise in thinking of counterexamples as result of coping with problems of a certain sort. One other factor is important. When we draw our own conclusions, we have to base them on the models of the premises, and this procedure may make a search for anti-models difficult.

* * *

What is the appropriate criterion to assess the rationality of our deductive reasoning? Most theories presuppose that it is validity—that a conclusion must be true given that the premises are. But, two psychologists Mike Oaksford and Nick Chater disagree. They have argued that the right criterion to assess our everyday reasoning and our deductions in the psychological laboratory is the probability calculus. They even claim that this calculus *describes* our deductions. They believe that our reasoning is a rational adaptation to the world, and that it depends on a tractable process. Because the probability calculus isn't tractable, they add a rider: we use heuristics rather than the intricate computations that the calculus demands. Yet, they reject Tversky and Kahneman's findings that heuristics can lead us into errors in probabilistic thinking. They advocate instead different heuristics, which they claim are rational. Their theory is ingenious, and, granted certain assumptions about the interpretations of premises, it gives a good account of the frequencies with which participants draw various syllogistic conclusions. For example, given the premises:

> Some of the authors are bakers.
>
> Some of the bakers are cricketers.

some of us do draw the conclusion:

> Some of the authors are cricketers.

It isn't valid, but it does follow in the probability calculus. And so when we reason, on this account, we draw conclusions that are possible and sometimes in addition necessary.

The majority of the participants in the experiments I described earlier constructed a counterexample to the syllogism above. If the probability calculus is the appropriate norm to assess reasoning, they were irrational to do so. But this claim is odd. The dilemma for the theory is that some of us reject invalid deductions and some of us do not. If we're right to reject them, we're irrational to accept them; and if we're right to accept them, then we're irrational to reject them. No consistent account of rationality can have it both ways.

In fact, the probability calculus provides a poor description of our deductive reasoning. We are not aware of thinking about probabilities when we make syllogistic or propositional deductions. We don't mention them when we think aloud. Recent studies have shown that when we assess whether a conclusion is necessarily true, probably true, or possibly true, our performance differs from one task to the other. Here's a simple example to sharpen the contrast:

> There is a red marble or a green marble, or both, in the box.
>
> Therefore, there is a red marble and a green marble in the box.

Do you think that the conclusion follows from the premise? I doubt it. Yet, it follows in the probability calculus, and so on the probabilistic account you ought to accept that the conclusion follows from the premises. In fact, the participants in the experiments with propositional connectives, which I described earlier in the chapter, spontaneously used counterexamples to refute inferences of this sort. Hence, validity *is* central to their reasoning. Logicians and psychologists, including Oaksford and Chater themselves, also grasp the notion of validity, and so we can be sure that at least some of us have it. In fact, our ability to meet the criterion of deductive validity correlates with measures of our intelligence. The smarter we are, the more we draw valid deductions and refrain from invalid deductions. The extent to which our deductions yield probable rather than valid conclusions is a measure of our stupidity.

* * *

Our everyday reasoning often begins outside our awareness. It is rapid, automatic, and often leads us to true conclusions. We guess right, as Peirce pointed out. But, is it rational? Some psychologists say it must be because we tend to achieve our goals, and they distinguish between one sort of rationality for everyday reasoning and another sort for our deliberate deductions. But, the mere fact of achieving a goal is no evidence for any sort of rationality unless one is prepared to ascribe rationality to all living creatures. Bees, for example, have been around for millions of years longer than we have. They achieve their goals, and yet their preferences for sources of nectar violate a simple logical principle. Experiments have shown that in certain cases they prefer source A to source B, and source B to source C, and yet prefer source C to source A. Likewise, our explanatory ability leads us to blatant inconsistencies with the probability calculus. Why, for instance, do highly intelligent women marry less intelligent men? As you will recall, we offer explanations instead of recognizing a case of regression to the mean. And we sometimes find conjunctions more probable than their constituent propositions. Best to own up and to say that we make mistakes too.

   The chapter began with three questions that I can now answer. First, we do recognize the force of counterexamples. We grasp the principle that a valid inference has no counterexamples. This understanding, however, does not inoculate us against errors. We often survive—though not always—despite our irrational errors. We do even better when we are rational in our reasoning. Second, the best recipe to elicit counterexamples appears to be to ask us to evaluate someone else's conclusion, to use simple premises that elicit multiple models of possibilities, and to ensure that the conclusion holds in at least one of these models. Finally, the model theory appears to explain our performance. We are likely to adopt a critical attitude to someone else's conclusion, and when we don't have to formulate the conclusion for ourselves, it tends not to clutter up our working memory. Invalid conclusions that are consistent with the premises are more likely to elicit counterexamples, whereas those that are inconsistent with the premises are more likely to elicit the detection of the contradiction. We don't have a fixed procedure for searching for counterexamples, and the present chapter has shown that we make predictable mistakes in our searches for them.

Chapter 17

Truth, Lies, and the Higher Reasoning

What is truth? Pontius Pilate posed the question to Jesus (John 18:37), but Jesus didn't say. Jesting Pilate, wrote Francis Bacon, the sixteenth century philosopher, would not stay for an answer. The question comes down to us with such a mystique that many suppose, like Pilate, that it is too deep to be answered. Yet, its broad outlines are not so mysterious. If we ask people, "what does it mean to say that a proposition is true?" then the most frequent answer is: the proposition describes a situation that corresponds to the facts. This "correspondence" theory, which has a long philosophical history, is correct. A proposition is true when it corresponds to the way the world is; and it is false when it doesn't correspond to the way the world is. All legal systems would collapse if we didn't accept this principle.

The difficulty in formulating the correspondence account is to put into words what it is that the correspondence holds between. Logicians separate the language for talking about logic, which they refer to as the "metalanguage", from logic itself, which has its own language, the "object" language. Hence, the solution in logic to the correspondence is to say, for example, that the sentence "snow is white" is true if snow is white. Which seems vacuous, but which does illustrate the difference between a claim in the metalanguage: *"snow is white" is true*, and a claim in the language under analysis, the object language: *snow is white*. Logicians talk of *sentences* as being true or false, but you will remember that earlier in the book I distinguished between a sentence such as, "I can hear you now", and the many propositions that it expresses, depending on who says it, to whom it is said, and the context of its utterance. So, on one side of the correspondence is a proposition expressed by the use of a sentence in a particular context, and on the other side of the correspondence is a state of affairs in the world. I can try to identify a particular proposition in this way: the proposition expressed by the sentence "I can hear you now" when Pat O'Brian said it to Viv Waugh on the telephone at 9 a.m. on Monday January 10, 2005 on the corner of Bleecker Street and Broadway in Manhattan. The proposition is true if indeed Pat could hear Viv on this occasion. This claim seems to be accurate, but it's hard to generalize it. Perhaps the best one can say is that a proposition refers to certain individuals or entities, and ascribes properties or relations to them. It is true when those individuals or entities have the ascribed properties or relations. I imagine that when robots can perceive the world and describe it, this principle will be embodied in their software.

The Romantic poet John Keats wrote in a letter to a friend, "I have never yet been able to perceive how anything can be known for truth by consecutive reasoning—and yet it must be". But, granted that a set of propositions is true, any other proposition that is their valid consequence is also true. And this fact resolves Keats's puzzlement about how "consecutive reasoning" leads to the truth. It does so by being sound, that is, a valid inference from true premises. Some philosophers have promoted the inferential view into a full-fledged theory of truth, the so-called "coherence" theory, in which a proposition is true if it coheres with other propositions known to be true. But, coherence seems to be parasitic on consecutive reasoning from truths of correspondence.

Communication works because a fundamental convention is that speakers tell the truth. Without this convention, discourse would be pointless. Listeners would have to check the truth of every proposition. Likewise, without the convention, lies wouldn't work. But, only on occasion can we check the veracity of a communication. As a result, we may discover that a proposition is true. We then *know* that it is true, and may in turn testify to it. Most propositions, however, we take on trust.

Truth matters to us because communications about the world are worth more to us, and are a more useful guide to our actions, if they are true rather than false. Of course, if we *know* that a proposition is false, then its negation is true, and negations can be informative. Often, however, we do not know whether propositions are true. But, if they are true, we know how the world is, and we know it by proxy. That is, we haven't witnessed the state of the world, but someone else has, and they have described it to us. When two young engineers at Chernobyl went to investigate the fate of the reactor after the explosion, they saw that it had been destroyed, and they went back to the control room to describe what had happened. The two young men later paid for their observations with death from radiation sickness, but their description at last convinced the engineers in charge that the reactor had been destroyed. The engineers notified the authorities in Moscow, and the evacuation of the town at last began, some hours after the accident. A true description saved lives.

* * *

Truth is simpler in logic than in life. A sentence in a logical calculus is true when it corresponds to some domain of interpretation; otherwise, it is false. If we know the truth values of a set of elementary propositions, then it is simple in principle to determine the truth value of a compound sentence made up from these propositions using logical connectives. Logicians have generalized this idea to show how to determine the truth values of sentences in a logical language that contains quantifiers, i.e., the logical analogues of "any" and "some".

One tricky issue about propositions in life is whether every proposition is either true or false. The meaning of negation works in a simple way granted this assumption. As Aristotle pointed out, if an affirmative proposition is true then its negation is false, and if an affirmative proposition is false then its negation is true. For instance, if it is true that you are reading this book, then it is false that you are *not* reading this book. But, certain sentences give rise to problematical propositions. I say to you: My wife has stopped smoking. But, suppose that my wife has never smoked in her life. Is my proposition true or false? If you say it's false, then its negation should be true: my wife hasn't stopped smoking. But that proposition implies that she's still smoking. Another problematical proposition, which Bertrand Russell made famous, is: "The present king of France is bald." There is no present king of France. So, is the proposition true or false? If you say that it's false, then again its negation should be true: "The present king of France isn't bald". Logicians are sometimes prepared to swallow these unpalatable consequences. In everyday life, however, some sentences depend on *presuppositions* in order to express propositions. The proposition about my wife's smoking presupposes that at one time she did smoke. The sentence about the king of France presupposes that there is a king of France. If these presuppositions are false, then neither the sentences nor their negations express propositions. They are neither true nor false. This claim doesn't imply the existence of some third sort of truth value, beyond truth and falsity. The sentences fail to have a truth value, just as division by zero fails to yield a result.

* * *

If our spouse tells us, looking out of the window, "There's a unicorn in the garden," we can decide whether or not the proposition is true by looking out of the window too. We understand the proposition: our interpretative systems construct a mental model of the possibility that it describes. A verification procedure compares our model of the proposition with the perceptual model that our visual system constructs of the scene. The mechanisms underlying this process are not well understood, but *what* they have to do is to map referents from our model of a possibility on to objects in our perceptual model, and to determine whether the properties and relations map from one model into

234 | HOW WE REASON

the other. Models of the propositions expressed in language are rudimentary in comparison with perceptual models of the world, which contain much more information—many more referents, properties, and relations. So, if the proposition is true, the model based on the proposition maps into part of the model based on perception: all of the referents, properties, and relations, in the propositional model map into the perceptual model, which contains much else besides.

The process is fallible. We may misunderstand the proposition and construct the wrong model; we may misperceive the world and construct the wrong model; our mapping may go wrong and misidentify a referent, a property, or a relation. But, the process is right often enough for us to be confident either that a proposition is true, or that it is false. Many propositions, alas, cannot be perceived to be either true or false. An example is the proposition: President George W. Bush owns a ranch. We cannot perceive its truth value. At most we can perceive evidence pertinent to its truth value, e.g., he produces the records of his purchase. We can't thereby *know* that he owns a ranch, but we may come to believe the proposition.

* * *

"True" and "false" are terms that can refer to the relation between propositions and the world. Hence, a proposition, such as:

> It is false that David Thomson is a theatre critic

asserts a proposition about a proposition. It is a *metalinguistic* proposition. Certain inferences concern claims about the truth or falsity of propositions. Consider, for instance, this brief dialogue:

> Galileo says: I recant and aver that the earth is the center of the universe.
>
> The inquisitor says: That's a lie.

We infer that if the inquisitor is sincere then he believes that Galileo hasn't recanted or doesn't aver that the earth is the center of the universe, or neither.

Inferences from discourse about truth and falsity are common in life. But, they can yield deep paradoxes. The most famous is the paradox of the "liar", which St. Paul alludes to in his *Epistle to Titus I*:

> One of themselves, a prophet of their own, said, Cretans *are* always liars, evil beasts, slow bellies. This witness is true.

Paul appears to be referring to Epimenides, a Cretan prophet, and to be making a moral judgment rather than a claim about paradoxes in language. Yet, the implication is that, as a Cretan, Epimenides is lying when he says that Cretans are always liars. And so his claim is false. No real paradox follows, but just that Cretans don't always lie. A genuine paradoxical version of the "liar" paradox condenses it into a single sentence that refers to itself:

This sentence is false.

If the preceding sentence is true, then it is false; if it is false, then it is true. Logicians abhor sentences of this sort, just as they abhor any paradox that threatens the consistency of a system. Some analysts locate the root of the "liar" paradox in the fact that the sentence refers to itself. But, self-reference isn't always paradoxical (see the first—and only—footnote in this book). The paradoxes occur in natural language because it is its own metalanguage. That is, we can use English sentences to talk about the relations between English sentences and the world. As I remarked earlier, logicians keep the language for talking about a logic, the metalanguage, separate from the language of the logic itself. In this way, they prevent the liar paradox in logic.

Because a natural language is its own metalanguage, we can reason about the consequences of truth and falsity. For example, given the pair of sentences:

It is false that the next sentence is true.

Adolf lives in Argentina.

the first sentence implies that the second sentence is false, and so it follows that Adolf doesn't live in Argentina. As you can imagine, these puzzles can be very complicated. They resemble the marginalia on school textbooks (the *Shorter Latin Primer* in my day), such as: "Turn to page 183". When we turn to this page, it gives a further instruction to turn to another page, and so on and on— until we reach a page with a rude message, or are referred back to page 183 so that we can go into an infinite loop of page turning.

Metalinguistic puzzles often concern individuals who assert the truth or falsity of their own assertions, e.g.:

Lance says: I am lying and Art is lying.

Art says: Lance is lying.

Who is telling the truth?

Lance cannot assert without paradox that he is lying unless he asserts something else in conjunction with his claim. But, he does assert something else— that Art is lying. Granted that this second clause is false, Lance's conjunction as a whole *is* false, and so his claim that he is lying is true. It follows that Art, the second speaker, is not lying but telling the truth, and indeed he *is* telling the truth because he asserts that Lance is lying. The reasoning is a little dizzying, but if you think it through, you'll see that it is right.

Problems of this sort are often couched as "knight-and-knave" puzzles. Here's the same problem in this guise:

> There are two sorts of individual, knights and knaves. Knights always tell the truth, whereas knaves always lie.
>
> Lancelot says: I am a knave and Arthur is a knave.
>
> Arthur says: Lancelot is a knave.
>
> What is the status of Lancelot and Arthur: knight, knave, or impossible to tell?

The solution is analogous to the preceding problem: Lancelot is a knave and Arthur is a knight.

The first psychologist to study these problems was Lance Rips. He postulated that we use a single procedure to solve them, and he posed them as a challenge to the model theory. According to his account, we suppose that the first individual in a puzzle is telling the truth, and then use formal procedures to draw as many inferences as possible. We can also suppose that the first individual is telling a lie and pursue the consequences of this assumption. Each inferential step is based on a formal procedure. To deal with these problems, however, Rips adopts some content-specific rules for making inferences about knights (and what is true) and about knaves (and what is false). Box 17.1 describes the system. It is supported by the finding that reasoners make more errors and take longer to solve problems that require more formal steps in their derivations. There is an irony, however, in applying formal procedures to matters of truth and falsity. Formal approaches to logic contrast with approaches based on truth and falsity, and as I mentioned in Chapter 1, an irremovable wedge exists between them.

The model theory proposes that we do not use a single method for solving these problems. Indeed, most of us arrive at the psychological laboratory with no prior method for them and have to learn on the job. Our first efforts are tentative. But, we can develop a variety of procedures for dealing with the problems, or at least with those of them that are within our competence. The particular problems that we encounter therefore influence the particular methods that we develop. One method, like the one proposed in Rips's account, makes use of suppositions.

A different method depends on premises that are "circular", i.e., those that refute the status of those who make them, as in the earlier example:

Box 17.1 Rips's formal rules for knight-and-knave problems

The formal procedures for reasoning are supplemented with rules to deal with knights and knaves. Consider the valid inference:

A says that B is a knave. A is a knight. ∴ B is a knave.

This formal rule yields the inference:

1. x says: p
   x is a knight
   ∴ p
   I have here simplified Rips's syntax. Likewise, to derive the valid inference:

   A say that B is a knave. A is a knave. ∴ B is not a knave.

   the theory has this rule:

2. x says: p
   x is a knave
   ∴ not p

   There are also rules to infer that if x is not a knight then x is a knave, and that if x is not a knave then x is a knight.

Here is an example of a formal proof using Rips's single procedure based on suppositions. The problem is:

A says: B is a knave.

B says: A is a knight if and only if C is a knight.

What is C?

The answer is derived from this proof:

Suppose A is a knight.

∴ B is a knave. [from rule 1 above]

∴ Not(A is a knight if and only C is a knight) [from rule 2 above]

∴ C is a not a knight. [from the supposition and the previous line]

∴ C is a knave. [from the rule interdefining them]

At this point, the program makes a new supposition:

Box 17.1 (*continued*)

Suppose A is a not a knight.

∴ A is a knave.

∴ B is not a knave.

∴ B is a knight.

∴ A is a knight if and only if C is a knight.

∴ C is a not a knight.

∴ C is a knave.

From either assumption about A, it follows that C is a knave, and so C is a knave (and Rips's program has a general rule for making an inference of this sort).

> Lancelot says: I am a knave and Arthur is a knave.

Circular premises catch our attention. Almost all of us grasp that they appear to be self-refuting. Many of us can go no further, but some of us do realize that Lancelot's premise cannot be true as a whole. He must be a knave. Granted, then, that his premise is false, its first clause is true, and so its second clause must be false. Hence, it follows that:

> Lancelot is a knave and Arthur is a knight.

A third method may develop from encounters with premises of this sort:

> Gawaine asserts that Percivale is a knave.
>
> Bedivere asserts that Percivale is a knave.
>
> Percivale asserts that Gawaine is knight and Bedivere is a knave.

We may notice that as Gawaine and Bedivere assert the same proposition, they are either both knights or else both knaves. Percivale, however, assigns them to different categories. Hence, Percivale must be a knave. It follows that both Gawaine's and Bedivere's propositions are true: they are knights. The method also detects where two individuals assert opposing propositions about the same individual, and assigns falsity to any premise that treats the two individuals as of the same status.

Ruth Byrne and her colleagues have shown that participants do develop their own methods for these problems during the course of an experiment. They become faster and more accurate even though they don't receive any information about the accuracy of their performance. Those who develop a method that is applicable to a narrow range of problems do less well when they encounter problems to which the method does not apply. Those who make use of the general method based on suppositions are less hindered when they encounter problems tailor-made for another method. They don't have to learn a new method for them, but can continue to use the more general method. And different participants do develop various methods. They may pursue the consequences of suppositions, they may grasp the consequences of circular premises, or they may notice certain interesting patterns in the premises.

Knight-and-knave problems are straight out of puzzle books. They don't occur in the workaday world, and so it is easy to dismiss them. But, you should remember that they are just an abbreviated way of stating arguments, such as:

> I lied when I told you that Pat was lying.

> She said that she *had* posted the letter and that I was a liar.

The use of models for propositional reasoning cannot alone cope with propositions of this sort. They call for a higher-level ability to deal with truth and falsity. This ability is essential for the development of formal logic as an intellectual discipline because it enables us to relate formal patterns to matters of truth and falsity.

Psychologists can go beyond metalinguistic puzzles to formulate puzzles that are metalogical, e.g.:

> There are two sorts of persons: logicians who always make valid deductions and politicians who never make valid deductions. Abe says that either Bob is telling the truth or else Bob is a politician but not both. Bob says that Abe is telling the truth. Cal infers that Bob is a politician. Is Cal a logician or a politician?

To solve this problem, let's start with the supposition that Abe is telling the truth. It follows there are two possibilities: Bob is telling the truth and not a politician, or Bob is not telling the truth but is a politician. In the first possibility, it follows from what Bob says that Abe is telling the truth. Which is consistent with the supposition and supports the conclusion that Bob is not a politician. In the second possibility, it follows from what Bob says that Abe is not telling the truth, which is inconsistent with the supposition that he is.So, this second possibility can be eliminated, and we know from the assumption that Abe is telling the truth that it follows that Bob is not a politician. Now, let's make the supposition that Abe is not telling the truth. One possibility is that Bob is telling the truth and is a politician, but he asserts that Abe is telling the truth. Which is inconsistent with the supposition, and so we can eliminate this possibility. The other possibility is that Bob is neither telling the truth nor a politician. It now follows from the falsity of Bob's proposition that Abe is not telling the truth. Which is consistent with the supposition. And so we know that from the assumption that Abe is not telling the truth that it follows that Bob is not a politician. Both suppositions, which are exhaustive, yield the valid conclusion that Bob is not a politician. However, Cal infers that Bob is a politician, and so Cal's inference is invalid. Hence, Cal is a politician. Simple, isn't it?

* * *

We often reason about our own or others' reasoning. One circumstance in which we carry out this metareasoning, or "higher reasoning" as I refer to it, is when we're concerned about what other people will think. If we're loitering in a public place waiting to meet someone then we may worry that other people will suspect that we're up to no good. So, to allay their suspicions, we keep looking at our watch and frowning with impatience in a conspicuous way so that others will infer that we're waiting for someone who is late for an appointment, and that our loitering has no malicious intent. Ervin Goffman considered these cases as public behavior designed to elicit certain inferences in others. Conjurors, as I mentioned earlier in the book, are always trying to imagine how their audiences will reason, and to think of possibilities that they will not infer. The whole business of co-operating with other people, or competing with them, also hinges on making inferences about what they will infer.

George Erdos has examined metareasoning in an experiment, using a well-known puzzle:

> Three women, Ann, Beth, and Cath, sit in a line one behind the other. The milliner has five hats: three white hats and two black hats. She puts a hat on each woman's head without the woman seeing the color of her hat. But, Ann can see Beth's and Cath's hats, and Beth can see Cath's hat. Cath, of course, can see no one's hat. The women know what the milliner has done. They are honest, and they can reason validly. The milliner asks them to say, "yes" if they know the color of the hat they are wearing, and "no" otherwise. Ann says, "No". Beth says, "No". What does Cath say, and why?

To explain how we solve this problem and carry out metareasoning in general, the model theory needs an additional component. It enables our reasoning system to construct a model of how other individuals reason. Consider, for a moment, how we solve the problem.

The first step is to understand the initial set-up. There are five hats, three white and two black. Three individuals each wear one of the hats. Hence, there are seven different possibilities: each woman wears a white hat, Ann and Beth wear white hats and Cath wears a black hat, and so on. To solve this problem, we have to reason about how each of the women reasoned. Ann reasoned: if I see two black hats, then I would be wearing a white hat, because there were just two black hats in the set of five. But, since she said, "no", she didn't know the color of her hat, and so she didn't see two black hats. Beth and Cath both make this inference. So they both infer that Ann sees at least one white hat, and so there are three possibilities: Beth is wearing a white hat or Cath is wearing a white hat, or both of them are. Beth reasons further from these three possibilities: if I see that Cath is wearing a black hat, then I must be wearing a white hat. But, because she said, "no", she didn't see a black hat. Cath made this inference, and she reasons further: I am wearing a white hat, and so I respond, "yes".

The problem is difficult. It is not easy to reason about other people's reasoning, because we have to construct models of their models. And this particular problem calls for us to think about models of three distinct possibilities when we reason about Beth and Cath's reasoning. Three possibilities are difficult to hold in mind.

Hat problems and their analogues can be generalized to any number of individuals. For example, there is a hat problem about four individuals and four white hats and three black hats, and a hat problem about 100 individuals and 100 white and 99 black hats, and so on. There is also a hat problem about two individuals and three hats: two white and one black. In this case, Ann says, "No", and Beth can infer that Ann doesn't see the black hat, because if she had done so, she would have inferred that she was wearing a white hat. Ergo Beth is wearing a white hat. This problem is easier, as Erdos showed in an experiment, because we need to consider just how one individual reasoned about how another reasoned, and the consequences yield a single model of a possibility—equivalent to the final step of the three-person problem.

To outwit an opponent, or to make the best of co-operation with a partner, we need to think about what this other individual is likely to do. This sort of thinking is known as *strategic*, and it is ubiquitous in business, politics, and daily life. If you read the transcript of the Kennedy tapes, which records the conversations between President Kennedy and his advisers during the Cuban missile crisis in October 1962, you'll be struck by how often the participants tried to fathom what was going on in Soviet Premier Khrushchev's mind and in the minds of his advisers. A typical remark early in the crisis describes how the then head of the CIA, John A. McCone, reasoned:

> Mr. McCone's reasoning ... was: If this is so, then what possible reason have they [the Soviets] got for going into Cuba in the manner in which they are, with surface-to-air missiles and cruise-type missiles? He just couldn't understand *why* the Soviets were so heavily bolstering Cuba's defensive posture. There must be something behind it. Which led him then to the belief that they must be coming in with MRBMs [medium range ballistic missiles].

The puzzle was why Khrushchev had ordered the MRBMs delivered to Cuba. Was it to persuade President Kennedy to loosen his ties to Berlin, to widen the coverage of the Soviets' missiles, to discourage the USA from invading Cuba— Khrushchev's ostensible reason, or a consequence of arguments between different factions within the Kremlin? We know now that it was Khrushchev's decision, but that only makes it harder to know which of the remaining possibilities motivated him. As Ernest May and Philip Zelikow, the editors of the transcripts of the tapes, remark, "Kennedy and his advisers understood the reasoning in the Kremlin better than have most scholars writing about the crisis in retrospect".

The theory that describes how we ought to reason strategically is the mathematical theory of games, which includes John Nash's theorem about the strategies that are optimal for all players, based on rational predictions of other players' choices. But, as Reinhard Selten, co-winner of the Nobel prize for economics with Nash in 1994, remarked at an international meeting four years later, "game theory is rational theology". What he meant is that we are often irrational in daily life, and so game theory is poor at predicting how we engage in strategic interactions with others. Thinking about what other people are thinking is indeed difficult, because it calls for a representation, not only of our own state of mind, but also of the other person's state of mind. No general psychological theory exists of how we carry out such reasoning, but a striking result concerns simple experimental games. You have a choice, say, of choosing option A or option B, and so does the other player. You each gain a certain amount of money depending on your joint choice, but one of you may gain more than the other. If you can predict your opponent's choice, then you can make a more prudent choice. A study showed, however, that participants would play these games without even asking what the other player's pay-offs were for the various options.

* * *

One of the unsung abilities of participants in psychological experiments is that they can understand the experimenter's instructions about what they are supposed to do, and (usually) figure out how to do it. John Duncan in some unpublished studies has shown that the ability to follow instructions when one task is embedded in another correlates with a measure of the participants' intelligence. The low-level task was to read aloud just the letters in a vertical column of letters and numbers. There were two of these columns and the high-level task was to shift from one-column to the other in the direction signaled by an arrow, though the arrows appeared only from time to time. Intelligent participants coped with the task. But, less intelligent participants knew what they were supposed to do, but they forgot to switch from one column to another once they were in the thick of things.

The ability to understand instructions is remarkable in the case of experiments about reasoning. The experimenter tells us, for instance:

> Your task in this experiment is to provide a missing premise to an argument. Together with a given premise, it should imply the conclusion.

She shows us an example:

> All critics who admire Hitchcock think that his movie *Vertigo* is terrific.
>
> Therefore, David Thomson thinks that his movie *Vertigo* is terrific.

Our task is to provide the missing premise that yields the conclusion. Once we understand the task, it isn't too difficult. The missing premise is:

> David Thomson is a critic who admires Hitchcock.

The ability to understand the instructions in reasoning experiments depends on a grasp of certain concepts, such as *premise, conclusion, imply,* along with more mundane notions, including the conventions of an experiment. These concepts and an ability to do higher reasoning enable the participants to figure out what they are supposed to do. In the preceding case, there's a set of premises, a conclusion, and a missing premise that makes an inference valid. For a logician, there's a trivial solution: make the missing premise the conclusion itself. Sensible persons in a psychological experiment don't make this response. They infer that they should think of a premise that states something new and that yields the conclusion only in conjunction with the given premise. They also have to work out how to perform this task. They have to use their knowledge to work out a method that enables them in principle to solve these problems. They have to reason about reasoning. The premise in the example above was: all critics who admire Hitchcock think that his movie *Vertigo* is terrific. So, they can imagine a model of this premise in which they represent each critic who admires Hitchcock as thinking that *Vertigo* is terrific. To ensure that a person, such as David Thomson admires *Vertigo*, it is necessary to represent him as a critic who admires Hitchcock. Hence, they infer that the missing premise is, indeed, that David Thomson is a critic who admires Hitchcock.

An interesting challenge is to devise a computer program that could infer how to carry out any sort of reasoning problem, e.g., to determine whether a set of sentences could all be true, to provide premises that yield a valid inference in a parsimonious way, to evaluate whether a given conclusion follows from a set of premises, to evaluate whether a given conclusion could be true given a set of premises, and so on. We can figure out how to do any of these tasks, and so we can reason about reasoning. Likewise, when we carry out a sequence of deductive inferences, we often start to notice some of their formal properties. For example, given a sequence of syllogisms, we may notice that nothing follows when both premises contain the quantifier "some". This nascent formal knowledge arises from reasoning about reasoning. The formal principles that we infer fall far short of the actual inferences that we can make, and they are sometimes mistaken. For example, someone claimed after an experiment on conditional reasoning that "nothing follows from two conditional premises." The claim was true for the experiment, but it is false in general. The two conditionals: *If Pat goes to the party then Viv won't go* and *if Pat doesn't go to the party then Viv won't go* yield the valid inference that *Viv won't go*. Nevertheless, the observation that we can develop our own formal rules shows that we have the ability to abstract them from content. It also shows we don't come to the experiment already armed with these rules.

* * *

We all understand what it means to say that a proposition is true: it corresponds to the facts. Because natural languages include terms such as "true" and "false", paradoxical propositions can be framed within them. But, we can also reason from premises that include these metalinguistic terms. The model theory can be extended to explain these inferences, and, as in simpler reasoning, it predicts that we can develop various methods to deal with them—a prediction that has received experimental corroboration. Working memory restricts the methods that we can develop for metalinguistic reasoning. For instance, those methods that follow up the consequences of assumptions do so only to a limited extent. More complex tasks call for reasoning about reasoning. We also reason in this way in order to understand the instructions for experiments on reasoning, and to figure out how to carry them out.

Psychology has a property that is unique in science. It needs to explain its own origin. Hence, a theory of higher reasoning should provide some insight into its own development. The model theory postulates a capacity to think about the truth and falsity of premises, and indirect reflections of them in the guise of knights and knaves, which in turn depends on an ability to reflect about problems and processes of thought. Cognitive scientists can use this ability to help to construct theories of reasoning. Logicians likewise use the same component of thinking in order to create formal calculi, and to reflect on the relations between these calculi and their meanings.

Part VI

How We Develop Our Ability to Reason

... in a culture which put a high value on imagination and a low one on logic, children might well appear to be more rational than adults, for a child is not, by nature, more *anything*.

Auden

Chapter 18

On Development

How do we acquire the ability to reason? This question is so puzzling that no one has a satisfactory answer. The Platonic doctrine is that everything is innate, including all our concepts and intellectual abilities, and all that happens in our development is that experiences trigger this innate knowledge. Yet, we do have to learn some things. We have to learn how to read, how to ride a bicycle, how to cook. We have to learn that the earth is round, that it rotates and goes round the sun, and that its climate is getting warmer. A case can be made— and I'll make it in a moment—that innate factors underlie the development of language. But, variations in reasoning ability are much greater than the variations in linguistic ability. I refer here not to eloquence, but to the mere competence to make and to understand utterances in our native tongue. So, the doctrine of innate ideas must be tempered a little. Nevertheless, some modern philosophers believe that all our concepts, from *bicycles* to *chicken marengo*, are innate, and await only the appropriate experiences in life to trigger them. The trouble is that these philosophers prove too much. They argue that we cannot learn concepts, and so they must be innate. Innate concepts, however, must have evolved, and evolution itself is a form of learning. It can be mimicked in computer programs that learn solutions to problems.

The antithesis is the Empiricists' blank slate. Nothing is innate on this account apart from a powerful learning program, and our experiences trigger this program so that we learn all our concepts and intellectual abilities. Indeed, the learning program may even enable us to learn other more specialized learning programs. We learn to learn. The trouble is that no one has explained how the powerful learning program works. A program simulating evolution would be far too inefficient to explain, say, the rapidity with which children learn the meanings of words. A "connectionist" program simulating learning in a network of brain cells learns complex associations. But, these programs as yet cannot learn how the meanings of sentences are composed from the meanings of words, or how to make anything beyond the simplest of inferences—the sort that I earlier postulated as unconscious.

* * *

Proud parents often suppose that their offspring *learn* to talk. Psychologists, and behaviorists in particular, used to encourage them in this view. Chomsky's revolution in linguistics inspired an about-turn. As he argued, sentences do not wear their grammatical structures on their sleeves, children receive almost no instruction in grammar, and yet they acquire their native tongue from mere exposure to the language. There must therefore be inborn constraints on the set of possible grammars for natural languages. These constraints make up a "universal grammar", which provides a number of options for each of the grammatical components in languages. One component, for example, concerns the order of subject, object, and verb; another component concerns whether adjectives come before or after the nouns they modify; and so on. Hence, in terms of grammar, only a finite number of natural languages are possible. Children exposed to their native tongue have only to identify its particular grammatical options.

Innate constraints could also enable us to acquire the principles governing meaning and truth. The principles compose the meanings of sentences from the meanings of their parts according to the grammatical relations among them. They enable us to construct representations of what a sentence refers to, to imagine what is possible according to its significance, and to evaluate truth and falsity from a comparison of these models with models of the world.

You might wonder why language evolved. One plausible notion is that the ability to communicate gave human beings an advantage in the struggle to survive and to reproduce. Some psychologists have made this argument. Chomsky does not. Indeed, he suggests that the function of language could be to allow us, not to communicate, but to externalize our thoughts. We may never know what led to the evolution of language. Meanwhile, the slate cannot be a complete blank.

* * *

The correct synthesis that explains intellectual development must combine genes and experience. Jean Piaget, one of the great pioneering investigators of children, was the first to propose this sort of theory of reasoning. His view was that a series of mental processes, culminating around the age of twelve, yields rules for reasoning that operate on the form of propositions. A central concept in his thinking was the notion of a reversible operation. I can illustrate this notion in some typical Piagetian experiments on the topic of "conservation". The experimenter takes a ball of plasticene and rolls it out into a long cylinder. Is there still the same amount of plasticene? Children of five or six say, "No, there's more plasticene now, because it's longer". The experimenter takes a beaker of water and pours it into a thinner and taller glass. The children say, "there's more water now, because it comes up higher." The experimenter re-arranges a line of six vases so that they are now spread out in a longer line. The children say, "there are more vases now, because the row is longer." Unlike adults, children at this age do not understand that these quantities remain the same under certain operations. They have an imperfect grasp of conservation.

The observations were striking. No one knew of children's ignorance of conservation until Piaget demonstrated it. His work had an impact on educators, though he himself was not interested in pedagogy. He said that children failed tests of conservation because they had yet to master the concept that certain operations can be reversed to get back to the status quo. The experimenter can roll the plasticene back into a ball, pour the water back into the fatter beaker, and move the vases back into their original line.

Piaget asked the right questions but, with hindsight, his answers were wrong. And his theorizing was tendentious: he aimed for an equivalence between mental structures and the mathematical structures postulated by a group of mathematicians who published under the collective pseudonym of "Bourbaki". Our intellectual development ends with these structures, Piaget argued, and they explain how it is possible for us to master abstract mathematics. Box 18.1 summarizes his theory.

It is not always easy to understand Piaget's theory, it makes some erroneous predictions, and some notable proponents of formal rules have given up on it. Contrary to the theory, infants of less than eight months do grasp that a physical object continues to exist when it is out of sight, children can make deductions long before their eleventh birthday, and, as I showed earlier in the book, not even adults have a complete mastery of the logic of "if", "or", and "and".

* * *

If Piaget is wrong too, what then? The first move is to pin down what develops. The evidence for the development of a set of formal rules for reasoning was equivocal at best. But, because it was the one view on offer, psychologists continued to believe it for a long time. Some still do. Of course, we can all learn formal rules—in a course on logic, for example. But, the model theory postulates a different terminus for our intellectual development:

> Reasoning is the ability to construct models from perception, description, and knowledge, to formulate novel but parsimonious conclusions from these models, and to grasp the force of counterexamples to these conclusions.

I am going to treat this account of reasoning as the answer to what develops. And I am going to outline a theory of how it develops. The theory

Box 18.1 Piaget's theory of intellectual development

- ◆ Knowledge evolves governed by (Lamarckian!) evolutionary principles. Protozoa and minds alike assimilate reality or transform themselves to accommodate it.

- ◆ Development is a result of an innate and automatic tendency to self-regulation called "equilibration". Each new equilibrium is the outcome of reversible operations, but each is also an occasion for further correction in case of conflicts. Development accordingly passes through four main stages:

  1. During their first two years, children develop a "sensorimotor" intelligence from acting on the world. They attain the concept of simple causation and the concept that objects that are out of sight continue to exist.

  2. About the age of two, they start to acquire language. They internalize their actions on the world, but they lack the full concept of reversible operations, and so they fail the conservation tasks that I describe in the text. They have only "pre-operational" intelligence. They fail to distinguish between their "egocentric" conceptions and reality.

  3. At the age of about seven, they master reversible operations and the concept of number, and thereby attain the stage of "concrete operations". They conserve quantities.

  4. After the age of eleven, they attain the stage of "formal operations" in which they are able to frame hypotheses, to calculate combinations, and to reason using a formal logic corresponding to the logical meanings of negation, *if*, *or*, and *and* (see Chapter 8). They have acquired three sorts of mental structures: groups, serial relations, and topological spaces. These structures are fundamental for mathematics (according to Bourbaki).

has three principal components: children's innate abilities, their acquisition of knowledge about both language and the world, and an increase in the computational power of their thinking.

* * *

What have the rich got that we haven't, Scott Fitzgerald asked. And Ernest Hemingway replied: more money. What have adults got that children haven't, you ask. And I reply: more knowledge. That's true, though it's not the whole truth. Evolution has equipped infants with what they need to acquire knowledge. But, they also develop computational power, and its growth enables them to make more complicated computations. You might imagine that the way to increase this power is to develop some new and more sophisticated procedures. In fact, a small set of basic procedures and ways of combining them suffice for any computation. An increase in computational power depends on developing a working memory of a greater capacity. Indeed, I suspect that the vast differences in the ability to reason from one person to another are attributable to two factors: differences in knowledge and differences in computational power.

* * *

Most of what it takes to acquire the ability to reason may be "wired into the nervous system", that is, a consequence of human genes. Babies have many more cognitive abilities than a blank slate. Cunning psychological investigators have established this point from the length of time that babies spend looking at various events. Unusual events attract their attention for longer. Experiments have to ensure that they are familiar with the final state of affairs after an event has happened—it shouldn't be this state that alone surprises them, but the sequence of events leading up to it. If an object moves sideways, is hidden for a moment, and then by magic arrives on the other side of a fixed barrier, infants of three months look longer at the display than if the barrier stops the object's movement. One solid object shouldn't pass through another, and so the first event is unusual. But, for infants to register that the event is unusual, they must compare it with what is usual. Hence, they expect one possibility—that the barrier will block the object—but this possibility does not occur. The infants therefore perceive that the same object is moving before and after it is hidden from view for a moment. They do grasp the permanence of objects. This result refutes Piaget's claim: he inferred that infants don't have the concept of permanent objects, because they don't reach for hidden objects.

During their first year, infants reveal that they have a whole world of "naïve physics" in their minds—a common-sense world in which solid objects do not pass through holes smaller than them, do not remain floating in mid-air if they are unsupported, and are not deflected from their trajectory if nothing bumps into them. When the experimenter arranges tricks that violate these principles, infants look longer at the display, just as the spectators look longer at the stage after the magician David Devant makes the "Mascot moth" disappear (see Chapter 3).

Knowledge of naïve physics develops so soon after birth that an innate predisposition to construct it must exist. Experiences are critical, but they seem to be triggers that evoke this predisposition. Infants do not need to learn by trial and error that large objects cannot pass through small holes. Likewise, their machinery for comparing what happens with what should happen must be inborn. They have an innate ability to imagine possibilities.

Do infants have the ability to reason? The psychologist Justin Halberda has argued that two-year olds can make disjunctive inferences. For example, they watch a race between two animals and hear either a positive statement, "the winner is the lion," or a negative statement, "the winner is not the elephant". In either case, they are able to pick the winner. In effect, they make the inference:

Either the winner is the lion or else the winner is the elephant.

The winner is not the elephant.

Therefore, the winner is the lion.

In another task, they play a game in which they learn what several animals like to do, e.g., the lion likes swimming, the elephant likes cookies, and so on. On critical trials, they see an animal whose preference they know, such as the lion, and an animal that they haven't seen before, such as a dog. They hear the sentence, "I like applesauce", and they are asked, "who said that?" The children are not told that each animal can like just one thing, but every child jumps to this conclusion, and infers that it is the new animal, the dog, that likes applesauce. The children are rejecting one alternative in order to infer the other.

Do infants reason before they understand language? The Stoic logician Chrysippus described a dog chasing its prey, and, when it arrived at a spot where three roads met, it sniffed one road, sniffed another road, and then at once rushed off down the third road without stopping to sniff. The dog, he claimed, made a disjunctive inference: there was no scent of the prey at the first two roads, and so it must have run down the third road. Alas, dogs have no such ability according to a recent study. Infants might be able to make the disjunctive inference, but an experiment has yet to demonstrate this ability. At the age of about twelve months before they have acquired language, they can make simple inductions. If they see an adult giving water to a toy dog, then they will imitate the action with another animal, such as toy cat, but not with entities in other categories, such as a toy car. They have a concept of animal and it constrains their inferences.

* * *

Children attribute minds to other human beings, to animals, and even to the inanimate objects of their play. This propensity may be the foundation of our models of other individuals, and our beliefs about them, including our beliefs about their beliefs. But, our ability to grasp beliefs about beliefs takes some time to develop. Here's a dialogue that illustrates its delay:

Experimenter, showing a child a matchbox: What do you think is in here?
Child: Matches.
Experimenter opens the matchbox to show the child that it contains M&M's (also known in the UK as "Smarties"). A second child, Pat, arrives.
Experimenter: What will Pat think is in here?
Child: M&M's.

This response is typical of the egocentric thinking of three year-olds. They cannot hold in mind the difference between what they know and what others know. But, a year later, children can make the correct answer. They separate their own belief from the false belief of the child who did not see that the matchbox contained M&M's.

Yet, four year-olds still go wrong with Pat's beliefs about another person's beliefs—a so-called "second order" belief. Suppose you are a four-year old in the experiment. You grasp that Pat believes that the matchbox contains matches, because she didn't see the experimenter reveal its true contents to you. If a third child, Viv, enters the room, then Pat will believe that Viv also believes that the matchbox contains matches. But, suppose that unbeknownst to Pat, you see the experimenter show Viv that the matchbox contains M&M's. Here's the state of play:

You believe that the matchbox contains M&M's.

You believe that Pat believes that it contains matches.

You believe that Viv believes that it contains M&M's.

You believe that Pat believes that Viv believes that it contains matches.

You believe that this second-order belief of Pat's is false. Why? Because you know that Viv believes that it contain M&M's.

That's a lot of information to hold in mind. Indeed, children don't master second-order beliefs, and their potential falsity, until they are seven years old. Until then, they are inclined to think that Pat believes, as they do, that Viv believes that the matchbox contains M&M's.

To understand beliefs about what others believe seems to depend on the ability to ascribe states of mind to others. That in turn seems to have an innate basis, because autistic children are impaired in this ability. They fail tests of first-order and second-order beliefs. Yet, they can carry out inferences of the same sort about maps or pictures. They can grasp that a photograph is out of date. It no longer corresponds to reality just as an obsolete belief no longer does. To cope with second-order beliefs, however, you need computational power—a working memory with a large enough capacity to hold all the relevant information. And a lack of capacity may be responsible for the problem of understanding beliefs about beliefs. Indeed, some social scientists argue that the problem reflects the "curse of knowledge", that is, our difficulty in re-capturing our intellectual innocence once we have acquired knowledge about a situation.

* * *

The way to increase computational power is to increase working memory. A superhuman being would have an unlimited memory for the results obtained during a computation, such as the intermediate products that we need to remember if we try to do long multiplication in our heads. Indeed, as the capacity of children's working memory increases so they are capable of more complex processes. As an example consider another Piagetian task in which children have to put a set of rods into order according to their lengths. Four year-old children cannot do this task. Their arrangements show just a rough approximation to the proper serial order. They can put down a long rod to start an array, and put the next rod they pick up in its proper place. But, thereafter their performance is hit or miss, and they have difficulty in interpolating a new rod between rods already in the array. The interpolation calls for them to reason about relations. They need to reason that because the new rod is longer than one rod and shorter than the other, it should be put between them. This inference is impossible if at any one time our working memory cannot hold more than one binary relation between two objects. By the age of five, however, the capacity of children's working memory has increased, and they can arrange the rods in the correct order, though they still have difficulty in interpolating rods. They tend instead to rearrange adjacent pairs of rods, and their rearrangements ripple through the whole series until it is in the correct order. By the age of seven or so, their working memory is still larger, and they can make a systematic arrangement of the rods, and cope with interpolations.

Psychologists measure the capacity of working memory in various ways. The simplest way is to measure how many digits a child can hold in mind for a few seconds. You and I can cope with a telephone number of about seven digits, sometimes more, sometimes less. A three-year-old child, however, can cope only with about three digits. By four years, a child can cope with four digits. This improvement in working memory appears to be a consequence of the maturation of the brain, but also a consequence of the development of knowledge. Children acquire more efficient ways to represent information in working memory. I turn next to a different aspect of mental architecture.

* * *

Evolution cannot have shaped a mind that depended on one homogeneous glob. It must tinker with a large set of separate mental "organs", and so the mind may be divided into separate modules, for much the same reason that programmers develop their programs in separate routines. Programmers want to work on one routine without having to think about all of them at the same time. Hence, a division into separate routines is helpful in programming. Likewise, if the brain were a single glob of undifferentiated neurons, evolution couldn't tinker in an adaptive way. Tinkering can be adaptive because it affects one module but not all of them. A variation in a module for the perception of color could lead to a better performance without having adverse effects on any other module. Those individuals with this variation would have a better chance of surviving and reproducing, and so their genes would become more frequent in the population.

A recent group of theorists, "evolutionary psychologists", has gone one step further. They imagine what would have been adaptive for our hunter-gatherer ancestors about 120,000 years ago, postulate an innate module for computing it, and then carry out experiments to see whether the module still exists in our thinking. One innate module, they say, is for reasoning about whether someone is cheating us. It would have arisen because social exchanges would have been important for our ancestors. Another module, they say, is for reasoning about precautions against risks.

Reasoning does have a modular structure. Each of the procedures that I described for reasoning with models (see Box 9.2) is a separate module in the program simulating the theory. For example, there is a module for starting the construction of a model, one for updating it, and so on. And modules of this sort can be used in different ways for deduction, induction, and abduction. But are there separate modules for reasoning about different topics? That is, processes that differ depending, say, on whether we are reasoning about people who may be cheating us, or about how to avoid contracting cholera? We know that content matters. For example, I described earlier how content affects the selection task (in Chapter 1). And so you might suppose that there must be different modules for different contents. An alternative hypothesis, however, is that a single process of reasoning carries out different operations depending on differences in content. Content can block the construction of possibilities, add information to a model, and bring to mind a familiar counterexample.

Is there an innate module for reasoning about cheating? Perhaps not, because the notion of cheating is vague. Is lying cheating? Is polygamy cheating? Is murdering a rival cheating? The problem for the theory is to explain what triggers the use of an appropriate module. Evolutionary psychologists need to formulate a comprehensive list of innate modules, an account of what triggers each of them, and a description of the different ways in which they work. The support for the evolutionary theory of reasoning at present depends on the selection task. But, critics point out that the results can be explained in other ways. And content doesn't always affect reasoning. Several studies have failed to find any significant differences between reasoning about facts and reasoning about obligations. No decisive evidence exists that calls for innate modules that reason about different contents. Human beings have only about thirty thousand genes, and to use them to encode modules for reasoning about particular topics would seem rather prodigal.

No doubt the human mind has been shaped by evolution. But, it is hard to tell in what ways, beyond modules such as those for hearing and vision, which evolved long before human beings did. As critics of evolutionary psychology say, we cannot go back to the Stone Age to test natural selection at work. The best we can do is to tell a "just so" story about what should have been adaptive for our ancestors, and test whether it predicts how our minds work now. Evolutionary psychologists do indeed spin some entertaining stories— from how humans got their taste for floral wallpaper to why siblings get into spats. But, what should they do when a "just so" story just isn't so? They can allow—and do—that not all mental functions are adaptations, or they can rewrite the story to fit the facts. Evolutionary psychology is a useful heuristic for generating hypotheses. They can be tested, but it is hard to see how to test the theory as a whole.

* * *

Much of our reasoning may have developed from innate abilities. They under-lie the construction of models from perception, imagination, and language. Hence, infants focus on violations of naïve physics, and children can reason about what's in the minds of others. Perhaps, all the fundamental mechanisms of reasoning are innate. Yet, the reasoning ability of a newborn babe is very different from that of a mature Einstein. So, how do we get from one to the other?

One factor is the growth of knowledge. In a nice irony, the evidence comes from a line of research that was intended to show something different, namely,

Piaget's studies of conservation. Mastery of reversible operations, Piaget said, depends on a general restructuring of the mind that occurs around the age of seven (see Box 18.1). But, an alternative possibility is that children do not acquire a general principle of reversible operations, but just the piecemeal knowledge that rolling plasticene, pouring water, or rearranging vases, has no effect on quantity. The invariants are not logical necessities. Children have to learn them one by one, just as they have to learn that when water freezes it *increases* in volume. As an example, consider this demonstration. I take a loop of string and hold it over my thumbs and index fingers to form the shape of a square. Next, keeping the string taught at all times, I move my hands further apart but my thumbs and fingers closer together so that the shape of the string becomes a rectangle. Does the string still enclose the same area? Most people say, "yes". Conservation is the norm. But the correct answer is: "no". You can work it out using arithmetic, or you can imagine that I extend the string so that the height of the rectangle becomes so tiny that its invisible, and in this case the area of the rectangle must be smaller. If you don't know about loops of string, no general mental restructuring is needed to acquire this knowledge, just the piecemeal acquisition of a small fact about the world. Other evidence for this piecemeal view is that when knowledge does matter children acquire it earlier. Children of aboriginal Australians living in the outback cannot afford to get lost, and they learn to conserve spatial relations from one view of a landscape to another earlier than city dwellers do.

Psychologists have investigated how knowledge develops. Children categorize entities at first on superficial features. If it walks like a duck and talks like a duck, then it is a duck. Later, they begin to grasp the importance of hidden causal factors. If it is the offspring of a duck, then it's a duck even if it doesn't walk the walk or talk the talk. Likewise, their conceptions of the earth and the solar system start from oversimplified models, or fragments of knowledge, and move towards more mature conceptions.

How children progress from one model of the world to another is not well understood and so far has not been simulated in a computer program. The developmental psychologist Susan Carey likens the process to the overthrow of one scientific theory by another. The proponents of one theory have difficulty in understanding the rival theory. It is not impossible for them to do so, but it's hard work, because the theories seem to be incommensurable. For example, Goethe had problems in understanding Newton's theory of color. Newton's goal was to test his theory by splitting light into the colors of the spectrum, and by mixing colors together using rotating wheels with segments of different colors. In contrast, Goethe's experiments were exploratory and of a more psychological nature. Newton treated the colors in the spectrum as fundamental, but Goethe allowed that nonspectral colors, such as magenta, were also fundamental. Carey has noted a similar incommensurability between young children's concepts and adult concepts. She reported this dialogue with her daughter of three and a half:

Eliza: How do dead people go to the bathroom?
Carey: What?
Eliza: Maybe they have bathrooms under the ground?
Carey: Dead people don't go to the bathroom. They don't do anything; they just lie there. They don't eat or drink, so they don't have to go to the bathroom.
Eliza: But they ate or drank before they died—[triumphant] they have to go to the bathroom from just before they died!

Eliza thought that the dead live on underground in altered circumstances. It is no easier to shake children out of their misconceptions than to shake scientists out of their pet theories.

* * *

Those of us without scientific training carry over our "naïve physics" from childhood to adulthood. Studies in Italy and later in the USA showed a striking resemblance between adult misconceptions of physics and Aristotle's views and those of his Medieval followers. Aristotle thought of motion as a change of place. Two sorts of motion occurred: natural motions, such as the fall of weighty objects to the earth; and unnatural motions, such as the movement of one object pushed by another. Aristotle's notion of speed was that the quicker of two moving objects goes further in an equal time, and the same distance in less time. These ideas are similar to common sense. Motion *is* a change of location over time. Some objects move naturally; others move because of the actions of other objects on them. We tend to think that an object that has been given a push has an "impetus" that peters out, and so the object slows down and at length stops. Likewise, consider how we think about an object swinging around in a circle at the end of a piece of string when the string breaks. Many of us imagine that the object continues in a spiral trajectory that slowly opens up until it is traveling in a straight line. The circular "impetus", we suppose, unwinds. We make a similar error about the trajectory of a ball that comes out of a C-shaped tube. We refrain from this error, however, with a jet of water, perhaps because we've observed water jetting out of a curved faucet. According to Newtonian mechanics, a centripetal force accelerates the object on the string or in the curved tube towards the center of its rotation. When the string breaks or the object comes out of the tube, the acceleration ceases. The first law of motion then applies: an object remains at rest or else moves at a uniform velocity in a straight line unless a force acts on it. So, the object flies off in a straight line.

Our common sense conception of speed also confuses us. Like Aristotle, we conceive one object as moving faster than another if at one time they are lined up together and at a later time one object is ahead of the other. But, we can also tell that an object is moving at high speed if it appears blurred. The greater the blur, the faster is its speed. Our mental models embody both notions: one object overtakes another (it has a higher average speed), and it moves faster because it is more blurred (instantaneous speed).

The scientific revisions to these conceptions took many centuries. Newtonian mechanics applies to both of Aristotle's two sorts of motion, natural and unnatural. Common sense draws an unnecessary distinction. Likewise, the common sense conception of speed is incoherent. Its confusions are illustrated in this dialogue adapted from the late Richard Feynman's lectures on physics:

Policeman: You were going at 60 miles an hour.
Driver: That's impossible. I was traveling just for seven minutes. How can I go 60 miles an hour when I wasn't going for an hour?
Policeman: What I mean is that if you kept going the same way as you were going, then in the next hour you would go 60 miles.
Driver: The car was slowing down, so if I kept on going that way it would not go 60 miles. And in any case, if I had kept on going, I would have run into the wall at the end of the street!
Policeman: What I mean is if you went one second, you would go 88 feet.
Driver: There is no law against going 88 feet per second.
Policeman: Tell that to the judge!

The policeman could have replied instead that 88 feet per second is the same as 60 miles per hour. Indeed, the driver's speed at the moment the radar beam was reflected back from the car was 60 miles per hour. This concept of instantaneous speed must be distinguished from our common sense notion of average speed. Instantaneous speed depends on Newton's mathematical conception of "differentiation", that is, we divide distance by time while making the interval of time smaller and smaller, and observing the result as the interval tends towards the infinitesimal. In this case, a single inchoate notion is refined into two distinct concepts: instantaneous speed and average speed.

In Newton's theory, the mass of a moving object is constant, where mass is the inertia of an object, i.e., how hard it is to get the object to move by applying a force to it. But, in Einstein's special theory of relativity, the mass of an object is no longer constant, but increases with its velocity. As that velocity approaches the speed of light, the object's mass approaches infinity. Hence, it cannot go faster than light. This new concept overlaps with the old one. They share the concept of inertia, but differ on how it is affected by motion. But, these concepts are those of expert physicists, and I shall pursue them no further.

A revolution in science leads to a new sort of model, which often embodies concepts that are not observable in the world. It may lead to various sorts of conceptual changes: the merging of two separate notions, or the splitting of a single inchoate concept into two distinct concepts, or the maintenance of some components of a concept and the modification of others. Our intellectual development is analogous, but unless we have an education in science, many of our concepts remain incoherent.

* * *

If we don't know the meanings of connectives or quantifiers, we will go wrong in making inferences based on them. We may fail to realize that a sentence such as:

All the artists are beekeepers

doesn't mean that:

All the beekeepers are artists.

We may adopt the simplest hypothesis, namely, that those who are artists are beekeepers, and vice versa. Our hypothesis is useful because it minimizes the number of distinct referents that we have to hold in mind. But, it leads us astray. We infer that all the beekeepers are artists because all the artists are beekeepers. We go wrong because of our lack of knowledge about the meanings of quantifiers. Likewise, if we lack the knowledge that would enable us to modulate the interpretation of a term, we will also fail to draw correct inferences.

An increase in the capacity of working memory also yields better reasoning. The French psychologist Pierre Barrouillet and his colleagues have shown that when children are asked to list the possibilities compatible with a conditional, such as:

If there is a triangle then there is a circle

they tend to list just one possibility in which there is a both triangle and a circle. They treat the conditional as though it were a conjunction. As children grow older, they list two possibilities: one in which there is both the triangle and the circle, and one in which there is neither a triangle nor a circle. And, as they approach maturity, they list three possibilities compatible with the "logical" meaning of the conditional: they add the case in which there isn't a triangle but there is a circle. The better predictor of the number of possibilities that children think of is, not their age, but the capacity of their working memory.

Effects of working memory also occur when children draw their own conclusions from premises, such as:

Some of the parents are teachers.

All the teachers are drivers.

This inference calls for the construction of a single mental model, and children as young as seven years can draw the conclusion:

Some of the parents are drivers.

Contrary to Piagetian theory, they cope with these inferences better than chance. However, when inferences call for multiple models, they defeat most of us. The ability to make inferences improves with age from seven to adulthood, and this improvement correlates with an increase in the capacity of working memory.

* * *

The development of language depends on both nature and nurture. Infants of a few days have already become attuned to their mother tongue and attend more to it than to some other language. But, if they grow up unable ever to hear any language or to see any sign language, then, as in the handful of tragic cases of "wolf children", they never master a language. Hence, both genetic endowment and environment matter. They *interact*. Reasoning may also depend on an innate basis for imagining possibilities, and for manipulating models of them. Its development, as I have argued, rests on the growth of knowledge, including concepts and meanings, and on an increase in the capacity of working memory. How knowledge grows is puzzling. It is not the mere accretion of facts. It calls for revisions in concepts, and perhaps for changes in our models of reality. The process is a mystery, and at present beyond the ability of cognitive scientists to explain.

Chapter 19

Strategies and Cultures

Some years ago, a distinguished cognitive scientist came to Princeton to give a talk. He arrived early for an appointment to chat with me, but I wasn't in my office, and so to entertain him a postdoctoral student gave him one of the illusory inferences that we were working on. Most people get it wrong, and he got it wrong too. Later, he explained to me:

> I said to myself, "This is one of Phil's silly inference problems, and so I've got to be careful". But I *still* got it wrong!

His remarks illustrate reasoning about reasoning—what I referred to earlier as "metareasoning". Despite his insight, however, he failed to come up with an appropriate strategy for dealing with the inference. In this chapter, I am going to consider a special sort of development, the short-term development of strategies for reasoning, which occurs when we tackle a novel series of reasoning problems. A *strategy* is a sequence of steps that enables us to infer the answer to a deductive problem. Earlier in the book, when I referred to a method or procedure for making an inference, I was talking about a strategy. When we think aloud in making an inference, we describe each step in our strategy, and each step is what I will refer to as a *tactic*. We are aware of our tactics, and the sequence in which they occur, but we are not aware of the mechanisms underlying them. These mechanisms, I argue, are rooted in mental models, but they include mechanisms for grammar and for detecting formal regularities.

In life, we reason all the time, but our inferences are simple, embedded in a sensible context, invoke our knowledge, and are not a matter of chopping logic. We learn, for instance, that flu vaccine will be available only for individuals who are at risk, such as infants and seniors. We know that we are not at risk, and so we realize—infer, to be precise—that we won't receive a shot. Our strategies are simple unless we've learned to cope with inferences of a certain sort, such as medical diagnosis, fixing broken radios, or reverse engineering toaster-ovens. In experiments, we are presented with a series of problems that are standardized, isolated from any everyday context, and cut off from general knowledge. When we encounter an inference of this sort for the first time, we are nonplussed for a moment. But, we tend to be able to work out its solution. Over the course of a few inferences of a similar sort, we develop a strategy for coping with them. But, as we'll see, we differ from one another in the strategies we acquire. An obvious corollary is that don't come to the psychological laboratory already equipped with a strategy for these inferences. As we develop a strategy, our performance improves. We learn to reason better.

In the past, psychologists have investigated reasoners' strategies, but using problems based on simple relational premises, such as: *Pat is taller than Viv.* When participants tackle problems based on five premises of this sort, they soon develop short cuts. For example, given a problem with premises that each contain the same relation, such as:

Beth is taller than Cath.

Ann is taller than Beth.

Dot is taller than Eve.

Cath is taller than Dot.

Eve is taller than Fran.

Who is tallest?

the participants look to see whether a term occurs only on the left-hand side of a single premise. It denotes the tallest individual—Ann in the present case. When a question is posed in a problem, such as, "Is Cath taller than Eve?" the participants can use it to select just those premises they need to construct a chain linking these two individuals. And, when an inference has two premises, they sometimes try to answer the question just from the information in the first premise. It sometimes works, but it can backfire.

Some psychologists argue that all our deductive reasoning depends on a single strategy. But, over the years, experiments have discovered various embarrassments to this view. The order of the premises, for instance, has robust effects on inferences from conditional premises. These effects appeared to be inconsistent with a single strategy. And the hypothesis seemed to have survived because experiments were not sensitive enough to detect strategies. They used no more than two premises, examined just the conclusions that the participants drew, and sometimes the speed of their responses. These results could not reveal *how* the participants reached their conclusions, and so psychologists neglected the possibility that they developed various strategies.

My aim is to make good this neglect. And so I am going to describe some studies that do reveal strategies in various sorts of reasoning. These studies corroborate the existence of four different "levels" of reasoning. At the highest level is the metareasoning exemplified in my visitor's remarks. At the lowest level are the unconscious mechanisms that I described in Part II of book. My concerns now are the two levels between: strategies and their component tactics. The psychologist Robert Sternberg pioneered the study of component tactics in his studies of analogies, numerical series problems, and syllogisms. Later in the chapter, I argue that strategies are central to the debate about differences in reasoning from one culture to another.

* * *

A recent world-wide craze that started in Japan is for Sudoku puzzles—the name is a Japanese abbreviation for "a unique number". The puzzles were introduced into Britain in November 2004 in the *Times* of London. They spread to many British national newspapers and then to other countries in Europe, to Canada and Australia, and to the *New York Post* in July 2005. I dare say that by the time you're reading this paragraph they are everywhere or, as is the way with crazes, nowhere. They are wonderful for the student of reasoning because they are the first popular puzzles that depend on pure deduction. They are Hans Anderson's "Ice Puzzles of Reason" for whose solution the Snow Queen promised to give little Kay, "the whole world and a new pair of skates".

Figure 19.1 is an example of a Sudoku puzzle. In case you've never encountered one before, I will explain how they work. Even though they contain

7		1			3		6	5
		4	6				3	
			5	1	9			
	4	3	9			6		7
6				5				1
2		9			7	8	5	
			1	9	6			
	3				8	4		
1	8		4			9		2

Fig. 19.1 An easy Sudoku puzzle (its solution is in the notes to the chapter).

numbers, they call for no knowledge of arithmetic—letters of the alphabet would do just as well. The task is to fill in the missing numbers in the array according to three rules:

> Every horizontal row in the puzzle must contain just one instance of each of the digits 1 through 9.
>
> Every vertical column in the puzzle must contain just one instance of each of the digits 1 through 9.
>
> Every three-by-three box in the puzzle—there are nine such boxes outlined in bold in the puzzle—must contain just one instance of each of the digits 1 through 9.

Each of these rules depends on three quantifiers: *every, just one,* and *each*: they are rules containing multiple quantifiers.

Sudoku puzzles are natural experiments in reasoning and they establish three facts. *Item:* many of us, even though we have had no training in logic, are able to make deductions that depend on multiple quantifiers. We enjoy challenging deductions of this sort. This fact is contrary to the view that without logical training we are incapable of valid deductions based on quantifiers, and to the view that validity is an inappropriate criterion for our deductions. *Item:* deductive ability is common to peoples all over the world. It is contrary to the hypothesis that deductions are the prerogative of Westerners, whereas East Asians shun them in favor of "holistic" thinking. *Item:* when we tackle a series of Sudoku puzzles, we develop strategies for dealing with them based on our acquisition of particular deductive tactics, and, as a result, we learn how to solve more difficult puzzles. This observation is contrary to the thesis that we all reason using the same fixed strategy, and it is also contrary to the view that our reasoning ability cannot improve.

Sudoku puzzles come in five levels of difficulty: trivial, which are never published but are simple to make up, easy, mild, difficult, and fiendish (or, as Italian newspapers refer to them, "diabolico"). The devisers of the puzzles set these levels, but they know what they're talking about. For a competent solver, an easy puzzle can be solved in about ten minutes, whereas a fiendish puzzle can take the best part of two hours. Part of the attraction of the puzzles may be this large difference in difficulty, so that as we master easier puzzles we can move on to more difficult ones. When we tackle our very first Sudoku puzzle, as an experiment confirmed, we tend to use simple tactics. They enable us to infer the definite identity of a digit in a single step. For example, when all but one of the digits in a box or a line have been filled in, then the value of the missing cell is whatever digit from 1 to 9 remains to be filled in. We soon acquire other simple tactics. Consider, for example, the top left-hand 3 × 3 box in Figure 19.1. It already contains 1, 4, and 7, and the general rule for boxes implies that a 3 must occur somewhere in the box. There are already 3's in the top two rows intersecting the box, and so the 3 must occur in the bottom row of the box. But, 3's in the columns below the box rule out all possible cells except the bottom left-hand corner of the box. Hence, 3 must occur in this cell as a result of these five separate constraints (the box itself, two rows, and two columns). The simple tactics differ in difficulty as a consequence of the number of constraints that we have to take into account, which vary from one to five. Psychologists refer to the number of constraints on an inference as its "relational complexity", and an experiment showed that participants do tend to take longer to use simple Sudoku tactics as the number of constraints increases, though five constraints are a little easier than four, perhaps because four instances of the same digit (in the case of five constraints) are easier to spot in the array than three digits (in the case of four constraints).

Simple tactics enable us to make progress in Sudoku puzzles of all levels of difficulty, and they suffice to solve most easy and mild problems. However, we have to make a major shift in strategy in order to solve the difficult and fiendish puzzles. We have to learn to list the *possible* digits in cells. Only when we do so can we develop advanced tactics. They enable us to eliminate possible values from cells. For example, suppose a pair of cells in a line or box can have just two possible values, e.g., 4 or 8. One cell must contain 4, and the other cell must contain 8, though we don't know which cell is which. It then follows that these two digits can be eliminated as possibilities from all other cells in the same line or box.

You might think that the difference in difficulty among puzzles depends on the number of empty cells in the initial array. A slight tendency does exist for harder puzzles to have a greater number of missing digits, but that in itself is not a major cause of difficulty. Puzzles with the same number of missing digits can vary vastly in difficulty. Even when solvers have completed many digits in a fiendish puzzle, they may run into an almost impossible stage. And, at the start of a puzzle, the initial tactical steps often do not differ in difficulty from one level of puzzle to another.

If a puzzle is at a particular *stage* in its solution, a certain number of digits have been solved, and a certain number of deductions about the remaining cells can be made independently of one another. Some of these deductions may yield definite digits for cells, and some of them may eliminate possible values for digits in cells. A stage ends when all these deductions have been made to update the possibilities in the array. A new set of independent deductions can then be made at the next stage, taking into account the previous deductions, and so on. We don't tend to make all the deductions that are inferrable at each stage. Some of us make some deductions, others of us make other deductions, and the sequence differs from one person to another at least until the final stages. Nevertheless, the easier that a puzzle is the higher on average should be the number of definite digits that can be deduced at any stage. I wrote a computer program to solve Sudoku puzzles, and used it to test this prediction. I took a random sample of ten puzzles at each of the four levels of difficulty (easy, mild, difficult, and fiendish) from a compendium of puzzles. The program worked out that the average numbers of definite digits that could be inferred at each stage in the solution of the problems, and the results were 4.3 for the easy puzzles, 2.3 for mild puzzles, 1.8 for difficult puzzles, and 1.3 for fiendish puzzles. This trend was most improbable by chance. Hence, at each stage in a puzzle, more definite digits can be inferred in the easier puzzles than in the harder puzzles. A corollary is that if we make all possible deductions at every stage then the easy puzzles take on average fewer stages than mild puzzles, and so on. The simple tactics alone, however, cannot solve the difficult or fiendish puzzles. Sudoku are a vivid demonstration that we develop reasoning strategies, which in turn enable us to improve our ability to deduce their solutions. But, to track *how* we develop strategies, I am going to consider much simpler deductions.

* * *

Box 19.1 presents a typical example of the sort of problem used in experiments on deductive reasoning, except that it has several premises in comparison with the one or two that psychologists favor. If, as I imagine, you haven't bothered to solve the problem, then please do tackle it now. It is easy. You can use pencil and paper, but do try to think aloud as you reason—so that later you'll have some idea of *your* strategy.

The correct answer to the problem is: yes, if there isn't a red marble in the box then there is a black marble. An experiment based on problems of this sort examined the strategies that the participants developed for themselves. The premises of each problem were compatible with just two possibilities, and half of the problems were presented with a valid conclusion and half of them were presented with an invalid conclusion. The participants had to think aloud as they reasoned, and they were allowed to use paper and pencil. A video-camera was above them and focused down on the desk on which they were writing. They soon adapted to its presence. Introspection can be an unreliable guide to our thinking, because we may rationalize. But, when the participants thought aloud as they were reasoning, what they said did reveal their main steps— the sequence of their tactics—from which it is possible to reconstruct their strategies. However, they never said anything about their strategies, nothing

Box 19.1 A typical problem used in a study of reasoning strategies

There is a red marble in the box if and only if there is a brown marble in the box.

Either there is a brown marble in the box or else there is a gray marble in the box, but not both.

There is a gray marble in the box if and only if there is a black marble in the box.

Does it follow that: If there is not a red marble in the box then there is a black marble in the box?

(Well, does it? Try thinking aloud as you tackle this problem.)

along these lines, "my aim is to build a single diagram based on all the premises from which I can check whether the conclusion follows". And, as you would expect, they said nothing about the mechanisms underlying their tactical steps—they couldn't because the mechanisms are unconscious.

All the participants were correct for every problem, and their strategies were clear for almost every problem, though they did sometimes change from one strategy to another in the middle of a problem. This experiment, and subsequent ones, showed that participants tend to develop five main strategies for reasoning based on propositional connectives, such as the inference in Box 19.1. Box 19.2 summarizes the five strategies. Most of the participants developed one or two of them during an experimental session.

To give you the flavor of what the participants had to say, let's consider a protocol from a participant using the most frequent strategy, which was to draw a single diagram representing the possibilities compatible with the premises. With the problem in Box 19.1, the participant read the first premise aloud: "There's a red marble if and only if there's a brown marble", and then made an immediate inference from it to the conclusion, "If brown then red". He then drew a diagram of a possibility compatible with this proposition:

Brown   Red

He read the second premise aloud, "Brown or else gray", and added an element to his diagram to represent an alternative possibility:

Box 19.2 Five strategies for reasoning based on sentential connectives

1. Single diagram: Draw a diagram that keeps track of the separate possibilities consistent with the premises.

2. Single possibility: Follow up step by step the consequences of a single possibility. If a problem includes a premise that makes a categorical assertion, then follow up its consequences. Otherwise, make a supposition to start the strategy rolling, either one suggested by a premise, or perhaps one that is a counterexample to a given conclusion.

3. Chain: construct a chain of conditionals leading from one clause in a conditional conclusion to its other clause, converting any premise into an appropriate conditional so that it leads from one conditional in the chain to the next.

4. Compound: drew a compound conclusion from a pair of compound premises, where "compound" means that an assertion contains a connective. Combine the conclusion with a new compound premise, and so on, until the conclusion is reached.

5. Concatenation: concatenate two or more premises in order to form a conclusion, e.g., premises of the form: *A if and only if B; Either B or else C; C if and only if D*; yield five possible concatenations, but individuals tend to form the one that fits the mental models of the premises: *(A if and only if B) or else (C if and only if D)*.

Gray

Brown   Red

He represented separate possibilities on separate horizontal rows in this way. He read the third premise: "There's a gray marble if and only if there's a black marble", and he inferred: "If gray then black". He added a new referent to his diagram:

Gray   Black

Brown   Red

The diagram supports the conclusion: if not red then black. He accepted it by saying: "Yes". He then checked the inference, working through the premises again, and comparing them with his diagram of the two possibilities. Some participants who used this strategy drew a vertical line down the page and wrote down the colors of the marbles in the two possibilities on either side of it. Others, as in the present case, arranged the possibilities in horizontal rows. One participant drew circles around the terms in the premises themselves to pick out one of the two possibilities. A tell-tale sign of the strategy was that the participants worked through the premises in the order in which they were stated, and they included in their diagrams information from premises that were irrelevant to evaluating the conclusion.

Another frequent strategy was to follow up the consequences of a single possibility, either one that was a categorical proposition in the premises, or one that a participant imagined in a supposition. In life, we often suppose that some proposition holds and then draw out the consequences of this supposition. Suppose that inflation increases as the economy picks up, what then? We use our general knowledge to infer various consequences, e.g., our savings will lose value. When we make a supposition, our conclusion should embody it. We should conclude: *if* inflation increases, then our savings will lose value. But, sometimes, our conclusion may feed back to show that our supposition must be false. Suppose, for example, we want to go to a movie but we also need some exercise. We think:

> If I go to a movie tonight then I'll go for a walk tomorrow.

But, we're very busy, and so we don't have time to do both, and so we think:

> Either I'll go to a movie tonight, or else I'll go for a walk tomorrow.

We may then think: Suppose I go to a movie tonight. We can use our mental models of our conditional premise to infer that we'll go for a walk tomorrow. But, this conclusion and our mental models of our disjunctive premise yield the conclusion that we will *not* go to a movie tonight. So, our reasoning has led us to the negation of our supposition: *if I go to a movie tonight I will not go to a movie tonight.* The conjunction of going and not going to a movie yields the null or empty model, which you may recall represents contradictions. But, if we flesh out the models of our conditional conclusion into complete models, they yield the negation of our supposition. We have "reduced" our supposition of going to a movie to an absurdity, and logicians refer to this form of argument as a reductio ad absurdum. Psychologists sometimes assume that we need a formal rule of inference to make it. But, as I have just demonstrated, we can make it using models, though we do need complete models to appreciate the force of the contradiction. Hence, the inference isn't trivial, but it shows that we must reject our supposition. In turn, its negation leads from our disjunctive premise to the further conclusion that we will go for a walk tomorrow.

We aren't always logical in our use of suppositions. Given a conclusion to evaluate, such as: "If there's a red marble then there's a black marble", the correct procedure in logic is to make the supposition that there's a red marble and then to try to show that it follows that there's a black marble. A common error is to work in the opposite direction: to make the supposition that there's a black marble and to show that it follows that there's a red marble. This procedure shows that if there's a black marble then there's a red marble, but the conclusion to be proved is its converse. We don't just make suppositions of clauses in conditionals. We sometimes make suppositions based on disjunctions too. We differ from one another in our propensity to make suppositions. In experiments at least, some of us seldom make them, whereas others are profligate in their use, even making them when there are categorical premises.

The compound strategy is difficult because it calls for us to keep a considerable amount of information in mind. It yields conclusions from pairs of compound premises, that is, those containing a propositional connective. One feature of the strategy is that even when neither the premises nor the conclusion made use of the word, "possibly", the participants often drew conclusions about one possibility. For instance, one participant made this compound inference:

> Either there's a red marble or else a blue marble.
>
> Either there's a blue marble or else a gray marble.
>
> Therefore, possibly there's a gray marble and a red marble.

The conclusion refers to just one of the two possibilities consistent with the premises. It reduces the amount of information that the participants have to hold in mind.

The chain strategy calls for converting all the premises, including disjunctions, into conditionals. It is easier to make inferences from conditionals than from disjunctions, because conditionals have one explicit mental model, whereas disjunctions have at least two explicit mental models. Hence, the model theory predicts that we should construct chains of conditionals rather than chains of disjunctions, though the latter are used in certain theorem-proving computer programs. In fact, so far, no participant has ever converted a set of premises into a chain of disjunctions.

All five strategies can be used with any propositional inference. But, depending on the sorts of problems in an experiment, the different strategies vary in their frequencies of use. For example, participants tend to use the chain strategy to evaluate conditional conclusions, whereas they tend to use the concatenation strategy to formulate their own conclusions. In all the experiments, however, the most frequent strategy was to construct a single diagram of the possibilities consistent with the premises. Participants do mix strategies, and switch from one strategy to another in unpredictable ways. Sometimes they switch in the middle of a problem; sometimes from one problem to another. There are no fixed sequences of steps that anyone followed. They are not following a single deterministic strategy.

* * *

How do we develop strategies? My first assumption (from Chapter 1) is that reasoning is not a deterministic process that unwinds like clockwork. It is governed by constraints, but they seldom yield just a single path it must follow. It varies in ways that can be captured only in an account that is not deterministic. The brain itself may or may not be deterministic. It could be our ignorance that makes it appear not to be. But, the assumption that reasoning cannot be explained in a deterministic way is corroborated at two levels. At a high level, we develop diverse strategies. At a low level, there is variation within our own reasoning. When we follow a particular strategy, we don't go through a fixed sequence of tactical steps in every inference. For example, we vary in whether we read a premise once or twice, in which proposition, if any, we use as a supposition, and in whether or not we draw a diagram to represent a premise. We come to the psychological laboratory already equipped with a set of inferential tactics. We can construct a diagram or a mental model, update it, make suppositions, formulate conclusions, and so on. When we try to reason about a problem, we try out various sequences of these tactical steps. We are not governed by any over-arching plan, thought out in advance, but we are not flailing around at random, either. We are constrained by the task, and by the results of our inferential tactics. If, say, we draw a conclusion from a supposition and a premise, this conclusion constrains us to see whether we can use it in drawing a further conclusion. We explore different sequences of tactics. These explorations can lead us, not just to the solution of a problem, but also to a new reasoning strategy.

In the jargon of cognitive science, we assemble a strategy "bottom up" from our explorations of problems using our inferential tactics. This method contrasts with the "top down" development of a strategy using high-level planning. A top-down method may be possible for experts who think in a self-conscious way about a branch of logic. But, we develop a strategy bottom up. Once we have mastered its use in a number of problems, it can then constrain our reasoning in a top-down way. Evidence corroborates this hypothesis. One crucial datum is that we learn from our mistakes. That is, we may use a tactical step that leads nowhere in a particular problem, but we learn about the tactic, and later it may come in handy for solving another problem.

One consequence of this account is that the set of possible strategies is defined by the different orders in which inferential tactics can be used to make inferences. Hence, if psychologists can enumerate all our tactics for a particular sort of problem, then they have the basis for all our feasible strategies for these problems. But, where do the tactics themselves come from?

* * *

The model theory postulates that each inferential tactic is based on models. This consequence does not rule out the development of formal rules, granted the existence of tactics that detect similarities in *logical form* from one proposition to another. What it does imply, however, is that our reasoning depends at first on models, and later it may depend on formal rules. Another consequence of the theory is that the sort of problems that we encounter should bias us to develop particular strategies.

Experiments have supported this prediction. One way to inculcate the use of a single diagram, for instance, is to use premises that force participants to think about alternative possibilities. The connective "or" is an obvious candidate, and it does predispose reasoners to adopt the diagrammatic strategy. In contrast, conditional premises yield one explicit mental model, and so they tend to elicit the chain strategy or the strategy of following up a single possibility. An experiment showed that the diagram strategy increased in use when the participants switched from problems based on conditionals to those based on disjunctions, but did not decline in use when they switched in the opposite direction. The diagram strategy is more flexible than the other strategies, which are dependent on conditional premises. Another experiment showed that regardless of strategy, the difficulty of an inference depends on the number of models that it calls for: there were eight percent of errors with one-model problems, fifteen percent of errors with two-model problems, and twenty percent of errors with three model problems.

* * *

During the 2004 US Presidential election, researchers reported:

> Kerry supporters are better informed about Kerry's views than Bush supporters are about Bush's views.

This claim asserts a relation between relations. It says, in effect, Kerry supporters are informed to some extent about Kerry's views, Bush supporters are informed to some extent about Bush's views, and the first extent is greater than the second extent. These sorts of proposition are common, e.g., *I like opera more than ballet*. Relations between relations are a good "test bed" for my hypothesis about the development of strategies because participants are not likely to have developed a strategy for them before they enter the psychological laboratory. Experiments have therefore posed relational problems of this sort:

> Art is taller than Cal to a greater extent than Bob is taller than Dan.
>
> Bob is taller than Dan to a greater extent than Cal is taller than Dan.
>
> What is the order of the four individuals in terms of their height?

The answer in this case, with the tallest first, is: Art, Bob, Cal, Dan. One strategy for solving the problem is to realize that the second premise establishes the order:

> Bob   Cal   Dan

and then to use the first premise to add Art in his appropriate place. If you doubt whether Art is taller than Bob, you should work out the consequences of the supposition that they're the same height. It is then impossible for the first premise to be true, because *Bob* would also have to be taller than Cal to a greater extent than Bob is taller than Dan, and that would conflict with the order of the three of them above.

The experiments showed that participants develop various strategies for coping with relations between relations. They switch from one strategy to another in an unpredictable way, and particular sorts of premise can bias them to develop one strategy rather than another. In theory, there are no bounds on the complexity of relations between relations. For example, there can be a relation between relations between relations:

> The degree to which Abe is taller than Ben to a greater extent than Cal is taller than Dan is larger than the degree to which Eve is taller than Faith to a greater extent than Gerd is taller than Hope.

Once again, language can carry us beyond our ability to think.

The direct evidence about strategies comes from studies in which the participants think aloud. Psychologists worry that the task of having to speak our thoughts aloud may affect how we think. We could develop a strategy that we would never use in reasoning without speaking. It is hard to rule out this possibility, because when we reason in a silent way, experimenters cannot tell what strategy we are using. However, when we describe our strategies later, we tell much the same story as the thoughts we speak aloud, and the patterns in the speed and accuracy of our inferences are much the same in both regimens.

* * *

Do Kpelle rice farmers in Liberia reason in the same way as villagers in remote Uzbekistan? Do Asians reason in the same way as Europeans? Do we reason in the same way as our ancestors? Social scientists argue about these questions. Some say that human beings reason much the same the world over and always have done so; their opponents say that human beings differ in how they reason depending on their culture. Some argue that the norms of rationality should be the same for all cultures; their opponents—so-called "relativists"—argue that norms should differ and depend on the local culture. Hence, what is rational for the Azande of Central Africa is irrational for Evans-Pritchard, the English anthropologist who studied them, and vice versa. It is hard to resolve controversies about norms, but the educability of peoples from all over the world suggests that no profound differences in reasoning exist from one culture to another. The debate has often been couched in terms of formal rules of inference. No formal rules are universal, relativists say. But, their argument presupposes that we use formal rules. From the standpoint of the model theory, the question to pose is: do all cultures realize the force of a counterexample? Show me a culture that does not, and I will concede that relativism is right for some cultures, though not for mine.

Relativism has an aura of self-refutation (like my last remark), because relativists must allow that there is a subculture of rationalists, who believe that the principles of reasoning are universal. Suppose relativists claim that rationalism is right in its subculture. It follows that the principles of reasoning *are* universal, because that's what rationalists believe. And so relativism is wrong. Suppose rationalism is not right in its subculture. It follows that there's a culture whose principles of reasoning are not right, and so relativism is wrong. Either way, it follows that relativism is wrong.

* * *

Are there differences in the mental processes of reasoning from one culture to another? Two strands of psychological evidence are striking. One strand shows that peoples from subcultures with no writing or schooling are reluctant to make inferences about hypothetical individuals. For instance, a nonliterate Kpelle rice farmer in Liberia was given, in translation, this problem:

All Kpelle men are rice farmers.

Mr. Smith is not a rice farmer.

Is he a Kpelle man?

You or I would respond: no. But the farmer replied: "If I know him in person, I can answer that question, but since I do not know him in person, I cannot answer that question". This answer is typical of those individuals in cultures that have no writing. They tend to make inferences based on knowledge and experience rather than logical acumen. But, even the farmer's remarks show that he is able to make deductions. He is arguing: I can reason about a man only if I know him; I don't know Mr. Smith; therefore, I can't reason about him. Preschool children and unschooled adults in Recife, Brazil, have the same bias. Yet, when an inference is couched in the context of a distant planet, where no one could have any relevant knowledge, the bias disappears and the participants reason in a competent way about hypothetical individuals. Likewise, the effect of schooling and of learning to read and write is to make people in these cultures much more amenable to psychological experiments on reasoning. The difference is not so much in the process of reasoning but more in the contents about which people are prepared to reason.

The second strand of evidence is due to the psychologist Richard Nisbett. He and his colleagues have observed differences in thinking between Westerners and East Asians—Chinese, Japanese, and Koreans. They are a consequence, Nisbett says, of long-standing cultural differences. Analytical thinking and deductive reasoning are the prerogative of Westerners, whereas intuitive, holistic, reasoning with a tolerance for contradictions, is the prerogative of East Asians. These investigators reported studies that led them to conclude that Westerners make formal inferences more often than East Asians, who, like the Kpelle, tend to reason from their knowledge and experience.

A re-analysis of some of these results has cast doubt on them. Likewise, some unpublished studies have been unable to detect any differences in reasoning between Chinese speakers in Hong Kong and Western students in Princeton. Here is one trial from a task that was instructive:

> If a pilot falls from a plane without a parachute the pilot dies.
>
> This pilot didn't die.
>
> How come?

Participants can respond either with a deduction:

> The pilot didn't fall from a plane without a parachute.

or with an abduction based on their knowledge, such as:

> The plane was on the ground.

Most people make an abductive response to these problems. The bias occurred in the responses of the Chinese and the Americans, and the two groups didn't differ in a statistical test. Both groups, however, were more likely to make the deduction if they had just carried out an unrelated deductive experiment. Insofar as cultural differences in reasoning do exist, they seem to be in strategy rather than in underlying mechanisms of reasoning. Nisbett himself has commented that the differences are matters of habit.

* * *

We develop our reasoning in the short term when we have to make a sequence of inferences. We discover strategies, not by laying out some grand design for reasoning, but by trying out different tactical steps until we find a strategy that reaches a conclusion. As this hypothesis predicts, the particular nature of problems biases us in favor of one sort of strategy as opposed to another. Regardless of our strategy, however, one invariant is that the number of models required for an inference affects its difficulty. This observation suggests that the mechanisms underlying tactics are sensitive to the number of possibilities compatible with the premises. But, it doesn't imply that we use only models. It is also possible for us to develop a strategy that exploits some formal rules. However, the invention of formal logic is the ultimate strategy of only a handful of exceptional individuals.

Our reasoning is organized on different levels. At the highest level is metareasoning—the sort that leads us to evaluate our own performance. It is rare in the protocols from experiments. No one remarked, for example, "I see now how I can solve these problems", and went on to describe an insightful strategy. But, remarks about metareasoning do occur in some circumstances, such as when we instruct others on how to reason. The second level is strategic. Once we have developed a strategy, its mental representation allows it to be used in future. This mental representation governs the sequences of tactics observable in experiments. The third level is tactical. It consists in individual tactics, such as drawing a diagram of a premise, or adding information from a premise to an existing model. The fourth, and lowest level, consists in the mechanisms that underlie tactics. We are not aware of them. They are comparable with the "instruction set" of a computer chip, i.e., the fundamental operations that the chip carries out, and into which all computer programs must be translated. The nature of our reasoning mechanisms is controversial, but the evidence supports the existence of mechanisms that construct and manipulate models.

Psychologists cannot predict what strategy we will develop in tackling a set of problems. Once we have a strategy, some of us seem set in our ways, but then we make a sudden change in strategy; others of us do not even settle down to a consistent choice. Even our tactical choices are uncertain. We read a premise aloud, for instance, and proceed to the next premise, or we may read the premise again, and even again, before we move on. Psychologists must settle for theories that are not deterministic from top to bottom.

Is there a culture that is incapable of reasoning? I doubt it. If anthropologists had discovered one, it would be as famous by now as those cultures that have no numbers beyond "roughly one", "roughly two", and "many". Insofar as cultural differences do occur in reasoning they too appear to be strategic rather than deep-seated. The popularity of Sudoku in certain parts of East Asia suggests that people there have no problem in deductive reasoning contrary to the hypothesis that it is the prerogative of Westerners.

Why then do big differences occur in world-view from one culture to another? Many cultures still believe in witchcraft, in magic, and in forces that have no scientific warrant. Cultures differ in their beliefs, and no simple antidote to erroneous beliefs exists. We have to be credulous in order to make inductions, and all inductive mechanisms are bound to be fallible. Magical thinking, as I argued earlier in the book, is universal to all cultures. The one corrective known to us is scientific investigation, but that is expensive and itself depends on knowledge that has still to reach many parts of the world. Yet, we find the seeds of science and technology in a core of rational principles common, it seems, to all cultures. They show up in Micronesian navigation, the hunting techniques of Kalahari bushmen, and the indigenous Americans' method of fashioning stone arrowheads. No strong case exists for cultural differences in the *process* of thinking.

Chapter 20

How We can Improve our Reasoning

Superhuman intelligences, as I have remarked several times before, would have an almost unlimited working memory for holding information in mind while they reasoned about it, and they would think at a much greater speed than we do. They would be able to think about many alternative possibilities, and about both what is true and what is false. They would out-reason us. They would believe that our mental abilities were defective; we would despise them for their uncanny powers. They would get perfect scores on all our tests of reasoning and intelligence. Indeed, they would be much more intelligent than we are. Yet, if we could improve our reasoning, we too would perform better on tests, and we would be better at the skills that the tests predict. We would be able to solve problems that at present defeat us. We would be able to avoid some of the disasters and catastrophes that at present threaten us. We would live longer—intelligent individuals do. And we might even be wiser and live in better societies than we do now.

Skeptics might argue to the contrary that our mistakes in reasoning, which I've described throughout this book, don't matter much. We get by. We survive from day to day, and when we notice our mistakes, we recover from them. Our continued existence proves it. Errors in reasoning, they would say, are a matter of academic interest only. They would be wrong. The Darwin awards are compendia of cases in which individuals have, in the hard-hearted words of Wendy Northcutt, "improved the gene pool by eliminating themselves from the human race in an astonishingly stupid way." Like the man who peered into a gasoline can using a cigarette lighter, they do so by failing to think of a possibility. Many major catastrophes have the same cause. Consider just one example that I mentioned earlier, the sinking of *The Herald of Free Enterprise*. This car ferry sank because its bow doors had been left open when it put out to sea. The folly of running a ship in a way that allowed this incredible blunder is attributable to one cause: those responsible did not reason well. They had set up a system of "negative reporting" in which the crew reported just those events that had gone wrong. A failure to make such a report is a disaster in the making, and the antidote is to demand positive reports that actions have been carried out too, e.g., "the bow doors have been closed". The failure to make this report would have alerted the master of the vessel to the oversight.

Is it possible for us to improve our reasoning? The previous chapter showed that we get better as we develop strategies. Give us a fiendish Sudoku puzzle, and we'll fail to solve it. But, let us work our way through easier ones, and we will develop the strategy and tactics—if we persevere—to have a good chance of solving it. So, what can we do to improve our reasoning—are there any general strategies that can help us?

Methods purporting to enhance reasoning are as numerous as diets, and perhaps no more effective. Some are grandiose like the project in the 1980s to increase the intelligence of the entire population of Venezuela; some are as miniscule as self-help books. Our best hope—as with a diet—is to ask: does any robust evidence show that the regimen works? If not, we're not bound to commit it to the flames, but we should think twice before investing in it.

* * *

What about logic? Some extremists say that we can't reason unless we learn logic. The Sudoku craze shows that this claim is false. Perhaps logic is a key to *good* reasoning. But, would the study of economics improve our ability to manage money? Some economists have become expert investors—John Maynard Keynes, for instance—but others have been disastrous, such as the Nobel prizewinners who bankrupted a hedge fund. A theoretical understanding of how we ought to reason might be not so useful in practice.

We can use logic to evaluate arguments. Thomas Paine, the Revolutionary pamphleteer, once made this argument:

> With respect to what are called denominations of religion, if everyone is left to judge of his own religion, there is no such thing as a religion that is wrong; but if they are to judge each other's religion, there is no such thing as a religion that is right; and therefore all the world is right, or all the world is wrong.

Is the argument a good one? Most methods of logic use formal proofs, and Box 20.1 illustrates how to analyze the argument this way. It takes three steps: we summarize the argument; we recover its logical form and stipulate any missing premises; we prove that the conclusion follows from the premises using formal rules. All three steps can be difficult. My analysis was inspired by one due to Geoffrey Keene, but his analysis is different. Which analysis is

Box 20.1 The analysis of Paine's informal argument using formal logic

Step 1: Summarize the argument to bring out its logical form:

1. If everyone judges his own religion then no religion is wrong.
2. If everyone judges others' religion then no religion is right.

Therefore, all the world is right, or all the world is wrong.

Step 2: Symbolize the logical form of the argument, though here I have avoided the use of logical notation, and state any missing premises:

1. If and only if everyone judges his own religion then no religion is wrong.
2. If and only if everyone judges others' religion then no religion is right.
3. Either everyone judges his own religion or else everyone judges others' religion.
4. If and only if no religion is wrong then all the world is right.
5. If and only if no religion is right then all the world is wrong.

Step 3: Prove the argument using formal rules of inference:

1. Suppose that everyone judges his own religion.
2. It follows from the first premise that no religion is wrong.
3. It follows from the preceding line and the fourth premise that all the world is right.
4. Now suppose that everyone does *not* judge his own religion.
5. It follows from the third premise that everyone judges others' religion.
6. It follows from the preceding line and the second premise that no religion is right.
7. It follows from the preceding line and the fifth premise that all the world is wrong.
8. It follows that all the world is right or else that all the world is wrong, because one supposition or the other holds (an inference of a form known as a *dilemma*).

So, the inference is valid: if its premises are true, then its conclusion is true too. But, is its third premise true?

correct? They both strike me as plausible, and no method exists to decide on their respective merits. The proof in the box is easy to find; other proofs—sometimes of simple inferences—can be very difficult to discover. An alternative method for the analysis of arguments is to use complete models, and Box 20.2 shows the output of my program to the argument when it uses complete models.

As both boxes show, Paine's argument has an analysis in which it is valid. Is its conclusion true? As ever, we shouldn't confuse a valid conclusion with a true conclusion. It also depends on whether the premises are true, and one of the premises I had to add to the argument was: Either everyone judges his own religion or else everyone judges others' religion. This premise is false: plenty of people don't judge any religion, and some may judge both their own and others' religions. The world is grayer than Paine imagined.

A problem in using logic is that we have to invest time and effort to learn it. Most methods of teaching it emphasize formal proofs, and so we also need to acquire the ability to extract the logical form of everyday arguments. A contrasting method of teaching logic, pioneered by the late Jon Barwise and John Etchemendy, is to emphasize content rather than form. They and their colleagues wrote a computer program, "Hyperproof", that allows students to construct sentences in a logical calculus and to evaluate whether they are true or false in relation to a model of blocks laid out on a chess board. A psychological study of the efficacy of Hyperproof as a way to teach logic has shown that it works for some students, but not for others, perhaps because of differences in their style of thinking.

No one knows whether a course in logic would improve our reasoning in life. It shouldn't harm us, but the evidence shows that its improving effects may be limited. When participants took a semester's course in propositional logic (dealing with the logic of "if", "or", and "and"), their ability to cope with a reasoning task based on conditionals—the selection task—was better than that of a group who took no course in logic. Given a conditional, "If there's an A on one side of a card then there's a 2 on the other side", the logically trained participants understood the relevance of a card bearing a 3 as a potential counterexample to the conditional. However, when the general statement was couched in terms of a quantifier, "Every card with an A on one side has a 3 on the other side," their advantage evaporated and they did no better than the group untrained in logic. The course in logic hadn't dealt with quantifiers, and the participants who took the course were unable to see that the quantified proposition called for the same tests as the conditional proposition.

Box 20.2 The analysis of Paine's informal argument using complete models

The premises and the conclusion, where "iff" stands for "if and only if" and "ore" stands for "or else" (an exclusive disjunction) are as follows:

Everyone judges his own religion ore everyone judges others' religion.

Iff everyone judges his own religion then no religion is wrong.

Iff everyone judges others' religion then no religion is right.

Iff no religion is wrong then all the world is right.

Iff no religion is right then all the world is wrong.

All the world is right ore all the world is wrong. (The conclusion)

The output of the program to each premise and conclusion (in abbreviated form in which '¬' stands for 'not'):

Judges own ore judges others, yields the complete models:

    judges-own   ¬ judges-others

     ¬ judges-own   judges-others

Iff judges own then none wrong, updates the models to:

    judges-own   ¬ judges-others   none-wrong

     ¬ judges-own   judges-others   ¬ none-wrong

Iff judges others then none right, updates the models to:

    judges-own   ¬ judges-others   none-wrong   ¬ none-right

     ¬ judges-own   judges-others   ¬ none-wrong   none-right

Iff none wrong then all right, updates the models to:

    judges-own   ¬ judges-others   none-wrong   ¬ none-right   all-right

     ¬ judges-own   judges-others   ¬ none-wrong   none-right   ¬ all-right

Iff none right then all wrong, updates models to:

judges-own ¬ judges-others   none-wrong ¬ none-right   all-right ¬ all-wrong

¬ judges-own   judges-others ¬ none-wrong   none-right ¬ all-right   all-wrong

All right ore all wrong, yields the output:

Your argument VALIDLY implies the assertion: All right ore all wrong.

Should the engineers in charge at Three Mile Island when the turbine "tripped" on March 28, 1979 have translated their knowledge into a logical calculus and sought a proof of the cause of the emergency? The idea is preposterous. Logic is far too time consuming for use in emergencies. We have to think on our feet. But, skepticism about logic as an aid to reasoning should not be confused with the downright hostility of some commentators. They write about the dangers of applying logic to human affairs, blinkered deductions, and unreasonable conclusions. Much of their rhetoric rests on nothing more than a confusion between truth and validity. Rubbish in, rubbish out—even if a deduction is valid.

* * *

Many of those who teach students to reason have abandoned logic as a useful tool. One of their legitimate concerns is the sheer difficulty of logical analysis. Another is the gap between logic and everyday inferences. The philosopher Stephen Toulmin argued that logic is inappropriate for the analysis of real arguments. Premises, he said, have different roles in arguments, and logic fails to distinguish them. Many pedagogues shared his skepticism, and they formed an association for informal logic and critical thinking (AILACT). Its members advocate all sorts of methods of analysis—the identification of fallacies, the use of special diagrams or computer programs, and much else besides. These various approaches are not mutually exclusive, but they have been mutually explosive. Proponents of one system find other systems unworkable. And no one appears to have demonstrated robust improvements in reasoning as a result of any of them.

* * *

Many authors have argued that diagrams can help us to reason. The question of how they might do so has a long history. I have already described Euler circles and Venn diagrams for representing syllogisms. Lewis Carroll developed a game of logic for the same domain. By far the most powerful diagrammatic system, however, is due to Peirce. He devised it, not for pedagogical purposes, but to display the steps in our thinking. Once again, no one knows whether our reasoning will benefit from learning any of these systems.

In a pioneering psychological study, the late Herb Simon and his colleagues distinguished several ways in which diagrams could be helpful. They can make it easy to find relevant information, because we can scan them quickly. They can make it easy to identify instances of a concept, because we can recognize an icon faster than a description. But, according to Simon, they shouldn't make any difference to reasoning. It should proceed in much the same way whether the premises are sentences or diagrams. Barwise and Etchemendy also argued that diagrams can present a wealth of details that hold in conjunctions, e.g., the vehicle has six wheels *and* a rear-mounted turret *and* an open top *and* a large front bumper. But, they said, diagrams are poor at representing negative or disjunctive premises (based on "or"), which are better presented in sentences. Their program *Hyperproof* uses this division of labor between diagrams and sentences.

The model theory makes a very different prediction. The mere use of a diagram is no guarantee that our reasoning will be better. But, diagrams that help us to imagine different possibilities should improve our reasoning, even from negations and disjunctions. I can illustrate this point with taxing inferences from pairs of disjunctive premises, such as:

> Julia is in Atlanta or Raphael is in Tacoma, or both.
>
> Julia is in Seattle or Paul is in Philadelphia, or both.
>
> What, if anything, follows?

Granted that Julia can't be in both Atlanta and Seattle, it follows that Raphael is in Tacoma or Paul is in Philadelphia, or both. But, the inference is hard, because we have too many possibilities to hold in mind. Could a diagram make it easier?

An initial study compared inferences from verbal premises with those from diagrams. Figure 20.1 shows one of the diagrams from the experiment, which represents the preceding premises. The ellipses represent the location of a person in a city, and the two lines connecting the ellipses intersect at a square. The square represents an inclusive disjunction, which allows both possibilities. A different symbol, not shown in the figure, represents an exclusive disjunction, which does not allow both possibilities to occur. The experiment confirmed that exclusive disjunctions, which yield two possibilities, are easier than inclusive disjunctions, which yield three possibilities. The diagrams, however, did not improve reasoning. If you look again at Figure 20.1, you can see that they fail to make explicit the different possibilities compatible with the premises. And they fail to make explicit the force of an implicit negation: there's nothing in the diagram to represent that if Julia is in Atlanta, then she is *not* in Seattle, and vice versa.

A second experiment used very different diagrams in order to correct these shortcomings. One group of participants reasoned from the new diagrams and another group of participants reasoned from verbal premises. The participants were told that the premises had to be true for a certain event to

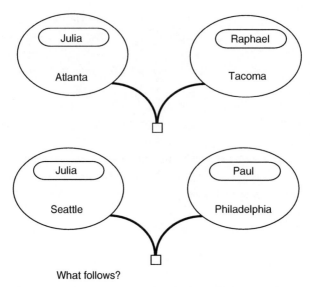

What follows?

Fig. 20.1 A diagram used to present premises in the preliminary study.

occur. Figure 20.2 shows the diagram presenting the same problem as before. The participants knew that they had to complete a path from one side of the figure to the other by inserting the shapes representing people into the slots representing places. As the figure shows, the shape standing for a person can fit only into the same shaped slot corresponding to a place. Hence, the shape standing for Raphael can be in Tacoma or not, the shape standing for Paul can be in Philadelphia or not, and the shape standing for Julia can be in Atlanta or Seattle, or in neither.

The new diagrams increased accuracy in a striking way. The participants drew seventy-four percent correct conclusions from them as opposed to forty-six percent correct conclusions from the equivalent verbal premises. They were also much faster to respond to the diagrams (on average 99 seconds) than to respond to the verbal premises (on average, 135 seconds). In both conditions, exclusive disjunctions (two possibilities) were easier than inclusive disjunctions (three possibilities), and affirmative problems were easier than the problems containing an implicit negation. These patterns were evident in both the percentages of correct responses and the response times. Erroneous conclusions tended to be consistent with *some* of the possibilities compatible with the premises. This tendency was greater for the diagrammatic problems than for the verbal problems. Once again, the diagrams made it easier to grasp at least some of the possibilities.

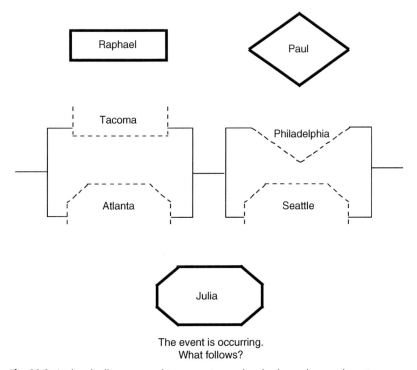

Fig. 20.2 An iconic diagram used to present premises in the main experiment.

Why are these diagrams so helpful? Figure 20.2 is iconic, and so it makes it easy for us to imagine the *possible* routes from one side of a diagram to the other. The diagrams are static, but we can imagine moving this piece or that into its appropriate slot. They display negative states of affairs, but we can imagine sliding a piece into its appropriate slot, to represent the corresponding affirmative proposition. In short, the diagrams enable us to visualize the possibilities inherent in the premises: they translate disjunction and negation into spatial analogs.

When we reason from a disjunction, we have to grasp its meaning and use it to construct models of the alternative possibilities. We have to update these models with the alternatives from subsequent premises. This process is taxing, and we can lose track of where we are. With a diagram, however, we form an iconic representation, and in our mind's eye we can visualize moving the pieces into their slots. We carry out a *visual* transformation, but it is equivalent to imagining a possibility. We visualize moving the lozenge designating Julia into the slot representing Atlanta, and we know that the result represents the proposition that Julia is in Atlanta. We can describe this possibility in our conclusion. The process is faster and more accurate than one based on verbal premises. In summary, not every sort of diagram improves reasoning, but those that make it easier for us to imagine possibilities are helpful.

* * *

To improve our reasoning, we need a more capacious working memory and perhaps faster mental processes. We need to improve our understanding of premises, our ability to think of all the possibilities compatible with them, our power to formulate conclusions capturing what is common to these possibilities, and our skill in finding counterexamples to conclusions. Above all, we need more imagination in envisaging what is possible: Julia may not be in Atlanta; the bow doors may not have been closed.

We can learn more efficient ways to encode information in working memory but the procedure calls for much practice and works only for limited sets of materials. We cannot, it seems, increase the processing capacity of working memory itself or the speed of our neural responses. They appear to be a consequence of the make-up of our brains. Hence, we need a panacea. We need a practical method that takes a few minutes to learn and is easy to use, that is rooted in what is natural for us, that requires no apparatus—not even pencil and paper, that improves our reasoning, that has lasting effects, and that works for any domain. I will describe the best method I know that comes some way to meeting these targets.

When we develop strategies for reasoning, some of us spontaneously use a single diagram that represents all the possibilities compatible with the premises. As the previous chapter described, we draw these diagrams in various ways. Some of us draw a line down the middle of the piece of paper to separate possibilities. Some of us draw a horizontal line. Some of us draw circles round those items in the premises that occur in one of the possibilities. This strategy of reasoning is based on a diagram designed to keep track of possibilities. And the evidence showed that it was a more flexible strategy than others. We can learn a method of reasoning based on this strategy in a couple of minutes. This so-called "model method" consists of one command: *Try to construct all the possibilities consistent with the given information.* We can put this precept into practice in a simple way, which I'll illustrate with an example.

Imagine that a course is to be taught by certain professors, and that these premises govern who lectures on the course:

Dr. Comer lectures or Dr. Sugarman lectures, or they both lecture.

If Dr. Sugarman does not lecture then Dr. Glucksberg lectures.

Dr. Hoebel lectures if and only if Dr. Sugarman lectures.

Dr. Prentice lectures.

Dr. Glucksberg has another class and so cannot lecture.

Who lectures?

There are three possibilities consistent with the first premise, and we can represent them in three columns separated by vertical lines using the first letter of each name:

$$
\begin{array}{c|c|c}
C & & C \\
& S & S
\end{array}
$$

The second premise calls for Dr. Glucksberg to be at least added to any possibility in which Dr. Sugarman does not occur:

$$
\begin{array}{c|c|c}
C & & C \\
& S & S \\
G & &
\end{array}
$$

The third premise calls for Dr. Hoebel to be added to any possibility in which Dr. Sugarman does occur:

$$
\begin{array}{c|c|c}
C & & C \\
& S & S \\
G & & \\
& H & H
\end{array}
$$

The fourth premise calls for Dr. Prentice to added to all possibilities:

$$
\begin{array}{c|c|c}
C & & C \\
& S & S \\
G & & \\
& H & H \\
P & P & P
\end{array}
$$

The final premise eliminates any possibility in which Dr. Glucksberg occurs, and so it can be deleted, and so I've crossed out the left-hand column:

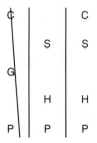

This diagram yields a valid conclusion:

> Drs. Sugarman, Hoebel, and Prentice must lecture, and Dr. Comer may lecture.

That's the end of the account of the method.

To see whether the method was effective, an experiment tested participants in two blocks of reasoning problems in which they evaluated given conclusions. One group of participants was left to their own devices in both blocks; one group was taught the model method (in almost identical words to those above) after the first block of problems; and one group was taught it before the first block of problems. The effects were striking. Without the benefit of the model method, the participants were right on about two-thirds of the trials, and they took an average of twenty-four seconds to evaluate each inference. With the benefit of the method, however, they were right on ninety-five percent of the inferences, and they took an average of fifteen seconds to evaluate each inference.

A subsequent experiment demonstrated a comparable improvement when the participants were not allowed to use paper and pencil. They were taught the method as before, but then they were told to imagine the different possibilities. The problems were a little easier than those in the first experiment, and the group who were left to their own devices were right for eighty percent of the inferences. The group who were taught the model method did better: they were right on ninety-three percent of the inferences. Some problems were based in part on biconditional premises ("if and only if") and others were based in part on exclusive disjunctions ("or else"). As the model theory predicts, inferences from the biconditionals were faster than those from the disjunctions. However, the effect of learning the model method speeded up responses more for the disjunctive premises. It is hard to hold two alternative possibilities in mind, and so it helps if we have been instructed to try to keep track of possibilities.

Consider this problem:

> Allan is on the committee or else Bobby is.
>
> Bobby is on the committee or else Nigel is.
>
> Nigel is on the committee if and only if Wally is.
>
> Does it follow that Allan is on the committee if and only if Wally is?

An alternative method for evaluating conclusions is based on making suppositions. Suppose, for instance, that Allan *is* on the committee. It follows from the first premise that Bobby isn't on the committee. It follows from this conclusion and the second premise that Nigel is on the committee. It follows from this conclusion and the third premise that Wally is on the committee. Hence, we have established that if Allan is on the committee then Wally is. But, the conclusion also asserts that Allan is on the committee *only* if Wally is. To check this claim, we need to make a further supposition. One way to proceed is to suppose that Wally is on the committee. It follows from this supposition and the third premise that Nigel is on the committee. It follows from this conclusion and the second premise that Bobby is not on the committee. It follows from this conclusion and the first premise that Allan is on the committee. So now we know that if Wally is on the committee then Allan is too. We have shown that the conclusion follows from the premises.

An experiment examined the efficacy of teaching the participants to use suppositions, because some of us have a natural tendency to use this strategy. The experiment showed that those who were taught the model method were the most accurate (over ninety percent correct). Those who were taught to use suppositions were the next most accurate (about eighty percent correct). And those were left to their own devices were the least accurate (about sixty-five percent correct).

The experiments so far called for the participants to evaluate given conclusions, but a further experiment showed that the model method was also helpful when the participants had to formulate their own conclusions. The inferences were all based on two premises, one containing a propositional connective, and one a simple categorical proposition. Those participants who were taught the model method drew many more valid conclusions (eighty percent) than those who were left to their own devices (fifty-two percent).

The conclusion from these studies is that the model method, though it takes only a few minutes to teach, has robust effects on both the accuracy and speed of reasoning. It helps us to bear in mind the alternative possibilities compatible with the premises. It is not just a generalized effect of instruction, because it leads to a bigger improvement in reasoning than instruction in the use of suppositions. I don't know whether it yields a long-lasting improvement, because the studies did not address this question, but the method is efficient and effective in the short term. It is not fool-proof, but it does exploit the tendency that we all have to think about possibilities.

* * *

Despite the existence of many systems for improving reasoning, few empirical studies have examined their worth. Psychologists do not even know whether we reason better in life as a result of learning logic. The study that I described showed that any beneficial effect failed to transfer to inferences of the same logical form but different wording. This lack of evidence has led the proponents of "informal logic and critical thinking" to advocate other ways to assess arguments. Some of these systems use diagrams to represent arguments, just as many systems of logical analysis do. The results that I have reported suggest that only certain sorts of diagram should be helpful. To be effective, they need to help us to imagine the possibilities compatible with the premises. Other diagrams that lacked this iconic property had no beneficial effects. The "model method" depends on teaching us to think about the possibilities compatible with the premises. It has the virtues of simplicity and efficacy. We soon learn the method—it builds on our natural propensity to think about possibilities—and it improves both our accuracy and speed of reasoning. Most of us should benefit from this method.

Part VII

Knowledge, Beliefs, and Problems

All knowledge that conflicts with itself is Poetic Fiction.

Auden

Chapter 21

The Puzzles of *If*

"Even the crows on the roof caw about the nature of conditionals", wrote Callimachus, the librarian of Alexandria in the third century BC. So, "if" has been under discussion for some time. It *is* a puzzling word. I have described the main principles of the model theory of reasoning—from the mechanisms that construct models to the development of strategies, and my aim in this part of the book is to show how the theory can be used to solve various puzzles. I begin with the puzzles of *if*.

Suppose that you are an engineer carrying out a test of a complex system and you know that if the test is to continue then the system must not have reached the critical level. You then observe that it has reached the critical level. What should you do? It seems obvious that you should stop the test. The engineers in charge at Chernobyl were in this position, but they continued the test. Why they continued is perplexing, because the test was not just dangerous, but pointless. It led to the disaster.

For several years, I have given engineering students premises of a similar sort to those that confronted the operators of the nuclear reactor at Chernobyl, but with a more abstract content:

> If there is a triangle on the board then there is a circle on the board.
>
> There isn't a circle on the board.
>
> What, if anything, follows?

Your first thought might be that nothing follows from these premises. Every year, at least half of the engineers think so too. Perhaps the engineers at Chernobyl were in a similar state of mind. In fact, there *is* a valid inference. It follows that there is not a triangle on the board. The inference is quite difficult for the students, but not because they are reluctant to make inferences from conditionals. With premises of this sort:

> If there is a triangle on the board then there is a circle on the board.
>
> There is a triangle on the board.

almost all of them draw the valid conclusion that there is a circle on the board. The difference in difficulty between the two sorts of inference—this one and the Chernobyl inference—is one of the most robust effects in experiments on reasoning. A myriad of experiments has corroborated it.

Reasoning from *if* is commonplace, because so much of our knowledge is conditional in form. If we get caught speeding then we pay a fine. If we have an operation then we need time to recuperate. If we have money in our bank account then we can cash a check. So, why do the engineers in the laboratory and in the control room sometimes go wrong? That is the first puzzle of *if*.

There is a deeper puzzle. As Callimachus implied, conditional propositions are perplexing. They have continued to perplex philosophers, linguists, and psychologists. No other little word has provoked so many books. The root of the problem is simple to state: what do conditionals mean? You may retort: it's obvious what they mean—even little children know that. They understand very well when a parent says to them: "If you're good then you can have popcorn." A three-year old responded to this promise from her father with the remark: "I am good", inviting him to draw the obvious conclusion. Hence, I am sympathetic to your skepticism. Children do understand conditionals. The people who don't are philosophers, linguists, and psychologists. Indeed, everyone understands conditionals in the flow of conversation, but no one seems to understand them in reflecting on them in analytical tranquility.

Conditionals are inconstant. Sometimes they mean one thing; sometimes they mean another. As an example, consider the difference between *if he owned the car then he drove it*, and *if he drove the car then he crashed it*. They seem similar, but they're quite different. The first conditional is consistent with three possibilities:

He owned the car.	He drove it.
He didn't own the car.	He drove it.
He didn't own the car.	He didn't drive it.

But, the second conditional is consistent with just two possibilities:

He drove the car.	He crashed it.
He didn't drive the car.	He didn't crash it.

The difference is that he can't have crashed the car if he didn't drive it, whereas he could have driven it if he didn't own it. We seldom notice these differences, because our mental models of conditionals make explicit just one possibility, e.g.:

> He owned the car.   He drove the car.
>   ...

We represent the other possibilities in a model that has no explicit content (denoted by the ellipsis), and so we don't notice that they differ from one conditional to another.

There are plenty of other interpretations of conditionals, and their chameleon-like behavior has led some theorists to propose that the word *if* is ambiguous, though the ambiguities are not ones that dictionary-makers recognize. Others have treated conditionals in the same way that Procrustes treated his victims. They lop off the bits that don't fit their theories. Almost everyone has thought of conditionals as unique, and that is why there are books on *if*, but not on *or*.

The resolution of the puzzle, I believe, is that *if* has diverse interpretations because several simple components in its interpretation interact. These components also occur in different combinations in the interpretation of other connectives. Once I have pinned down the meaning of *if* in this way, a straight-forward account of reasoning emerges to explain why the Chernobyl inference is difficult. I'll describe these components, sketching some alternative accounts to throw them into relief, and summarize some evidence that helps to clarify the theory.

* * *

The first component that influences conditionals is grammar. *If* differs from *and* and *or*. They can connect main clauses, e.g.: *she moved and the X-ray is blurred*. But, conditionals have a subordinate if-clause and a main then-clause. One consequence is that expressions that seem to apply to a conditional as a whole in fact apply only to its main clause. Sentences such as:

> It is likely that if she moved then the X-ray is blurred
>
> It is obligatory that if he earned a salary then he pays taxes.

therefore have the same meanings as:

> If she moved then it is likely that the X-ray is blurred.
>
> If he earned a salary then it is obligatory that he pays taxes.

In contrast, the conjunction, *it is likely that she moved and the X-ray is blurred*, is not synonymous with *she moved and it is likely that the X-ray is blurred*. The first sentence asserts only that is likely that she moved, but the second sentence asserts that she did move. This migration of qualifications from sentences as a whole to their main clauses occurs with other sorts of sentence containing subordinate clauses, e.g., *it is obligatory that after you emigrate you register with the police* means the same as *after you emigrate it is obligatory that you register with the police.* We'll see later that the facts of migration may have misled theorists about the meaning of conditionals.

The if-clause in a conditional describes a possibility, almost always in an incomplete way. The then-clause is interpreted as though it were an isolated main clause in the context of this possibility. It follows that the if-clause must be declarative in order to *describe* a possibility. But, the then-clause is not restricted in this way: it can be interrogative and ask a question, or it can be imperative and make a request, e.g., *If she moved then take another X-ray.* No such restriction occurs in conjunctions and disjunctions.

The auxiliary verbs that occur in conditionals are also special. The past tense of "have" and "will" have a special meaning in conditionals, e.g.: *If it had rained yesterday then there would have been puddles in the road.* One interpretation of this example is that whether or not it rained is an open question. Another interpretation is that it did *not* rain, and the then-clause describes what would have happened in the "counterfactual" possibility in which it did rain.

* * *

The core interpretation of conditionals is the one that I referred to earlier in the book as "logical". The conditional above, *if he owned the car then he drove it,* has this interpretation. It occurs for various conditionals, and in particular for those that don't depend on their context for their interpretation and that don't evoke any sort of relation between the if-clause and the then-clause over and above their co-occurrence in the same conditional. The logical interpretation therefore occurs for the proposition:

If there's a circle on the board then there's a triangle on the board.

The most salient possibility compatible with this proposition is the one corresponding to its explicit mental model:

There's a circle and a triangle on the board.

But, the conditional allows there may not be a circle on the board, and so with a little thought most of us can think of two further possibilities:

There is not a circle and there is a triangle.

There is not a circle and there is not a triangle.

These three possibilities correspond to the complete models of the logical interpretation of conditionals, and you may recall that we tend to list them when we we're asked what is possible given the conditional.

We make a different sort of judgment when we evaluate the *truth* or *falsity* of the same conditional (If there's a circle on the board then there's a triangle on the board). If we see a circle and a triangle on the board, we judge that the conditional is true. If instead we see a circle without a triangle, we judge that the conditional is false. But, suppose we see just a square, or a square and a triangle, what do we say then? Most of us say that these cases are irrelevant to the truth or falsity of the conditional, even though we list them as possible when we're told that the conditional is true. That's another puzzle about *if*: what we think is possible given a conditional doesn't quite tally with what we think makes a conditional true.

The model theory explains the difference. To list the possibilities, all we have to do is to understand a conditional and to think of what is possible. We enumerate the complete models of the conditional. To evaluate whether a conditional is true or false, however, we have to compare it with a state of affairs that we see, and we also have to understand the "metalinguistic" terms *true* and *false*. We are more likely in this case to rely on mental models than complete models. The mental models of the conditional above are:

$$\bigcirc \qquad \triangle$$
$$\cdots$$

where the ellipsis denotes an implicit model representing the possibilities in which the if-clause is false. Hence, we judge any situation in which the if-clause is true as making the conditional true or false depending on whether or not the situation matches the explicit mental model. And we judge any state of affairs in which the if-clause is false as irrelevant to the truth or falsity of the conditional, because the situation corresponds to a model with no explicit content (symbolized by the ellipsis).

Consider again the Chernobyl inference of the sort I gave to the engineering students:

> If there is a circle on the board then there is a triangle on the board.
>
> There isn't a triangle on the board.
>
> What, if anything, follows?

If we reason using the mental models of the conditional, the categorical premise that there isn't a triangle eliminates the explicit model of the conditional and leaves just the model with no explicit content. Hence, it seems that nothing follows from the premises, which is what many of the students said. One way to reach the valid conclusion that there isn't a circle is to flesh out the models of the conditional to include the possibility:

> There is not a circle and there is not a triangle.

Another way is to make a supposition that there's a circle on the board. It follows from the explicit model of the conditional that there's a triangle on the board. This conclusion contradicts the categorical premise, and so a further model-based inference yields a denial of the supposition. Still another way is to think about the case that the conditional rules out, i.e., its anti-model in which there is a circle and not a triangle, and to infer from the fact that there is not a triangle that there cannot be a circle. None of these methods is simple, and that is why the Chernobyl inference is difficult. The if-clause of a conditional often invokes reasoning from its supposition, and some psychologists have argued that we always reason in a hypothetical way from conditionals. However, some if-clauses assert facts, e.g., "If it's as hot as this now, it's going to be even hotter in July".

* * *

Another puzzle about conditionals is the root of a long controversy. It concerns their logical interpretation, and the puzzle is that a categorical premise, such as:

> There is a triangle

implies any conditional whatsoever provided that the categorical premise is also its then-clause, e.g.:

> If there is a circle then there is a triangle.

The reason is that the logical interpretation of a conditional can be false only when its then-clause is false, but the categorical premise rules out this possibility. A categorical premise such as:

> There isn't a circle

also implies any conditional whatsoever, including the previous one, provided that the categorical premise negates its if-clause. The reason is that the logical interpretation of a conditional cannot be false when the conditional's if-clause is false. These inferences are so bizarre that some authors have dubbed them "paradoxes", and refused to accept any theory of conditionals that allows them.

The two paradoxes are analogous to inferences based on inclusive disjunctions:

> There is a triangle.
>
> Therefore, there isn't a circle or there is a triangle.

and:

> There isn't a circle.
>
> Therefore, there isn't a circle or there is a triangle.

We also baulk at these inferences. What is common to them and to the conditional paradoxes is that they all throw information away by adding alternative possibilities to those conveyed by their categorical premises. No theorist, however, has rejected the logical meaning of disjunctions on the grounds that they yield quasi-paradoxical conclusions. The model theory, as you'll soon see, predicts that some occurrences of the conditional paradoxes are more acceptable than others.

* * *

Meaning and knowledge can modulate the interpretation of propositional connectives. One effect is to block the construction of models. The earlier example: "If he drove the car then he crashed it", illustrates this effect, because knowledge blocks the construction of a model in which he didn't drive the car, and yet he crashed it. We know that to crash a car a person has to be driving it. Even an engineer controlling a test crash has to be driving the car, albeit at a distance, in order to crash it. An example in which a different sort of model is blocked is shown here:

> If you put your toe in the pool then the water's hot.

You know that putting your toe in the pool isn't sufficient in itself to make the water hot. It's hot regardless of whether you put a toe in. Hence, modulation blocks the possibility in which you don't put a toe in and the water isn't hot. The conditional means, in effect: the water's hot, as you'll discover if you put a toe in the pool. The varied effects of modulation have been corroborated in experiments in which the participants listed what is possible for conditionals with different contents. The interpretations in turn have predictable effects on reasoning.

Irony can block two out of the three models of a logical conditional. For example,

> If he's here then I'll jump in the lake.

means that he isn't here (and, as you know, I won't jump in the lake). The conditional:

If my name is Phil then he's here

means that he's here (and, as you know, my name is Phil).

A second effect of modulation is to add information to models. It may introduce various relations between the events referred to in the conditional. In the conditional, "If he put the book on the shelf then it fell off", the first event occurred before the second event, and the book finished up lower than its position on the shelf. Temporal relations call for models of possibilities at different times. They may be organized so that one model occurs after another in a mental sequence of events, or in a static way akin to a diagram or graph.

Another modulation of this sort adds a putative causal *mechanism* to an interpretation:

If you lift the switch then the light bulb comes on.

Given that we have the appropriate knowledge, we tend to infer that the switch is in an electrical circuit, that lifting it closes the circuit to cause electricity to flow through the circuit and hence through the filament of the light bulb, which in turn causes it to emit light. As the example shows, the mechanism itself consists of causal relations on a smaller scale.

A third effect of modulation is to help us to construct *complete* models, that is, those that list both what is true and what is false in the possibilities consistent with propositions. For example, the premise:

If Bill is in Rio de Janeiro then he is in Brazil

expresses common knowledge about a geographical relation. We know that Rio is in Brazil. Hence, we realize that if Bill is not in Brazil, he cannot be in Rio. A corollary is that we should make the "Chernobyl" inference with ease:

If Bill is in Rio de Janeiro then he is in Brazil.

Bill is not in Brazil.

Therefore, he is not in Rio de Janeiro.

In contrast, spatial exclusions should inhibit this sort of inference, and so given the premises:

If Bill is in Brazil then he is not in Rio de Janeiro.

Bill is in Rio de Janeiro.

we should baulk at the conclusion:

> Bill is not in Brazil.

We know that if Bill is in Rio then he must be in Brazil. With familiar contents of this sort, participants in an experiment drew many more conclusions (ninety-two percent) with the spatial inclusions than with the spatial exclusions (thirty-four percent). These effects occur with modulations that depend on general knowledge or on meaning, and they also affect other sorts of conditional reasoning.

* * *

Modulation solves several other well-known puzzles. *Item:* reference in conditionals. Reference can be so problematical for logical analyses that certain examples are known in some quarters as "donkey" sentences from the original example of the puzzle. A simplified version of it is illustrated here:

> If Joe owns a donkey then he beats it.

What does "it" refer to here? If Joe owns a donkey, the pronoun refers to the donkey, but if he doesn't own a donkey, the pronoun doesn't refer to anything. The conditional is compatible with just two possibilities:

> Joe owns a donkey and beats it.

> Joe does not own a donkey.

Item: according to the logical meaning of conditionals this sort of inference, known as "strengthening the antecedent", is valid:

> If you strike a match properly then it lights.

> Therefore, if a match is soaking wet and you strike it properly then it lights.

Analogous conundrums occur with disjunctive propositions, e.g.:

> You put sugar in your coffee or it doesn't taste sweet.

> Therefore, you put sugar or diesel oil in your coffee, or it doesn't taste sweet.

You may think that the trouble arises because the premises in these examples are untrue, and that the solution is to reformulate them, taking pains to state all the relevant conditions, e.g.:

> If a match has not been soaked in water, is chemically intact, is in an atmosphere containing oxygen ... and is struck properly then it lights.

Can you guarantee to state all the relevant conditions? Probably, not. Hence, this solution may degenerate into a vacuous circle:

> If a match is in a state that it lights when it is struck properly and it is struck properly then it lights.

If you like this sort of solution, then this solution is the sort you like. When we reason in life, we almost always reason in the absence of complete information. We jump to a conclusion that reality may overturn. But, our conclusions are often true. And so our belief, say, that properly struck matches light is an idealization that is a useful springboard for inferences.

When this puzzle first came to the attention of practitioners of artificial intelligence—those scientists who try to write computer programs to do intelligent things—one of the leading figures in the field, Marvin Minsky, introduced the idea of a default assumption. That is, an assumption that can be made provided that no evidence exists to overrule it. If a match is struck properly and there is no information to the contrary then, by default, it lights. To soak a match in water is just one way in which to overrule this default assumption. A more psychological approach to the problem, however, is to allow that knowledge can modulate the interpretation of propositional connectives. Consider the inference again:

> If you strike a match properly then it lights.

> Therefore, if a match is soaking wet and you strike it properly then it lights.

The logical interpretation of the conclusion yields a model of a possibility in which the match is soaking wet, it was struck properly, and it lit. However, the proposition that the match is soaking wet triggers our knowledge that soaking wet matches do not light. Knowledge takes precedence over the meaning of sentences, and so this model rules out the "then" clause to yield an alternative possibility: the match is soaking wet, it is struck properly, and it does *not* light. This possibility is a counterexample to the conditional premise, and so the conclusion doesn't follow from the premise.

I wrote a computer program that uses a "data-base" of knowledge in just this way. If the program is given the premises:

> If the match is struck then the match lights.

> The match is soaked and the match is struck.

then the clause that the match is soaked triggers a matching possibility in the data-base that the match does not light. This knowledge has precedence, and blocks the conclusion that the match lights.

Item: the "paradoxes" of the logical interpretation of conditionals. Some authors, as I mentioned, reject the paradoxes along with any theory that warrants them. In contrast, the model theory predicts that they should be acceptable in some cases. One case is when a conditional is modulated so that there is no doubt about the falsity of its if-clause, e.g.:

> The experiment won't work.
>
> Therefore, if the experiment works then I'll eat my shorts.

The other sort of paradox should be acceptable when the conditional is modulated so that there is no doubt about the truth of its then-clause, e.g.:

> They didn't play soccer.
>
> Therefore, if they played a game then they didn't play soccer.

These inferences are plausible, and so theories that reject all cases of the paradoxes may be in error.

Item: conjunctions and disjunctions of conditionals. Consider this premise:

> If there is a circle then there is a triangle and if there is a diamond then there is a star.

What are the possibilities compatible with it? We tend to list three possibilities: one in which there is a circle and a triangle, another in which there is diamond and a star, and one in which all four shapes are present. Now, consider this alternative premise:

> If there is a circle then there is a triangle *or* if there is a diamond then there is a star.

What are the possibilities compatible with it? We tend to list the same three possibilities. There's a difference in meaning between *and* and *or*, so why do we list the same possibilities? The answer is that the two sentences have the same mental models, because mental models don't represent propositions that are false in possibilities. However, the complete models of the two assertions, which take into account the falsity of clauses, yield nine possibilities for the conjunction and fifteen possibilities for the disjunction. No one in any experiment has ever come anywhere near to listing all these possibilities.

* * *

Is this conditional true or false?

> If the US constitution is *not* amended to allow that people born outside the country can be elected President, then Arnold Schwarzenegger will be President of Austria one day.

We can't tell now. Nevertheless, we may believe the conditional to a greater or lesser degree, and we can adduce evidence to support our position. We may think to ourselves on these lines:

> Well, it is possible. Mr. Schwarzenegger is quite a skillful politician; it's no secret that he'd like to run for US Presidency, but that would call for a constitutional amendment. So, if no amendment is passed, and I rather doubt that it would be, then he might return to his native country, and be a successful politician there. On the other hand, there are many imponderables, and so it's by no means certain.

We may not judge that the conditional is true or false for certain. But, what puzzles psychologists are the mechanisms that fix the strength of our belief in it.

A seminal view goes back to the English logician Frank Ramsey. He addressed this question in a footnote to a paper, one of the most quoted footnotes in all of philosophy:

> If two people are arguing 'If p will q?' and both are in doubt as to p, they are adding p hypothetically to their stock of knowledge and arguing on that basis about q; so that in a sense 'If p, q' and 'If p, not q' are contradictories. We can say they are fixing their degrees of belief in q given p. If p turns out to be false, these degrees of belief are rendered *void*.

On Ramsey's account, we add the if-clause to our beliefs and then determine whether we believe the then-clause. And how do we do that? It's not obvious. We could use our knowledge to construct a chain of implications, perhaps causal in nature, as illustrated above in the example about Mr. Schwarzenegger. Several modern philosophers, however, have transformed Ramsey's test into a theory, not of belief, but of the *meaning* of conditionals. They take a conditional to be true if, in any "possible world" in which its if-clause is true, and which resembles the real world as closely as possible, then its then-clause is also true. This theory allows that the if-clause may be false, and so a possible world in which the if-clause does hold and which resembles the real world is a philosophical idealization. The theory cannot be put into practice to determine whether an actual conditional is true or false. What is more worrying is that when we know that a conditional is true, e.g., *If my next paper is accepted for publication then I'll be pleased*, we cannot ascertain that it is true according to the principles of this account.

To return to degrees of belief, Ramsey's footnote is plausible, though psychologists don't have a working model of it. But, it does not appear to be the full story. Consider this claim:

> If Bacon wrote *Hamlet*, then Shakespeare didn't.

I believe it, even though I think its if-clause—that Bacon wrote *Hamlet*—is false. Ramsey's test doesn't apply in this case, but, taking our cue from its philosophical idealizations, we could say that I add the if-clause to my beliefs, adjust them to accommodate this intruder, and then figure out whether I believe the then-clause. In fact, to reach my belief that the conditional is true, I didn't for one moment believe that Bacon wrote *Hamlet*. I merely thought:

> Bacon and Shakespeare were two different individuals.
>
> *Hamlet* was the work of one individual.

Ergo, if Bacon wrote *Hamlet*, Shakespeare didn't.

* * *

We often reason about what didn't happen. We enter an imaginary world in which an event that was once possible failed to occur. Sometimes our thoughts concern trivial events—if the Viennese had had three legs then they would have marched to waltzes. Sometimes they concern matters of life and death. The military historian Max Hastings, for instance, wrote about the debacle of Arnhem in World War II:

> Many accounts... have concentrated on the 'might-have-beens' of British failure at Arnhem. Yet it seems at least as relevant to examine those at Nijmegen. If elements of the 82nd Airborne had been landed closer to the bridge, and if the vast Allied force of fighter-bombers had been used to block German armoured vehicles dashing into battle along open Dutch roads, that crossing could have been taken on the first day.

Ruth Byrne's outstanding book *The Rational Imagination* reports her and her colleagues' major investigation into this topic of "counterfactual" conditionals. Her starting point is that individuals tend to alter the same sorts of things when they imagine alternatives to reality. She argues that our thinking about counterfactual possibilities is governed by a small set of tacit principles. We tend to undo voluntary actions, and those that are unacceptable but that had a causal influence on the outcome. In the short term, we tend to regret our actions rather than our inactions, but in the long term—say, when we think about our life as a whole, we regret more our missed actions.

A conditional, such as:

> If he had left home earlier than 6am then he wouldn't have run into a traffic jam

can be used to make a counterfactual claim. And when we understand it in this way, we entertain two possibilities. One possibility is what the speaker presupposes to have happened, i.e., the facts of the matter:

He didn't leave home earlier than 6am. He ran into the traffic jam.

The other is a counterfactual possibility, i.e., it is something that once was a real possibility, but that in fact did not happen:

He left home earlier than 6am. He didn't run into the traffic jam.

As Byrne and her colleagues have shown, a consequence of this sort of representation is that it makes it easier for us to draw the Chernobyl sort of inference. That is, from the further premise:

In fact, he did run into a traffic jam

we tend to draw the conclusion:

He didn't leave earlier than 6am.

These inferences are easier than their counterparts based on ordinary conditionals, because we have constructed an explicit mental model corresponding to the falsity of the if-clause.

* * *

Contrasts with alternative accounts of conditionals throw the model theory into sharper relief. One account dovetails with naïve judgments about truth and falsity, which I described earlier. It postulates that a conditional, such as:

If there is a circle on the board then there is a triangle on the board

is true or false only when its if-clause is true. If its if-clause is false, the conditional is neither true nor false. It has, as philosophers say, no truth value. One reason to doubt the theory comes from a study that Tom Ormerod and his colleagues carried out. They showed that we infer disjunctions from conditionals, and conditionals from disjunctions. Yet, no one supposes that a disjunction has no truth value because one of its clauses is false. Another blow to this theory comes from conditionals that we know to be true. Consider the conditional:

If Phil's next grant application is going to be funded then he will be delighted.

It is true (believe me). But, if conditionals have no truth value when the if-clauses are false, it follows that the if-clause of this conditional must be true:

Phil's next grant application is going to be funded.

This miraculous inference follows from the theory because the only way that a conditional can be true is for its if-clause to be true. What a wonderful recipe for wishful thinking! It's far too good to be true; and far too good for the theory of a missing truth value not to have a truth value. It's false.

Another account of conditionals concerns when we are justified in asserting them. On this account, we are justified in asserting the conditional:

> If there's a circle then there's a triangle.

when the probability that:

> There's a triangle given that there's a circle

is greater than the probability that:

> There's not a triangle given that there's a circle.

The appeal of this account, I suspect, relies on the migration effect that I described earlier. Someone asks us:

> What's the probability that if there is a circle then there is a triangle?

Migration leads us to construe the question as equivalent to:

> If there is a circle then what's the probability that there is triangle?

This construal converts the original question into a direct request for a conditional probability. It is hard to resist this construal because it's warranted by the grammar of subordinate clauses. Yet, it is misleading, because of the equivalence between conditionals of this sort and disjunctions, and the probability of disjunctions depends, not on a conditional probability, but on the possibilities in which they hold.

* * *

What are the solutions to the puzzles of conditionals? They depend on three essential points:

First, we understand a conditional as referring to a set of possibilities, but we seldom think about all of them. The Chernobyl inference is difficult because we tend not to represent the possibilities in which the conditional's if-clause is false.

Second, a conditional often elicits temporal, spatial, or other sorts of relation, between the situation described in its if-clause and the situation described in its then-clause. Our grasp of their content, our knowledge, and even our imagination, all contribute to interpretations that yield these relations. Hence, conditionals have an indefinite number of different sorts of interpretation.

Third, the logical interpretation of a conditional can occur, and modulation can even make some of its paradoxical consequences more plausible. But, the process of interpretation transcends the logic of the propositional calculus, because we must always be on the lookout for effects of modulation.

The complexity of conditionals has simple causes. Their chameleon-like characteristics arise from interactions among a set of elementary components: their grammar, their core logical meaning, their representation in models, and their modulation by content and knowledge. What remains a mystery is how we determine our belief in a conditional. Ask yourself one last time whether you believe the proposition:

> If the US constitution is *not* amended to allow that people born elsewhere can be elected President, then Arnold Schwarzenegger will be President of Austria one day.

You may have thought about what would happen if the constitution were not amended, given Mr. Schwarzenegger's ambitions, and then you conceded that the then-clause is possible. Ramsey was right. But, didn't you also think—just for a moment—about what might happen if the US constitution *is* amended? Arnold as President of the USA? Or runs, loses, and returns to native land? If so, Ramsey told us just part of the story. No existing psychological theory describes the mechanisms that enable us to assign a number to our degree of belief in a conditional. That nasty little word, "if", is going to continue to irritate us for a while longer.

Chapter 22

Causes and Obligations

Earlier in the book, I described how a sewing machine works. The needle makes a hole through the garment, and pushes a loop of thread through it. The bobbin's rotation enables the notch on it to snag the loop, and causes it to be pulled round the bobbin, which contains a separate lower thread. One end of this thread comes from the garments—it has already between stitched into them, but the other end of the thread is free—it is wound round the bobbin. After the loop comes up on the other side of the bobbin, the needle is moving upwards and so it drags the loop containing the lower thread up from the bobbin, so that the thread is pulled up against the underside of the garments. And the whole cycle is ready to repeat.

This account describes the causal mechanism—down to the level of simple mechanical actions—of a modern sewing machine. If you look back at the description, you'll see that it contains a number of verbs that express causation either explicitly, as in *make* and *cause*, or implicitly, as in *push* and *pull*. Hume wrote: "All reasonings concerning matters of fact seem to be founded on the relation of Cause and Effect". His claim seems plausible, but not everyone agrees, and some authors have even argued that there's no such thing as causation. The concept, they say, is incoherent. Yet, it is built into so many verbs, such as *push* and *pull*, that its incoherence seems improbable.

A parallel exists between causal relations and deontic relations, i.e., those that concern obligatory and permissible actions. If one event *causes* another, then the occurrence of the first event makes the second event a physical necessity. If one action *obligates* another, then the occurrence of the first action makes the second action a moral necessity. Physical and moral necessity differ in meaning. A physical necessity is bound to occur, but a moral necessity is not bound to occur—individuals have been known to fail to carry out their obligations. A sentence such as, "It must happen", is ambiguous between the two meanings. The language of causation is close, though not identical, to the language of obligation.

What do causal and deontic propositions mean? Those are the puzzles that I hope to elucidate in order to explain our reasoning with them. Causes, which are the topic of the first half of the chapter, can be actions, events, or mere states of affairs—as Benjamin Franklin wrote, "for want of a nail the shoe was lost". Obligations, which are the topic of the second half of the chapter, concern possible and permissible states of affairs.

* * *

Our everyday beliefs about causation *are* sometimes incoherent. We assume that we can initiate a causal chain. We serve in tennis; our opponent returns the ball; and we play to and fro until the rally ends. We serve again, and so on. Each serve is the start of a causal chain, which ends when the point is decided. Likewise, a typical psychological experiment has a series of "trials". On some trials, the experimenter presents us, say, with a cup of tea in which the milk was poured in first, and on other trials, she presents us with a cup of tea in which the milk was poured in second, we taste the tea and try to identify whether the milk went in first or second. Each trial is a separate causal chain; and the experimenter is interested in whether we can tell the difference between the two sorts of tea. Nature too can intervene to initiate and end a causal chain. A child is flying a kite, when a gust of wind snaps the string, and the kite plunges to the ground. The notion of an intervention initiating a causal chain seems sensible. In contrast, however, we often assume that every event has a cause. The screen on our computer flickers and goes dead. We infer that something has gone wrong: perhaps, the battery is dead and needs to be re-charged. But, if every event has a cause, then an action that appears to start a causal chain has a cause itself, and so it is not the start of the chain. This view leads us back to the origins of the universe, which is the uncaused cause that initiated all causal chains. But, if a tennis player, a psychologist, and a gust of wind, can all initiate causal chains, then we are treating each of the initiating actions as causeless. We cannot have it both ways: either we can initiate a causal chain or else every event has a cause. However, these are tacit assumptions about causation, and should not be confused with the meaning of the term, which I will analyze in a moment. When we think about the start of a causal chain, we discount its previous causes for the sake of simplicity.

The initiation of a causal chain, or an *intervention* for short, is sometimes said to have its own special logic. But, as an example, consider the causal claim that overeating causes indigestion. Granted its truth, if we were to observe that Phil didn't have indigestion, then we'd infer that he hadn't overeaten. But, suppose that Phil had made an intervention: he took a pill that prevented indigestion. Now, we would no longer infer from his lack of indigestion that he hadn't eaten too much. His intervention initiated a new causal chain that negates the effects of overeating. No special logic is required, but just our ability to understand the premises:

Overeating causes indigestion.

Taking an indigestion pill prevents indigestion.

and to realize—as in the case of modulation—that the second premise takes precedence over the first.

* * *

A proposition, such as:

The use of the fertilizer will cause the plants to grow

makes a claim about a particular causal relation. It is equivalent to the conditional proposition:

If the fertilizer is used then the plants will grow.

That is to say, the meaning of both sentences is consistent with the same three possibilities: the fertilizer is used and the plants grow, the fertilizer is not used and the plants don't grow, and the fertilizer is not used but the plants grow anyway. What is impossible according to both propositions is that the fertilizer is used and the plants don't grow. So, use the fertilizer, and there's just one possibility: the plants must grow.

When the outcome is known, the claim is direct:

The use of the fertilizer caused the plants to grow.

The corresponding conditional is "counterfactual" in the sense that I discussed in the previous chapter:

If the fertilizer hadn't been used then the plants wouldn't, or mightn't, have grown.

The facts are that the fertilizer was used and the plants did grow, whereas the counterfactual possibilities are that the fertilizer wasn't used and the plants didn't grow or they grew for some other reason. What wasn't possible was that the fertilizer was used and the plants didn't grow.

This analysis is not original. Hume made much the same claim when he wrote: "We may define a cause to be *an object followed by another, and where all the objects, similar to the first, are followed by objects similar to the second. Or in other words, where, if the first object had not been, the second never had existed.*" Why then does the present account of causation not end here? The answer in a word is: complications.

* * *

The fact that causal claims can be paraphrased in conditionals does not imply that all conditionals express causal claims. The reason is that modulation allows conditionals to express a variety of different sorts of proposition. You might suppose that the preceding analysis uses conditionals in their logical meaning in which they are compatible with three possibilities. A normal constraint, however, is that an effect does not precede its cause. This temporal constraint allows a cause to be contemporaneous with its effect—squeezing the toothpaste tube occurs at the same time as the toothpaste comes out of the tube. Hume in his *Treatise on Human Nature* argued that the cause precedes the effect, and rejected contemporaneity. But, he declared that the matter was of no great importance. Yet, a causal interpretation of a sentence such as *the moon causes the tides*, from the standpoint of Newton's theory of gravitation, calls for instantaneous action at a distance. Modern quantum mechanics also calls for action at a distance. And physicists and philosophers go a step further when they discuss time travel and assert that a present event caused a past event. Yet the temporal constraint seems to be true for everyday factual propositions.

When we see one billiard ball bump into another, and knock it away, the right timing yields an irresistible impression that the first ball caused the second one to move. Yet, our concept of causation is much broader and more abstract than the perceptions of billiard balls bouncing off each other. A cause doesn't need to bump into its effect. We can assert, for example, that Pat's rudeness caused Viv to lose her temper, without having to imagine a chain of events contiguous in space and time leading from the cause to the effect. There may be such a chain, that is, a causal *mechanism* linking the two, but, as we'll see, its existence is not part of the everyday meaning of causal propositions.

* * *

The claim that a cause causes an effect is compatible with three temporally constrained possibilities:

cause	effect
no cause	effect
no cause	no effect

Given the cause, as Kant argued, the effect is therefore necessary. But, another sort of causal relation exists in life. Public television in the USA often transmits the message, "This program was made possible by viewers like you". It means, not that the viewers made the program—that is, caused it to come into existence—but that they enabled it to be made. The relation is therefore one in which one state enables another to occur. Hence, the proposition:

Keeping to this diet will enable (or allow) you to lose weight

means, not that the diet will cause you to lose weight, but rather that it will make it possible for you to lose weight. You could also lose weight even if you didn't keep to the diet. In other words, all cases are possible: you could lose weight or not, regardless of whether you kept to the diet or not. Often, however, we mean that you won't lose weight unless you follow the diet. In this stronger sense, the proposition is more informative. It is compatible with just three possibilities, but a different set from those of a causal claim:

enabler	effect
enabler	no effect
no enabler	no effect

With a cause the effect is necessary; with an enabler it is possible.

The two concepts can be defined in terms of one another. If *light causes the alarm to ring* then *light doesn't allow the alarm not to ring*. Likewise, if *light allows the alarm to ring* then *light doesn't cause the alarm not to ring*, i.e., it doesn't prevent it from ringing. These definitions work because buried inside necessity and possibility are appeals to "all" and "some": an event is necessary if it holds in all possible states, and it is possible if it holds in at least one such state. And "all" and "some" are interdefinable: *all A are B* means that *it is not the case that some A are not a B*, and *some A are B* means that *it is not the case that all A are not B*.

The proposition that a diet causes you to lose weight is a weak causal relation in that there are other ways in which you can lose weight. You can take regular exercise, for example. Sometimes, however, a causal proposition is stronger in that it picks out a unique cause, as in: drinking too much alcohol causes you to get drunk. Alcohol is sufficient to make you drunk, but it is also necessary: there is no other way to get drunk as far as I know. We understand propositions about causes and enabling conditions, but we cannot hold in mind all the possibilities consistent with them. The model theory postulates that both sorts of proposition have the same salient mental model—in which the cause or enabler and the effect occur. One consequence is that we have difficulty in distinguishing between the two. Likewise, many theorists, beginning with the nineteenth century philosopher John Stuart Mill, have denied that there is any difference in meaning between causes and enabling conditions. Modern accounts offer all sorts of other distinctions between them: the cause is an unusual state and the enabling condition is the usual state, the cause is inconstant, whereas the enabling state is constant, the cause violates a norm, whereas the enabling condition does not, and so on. Why have theorists followed Mill on this matter? The answer, I suspect, is that it is hard to bear in mind the five different possibilities referred to in descriptions of how a cause and an enabler work together to bring about an effect (see Box 22.1 below), and all too easy to think of cases of two joint causes.

Nevertheless, experiments have shown that we have some sensitivity to the difference between causes and enabling conditions. We tend to list different possibilities for them, in line with the theory. We take a statement of the form, *A will cause B*, to rule out as impossible a case in which *A* occurred but *B* did not, whereas we take a statement of the form, *A will allow B*, to be compatible with this possibility—if it rules out anything, it is the possibility that *B* occurred in the absence of *A*. Hence, we should draw different deductive conclusions from the two sorts of claim. And an experiment corroborated this prediction too. Given the premises:

> Eating protein will cause her to gain weight.
>
> She will eat protein.

the participants tended to draw the conclusion: She will gain weight. But, as the theory predicts, they tended not to draw this conclusion from the premises:

> Eating protein will allow her to gain weight.
>
> She will eat protein.

In contrast, given the premises:

> Eating protein will allow her to gain weight.
>
> She won't eat protein.

the participants tended to draw the conclusion: She won't gain weight. But, they tended not to draw this conclusion from the premises:

> Eating protein will cause her to gain weight.
>
> She won't eat protein.

We rely on mental models of causal relations, which represent the salient possibilities, just as they do for conditionals. One consequence is that we should succumb to illusory inferences from certain causal premises. A sentence of the form, *A causes B*, has one explicit mental model that represents the case in which *A* and *B* occur; and a sentence of the form, *A prevents B*, has one explicit mental model that represents the case in which *A* occurs and *B* does not occur. Hence, premises of the form:

A prevents B.

B causes C.

yield explicit mental models of two possibilities. In one possibility, *A* occurs, and *B* and *C* do not. In the other possibility, *A* does not occur, but *B* and *C* do occur. Hence, we should infer that *A* prevents *C*. In an experiment using sensible everyday contents, the participants did indeed make this inference. But, it is an illusion: *C* could have a cause other than *B*, and so when *A* occurs this other cause could still bring about *C*. The control problem for this illusion was of the form:

A causes B.

B prevents C.

In this case, it does follow that *A* prevents *C*, and the participants drew this conclusion too. The experiment examined a variety of these matching pairs of problems, and showed that the participants succumbed to the illusions, but were accurate in reasoning from their controls.

* * *

A strange thing happened in the twentieth century. Theorists proposed that causation is a probabilistic notion. Some general claims, such as: *smoking causes smoke*, are true, but other general claims, such as: *smoking causes cancer*, are not strictly true. Not everyone who smokes gets cancer. Smokers, I have noticed, stand ready to name exceptions. The philosopher Hans Reichenbach did not reject these generalizations as false, but instead postulated that causation is probabilistic. The proposition that *smoking causes cancer,* he would have claimed, means that the probability of cancer given that a person smokes is greater than the probability of cancer given that a person doesn't smoke. But, there is more to the meaning of causation than this difference between two conditional probabilities. Consider the preposterous idea that lung cancer causes us to smoke. The probability of smoking given that a person has lung cancer is greater than the probability of smoking given that a person doesn't have lung cancer. Yet, we don't infer that lung cancer causes smoking. Nevertheless, many philosophers and psychologists have followed in Reichenbach's path. But his view would have astonished Hume, who took causation to mean a constant conjunction of cause and effect, and it would have astonished

Kant and Mill, who took causation to imply a necessary connection. We can paraphrase a causal claim in this way: *If a person smokes then there must be smoke*. Are we to assume that "must" has a probabilistic interpretation? The assumption would infect our moral duties with a dangerous probabilistic qualification. If you lend me money then I *must* pay it back to you. How convenient for the dissolute borrower if his obligation is only probable.

The probabilistic approach might be justifiable for scientific conceptions of causation in quantum mechanics. But, it is implausible as an account of everyday causation. Three strands of evidence count against it. One strand is that we interpret causal propositions to mean that certain states are impossible. For instance, experiments have shown that given the sentence: *Running the new application will cause the computer to crash*, participants tend to list as impossible the case in which the new application is run and the computer does not crash. This result is contrary to a probabilistic theory, which allows that all cases are possible: it is their probabilities that matter. The use of claims about particular events might have discouraged probabilistic interpretations, but a replication showed the same effect for general causal claims.

A second strand of evidence comes from the inferences that I described earlier. Given premises such as: Eating protein will cause her to gain weight, and she will eat protein, we tend infer that she will gain weight. The inference is unwarranted if the first premise states a probability—unless the probability is 100 percent. But, if we assume this probability in the case of a novel causal relation, then the probabilistic analysis is superfluous.

A third strand of evidence is summarized in Box 22.1. It shows that probabilistic accounts have no obvious way to draw a distinction between causes and enabling conditions. Yet, we make this distinction in the meanings of the two relations, and the difference in turn affects which conclusions we infer. Why do we so often assent to causal generalizations to which we know there are exceptions? One reason may be that we treat them as useful idealizations, like the earlier example: *striking a match properly causes it to light*. We are aware that many causes in everyday life yield their effects only if unknown enabling conditions are present and disabling conditions are absent. Hence, when we assert generalizations, such as, *smoking causes cancer*, we are asserting that smoking causes cancer in some people. It is a way of speaking akin to other sorts of generalization, such as: *all food in Italy is good*, or *everyone is wearing pink this season*. Another reason for our causal generalizations is that we often induce them from probabilistic data. Scientists record co-occurrences between events, sometimes to test conjectures, sometimes to induce causal laws. Probabilities are useful in capturing

---

Box 22.1 Probabilities cannot distinguish between causes and enabling conditions

1. Suppose you observe the frequencies of various events depending on the occurrence of sunlight, the use of fertilizer, and the growth of plants. And suppose further that each of the following five possibilities occurs equally often, say, twenty occurrences each in 100 observations:

sunlight	fertilizer	growth	20
sunlight	no fertilizer	growth	20
sunlight	no fertilizer	no growth	20
no sunlight	fertilizer	no growth	20
no sunlight	no fertilizer	no growth	20

2. The probability of growth given sunlight ($40/60 = 2/3$) is greater than the probability of growth without sunlight ($0/40 = 0$).

3. The probability of growth given fertilizer ($20/40 = 1/2$) is greater than the probability of growth without fertilizer ($20/60 = 1/3$).

4. Hence, on a probabilistic analysis both sunlight and fertilizer are causes, and sunlight is the stronger candidate. Yet, from a description of these possibilities, such as: *if there is sunlight, the plants grow if the fertilizer is used, but if there is no sunlight then the plants do not grow even if the fertilizer is used*, we should judge sunlight to be the condition that enables the fertilizer to cause the growth.

5. The table above presents all the information necessary for assessing any probability about the domain. Hence, a probabilistic theory obliterates the distinction in meaning between causes and enabling conditions.

---

the relation between co-occurring events, so that we can induce causes from data.

* * *

A causal mechanism, as the example of the sewing machine shows, is nothing more than a set of further causal relations interpolated in the chain from cause to effect. You could ask for the mechanism underlying the simple physical effects of the bobbin on threads, and I could refer you to mechanical principles. You could ask for the mechanism underlying them, and so on.

But, there cannot be causes all the way down, any more than the earth can be supported by a turtle, which is supported by a turtle, and so on with turtles all the way down. Hence, some causal relations have no underlying causal mechanisms, but just happen. It follows that when we make a causal claim, its meaning does not imply the existence of a causal mechanism. An analogous argument can be made about so-called causal "powers"—the idea that some things have a power to bring about effects. As Hume anticipated, no one has succeeded in formulating a satisfactory definition of a causal power that does not presuppose the concept of causality.

When we can think of a causal mechanism, it tends to override data about the frequencies of events both in experiments and in life. This tendency can mislead us. For example, noxious miasmas were thought to be the cause of cholera and other diseases. The mechanism was obvious: you breathed in the bad air, and it infected you by contagion. Likewise, for far too long, maternal rejection was thought to be the cause of autism. It was a plausible mechanism—even parents of autistic children could think of instances in which they had neglected their children. These erroneous mechanisms are compelling, because they can be eliminated only by careful scientific investigation. The overthrow of the miasma theory is a topic to which I return in the penultimate chapter of the book.

* * *

One practical puzzle that the present account resolves is the problematic role of enabling conditions in the law. Causation lies at the heart of the law because those who cause harm to others are liable to punishment or to pay damages. In the past, legal theorists have agreed with John Stuart Mill that the difference between causes and enabling conditions is unprincipled and capricious, and so it is often overlooked or blurred in legal judgments. Consider this case:

> The defendant, a builder, negligently left open an unguarded lift shaft, and a young lad knowing that the lift was not there impersonated the lift attendant and invited the plaintiff to step into it. Did the builder cause the plaintiff's resulting injuries?

The court decided that the free action of a third party, the young lad, blocked the causal connection, and so the builder was not liable for damages.

A contrasting case concerned US gun manufacturers:

> The defendants, the manufacturers of guns, negligently oversupplied shops in states with weak gun laws. Criminals came into possession of these guns and murdered relatives of the plaintiffs. Did the defendants cause the homicides?

The court decided that at least some of the defendants were the cause of the homicides, and so they were liable for damages. (The court held that they were the "proximate cause" of the homicides. The phrase is used in common law, but quite what it means puzzles legal scholars.) In both cases, the defendants *enabled* the harmful events to occur. The builder's negligent action enabled the boy to cause the accident. The gun manufacturers' negligent actions enabled the criminals to murder their victims. It is a pity that the law of tort in the English-speaking world has no conception that those whose negligence enables harm to occur, as well as those who cause the harm, should be liable to pay damages. Instead, as in the case about guns, courts strain to find a cause where only an enabling action occurred.

* * *

If your serve in tennis touches the net cord, you're obligated to serve again. It's a rule of tennis. Is it your moral duty to serve again? It seems odd to say so. But, if your desire to win Wimbledon leads you to cheat, then you have infringed a moral code, if not the laws of the game. If you go to Wimbledon as a spectator then you ought to see a match on the Centre Court. It's not a rule or a moral obligation, but a recommendation. And if you go to the Centre Court to see the finals of the Championship, you ought to have a ticket. It's a moral and a legal obligation. You will be the defendant in a criminal prosecution if the authorities discover that you got in without one. These uses of "ought" are all deontic. What differs among them are the principles to which the verb makes a tacit appeal—from the rules of tennis to the criminal laws of Britain. I am now going to consider the foundations of deontics, and I aim to show that underlying the puzzling variety of deontic topics are simple concepts.

* * *

Logicians have developed deontic logics based on the two central concepts of obligation and permissibility. Like their parallels in the causal domain—causes and enabling conditions, they depend on the concepts of necessity and possibility. What we're obligated to do, we have a moral necessity to do. And what we're permitted to do, we have a moral possibility of doing. But, a crucial difference exists: what is necessary in the causal domain *is* the case; but what is obligatory in the deontic domain may not be the case, because we may fail to meet our obligations. The two deontic concepts, like the two causal concepts, can be defined in terms of one another. If we're *obligated* to leave, then it's not permissible for us not to leave. Likewise, if we're *permitted* to leave, then we're not obligated not to leave.

The model theory postulates that possibilities are central to reasoning, and so a simple extrapolation is that deontic propositions concern deontic possibilities, i.e., permissible states. Each model of a deontic proposition represents either a permissible or in some cases an impermissible state. If one action is common to all models of what is permissible, then it is obligatory. Some deontic propositions are categorical, such as Kant's categorical imperative: *act according to a maxim that you can will to become a general law*. But, many propositions state a relation between possible and permissible states: *if your serve hits the net cord then you must serve again*.

* * *

Children begin to understand deontic utterances at a young age, and most of them start to make such utterances before they are three years old. They tend to learn what they should *not* do earlier than what they should do, and this observation yields a prediction about adult reasoning that I'll get to in due course.

A proposition such as:

Earning a salary obligates you to pay taxes

is compatible with three states in which the first item in each state is a possibility and the second item is what's permissible:

Possible states	Permissible states
earning salary	pay taxes
not earning salary	pay taxes
not earning salary	not pay taxes

You may remember that models always have some sort of epistemic status. They call for a labeling system that our mental processes are sensitive to. I won't label the models any further in this chapter, but you should bear in mind their status. You should also bear in mind that in many cases the first state in a deontic model is both possible and permissible. Alas, this status is not universal, and an example such as, *fiddling his taxes obligates him to confess*, has an initial state that is possible but not permissible.

The theory postulates that mental models do not represent all the possible and permissible states that a deontic proposition refers to. Our mental models of a proposition, such as: *Earning a salary obligates you to pay taxes*, make most salient this case:

earning salary   pay taxes

...

The ellipsis denotes other cases in which one doesn't earn a salary. The next most salient case is what's not permissible: earning a salary and not paying taxes. Prohibitions are similar in that a prohibition is an obligation not to do something, but their mental models make most salient the case that is *not* permissible. Hence, a proposition such as:

Paying taxes prohibits you from taking a pension

has a mental model conjoining a possibility with what is not permissible (italicized here):

paying taxes   *taking pension*

The next most salient model is of the permissible case:

paying taxes   not taking pension

The mental models of a statement of permission also represent the action that renders a state of affairs permissible, but we know that other situations in which the action occurs are also possible. Experiments have corroborated these claims, and the first state that the participants thought of corresponded to the first explicit mental model of the various propositions.

* * *

Once propositions have been represented in mental models, the usual principles of the model theory apply. We can draw conclusions that correspond to novel relations in the resulting models. Consider, for instance, how we might draw a conclusion from these premises:

Earning a salary obligates you to pay taxes.

Paying taxes prohibits you from taking a pension.

The principles summarized earlier in the book (in Box 8.2) can be extended to deal with permissible and impermissible states. They yield a salient mental model of the two premises:

earning salary   paying taxes   *taking pension*

in which the italics indicate an impermissible state of affairs. Hence, the premises yield the conclusion:

Earning a salary prohibits you from taking a pension.

Complete models of the same premises, which I spare you, yield the same conclusion, and so it is valid.

A contrasting inference is based on premises of this sort:

> Taking a pension prohibits you from paying taxes.
>
> Paying taxes obligates you to earn a salary

The initial mental model of the first premise is:

> taking pension   *paying taxes*

and this model can be updated according to the second premise as follows:

> taking pension   *paying taxes*   *earning salary*

This model yields the invalid conclusion:

> Taking a pension prohibits you from earning a salary.

Because the model of the first premise concerns what's forbidden, whereas the model of the second premise does not, we might construct a model of what's permissible from the first premise:

> taking pension   not paying taxes

and then update this model according to the second premise to yield two mental models:

> taking pension   not paying taxes
>
>   paying taxes   earning salary

These models don't support the previous conclusion, but instead yield the conclusion:

> Taking a pension permits you not to earn a salary.

This conclusion, unlike the previous one, is a valid inference from the premises. But, inferences based on multiple models are harder, and may defeat us. In an experiment, the participants drew their own conclusions in their own words, and they tackled sixteen logically distinct problems. Their conclusions, right or wrong, corroborated the model theory, which predicted ninety-one percent of their responses. Problems that elicit multiple models, such as the previous example, ought to elicit more responses of the form, "nothing follows", because it is hard for us to determine what conclusion, if any, holds in multiple models. The results also corroborated this prediction: the response "nothing follows" occurred for thirty-one percent of the multiple-model problems but only for two percent of the one-model problems.

Is there any way to clinch the claim that we use mental models in deontic reasoning? Consider the problem:

You are permitted to carry out only one of the following actions:

Action 1: Take the apple or the orange, or both.

Action 2: Take the pear or the orange, or both.

Are you permitted to take the orange?

You are allowed to carry out either action 1 or else action 2, but not both. The mental models of action 1 represent what it is permissible to take:

Apple

       Orange

Apple   Orange

They support the conclusion that it is permissible to take the orange. Likewise, the mental models of action 2 support the same conclusion. Hence, if we use mental models, then we should respond: "Yes, I'm permitted to take the orange". However, the response is an illusion. If we were to take the orange then we would have carried out both action 1 and action 2, contrary to the rubric that we are permitted to carry out only one of them. Unlike mental models, the *complete* models of the problem take into account that when one action is permissible the other action is not. These models show that two states are permissible: you either take the apple alone, or else you take the pear alone. Hence, you cannot take the orange, and so the correct response to the problem is: "No".

A simple control problem for the illusion has the same premises, but poses the question:

Are you permitted to take the pear?

The mental models of action 2 yield the answer: "yes", and this answer is correct. Hence, reasoners should be correct even if they fail to consider that if they carry out one action, they must not carry out the other action.

The participants in an experiment carried out two illusory and two control problems. They made many more correct responses to the control problems (ninety percent) than to the illusions (seven percent): 229 of the participants performed better with the control problems than with the illusory problems, eight did equally well, and just three performed worse with the control problems than the illusory problems.

I have reported other studies of illusory inferences earlier in the book. It has been difficult to find an effective antidote to them, other than to teach participants to consider both what is true and what is false in the case of factual propositions. Deontic reasoning, however, offers a possibility for an effective antidote. Problems couched in terms of prohibitions should lead participants to think about what is forbidden, because the salient mental model represents this case. This problem is equivalent to the illusory problem above:

> You are prohibited from carrying out more than one of the following actions:
>
> Action 1: To take the apple or the orange, or both.
>
> Action 2: To take the pear or the orange, or both.
>
> Are you permitted to take the orange?

Reasoners should construct the mental models of what it is *impermissible* to take:

Apple   Pear

      Orange

As these models show, it is not permissible to take the orange, and so the participants should make the correct response, "No". It follows that prohibitions should reduce illusory inferences.

The corresponding control problem couched in terms of *prohibits* has the preceding premises, but the question is:

> Are you permitted to take the pear?

The mental models of what is impermissible do not include the state of taking the pear alone, and so reasoners should make the right response, "Yes". But, the task should be harder than a control problem based on *permits*, which yields a model that represents the permissibility of taking the pear. Hence, the model theory predicts that illusory problems should yield a better performance with *prohibits* than with *permits*, but control problems should yield a better performance with *permits* than with *prohibits*.

An experiment corroborated these predictions. Illusory problems yielded a better performance with *prohibits* than *permits* (an improvement of twenty-eight percent in accuracy), whereas the opposite was true for the control problems (a decline of thirty-seven percent in accuracy). Hence, although the verb *prohibits* alleviated the illusions, it did so at a cost of impairing performance with the control problems.

You may suspect that illusory inferences lead reasoners astray because the problems are unusual, unnatural, artificial. Reasoners assume that they are dealing with normal discourse, not subtle problems that are deceptive. Your criticism seems plausible, but it doesn't withstand scrutiny. For example, the participants do very well with the control problems, which are based on the same premises, and ask a similar question. The theory of mental models predicts both inaccurate performance with the illusory inferences and accurate performance with the control inferences. It also predicts that the illusions should be reduced for problems couched in terms of prohibitions.

You won't be too surprised to learn that alternative theories of deontic reasoning exist. Some of them are based on formal rules of inference; others are based on rules with a specific content or on the invocation of innate "modules" in the mind that are specialized for reasoning about cheating—the view of the evolutionary psychologists, which I discussed earlier (in Chapter 18). These theories were advanced to explain performance in the selection task—the task in which participants have to select evidence pertinent to establishing violations of general principles. This task has skewed theories of deontic reasoning so that many of them tend not to consider any other sort of reasoning. The observations that I have described in the present chapter therefore present a challenge to these other theories. They need to account for the meanings of modal terms, for the salience of some permissible situations over others, and for the occurrence of illusory inferences. This last problem is severe for theories based on general rules. If the rules yield only valid conclusions, they cannot account for illusory inferences; if they yield invalid conclusions, they run the risk of internal inconsistency.

* * *

A rational deontic system, whether it is the rules of a game such as soccer, common law, or an ethical system, should at the very least be founded on consistent principles. Granted a viable system of valid reasoning, these principles yield deontic conclusions. They may fail to do so in certain cases if the principles don't cover every eventuality, but they should not lead to conflicts about what is permissible or obligatory. In fact, no matter how hard we try, it is almost impossible for us to devise consistent and complete deontic principles. The rules of many games are incomplete. For example, once in the World Cup Soccer competition, English fans complained about the size of the German goal-keeper's gloves. The rules of soccer, alas, have nothing to say about the goal-keeper's gloves, though the rules are at least consistent and free from paradox. Legal systems are not. An English judge, Lord Halsbury, made the prudent remark:

> A case is only authority for what it actually decides. I entirely deny that it can be quoted for a proposition that may seem to follow logically from it. Such a mode of reasoning assumes that the law is necessarily a logical code, whereas every lawyer must acknowledge that the law is not always logical at all.

In Joseph Heller's great novel, *Catch-22*, the protagonist Captain Yossarian is a bombardier flying missions in World War II in Italy (just as Heller himself had done). His tent-mate Orr is driven insane by combat, and insanity is grounds for being excused from combat duty. As Heller writes:

> There was only one catch, and that was Catch-22, which specified that a concern for one's safety in the face of dangers that were real and immediate was the process of a rational mind. Orr was crazy and could be grounded. All he had to do was ask; and as soon as he did, he would no longer be crazy and he would have to fly more missions. Orr would be crazy to fly more missions and sane if he didn't, but if he was sane he had to fly them. If he flew them he was crazy and didn't have to, but if he didn't want to, he was sane and had to. Yossarian was moved very deeply by the absolute simplicity of this clause of Catch-22 and let out a respectful whistle.

The final irony in the novel is that Catch-22 doesn't exist, but everyone believes it does. That makes it worse, because there's no way to refute it.

Some aspects of the law are analogous to *Catch-22*. For example, in the case of Douglas v. The State of California (1963), a California rule gave indigents the right for counsel to represent them on appeal. But, this right was available only if the appeal court judged that the indigent's case had merit. The court had to decide whether the case had merit in order to allow the indigent to be represented while the court decided whether the case had merit. In Dobner v. Peters (a case heard in the Court of Appeal in New York, 1921), the court determined that infants maimed while a fetus had no cause for legal action. Thirty years later, the court reversed its decision. It determined that Dobner v. Peters was no longer good law, because its chief basis had been the lack of a precedent. However, there was now a precedent, namely, Dobner v. Peters.

In W.E. Bowman's spoof of a British mountaineering expedition, *The Ascent of Rum Doodle*, intrepid climbers tackle a little known mountain called Rum Doodle, which is 40,000 and one half feet tall. They aim to establish a base camp for two climbers at 39,000 feet. The book outlines their plan:

> The equipment for this camp had to be carried from the railhead at Chaikhosi, a distance of five hundred miles. Five porters would be needed for this. Two porters would be needed to carry the food for these five, and another would carry the food for these two. His food would be carried by a boy. The boy would carry his own food.

This sort of reasoning led the climbers to infer that the expedition as a whole would need 3000 porters and 375 boys. It also leads to rules, such as the one governing US income tax:

> If your employer pays your income tax, then this money is extra income for you. Hence, it is taxable. If your employer pays the tax on this extra amount, then that's

also income and so you must pay tax on it. If your employer pays this tax, then … and so on ad infinitum.

The series can be summed, however, and the amount of tax you owe turns out to be more than you would owe if you paid your own income tax.

* * *

We reason to determine the deontic status of an action. It may be permissible, obligatory, or forbidden. We also reason to determine whether we have broken a rule or violated a moral principle. Our reasoning has its limits, and it cannot always help us to resolve our competing obligations. We have a duty to look after our children, and we have a duty to be honest. Suppose that we don't have enough money to pay for a medical operation that is vital for one of our children, but then we find a criminal's cache of illegal money. We may be in a dilemma about whether to hand it in to the police or to keep it. We try to deal with these conflicts by reasoning. We think to ourselves, for instance:

> This is a massive amount of ill-gotten money and it's my duty to hand it over to the police. But, I could hand back all but the amount that I need for the operation. Where's the harm in that? The harm is that it's wrong, and I shouldn't do it. Yet, the money comes from criminals, so why shouldn't I defraud them of a small proportion that no one else needs? Because it's wrong. Yet I have a moral duty to look after my family, and that duty is more important than any other. If I fail to keep the money, my child will suffer and may even die, and it will be my responsibility.

Reasoning has led us to two incompatible conclusions. We all experience these conflicts, and authors from Plato to the creators of Tom and Jerry cartoons have depicted our struggles with them. If a valid system of reasoning starts from consistent premises, conflicts are impossible. To suppose that we are incapable of valid reasoning would be to posit chaos in our minds. Conflicts about what we ought to do therefore occur because our starting point is not a single consistent set of deontic beliefs, but rather, as in the case of causation, various incoherent intuitions and beliefs.

Sydney Smith, the eighteenth century wit and Anglican cleric, was walking through the city of a London with a friend. They came to a narrow street in which the upper stories of the houses on opposite sides leaned out close to each another, and from facing windows two women were screaming abuse at each other in a vicious argument. Smith remarked to his friend, "They'll never agree—they're arguing from different premises". In an argument between Buddha and Nietzsche, which Bertrand Russell imagined, the two of them also argued from different premises. Buddha's premise was that anyone's suffering was a matter for his concern; Nietzsche's premise was that the suffering of only certain individuals was a matter for his concern. Because their premises were different, as Russell pointed out, their conflict could not be resolved in a rational way.

Most of us have a little bit of Buddha and a little bit of Nietzsche in our make up. Our arguments with ourselves proceed from principles that concern everyone and principles that concern certain special people in our lives. And so reasoning cannot always resolve our moral conflicts either. That may not be a bad thing. Some of the most frightening individuals are those who lead their lives guided by single unbending dogmas: Torquemada, Robespierre, Hitler, Pol Pot, Bin Laden.

Most of us have immediate moral intuitions deriving from unconscious inferences of the sort that I described in Part II of this book. These inferences are more rudimentary computations than those of conscious inferences. Intuitions themselves may not be free from conflict, and they can allow us to fudge our responsibility or to disengage our sense of morality from unpleasant actions that we have a duty to perform. When our intuitions are uniform, however, they may sway us from our reasoned decisions. Indeed, some authors treat them as prime movers in our moral judgments.

Psychologists, including some of my Princeton colleagues, have examined our moral intuitions. They have contrasted dilemmas in which we can act in an impersonal way like a bombardier dropping bombs with dilemmas in which we have to act like a soldier using an edged weapon in a bloody battle. An example of the first sort of dilemma is:

> A runaway trolley is about to run over and kill five people. You can hit a switch that will divert the trolley onto a different set of tracks where it will kill one person instead of five. Would you hit the switch?

Most people say, "yes". But, suppose the only way to save the five people is for you to push a person in front of the trolley, so that he is killed instead of the five. Would you do it? Most people say, "no". This difference may arise because our conscious moral reasoning can follow the Utilitarian maxim of "the greatest good for the greatest number". But, the thought of having to push someone to his death elicits an emotion, and it affects our decision. This difference showed up in a brain-imaging study: different regions of the brain were active when participants had to make the two sorts of decision. Indeed, our emotions may overwhelm our reasoned decisions or even pre-empt them, because they can elicit a response before we have finished reasoning.

My earlier example of the conflict between honesty and the money for a child's operation arises because our moral intuitions or conscious principles are inconsistent. Both alternatives have their emotional supports. However we resolve the conflict, we can infer that we were wrong. In one case, we have been dishonest and that is wrong; in the other case, we have sacrificed a child for our principles and that too is wrong. Either way, we may feel that we have done wrong.

* * *

The machinery for reasoning about causation and obligation seems to be the same as the machinery for reasoning about any other matters. We construct models, we derive conclusions from them, and, perhaps, we search for counterexamples to them—especially if others provide us with conclusions to evaluate. Hence, no special processes of causal or deontic reasoning appear to exist. It is business as usual. Yet, some aspects of these sorts of reasoning seem special. The assumptions from which we reason are fraught with conflicts, which may be more frequent than in other domains of reasoning. And moral decisions seem more likely to elicit emotions. What is worse, we have no systematic way to resolve our moral dilemmas. Conflict and emotion make deontic reasoning different from reasoning about Sudoku puzzles.

Chapter 23

Beliefs, Heresies, and Changes in Mind

As a child, Sir Edmund Gosse, the Edwardian man of letters, was raised as a member of a strict Christian sect. His father was the author of *Omphalos*, a critique of the theory of evolution, which argued that when God created the world, he included fossils, geological strata, tree rings, and many other entities such as Adam's navel (the title of the book is the Greek for navel), that were not a real record of the earth's origin. His father told young Edmund that the worse sin of all was idolatry. One day when Edmund was alone in the house, he put a chair on top of a desk, and bowed down and declared, "I worship thee, O chair". He expected to be struck down by lightning for his impiety. He looked out of the window. The sun continued to shine in the clear blue sky. And nothing happened.

What conclusion do you suppose that Edmund drew from this experience?

His religious faith was unaffected. But, as he later wrote, he concluded that his father might not be right about everything.

The leader of an American doomsday cult announced that the world was coming to end. On the appointed day, many of the faithful assembled to pray with her on a mountain top. The dread hour approached; it passed. And nothing happened.

What conclusion do you suppose that the faithful drew from this experience?

The leader announced that the world had been saved thanks to their prayers, and they became even more devout believers, and proselytized still harder on behalf of the movement. Only those who had not been on the mountain top showed a weakening in conviction.

You and I both see a chicken cross the road. And so we both believe that the chicken crossed the road. We know that our perceptions can be fallible, but the fact that we both witnessed the same event corroborates our mutual belief. But, a more potent source of beliefs is, not what we perceive, but what others tell us. We don't sacrifice our lives for a belief about something we saw. But, we might make this sacrifice for a belief based on the testimony of others. Vital testimony concerns faith as St. Paul described it: "the substance of things hoped for, the evidence of things unseen." Things unseen, by definition, cannot be overturned by observation. Indeed, some early Christians rejoiced in the impossibility of their beliefs. We believe, because others believe. Or, as William James remarked: "Our faith is faith in someone else's faith". If we want to create a religion, we should believe the testimony that we give and our disciples should be predisposed to believe us. We should be credible: they should be credulous. We can be as convincing as we like in trying to persuade them that there's a star made of cardboard, but who cares? Faith is about important matters. We need to provide a world-view that gives a reason for living, consolation for loss, and hopes for a live hereafter. St. Ignatius of Loyola, the founder of the Jesuit order, said: "Give me a child until he is seven and he is mine for life". So, we should start with young children. We should surround our novices with other convinced believers to provide emotional support and pressure to conform. We should isolate older novices from nonbelievers. We should give them a new name, a new identity, a new faith. This new faith should include symbolic rites that have an emotional significance. It should also threaten back-sliders with retribution.

We should promulgate a set of beliefs that are consistent, self-supporting, and impossible to refute. As an example, consider the central tenets of terrorist sects, whether they are Muslim, Jewish, or Christian:

- Our aim is to bring about a perfect world.
- Our land is sacred.
- We must protect it.
- Our enemies threaten it.
- We must kill them.
- They are Satan's followers.
- Their deaths purify the world.
- Our cause demands our sacrifice.
- Our sacrifice is our highest goal.
- We will get our reward in heaven.

The spread of a world-view begins in a sect. A successful sect becomes a religion. An unsuccessful sect becomes a heresy. Its failure seldom depends on a failure of faith, but on the power of the orthodoxy. The heterodox will lay down their lives for the heresy. To those outside the battle of beliefs, the differences don't seem to be a matter of life and death. Consider, for example, these different articles of faith:

Jesus was two persons, one divine and one human.

Jesus had two natures, one human and one divine.

Jesus had only one nature, and was divine.

Jesus had only one nature, and was a human agent for God.

There are many other views about the nature of Christ, but which of the above beliefs is orthodox, and which of them are heresies? If you are a Christian, you should know, but you can check the answer in the notes to the chapter. If you are not a Christian, you might wonder how anyone could have ascertained the correct view. The answer is human reasoning.

Heresies demonstrate the power of beliefs, because steadfast adherents die for their doctrines. In Medieval times, the greatest threat to the Catholic church was the Albigensian heresy. Its adherents lived in Languedoc in what is now the south-west corner of France, and they were known as Cathars. They had the Gnostic belief that the tangible world was the work of the devil, and so Jesus just seemed to have a human body. The true God was invisible. The Cathars tried to make themselves perfect moral beings. If they failed, they would be reincarnated again and again until they succeeded. Some "perfects" did exist, and they preached the path to sainthood.

The heresy threatened Catholicism, because it rejected the church's spiritual and temporal claims. Pope Innocent III declared a Holy war against the Cathars. It was the first Crusade. And in 1209 a Norman army swept down on Languedoc to deal with the Cathars. The army besieged the town of Béziers, a centre for the heresy, and demanded that the citizens hand over the perfects. The citizens refused to do so. When the siege was broken, the commander of the Norman army asked the Cistercian monk in charge of the crusade what to do. He is said to have replied, "Kill them all, God will know his own". In a morning's work, the Crusaders slaughtered some fifteen to twenty thousand men, women, and children. Both sides of the dispute were in thrall to religious beliefs. The Pope then created the Inquisition in order to extirpate the Cathars. It succeeded, but it took over a century until the heresy was dead.

Why are these untestable beliefs so powerful that those who hold them would sooner die than abandon them? The answer, I propose, depends on an unconscious transition to an emotion. The beliefs concern how we should live, the nature of death, and survival beyond it. These matters have an extraordinary capacity to invoke a basic emotion of attachment. We become attached to God the father and mother church. And basic emotions, as I argued earlier in the book, are created by the simple evaluations leading to unconscious transitions. Any challenge to these primeval beliefs is a deep threat, and it will be resisted.

We experience this consequence if we criticize any untestable ethos, whether it is a religious doctrine, a political view such as Marxism or laissez-fair capitalism, a moral proposition about euthanasia or vivisection, or even a scientific theory that has become a quasi-religion—as Oscar Wilde remarked, science is the history of dead religions. Its proponents have an emotional reaction. The threat can yield an unconscious transition to intense anger, and a rational interchange of ideas ceases to be possible.

So, what does it take for us to change our beliefs? Saul on the road to Damascus—with the intention to persecute Christians—was surrounded by a bright light, and heard the voice of Jesus admonishing him. He was blind for three days, and without food or drink. And then "the scales fell from his eyes", and he became Paul, the Christian Apostle. Beliefs about things unseen are exceptional.

* * *

Some beliefs to which we have an emotional tie *are* testable. And sometimes we persist with them regardless of the evidence. The dispassionate psychologist says that we have a stereotype. Suppose, for instance, that I believe that women are bad drivers. I may not be shaken from my conviction if you point out that insurance companies charge smaller premiums for women drivers than for men, because women have fewer accidents. Women, I might argue, don't drive as many miles as men, and so they are less often in accidents. Stereotypes about the sexes, races, and social groups, persist in the face of conflicting evidence. And some stereotypes have a logic that makes them hard to refute. I see a piece of bad driving; and I look to see the sex of the driver. If the driver is a woman, I say, "typical!" And my prejudice is strengthened. If the driver is a man, I say, "Well, some men are bad drivers too". So, what could I observe that might shake me from my stereotype? It isn't obvious. But, in fact, I have to observe women driving well. Good driving, however, is not so conspicuous as bad driving. The best evidence for the long-term quality of driving is actuarial; we are back to insurance premiums. They lack all conviction to shift a stubborn skeptic.

Our culture provides us with norms, and it can be hard for us to accept that they do things differently elsewhere. The bias is difficult to study in the psychological laboratory, but it is corroborated by many anthropological observations. A short distance in geography can be long way in culture. In Italy, a document called a "residenza" is an official register of where you live. It enables you to vote, to get a doctor in the national health system, to register your car, and to do much else besides. The author Tim Parks tried to explain to an Italian policeman that no document of this sort exists in the UK. They had this dialogue, which began with the policeman asking the question:

> So what do you do when you move?
>
> You move.
>
> And the registration plates on the car?
>
> You leave them as they are.
>
> And your identity card?
>
> There are no identity cards.
>
> And the doctor?
>
> You go and register at the nearest doctor's office.

He didn't believe Parks: moving couldn't be that easy.

Another mechanism that protects our beliefs from revision is the way we reason. Ask yourself, for example, what follows from these premises:

> All the Frenchmen in the restaurant are gourmets.
>
> Some of the gourmets are wine-drinkers.

Most people draw the conclusion:

> Some of the Frenchmen in the restaurant are wine-drinkers.

It's a plausible conclusion, because it fits our stereotype about Frenchmen. But, now ask yourself what follows from these premises:

> All the Frenchmen in the restaurant are gourmets.
>
> Some of the gourmets are Italians.

You're unlikely to infer that some of the Frenchmen are Italians.

Experiments have corroborated this difference, and the model theory predicts it. In the first case, we construct a model of the premises that yields the conclusion: some of the Frenchmen are wine drinkers. The conclusion is credible, and so we make the inference without noticing that it's invalid. In the second case, we construct an analogous model and it yields the conclusion that some of the Frenchmen are Italians. The conclusion is preposterous, notwithstanding the existence of the European Union, and so we search harder for a counterexample in which it doesn't hold. We find one: the gourmets who are French could be distinct from the gourmets who are Italian. This model refutes our conclusion, and so we do not draw it. Of course, a similar model rebuts our conclusion in the first example: the gourmets who are French are distinct from the gourmets who are wine-drinkers. But, we never looked for this counterexample, because we were satisfied with our initial conclusion. In general, we search harder for counterexamples to incredible conclusions than for counterexamples to credible conclusions. Hence, our method of reasoning is liable to leave our strong beliefs unscathed by counterexamples even in those cases where they exist, though our beliefs can also make it difficult for us to construct a model in the first place.

* * *

We all harbor beliefs that resist revision; but we also have many beliefs that are easy to change. Consider this typical episode:

> I am sitting with Maria outside a pleasant café in Provence in Southern France. We know that Paolo and Vittorio went to get the car to pick us up. We also know that if they went to get the car then they should be back soon, because we left it just a short walk away up a hill. Ten minutes go by, and then another ten, with no sign of the car.

Something unexpected has happened: life, alas, has led to a conflict with a valid consequence of our beliefs. There is no doubting the facts of the matter. We inferred that they would be back soon; and they're not. So, something has to give. At the very least, our conclusion is false, and we must retract it. It was a valid consequence of our beliefs, so at least one of them must be false too. Either they didn't go to get the car, or if they did, then it doesn't take a few minutes to return.

A more pressing issue is what has gone wrong and what we should do. Should we go in search of them or remain where we are? The car is an old and comfortable Citroen. We suspect that Paolo and Vittorio may have had trouble in starting it, because it has been showing signs of its age. So, should we walk up the hill to help them? No, we decide, we should stay put, because if they do get the car started, they will come to the café to pick us up, and they may come by another route. We'd better be waiting for them outside the café. And if there is some other problem—perhaps a complex one-way system that has forced them out of the town, we had also better be waiting for them. So, our reasoning, based on, a few pieces of general knowledge, leads us to sit tight, admiring the view of Mont Sainte-Victoire and the chateau where Picasso used to live. Sure enough, after another ten minutes, the car comes spluttering into view. They had needed a tow to get it started.

The example is typical. An inconsistency occurs between our beliefs and an incontrovertible fact, and we are bound to modify our beliefs. The same sorts of inconsistency occur in science. We believe, say, that heat is a substance and that substances have weight. We heat an object, but discover that it is no heavier. We need to account for this inconsistency, and the solution calls for reasoning. We have to revise at least one of our beliefs. We also have to try to reason our way back to consistency. We need to make an abduction that resolves the inconsistency. Our reasoning is no mere academic exercise. It affects what we decide to do. These three steps—the detection of an inconsistency, the revision of beliefs, and the explanation of the inconsistency—provide the psychologist with an agenda for the study of changes in mind.

* * *

When we read a description of some events, we build a model of what happened. If at some point the description is inconsistent with our model of the situation, we may notice the discrepancy. Daniel Defoe's novel *Robinson Crusoe* describes the eponymous hero as stripping off his clothes and swimming out to his wrecked ship to rescue items of value. Not long after he's on board, Defoe has him "stuffing his pockets with biskit". But, if Crusoe is naked, he has no pockets. The literary critic John Sutherland noticed this inconsistency, and he has assembled several books of comic slips that occurred in well-known novels. A close reading of the Bible also reveals apparent inconsistencies. Genesis, for example, implies both that God created trees before man and that God created trees after man. Frank Kermode, the doyen of literary critics, has pointed out other trivial errors that novelists have made. Tolstoy muddled dates in *War and Peace*. Dickens, despite keeping careful memoranda about his characters, forgot the dog Diogenes in the final part of *Dombey and Son*. As Kermode remarks, gross inconsistencies occur in great literature, though sometimes they are used for literary effect. We need an eye of a hawk and an elephant's memory to detect them. Perhaps Sutherland adopted a critical attitude in which he made a deliberate search for them—I hope he did, because it would be awful to be unable to read in any other way. Kermode talks of the "abnormally close attention" with which literary scholars read.

We attend to consistency with varying success. Life is always surprising us, and a surprise is something inconsistent with our beliefs or their consequences. And it may be vital to change our mind in the light of a surprise. If our reasoning has been impeccable—and it may not have been, then at least one of our beliefs is false. Logic, alas, does not tell us which is the offending belief.

* * *

To say that a set of propositions is *consistent* means that it is possible for all of them to be true. As a corollary, a set of propositions is inconsistent if it is impossible for all of them to be true. A special case of inconsistency is a self-contradiction. Yogi Berra, the famous Yankee baseball player, specializes in utterances of this sort, such as, "I didn't really say everything I said". If a set of propositions is inconsistent, then at least one proposition in the set is false. And if we act on a false belief, disaster may follow.

In logic, inconsistency has drastic consequences: we can prove any proposition whatsoever starting from an inconsistency. Bertrand Russell dining at high table at Trinity College, Cambridge, encountered a skeptical enquirer, who asked him whether this consequence of contradictions was true. Russell replied that it was. In that case, the skeptic said, prove that I am the Pope from 1 + 1 = 1. And Russell said: You are one. The Pope is one. One plus one equals one, and so you and the Pope are one. A witty riposte, though the real proof that inconsistencies imply any proposition is a little more technical.

* * *

So far, you may have assumed that inconsistency occurs only when one proposition conflicts with another. But, it can also occur among a set of propositions in which no two propositions conflict. Here's a simple example:

> If Alan is at my party then Betty is too.
>
> If Betty is at my party then Chuck is too.
>
> Alan is at my party but Chuck isn't.

A moment's thought should convince you that the three propositions can't all be true, but any pair of them can be. We can replay this example with a thousand propositions or a million, with the proviso that as soon as we remove a single proposition, then the remaining 999 or 999,999 propositions, whatever they are, make up a consistent set.

The propositions asserted in this book are inconsistent. I thought it best to make this point to forestall my critics. The claim must be true, because if all other propositions in the book are consistent, then the claim itself is inconsistent with them, and therefore true. And if all the other propositions are themselves inconsistent, then the proposition is also true. The book contains thousands of simple propositions, such as "Tolstoy muddled dates in *War and Peace*", and the book asserts various relations among them. It is consistent if all these relations are true in at least one possibility. A hundred simple propositions yield zillions of possibilities, because each proposition can be either true or false. In the worst case, we might have to search through all these possibilities. The number seems innocuous, but it isn't. It is so vast that even if we could check each possibility in a millionth of a second, it would still take us over forty thousand million million years to check them all. Hence, tests of consistency are intractable. They make bigger and bigger demands on time and memory as the number of different simple propositions increases. Good luck with the test of whether the propositions in this book are consistent!

The intractability of a domain does not mean that every problem within it is impossible to solve. Small-scale problems are solvable both in our minds and in computers. One obvious economy is that our beliefs tend to be segregated into separate sets. Our beliefs, say, about Jesus are independent of our beliefs about the rules of tennis. (Now, of course, you do have a belief about both of them—a second-order belief that you don't have any first-order beliefs about both of them.) This segregation also allows us to maintain isolated but inconsistent world-views. Whole cultures seem to entertain such views; and we do too. I have met an experimental psychologist who believes in faith healing, an engineer who believes in ESP, and a physicist who believes in spoon bending. And who knows what strange agglomerations are to be found in your mind and mine? Perhaps the poet Walt Whitman was rejoicing in this multifariousness when he wrote: "Do I contradict myself? Very well I contradict myself..."

* * *

We notice glaring inconsistencies, but how do we detect more subtle ones? The evidence suggests that we use mental models. We search for a model of a possibility in which all the propositions are true. If we find such a model, then we evaluate the propositions as consistent; if we fail to find such a model, then we evaluate the propositions as inconsistent. Granted that we can deal with just a handful of propositions at most, one strategy is to start with a model of a possibility that satisfies the first proposition in a set, and then to check it against each successive proposition. If we encounter a proposition that rules out the possibility that we have in mind, then we start over. Box 23.1 illustrates the model theory's account of how we carry out the task, using a procedure that I have also implemented in a computer program.

Box 23.1 Tests of consistency using mental models of possibilities

1. The task is to decide whether or not a set of sentences is consistent. Given the following set of sentences describing fruit on a tabletop:

   If there isn't an apple then there is a banana.

   If there is a banana then there is a cherry.

   There isn't an apple and there is a cherry.

Box 23.1 *(continued)*

we construct a mental model of the salient possibility for the first sentence:

> no apple   banana

This model is compatible with the second sentence, which updates it:

> no apple   banana   cherry

This model is compatible with the third sentence, and so we judge that the sentences are consistent.

2. Given a set of sentences, logically equivalent to the first example:

> There is an apple or there is a banana, or both.
>
> There isn't a banana or there is a cherry, or both.
>
> There isn't an apple and there is a cherry.

we construct a mental model of the salient possibility for the first sentence:

> apple

The absence of a banana in this model is consistent with the second sentence, which updates the model:

> apple   no banana

This model is not consistent with the third sentence, and so we have to back up and to construct a new model of the first sentence:

> banana

which the second premise updates:

> banana   cherry

This model is compatible with the third sentence, which updates it:

> no apple   banana   cherry

The need to search for an alternative possibility predicts that this problem should be harder than the first one.

The evidence supports the account in the box. Participants in an experiment had to decide whether it was possible for all the sentences in a set to be true—to decide, in effect, whether the sentences were consistent. They were more accurate with sets of conditionals such as those in the box than with sets of disjunctions such as those in the box. This result suggests that they tried out one model at a time, and had to go back to search for an alternative model for the disjunctive problems. When the sentences were inconsistent, the task was a little harder, as the model theory also predicts, but the difference between the two sorts of problem narrowed. Another study corroborated the use of mental models by showing that the participants succumbed to illusory inferences. The problems had an initial rubric that made clear that one sentence was true and one sentence was false, e.g.:

> Only one of the following propositions is true:
>
> > The tray is heavy or elegant, or both.
> >
> > The tray is elegant and portable.
>
> The following proposition is definitely true:
>
> > The tray is elegant and portable.
>
> Write a description of the tray _____

The participants wrote a description if they evaluated the premises as consistent. As the mental models of the premises predict, they tended to judge that the premises were consistent in this case and to describe the tray as: *light, elegant, and portable*. In fact, the premises are inconsistent. If the tray were elegant and portable, both sentences in the initial disjunction would be true, contrary to the rubric that only one of them is true. In the experiment, the participants succumbed to the illusions, but performed well with control problems. They produced descriptions for the illusions and their controls that corresponded to the mental models of the propositions.

* * *

What should we do when we detect an inconsistency? In logic, a surprising fact is that if a conclusion follows from some premises, then no additional premises can ever undo the validity of its inference. In my earlier example, Maria and I made the valid deduction:

> Paolo and Vittorio have gone to get the car.
>
> If Paolo and Vittorio have gone to get the car then they will be back soon.
>
> Therefore, Paolo and Vittorio will be back soon.

What additional premise could invalidate this inference? You might think: well, the fact that Paolo and Vittorio are *not* back soon. But, no, the addition of this premise yields a contradictory set of premises, and in logic any conclusion whatsoever follows from contradictory premises. And so, of course, the conclusion above also follows from them. Hence, as we add new premises to an existing set, all that happens is that we can draw new conclusions. Logicians use some jargon for this fact. They say: logic is *monotonic*, because with each additional premise, further conclusions follow from the premises. Logic, not love, means never having to say sorry. We never have to retract anything.

In life, we are inclined to withdraw a conclusion if it runs into the ugly brick wall of an inconsistent fact. To use another term of art, our reasoning is *nonmonotonic*. We withdraw a previous conclusion, even if its inference is valid, in the light of a subsequent conflict with reality. The retraction of conclusions is pervasive in life, because events so often conspire to defeat our inferences. But, which of our beliefs do we give up?

In some cases, we can sidestep this question. We often reason from idealizations, such as: a dog has four legs. We take our idealizations to be true unless there are facts to the contrary. If there is a fact to the contrary—my dog Fido, for instance, has just three legs, we abandon the consequences in this case, but keep the idealization.

The inference about Paolo, Vittorio, and the car, did not depend on any default assumptions. Maria and I had no option but to revise our beliefs, and logic cannot tell us which premise we should retract. One of our premises was conditional: if Paolo and Vittorio have gone to get the car, then they will be back soon. The other was categorical: Paolo and Vittorio have gone to get the car. If we combine our conditional premise with the fact that they are not back soon, then it follows that they did not go to get the car. We could therefore retract our categorical premise. Another possibility, however, is that the conditional premise itself is false.

Beliefs differ in how *entrenched* they are. I have already talked about emotional investments in beliefs, and so I use the word "entrenchment" to refer solely to the intellectual basis for a belief, such as its coherence with other beliefs, the existence of reasons that support it, its probability, and so on. If one belief is less entrenched than others, perhaps we should abandon it in the face of a conflict. We can detect a weak belief of this sort. Suppose, for example, that Maria and I had known that Paolo and Vittorio were avid lepidopterists, and always rushing off to chase new butterflies to add to their collections. When they didn't return soon, we might have thought that they had seen an attractive butterfly and went in chase. We therefore give up our belief that they went to get the car. Psychologists have tested analogues of this idea in experiments, and corroborated their occurrence.

A similar effect occurs with general knowledge. On the whole, if we're faced with a choice of giving up a general principle or giving up a particular, but alleged, fact, then we abandon the alleged fact. We know that water freezes into ice. We have many reasons to believe this proposition. It fits with our other beliefs about winter, refrigerators, and mountaineering, and we have many observations to support it. Hence, if someone tells us: I froze some water, but it didn't turn into ice. We tend to doubt the claim that they froze water rather than the general principle that freezing water turns it into ice.

Is there perhaps an effect of the form of propositions? Some psychologists believe so. Suppose someone tells us:

> If it was raining then Pat went to the cinema.
>
> It was raining.

Given a conflict, because Pat didn't go to the cinema, which of these two propositions do we give up if they are equally entrenched? Suppose someone tells us:

> Either Viv was late or else she didn't go to the cinema.
>
> Viv wasn't late.

Given a conflict, because Viv did go to the cinema, which of these propositions do we give up? The psychological evidence suggests that we tend to give up the conditional in the first case, and the disjunction in the second case. What is odd, however, is that conditionals and disjunctions are consistent with more possibilities than categorical propositions, and so they have a greater probability of being true. One reason for our judgment may be that we believe that speakers are less likely to be wrong about simple categorical facts. Their truth can be a matter of observation rather than inference. Hence, categorical propositions have an aura of certainty lacking from more complex assertions about relations between propositions.

In sum, the entrenchment of a statement depends on its form, its meaning, and its relation to other knowledge. These effects do not ascribe any role to the reasoning processes through which we recognize and resolve inconsistencies. These processes, however, do have effects of their own.

* * *

Conflicts matter. In several experiments, participants rated their respective beliefs in pairs of propositions. They were then confronted with facts that were inconsistent with the consequences of the pairs, and they rated their beliefs again. Depending on the nature of the inconsistency, they often gave up the member of a pair that they had rated earlier as more believable. Entrenchment alone is no guide to the revision of beliefs.

I am going to describe a general "mismatch" principle that affects which proposition we abandon in the case of a conflict with a fact. If the fact is inconsistent with a single belief, then no matter how entrenched the belief is we should abandon it. We would go on oath that there's some milk in the refrigerator. We open the refrigerator and there's none. We may be very surprised, but we give up our belief. The case doesn't need experimental corroboration. But, subtler cases do. Suppose Pat, a friend of ours, tells us:

> If the President owns a villa and a swimming pool, then he owns a plane.

And another friend, Viv, tells us:

> The President owns a villa and a swimming pool.

But we know that the President does not own a plane. Our knowledge conflicts with a consequence of Pat and Viv's remarks. Which of the two speakers was wrong? Most participants in an experiment rejected Pat's assertion, and so perhaps they were biased against complex propositions. But, consider this different case:

> Pat says: The President owns a villa and a swimming pool, or else he owns a plane.

> Viv says: The President owns a villa and a swimming pool.

But, we know that the President owns a plane. Which of the two speakers is wrong? Now, most of the participants rejected Viv's assertion. No general bias against complicated propositions occurred, so what's going on?

The model theory predicts the responses, because we should be susceptible to illusory reasoning in this task too. When a proposition has at least one mental model that conflicts with the unequivocal fact, the proposition seems to "mismatch" the fact. There may be no real inconsistency, because a possibility not represented in the proposition's mental models may be compatible with the fact. But, to discover this possibility, we have to flesh out our mental models into complete models. We tend not do so, and so we doubt the proposition. In the first example above, the participants knew that the president does not own a plane, and this fact conflicts with the one explicit mental model of Pat's conditional proposition. This model represents that the President owns a villa, a swimming pool, and a plane.

In the second example, the participants knew that the President owns a plane, and this fact matches one of the explicit models of what the President owns according to Pat's disjunctive proposition: the President owns a villa and a swimming pool, or else he owns a plane. Hence, the fact is consistent with this proposition. But, it is not represented in the model of Viv's proposition that the President owns a villa and a swimming pool. And so participants tend to reject Viv's proposition.

So far, the mismatch might be between the grammatical forms of *sentences*. For example, "the President does not own a plane," fails to match, "the President owns a plane". But, the effect hinges, not on form, but on models. Consider, for example, these assertions:

> Pat says: If the President owns a villa and a swimming pool then either he owns a plane or else a Ferrari".
>
> Viv says: The President owns a villa and a swimming pool".

But, we know that he owns both a plane and a Ferrari. We should perceive the inconsistency, and the mismatch principle predicts what then happens: we retract Pat's proposition. But, we cannot do so on the basis of grammatical form. The two clauses in the facts—he owns a plane, he owns a Ferrari— match the two clauses in Pat's proposition. We have to grasp that their conjunction in the facts is inconsistent with their exclusive disjunction in Pat's proposition. A mere grammatical mismatch between "and" and "or else" isn't enough to establish an inconsistency, because a conjunction *is* consistent with other connectives, such as an *inclusive* disjunction. Hence, we have to infer the inconsistency. And that task, as I have argued, depends on mental models.

* * *

The resolution of inconsistencies is not just a matter of changing our beliefs. We want to understand what gave rise to the inconsistency in the first place. It will help us to decide what to do. The list of possibilities is almost always long. However, we eliminate probable causes, if we can, before we entertain improbable ones. The process of narrowing down the list may yield one overwhelming possibility, but often it will yield competing alternatives. Sometimes, it may fail to yield any possible explanation at all—the Mary Celeste effect again (see Chapter 14). A major process in the resolution of inconsistency is therefore the attempt to think of a causal scenario—a diagnosis—that makes sense of the situation.

The process is abductive. We reason backwards from an inconsistency to a cause that explains it. Earlier in the book, I described how the best explanations are causal chains—a cause and an effect—and how we use general knowledge to construct these chains, a process that is simulated in a computer program. The same mechanism can account for the abduction of causal resolutions of inconsistencies. As an example, consider the inconsistency:

> If someone pulled the trigger, then the gun fired.
>
> Someone pulled the trigger.
>
> But the gun did not fire.

A minimal explanation would be:

> There were no bullets in the chamber.

But, a better explanation provides a motivation in terms of a cause:

> A prudent person unloaded the gun and there were no bullets in the chamber.

Of course, one might also ask for an explanation of this cause, but the longer a causal chain, the more improbable it becomes, and so a cause and an effect should be optimal.

This hypothesis about optimal explanations violates a common assumption. Philosophers have argued for a long time that changes to beliefs in the face of an inconsistency should be as *minimal* as possible. William James wrote: "[The new fact] preserves the older stock of truths with a minimum of modification, stretching them just enough to make them admit the novelty". Most recent theorists have agreed; but if the model theory is correct, this principle is wrong. We don't just take on board a single new proposition—an effect—we also accommodate its cause.

A program implementing this account uses mental models to detect an inconsistency, and it then uses the mismatch principle to reject a premise. In the gun example, the result is a model of this situation:

> Someone pulled the trigger and the gun did not fire.

This model elicits several possibilities in the program's knowledge base, and the program makes an arbitrary choice among them, and extends its model accordingly:

> The gun was broken and someone pulled the trigger and the gun did not fire.

According to the theory, the new conjecture stands in need of explanation. The program constructs such a cause, by using the preceding model to search its knowledge base for a possibility that accounts for the breaking of the gun.

Among its knowledge is the notion that if someone drops a gun then it may break, and so its if-clause is added to the model of the situation.

> Someone dropped the gun and the gun was broken and someone pulled the trigger and the gun did not fire.

The program has constructed a causal chain of the sort that the theory postulates should resolve inconsistencies. The program also works with complete models of the premises, which yield a different resolution of the inconsistency.

Several experiments have confirmed that participants prefer explanations that go beyond the minimal. In a preliminary study, the participants tackled a series of twenty different problems from various domains. Each problem was based on a blatant inconsistency, such as the one above about the gun. The participants' task was to explain what had happened in their own words. Each problem elicited a variety of different explanations, with an average of just under five explanations per problem. As the mismatch principle predicts, however, the vast majority of explanations amounted to retractions of the conditional proposition (ninety percent of trials) rather than the categorical proposition. On two percent of trials, the participants were unable to come up with any explanation (the Mary Celeste phenomenon).

In a second experiment, a new set of participants had to evaluate sets of putative explanations of the twenty inconsistencies. Their task was to select the most probable explanation, then the next most probable one, and so on, until in effect they had put the explanations into an order according to their probabilities. The explanations were constructed from those collected in the previous study. As the model theory predicts, the participants showed an overwhelming tendency to evaluate a cause and effect as the most probable explanation. For instance, they put the putative explanations for the failure of the gun to fire in this order, starting with the most probable explanation:

1. A prudent person had unloaded the gun and there were no bullets in the chamber. (Cause and effect)
2. A prudent person had unloaded the gun. (Cause alone)
3. There were no bullets in the chamber. (Effect alone)
4. The person didn't really pull the trigger. (Rejection of the categorical proposition)
5. The gun was heavy and there were no bullets in the chamber. (Noncausal conjunction)

The theory also predicted that a cause alone should be more convincing than the effect alone, because knowledge makes it easier to infer an effect from a cause than vice versa. The cause and effect is a conjunction, and so the non-causal conjunction was included as a control. One weakness of the experiment was that all the participants received the twenty scenarios in the same order. However, the same pattern of results occurred in a subsequent experiment in which they were presented in four different orders. It also occurred in an experiment in which the putative explanations ruled out the categorical premise, e.g.:

> The person was semi-paralyzed and he was not able to move his fingers with sufficient strength.

We don't always accommodate a new belief by making as small a change as possible to our old beliefs. The acceptance of a conjunction calls for a greater change than the acceptance of just one of its propositions. The preference for the conjunction is surprising in another way. Its rating as more probable than either of its constituents is contrary to the norms of probability: a conjunction cannot be more probable than one of its constituents. The best explanation is not always the minimal and most probable proposition.

* * *

How does reasoning influence our beliefs? Unconscious inferences lead us to have an emotional tie to beliefs about things unseen. These beliefs are vital to us, and our tie to them often renders them immune to reasoned argument. Our stereotypes can be benign—most dogs do have four legs. But, they can also be malign—women are *not* poorer drivers than men. When they are part of our world-view, they can be hard to change. Our belief in them may inhibit us from searching for counterexamples to inferences that support them. We do modify our mundane beliefs, however, in the case of a clash with the facts. We give up beliefs that conflict with the facts, or those that appear to do so— an appearance that a mismatch with mental models can explain. We try to reason our way to a resolution of the inconsistency. Our ability to make these abductions is far superior to any existing computer program, but it isn't, and can't be, perfect. From time to time, we are unable to create an explanation that resolves an inconsistency. And we often modify our beliefs by accepting changes to them that are not as minimal as possible. In a small way, we too walk the road to Damascus.

Chapter 24

How we Solve Problems

Suppose you did a painting of the famous Baptistery in Florence, and you wanted to check its accuracy. How would you do it? When I asked a group of students this question, they suggested that you should make measurements of the building and compare their ratios with those in your painting. That would work for an architect's drawing of the façade, but your painting is of how the building looks from a particular point of view, and lines that are parallel in the building ought to converge in a painting. So, how could you check that you'd got them right? The students suggested a comparison with a photograph from the same point of view. Fair enough; but suppose you made your painting in the fifteenth century long before the invention of photography. This problem confronted the great Renaissance artist and architect, Filippo Brunelleschi, and he solved it with an extraordinary insight. He made a pinhole in the centre of his painting, turned the picture towards the building, and peeped through the hole. He saw how the building looked from his point of view. And then he moved a mirror facing him between his picture and the building so that it reflected his picture back at him through the pinhole. By moving the mirror into and out of his line of sight, he could make an almost immediate comparison between his picture and the building itself. In this way, Brunelleschi discovered the principles of perspective and the use of "vanishing" points.

We don't know how Brunelleschi thought of his deep trick with a mirror, but I fancy that he struggled with the problem, and then had a burst of inspiration from which the solution popped into his mind as if from nowhere. We all have had such experiences. "Eureka, I have it," we say, as Archimedes is supposed to have done when he thought of how to measure the volume of the King of Syracuse's crown. We do not, however, leap from our bath and run naked through the streets. Such insights seem different from the normal process of thought in which we advance step by step towards the solution to a problem, as when we use a map to work out how to get from one place to another. Indeed, there is a long tradition in psychology that insight is unique. The experience *is* special, but does it depend on a special sort of thinking? Skeptics doubt it. If we search for the number that opens a combination lock, its discovery is bound to be sudden, but it does not depend on a process that differs from the previous steps that failed. We just try a new combination, and it works. Yet, some evidence suggests that insight is different from the humdrum application of habitual methods. When we proceed in this routine way, we sense when we are getting nearer to a solution. But, an insight is not presaged by any sense of increasing "warmth". One moment we have no idea of the solution; the next moment we have it. Evidence from brain-imaging studies even suggests that special parts of the brain become active during an insight. No one, however, has succeeded in pinning down what counts as an insight or what mental processes underlie it. Hence, I side-step these puzzles for a while. Instead, I consider *reasoning*, and its use in solving problems. Afterwards I come back to insight.

Students of creativity often argue that we are too logical to be as creative as we could be. We need to stop thinking in a straight-laced way. We need to think "laterally" and "out of the box". Students of reasoning, on the contrary, argue that we are too creative to be as logical as we could be. We need to stop thinking in an undisciplined way and to start thinking more "linearly". The truth of the matter is that imagination helps us to reason, and reasoning helps us to imagine. Theorists can draw a line between deduction and other sorts of reasoning: deduction yields conclusions that must be true given the premises. But, abductive reasoning is an exercise in imagination. And so the present chapter outlines a theory of how reasoning, both deductive and abductive, helps us to solve problems. It is a precursor to an examination of expertise in the final part of the book.

* * *

What does it mean to say that a process is creative? The proof of the pudding is in the eating. We examine the results. They should be novel—at the very least we shouldn't have had the same idea before and recalled it, and, with luck, they might even be novel for the world at large. That's an option, because if we have thought of the idea for ourselves, we were creative even if someone else had anticipated us. Perhaps that notion underlies Borges's strange story, *Pierre Menard, Author of the Quixote*, in which a French symbolist author is trying to rewrite Cervantes' *Don Quixote* word for word, not by plagiarizing it, but as a result of his own creative process. As I argued earlier in the book, thinking isn't deterministic, and so the creative process isn't, either. Abduction can create ideas with propositional content, i.e., we can ask whether the results are true or false. Other sorts of creation, such as musical composition, yield artifacts that have no propositional content.

When we make abductions, we work within a recognized paradigm in science, or within a recognized genre in art. We create a scientific hypothesis or a work of art. As a consequence, the process is constrained by our knowledge of the domain, though we may not be aware of much of this knowledge. Our minds contain unconscious constraints, which I discussed earlier in the book, and they govern our efforts to create. We are about as aware of them as we are aware of the rules of grammar of our native tongue. That is, we are aware of some rules—for example, that the subject of a sentence should agree in number with its verb. But, we are oblivious of most rules, which is why the discipline of linguistics exists. Likewise, we are aware of some constraints governing a paradigm or a genre. The velocity of light is constant. Genes encode proteins. A sonnet has fourteen lines. But, we are ignorant of many constraints that guide us in the process of abduction. If it were otherwise, it would be easy to program a computer to mimic our thoughts, or to prove that the process is not computable. What we *are* aware of is the set of elements that we put together to create. Science is made from concepts, such as genes and proteins; music is made from notes; and poems—as Mallarmé reminded the painter Degas—are made, not from ideas, but from words.

I have now described the five components of a working definition of creativity, the so-called "NONCE" definition: *N*ovelty for us, *O*ptional novelty for society, a *N*ondeterministic process, the *C*onstraints of the paradigm or genre, and the use of existing *E*lements. The definition demarcates what counts as creative, but it errs on the generous side. So far, however, no one has come up with a case of genuine creativity that falls outside the definition. The discovery of a mathematical proof is the strongest candidate, but those who invoke it confuse the apparent determinism of a proof with the very different process of its discovery—even computer programs that create proofs simulate processes that are not deterministic. Granted the NONCE definition and the assumption that abduction is a computable process, it follows that there are just three sorts of computational process that could create new ideas.

The first process mimics the evolution of species. Like genes, existing concepts are shuffled at random to generate new ideas. Like natural selection, constraints based on knowledge and experience sort out what, if anything, is viable—to which the entire process can be applied again and again until perhaps something useful emerges. Nowadays computer programs simulate this evolution of ideas, and they can approach optimal solutions to certain problems, such as minimizing the length of connections in an integrated circuit. Most psychologists who have thought about creativity defend this "neo-Darwinian" account of it. But, the process couldn't be more inefficient. Evolution works this way only because the experiences of an individual organism cannot be encoded in the genes that it passes on to its offspring. Our creativity is seldom trial and error of this sort, with knowledge acting as a mere sieve.

The second process is more efficient. It uses some constraints in the generation of ideas. Other constraints are used to evaluate the results and to make changes to them, and the results can be fed back to the generative stage for further work. Because constraints govern generation, the procedure is no longer pure trial and error, but matches the usual business of generating initial ideas, revising them, revising again, and so on, in multiple drafts. Creation of this sort is a "multi-stage" affair. The generative stage, like all mental processes, is unconscious. The evaluative stage can apply conscious constraints.

The third sort of process takes the multi-stage procedure to an extreme. All the constraints that we have govern the generation of ideas. So, if the constraints are viable, the output needs no revision. By definition, no other constraints exist to evaluate it. At various points in the procedure, there may be more than one option, because constraints seldom yield just one possible next step. But, because we have used all the constraints that we have, a choice among the options must be arbitrary. The choice is where the nondeterminism of creativity enters into this process. It is "neo-Lamarckian" by analogy to Lamarck's theory of evolution, because all the constraints that we have acquired from experience come to govern the generative stage. With a viable set of constraints, a neo-Lamarckian process is very efficient. It allows us to create in real time, and so it underlies any sort of improvisatory art. For example, jazz musicians, who improvise for a living, cannot go back to revise a phrase that they have just played. They therefore need to develop a tacit knowledge of the constraints of the genre, which they can use to create music. When we master a method of solving certain sorts of problem without ever making any false steps, we too have abduced a neo-Lamarckian process. Figure 24.1 summarizes the three sorts of creative process.

* * *

Most problems in life call for a multi-stage process. We use some constraints to generate a putative solution, and other constraints, such as the goal of the problem, to criticize and to amend the results. If our efforts are no good, then we work on them some more, and so on, until we either succeed or give up. Success depends on our having the requisite knowledge and being able to bring it to mind. Problems that call for an insight are often of this sort. For instance, in the candle problem (see Chapter 6), we have a candle and a box of thumbtacks (drawing pins), and without using anything else our task is to fix the candle to the wall. We push a thumbtack through the candle, but it doesn't stick out far enough on the other side to pin the candle to the wall. Most of us are stumped at this point. The solution depends on an insight: we can pin the box that contained the thumbtacks to the wall, and use it to support the

1. Neo-Darwinian

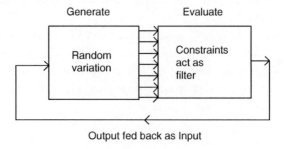

Output fed back as Input

2. Multi-stage

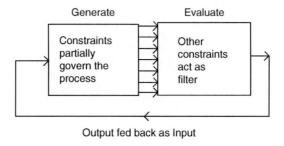

Output fed back as Input

3. Neo-Lamarckian

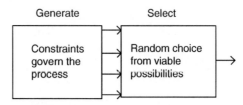

Fig. 24.1 Three sorts of creative process.

candle. The solution seems trivial once we know it, but it isn't easy to discover. We have the requisite knowledge, but we also need the insight that an object that serves one function can also serve another. We tend to be fixed in our thoughts about what an object can do, and so the problem is difficult.

Many problems defeat us because we lack the knowledge to solve them. When the TV fails, the computer won't boot, or the telephone goes dead, we may need experts to fix them. But, we can develop an expertise of our own if we have got the rudiments needed to find a solution. Once we have solved the candle problem, we retain our knowledge of its solution, and so any other instance of the problem is trivial. But, other sorts of problem are not one of a kind, but come in many varieties that each call for thought. To plan a journey, to write a computer program, and to fill in a tax form, are all examples of problems that some of us have to solve over and over. When we tackle one of these problems for the first time, we don't know what to do. We flail around trying one tactical move then another with few constraints governing our choices. We have no *strategy* for solving the problem, where a strategy is a set of systematic constraints that guide our generation of elementary tactical moves to lead us to a solution (see Chapter 19).

We learn from our mistakes. The point is obvious to everyone except those psychologists who argue that we should be taught in a way that prevents us from making errors. Anyone who has learned to write computer programs knows that this goal is both impossible and inadvisable. We learn from correct tactical moves too. This point is obvious to everyone except those psychologists who advocate theories in which learning occurs only when we err. We generate a tactical move, and we evaluate its consequences. We deduce that it is useless because it does not advance us towards a solution. Or, we deduce that it is useful. In either case, we can learn the consequences of the tactical move. Hence, even though the move may have been futile and we need to undo it later, we may have learned something that will be useful in future.

A key assumption of the theory that I propose is that our system for solving problems can shift knowledge from the evaluative stage of the process to the generative stage. Hence, knowledge that we deduce about a tactical move can shift so that it starts to constrain our generation of moves—we're progressing towards a neo-Lamarckian process. The shift depends on experience, but it enables us to avoid mistakes that we would later have to undo. Let us look at some examples that support this theory.

* * *

"Shape" problems call for us to modify a shape by the addition, removal, or re-arrangement of some of its component pieces. They illustrate many of the features of how we solve problems that don't in general call for insight, and here is an example of the sort that I am going to focus on. Given the six squares below, remove five pieces to leave exactly three squares with no loose ends, i.e., pieces that are not connected to any other piece at one or other end:

You are invited to tackle this problem for yourself either in your mind's eye or using an external model made from matches or toothpicks.

Those of us who have never done one of these problems before tend to try one or two experimental moves using a neo-Darwinian strategy. Suppose that we remove a piece from the middle row:

We removed one piece and eliminated two squares. And, as we can deduce, the move transforms the problem into a new one: we now have to remove four pieces from the resulting array to leave exactly three squares with no loose ends. So, is our move a good one or not? We have no way to answer this question without carrying out some further moves, perhaps in our mind's eye, and evaluating their consequences. Hence, we have no immediate way to assess whether a move is useful, and so we have to continue to try out moves.

When we look at the initial array of squares above, we see at once a symmetrical arrangement of squares in a rectangle. Certain parts of the figure are more salient than others, and in particular those parts where its external contour changes direction. The four corners are therefore the most salient. Both symmetry and saliency should affect the moves that we make, because we focus on salient pieces, and symmetry encourages us to aim for symmetrical solutions. The computer program that I wrote for applying a neo-Darwinian process to these problems works in a plodding serial way to identify squares in the array. It has a template for a square, and it identifies squares by comparing this template with each cell in the array. It plonks the template on a cell in the array, and checks one at a time whether each piece in the template has a corresponding piece in the array. If so, it has identified a square, and it moves on to the next cell in the array. It identifies other shapes, such as corners of squares, using templates for them in the same way, though it can rotate the template too. In contrast, our vision carries out a vast number of these operations in parallel, and that is why we see at a glance an array of squares. What we don't notice at first is that some pieces are parts of two squares.

As we try out moves, we learn their tactical consequences. Our previous move, for instance, removed a *middle* piece that was part of two squares, so we removed one piece but eliminated two squares. If we decide that the move was a dead end, we replace the piece and try a different move:

We now have to remove the remaining loose end to yield:

We learn that another way to eliminate a square is to remove the two pieces making up a *corner*. We can deduce that we now have to remove three pieces and to eliminate two squares. Suppose we remove another corner:

We deduce that we now have to remove one piece to eliminate one square. We can succeed:

Once more, we learn that we can eliminate a square by removing an outer piece, i.e., a piece in a square that has middles of squares at both ends, but that is not itself a middle. With sufficient experience, we learn the effects of the other tactical moves: we can remove an isolated square, a U-shape of three pieces, or a join that is not part of a square but is connected at both ends to other pieces.

Video-recordings of participants solving these problems showed that they did indeed acquire tactical knowledge—they made fewer false moves with increasing experience. They used strategies in which they tackled each problem in two phases. The first phase was exploratory: they tried out various tactical moves, which they later had to undo. But, they were learning the effects of various tactical moves, and deducing their consequences for their progress towards a solution. The duration of this phase depended on the participants' experience, and so it shrank in proportion over the problems as the participants acquired knowledge. The second phase of the strategy was the abductive application of tactical knowledge. A key factor was the ratio of the number of pieces to be removed to the number of squares to be eliminated. The participants deduced this ratio and used it to constrain their selection of appropriate tactical moves. However, its optimal use depends on knowledge of the full variety of tactical moves. The participants grasped their relevance, but seldom in a complete way.

* * *

Suppose that you work for a company that manufactures toaster ovens, and a rival company has put an ingenious new model on the market. Your boss presents you with one of them, and says, "Figure out how it works, so that we can make something similar without infringing their patent". Your task is to take the thing to pieces, and to use your knowledge of how its components work to infer by a series of abductions how the device functions as a whole. You have to construct a model that simulates its operations. You may also have to discover how the components work too. They were assembled to meet a specification of what should happen when the person using the device selects various settings of the controls. You can read about these settings in the instruction manual, and you have to work backwards from them to infer how the device implements these various functions. You have to abduce possible ways to fit the components together, using a generative procedure constrained by your available knowledge. You then evaluate the results by deducing the consequences of the system you've assembled. You compare the result with the required one, and in this way you deduce whether the device is doing what it's supposed to. In short, your task is to "reverse engineer" the toaster oven. And my task is to reverse engineer how you do it.

* * *

What sort of domain makes a suitable test-bed for reverse engineering? Toaster-ovens and their controls are not ideal, because they depend on too specialized knowledge. A domain that turns out to be ideal—not too simple and not too complicated—is one that implements Boolean logic, which I introduced earlier in the book (see Chapter 8). It concerns the logic of *not*, *and*, and *or*, which the nineteenth century logician George Boole was the first to formalize. The processing unit for a computer is made up of Boolean components, because they suffice for doing arithmetic too. A simpler example of a Boolean problem is an electrical circuit that controls whether or not a light comes on. Suppose, for example, there are two switches, and the light comes on when one switch *or* the other switch is in the down position, or both of them are. Your task is to reverse engineer a circuit for this "or" problem, that is, to infer how to wire up the two switches, the battery, and the light bulb, so that the circuit works in the required way. The two switches that you have at your disposal are of the sort illustrated in Figure 24.2. They have one terminal on one side and two terminals on the other side, and the switch connects the single terminal on one side either to the upper or lower terminal on the other side. If you wire up one of the two terminals on their side of the switch, then you have a simple "make or break" switch; if you wire up both terminals, then the switch is part of two alternative circuits, and when it makes one circuit it breaks the other circuit. Just for fun, you might like to see whether you can solve the "or" problem, assuming that you're not an electrical engineer who

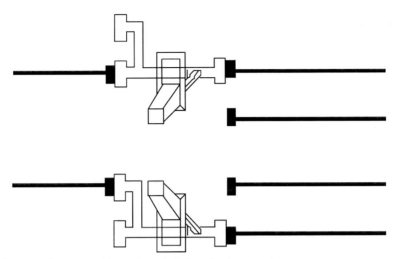

Fig. 24.2 The two positions of a switch for a Boolean circuit.

already knows the answer. Once again, you can tackle the problem using an external model, such as a diagram or a toy circuit of wires and a bulb. You can wire up the two switches in any way you like provided that the light comes on when one switch or the other is in the down position, or both of them are.

How did you go about it? You might like to compare your performance with the theory I am going to outline of how we solve these problems. The theory takes for granted that we understand the problem—in this case the possible switch positions and their resulting effects on the bulb. Just to be sure that you understand the problem too, I'll spell out the four possibilities:

Switch 1	Switch 2	Bulb
Down	Down	On
Down	Up	On
Up	Down	On
Up	Up	Off

As you see, I've adopted the European convention that the "on" position of a switch is when it's down. The theory also assumes that we have some rudimentary knowledge of electrical circuits and that we understand how the components work—in this case what the two positions of the switch do. We also need some idea of the tactical moves that we can use to wire up a circuit, e.g., connecting a wire to a battery or to a switch.

The theory postulates that we use some constraints to abduce possible moves towards a solution and other constraints to deduce the consequences of these moves. That is, we use a multi-stage process. The first stage is abductive and the second stage is deductive, and we cycle round from one stage to the other until we solve the problem or give up. The components of the wiring problem are of two sorts: the static components of wires and the battery, and the variable components of switches and the bulb, which can each be in one of two states. One state of a switch is shown here in a simplified diagram:

The other state is:

This state breaks the lower circuit and, if necessary, it makes a circuit to the upper terminal. The states of the two switches are the input to the system. The state of the remaining variable, the bulb, is the output.

There are two main sorts of strategy that we can develop to reverse engineer a system. We can focus either on the outputs of the device or on its inputs. With outputs, we focus first on those that are positive, i.e., the bulb comes on. One possibility for the "or" problem is that both switches are down and the bulb comes on. We construct the simplest possible circuit with two switches:

For simplicity, I assume that in these diagrams the two ends of this wire are connected to the battery and the bulb in order to make up the rest of the circuit. We can deduce that the bulb comes on when both switches are down, and that it does not come on when both switches are up. But, as we can also deduce, the bulb comes on only when *both* switches are on. I refer to this sort of circuit as an "and" circuit because the first switch *and* the second switch have to be down for the light to come on. Electricians say that the two switches are wired up in "series". We generate an amended circuit including a T-junction, such as:

We deduce that this circuit accounts for three of the possibilities: both switches down and the bulb is on, both switches up and the bulb is off, and the first switch is down and the second switch is up and the bulb is on. But, it fails to account for the fourth possibility in which the first switch is up and the second is down and the bulb comes on. We could try various alternatives, such as wiring up the first switch in the same way as the second in the preceding diagram. Alas, the bulb comes on regardless of the positions of the switches. And so we seem to have reached a dead end.

One way round the impasse is to consider the outputs in a different order. Indeed, we could have started with a different order from the one that I described above. We start again with the case in which both switches are down and the bulb comes on, and we construct the "and" circuit that I illustrated earlier. We extend the circuit to deal with the possibility in which the bulb comes on when the first switch is up and the second switch is down:

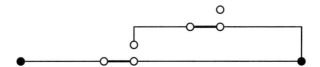

The bulb now comes on in three possibilities, but, as we can deduce, not the correct ones. We can try moving the switch to the upper circuit:

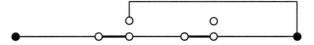

At last, as we can deduce, the bulb comes on when both switches are down, and when one switch is down and the other is up. And it does not come on when both switches are up. This circuit is one way to solve the problem—not the electrician's standard way, and it has the consequence that when the first switch is down, the second switch is irrelevant.

If instead we focus on the input components, we start with one switch and try to wire it up so that its positions yield the correct outputs. This circuit is the simplest starting point:

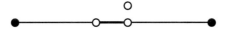

But, we can deduce that the bulb cannot come on when the switch is up, and so it fails to allow that the bulb can come on in some cases in which the switch *is* up. At this point, we may infer that each switch lights up the bulb without depending on the other switch, and so we need to consider a separate independent circuit for the second switch:

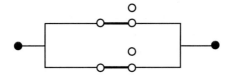

This standard "parallel" circuit solves the problem: we deduce that the bulb comes on provided at least one switch is down.

The strategies do not dictate the order in which we consider possibilities or how we deal with them. We may even change from one strategy to the other and back again. The process is not deterministic. But, each time we add a switch or a wire to the circuit, whether or not the result is useful, we should deduce at least one consequence of the move. This knowledge, which is acquired from deduction, transfers so that it constrains the generative stage of abducing a move. As with the shape problems, a strategic shift occurs as knowledge from the evaluative stage is used in the generative stage.

* * *

The theory predicts the difficulty of reverse engineering Boolean circuits. One source of difficulty is the number of variable components, whether they are input or output components. A problem with fifteen switches and twenty bulbs will be well-nigh impossible for all but experts unless the switches have to be wired up in a single series to switch all the bulbs on like a Christmas decoration. These numbers constrain the number of possibilities that we have to take into account. But, the number of *positive* outcomes in which the bulb comes on is a second factor in the difficulty of a problem. An "and" problem should be easier than an "or" problem, because an "and" problem has one positive possibility, whereas an "or" problem has three. Experiments have corroborated this prediction both with electrical circuits and with equivalent problems in other domains, such as the control of the flow of water with faucets. In general, the easiest problems are those in which there is one possibility in which the system produces a positive output, and as the number of positive possibilities increases so, other things being equal, does the difficulty of the task. With experience, we may realize that it can pay to focus on the negative outcomes if they are far fewer than the positive outcomes.

A third factor is subtle, but crucial. It is the extent to which we can separate the system into independent subsystems or components. A component is independent when its effects on the output are not affected by the status of other components. As an example, consider again a circuit with two switches. You control one of them and I control the other. If they are wired up in an "or" circuit, then each of us can switch on the bulb regardless of the other. If you put your switch on, the bulb lights up and nothing I can do turns it off. The same applies for me. To turn the bulb off, however, both of us must put our switches off. A circuit with the two switches in series—an "and" circuit—is a mirror image of this situation. You have a guaranteed way of switching the bulb off: you push your switch up, and nothing that I can do turns the bulb on. The same applies for me. To light up the bulb, however, both of us must put our switches on.

We cannot both have absolute independence. If you switch the bulb on, and I switch it off, what would happen in that case? It is impossible for the bulb to be in both states, and so one of us has to be dependent on the other. Independence within the same system concerns either the positive or the negative outcomes. For both of us to have absolute power, we must be dictators and control separate systems.

The light in my hall at home is controlled by two switches. One switch is at the bottom of the stairs and another switch at the top of the stairs. Whichever switch I throw, the state of the light changes. Aren't the two switches independent of one another? No, far from it. If you switch the light on at the bottom of the stairs, then I can at once switch it off at the top of the stairs, and vice versa. You cannot guarantee to switch the light on for more than the fraction of a second that it takes me to overrule you, and vice versa. Here's a diagram of the circuit:

As you can deduce, the light comes on when your switch is down *or else* my switch is down, but not both. The circuit has the logic of an exclusive disjunction. Hence, the effect of the position of my switch depends on the position of your switch, and vice versa. The effects of the two switches are *dependent* on one another rather than independent. Unlike an "and" or an "or" problem, the circuit cannot be decomposed into independent components. But, if a system cannot be decomposed into independent components, we pay a penalty if we think about the effects of one component while ignoring the others. It follows that dependent systems, such as an "or else" circuit, should be harder to reverse engineer than independent systems, such as an "or" circuit. With an "or else" circuit, we need to think about the positions of both switches together whether we focus on input components or possible outputs.

Experiments have corroborated this prediction: "or else" systems were harder than "and" and "or" systems. Naïve participants took longer and were less likely to solve them. Three factors therefore affect the difficulty of reverse engineering Boolean systems: the number of variable components, the number of possibilities yielding positive outputs, and the relative independence of the components in determining either sort of outcome. A reasonable conjecture is that the same principles hold for any domain, even the reverse engineering of toaster ovens.

* * *

A natural strategy that we tend to adopt for solving problems is to work forwards from the initial state towards a solution, constrained by whatever knowledge we have. Other sorts of problem inculcate other sorts of strategy. One well-known strategy, which goes back to Plato, is to start with the required solution, and to work backwards towards the initial state. This strategy is known as "means-ends" analysis because it depends on knowledge of the means available to achieve our ends. There is a hole in our bucket that we need to mend. The means, as we know, is to make a bung out of straw. But, we can't use the straw because it is too long. So, we need a knife. The knife is blunt, and so we need to sharpen it. We can sharpen it on a stone. But, the stone is dry, and so we need to wet it. At this point, we must be careful to avoid the problem that arises in the folk song that Harry Belafonte made popular. We shouldn't try to fetch the water in our bucket. (There's a hole in it.) We should take the stone to the river.

The means-ends strategy has been influential in both the study of how we solve problems and the development of intelligent computer programs. However, it is not applicable to shape problems or to switch problems. We can have no models of their final goals, and work backwards from them, because the final goals are the solutions to the problems. Yet another strategy, which mathematicians use in trying to prove equations, is a compromise between working forwards and working backwards. They start to work from one side of the equation to the other and then switch to working in the opposite direction if they get stuck. A theoretical goal for psychologists is to formulate an account of all our possible strategies for solving problems. The difficulty, however, is to take into account every sort of problem.

* * *

What about insight—does it depend on a special mental process? To try to answer this question, I will propose a broad description of insight as an event, and then tackle its underlying mental processes. I start with an illustrative problem:

> A shape consists of exactly four squares of the same size. Remove one piece to eliminate all of them with no loose ends.

If an experimenter gives this problem to unsuspecting participants who have just solved a bunch of shape problems of the earlier sort, then they are stumped at first. It is a difficult problem. You can try it for yourself before you read on.

If you didn't already know the solution to the problem, you are likely to have been blocked for a while or else to have given up. But, if you persevered and solved the problem, then you may have had a sudden realization that a shape problem could be three-dimensional. You then imagined an arrangement of squares akin to the one in Figure 24.3. You removed the central vertical piece, and you thereby eliminated all four squares, because they became two rectangles. The problem is typical of those that psychologists have studied as instances of insight. It also has the hallmarks of problems in life that hinge on an insight.

When we have an insight, at one moment we are at an impasse unable to solve a problem, and at the next moment we are aware of the solution. We feel that the scales have fallen from our eyes, that is, there was a discontinuity in which a fundamental change occurred in our thinking. If you solved the preceding problem, a change in your thinking may have occurred, and you can describe what it is: you were thinking in two dimensions, and then you thought in three dimensions. You were not aware of the process that led to the switch, but you were aware of the switch and of the solution to which it led. You realize what the significant change was, and you can describe it to other individuals or give them hints that may enable them to have the insight too. All but the most adamant skeptics should allow that these changes do occur. Their description entails that some sorts of problem may depend on an insight for their solution, whereas other sorts of problem do not. But, the occurrence of an insight is a subjective matter: it depends on whether we solved the problem, and on whether it was a result of a discontinuity in our thinking yielding a significant change of which we were aware.

The theory of how we solve problems described in this chapter contains a mechanism that would give rise to insight. The precondition is that the current constraints that the generative procedure uses fail to solve the problem. The result is an impasse. The abductive system registers the impasse, and so it sets up an attempt to modify the constraints. The process may start in consciousness, but it proceeds in the unconscious generative stage. This stage may alter the constraints, and the modified constraints may yield a solution. In the case of a false insight, we think that we have a solution, but, despite the change in constraints, we later deduce that we were wrong. A genuine insight is therefore an initial failure to solve a problem, followed by a change in constraints, followed by a solution. Once an insight has occurred, it may be used henceforth to constrain the generative stage itself: we look at once for a three-dimensional solution when two-dimensional attempts fail. A change

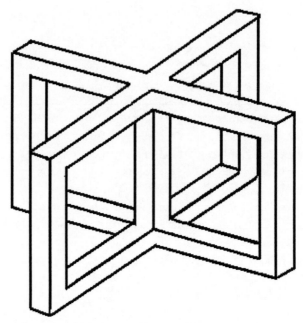

Fig. 24.3 A three-dimensional solution to a shape problem.

in constraints is bound to be discontinuous, but it may be preceded by useless changes. A special case of a change in constraints yields a new representation of a problem, e.g., a switch from two to three dimensions, and some psychologists have argued that it is this sort of change that is crucial for insight. Yet, other shape problems that meet my description of an insight depend only on relaxing the constraint that squares should be of the same size.

Part VIII

Expert Reasoning in Technology, Logic, and Science

A scientific hypothesis is a provisional framework for organizing future experience.

Auden

Chapter 25

Flying Bicycles: How the Wright Brothers Invented the Airplane

The Wright brothers took less than five years to invent a heavier-than-air craft that flew under its own power and the pilot's control. They designed and built their "flyer" and its internal combustion engine. Their first flights were just over a hundred years ago near Kitty Hawk on the Outer Banks of North Carolina. They had developed the machine from a kite and three man-carrying gliders. Why did they succeed when so many failed? There have been many conjectures, ranging from their exceptional mechanical ability to the psychodynamics of their lives as bachelors unencumbered by any sexual relationships. As with any historical puzzle, we can never know for certain. One view, of course, is that genius is inexplicable and the Wrights were geniuses. They would have had some wry humor with this idea. They were level-headed practical men from Dayton, Ohio. Wilbur himself thought that they had no exceptional abilities, and that if time had been turned back to the start of their efforts in 1899, and then rerun, they were unlikely to have succeeded the second time around. He was impressed only by the short time it had taken them. But, he thought that they'd been lucky. They *were* lucky; but they weren't only lucky.

* * *

In this part of the book, I am going to consider three cases of expert reasoning—in technology, logic, and science—in order to try to understand them through the lens of the model theory. I begin with the Wright brothers. What shows that they were outstanding is the exceptional lead that they established over their rivals. Long after they had discovered the principles of flight, others were either stealing their ideas or crashing aircraft with fatal regularity. We can eliminate at once a number of factors for their success—some because the Wrights lacked them, some because their rivals possessed them. The Wrights had no education beyond high school, and no scientific training. They were not rich. Their bicycle business enabled them to take time off for their experiments and to pay for their machines, which were not very expensive. Their first successful aircraft cost less than $1000, they reckoned. They were skillful in making and repairing machines; Orville had already devised a printing press and a calculating machine of his own designs. They were conscientious, stubborn, persistent. Yet, their rivals included trained engineers with skill, persistence, time, and money. Samuel Langley, the secretary of the Smithsonian Institution in Washington, received $150,000 of taxpayers' money to build a plane, but failed.

What I am going to argue is that the Wrights succeeded because they were better reasoners than their rivals. You may say instead that the Wrights were more *intelligent* than their rivals. But, we agree in this case, because intelligence depends on reasoning ability (see Chapter 1). The Wrights seldom said anything about their methods—they were too busy reasoning to have time to reflect on *how* they were reasoning. Moreover, as I have argued, the processes of reasoning are unconscious. Only its results can be conscious. My main aim is to show they were superb in reasoning and in drawing fruitful analogies. Any attempt to reconstruct an individual's thinking is bound to be speculative, but I am armed with scattered clues from the brothers' writings and with a theory of reasoning.

* * *

The Wrights' aim was to build an aircraft, not to acquire scientific knowledge. In the late nineteenth century, scientists looked askance at aeronautical explorations. The physicist Lord Kelvin wrote in 1898 that efforts in aviation "could only lead to disappointment, if carried out with any expectation of leading to a useful flying machine". The brothers' interest in the principles of flight was practical. In the previous chapter, I distinguished three sorts of process for creative thinking. The history of the Wrights' reasoning makes clear that they tried to reduce "trial and error" to a minimum: they didn't use a neo-Darwinian strategy. But, no inventor starts with a knowledge of all the constraints necessary to produce the successful invention. To have this knowledge would be to have the invention already in mind. And the Wrights did not work in this neo-Lamarckian way, either. They used some prior constraints in creating their various aircraft, but they also tested their ideas in practice to see whether they met other constraints, returning the results for further work, re-evaluating these results, and so on and on. They cycled through these creative and evaluative stages many times: they used a "multi-stage" strategy. Like many original thinkers, they thought hard about what it was that they wanted to invent, and then used these criteria to measure their success.

To avoid trial and error, one needs knowledge, and so if the Wrights could find the knowledge they needed in the literature, then their designs met the criteria that it set. If they could not find it in the literature, then they developed it for themselves. And, as they discovered, the literature is not always right. Wilbur took the first step towards flight in May 1899 when he wrote to the Smithsonian requesting papers on flying and a list of recommended readings. His immediate inspirations were a recent book on ornithology, and the death a few years earlier of the German glider pioneer Otto Lilienthal, who had crashed and killed himself in one of his own machines.

After three months of reading aeronautical history, Wilbur realized that much theorizing was half-baked. The lesson that he took from the literature was that an airplane depends on three components: wings to provide it with lift, an engine to propel it, and a system that enables a pilot to control it. Sir George Cayley, the English glider pioneer of the early nineteenth century, had made this analysis. But which component was the most important?

* * *

Many of the Wrights' contemporaries believed that all that was lacking for success was a light but powerful motor. I quoted Sir Hiram Maxim on this question in Chapter 1: "Give us a motor," he said, "and we will very soon give you a successful flying machine." But, two powerful steam engines hadn't prevented his plane from crashing. Wilbur put no priority on motors. In an epitome of the airplane's invention, he wrote, "It is possible to fly without motors, but not without knowledge & skill". With hindsight, the claim is obvious, but consider Wilbur's reasoning:

1. Engines fail from time to time. Hence, airplanes' engines are liable to fail.

Here, he made a plausible induction: engines do fail from time to time, and so an airplane's engine is liable to fail. It was possible, but improbable as far as he knew, that engineers might build an engine that never failed.

2. If the engine fails and the pilot has no control of the aircraft, then it will crash and the pilot is likely to be killed.

He had found a clear counterexample to the view that an engine would solve the problem. It can be hard to find counterexamples (see Chapter 16), but Wilbur had little difficulty. One of his few remarks about mental ability was: "It is a characteristic of all our family to be able to see the weak points of anything...". His argument about the priority of control was also an induction from the fate of Lilienthal and other glider pilots such as the Englishman Percy Pilcher, who had died in the same way as Lilienthal. Both lacked control of their gliders. Wilber inferred by analogy that a plane with an engine that has failed *is* a glider.

3. If the engine fails but the pilot has control of the aircraft, then he will be able to land the craft in safety. Therefore, control of an aircraft must come before the development of engines.

The conclusion is a valid inference from the premises (1 through 3) given the assumption that a safe landing is preferable to a disaster.

A remarkable feature of Wilbur's thinking is how few aeronautical pioneers thought in the same way. They wanted to fly first, and reason later. Many of them did not survive, or else were intelligent enough to pay someone else to do their flying for them. One who put flying ahead of reasoning was John J. Montgomery, the first person to fly a glider in the USA. The design of his gliders embodied little knowledge of the principles of control. One was cut adrift from a balloon at several thousand feet, and, after one or two flights, it went out of control sending its pilot to his death. Montgomery himself died the same way, later. Wilbur knew Montgomery, foresaw catastrophe, but had no way to avert it.

There is an unending controversy about who first invented the airplane. One reason is that other contenders formulated less stringent criteria than Wilbur's for what should count as an airplane. If success were just a matter of getting a heavier-than-air machine aloft, then others such as Maxim, Langley, or Richard Pearse, the New Zealand pioneer, could be said to have been the first to fly. But, an old flying adage is that a *good* landing is one that the pilot can walk away from, and a *great* landing is one that leaves the machine fit for someone else to fly. There were no good landings, let alone great ones, until the flights at Kitty Hawk just over a century ago. They were the first in which the pilot controlled the craft.

* * *

The brothers set maneuverability under the pilot's control as the decisive criterion for a successful airplane, and they differed from other aeronauts on the nature of control. Rivals such as Maxim and Langley aimed for a machine that would fly in a stable equilibrium—in a straight undeviating line that we now hope for in a cruising airliner. Cars, coaches, buses, trains, and trucks, move us from one place to another, and they are stable. They wobble, but they seldom topple. It was natural for inventors to transfer this characteristic to the design of aircraft. They sought stability, for example, in a dihedral configuration of the craft's wings—wings that pointed upwards in a slight V-shape. If a gust of wind rolled the plane to one side, then they supposed that the lower wing would generate more lift than the higher wing and thereby cause a compensatory return to level flight. Still others tried to develop mechanical methods for maintaining stability.

The Wrights did not even aim for stability. Wilbur drew an analogy from the "safety" bicycle with its wheels of equal size. It was a recent craze. The brothers were keen cyclists, and their business was repairing, selling, and manufacturing bicycles. A bicycle, however, is not a stable vehicle. With practice, a rider learns to balance and to control it. Wilbur argued that the essence of equilibrium in an aircraft should also be control rather than stability. Like many profound analogies, his concerned not the superficial characteristics of the source of the analogy—the fact, say, that bicycles are made of metal, or that they have two wheels—but instead a complex structure of relations of the sort that psychologists have postulated as underlying analogies. Riders balance a bicycle, and control it on two axes: steering it left or right, and leaning it to one side or the other. Pilots should have an analogous control of an aircraft on its three axes. They should steer it left or right, bank it to one side or the other, and nose it up or down.

Analogies are a useful tool for abduction, and they can be between models of the world (see Chapter 14). Wilbur's analogy has a corollary. Just as cyclists have to learn how to maintain the equilibrium of their machines, so too pilots would have to learn how to control their aircraft. It was crucial, as he realized, for the brothers to develop this expertise. They would need to have acquired it long before they added a motor. Hence, they should begin with gliders.

Analogies were a powerful tool in the Wrights' thinking, and they drew often on the bicycle as a source. In many ways, their flyer *was* a flying bicycle. The Wrights also drew many "local" analogies between one glider and another. But, the analogy between the control of bicycles and the control of aircraft is altogether deeper. It crosses from one domain to another, though the two domains are members of the same higher category of vehicles. Analogies of this sort concern, not superficial properties, but complicated matters such as causal relations. We don't always grasp the import of an analogy, however. And what is still harder is to find the right analogy among all the knowledge that we possess about the world. The task of comparing a problem to all analogies that might be fruitful isn't tractable. The Wrights, however, were in an ideal position to see many analogies between bicycles and aircraft.

* * *

The pilots of early gliders, such as Lilienthal, hung from their craft and exercised control by swinging their bodies around to change the center of gravity. With his eye on the goal, Wilbur realized that a powered aircraft would be too heavy to be controlled in this way. A horizontal "rudder", or elevator, could be lifted up or down to control climbing and diving. But, how could banking or turning be controlled? In the summer of 1899, Wilbur had a key insight from an analogy with birds. He wrote about buzzards: "If the rear edge of the right wing tip is twisted upward and the left downward the bird becomes an animated windmill and instantly begins a turn, a line from its head to its tail being the axis... In the apparatus I intend to employ I make use of the torsion principle." His idea was to twist the left and right wings of the craft in opposite directions so that one presented its leading edge at a greater angle to the oncoming air than the other. As the result of this wing "warping", the two wings would differ in the lift that they generated and so the machine would bank and turn. Here, again, the bicycle reappears. Some early aeronauts had assumed that aircraft would turn on a horizontal plane like automobiles. The brothers realized that the bicycle was a better analogy. To turn, a rider must lean a bicycle: a pilot must bank an aircraft. Orville, who had by now joined Wilbur's project, suggested that the outer ends of the wings could pivot on metal shafts, which would be geared to move in opposite directions when the pilot pulled a lever. This system anticipated modern ailerons, but metal shafts and gears would have been too heavy for the Wrights' glider.

The next step in Wilbur's thinking depended on an analogy that I described earlier (in Chapter 14). For wings to be warped in opposite directions, they must be flexible. But, if wings are flexible, their ends could flap up and down in ways that would be worse than embarrassing. The solution to this problem came when Wilbur saw an analogy between an inner tube box that he happened to twist and the wings of a biplane. He wrote later, "If you will make a square cardboard tube two inches in diameter and eight or ten long and choose two sides for your planes you will at once see the torsional effect of moving one end of the upper plane forward and the other backward, and how this effect is attained without sacrificing lateral stiffness". The solution was to construct a biplane. Its entire wings could be twisted to produce the opposite warping on the right and the left wings without any danger that they would flap around. Chance favors the prepared mind, as Pasteur is supposed to have said. Wilbur was prepared for his insight, because he had been thinking about how to warp the wings of a plane. It depended on visualizing the upper and lower sides of the twisted box as a biplane. He had an unusual ability to visualize solutions to problems. He himself wrote: "My imagination pictures things more vividly than my eyes". Computer programs have been written to draw analogies, but, as I mentioned earlier in the book in discussing this example, they represent knowledge in a linguistic way. Experts in making analogies, however, use models of the world rather than linguistic representations.

The brothers made a real model of the wings out of bamboo and tissue paper. The design seemed feasible, and so they set to work in July 1899 to construct a biplane kite of the same design with a wingspan of five feet. The operator controlled the kite with a stick in each hand from which ran two cords, one to the top wing and the other to the bottom wing, so that the ends of the wings could be twisted in opposite directions. Wilbur tested the kite and confirmed that wing warping worked. It banked the kite from one side to the other in just the way that he had imagined.

The Wrights conceived a man-carrying glider on the same principles, and turned to the design of its wings. The wings of an aircraft produce lift: the air travels at the same velocity both over and under the wing. It takes a longer route over the top of the cambered surface of the wing than under the wing, and so the air pressure is less above the wing than under it. This difference in pressure lifts the wing. Of course, there is more to the story, because planes can fly upside down: what also matters is the angle of the wing to the oncoming air. The wing also resists the passage of air, as does the body of the aircraft. This resistance is known as *drag*. Every wing passing through the air produces both lift, the force at right angles to the flow of air, and drag, the force pushing the wing backwards and therefore in the same direction as the flow of air. The amounts of these forces vary depending on the cross-sectional shape of the wing and its angle to the air. Lilienthal had published a table of these data for his glider's wings, and the brothers used this table in their design. It was a biplane with a horizontal "rudder" sticking out in front that the pilot could flex up or down to control climbing and diving. It should lift a man aloft in a moderate wind.

* * *

In those days, a glider was flown from the crest of a hill or dropped from a balloon so that gravity accelerated the craft through the air. Wilbur knew that the procedure was dangerous because the craft was soon high above the ground. Lilienthal had died in such a crash. But, was a launch from the top of a hill the only method to get a glider into the air?

Wilbur solved the problem using the method of switching "ground" to "figure". When we look at a picture of an object, we see the object—the figure— against its background. But, with a mild effort, we can switch ground to figure and focus on the background and the shape that the figure makes in it. To glide, air has to move over a glider's wing fast enough to produce lift. Wilbur reasoned that there were two possibilities: either the glider could speed through the air—a focus on the figure, or else the air could speed past the glider—a focus on the ground. The first possibility might rely on gravity, but that was dangerous. It would be better to use a catapult to launch the glider through the air. That would be safer, but the design of an effective catapult would be a challenge. The second possibility was to speed the air past the glider. That would also be safer, because the glider could stay closer to the ground, and perhaps it could also be tethered to a tower with a counterweight to break its fall. But, how could air be speeded past the wings?

We might think of a large propeller or some sort of wind tunnel. Wilbur had a simpler idea. He consulted the National Weather Bureau's tables of average wind speeds at different places. He chose Kitty Hawk on the Outer Banks of North Carolina, a long isolated strip of beach off the coast, lying between a sound and the ocean, because the prevailing winds there averaged from fifteen to twenty miles per hour. After a busy year in the bicycle shop, Wilbur got to Kitty Hawk in September 1900 after a long journey, including a perilous sea trip across the sound in a rotting schooner. He had bought the spars for the glider's wings in a local shop, and the longest he could get were two feet shorter than their specification in the design. The rest of the parts arrived, as did Orville, and the brothers assembled the glider, adjusting the fabric to match the shorter spars. In October, they flew the glider, first as a kite, then with Wilbur as a pilot of a tethered glider, and then with him as a pilot in free flights. He lay on its lower wing to operate the controls. It looked dangerous, but the brothers soon discovered that it was safe. It had the advantage of reducing drag in comparison with a pilot sitting upright. Wilbur spent a total time of about two minutes in free flight. As I mentioned, he believed that it was vital for inventors to learn how to fly their craft as they developed them (without killing themselves). For a long time, he was the sole pilot. And, for safety's sake, the brothers flew together just once, many years later after Orville had taken their father for his first flight in a powered flyer.

According to Lilienthal's table, the glider should have lifted Wilbur in a wind of just over twenty miles an hour with the wings at an angle to the wind of about three degrees. In fact, the wind had to be over twenty-five miles an hour and the wings at an angle of almost twenty degrees. From his knowledge of aeronautics, Wilbur deduced that there were two possibilities that could account for the poor lift: the fact that the brothers had used a less cambered cross-section than Lilienthal's wing, or that they used smaller wings than those in their original design. Towards the end of October, they left the glider in Kitty Hawk to be cannibalized by the locals—the sateen fabric was used for dresses for two young girls—and went back to Dayton.

* * *

They returned to Kitty Hawk in early July 1901. They had designed a second glider, which took into account the prevailing winds at Kitty Hawk. With a wingspan of twenty-two feet, it was the largest glider that had ever been built. They gambled by making two untested changes to the wings. They introduced

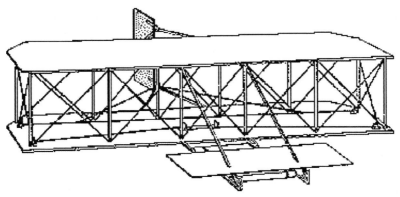

Fig. 25.1 A diagram based on the Wright's patent application of 1903. It shows the generic design of their craft with the horizontal elevator in front and the vertical rudder at the back.

a blunt leading edge, and they reverted to Lilienthal's camber. The glider was a huge disappointment. Its flight was erratic, its lift was a third of the predicted amount, and its control was capricious. It often dipped into the ground or else, when Wilbur tried to correct the dip, it stalled. A stall occurs when the angle of an aircraft's wings to the airflow becomes too great, turbulence sets in above them, they lose all lift, and the craft takes on the flight characteristics of a real bicycle. Unlike almost all modern planes, the Wrights' aircraft had a design in which the elevator—the horizontal rudder controlling climbing and diving—stuck out in front of the wings like a duck's neck. This configuration is indeed known in French as the "canard" design. It is illustrated in Figure 25.1, which is based on the drawing that the Wrights submitted with their 1903 patent application for wing warping. The brothers later used this same configuration for their powered craft. They discovered that it had an unforeseen advantage. When a craft stalled, it did not make a lethal nose-dive into the ground like Lilienthal's glider but dropped flat like a parachute. The canard saved its pilot's neck several times.

At the core of the second glider's problems was the difficulty of controlling the center of air pressure. The air pressure under the wing differs from one part of the wing to another, and it has center around which all the other air pressures are in an even distribution. For perfect equilibrium, the center of air pressure needs to coincide with an aircraft's center of gravity. But, as Wilbur said, the two had "an almost boundless incompatibility of temper which prevents their remaining peaceably together for a single instant, so that the operator, who in this case acts as a peacemaker, often suffers injury to himself while attempting to bring them together". The design of the wings, they thought, should have minimized these problems, but perhaps it had been a mistake to revert to Lilienthal's camber.

The Wrights stopped flying the glider to check what was happening to the center of air pressure. But, how? You might pause for a moment to think what you would do, and to pit your ability against the brothers' ingenuity. The problem is to determine where the center of air pressure is in relation to the wings' center of gravity, when all you have are a few rudimentary materials and tools, you are miles from anywhere, and a powerful wind batters you without pause. No one to whom I have put this problem has so far solved it. The solution is summarized in Box 25.1.

The brothers retrussed the wings to change the camber to a shallower one, and they made a sharper leading edge. The modifications solved the problem of control. Wilbur could now skim over the ground using the elevator to follow its

Box 25.1 How the Wrights determined the movement of the centre of air pressure in their second glider's wings

1. They dismantled the glider, and flew the upper wing alone as a kite using two cords attached to its leading edge.

2. They flew it in a light wind, and observed that the front of the wing angled up, pulling the cords up nearly vertically from their hands. They inferred that the center of pressure had moved in front of the wing's center of gravity, pushing up its front edge.

3. They flew it in a fresher wind, and observed that the wing's angle to the wind was smaller and the cords streamed out nearly horizontally from their hands to the wing's leading edge. They inferred that the center of pressure coincided with the center of gravity, and the wing was in equilibrium.

4. They flew it in a strong wind, and observed that the front of the wing dipped down and pulled the cords down from their hands to its leading edge. They inferred that the center of pressure had moved behind the center of gravity, pushing the rear of the wing upwards. It was this last movement of the center of pressure towards the rear of the wing that would suddenly push their glider downwards.

5. They inferred that the deep camber of Lilienthal's design caused these shifts in the center of air pressure.

undulations. They now tried wing warping to control banking. It didn't work. When Wilbur warped the biplanes' wings to bank to the left, the wings on the right came up and the wings on the left went down. But, the maneuver was followed by a bizarre consequence. The downward wings now moved through the air faster than the upward wings, and so the craft slewed round to the right even though it was banked to the left. This effect upset both the plane and the brothers' theory of wing warping.

They returned to Dayton dispirited. The lift of the glider was far too low; wing warping had failed. Wilbur is supposed to have said on the train going home: "Not within a thousand years would man ever fly".

* * *

The glider had failed to produce the predicted lift. The brothers had encountered a discrepancy between the consequences of their beliefs and incontrovertible evidence. They had to reason back from the inconsistency to a consistent explanation of what was going on (see Chapter 23). Wilbur inferred three possible causes for the poor lift: the brothers had changed the wings to a shallow camber, the fabric on the wings may not have been airtight enough, or the data in Lilienthal's table that predicted the lift may have been wrong.

In September 1901, Wilbur gave his first public talk. He was the brothers' official spokesman and for many years their designated writer; Orville never spoke in public in his life. Wilbur's talk was on "Some aeronautical experiments" and he gave it to the Western Society of Engineers in Chicago. Its preparation led him to ruminate on the problem of lift. The brothers wanted to check Lilienthal's table, which was based on his measurements using a whirling arm with a small section of wing on one end and a counterweight on the other end. The method might not have been reliable.

The brothers needed a way to measure the lift produced by various sorts of wing. Their next step depended on their ability to imagine a mechanical device that would yield the answer to a theoretical puzzle. They abandoned gravity as the countervailing force, and used drag instead. They imagined a small flat surface facing at right angles into the wind. It would produce no lift whatsoever, but pure drag. They would balance it against a vertical cambered wing presented edge on at various angles to the wind. Lilienthal's table would predict the angle to the wind at which the lift (and drag) created by the wing should balance the drag created by the flat plate. They mounted the flat plate and the wing on a horizontal bicycle wheel. The plate and the wing stuck up vertically and were separated by a quarter of the wheel's circumference. If the wind were constant, the device would answer: when the forces balanced, the wheel would be stationary; when they did not balance, it would rotate.

The winds in Dayton, however, were not constant. So, they mounted the wheel horizontally on an axle in front of the handlebars of a bicycle, and surprised the locals by pedaling the contraption about the town at uniform speed, both into the wind and against it. They discovered that the wing's angle to the wind had to be much greater than Lilienthal's predictions in order to balance the drag on the flat plate. His data seemed to be wrong, but their method may have been no more reliable than his whirling wing.

They constructed a small wind tunnel, and then a larger one, taking a month to ensure that the air flowed in a constant and uniform direction. Within the wind tunnel, they inserted a new balance system that again compared a wing with a flat surface. A single flat surface created too much turbulence, and so they used instead four narrow strips. The wing was mounted above these strips, and connected to them by a system of bicycle spokes so that the wing's lift and drag could be balanced against the drag of the strips. After each initial reading, they re-adjusted the balance to correct for the wing's drag, and measured its lift alone. A second balance measured the ratio of lift to drag to enable them to calculate the wing's drag.

Wind tunnels are no longer necessary in aircraft design. Instead, computer programs model the flow of air over the surfaces of an airplane. The Wrights had an analogous ability to imagine the flow of air over surfaces. This ability was sufficient for them to construct wind-tunnel balances that yielded accurate measures from which they could compute lift and drag. They ran a series of systematic tests of different cross-sectional wing shapes at varying angles to the air flow. These observations clinched the fact that Lilienthal's data were wrong. The brothers also discovered that a long thin wing yielded more lift than a short wide wing of the same area. Others had built wind tunnels before, but they were the first to use them to make accurate measurements. When the time they had allotted for these experiments came to an end, they stopped them, and returned to their business.

The brothers designed their third glider, taking into account their wind-tunnel results. They also had to correct the problem with wing warping. It banked the glider to one side, but then the downward wings overtook the upward wings and the craft slewed round in the wrong direction. They needed a way to decelerate the downward wings. Once again, they imagined the flow of air over their glider. Some surface on the plane would have to act as an air break on whichever side was lower when the plane banked. They imagined two fixed vertical tails behind the wings. As the glider banked to one side, the tails would tip into the wind to impede the downward wings.

In late August 1902, they traveled once more to Kitty Hawk. They assembled their third glider, and tested it, as usual, as a kite and then in short glides.

On their first trip to the area, Wilbur had recorded his observations of birds. He noted, for example, that the buzzard with its wings in a dihedral angle had greater difficulty in maintaining equilibrium in strong winds than eagles and hawks that hold their wings level. The dihedral angle increased the disturbance produced by side gusts. The brothers had trussed their first glider with a dihedral angle, and found it unsatisfactory. They retrussed the wings on their current glider so that their ends drooped a little to make them less susceptible to side gusts—a feature more appropriate to the strong winds of Kitty Hawk than elsewhere. For the first time, Orville began to pilot the glider. He crashed, damaging the craft but not himself. After repairs, they flew again, and outdistanced the previous year's glides. Yet, the wing warping still was not right, and sometimes the fixed tails led to a new problem. The glider was no longer pirouetting around its upward wings, but instead side-slipping in the direction of the downward wings until it started to rotate around them and gouge into the sand like a drill. The brothers had discovered a new danger in flying—the tail spin.

The fixed tails were too effective. The downward wings now moved too slowly, and so they had less lift than the upward wings. Their speed was therefore further reduced, and so on ... until the machine spun into the sand. They tried removing one of the fixed tails. It made little difference. After a sleepless night, Orville hit on a solution: if the pilot could *control* the vertical tails, then he could turn them to relieve the pressure on their lower sides. He could balance the lift of the upward and downward wings, and thereby steer the craft out of the spin. As they were converting the fixed vanes into a steerable rudder, they had the further idea of connecting the wires that controlled them to those that operated the wing warping. In this way, whenever the pilot warped the wings, the rudder would turn in the appropriate direction.

The solution worked. They could glide for over 500 feet with excellent command of the craft. They could bank and turn. They could fly with the wind coming from the side. And they could land in safety. They had at last established a full system of control for an aircraft: the forward elevator controlled climbing and diving, and wing-warping and the vertical rudders controlled banking and turning. In late October, after much practice in gliding, they returned to Dayton. Before the end of 1902, they had applied for a patent for their aircraft and its system of control.

* * *

The Wrights needed an engine and propellers. They assumed that marine engineers had solved the theoretical problems of designing propellers. In fact, no theory existed. So, what should the theory be? They later wrote:

What at first seemed a simple problem became more complex the longer we studied it. With the machine moving forward, the air flying backward, the propellers turning sideways, and nothing standing still, it seemed impossible to find a starting-point from which to trace the various simultaneous reactions. Contemplation of it was confusing. After long arguments, we often found ourselves in the ludicrous position of each having been converted to the other's side, with no more agreement than when the discussion began.

The brothers developed their own theory. A propeller moves a ship by displacing a volume of water. It bites into the water in the same way that a corkscrew bites into a cork. Many of the Wrights' rivals supposed that an airplane's propeller should be a flat blade that would cut into the air. But, the analogy is false. Unlike water, air is very compressible. So, what shape should a propeller be? The brothers drew a brilliant analogy. A propeller is a *wing* traveling in a spiral course. The analogy depends on envisaging a model of a wing, carrying out a mental rotation, and observing that it corresponds to half of a rotating propeller. As the wing rotates, it generates, not lift, but *thrust*. A flat blade, like those on Maxim's or Langley's propellers, does not generate much thrust. The blade should instead be cambered like a wing, and the principles for lift apply to the thrust of propellers too.

They designed a propeller for their flyer. It was much more efficient than any other existing propeller in converting energy into thrust. And their theory predicted its thrust to within one per cent. They were far ahead of their rivals, who continued to rely on trial and error in their designs of propellers. After the brothers had made and tested a prototype, they constructed two wooden propellers. They would use both of them, rotating in opposite directions to balance torque, and mount them behind the wings of their flyer to minimize turbulence.

* * *

The Wrights' rivals sought the lightest and most powerful engines they could get. Langley's engine, for example, was a marvel of economy. It delivered almost fifty-five horsepower, and weighed just over 200 pounds. The Wrights in one of their marathon series of calculations worked out the bare minimum that they could get away with. They estimated the area of the powered flyer's wings (500 square feet), and its total weight (625 pounds) complete with engine (200 pounds) and pilot (140–145 pounds). They then calculated the minimum velocity that would lift the machine into the air (twenty-three miles per hour). From this velocity, they calculated the total drag of the wings and the frontal area of the machine (ninety pounds). Hence, the engine needed to produce ninety pounds of thrust. And, at last, from the velocity and drag, they calculated that the engine needed to have eight horsepower. They wrote to various commercial manufacturers with a request for a 180 pound internal combustion engine that would generate eight to nine horsepower. No manufacturer could meet this specification at a reasonable cost, and so they designed their own engine.

Charlie Taylor, who was a skilled machinist working for them, built it in their cycle workshop. The fuel was gravity fed; it was vaporized in a steel can through which air passed; ignition was by way of make-and-break contacts driven by cams; and the four cylinders were water-cooled. They tested the engine, but the next day the crankcase fractured. They made a new engine. It weighed less than 180 pounds, and delivered just under twelve horsepower, more than the minimum.

* * *

The brothers had an engine and two propellers, but how could they connect them? It was no easy matter, Orville wrote, to transmit power from one motor to two propellers rotating in opposite directions. The Wrights were expert at manipulating mental models of mechanical systems; and the reader should be able to guess the source of their design for the transmission. Once again, it was the bicycle. They used an arrangement of sprockets and chains to transmit the rotation of the engine's shaft to the two propeller shafts. To ensure that one propeller rotated in the opposite direction to the other, they twisted its chain once (in the same way as the belts in Figure 2.5).

By midsummer of 1903, they had completed the transmission, and were busy making the flyer's parts. It was in the canard configuration, but on a larger scale with a wingspan of just over forty feet. The machine exceeded its estimated weight, but they calculated that the wings should just about lift it into the air under the power of the engine.

* * *

In late September, they left for their fourth trip to Kitty Hawk with their fourth machine, the powered flyer. The next month they honed their flying skills, practicing on the glider that they had left behind the previous year. They had news of Langley's maiden flight. His aircraft, the *Great Aerodrome*, had dived straight into the Potomac river—an outcome that would not have surprised them had they known that Langley had neglected control, and scaled up a model aircraft to a size large enough to carry a man. Their flyer was ready, but a trial of the engine damaged the propellers' shafts. In new trials of the engine, one of the repaired shafts developed a hairline fracture. Orville went back to Dayton, and returned with new shafts made from solid steel and the latest news of Langley's aerodrome. On its second flight, it broke up in midair and fell again into the Potomac. The pilot managed to escape drowning.

With help from the locals, the brothers moved the flyer to its launch site, where a rail was laid out for it to run on. Wilbur won the toss, and so he was to make the first try. They started the engine, and, after an initial problem in releasing the restraining wire, the flyer ran down the rail. Before it had come to the end of the rail's final section, it was moving faster than Orville could run. Wilbur pulled the plane up, but too steeply. It reached a height of about fifteen feet, but then stalled, settling hard on the ground and damaging the skids and some struts. They soon repaired it. But the weather delayed them for a couple of days. On Thursday, December 17, 1903, they woke to winds of thirty miles an hour. It seemed to be their last chance for the year, and so they laid out the launching track again. Four locals turned up to help them move the flyer out from the hangar. They started the engine. It was Orville's turn to fly first. On his signal at about 10.35 a.m., the flyer ran down the track with Wilbur at the tip of the right wing. Figure 25.2 is the famous photograph of the flyer just after take off. It rose into the air and flew for twelve seconds under Orville's control at a speed of about thirty miles per hour. It covered a distance of 120 feet over the ground, and landed at a position no lower than its point of take off. Three other flights followed the same day. In the longest, Wilbur flew for 852 feet in 59 seconds.

Fig. 25.2 The flyer just after take off on its first successful flight, December 17, 1903. Orville is lying on the wing at the controls; Wilbur is to the right of the machine. The two bicycle chains transmitting power from the engine to the propellers are visible.

In subsequent years, the brothers made many improvements to the design of their flyers, and they separated the controls of the rudder and of wing warping. There was a hiatus of several years in which they made no flights while they tried to sell their machines first to the US War Department, and then, when they were snubbed, to European governments. Their rivals did not catch up. Wilbur took a flyer to France and astounded the French aeronauts, who had deluded themselves that they were leading the race to flight. Orville, at last, demonstrated a flyer to the US military. During the trials, a propeller fractured, and he crashed killing his passenger—the first fatality in an airplane. Their patent was good, but they found themselves in extensive litigation to enforce their rights. They won every case; but Wilbur was worn out. He died of typhoid in 1912.

Orville lived on. He saw almost all the major innovations in aircraft. The development of ailerons, single-winged planes, and powerful engines, which soon outpaced their flyer. He invented the split flap, which is still used by planes as they land. And he noted that their discoveries about the control of aircraft and the design of propellers were not outmoded. One development that he did not live to see would have pleased him. It was the *Gossamer Condor*—an ultra-light aircraft designed by Paul MacCready. Its propeller was driven, not by an engine, but by a very fit bicyclist pedaling prone in the streamlined cockpit.

* * *

Soon after the Wrights had begun their work, they realized that flight was not a puzzle that trial and error could solve. It called for systematic thought about many problems. "Isn't it astonishing," Orville wrote, "that all these secrets have been preserved for so many years just so that we could discover them". Why did they succeed in flying when so many others failed? They had some luck, great perseverance, skill with their hands, but above all, they were exceptional thinkers. Their rivals had the wrong priorities; they scaled up toy models; they tried to fly without understanding first principles. The Wrights flew before their rivals because they out-thought their rivals.

We can make sense of their thinking, and we can understand the mechanisms on which it depends. They were adept at finding counterexamples to arguments: the consequences of engine failure showed that control was more important than power. They could resolve inconsistencies by creating possible diagnoses. In solving problems, they could calculate, they could make deductions, and they could visualize mechanical devices that solved theoretical problems. In their minds, they could simulate the behavior of processes, such as the flow of air over a wing or tail. Above all, they were masters of analogy.

They used five major analogies in their invention of the airplane: the bicycle showed that control mattered more than stability; buzzards showed that wing warping would turn and bank a plane; an inner-tube box showed how to warp wings without loss of lateral stiffness; a rotating wing showed how to design a propeller; and a bicycle chain showed how to transmit power from the engine to the propellers. They had a genius for visualization. But, it depended on the ability to construct mental models of three-dimensional entities. They could animate these representations to work out the flow of air over an aircraft, or to design a transmission system. And they were most adroit in using a model of one thing, a bicycle, as an analogy for another, an aircraft.

Chapter 26

Unwrapping an Enigma

During World War II, a major Allied triumph was to break the German's Enigma cipher. The cipher depended on a machine, the Enigma, which was used by all the German forces. The Allies' ability to read the secret messages between the Nazi High Command and the German armies, navies, and air forces, had a major effect on hastening the end of the war in Europe. Various individuals and groups of individuals played a part in this story—the Polish cryptanalysts, in particular Marian Rejewski, who was the first to break the code, and Alan Turing, who had laid out the abstract logic of programmable computers in 1936. He formulated a complete theory of Enigma for the British code-breakers working in the Government Code and Cypher School in Bletchley Park about fifty miles North of London.

For psychologists, the breaking of the code is a wonderful instance of how reasoning can solve a problem. Most of those who broke the code left us no account of how they did so. But, one of Turing's colleagues, Gordon Welchman, also a brilliant mathematician, did describe the steps in his thinking, albeit many years later. He broke the code during October and November 1939, soon after the war had begun. He worked alone, and ignorant of his precursors. When he reported his success, his boss at Bletchley Park was furious because the code had already been broken. Welchman learned for the first time that others—the Polish cryptanalysts—had broken the code, and that a punch-card system similar to his proposal was already in progress. Yet, his work on solving the Enigma helped him to prepare to organize the massive traffic in decodes. And his account provides us with an insight into the extraordinary mind of a successful code-breaker.

Welchman's reasoning depended on his knowledge of the Enigma machine and of the German protocol for its use. At the heart of his thinking was an exemplary sequence of deductions, including some that depended on probabilities, and so I am going to describe how the model theory of deduction elucidates his mental processes. To understand these processes, however, it is first necessary to know what Welchman already knew when he began to think about the problem. Hence, I start with a description of ciphers and the Enigma machine, and the German protocol for setting up the machine before encoding or decoding a message. It was here that they made one fateful error. And then I analyze Welchman's thinking as he broke the code.

* * *

At the outset of World War II, the German strategy of *Blitzkrieg*—lightning war—called for generals to fight near the front line of their mobile troops. The success of this strategy depended on a rapid and secure method of communication. The messages were not just a secret from the outside world, but also from one unit to another among the ground, air, and naval forces, Hitler's private army (the SS), and German intelligence units. The Germans used Enigma machines to encrypt their secret messages. General Guderian's panzers, for instance, were equipped with these machines during the invasion of France in 1940. Figure 26.1 is photograph of the general in an armed personnel carrier during this invasion, and an Enigma machine is visible in the left foreground of the picture.

Ciphers are almost as old as war. Augustus Caesar relied on a simple "Caesarian" code in which the letters of the alphabet were displaced by a fixed number of letters to encode a message. If the displacement is, say, three letters, then A is coded as D, B as E, and so on. Because the code is easy to crack, a better procedure is to map each letter to a letter selected at random, e.g., A is coded as W, B as A, and so on until each letter is assigned a different code. If you have read Edgar Allan Poe's short story, *The Gold Bug*, then you will know that this sort of code is also easy to crack. We match the frequency with which each letter occurs in a set of encrypted messages with the known frequencies of the letters in the original language, or "plain text," of the messages. The most frequent letter in English texts is E. Hence, if S is the most frequent letter in messages encrypted from English, we can infer that E is encrypted as S in the cipher. The second most frequent letter can be decoded as T in English in a similar way, and so on. We need to know only the relative frequencies with which the letters of the alphabet occur in the written language of the plain texts.

One way to obviate a frequency analysis is to use a "one-time pad". The cipher uses a different Caesarian coding for each letter in a message. The first letter in the plain text of a message, whatever it is, is encoded as, say, one five letters away, the second letter in the message as one 22 letters away, and so on, throughout the entire message. The one-time pad, which specifies the cipher, therefore has to be as long as the plain text of the message, and each occurrence of a particular letter, such as "E", tends to have a different encoding. The cipher is unbreakable except by brute force, that is, by trying every possible encoding for every possible letter. If no letter is encoded as itself, then there are

Fig. 26.1 General Guderian, standing with field glasses, in an armed personnel carrier in 1940 during the invasion of France. In the foreground are two cipher clerks and a radio operator. The Enigma machine (with three rotors) is in the left foreground.

twenty-five possible encodings for each letter in a message. Given a message of, say, twenty letters, the code-breakers in the worst case will have to examine a vast number (25^{20}) of possible encodings to crack the message. Even if they could examine each possible encoding in a millionth of a second, then it could take almost three hundred million million years to break the code. The code is

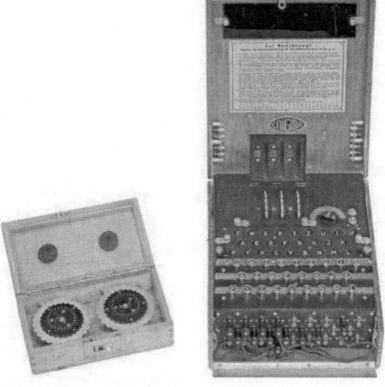

Fig. 26.2 An Enigma machine and its two spare rotors. (© Deutsches Museum, 80306 München, Germany).

unbreakable, but at a cost. Both the encoder of a message and its decoder must have the same one-time pad, and plenty of time both to cipher and to decipher messages. General Guderian couldn't have communicated with his troops in this way. What he needed was a rapid, but impregnable, system of encryption. What he needed was a machine to do the job.

Figure 26.2 is a picture of an Enigma machine. It looks like a combination of a portable typewriter and an old-fashioned desk calculator. At its front end, you can see wires plugged into various sockets. The keyboard has keys for the twenty-six capital letters of the alphabet. Beyond them is a set of lights for each letter in the alphabet in the same spatial arrangement as the keys on the keyboard. Towards the rear of the machine are three rotors. (Later in the war, the machines had four rotors.) The central feature of the machine is that it does not rely on a constant system of encodings. If we type a letter, such as Q, then what lights up is some other letter, such as V. If we type Q again, then a different letter lights up, such as E. Still another letter lights up the next time we type Q, and so on. The Enigma is therefore armed against cryptanalysis based on the frequencies of occurrence of the different letters. The method is useless, because the Enigma's mapping from letters in the plain text to their encrypted versions shifts each time a character is typed on the keyboard. The machine is an automated one-time pad.

The encodings are symmetrical, i.e., if we type Q and the letter V lights up, then if we had typed V instead, the letter Q would have lit up. This property was crucial for decoding messages. The encoding clerk set up his machine in a particular state and encoded a message. The first letter of the plain text of the original message was Q, and so the clerk typed Q and the letter V lit up. That was the first letter in the encoded message. The decoding clerk set up his machine in the same initial state and typed the encrypted message on his machine. What lit up was the sequence of letters in the original plain text. The first letter in the encoded message was V. He typed V and the letter Q lit up. That was the first letter in the plain text of the original. The symmetry of the machine ensured that encoding and decoding were symmetrical operations.

The machine depended on two separate components. The plug-board at the front of the machine allowed a cipher clerk to make arbitrary connections between the keys and the letters that lit up. Because of the need for symmetry, when the clerk used the special cables to wire up the plug-board, a symmetrical relation was created, i.e., if the A key lit up the R light, then the R key lit up the A light. There were eleven symmetrical pairs of letters. The remaining four letters of the alphabet were not affected by the plug-board's wiring. In effect, they were wired to themselves. There were more than 200 million million ways in which the clerk could wire up the plug-board. Once he had wired it up, it remained unchanged for twenty-four hours.

The second component was the system of rotors at the back of the machine known as the scrambler. It had terminals for the twenty-six letters. When the clerk pushed down a letter key, current flowed from the battery through the key, and then through the plug-board to the appropriate terminal of the scrambler. It flowed through the scrambler in a complex way that I will describe in a moment, turned around and flowed out by way of a different route until it reached a different terminal on the scrambler. It then flowed back through the plug-board (by a different route and in the opposite direction to the one by which it entered) and lit up one of the lights for a letter. That letter was the encoding of the letter that the clerk had typed. This route is shown in Figure 26.3.

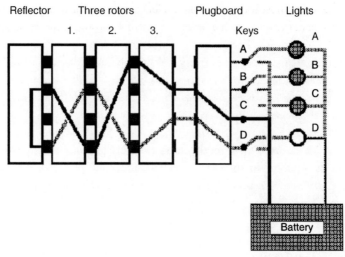

Fig. 26.3 A diagram of the wiring of an Enigma machine. It shows just four keys and lights. Key C has been pushed down, and the diagram shows the flow of current that completes the circuit to light up the letter D.

The terminals on the input to the scrambler were arranged in a circle. They were in physical contact with the adjacent rotor. Each rotor was wired so that the input for one letter led to an output corresponding to a different letter. Figure 26.4 is a simplified diagram of a single rotor, showing the wiring for just four letters of the alphabet. The rotor receiving the input was adjacent to the next rotor, which was wired in an analogous way, and so on and on, until the current came back through a static reflector and passed through the rotors in reverse order until it emerged to light up a letter.

The scrambler was thus a device that took a letter as input and delivered another letter as output. Each of the three rotors had different cross-wirings

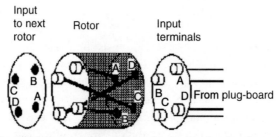

Fig. 26.4 A simplified diagram of the wiring of a single rotor, showing only four letters. Each input terminal on the rotor is wired to a different output terminal. The typed input of C, for example, maps to the input of B on the rotor and thence to A on the next rotor.

from one letter position to another. Hence, there was a complex set of mappings from the input to the first rotor, from this rotor to the second rotor, and so on, all the way back to the output. When the clerk typed a key, the first rotor rotated one position, and so now there was a different set of routes through the scrambler. The first rotor continued to rotate one step with each new keystroke until it reached a position, akin to one on an odometer, when both it and the second rotor rotated one step together. Likewise, the second rotor at length reached a position when it triggered the third rotor, and all three rotors rotated together. In the machine in use at the start of the war, the rotors did not return to their initial positions until they had gone through a large number of positions corresponding to the same number of keystrokes ($26 \times 26 \times 26 = 26^3 = 17{,}576$). Each position yielded a different encryption of the alphabet.

The initial position of a rotor at the start of encoding a message did not have to correspond to the letter A. There was a separate ring attached to the rotor that listed the letters in alphabetical order, and the cipher clerk could turn this ring and lock it into position in order to assign the initial position of the rotor to any letter of the alphabet. All the rotors had these rings.

In summary, the Enigma machine had two separate components that created its encodings. A plug-board that was wired up by hand before encoding or decoding messages, and a set of three rotors—later in the war, four rotors— that also produced a random code with the property that each time a key was typed, the scrambler rotated to change the code for the next letter. In order to produce a still greater number of possible encodings, the three rotors in the scrambler came from a set of five, and could be inserted into the machine in any order. These possibilities created a myriad of different settings (sixty possible sets of three rotors multiplied by 26^3 positions for the rings). These possibilities multiplied by those from the wiring of the plugboard yielded a total number of possible codes of over two hundred million million million. This number was large enough to make Enigma seem impregnable.

* * *

In order for a message to be sent from high command in Berlin to General Guderian sitting in his armored vehicle, a number of steps had to be taken to ensure success. The machine in Berlin and the machine in the vehicle had to be set-up in identical initial positions. Their plug-boards had to be wired in the same way; they had to have the same rotors in the same positions in the scrambler; the letter rings on these rotors had to be fixed on the rotors in the same positions; and the rotors with their rings fixed in position had to be turned to the same initial positions on both machines. Only if this set-up was carried out correctly were both machines in the same initial state. The clerk in Berlin typed the plain text into his machine, and the resulting sequence of letters that lit up was transmitted by radio in morse code. The radio operator in Guderian's armored car transcribed the sequence, and passed it to the cipher clerk sitting next to him. The cipher clerk typed the encoding into his machine, and the resulting sequence of letters that lit up, if no mistakes had occurred, was the plain text of the original message from Berlin. You can see the radio operator and two cipher clerks in the foreground of Figure 26.1.

How could the sending and receiving cipher clerks set up their separate machines so that they were in an identical initial state? The answer depended both on a code book that both clerks possessed and on the initial signals in the radio transmission. The code books, which differed from one military unit to another, contained a *key* that specified which three rotors to use, their order in the scrambler, the settings of the three alphabet rings on them, and the wiring of the plug-board. The key was valid for twenty-four hours, and so it would be used for many messages, though it was restricted to a particular sort of military unit. Welchman had studied the radio traffic, and he knew that the Germans were transmitting at least a hundred messages per day using a given key. Each key had a number, and this number was transmitted in plain text at the start of each radio message, so a receiving clerk could check whether it was in his code book. If it wasn't, the message wasn't meant for his unit, and he couldn't decode it. The British analysts, of course, could collect together all the messages sent using a particular key.

The one thing that the key did not specify was the initial positions of the rotors with their fixed rings at the start of a message. This matter was left to the discretion of the encoding clerks, who were supposed to choose a new position at random for every message. (The laziness of clerks was to become a great help to the code-breakers.) The Berlin clerk decided the initial positions of the rotors for encoding a message to Guderian. Suppose he decided that the initial positions of the three rotors should be respectively: MCR. He had to turn the rotors by hand so that he could see the initial letter M on the first rotor, C on the second rotor, and R on the third rotor. These letters were visible in small windows next to each rotor (see the open flap with three windows in Figure 26.2). He then had to transmit these positions of the three rotors so that the receiving clerk, who would already have his machine in the appropriate set-up, could turn the rotors on his machine to their correct initial positions. But, if the clerk transmitted their initial positions in plain text, it would give away vital information. Yet, he couldn't transmit them in a cipher, because they were part of the initial set-up necessary for the cipher. So, how was it done?

The Berlin clerk had chosen an initial rotor setting of MCR to encode a message. To communicate this setting, he spun the rotors to a position at random, say, NIV. This position was radioed in plain text before the ciphered text. From this position of NIV, he then typed the initial rotor setting for ciphering twice: MCRMCR. The result was, say, this encoding:

PUESQW

This sequence came next in the radio transmission. The transmitting clerk then set his rotors to the setting MCR, and encrypted the message, which was added to the radio signal.

Guderian's clerk received the following sequences of letters after the call signs and the identity of the key:

NIV—the plain text of the position chosen at random by the sending clerk to transmit the initial setting of the rotors for decoding the main message.

PUESQW—the encryption of the initial setting of the three rotors repeated twice.

The ciphered text of the message from the initial setting.

Guderian's clerk had already set up his machine according to the day's key. He turned his rotors to the position NIV, and then typed in the string PUESQW. This string lit up the letters MCRMCR, and so the clerk now knew the setting of the three rotors needed to decode the encrypted message. He turned his rotors to the setting MCR, and typed in the encrypted message, which the machine decoded. Only a clerk who had set up the machine in a correct way could decode PUESQW to reveal the initial settings of the rotors for decoding the main message.

You now know as much as Welchman knew. That is, you know all that is essential to understand how he broke the Enigma code, or even to try to anticipate his solution.

* * *

Suppose that an Enigma machine didn't have rotors in a scrambler but just the plug-board. It could produce millions and millions of different codes, but any of them would be child's play to break using an analysis in which the most frequent letter in the message was matched to the most frequent letter in the language of the plain text, and so on, as I described earlier. Suppose further that there were a mere 250 possible set-ups for an Enigma machine. It would be feasible to try each of them in turn to discover which one of them led to a successful decoding of the message, i.e., a sensible message in German emerged from a frequency analysis. And so at the heart of the problem is the task of reducing the number of possible set-ups of the machine to a manageable number. This procedure is indeed the one that Welchman followed. He described his thinking in a sequence of steps, which I will follow.

Step 1

What clue is there in how the Germans used the machine that might help to cut down the vast number of possible codes? Is there some information that they are giving away about the initial set-up of the machine? Sometimes when we play a game such as chess, we have a strong intuition about the right move to make even though we may be unable at first to see why it is the right move. (I described these intuitions in Part II of the book.) These intuitions often presage a solution. Welchman's first step was an intuition of this sort. He suspected, as you may well have done, that the clue might be in the double encoding of the initial setting of the scrambler rotors. The redundancy in the German's protocol was designed to minimize errors. Granted that the Berlin clerk had chosen MCR as the initial setting, he was then obliged to transmit their double encoding from some other arbitrary position of the rotors. The resulting encryption, PUESQW, means that the machine's set-up first encoded an unknown letter as P and then three keystrokes later as S. Similar relations exist between the other pairs of letters: U and Q, and E and W. These inferences are straightforward deductions from a mental model of the machine.

Step 2

The second step in Welchman's thinking depended on an examination of these double encodings of initial settings. Here are some typical examples. You should read them aloud, and see whether you notice any difference between the first one and the last two:

PUESQW

SPESNT

VBYQGY

I hope that you noticed that each of the last two strings contains a repeated letter. The critical property, however, is not just two occurrences of the same letter, but their positions. In the string *SPESNT*, the letter S occurs in the first and fourth positions. Hence, the machine repeats a letter to encode the *same* unknown letter in the description of the initial setting of the rotors. This repeated letter occurs three keystrokes apart. Likewise, the string VBYQGY encodes the third letter in the description of the unknown initial setting using

Y both times, three keystrokes apart. I will refer to these sorts of encodings as *repeats*, i.e., those for which the machine repeats the same letter three keystrokes apart in encoding the same given letter twice. Welchman's detection of repeats was inductive: he examined many double encodings, and noticed that some of them contained repeats. He reports that he began to think, by chance, about these repeats. The second step culminated in a subtle question: was it always possible to generate a repeat from any random choice of the position of the scrambler rotors? That is, does any set-up of the machine always yield for at least one letter of the alphabet the same encoding after two intervening encodings of letters?

Step 3

If a repeat isn't always possible, then an occurrence of a repeat rules out a certain number of possible set-ups for the machine. This conclusion calls for a subtler inference:

> Suppose that there is a property of an encryption, which I'll call property X, which is a consequence of the set-up of the machine. If *all* set-ups allow X to occur in *some* messages, then the occurrence of X in a message is compatible with *any* set-up. But, if *some* set-ups do not allow X to occur in *any* messages, then the occurrence of X in a message rules out these set-ups, i.e., X allows us to eliminate these set-ups. A repeat is a property such as X. Hence, if some set-ups do not allow repeats to occur in any messages, then the occurrence of a repeat in a message rules out these set-ups.

The deduction at the heart of this reasoning is one that hinges on premises that contain several quantifiers, which I have italicized above. They make deduction tricky, but a skilled reasoner can use models to make these inferences (see Chapter 11).

Welchman discovered that repeats couldn't occur in all possible settings. He examined examples of encodings for successive positions of a machine, and saw that in some set-ups no repeats occurred three keystrokes apart for any letter of the alphabet. That was his third step: repeats cannot always occur, and so the occurrence of a repeat rules out possible set-ups. As he wrote, this fact was the germ from which his success was to grow.

Step 4

His next step was to work out the probability that a repeat occurs in the double encryption of the initial setting of the rotors. Welchman tells us that the probability calculus was not one of his strong points, but that the calculations were elementary. They can be carried out from mental models of possibilities and the assumption of equiprobability (see Chapter 15). In each position of the rotors in the scrambler, the Enigma machine produces a symmetrical coding based on thirteen pairings of letters. Consider two different positions of the rotors, and suppose that in first of them A is coded as R (and therefore R is coded as A). The full set of pairs in the first position is, say:

A	B	C	D	E	F	H	I	J	K	M	N	V
|	|	|	|	|	|	|	|	|	|	|	|	|
R	G	L	Y	P	Z	U	W	T	S	O	Q	X

In the second position of the rotors, the probability that A is again coded as R is one in twenty-five, because there are twenty-five letters other than A to chose its encoding from. The same argument applies to each of the thirteen pairings, i.e., each of them has a probability of repeating of 1/25. So, the chances that at least one pair is repeated in the second position of the rotors are therefore thirteen out twenty-five.

The selection of any pair to encode the initial setting of the first rotor is one in thirteen. Hence, the probability that the encoding of the first rotor's setting yields a repeat is equal to the probability that at least one pair is repeated (13/25) multiplied by the probability of selecting that pair to encode the position of the first rotor's position (1/13), i.e., the probability is 1/25. The chances of a repeat in positions two and five are the same, as are the chances of a repeat in positions three in six. In sum, the chances that a repeat occurs are three in twenty-five, or about one in eight. The fourth step therefore showed that the chances of a repeat in an encoding of the initial setting of the rotors should be about one in eight.

Step 5

This step was a series of deductions. It began with the inference that the probability of a repeat depends on the positions of the rotors (and their internal cross-wirings). It is not affected in any way by the choice of wirings for the plug-board. That choice will change the particular letter that is repeated, but not the chances of a repeat. It follows further that the 200 million million possible ways of wiring the plug-board have no effect on the occurrence of repeats. All that matters are the rotors. As I explained earlier, there are sixty choices for the three rotors out of the set of five, and there are 17,576 distinct settings for their alphabet rings. Welchman's deductions therefore reduced the number of possible set-ups to be analyzed to the product of these two numbers, i.e., to just over a million.

A typical preamble to an Enigma message containing a repeat was:

KCX—the initial arbitrary positions in plain text

SPESNT—the double encoding of the subsequent setting of the rotors for the encoding or decoding of the message.

The analysts know that the rotors were turned to the position KCX, but they don't know the set-up of the scrambler—the choice of rotors or the settings of their alphabet rings. In theory, they could type KCX on a machine for each of the million or so settings. About half the settings will yield the required repeat of a letter in the first and fourth positions. Those settings that fail to produce a repeat can be eliminated. The same key is used for twenty-four hours, and each message contains the plain text of the arbitrary starting position of the three rings. It follows that each repeat in the preamble of a message allows us to eliminate about half the possibilities from the set of just over a million possible rotor and ring settings. Elementary arithmetic yielded the next inference: after the first repeat, there are just over half a million possible set-ups left. After the second repeat, there are just over a quarter of a million. And after twelve repeats, there are just 250 possible set-ups left. Each of them could be examined to check whether it was the correct setting, but that task was feasible.

Step 6

A repeat, as step 4 showed, should occur on average in one out of eight messages. In a hundred messages, there should be on average twelve repeats, and the Germans were transmitting each day at least a hundred messages for a given key. Hence, the sixth step concluded with the induction that there should be enough messages to reduce the number of possible set-ups of the machine using a given key to about 250.

We have now followed the six steps in Welchman's thinking that led him to see how to break the code. You should have understood how each occurrence of a repeat for a given key enables the number of possible initial settings to be halved, and that enough repeats should occur to reduce them to a manageable number. Welchman's remaining thoughts concerned the practical implementation of his solution in a pre-computer era. His idea was to examine once and for all whether a repeat occurred in each of the million or so possible settings of a machine, and to store the results in large punched sheets. Holes in the sheets represented repeats. The sheets could be piled up on top of a light table and aligned in an appropriate way. Whenever a light shone through all the sheets, it would indicate a possible alphabet ring setting and rotor arrangement used in the encoding. The testing of a machine and punching of the sheets would take several months. But, once it was done, they could be used every day. The stacking of the sheets and then isolating the correct setting among the 250 might take half a day. Welchman computed that an average of 760 stackings would do the job. Once the set-up of a machine was known, it could be used to type the encoded message. The result was a static unchanging cipher based solely on the plug-board, which could be cracked using a frequency analysis of the sort that I described earlier.

* * *

Each step in Welchman's reasoning can be explained in terms of the major processes of deductive and inductive reasoning that the model theory elucidates. His principal inductions are based on observations of the output of machines. His principal deductions could all be simulated in a computer program equipped with a working model of an Enigma machine. Box 26.1 summarizes his six steps from this standpoint. Each step can be accounted for in terms of the basic processes of inference. What presents a much greater challenge is to devise a computer program that would discover for itself the sequence of steps. It took Welchman a week of concentrated thinking to solve the problem. Each step prepared the way for the next step. He was working forwards towards the goal in the same sort of way in which we tackle simple problems of reverse engineering. But, I suspect, that a means-ends analysis yielded the overall break-down of the problem into two components: the reduction of the scrambler settings to a feasible number and the use of a frequency analysis to solve the plug-board wirings.

Box 26.1 The main steps in Welchman's reasoning

1. The double encoding of the initial rotor positions might be useful: an unconscious intuition.

2. Repeats occur in at least some set-ups: an induction. If repeats are impossible in other set-ups, then the occurrence of a repeat rules out these set-ups: a deduction.

3. Repeats are impossible in some set-ups of the scrambler: an induction.

4. The probability of a repeat is about one in every eight messages: a series of deductions.

5. This probability depends only on the scrambler position. Therefore, analysis can ignore the wirings of the plug-board: a deduction.

6. Twelve repeats for a given key reduce possible scrambler set ups to 250: a deduction. Traffic should yield this number for daily keys: an induction.

The initial cracking of the Enigma code, which Welchman duplicated, occurred at the same time that other methods for breaking it were under development. They led to the invention of various machines to aid analysis, culminating in Colossus, a precursor to the programmable digital computer. The computer has in turn led to the development of cipher systems that are impregnable... so far.

Chapter 27

On the Mode of the Communication of Cholera

In 1831 cholera came to England for the first time. The disease is terrible. At first, you feel a little queasy, as though you have eaten something that didn't agree with you. It soon gets worse. You start to suffer from excessive diarrhea, vomiting, chest and stomach pains, and muscle spasms. In a matter of hours, you age visibly. Your pulse becomes weak. Your circulation is sluggish. Your body grows cold. And your face, neck, and hands turn almost blue. Your chances of dying are about one in three. If you do die, you will succumb in a day or two. Doctors in England knew that the disease came from Asia. It was easy to diagnose: the diarrhea was a characteristic sign. The stools had little fecal color or smell. They were watery and contained small white grains. Hence, the name "rice water" stools.

The disease broke out in Sunderland and Newcastle-on-Tyne, ports nearby to each other on the north-east coast of England. But it spread quickly from one place to another, focusing on slums. Physicians had neither preventives nor palliatives. They tried every possible cure that they could imagine but had little success. They did not know the cause of the disease, its pathology, or how it spread. Some thought that it was contagious. Some thought that it came from a miasma in the air—noxious effluvia in the atmosphere— perhaps a result of the filth in the slums. Some thought that the weather caused the disease, for those with a susceptible constitution. And susceptibility, they believed, was a result of a strong emotion, such as fear. As a precaution against the miasma the streets of Newcastle were spread with lime. The places most at risk were supposed to be low-lying areas, and most of the city was at a safe altitude. Yet, the disease spread, even to the mining villages outside the city.

The man who solved the puzzle of cholera's mode of communication was Dr. John Snow, and his research laid the foundations for a new discipline— *epidemiology*, the study of the spread of diseases through populations. His theory, which he tested in ingenious ways, was not accepted during his lifetime. He endured ridicule from his peers and the public. His views, however, were vindicated after his death when cholera struck England again in 1866, in its fourth outbreak.

What I want to examine is how Snow reasoned. His reasoning was the secret that led him to discover the mechanism of cholera's transmission prior to any knowledge of bacteria. The history of medicine is a history of magical thinking. Doctors and patients alike are vulnerable to the fallacy of *post hoc ergo propter hoc* (after this, therefore on account of this). That is to say, patients recovered from illnesses despite bleeding, cupping, blisters, leeches, or other curious regimens of no proven curative powers, and so credulous individuals attributed the recovery to these treatments. Snow's work contrasts with this history. His thinking was an exemplary case of scientific reasoning.

Snow was born in 1813 in York in the north of England. His parents were poor, but they were able to send him to school. He started his medical training as an apprentice to a doctor in Newcastle-on-Tyne, and he was there during the first outbreak of cholera. He was sent to a mining village outside the city, and saw for himself miners brought up from the pits dying from the disease. During his years in Newcastle, he became a vegetarian and a believer in the virtues of pure water: drinking water should be distilled. And he became a public speaker in the cause of temperance.

After nine years as an apprentice to various doctors in the north east, he was able to go to London to finish his medical education at the University of London. He qualified in 1838 as a surgeon and an apothecary—a double qualification that was then necessary to practice medicine. He became a pioneer in the use of ether and then chloroform as anesthetics. He undertook intensive programs of research to examine their effects on animals in order to understand the physiology of their operation, and he mastered the known laws about the diffusion of gases in the atmosphere. He became best known in his lifetime as the doctor who in 1853 administered chloroform to Queen Victoria as she was delivering her eighth child—an event that led to the widespread use of anesthesia in the delivery room. By this time, he had made a successful career as a physician and anesthetist in London. His great achievement, however, was his elucidation of the pathology and communication of cholera. He died at the age of forty-five in 1858.

* * *

In the fall of 1848, as Snow was continuing his researches into anesthesia, cholera returned to England in a second epidemic. Within a year, while the outbreak continued, he had developed a theory of the pathology of the disease and its transmission. Many scientists in Snow's era were "inductivists". They believed that scientific investigation was just a matter of making inductive generalizations from observations—a view that persisted on the part of some scientists almost to the present day. Karl Popper, the twentieth century philosopher of science, dismissed induction altogether. Science, he argued, depends on conjectures and refutations. Conjectures are happy guesses, and refutations are observations that are inconsistent with the deductive consequences of conjectures. A scientific theory, however, is seldom a set of happy guesses. Indeed, a neo-Darwinian account of conjectures is out of the question. The processes underlying the creation of a scientific theory depend on an interplay between induction, abduction, and deduction. The same interplay occurs in everyday reasoning, as in my earlier example about Italian coffee bars (see Chapter 13). Hence, scientific thinking is not special, but grows out of our daily practices. Probabilities may also enter, as they do in the statistical analysis of data. The critical steps, however, are to abduce hypotheses and to test them in a systematic comparison of their deducible consequences with observations of the world. As Popper argued, what demarcates science from other domains is tests that could falsify hypotheses.

Snow understood the need to develop theories. They might be based in part on inductions, but it was also necessary to formulate explanatory hypotheses and to deduce testable consequences from them. This view of science had been formulated earlier in the nineteenth century, and it was sometimes known as the "hypothetico-deductive" method. Many modern cognitive scientists have argued for a model-based conception of scientific investigation. Scientists develop mental models of how the world works, and they use these models both to create their descriptions of theories and to infer testable consequences. The mental construction of models depends on abduction. It relies on a multi-stage process, and knowledge, which may be acquired from induction, serves as a major constraint. This account makes sense, as we'll see, of how Snow reasoned in pursuing a scientific understanding of cholera.

He began with a number of inductions from well-known observations:

◆ Cholera was a single specific disease.
◆ It was communicated somehow from one person to another. Its spread followed the trade routes, and the arrival of an infected person in a particular place often led to an outbreak of the disease.

He then reasoned that if it was communicated in this way in some cases, then the chances are that it was so in all other cases. In making this induction, Snow refers to the maxim, which I've cited before: "similar effects depend on similar causes". The induction is also a consequence of a strain of parsimony in Snow's thinking. He had a bias towards a single mode of communication. This bias, coupled with a known mechanism for some cases and an unknown mechanism for other cases, yields the induction that the unknown mechanism is the same as the known mechanism. Hence, his initial model of the disease posited a single mode for its communication.

Throughout his life, the parsimony of his theory attracted criticism. The industrial revolution in nineteenth century England led to a "Sanitarian" movement for the introduction of water closets in place of cesspits, for curbs on pollution from factories, and for other sanitary reforms. Its advocates never could accept Snow's account, and they argued for diverse modes of communication of the disease. They were much attracted to the idea that some general pollutant was present in the atmosphere. This "miasmal" theory, however, Snow was able to dismiss outright. His study of anesthetics had led him to an understanding of the gas laws, and so he deduced that the distribution of noxious particles in the air would be too diffuse to transmit the disease. As he later wrote: "As the gases given off by putrefying substances become diffused in the air, the quantity in a given space is inversely as the square of the distance from the source. Thus, a man working with his face one yard from offensive substances would breathe ten thousand times as much of the gas given off, as a person living a hundred yards from the spot".

An analogous view, however, was that the disease is transmitted from one person to another by the inhalation of some contagion in the air, which had emanated from the victims. Snow had begun with this view, but once he began his proper investigations of the disease, he reasoned that the mechanism was improbable. The poison would vary in its concentration in the air. Some people would have to resist high densities of it, because they were in contact with victims but did not succumb, whereas others would have to be susceptible to very low densities, because they were distant from anyone with the disease and yet succumbed. It was implausible that susceptibility to the poison could vary in so large a way.

To develop an account of the pathology of cholera, Snow reported that he drew an analogy with other diseases. Physicians knew that the ova of certain intestinal worms, if ingested, could infect the alimentary canal. Snow made an abductive inference by analogy with this mechanism: unknown poisonous particles of cholera could likewise be ingested and transmit the disease to the gut. These particles could be living organisms or not, but they were organized, and obeyed the laws of chemistry. He made a further abduction. The particles multiplied in the gut, and they inflamed its mucous membrane so that it pulled out salts and the watery part of the blood, which the patients then evacuated. This hypothesis explained two long-standing observations: patients became dehydrated and their blood became thick. This thickening, he inferred, also explained patients' circulatory problems and difficulty in breathing.

How did the hypothetical particles of cholera pass from one person to another? When the disease was transmitted within a household, a plausible abduction was that victims' diarrhea infected their clothing and bedding. Its lack of feculent color and smell could lead others to pick up this linen. If they then prepared food without washing their hands, then they could pass on the particles to food and drink. They and others would then ingest the particles.

But, the disease could also leap large distances. Snow's long-standing pre-occupation with purified drinking water may have led him to the abduction that cholera particles could enter the drinking water supply. If infected sewage contaminated the water supply, then the disease could be communicated over a wide area.

The construction of the theory depended on common knowledge and Snow's particular expertise about matters such as the gas laws. As in any scientific theory, he was guided by certain established results. He was prepared to make inductions to simplify the observations to be explained: he inferred that the mode of communication was singular rather than diverse. He used an analogy to abduce a key hypothesis: particles of cholera infected the gut just as ova of worms could infect it. The inflammation led to the extraction into the gut of salts and the watery part of blood. They were evacuated in the diarrhea of the victims.

Given this pathology, the communication of the disease called for causation by contact. Once he had ruled out the miasmal theory, there remained only the inhalation of the noxious particles or their ingestion. Inhalation failed to explain the spread of the disease from one locale to another unless one was prepared to make an implausible assumption about the susceptibility of individuals to the disease. Ingestion was plausible within a household, and so all that was left to explain was transmission over larger distances. Granted the constraint that fecal matter was the transmitter and the gut was the receiver, drinking water was a salient channel of communication. Indeed, it is hard to conceive of any other possibility.

Snow's theory established a chain of causation by physical contact that explained both the transmission of the disease and its pathology:

1. the excretions of cholera victims contained poisonous particles;
2. these particles could be communicated to others by physical contact with soiled clothing and they could enter the sewage;
3. in the latter case, if the sewage contaminated the water supply, then other people who drank the water would ingest the particles;

4. when the particles were ingested, they multiplied and inflamed the gut, causing the disease in the infected victims;

5. the inflammation caused the extraction of serum from the blood, i.e., salts and its watery part;

6. this extraction caused the blood to thicken, and it caused secondary problems in circulation (the blue appearance of patients) and in breathing, which could result in death;

7. the salts and watery part of the blood, together with poisonous particles of disease, entered the alimentary canal.

And so the cycle of infection continued.

The causal theory rested on both abduction and inductions from observations. It lacked just one component: the nature of the poisonous particles. But, it implied that a small number of them were sufficient to cause the disease, and so they were capable of multiplication. It also implied that they retained their potency and were not diluted in vast quantities of water. Snow inferred that they were organized entities, perhaps even living organisms.

* * *

The theory was plausible, and Snow deduced some testable consequences. The most salient was that if drinking water was the channel of communication, then cholera should tend to occur whenever the water supply could have been contaminated by sewage containing the poisonous particles. His pursuit of evidence on this point led him to become a pioneering epidemiologist, and after the cholera epidemic of 1848–49 he helped to set up the London Epidemiological Society.

At first, Snow gathered evidence in an anecdotal way. He described two reports that he read on the 1848 epidemic of cholera in London. The first described an outbreak in Horsleydown. In one set of buildings, the disease had been rampant; in another nearby set, there had been just a single case. The only difference between the two sets of buildings, the author of the report observed, was that the drinking water in the infected building was drawn from a well on the same level as a sewage drain. A second report described a similar difference in Albion Terrace in Wandsworth. Snow does not seem to have used maps to aid his thinking, though he did use them to help audiences draw deductive consequences from them. However, he often imagined the spatial layouts of drains and water pipes. In Albion Terrace, the brick drains and cesspools were higher than the pipe supplying drinking water. A severe rain storm had caused the drains to overflow, and two days later the first case of cholera occurred.

The overflow could have contaminated the water supply. Because no other outbreak occurred in the region, this case counted against the hypothesis that the cause of the disease was a miasma. Hence, the lack of the disease was contrary to a deductive consequence of the miasmal theory, and so counted as a counterexample to that theory.

His next step was to collect systematic data. He drew up a table of deaths from cholera in the principal regions of London. South of the river Thames the mortality rate from cholera was seven times greater than north of the river. South London had its water supply from companies that drew water from the tidal region of the Thames, below the city's main outflows of sewage. Hence, the water could have been contaminated by the poisonous particles of cholera. North London had its water supply from companies that drew water from the Thames higher up than the sewage outflows. Its water was much less likely to have been contaminated. The difference was suggestive, but not decisive. Snow continued to collect evidence for this theory after the publication of his monograph on the disease. He corresponded with many people around the country to gather data, both about the first epidemic of 1831 and the more recent one of 1848. He described cases where outbreaks occurred and cases where, according to rival theories, they had not occurred but should have done so. The critical difference, he argued, was whether or not sewage could have contaminated the water supply.

Perhaps the best of this evidence was a natural experiment concerning two English cities: Exeter and Hull. In the 1831 epidemic, Exeter had suffered, but its waterworks had then moved upstream of the sewage outflow. It had far fewer victims in the 1848 epidemic. The fate of Hull was the opposite: few victims in the first epidemic; its waterworks moved to a polluted region of the river; and it had many more victims in the second epidemic. Nevertheless, defenders of alternative theories were unconvinced, and continued to support the miasmal theory.

What was missing from Snow's analysis was a comprehensive study of water supply and cholera. When a third epidemic broke out in the summer of 1853, Snow was able to carry out a "grand experiment". Because height above sea level was important for the miasmal hypothesis, this crucial experiment had to pit the nature of the water supply against height above sea level in order to determine which variable predicted the rate of cholera victims. Snow noticed an interesting feature in the official figures of deaths from cholera. Some areas of London were supplied with water from two rival companies, one took its water from above the tidal region of the Thames, whereas the other did not. He analyzed the respective mortality rates. No one had died from cholera in those subdistricts supplied only by the upstream company, but the mortality rate in those subdistricts supplied only by the downstream company was 114 per 10,000. But, there was a snag. The subdistricts differed in character. The healthy ones were residential suburbs. The unhealthy ones were overcrowded and poverty-stricken parts of the inner city.

The crucial comparison could be made only in subdistricts supplied by both companies. In these subdistricts, pipes from both companies ran down all the streets, and so one house could receive water from one company while the house next door received it from the rival company. All that was necessary was to determine the mortality rates in the houses of the two sorts. Snow decided to focus on *deaths* from cholera, and then determine which company supplied water to the victims' houses. Cholera had waned towards the end of 1853, but it waxed strong again in the following summer. He cut down on his medical practice so that he could walk the streets of Kennington in South London to gather the relevant data. Of forty-four deaths there during the first five weeks of the renewed epidemic, thirty-eight were in houses supplied by the downstream company. This difference is most unlikely to occur by chance. If I tossed a coin forty-four times, and it came down heads thirty-eight, then you would have grounds for supposing that I was tricking you. Statistical tests had not been invented in Snow's era, but the actual chances of the result, or a more extreme one, given fair tosses of an unbiased coin, are that it should occur less than five times in ten million experiments in which the coin was tossed forty-four times.

Snow continued to gather evidence with a medical colleague. It wasn't easy to find out which company supplied the water to many houses, because absentee landlords often paid the water bills. But, Snow's chemical expertise helped him out. He was able to devise a simple chemical test that distinguished between the waters of the two companies, because they differed in saltiness. He and his colleague discovered that 286 deaths from cholera occurred in houses supplied by the downstream company, whereas just fourteen deaths from cholera occurred in houses supplied by the upstream company. Think of tossing a coin with that result!

As the epidemic continued, the difference should diminish because individuals were then at risk of catching the disease from other people rather than from contaminated water. Hence, Snow predicted that the difference in mortality rates between households supplied by the two companies should diminish. He corroborated this prediction, too. He was able to persuade those in charge of the register of births and deaths to gather data for him. These data were bound to be less reliable than his own results. They couldn't carry out the test to determine which company supplied a house if the occupants did not know. Yet, their data showed a similar massive difference in risk between the two companies with a ratio of deaths of about five to one. Snow published these results in the second edition of his book in 1855. One irony was that London's improved drainage—thanks to the Sanitarians—had led to more sewage being flushed into the Thames, and as a result to an increase in deaths from cholera.

When Snow had collected all these data, he carried out a mathematical test of his theory. His basic assumption was that the most important factor in the disease's spread was the water supply, and so the number of deaths should correlate with the number of houses receiving polluted water. He examined thirty-one subdistricts of London. There had been 160 deaths per 10,000 houses supplied by the downstream company, and twenty-seven deaths per 10,000 houses supplied by the upstream company. His theory predicted that these ratios should also occur in each subdistrict, and he examined the difference between them and the actual numbers. He described the result as "a very close relation".

* * *

In contrast to the slow but decisive accumulation of statistical evidence, a single outbreak of cholera in Broad Street (now Broadwick Street) in Soho in the center of London was the most vivid episode in Snow's researches into cholera. When he heard of the outbreak, which was just a few minutes walk from his home, he at once suspected contamination in the water from a pump. He recalled a similar incident in the 1848 epidemic. As he later wrote, he went to Golden Square in Soho with this hypothesis in mind. He inspected the water from a pump in Broad Street, and both he and an expert microscopist detected organic matter in it. In pursuing his enquiries, one informant told him that the water had an offensive smell just before the outbreak began. But, this evidence was again no more than suggestive.

Snow was then able to infer another way to test his hypothesis. Individuals who lived nearer to the pump than to any other pump should have succumbed to the disease more often than those who lived nearer to another pump. He worked out the point on each street that was equidistant between the Broad Street pump and another pump. His house-to-house inquiries showed that most of the victims had lived in houses closer to the Broad Street pump than to any other. Snow presented himself at a meeting of the local authorities responsible for health, and persuaded them to have the pump's handle removed. The epidemic was declining, but there were no further cases after the removal of the handle.

Snow continued to investigate the outbreak. He discovered that a workhouse in the area had been largely spared: it had its own well. He joined forces with the local vicar, who helped to find members of the victims' families when they had fled the area. The overwhelming majority of victims had drunk water from the pump. The vicar also pinpointed the initial case: a five-month old infant who had died of "diarrhea" in one of the houses near to the pump. As she lay dying, others in the area began to fall ill. A careful inspection of the pump revealed that a nearby cesspool could have contaminated the well that supplied its water.

During the course of his investigations, Snow prepared two maps of the area, showing the number of deaths in each house. The first map, which he published in the second edition of *On the Mode of Communication of Cholera*, locates the Broad Street pump in the wrong place. The second map corrects this error, and it also contains an innovative feature. Snow drew a line round the area that demarcated those points equidistant between the Broad Street pump and some other pump. Figure 27.1 presents this map. Snow used it to make the

Fig. 27.1 John Snow's second map of the Broad Street cholera outbreak. The pump is near the middle of Broad Street. The dotted line, which I have enhanced along with some other electronic tidying up of a reproduction of the map, shows Snow's line of points equidistant between the Broad Street pump and other pumps. Each black rectangle represents a person who died during the outbreak.

simple deduction—for the benefit of an official inquiry into the outbreak—that deaths fell almost to zero outside the circumference of the line.

* * *

Snow realized that his theory implied practical measures to prevent the spread of the disease. It was necessary to block the fecal–oral route. An elementary deduction was that individuals in contact with victims needed to ensure that they did not ingest the cholera particles. A quarantine of victims might be effective, but, contrary to other theories, Snow's account did not require infected individuals to be sequestered. Hygiene, not quarantine, was needed. If caretakers had touched infected persons or their bedding, they needed to be scrupulous in washing their hands. If the channel of communication was the water supply, then people should boil water before they drank it, and avoid drinking any that might be contaminated. Water companies should draw their water upstream from any sewage outflows, and check that the pipes delivering water could not be contaminated by seepage from drains or cesspits. Like his theory, these proposals were not accepted during his lifetime.

* * *

Snow's elucidation of cholera was an exemplary case of scientific reasoning. He had some facts at his disposal, which yielded some inductions about the epidemic, such as that cholera was a single specific disease. These inductions were dependent on knowledge: doctors had long before discovered the existence of specific diseases. From this model of the disease, Snow formulated a parsimonious theory of its pathology, which explained its causal effects on those whom it infected. Likewise, by a process of abduction, he explained the transmission of the disease. A central analogy in his thinking was from the known transmission of worms to the unknown transmission of the hypothetical particles of cholera. In 1854 unbeknownst to Snow, the Italian Filippo Piccini identified *Vibrio cholerae*, the bacterium that causes the disease. The world took little notice of his work. Robert Koch, who rediscovered the bacterium, continues to be credited with its discovery. The final link in Snow's reasoning was an abduction about the communication of the particles. Given the assumption of causation by contact, a simple spatial model yields two routes: a short-range one via contact with contaminated clothing and a long-range and indirect one. The pathology of the disease supported the hypothesis of contamination of the water supply.

Once Snow had his theory, he deduced various testable consequences from it. These consequences implied a need for certain sorts of data, which Snow gathered. To a disinterested party, they made a decisive case in support of his theory and against its main rivals. Proponents of these accounts, who were in the majority in the medical and health professions, were not convinced, and it was only after Snow's death and on the arrival of the fourth cholera epidemic in 1866 that the professionals and the public began to accept his ideas.

In the sweltering summer of 1858, as John Snow lay dying, the river Thames began to give off a terrible smell. He died of a stroke on June 16. Two days later, the *Times* newspaper described the "great stink", reporting that it had driven members from the Houses of Parliament, and calling for legislation to deal with it. Lime-soaked curtains were hung as a protection in Parliament. Yet, contrary to the miasmaists, no epidemic diseases occurred. Snow's vindication had begun. There are some final ironies. The ardent teetotaler is now commemorated in Broadwick Street by a pub, *The John Snow*, and by a replica of the infamous pump located, of course, in the wrong place.

Chapter 28

How we Reason

Our ability to reason is vital. The better we reason the better our lives. We are healthier, we live longer, and we are more successful in the academy and the market place. In life, we make many simple inferences, and we make them almost without realizing that we are reasoning. I described what happened when I first went into an Italian coffee bar to get a cappuccino. I had to infer that one pays first then orders at the bar. This induction was supported by a deduction—that the bar wasn't exceptional, because if it had been then other customers would have had to make the same detour as me—to the bar, to the cash register, and back to the bar. Another sort of inference strengthened my induction. I made an abduction that explained the coffee bar's modus operandi. The place was too busy for the men at the bar to work a cash register. An efficient solution was for the customers to present receipts, which showed what they had paid for, and for the barmen to prepare the corresponding drinks.

How do we reason? It depends on how an inference begins. Some inferences are initiated unconsciously but yield conclusions of which we aware. We call them guesses, hunches, intuitions. They are rapid and often accurate, but they cope only with simple properties or simple relations. We look at photographs of two individuals, and at once form the impression that one of them appears more competent than the other (see Figure 4.1). We cannot articulate the reasons for this inference, but it is robust and made by most of us. Other inferences that we make are wholly unconscious—we are not even aware of any sort of conclusion—but, as experiments show, these inferences are betrayed by changes in our behavior. Just how much of our behavior has these unconscious roots is an open question, but a limit exists. To the annoyance of Madison Avenue, subliminal advertising doesn't even bias us into buying sodas let alone sports utility vehicles. Unconscious processes with no access to working memory are incapable of the complex inferences needed for these transactions.

In England, if I had been refused service at a bar, I would have been angry. But, by the time I went to the coffee bar, I had already made the intuitive induction that Italians were friendly, and so I didn't infer that the barman was being hostile, and I didn't get angry. Inferences can lead to emotions, but we are not aware of the transition from thought to feeling. Indeed, we are unconscious of all mental processes, even those that build the world in our conscious minds.

An influential view about psychological illnesses, such as phobias or obsessive compulsions, is that their cause is faulty reasoning. "Cognitive" therapy is based on this assumption. But, no one appeared to have tested this assumption until the studies I reported in Part II of the book. They compared participants with propensities to various sorts of neurosis with control groups without these propensities. What the results revealed was that those with neurotic propensities are *better* at deductive reasoning than the control participants, but only when they reason about topics relevant to their neuroses. The difference disappears with other topics, though those with a propensity to neurosis are not worse than the control participants.

If faulty reasoning doesn't cause neurotic signs and symptoms, what does? One possibility is abnormal emotional reactions. We make an unconscious transition to an emotion that is appropriate to our awareness of the situation but out of proportion in its intensity. An individual with no history of psychological illness entered an Indian "sweat lodge": it was pitch dark, and at once he was overcome with an anxiety that was so intense that he was forced to leave. Once outside, he reasoned to himself that his fear was unjustified, and that he was being foolish. He went back inside—only to be overcome once more with the same intense anxiety, and so he had to leave again. What caused the anxiety? He cannot say. In the past, this sort of intellectual vacuum has been filled in several ways. Psychoanalysts have filled it with appeals to repressed desires remote from the object of our emotions. Cognitive therapists have filled it with thoughts that become available to us if they persist in interrogating us. But, the hyper-emotion theory, as I call it, implies that the evaluation of the situation is sensible—dark places can be dangerous—and that what has gone awry is just the intensity of the emotion. Some of us are susceptible to these episodes as a result of genetic factors, and susceptibility can be exacerbated in stressful environments. When we have an aberrant emotion, we reason about it. Our reasoning focuses us on the problem, and thereby intensifies our emotion and generalizes its precipitating situations. If this theory is correct then therapy needs to re-educate the system of unconscious transitions that leads from cognition to emotion.

* * *

How do we reason? The philosophers of the Enlightenment argued that we follow the "laws of thought". These laws are made explicit in formal logic and the probability calculus. In logic, the laws of thought go back to the Greeks, and they include the law of noncontradiction: *nothing is both A and not-A*, where *A* is any property we care to think of. The laws are embodied in the formal rules of inference of logic, and we can learn to use these rules to make inferences. The question is whether those of us with no logical training rely on form or content to reason. We understand the meaning and significance of what we reason about. Hence, we may be skeptical that we use rules of inference that apply willy-nilly to any premises of the appropriate logical form. The process would call for us to recover form and to throw away content, like a politician who learned to mouth perfect answers to journalists' questions without understanding the meaning of what he said. Our intuitions about mental processes are not worth much, but psychologists can go beyond their intuitions to carry out experiments. And I reported many results that imply that we don't reason on the basis of logical form.

One observation is the extraordinary difficulty we have both in couching and analyzing arguments in a logical format. As I illustrated, different people tend to make different logical analyses of the same argument. The difficulty is odd if our reasoning is formal. Our first nature ought to be to construct and deconstruct arguments in formal terms.

Another observation is that the inferential properties of connectives, relations, and quantifiers, are impossible to capture in a simple way. We use our knowledge of meaning, reference, and the world, to modulate their interpretation. Hence, no propositional connectives in everyday language, such as "if" or "or", can be treated as they are in logic. For example, the truth of a conjunction such as, "He fell off his bicycle and he broke his leg," depends on more than the truth of its two clauses: the events must also be in the correct temporal order for the proposition to be true. Likewise, a disjunction such as, "Either he's in Rio or in Brazil", triggers an interpretation in which he is in Brazil and may, or may not, be in Rio. The same problem infects the project of capturing in axioms the logical properties of relational terms, such as "taller than". It's an almost impossible task, because these properties are so dependent on context. If we learn that the Queen of Hearts was taller than the White Rabbit, who was taller than Alice, we may infer that the Queen is taller than Alice. But, all bets are off if the premise continues: *until Alice drank the magic potion*. Again, one wonders why, if reasoning is based on form, language is so profligate in its departures from formality.

Yet, another observation is that people make systematic errors in reasoning in life. As I mentioned, the engineers in charge of the Chernobyl nuclear power station went ahead with their disastrous experiment. They knew that if the experiment was to continue then the turbines had to be rotating fast enough to generate emergency electricity, and they also knew that the turbines were not rotating fast enough to do so. They should have inferred that they should not continue with the experiment. But, as psychological studies have shown, the inference isn't easy.

Formal rules of inference don't allow for systematic errors. They yield valid inferences, and so, as a leading proponent of the approach has said, whatever errors occur should be sporadic and haphazard—a result of an "accident" in the mind rather than a consequence of its basic principles. In fact, experiments show that we do make systematic mistakes in our reasoning. And there are big differences in reasoning ability from one person to another. In many experiments, they couldn't be any bigger. That's bad news for the laws of thought. If the laws are in our minds, then they would have to be part of our innate knowledge because most of us receive no instruction in them. We should therefore all be endowed with them, just as we are all endowed with the wherewithal to acquire a natural language. And so we should all acquire a comparable ability in reasoning just as we do in speaking our native tongue, which we acquire without any instruction.

Perhaps there are no laws of thought in our minds unless we have studied them in the works of George Boole and other logicians, or else had an opportunity to develop some formal generalizations as a result of experience in experiments on reasoning. You might suppose instead, as have evolutionary psychologists, that the brain has evolved a large set of diverse intellectual tools—like one of those knives that has twenty gadgets on it, from a nail file to a device for removing stones from horses' hooves (a "hoof pick"). But, that doesn't seem right either, because our inferential mechanisms seem coherent whether we are reasoning about coffee bars or cholera, and we don't seem to run into conflicting principles when we reason about the risk of catching cholera from someone who has cheated us. The conflicts that do occur in our reasoning are between our unconscious intuitions and our conscious inferences.

* * *

If we rely neither on form nor on intellectual Swiss Army knives, then how do we reason? I was led to the theory that we rely on content. We use perception, the meanings of words and sentences, the significance of the propositions that they express, and our knowledge. Indeed, we use everything we've got to think of possibilities, and we represent each possibility in a mental model of the world. In the ideal case, we would have to imagine only a single possibility, because our ability to cope with multiple possibilities falls off so rapidly. The use of models is *intractable*. The more models that we have to hold in mind, the worse our performance becomes—to the point that no finite device, such as the human brain or the digital computer, can cope with an inference in a practical amount of time.

A model isn't an image, but the abstract structure that underlies images and that represents contents that we cannot visualize. But, like an image, a model is "iconic", to use Peirce's term for a representation with a structure corresponding to the structure of the world—at least as we glean it from perception. An iconic model has the advantage that it can yield novel relations among the entities that it represents. These emergent relations are the stuff of conclusions. Not everything, however, can be represented in an icon. Negation, implicit possibilities, and the status of a model—whether, say, it represents a fact, a belief, a possibility, or even something that didn't happen—depend on propositional annotations that work in concert with the interpretative system.

The conclusions we draw depend on the models in which they hold. We infer that a conclusion is bound to be the case if it holds in all the models of our premises, probable if it holds in most of them, and possible if it holds in at least one of them. And, if we consider the proportion of models in which a conclusion holds, or represent their chances of occurrence, we can infer that a conclusion has a certain probability. Often, however, we go beyond the information given to us in order to make an induction, or we introduce new concepts beyond those in the premises in order to explain an event—we make an abduction. In all these cases, at the heart of our reasoning are mental models of possibilities.

* * *

The theory confronts two challenges that pull in opposite directions. It must account for the nature of the errors that we make in reasoning; and it must explain our potential for rationality. The model theory predicts several sources of human error, and I have described experiments corroborating them. One potent source of error is the need to consider multiple possibilities. This point is easy to establish in experiments: the more possibilities that we have to consider, the harder the task—it takes us longer, and we make more mistakes. Indeed, the more possibilities that we have to think about the more confused we tend to be. The same problem occurs in life. When the turbine tripped at Three Mile Island nuclear power station in 1979, as I mentioned earlier in the book, it took the operators a couple of hours to work out which of the many possibilities was responsible.

How many models are too many for us to grasp? Studies have shown that if we have to bear in mind just three new but distinct possibilities, then we are in trouble. If you doubt this point, ask yourself what follows from these two premises:

> Either you can have a bonus or else you can work fewer hours, but not both.

> Either you can work fewer hours or else you can have an increased pension, but not both.

Each premise yields two possibilities, but you have to combine them, and that isn't so easy. "Or else" means that one proposition is true and the other is false, but you don't know which is which. So, what are the possibilities? In fact, there are just two:

> You can have a bonus *and* an increased pension or else you can work fewer hours.

The inference defeats many of us.

A computer program simulating the model theory predicted our most compelling mistakes. They are the various sorts of illusory inference that I have described throughout the book. As a final example, consider a notice based on a chemistry professor's webpage for an undergraduate course:

> Either you get a "pass" grade if you don't take the final exam, or else if you do take it you get a numerical grade.

It sounds plausible, doesn't it? But, it doesn't say what the professor means. As I remarked a moment ago, the connective "or else" means that one proposition is true and the other is false. The professor doesn't mean that. He means that both propositions are true, but that they apply in different circumstances. Hence, what he should have said is:

> You get a "pass" grade if you don't take the final exam, *but* if you do take it then you get a numerical grade.

So, whenever you're in doubt about whether to say "or else" or to say "and", try saying "but". Its logical interpretation is equivalent to "and", but it allows for contrasting cases. The illusions arise from our system of reasoning. Because we can't hold in mind more than a few possibilities, we tend to focus on what's true at the expense of what's false. The same bias may underlie the difficulty of the Chernobyl inference from the conditional, "If the experiment is to continue then the turbine must be rotating fast enough to generate emergency electricity". We need to think about the possibilities in which its if-clause is false, and we fail to do so.

* * *

If humans err so much, how can they be rational enough to invent logic and mathematics, and science and technology? At the heart of human rationality are some simple principles that we all recognize: a conclusion must be the case if it holds in all the possibilities compatible with the premises. It doesn't follow from the premises if there is a counterexample to it, that is, a possibility that is consistent with the premises, but not with the conclusion. The foundation of rationality is our knowledge that a single counterexample overturns a conclusion about what must be the case.

* * *

Much of our everyday reasoning is hard to assess from a rational standpoint. We outperform our own computer programs in creating explanations that resolve inconsistencies. Our apparent fluency may lead you to think that we are using a tractable procedure. But, to determine whether a procedure is tractable, we need to know what it computes. We need to know the range of inputs and the appropriate outputs for them. We have no account of this sort for everyday reasoning. For instance, suppose you believe:

> If an old man is bitten by a deadly snake then he dies.
>
> This old man was bitten by a deadly snake.
>
> Yet, he didn't die.

And I ask you: how come? You might say:

> Because there was an antidote to the poison.

That seems to be an appropriate answer. Suppose, instead, you say:

> Because of a miracle.

or:

> I don't know.

Are these appropriate answers? That's the problem: we have no account of what everyday reasoning is supposed to yield. In our reasoning about the spatial layout of objects, we do know what the output should be: the spatial relations among the objects that a description implies. But, this domain *is* intractable. Hence, we can cope with small-scale problems, but large-scale problems defeat us. If spatial reasoning is part of everyday reasoning, then everyday reasoning is intractable too.

Some philosophers and psychologists—William James, for example—have argued that we should always make a minimal change to our beautiful beliefs to accommodate an ugly fact that clashes with them. I doubt whether we follow this procedure on every occasion, and I described experiments showing that participants violate it. Our abductive propensity to explain things often leads us to adopt quite grand changes to our beliefs. It even leads us to overlook simple statistical principles, such as regression to the mean.

* * *

Some of us reason better than others. You may say that the better reasoners are more intelligent. You're right in this sense: reasoning ability correlates with performance in intelligence tests. The trouble is no one knows what intelligence tests measure, and many of them include items that call for reasoning. So, the claim may be circular. Psychologists have so far isolated one factor that correlates with our ability to reason. It is the capacity of our working memory to hold information. This result makes sense because working memory retains information while we reason about it. That is why working memory lies at the heart of computational power. But, its capacity doesn't seem to explain all the differences in ability from one person to another. It could be as simple as practice. But, no one has yet discovered what else is responsible for these differences.

None of us is a superhuman reasoner. And the bottleneck is our working memory. To teach us the laws of logic doesn't help much to improve our reasoning. One may as well teach delinquents the criminal law to try to improve their behaviour. It doesn't tackle the fundamental problem. In contrast, I described a reliable way to improve our reasoning. The essential step is to ask ourselves: what are the possibilities compatible with the premises? We must then try to list them.

* * *

Models, I have argued, underlie deduction, induction, and abduction. But, what about scientific reasoning, mathematical reasoning, medical reasoning, legal reasoning, and all the other sorts of reasoning that merit chapters in textbooks on reasoning? Do they depend on different mental processes? The burden of this book is that they do not. The principal difference among them is in contents, not processes. We use the information given to us—the evidence of our senses, descriptions, and our knowledge—to imagine what may be going on. Of course, different processes of reasoning do occur. We may be asked to draw a conclusion, to assess whether or not a set of propositions is consistent, to challenge an argument, or to determine whether a given conclusion is reasonable in the light of the premises. Differences also occur among deduction, induction, and abduction. Induction depends on knowledge and heuristic constraints, and abduction depends on knowledge to create new concepts and explanations. But, no evidence that I know of corroborates the idea that scientists or jurists acquire special processes of reasoning, remote from those of everyday life.

My case histories of expert reasoning included nothing from the humanities, the professions, the arts. No tinkers, tailors, soldiers, sailors. No one doubts that the study of philosophy, history, language, or culture, depends on an ability to reason. Members of the professions reason, but they seldom mention it. Generals and admirals reason at every battle, but they say nothing about it. Ulysses S. Grant's memoirs, for example, are blank on the topic. I know of just one inference that the Duke of Wellington made. Before the battle of Assaye in India, which he won though outnumbered twenty to one, he inferred the existence of a ford between two villages because they were built on opposite sides of a river. Perhaps as a legacy of the Romantic movement, artists have seldom remarked on the need for reasoning in what they do. Like Walt Whitman, they sometimes praise the virtues of inconsistency, or, like James Joyce, they sometimes remain silent on their cunning. Authors tell us that they write lying in bed using a laptop, or standing at a lectern with a legal pad and a ballpoint pen, but they tell us almost nothing about how they think. A vast silence on their thinking emanates from painters, composers, playwrights, architects, choreographers.... There are only a handful of exceptions. W.H. Auden, who has been a touchstone throughout this book, discussed the topic in several essays. Stephen Spender described how he wrote a poem. Helen Vendler analyzed the patterns of thinking in four great poets. And Paul Valéry wrote an essay on the necessity of reasoning in the composition of poetry: "...if the poet were never anything but a poet, without the slightest hope of being able to reason abstractly, he would leave no poetic traces behind him." I conjecture that most artistic creation depends on abduction, induction, and deduction, just as most of the problems that we solve in life do.

* * *

At the start of this book, I advertised the fantasy that our minds could be recreated in computer programs for the dubious benefit of posterity. How far are we from that goal? One part of it is to be able to simulate the ways in which we reason. We have reached the end of the beginning of the research that makes simulations of our reasoning feasible. We have some idea of how we reason; and sufficient knowledge to implement computer programs that mimic the process.

It is time to draw to a conclusion. The argument of this book is that our reasoning depends on mental models, and that we can grasp that a conclusion follows from premises if it holds in every model of the premises. Is this theory correct? The chances are that it isn't. Few theories in science, if any, are correct in that they tell us the truth, and nothing but the truth. And no theories tell us the whole truth. So, we can be almost certain that the theory is false in some respects. Is it, then, nearer to the truth than other theories? Perhaps. If it is wrong, psychologists will discover a series of findings that are counterexamples to it. But, the theory itself argues that counterexamples are fundamental to our rationality. And so you can say this much for the theory: as it collapses, it will explain its own demise.

Glossary

Abduction: An inductive process yielding an explanation of an event or set of events.

Anti-model: A model of a possibility in which a proposition is false (*see also* Counterexample).

Artificial intelligence: The branch of computer science dedicated to the development of programs that carry out tasks calling for intelligence.

Atmosphere effect: The hypothesis that we are biased by the nature of the quantifiers in the premises of syllogisms, e.g., two premises containing the quantifier "all" bias us towards a conclusion containing "all". The hypothesis was proposed by Sells (1936), but has several modern variants.

Autonomic nervous system: The nervous system in all vertebrates that controls various organs, such as the heart and stomach, in situations of fight and flight, and rest and digestion. Its effects are involuntary.

Bayes's theorem: A theorem in the probability calculus relating one conditional probability to another (see Box 15.2).

Behaviorism: The doctrine, flourishing from about 1910 until 1956 in the USA, that psychology should concern external stimuli and responses, and establish laws interrelating them. The mind, in contrast, was a fit topic for conversation only among consenting adults in private.

Biconditional: A sentence formed with the connective, "if and only if", which is therefore equivalent to two conditionals, e.g.: *If A then B*, and *if B then A*.

Boolean logic: *See* Propositional calculus.

Complete models: akin to mental models but representing in addition what is false in each possibility.

Computational power: What a system is able to compute. A more powerful system can compute results that are beyond a less powerful system. Given a small repertoire of basic procedures including recursion, computational power depends solely on the nature of the working memory for the results of intermediate computations.

Conditional probability: The probability of one event given that another event occurs, e.g., the probability that it rains given that rain is forecast.

Conditional sentence: A sentence formed using the connective "if" to connect a subordinate clause *A* to a main clause *B*, and so the sentence has the grammatical form: *If A then B*, or equivalently: *B if A*.

Conjunction: A sentence formed using the connective "and" to connect two main clauses, and so of the grammatical form: *A and B*.

Connectionism: The doctrine that psychological theories should be implemented in computer models that simulate networks of idealized neurons in the brain. These networks can learn associations between stimuli and carry out simple inferences (see McClelland and Rumelhart, 1986). They can represent information either in individual neurons or distributed across many neurons in a way that resists damage to the system. One procedure for learning in these networks is the backwards propagation of error (from the mismatch between the actual output of a network and the required output).

Connective: In logic, a term that connects separate sentences to form a new sentence; in natural language, certain terms such as "if" and "or" serve an analogous function.

Conscious reasoning: A process initiated in consciousness that yields a conscious conclusion, though the process itself, like all mental processes, is unconscious.

Consistency: A set of propositions is consistent if and only if it is possible that each proposition in the set is true; otherwise, the set of propositions is inconsistent.

Content-specific rule of inference: A formal rule of inference that contains terms that are not from logic but that have a particular content.

Contradiction: In logic, one proposition contradicts another if and only if one proposition must be true and the other proposition must be false. Hence, a self-contradiction is a proposition such as: *The shape is a triangle and it is not a triangle.*

Contrary: In logic, one proposition is a contrary of another if and only if the two propositions cannot both be true. They could both be false, e.g., *The shape is a triangle and it is a circle.*

Counterexample: A counterexample to an inference is a possibility that is consistent with the premises but inconsistent with the conclusion, i.e., as represented in a model of the premises that is an anti-model of the conclusion.

A counterexample to a general proposition is an instance showing that the generalization is false.

Counterfactual conditional: A conditional that is interpreted as referring to a possibility that is contrary to fact, e.g., *If the Viennese had had three legs then they would have marched to waltzes.*

Deductive reasoning: The process of establishing that a conclusion is a valid inference from premises, i.e., it must be true given that they are true.

Default assumption: An assumption that can be taken for granted unless evidence overrules it, e.g., *dogs have four legs*. The idea is due to Marvin Minsky, and is embodied in certain computer programming languages.

Deontic reasoning: Reasoning about actions that are obligatory, permissible, or prohibited.

Determinism: A computational process is deterministic if and only if at each point in the process there is just one possible next step, which depends on the current input, if any, and the current state of the process. A process is nondeterministic if it violates this constraint, i.e., there is more than one possible next step and nothing in the process determines which steps occurs. Theorists often assume that the system makes the correct next step, i.e., "nondeterminism" is a euphemism for "by magic".

Disjunction: A sentence formed using the connective "or" to connect two main clauses. Inclusive disjunctions are made explicit in sentences of the grammatical form: *A or B, or both*. Exclusive disjunctions are made explicit in sentences of the grammatical form: *A or else B, but not both*.

Euler circles: A diagrammatic system invented by Leibniz (!) for representing quantified propositions about properties, e.g., "All beekeepers are chemists" (see Figure 10.1), and not be confused with the more efficient diagrams due to Venn (see Figure 10.2).

Evolutionary psychology: The doctrine that cognition depends on separate "modules" in the brain that evolved about 120,000 years ago because they conferred an advantage on our hunter-gatherer ancestors. One module, for instance, is supposed to check whether others are cheating us.

Formal rule of inference: A rule that can be used to derive a conclusion from premises in a way that takes into account only their logical form, not their content. Logical calculi are formalized using these rules, and several psychological theories of reasoning propose that we rely on them.

Functional Magnetic Resonance Imaging (fMRI): A procedure in which an experimental participant is tested with his or her head in a large magnet, and observations yield an indirect measure of the relative amounts of oxygen taken up by the various regions of the brain. Those regions that are more active require more oxygen.

Heuristic: A short cut or rule of thumb that yields a rough and ready answer, which may be correct, but which is often biased. Heuristics underlie many of our intuitive inferences.

Iconic representation: A representation with relations among its parts that correspond to those in what it represents, e.g., a visual image.

Illusory inferences: *See* Principle of truth.

Implicit model: A mental model acting as a placeholder and so with no explicit content.

Inductive reasoning: The process of deriving plausible conclusions that go beyond the information in the premises.

Intractability: A computational process is intractable if, as the size of some property of its input increases, the time and load on memory increases to the point that the computation ceases to be feasible for any finite device. For example, to test whether or not a set of propositions is consistent takes an intractable amount of time and memory as the number of atomic propositions in them increases. Atomic propositions contain neither negation nor propositional connectives, and so they are the constituents of other compound propositions. For a general introduction to computational intractability, see Garey and Johnson (1979).

Intuition: An unconscious heuristic process based on unconscious premises that yields a conscious conclusion.

Invalidity: An inference is invalid if its conclusion need not be true given that its premises are true. One sort of invalidity occurs when a conclusion is inconsistent with the premises, i.e., its negation is a valid inference from them. Another sort of invalidity occurs when a conclusion is consistent with the premises, but does not follow of necessity from them (*see also* Validity).

Logic: The science of implications among sentences (often in a formalized language). Logical calculi have systems of proof based on formal rules of inference ("proof theory") and a semantics (or "model theory").

Logical form: The logical form of a proposition represents the conditions in which it would be true, i.e., its significance. The use of a logical calculus to prove an inference in everyday language calls for the recovery of the logical forms of its propositions. No general procedure or computer program exists for carrying out this task. Linguists use "logical form" to refer to a representation of that part of the meaning of a sentence that depends solely on language and grammatical structure (see, e.g., Chomsky, 1995).

Magical thinking: The inductions of other cultures that yield conclusions that we don't believe.

Markov transitions: A sequence of events in which each event is drawn with a certain probability from a finite set of possibilities. The sets of possibilities may differ from one transition to the next. The probabilities may depend on the prior sequence of events. In principle, a process generating Markov transitions needs no working memory.

Mary Celeste phenomenon: The inability to explain a fact.

Meaning: The meaning of a sentence—idioms apart—depends on the meanings of its words and the grammatical relations among them. The meanings of words in principle enable us to pick out entities, properties, and relations.

Meaning postulate: An axiom used in logic to capture the logical property of a term, such as the transitivity of a relation.

Mental model: A representation of the world that is postulated to underlie human reasoning; a model represents what is true in one possibility, and so far as possible has an iconic structure. Mental models are the end result of perception and of understanding a description. Those of complex systems are a form of knowledge-representation in long-term memory.

Metalanguage: A language for talking about another language (the object language). In logic, the two languages are kept separate. But, a natural language, such as English, is its own metalanguage.

Metareasoning: Reasoning about reasoning.

Modulation: The use of knowledge about meaning, reference, or the world, to affect the interpretation of connectives or quantifiers.

Negation: A concept that can be expressed in English using the word, "not". A negative proposition is true if and only if the corresponding affirmative proposition is false, and vice versa.

Nondeterminism: *See* Determinism.

Nonmonotonic reasoning: Logic is monotonic because additional premises increase the number of valid inferences that follow from them. In everyday life, however, an additional premise may lead us to *withdraw* a conclusion: our reasoning is therefore said to be nonmonotonic.

Normative theory: A theory of how we ought to carry out a task, e.g., the probability calculus is a normative theory of how we ought reason about probabilities.

Object language: *See* Metalanguage.

Predicate calculus: *See* Quantificational calculus.

Presupposition: A proposition that has to be true in order for some other sentence to express a proposition, e.g., *my wife has stopped smoking,* and its negation both presuppose that *my wife smoked.*

Principle of truth: The assumption that mental models represent what is true, but not what is false. When falsity matters, the principle yields fallacious but compelling inferences, the so-called "illusory" inferences that are a hallmark of the use of mental models in reasoning.

Proposition: What a sentence expresses in context given that its presuppositions are true. A proposition is true or false.

Propositional attitude: A mental attitude to a proposition, e.g., belief.

Propositional calculus: A logic of idealized versions of "not", "and", and "or", and other connectives definable in terms of them. This logic is also known as the sentential calculus or Boolean logic.

Propositional representation: A representation with a syntactic structure in a mental language akin to a natural language.

Quantificational calculus: The logical calculus governing logical quantifiers analogous to "all" and "some" and incorporating the propositional calculus. It is also known as the "predicate calculus".

Quantifier: A term such as "all", "some", or "more than half".

Recursion: A loop of repeated operations, as when a procedure calls itself. It plays a central role in computation and in the processing of language. It depends on a working memory for the results of intermediate computations.

Reductio ad absurdum: An inference that leads from a supposition to a self-contradiction, and that therefore implies the denial of the supposition (see Chapter 19).

Relational complexity: The number of arguments in a relation, e.g., *Pat gave money to Viv* has three arguments: *Pat, money,* and *Viv.*

Reverse engineering: The task of inferring how a device or system works from a knowledge of its overt performance and of how its components work.

Selection task: A reasoning task that calls for the selection of evidence relevant to the truth or falsity of a proposition—a conditional proposition in most experiments (see Chapter 1).

Semantics: Pertaining to the meanings or truth-values of sentences.

Significance: Of a proposition, the conditions in which it would be true.

Strategy: A sequence of tactical steps that enables us to make an inference or to solve a problem.

Supposition: An assumption or hypothesis made for the sake of argument or inference.

Syllogism: An inference from two premises that both contain a single quantifier (see Chapter 10).

Tactic: A step in a strategy for making an inference or solving a problem. Tactics are based on unconscious mechanisms.

Transitive relation: A relation that yields a valid inference of the form: *A is related to B, B is related to C*, therefore, *A is related to C*.

Truth functionality: A connective has a truth-functional meaning if it yields a truth value that depends solely on the truth values of the propositions that it interconnects, e.g., a conjunction, *A and B*, is true if and only if A is true and B is true.

Truth table: A table used by logicians to lay out a set of possibilities compatible with one or more propositions. It can also be used to lay out the meaning of a truth-functional connective: the table specifies the truth or falsity of sentences formed with the connective in terms of the truth or falsity of the propositions it interconnects.

Truth values: A proposition has two possible truth-values: *true* or *false.*

Unconscious reasoning: An inferential process initiated and carried out without our awareness. It may yield a conscious conclusion—an intuition, or its consequences may be unconscious too.

Validity: An inference is valid if its conclusion must be true given that its premises are true. A valid inference from true premises yields a true conclusion; a valid inference from false premises may yield a true conclusion or a false one (*see also* invalidity).

Venn diagrams: An efficient diagram for representing quantified premises (see Figure 10.2), and not to be confused with Euler circles.

Visual images: An iconic representation of the appearance of an object or scene from a particular point of view.

Working memory: The short-term memory system that holds information in mind while we work on it. This memory is the heart of computational power, but ours is limited in its capacity and is therefore a bottleneck in our ability to reason.

Notes on the Chapters

Numbers refer to the relevant page numbers in the chapters.

Chapter 1: Introduction

1. Hooke estimates our memory capacity as a hundred million thoughts (Hooke 1705, p. 144; as cited by Dyson, 1997), von Neumann (1958) estimates it as 10^{20} bits, where a bit is the amount of information in one binary digit (a 1 or 0). Landauer (1986), like Hooke, allows for forgetting, and estimates a net gain over 70 years as about 10^9 bits. An alphabetical letter in a text takes eight bits, and so one novel is about 10^7 bits. A thousand novels is 10^{10} bits. Computers now have about the same amount of storage capacity, e.g., my Apple laptop has 4×10^9 bits of memory. Human memory works in a different way from computer memory, and is a process of reconstruction from shards of evidence.

2. The Church–Turing thesis is described in, e.g., Sieg (1999). Church identified "computations" with a particular logical calculus that he had devised; Turing identified them with those of abstract computational machines (now known as "Turing machines"). The two systems turned out to be equivalent in that what one system could do the other could do too. Subsequent theses about other systems have also converged on the same set of computations. Newell (1980) argues that the Church–Turing thesis is the foundation of the concept of a "physical symbol system", i.e., a physical system that can manipulate symbols, and that human beings are physical symbol systems. Likewise, Hunt (1999, 2002) treats the mind as a processor of information.

2. Descartes (1967) argues that free will makes a science of the mind impossible. Dostoyevsky's argument is in his *Notes from Underground* (1864). Koestler's bet was made in a British Sunday newspaper in the 1970s.

2. The concept of "associative" thinking goes back to Aristotle. The Victorian polymath, Francis Galton (1928) writes about his own associations: "Perhaps the strongest of the impressions ... regards the multifariousness of the work done by the mind in a state of half-consciousness, and the valid reason they afford for believing in the existence of still deeper strata of mental operations, sunk wholly below the level of consciousness ... "

3. My colleague the philosopher Gilbert Harman (1973) argues that thinking is not deterministic. Hopcroft and Ullman (1979) describe nondeterminism in computational theory.

3. The textbook definitions of deduction and induction go back to Aristotle. In his *Topics* (Aristotle, 1984, Vol. 1, 105a13), he writes, "induction is a passage from particulars to universals". He argues in his *Prior Analytics* (Book II, paragraph 23) that every belief comes either from deduction or induction, and that induction is from the particular to the general. Mill (1874, p. 210) writes: "Induction ... is that operation of the mind, by which we infer that what we know to be true in a particular case or cases, will be true in all cases which resemble the former in certain assignable respects".

4. The concept of information as ruling out possibilities goes back to medieval philosophers. Bar-Hillel and Carnap (1964) resuscitated the concept and put it on a precise foundation. They refer to it as "semantic information" to distinguish it from information in a statistical sense (see Shannon and Weaver, 1949).

4. Maxim's quote is cited in Jakab (1990, p. 26).

5. Henle (1978) writes: "I have never found errors which could unambiguously be attributed to faulty reasoning". Cohen (1981) argues that any errors that do occur are a result of local malfunctions in the system. These claims echo those of Leibniz (1765/1949), Kant (1800/1974), and Boole (1854).

5. Oaksford and Chater (1998) have by far the most ingenious view about reasoning and probabilities. I discuss their account in Chapter 16.

5. Revlis (1975) proposes that we do not reason, but follow the "atmosphere" created by the premises.

5. Gabrielle Lolli, an Italian logician, said at a meeting in Padua in 1999 that without training in logic we couldn't reason at all. Studies have shown that it does not help us with novel reasoning problems (Cheng *et al.*, 1986).

5. For variations in reasoning ability, see, e.g., Johnson-Laird (1983, p. 117 *et seq.*).

5. For an illustration of six-year-old children's reasoning ability, see Trabasso *et al.* (1975).

5. The evidence for my contention that counterexamples underlie our rational propensities is reviewed in Part V of the book.

5. Aristotle is supposed to have asserted: "Man is the rational animal". He believed it, but also that the mind contained an irrational part (cf. Aristotle, 1984, *Nichomachean Ethics*, Book X, Chapter 7).

5. Stanovich (1999) shows that the ability to reason (in experiments) correlates with intelligence (in mental tests).

6–7. The quotation about the LSAT test and the item in Box 1.1 are from the *Official LSAT PrepTest* published by the Law Schools Admission Council in 2000.

7. The expert witness from whose deposition I quote is my brother Andy Johnson-Laird, a forensic software analyst, an occupation that he invented. I am grateful to him for this example, which I have edited a little.

8. The quotation from Thesiger is from pages 65–66 of his book *Arabian Sands* first published in 1959 (see Thesiger, 1964), which describes his crossing of the "Empty Quarter" of Saudi Arabia before the discovery of oil in that country.

8. I owe the inferences from a patient with an "obsessive-compulsive" disorder to the psychiatrist, Francesco Mancini. I return to this topic in Chapter 7.

9. The quotation from LSAC is in the official *LSAT PrepTest*.

9. Aristotle's logic is in his *Organon*, a collection of texts including *Categories*, *Topics*, and the *Prior* and *Post Analytics* (see Aristotle, 1984). The great pioneers of formal systems of logic are Frege (1967, originally published in 1879) and Whitehead and Russell (1927). Jeffrey (1981) is an excellent introduction to modern logic, and discusses both form and content. In the symbolic language of a modern logic, sentences wear their logical forms on their sleeves.

9. Logicians take logical form to be a representation of the conditions in which a proposition would be true, i.e., it captures *significance* (e.g., Sainsbury, 2001, p. 343). Linguists, however, take logical form to be a representation of the *meaning* of sentences, which depends on language and grammatical structure (see, e.g., Chomsky, 1995, p. 21). No general procedure exists to recover logical form in either of these two senses from sentences in natural language.

10. Peirce (1931–1958) pioneered the semantic approach to logic. He invented truth tables, which are a systematic way to work out the interpretations of sentences containing negation and logical connectives, such as "if", "and", and "or" (see Berry, 1952; Johnson-Laird, 2002a). Wittgenstein (1922) reinvented them. Tarski (1956) extended the approach to logic as a whole, which contains quantifiers such as idealized versions of "any" and "some". Hintikka (1963) and Kripke (1963) extended it further to modal logic, which concerns such as operators as "possibly" and "necessarily". Montague (1974) showed how to apply it to natural language—an approach taken up by various linguists and philosophers. A central idea is that each rule of a grammar has a corresponding semantic rule. When the grammatical rule is used to parse the constituents of a phrase, the semantic rule can be used to "compose" the meanings of these constituents into the meaning of the phrase as a whole (see, e.g., Partee, 1995).

10. Boolos and Jeffrey (1989) outline the proofs relating formal calculi to interpretative systems.

10. Logicians who have taken context into account in their analyses of natural language include Kamp (1981; see also Kamp and Reyle, 1993) and Barwise (1987).

11. The quotation is from Hilbert (1928/1967, p. 475). The psychologists Inhelder and Piaget (1958, p. 305) write: "Reasoning is nothing more than the propositional calculus itself".

11. Ruth Byrne and I propose that human deductive reasoning maintains information, and yields parsimonious conclusions that state something new (Johnson-Laird and Byrne, 1991).

12. Sperber and his colleagues emphasize the importance of reasoners' goals (see, e.g., Sperber and Wilson, 1986; Sperber *et al.*, 1995).

12. The distinction between what the mind does and how it does it goes back to Lord Adrian, who argued that if we want to understand how the brain works, we must first understand what it is doing. Marr (1982) makes the same point in a seminal way.

13. The theory that reasoning depends on a memory for previous cases is explored in Stanfill and Waltz (1986), Riesbeck and Schank (1989), and Kolodner (1993).

14. Boole (1854) proposes a formal calculus for the mind. Piaget published many books and papers, but his writings are difficult to understand. The essence of his theory that reasoning depends on formal operations can be found in Inhelder and Piaget (1958) and Piaget (1965a). I summarize his theory of intellectual development in Chapter 18. Formal systems of human reasoning are described in Inhelder and Piaget (1958), Osherson (1974–6), Johnson-Laird (1975), Rips (1983, 1994), Braine (1978), Braine *et al.* (1984), Cherniak (1986), Macnamara (1986), Sperber and Wilson (1986), Pollock (1989), Smith *et al.* (1992), and Braine and O'Brien (1998). These theories differ in both the formal rules of inference that they postulate and in the procedures that they use to search for proofs. Fodor (1975) defends the formal view of the "language of the mind". Rips (1994), in addition, implemented his theory in a computer program, though

the program no longer contains all the rules. It could be used as a general-purpose programming language, and therefore to simulate any other theory. The theory in this general sense is thus hard to refute, that is, no empirical results could ever show it to be false unless they demonstrated that mental processes are not computable (Johnson-Laird, 1997). My concern here is, not with formal rules that underlie programming languages, but with those theories that postulate that we reason using formal rules of inference akin to those in logic.

14. Wason (1966) describes his first studies with the selection task (see also Wason and Johnson-Laird, 1972). Wason and Shapiro (1971) describe their study showing the effects of content on the selection task. A large literature exists on the task (for reviews, see, e.g., Evans *et al.*, 1993; Evans and Over, 2004, chapter 5).

15. Oaksford and Chater (e.g., 1998) argue that the selection task does not elicit deductive reasoning. Evidence exists to the contrary (Feeney and Handley, 2000).

15. The idea of content-specific rules was introduced in Hewitt (1969). For their use in so-called "expert systems", i.e., programs for medical diagnosis and other domains, see, e.g., Shortliffe (1976). The rule for pseudomas is from Norvig (1992, pp. 531–532) and is based on Shortliffe's program.

16. Searle (1980) argues that no computer program can understand the meaning of sentences.

16. The quotation about mental models is from Johnson-Laird (1970a). Craik (1943) introduced the notion into psychology, though he proposes that reasoning depends on verbal rules. Evidence for the use of models to represent discourse is reported in Garnham (1987, 2001) and Glenberg *et al.* (1987). The theory that reasoning depends on mental models was outlined in Johnson-Laird (1983). Ruth Byrne and I extended the theory to deal with propositional connectives, such as "if", and "or" (see Johnson-Laird and Byrne, 1991).

16. The last twenty years has seen an accumulation of experimental evidence corroborating mental models (for references, see the webpage developed by Byrne and her colleagues at Trinity College, University of Dublin: http://www.tcd.ie/Psychology/People/Ruth_Byrne/mental_models). Models have also played an increasing role in artificial intelligence, see, e.g., Halpern and Vardi (1991) and Glasgow (1993).

17. Shastri and his colleagues describe a "connectionist" system of simulating a network of idealized nerve cells capable of simple inferences (see, e.g., Shastri, 1988, and Shastri and Ajjanagadde, 1993).

17. Heidegger's views are described in his book, *What is Called Thinking*. His influence can be found in, e.g., Dreyfus's (1972) critique of artificial intelligence. Domestic hens appear to refute Heidegger because they remember where they ate food and what it was (Forkman, 2000), as do five-day old chicks (Cozzutti and Vallortigara, 2001).

Chapter 2: Icons and Images

19. The epigraph is from the poem, *Words* (Auden, 1976, p. 473).

21. Levinson (1996) reviews his work with the Guugu Yimithirr.

22. Gladwin (1970) reports his experiences learning to be a Caroline Islands' navigator. Oatley (1976) compares this skill with other methods of navigation.

22. Tolman (1948) argues that animals construct cognitive maps of their environment, and he carried out the experiment in which he blocked the dog-legged route to the food box. Hull (1934) argues for fractional anticipatory goal responses.

23. Von Frisch (1966) is the classic account of the "dancing" bees. For ethological observations of foraging animals and bees, see Gould and Gould (1994). Jumping spiders also have internal representations of routes that they have never taken (Jackson and Tarsitano, 1997).

23. Landau *et al.* (1984) showed that a blind child inferred new routes between objects as a result of walking between them. Her model of the world includes metric and geometric information within a framework of spatial co-ordinates.

23. Evidence suggests that regions of the hippocampus and of parietal cortex construct both egocentric and objective spatial representations (see O'Keefe and Nadel, 1978, and Bryant, 1992a,b). Likewise, birds that store food for future consumption have a larger hippocampus than genetically related birds that do not store food (see Rogers, 1997); and London taxi-drivers who have the "knowledge", i.e., know the lay-out of all the city's streets, also have enlarged hippocampi (Maguire *et al.*, 2000). Certain so-called "place" cells in an animal's hippocampus fire only if the animal is in a particular location (regardless of the cues to that location). Scoville and Milner (1957) describe the patient known as "H.M.", who had part of his hippocampus removed. Eichenbaum (1999) conjectures that the hippocampus represents relations among entities.

24. Bernard Shaw's description of Higgins's study occurs at the start of Act II of *Pygmalion* (see Shaw, 1965, pp. 720–721).

24. For evidence that models based on descriptions are similar to those based on perception, see, e.g., Bryant (1992a,b). Marr (1982) argues that vision yields a mental model that makes explicit what things are where in the scene.

25. The notion of "iconicity" is due to Peirce (e.g., 1931–1958, Vol. 4. paragraph 447). He argues that diagrams should be as iconic as possible (Vol. 4, paragraph 433), i.e., the parts of a diagram should be interrelated in the same way that the entities that it represents are interrelated (Vol. 4, paragraph 418). Other independent formulations of iconicity include Maxwell's (1911) account of diagrams, and Wittgenstein's (1922) "picture" theory of meaning, with its key proposition 2.15: "That the elements of the picture are combined with one another in a definite way, represents that the things [in the world] are so combined with one another." Another version of the same idea, when it is realized in a precise mathematical form, is known as a "homeomorphism".

26. A recent biography of Leonardo da Vinci is by Nicholl (2004).

26. The quotation is from Boltzmann (1974).

26. Ferguson (1992) criticizes engineers for their neglect of visualization.

26. The report of Kekulé's daydream is from Findlay (1937, p. 43). The claim that the anecdote is untrue is due to Wotiz and Rudofsky (1984, as cited by Gruber, 1994).

26. The questionnaire on imagery is reported in Galton (1928). Darwin's remark to Galton is in Darwin (1887, 3.239), and is cited by Keynes (2002, p. 213).

26–7. The quotation from Einstein is reported in Hadamard (1996). Wertheimer, a psychologist, interviewed Einstein, and corroborated his use of imagery (Wertheimer, 1961, p. 228; for corrections to historical inaccuracies, see Miller, 1984, chapter 5).

27. I owe the problems of the needles and the disks to Geoffrey Hinton.

28. Gleick (1992, p. 131) emphasizes the role of imagery in the late Richard Feynman's thinking.

28. The quotation about "habit" is from Auden (1977, p. 306).

28. Paivio (1971) postulates two modes of mental representation, one linguistic and the other imagistic.

29. I owe the account of Fisher and the tea-taster to Salsburg (2001).

29–30. The first study of mental rotation is reported in Shepard and Metzler (1971). Metzler and Shepard (1982, p. 45) write of their findings that rotations can be in depth: "These results seem to be consistent with the notion that ... subjects were performing their mental operations upon internal representations that were more analogous to three-dimensional objects portrayed in the two-dimensional pictures than to the two-dimensional pictures actually presented". Not all creatures appear to construct such models. Pigeons, for instance, pass the mental rotation test but do not show the effect of the disparity in angle of the main axis of the object from one picture to another (Hollard and Delius, 1982).

30. Hegarty (1992, 2004) reports her experiments on the simulation of simple mechanical devices. Differences in ability do occur from one individual to another (Hegarty and Sims, 1994). The gestures that we make in solving these problems appear to help us to keep track of where we are in a problem (Hegarty et al., 2005).

31. Tesla's power of imagery does seem to have been extraordinary. As a child, images got in the way of his thinking (see, e.g., O'Neill, 1944).

31. The study of scanning from one landmark to another in a mental image of a map is reported in Kosslyn et al. (1978; see also Kosslyn, 1980).

31. Pylyshyn expresses his skepticism about the causal role of imagery in several articles (see, e.g., Pylyshyn, 1973, 1981, 2003). Huxley (1893) coined the term, "epiphenomenon".

32. Proponents of representations rooted in perception include Barsalou (1999) and Markman and Dietrich (2000). The latter write (p. 472): "Theoretical arguments and experimental evidence suggest that cognitive science should eschew amodal representations".

32. Wittgenstein (1953) points out that an image of a large red cross doesn't in itself tell us that it represents negation. The times taken to evaluate affirmative and negative propositions were first studied by Wason (1959), and later by Clark and Chase (1972) and others. An affirmative proposition that is true, such as: "The square is on the right of the circle", is compatible with one sort of possibility. Its falsity is compatible with many sorts of possibility. In contrast, a negative proposition that is true, such as: "The square is not on the right of the circle", is compatible with many sorts of possibility. Its falsity is compatible with only one sort of possibility. This pattern may explain an odd observation: when we verify propositions, we judge that an affirmative proposition is true faster than we judge that is false, whereas we judge that a negative proposition is false faster than we judge that it is true (Wason and Johnson-Laird, 1972).

32. The notion that we think of all the positive possibilities equivalent to negation has experimental corroboration (Oaksford and Chater, 1994; Schroyens et al., 2001a).

32. Peirce developed two diagrammatic systems for logic, which exploit their iconic structure (for an account from a logical standpoint, see Shinn, 1994; and for account of their psychological implications, see Johnson-Laird, 2002a). To understand any system of representation, Anderson (1978) argues that it is necessary to know both the format of the representations and also the processes that operate on them.

33. Early studies of imagery show that it enhances reasoning about spatial relations (e.g., De Soto, London, and Handel, 1965; Shaver *et al.*, 1975). Studies showing no effect or an impeding effect tend to examine visual relations (e.g., Sternberg, 1980; Richardson, 1987; Clement and Falmagne, 1986). Egan and Grimes-Farraw (1982) observe that participants who report using imagery performed worse than those who did not. Farah *et al.* (1988) report evidence corroborating different systems for images and spatial representations. Knauff *et al.* (2001) examine the disruption of inferences by secondary tasks that were either visual or auditory, and either spatial or nonspatial. Only the spatial tasks disrupted inference, regardless of whether they were auditory or visual.

33–5. The experiment contrasting spatial and visual representations is from Knauff and Johnson-Laird (2002). The fMRI study is from Knauff *et al.* (2003): reasoning in general activated regions in the left hemisphere (the middle temporal gyrus), the right hemisphere (superior parietal cortex), and both hemispheres (the precuneus, and the middle and inferior frontal gyri in prefrontal cortices). Visual relations, as Figure 2.6 shows, activate areas in visual cortex. Knauff and May (2006) report the study of congenitally blind participants.

35. The research on the manipulation of images is described in Finke and Slayton (1988).

35–6. The analysis of Kekulé's problem relies on Findlay's (1937) account (see, p. 149).

36. The idea that each mental model represents a set of possibilities is due to Barwise (1993).

37. The quotation is from Golding (1955).

Chapter 3: Models of Possibilities: From Conjuring Tricks to Disasters

38. I wrote a draft of a paper on how to find lost objects—inspired by my experience with the lost notebook and also by Elizabeth Bishop's marvelous villanelle, *One art*, with its opening stanza:

> The art of losing isn't hard to master;
>
> so many things seem filled with the intent
>
> to be lost that their loss is no disaster.

Paolo Legrenzi asked me to join Maria Legrenzi and Vittorio Girotto in writing a paper in memory of the Italian psychologist, Mimma Peron (see Legrenzi *et al.*, 2001–2002). A similar view about how to find lost objects is in Klein (1998, pp. 267–268).

39. Philosophers hold diverse views about such propositional attitudes as belief and disbelief. Some dismiss them as myths of "folk psychology" (e.g., Stich, 1983), whereas others treat them as maps by which we steer (e.g., Fodor, 1981; Ramsey, 1990).

39. The labels on models are similar to Jackendoff's (1996) idea of "evaluations", which he treats as properties, such as "familiar" vs. "novel".

39. See the note in Chapter 1 for references to theories of reasoning based on formal rules of inference.

39. For a history of "modal" logics, which deal with possibilities, see, e.g., Kneale and Kneale (1962), and for an introduction to modern systems, see, e.g., Hughes and Cresswell (1996). My colleague Dan Osherson was one of the first psychologists to develop a formal theory of reasoning about possibilities (see Osherson, 1974–76).

40. The psychological literature on working memory is vast. An accessible account by one of its principal investigators is Baddeley (1986). For the relation between working memory and computational power, see, e.g., Johnson-Laird (1993). Simon (1983) points out that working memory is the bottleneck in reasoning.

40. Hopcroft and Ullman (1979) explain why computational power depends on a memory for the results of intermediate computations.

41. The experiments on reasoning from pairs of disjunctions are reported in Johnson-Laird *et al.* (1992) and Bauer and Johnson-Laird (1993).

42. The five possibilities compatible with the premises:

June is in Wales of Charles is in Scotland, or both.

Charles is in Scotland or Kate is in Ireland, or both

are:

June is in Wales	Charles is in Scotland	Kate is in Ireland
June is in Wales	Charles is in Scotland	
June is in Wales		Kate is in Ireland
	Charles is in Scotland	Kate is in Ireland
	Charles is in Scotland	

43. Rips (1994, pp. 365–369) reports his study of conjunctive and disjunctive inferences.

43–4. García-Madruga *et al.* (2001) report their experiments establishing that, for example, the conjunctive inferences are easier than the disjunctive ones unless participants can work back from the conclusions.

44. The model theory postulates that we can make suppositions, but we follow up their consequences in mental models (Van der Henst *et al.*, 2002). Victoria Bell carried out the unpublished study in which the participants answered questions about possible and necessary consequences of various hypothetical events.

45. The study of reasoning about one-on-one basketball games is from Bell and Johnson-Laird (1998). Unlike adults, children do not baulk at saying that an event might happen even though it is obvious that it must happen (Noveck, 2001). Children are more like logicians, because they are less sophisticated about the informative use of language.

46. The difficulty of learning concepts based on exclusive disjunctions is reported in, e.g., Neisser and Weene (1962). The difficulty of creating wiring diagrams for them is described in Chapter 24.

46. The difficulty of understanding documents such as the "Death grant" was shown in a study in Wason and Johnson-Laird (1972). Mrs. Thatcher abolished the grant, but at the time of writing it still exists in Jersey, one of the Channel Islands.

46. Studies showing that disjunctive alternatives lead to difficulties in making decisions were carried out by my colleague Eldar Shafir and the late Amos Tversky (Shafir and Tversky, 1992; Tversky and Shafir, 1992). Psychologists have known for some time that disjunctions create difficulties in reasoning and choice (Newstead and Griggs, 1983).

47. The Mascot moth is described in Steinmeyer (2003, p. 191–192).

47. Reason (1990) describes the psychological factors in the disaster at Three Mile Island nuclear power station.

Chapter 4: Mental Architecture and the Unconscious

49. The epigraph to Part II is from the poem, *The Maze* (Auden, 1976, p. 237).

51. Todorov *et al.* (2005) report the study of judgments of competence from photographs and their relation to election results.

52. Freud (1973) posits irrational (primary) and rational (secondary) thought processes.

52. Helmholz (1962) refers to unconscious inferences in perception (see also Whyte, 1978, for a history of the unconscious before Freud).

53. Pascal in his *Pensées* (1966, p. 211) writes: "It is rare for mathematicians to be intuitive or the intuitive to be mathematicians, because mathematicians try to treat intuitive matters mathematically, and make themselves ridiculous, by trying to begin with definitions followed by principles, which is not the way to proceed in this kind of reasoning. It is not that the mind does not do this, but it does so tacitly, naturally and artlessly, for it is beyond any man to express it and given to very few even to apprehend it."

53. Psychologists who defend dual systems of reasoning include Reitman (1965), Wason and Evans (1975), Johnson-Laird and Wason (1976, p. 5–6), Johnson-Laird (1983, pp. 127, et seq.), Sloman (1996), Stanovich (1999), Rader and Sloutsky (2002), and Kahneman and Frederick (2002). Evans and his colleagues, however, have made it their special province, see, e.g., Evans (1984, 1989, 2003), Evans and Over (1996). Nisbett (e.g., 2003) also distinguishes between "holistic" reasoning, which he supposes is the prerogative of East Asians, and "analytical" reasoning, which he supposes is the prerogative of Europeans. The great difficulty is to pin down the mechanism for the rapid, intuitive, and unconscious system. Evans and Over (1996), for example, distinguish between rationality$_1$, which achieves our daily goals, and rationality$_2$, which we achieve when we have reasons for our thoughts sanctioned by a normative theory. But, they do not specify what the system for rationality$_1$ computes or how it carries out these computations. They do, however, remark that it is: generally reliable and efficient for achieving one's goals, computationally extremely powerful, rapid, preconscious, of a connectionist nature, not all-or-none because it yields rationality$_1$ as a property that comes in degrees, almost automatic, shaped by past experience and beyond the control of consciousness, based

on tacit and parallel processes, and shared with animals who can be rational[1] (pp. 8, 10, 22, 35, 36, 96, 143, and 154). Rips (2002, p. 408) remarks: "It is not fair play to claim that something is a two-system theory, for example, when it is actually one well-defined theory [for deliberate reasoning] plus everything else (Bedford, 1997)."

53. Rips (2002, p. 396) points out the problem of getting evidence that corroborates two systems of reasoning as opposed to a single system operating at two different levels of efficiency (see also Sloman, 1996). The model theory provides two such levels (see Schroyens et al., 2003 for this idea). In Chapter 5, I propose a mechanism for unconscious inferences; unlike Evans and Over's proposal it is computationally weaker than the system for conscious inferences, but can cope with information in parallel.

53. The idea that we are not aware of any mental processes, but only their results, goes back to Lashley (1958). Jackendoff (1996) makes the same point.

54. The hierarchical architecture is described in Johnson-Laird (1983), which also posits mental models of the self and explains their role in intentional behavior. Oatley (1978) includes an outstanding review of the history of hierarchical ideas about the organization of the brain. My former colleague Marcia Johnson (1983) proposes a mental architecture that also has multiple processes in parallel. She and her colleagues argue that models with a single executive cannot do justice to various aspects of consciousness, such as awareness and control, and the ways in which consciousness breaks down (see, e.g., Johnson and Reeder, 1997). This view may be correct, but I won't pursue it further here. Where we agree is that unconscious processes are computationally less powerful than those that have access to consciousness. In particular, Johnson's model allows for recursive 'thinking about one's own thinking', and 'reflecting on one's own reflections', in terms of two interacting systems.

55. Hopcroft and Ullman (1979) show that serial and parallel computations do not differ in power, i.e., in what they can compute. These authors also describe intractable problems in computation (see also Poundstone, 1988).

55. Malthus published his *Essay on the Principle of Population* in 1798 (see Malthus, 2004).

57. For an account of the psychology of working memory, see, e.g., Baddeley (1986). Baddeley (2000) added a new component to working memory in his theory in order to explain certain phenomena of consciousness.

57. Minsky (1968) suggests that a self-describing computational device could use its own description to predict what it would do in hypothetical circumstances.

57. The psychoanalyst John Bowlby emphasizes the role of our mental models of ourselves as we develop (see, e.g., Bowlby, 1988).

58. The leading authority on facial expressions, Paul Ekman, distinguishes between voluntary and involuntary smiles (see, e.g., Ekman, 1980, 1992b). The spontaneous smile depends on contracting the muscles that lift the corners of the lips up and that wrinkle the eyes.

58. The "cocktail" party effect is described in Cherry (1980).

58. I discuss our inability to control our emotions in Chapter 6.

59. Paul Valéry's remark about cognition is in his *Analects* (see Valéry, 1970, p. 405).

Chapter 5: Intuitions and Unconscious Reasoning

60. The epigraph is from the poem, *New Year Letter* (Auden, 1976, p. 169).

61. Nisbett and Wilson (1977) argue that many introspections are rationalizations. Students of reasoning, however, have found that when participants in an experiment think aloud while they reason, their accounts seem to be accurate (Ericsson and Simon, 1980; Van der Henst, Yang, and Johnson-Laird, 2002).

61. Many psychologists propose "dual process" accounts of reasoning, contrasting intuitive with deliberate reasoning (see the notes to the previous chapter). The present account distinguishes four sorts of reasoning, because it includes wholly unconscious inferences.

61. Ekman (e.g., 1995) has studied the fleeting emotions that intrude for a moment when we try to suppress our true feelings.

61–2. The study in which words prime unconscious behavior, such as walking slowly, is reported in Bargh *et al.* (1996).

62. Steele and Aronson (1995) report the experiment in which identifying one's ethnicity can affect performance on the Graduate Record Examination. Shih *et al.* (1999) show that the priming was unconscious. One group of their female Asian-American participants was asked a question, such as: What languages do you speak at home? Another group was asked: Do you prefer coed or a single-sex floor? The first question primed the participants' ethnicity, whereas the second question primed their gender. Asian-Americans have the reputation of being good at math; but women have the reputation of being bad at math. The priming had the corresponding effects on the groups' subsequent performance in a mathematical test.

62–3. The study of associations between, e.g., "female" and "entrepreneur", is part of the Implicit Association Test (see Greenwald *et al.*, 2003). It measures your unconscious associations. You can take the test for yourself at http://moral.wjh.harvard.edu. For a skeptical assessment of it as a measure of implicit prejudice, see Blanton and Jaccard (2006).

63. Many studies have examined how participants control complex systems, such as simulations of a town or factory (see, e.g., Broadbent *et al.*, 1986). They can learn to control them without a conscious knowledge of how the system works, but they tend to err with systems depending on multiple variables (see Dörner, 1996).

63. The anecdote about Peirce is from Sebeok and Umiker-Sebeok (1983). For studies of immediate impressions of participants from brief descriptions or pictures, see, e.g., Fiedler and Schenck (2001), and Uleman *et al.* (2005).

63. Klein (1998) describes the immediate inferences of fire chiefs.

63–4. Hull (1920) describes the study of Chinese ideograms.

64. Maier (1931) reports the study in which the participants had to tie together two ropes hanging from the ceiling. Thinking aloud impairs insight into problems according to Schooler *et al.* (1993).

64. Inferences about the references of pronouns are discussed in Garnham (2001).

65. Working memory is discussed in Chapter 3.

65. I owe the example of Michael Frayn's *Tin Men* to George A. Miller, who uses it to describe a sort of grammar that he investigated in his "Grammarama" project (see

Miller, 1968, chapter 7). These so-called "regular" grammars can characterize the output of a Markov finite-state automaton.

66. Hopcroft and Ullman (1979) describe k-limited Markov finite-state automata.

67. Levesque (1986) discusses sentences based on conjunction and universal claims. He refers to them as "vivid" sentences, because we can form a single representation of them.

67. Chapter 22 describes how we construct causal chains out of the elementary links of causal knowledge in long-term memory.

67. The study of pigeons making attributions of paintings is due to Watanabe *et al.* (1995). It won the 1995 Ig Nobel prize for psychology. Ig Nobel prizes are awarded for studies that make people laugh, and then make them think.

67–8. The study of infants learning simple artificial languages is reported in Marcus *et al.* (1999). Marcus (2001, chapter 3) describes the difficulty of explaining these results using orthodox "connectionist" theories of learning that represent only particular syllables.

69. Inferences based on premises, such as, "Everyone is prejudiced against a prejudiced person," are described in Chapter 11.

69. For a study of subliminal advertising, see, e.g., Kihlstrom *et al.* (1992). According to William James (1890, p. 526), "We may lay it down for certain that every representation of a movement awakens in some degree the actual movement which is its object".

69. Michotte (1963) discovered the automatic inferences that one object causes another to move.

70. See Chapter 13 for the intractability of induction.

70. The classic description of magical thinking is in Fraser (1890). Scoditti (1984) studied the wood carvers on Kitawa. Evans-Pritchard (1937) reports his famous studies of the Azande. Bowker (2003) tells the story of Orwell and magic.

71. For examples of magical thinking in Western medicine, see Malleson (1973), and, though he does not draw attention to this aspect of doctors' thinking, Porter's (1997) outstanding history of medicine.

71. Sutherland (1976) recounts the case of the broken ECT machine.

71. Gigerenzer and his colleagues describe fast and frugal heuristics (see, e.g., Gigerenzer and Hug, 1992; Gigerenzer *et al.*, 1999; Gigerenzer and Selten, 2002).

72. Timothy Wilson and his colleagues have carried out various studies in which thinking about an option reduced individuals' satisfaction with it in comparison with not thinking about it, e.g., the choice of art posters. He writes: "The trick is to gather enough information to develop an informed gut reaction and then not analyze the feeling too much" (Wilson, 2002, p. 172). The similar study examining the participants' hypothetical choices among cars described in terms of four or twelve attributes is reported in Dijksterhuis *et al.* (2006). Gladwell (2005) describes judgments that occur in a blink. Tall (2006) is a parody: "You already know what this book is about. That is the power of BLANK: the power of not actually thinking at all. Using what scientific researchers call 'Extra-Lean Deli Slicing' (or would if they actually bothered to research it), your brain has already decided whether you're going to like BLANK, whether its cover goes with your shirt, and whether it will make you look smart if somebody sees you reading it on the train." I won't confess, as my brother told me,

that I didn't rush out not to buy a copy of the book so that I couldn't read it and benefit from not thinking about it.

72. The problems of running complex systems, such as simulations of economies, without sufficient thought are described in Dörner (1996). He refers to the "logic of failure" in our tendency, for instance, to focus on one thing at a time, and our inability to grasp dependencies. I return to the latter problem in Chapter 24 on how we solve problems.

Chapter 6: Emotions as Inferences

73. The epigraph is from the poem, *Natural linguistics* (Auden, 1976, p. 636).

73. Simon (1982) emphasizes the "bounded" nature of human rationality.

74. Chapter 4 discusses the intractability of reasoning (see also the Glossary). Neisser (1963) pointed out the problems that arise from multiple goals.

74. Aristotle's remark about insults making us angry is in his *Politics* (1984, line 1312b30 in Barnes's splendid edition). Aristotle is the great grandfather of the cognitive theory of emotions (see his account of emotions in his *Rhetoric*, Book II; and the *Nichomachean Ethics*, e.g., line 1106a3). He recognized that emotions have a characteristic facial expression (*Physiognomics*, line 805b1). He also argued that emotions can distort our perceptions (*On Dreams*, line 4601b) and our judgments (*Rhetoric*, Book I, line 1356a14). For modern accounts of Aristotle's cognitive analysis emotions, see Fortenbaugh (1975) and Elster (1999).

74. William James (1884) describes his theory of emotion. Bermond *et al.* (1991) show that paralysis can enhance emotions.

74. For the potential function of emotions, see, e.g., Minsky (1985), and Nesse, (1991). Plato in *Timaeus* (69d) offers a litany of complaints against emotions. Gurdjieff (1991), a twentieth century Russian mystic, argues that negative emotions, such as anger and fear, consume energy that could otherwise be devoted to positive emotions. A description of Tibetan Buddhist and Western psychological views of emotions is in Ekman *et al.* (2005). Stoics, both the Greek founders of the movement and its Roman followers, prized virtue above emotion. We should be kind to our children, not because we love them, but because that's the right thing to do (see Murray, 1915). Sartre (1948) argues that emotions are wishful thinking. Few of these authors have anything to say about emotions in social mammals apart from us.

75. Ekman (1980, 1992b) distinguishes between spontaneous smiles and voluntary efforts to reproduce them.

75. The quotation is from Darwin (1965).

75. The communicative theory of emotions is described in Oatley and Johnson-Laird (1987), and a revised version of the theory is in Oatley and Johnson-Laird (1996). The relations between innate basic emotions and emotions that depend on social norms in a culture are reviewed in Johnson-Laird and Oatley (2000).

75–6. Facial expressions of emotion appear to be universal, but with some local cultural modifications, see Ekman (e.g., 1980), and Marsh *et al.* (2003).

77. Many theorists postulate the existence of basic emotions, e.g., Ekman (1992a), Stein *et al.* (1993), and Power and Dalgleish (1997). But, others reject them, arguing that emotions are made up from components that cannot stand alone as emotions, such as

autonomic responses and cognitive appraisals (Ortony *et al.*, 1988; Ortony and Turner, 1990), prototypes (Russell, 1991), or tendencies towards certain actions (Frijda, 1986). Schacter and Singer (1962) propose that general arousal is common to all emotions. The opposing thesis, which Oatley and I defend, is that each basic emotion has its own pattern of nervous activity, neurotransmitters, and hormonal responses (see also Ekman, 1992a).

78. Freud (1915) argues that emotional feelings can never be unconscious.

78. Tranel (1997) describes the amygdala. LeDoux (1996) summarizes the evidence about the role of the amygdala in basic emotions. Calder *et al.* (1996) report the impairment in the recognition of facial expressions. Buchanan and Adolphs (2002) review the evidence concerning the amygdala and memory for emotional events.

79. LeDoux (1996) describes the two neural pathways to the amygdala that underlie fear.

79. Sifneos (1996) describes alexithymia. It is assessed using various self-report questionnaires, including the Toronto Alexithymia scale. Studies using functional magnetic resonance imaging (fMRI) have detected a significant reduction in the activity of a region in the brain, the posterior cingulate cortex, which is implicated in memory and emotion (see Aleman, 2005).

79. Rozin (1996) describes his work on disgust.

80. Darwin (1989) recounts his adventure with the potted meat (see the entry in his journal for January 19, 1833).

81. Bowlby (1988) describes the role of models of the self in the normal development of human beings.

81. Knight and Grabowecky (1995) emphasize the role of prefrontal cortex in dealing with "counterfactual" possibilities to what happened.

81. Phineas Gage has his own webpage: www.deakin.edu.au/hbs/GAGEPAGE/ maintained by the world's leading expert on his case, Malcolm Macmillan.

81. Damasio (1994) describes the modern patient similar to Phineas Gage, and discusses the role of the amygdala in basic emotions, which he refers to as "primary" emotions. They survive damage to the "ventromedial" region of the prefrontal lobes of the brain, whereas complex emotions do not. Damasio refers to complex emotions as "secondary", and he summarizes the relations between the two sorts of emotions in a way that corroborates the communicative theory. He writes: "The prefrontal, acquired dispositional representations needed for secondary emotions are a separate lot from the innate dispositional representations needed for primary emotions. But,... the former need the latter in order to express themselves" (Damasio, 1994, p. 137).

82. The study of prefrontal patients' decisions in the experimental gambling game is reported in Bechara *et al.* (1994).

82. Aristotle writes about our inability to choose which emotion to feel in his *Nichomachean Ethics* (Aristotle, 1984, line 1106a3).

82. St. Augustine's remarks about erections are in his *City of God* (see, e.g., 13.13, 14.16 of Augustine, 1950). The disobedience of the penis, he writes, is a fitting punishment for Adam's disobedience. (What about Eve?)

82. Some psychologists argue that we can control our emotions (see, e.g., Ochsner and Gross, 2005). We can sometimes distract ourselves from emotional events and sometimes reappraise them to modulate our feelings. A brilliant demonstration of this

sort of effect is a study combining the Implicit Association Test, which I described in the previous chapter, with brain imaging (Cunningham *et al.*, 2004). When white participants looked at pictures of black faces as opposed to pictures of white faces, their amygdala were more active. The effect was larger when the faces were presented for such a brief interval that the participants reported seeing only the display that followed a face. It was also larger for those individuals who showed a bigger bias in the Implicit Association Test, i.e., they associated "blacks" rather than "whites" with bad words. When the faces were presented for over half a second so that the participants could see what they were looking at, the regions of the frontal cortex, which mediate our ability to control ourselves, took over. They were more active when the participants looked at the black faces, and, the responses of the amygdala abated. The study shows that a basic emotion can be triggered by a very crude cognitive evaluation—one that we're not aware of, but that the ensuing emotion can be modulated by a conscious evaluation. Likewise, we have some voluntary control over the expression of our emotions. We may be able to suppress or enhance them using various cognitive strategies, such as distraction or reappraisal, but we appear to have no control over the onset of an emotion or over which basic emotion we feel. And we cannot switch an emotion off like a light.

82. For emotional "seepage", see Ekman (1995).

83. Shakespeare has Hamlet comment on real emotions to unreal events in the soliloquy about the player: "What's Hecuba to him, or he to Hecuba, That he should weep for her?" (*Hamlet*, Act II, Scene 2). Dadlez (1997) uses this remark as the title of her philosophical book on the topic.

83. Psychologists disagree about the role of inference in creating emotions. Zajonc (1980) argued that preferences do not depend on inferences, but Lazarus (1982) retorted that they do not depend on *conscious* inferences.

84. For studies showing that participants are wrong about their anticipated feelings, see, e.g., Schkade and Kahneman (1998), Gilbert *et al.* (1998), and Gilbert and Wilson (2000).

85. Kahneman and Tversky (1979) describe their "prospect" theory. Others who allow for the effects of emotions on decisions include Frank (1988) and Mellers *et al.* (1998). Evidence for the role of anticipated emotions in choice is reported in Bar-Hillel and Neter (1996) and Mellers and McGraw (2001).

85. I owe the whooping cough example to Baron (2000).

85. Reason (1988) describes the role of stress in cognitive errors.

85. Oaksford *et al.* (1996) demonstrate the preoccupying effects of watching emotional movies on the selection task. Blanchette and Richards (2004) show that emotional words in conditional premises have a similar preoccupying effect on reasoning.

86. Duncker (1945) describes the candle problem and "functional fixity". Isen *et al.* (1987) report the effect of emotional movies on its solution. Many studies by Isen and her colleagues and by others show that happiness improves creativity (see also, e.g., Greene and Noice, 1988).

86. Johnson and Tversky (1983) demonstrate the effects of anxiety on participants' assessments of risk. For studies of the effects of emotions on vigilance, see Broadbent and Broadbent (1988) and Mathews *et al.* (1997); and for their effects on memory, see Teasdale (1988).

86. Alloy and Abramson (1979, 1988) compare slightly depressed participants' estimates of their control over outcomes with those of participants who are not depressed.

86. Power and Wykes (1996) demonstrate the effects of depression on reasoning about positive and negative matters.

86–7. The study of the Russell Banks story was carried out by Oatley, Nundy, and Larocque (see Oatley, 1996). Nundy (1995) also showed that happy participants were more accurate in reasoning with syllogisms than sad participants. She induced the emotions using clips from movies.

87. Aristotle (1984) writes about anger in his *Rhetoric* (Book II, line 1378a).

87. Kahneman and Tversky (1982) discuss the counterfactual thoughts that one has when plans don't work, and the differences in imagining different sorts of counterfactual possibility (see also Kahneman, 1995). Girotto *et al.* (1991) show that participants tend to undo mentally the protagonist's intentional actions.

87. Ruth Byrne's (2005) book, *The Rational Imagination*, describes the work of the imagination in creating counterfactual possibilities. We are similar in what we undo in envisaging counterfactual possibilities (see also Byrne, 1996, 1997, 2002). We undo exceptional events or those under the control of the protagonist (Kahneman and Miller, 1986; Gavanski and Wells, 1989; Girotto *et al.*, 1991; Klauer *et al.*, 1995).

87. For the relations between complex emotions, such as regret and guilt, and thoughts about counterfactual possibilities (see, e.g., Kahneman and Tversky, 1982; Niedenthal, Tangney and Gavanski, 1994; Byrne and McEleney, 2000; Byrne, 2005). Medvec *et al.* (1995) show that such thoughts can ameliorate outcomes, e.g., if you've won only a bronze medal at the Olympics. Roese (1997) reports a study of the completion of counterfactual prompts after watching a sad clip from *Bambi*. Those who watched the clip were faster than control participants to complete a prompt of the form, "if only...," about their performance in an earlier test of their ability to solve anagrams.

88. Darwin (1965, p. 38) describes his adventure with the snake at London Zoo.

Chapter 7: Reasoning in Psychological Illnesses

89. The two vignettes come from a study carried out by an Italian psychiatrist Francesco Mancini and his colleague Amelia Gangemi in which 34 psychiatrists had to diagnose patients on the basis of these and other vignettes. The psychiatrists had no difficulty in identifying the nature of the psychological illness in the two vignettes. Mancini, Gangemi, and I, collaborated on the reasoning studies and in developing the theory of psychological illnesses described in this chapter (see Johnson-Laird *et al.*, 2006b).

90. Szasz (1974) is skeptical about the existence of mental illnesses.

90. The original concept of "neurosis" was of a mental illness that had a psychological cause rather than a neurological one, and that, unlike, say, schizophrenia, did not lead to an utter lack of contact with reality. The American Psychiatric Association, which no longer recognizes a category of "neuroses", publishes the *Diagnostic and Statistical Manual of Mental Disorders*, DSM-IV-TR (2000). The equivalents of neuroses are classified in many categories, including Disorders of Mood and Anxiety Disorders.

90. Descartes, the archetypal Dualist, argues that the pineal gland connects mind to body (see Descartes, 1984–91).

90. John Snow's research into the transmission of cholera is described in the penultimate chapter of the book.

91. Herink (1980) describes 250 different sorts of psychotherapy.

91. Various sorts of psychotherapy and of behavior therapy appear to be successful in reducing anxiety (Smith *et al.*, 1980). *Consumer Reports*, the journal that reports on manufactured products, gives a positive rating of psychotherapy (in its November 1995 issue). This report in turn has a positive assessment from Seligman (1995). Cognitive therapy for depression, as described in Beck *et al.* (1979) is said to be better than antidepressant drugs (Robinson *et al.*, 1990). Hollon *et al.* (2002) also review various forms of therapy for depression and report that cognitive-behavior therapy is more effective than a less intense version of Freudian psychoanalysis, and that it bolsters drug therapy.

91. Behavior therapy is described in Wolpe (1990). Auden was mordant on behaviorism: "Of course, Behaviorism 'works'. So does torture. Give me a no-nonsense, down-to-earth behaviorist, a few drugs, and simple electrical appliances, and in six months I will have him reciting the Athanasian Creed in public" (Auden, 1971).

91. Freud himself is unsurpassed for accounts of psychoanalysis (see, e.g., Freud, 1973). Erdelyi (1985) considers Freudian theory from the standpoint of cognitive psychology, and reports experimental tests of some of its hypotheses.

91. Beck (1976, 1991) claims that faulty reasoning leads to neuroses, see also Maslow (1938), Ellis (1962), Wells (2000), Cohen (2003), and Leahy (2004).

91–2. The quotation is from Auden (1977, p. 395).

92. Smeets and De Jong (2005) report a typical study of reasoning and psychological illness: its results are equivocal.

92. The woman worried about contracting HIV is a patient of Mancini's.

92. Personality tests show that people differ in their tendency to neuroticism, e.g., Eysenck's neuroticism scale (see, e.g., Eysenck and Eysenck, 1975), and the Minnesota Multiphasic Personality Inventory.

92. Studies of twins and their tendency towards neuroticism, or lack of it, are reported in Livesley *et al.* (1993) and Jang *et al.* (1998). These innate propensities are likely to be a consequence of multiple genes (cf. Eley and Plomin, 1997).

93. Oswald *et al.* (1970) report a relation between anxiety and breathlessness in asthma and bronchitis.

94–5. The case of "Ruth", the obsessive-compulsive patient, is described in Leon (1990). Studies of the reasoning of individuals with obsessive compulsions are reported by, e.g., Reed (1977) and Pélissier and O'Connor (2002).

95. According to Tversky and Koehler's (1994) "support theory", the description of an event in greater detail suggests more evidence in favor of it and thus leads to an increase in its judged probability.

95. The hypothesis of fusions in obsessive-compulsive thinking is due to several authors, including Wells (2000), Thodarson and Shafran (2002), and O'Connor and Aardema (2003).

96. The case of fleeting hypochondria is reported by Bruce S. Singh on his website: www.mja.com.au/public/mentalhealth/articles/singh/singh.html#case1.

96. Salkovskis (1996) argues that reasoning in hypochondria tends to corroborate the worst-case scenario.

96. Pascal's wager is in his *Pensées* (Pascal, 1966): "Let us weigh the gain and the loss in wagering that God is ... If you gain, you gain all; if you lose, you lose nothing. Wager, then, without hesitation that He is."

97. For the brain imaging studies of anxiety in individuals who are obsessive, see Breiter *et al.* (1996), of anxiety in social phobia, see Birbaumer *et al.* (1998), and of depression, see, e.g., Davidson *et al.* (2002).

97–8. The questionnaire study is from Johnson-Laird *et al.* (2006b).

98. The experiments on obsessive-compulsive disorder and depression are described in Johnson-Laird *et al.* (2006b).

98. The test for a tendency towards obsessive-compulsive disorder was the abridged Padua Inventory of obsessive-compulsive behaviors (Rhéaume *et al.*, 2000), which my colleagues gave to 290 students at Palermo University in order to select the fourteen who scored highest for obsessive-compulsive tendency and the fourteen who scored lowest.

100. The test for the tendency towards depression used the Beck Depression Inventory (see Beck *et al.*, 1979), which my colleagues gave to a new sample of 370 students at the University of Palermo in order to select the eighteen participants who scored highest for depression and the twenty-two who scored lowest. An unpublished study by Isabelle Blanchette and Michelle Campbell also showed an unexpected improvement in syllogistic reasoning. Military veterans from the first Gulf war reasoned better from premises that were emotional and specific to them, e.g., *Some friendly fire incidents result in death*, than from other sorts of premise. In a similar unpublished study, these authors tested the reasoning of individuals in three cities—London, Manchester, and the Canadian city of London, Ontario—about the terrorist bombing attacks in London. The task called for the participants to inhibit their beliefs in order to reach a valid conclusion. A week after the attacks, the participants in England were more accurate than the Canadian sample, but only with syllogisms pertaining to the terrorist attacks. No difference occurred with control syllogisms or syllogisms with a general emotional content. Six weeks later, the difference diminished, and only the London sample still had the advantage over the Canadian sample with the syllogisms about terrorism.

100. Beck (1976) discusses the thoughts of patients, which he treats as "automatic".

100. For accounts of "exposure" therapy, see Andrews *et al.* (2003) and Tryon (2005).

Chapter 8: Only Connections

103. The epigraph to Part III is from the poem, *New Year Letter* (Auden, 1976, p. 170).

105. The well-known movie of *Murder on the Orient Express* diverges from Agatha Christie's (1960) novel.

105. The number of possibilities with 100 suspects is 2^{100}, which is a vast number: 1, 267, 650, 600, 228, 229, 401, 496, 703, 205, 376, i.e., over a million million million million million.

107. George Boole (1815–1864) was born in Lincolnshire, England, but became a professor at the University of Galway in Ireland. His principal book is Boole (1854). Mary Boole's (1909) children's introduction to Boolean algebra devotes a chapter to

Macbeth. The psychological study of Boolean concepts has a large literature from Shepard *et al.* (1961) to Feldman (2004).

109. Truth tables are described in Jeffrey (1981). They were independently invented by Peirce and Wittgenstein.

109. For logics in which not all valid theorems can be proved in any consistent formal system, see Boolos and Jeffrey (1989). The predicate calculus can be formalized using a single rule of inference. But, another way is to use formal rules for each connective. This approach is called "natural deduction" (see Prawitz, 1965; Gentzen, 1969). Psychological theories of deductive reasoning based on formal rules of inference embody the same idea (see e.g., Braine and O'Brien, 1991; Rips, 1994).

109. Lord Kelvin's remark is in his Baltimore lectures (Kelvin, 1884, p. 270).

110. The computer program for reasoning with models is described in Johnson-Laird and Savary (1999).

112. Several methods for minimizing Boolean expressions exist. The Quine–McCluskey method is described in Quine (1955) and McCluskey (1956); other references include, e.g., Gimpel (1965), Arevalo and Bredeson (1978), and Dunne (1988). The intractability of minimizing Boolean expressions is described in Garey and Johnson (1979).

112. The idea that our system of reasoning constructs one model at a time was made vivid to me by two separate lines of research. One line is Tom Ormerod's studies of paraphrasing conditionals as disjunctions and vice versa (see, e.g., Richardson and Ormerod, 1997; Ormerod and Richardson, 2003). The second line is Vladimir Sloutsky's research showing that children tend to ignore the second clause of a premise formed with a propositional connective, so that the premise yields one mental model. They are more likely to ignore it in a disjunction, and less likely to in a conjunction (Morris and Sloutsky, 1998; Morris and Sloutsky, 2002). Likewise, adults tend to recall connectives as conjunctions (Rader and Sloutsky, 2001; Sloutsky and Goldvarg, 2004).

112. The principle of truth is introduced in Johnson-Laird and Savary (1999). Some critics have thought that the principle means that mental models represent only those clauses mentioned in the premises. This view, however, implies that sentences have the same models regardless of the connectives that occur in them. They don't. The connective "and" yields one model, whereas the connective "or" yields two or three depending on whether it is exclusive or inclusive.

112. Johnson-Laird and Byrne (1991, 2002) argue that we reason using mental models based on propositional connectives, but that mental footnotes allow us to construct complete models in simple cases.

113. Johnson-Laird and Tagart (1969) report a study in which the participants evaluated the truth or falsity of conditionals (see also Evans, 1972b; Oaksford and Stenning, 1992).

114. Chapter 2 makes the point that negation cannot be represented in an icon.

115–6. Clare Walsh carried out the experiments showing that participants succumbed to illusory inferences based on disjunctions (Walsh and Johnson-Laird, 2004). Illusions also occur in thinking about what is possible (Goldvarg and Johnson-Laird, 2000). The first studies of illusory inferences were reported in Johnson-Laird and Savary

(1996, 1999). Studies that have used procedures or instructions to reduce illusions include Newsome and Johnson-Laird (1996), Tabossi *et al.* (1998), Santamaría and Johnson-Laird (2000), and Yang and Johnson-Laird (2000a,b).

117. An unpublished paper of 1995 by Simon Handley and Ruth Byrne reports studies of the negation of conjunctions and disjunctions (Mimeo, University of Plymouth, England). The negation of a conjunction, *not both A and B*, has three complete models: not-A B, A not-B, not-A not-B. Barres and Johnson-Laird (2003) report that their participants had difficulty in imagining what is false given a complex proposition.

Chapter 9: I'm My Own Grandpa: Reasoning About Identities and Other Relations

119. I owe the story about Ernest Harrison to Littlewood (1953). The theory of reasoning with relations in this chapter is based on Goodwin and Johnson-Laird (2005a).

119. Professor Higgins's study is described in Chapter 2.

120. The logic of relations came to fruition as a result of the work of De Morgan, Peirce, and Schröder (see, e.g., Kneale and Kneale, 1962). Peirce analyzes the construction of complex relations, such as, *is the father of the mother of*, and their reduction into simpler relations (see, e.g., Peirce, 1931–58, Vol. 1, paragraph 66, i.e., the first paragraph of an article, "The logic of relatives", originally published in 1883). He devised diagrams of relations that anticipate so-called "semantic" networks (see Sowa, 1984), and he argues that any relation over any number of arguments can always be reduced to a set of relations in which no relation has more than three arguments. Tarski (1965, chapter V) gives a modern account of the logical properties of relations, such as transitivity.

120. Miller and Johnson-Laird (1976) discuss the case of small elephants.

120. The impossibility of treating relations as properties was known to nineteenth century logicians (Winkelmann, 1980). A relation such as, *father of,* is a special sort that is known to mathematicians as a "function". When a function is given values for its arguments, it delivers a single unique value as a result, just as the function of addition delivers a single unique value given the numbers to be added. Likewise, *father of George W. Bush* has a unique value: George H.W. Bush.

121. Halford (1993) argues that relations with more than four arguments tend to exceed our ability to understand them (see also Halford *et al.*, 1998). He refers to the number of arguments in a relation as its "relational complexity". We can adopt two methods to reduce the number of arguments in a relation that we need to consider at any one moment. One method reduces the number of arguments, as when we treat a relation as a property. The other method divides a task into different segments in order to avoid having to think about complicated relations (Birney and Halford, 2002).

121–2. Frames of reference are discussed in, e.g., Miller and Johnson-Laird (1976), O'Keefe and Nadel (1978), and Levinson (1996). Language and the intrinsic parts of objects are described in Fillmore (1971), Clark (1973), and Talmy (1983).

122. Inferences based on pairs of premises such as:

The triangle is on the right of the circle.

The circle is on the right of the diamond.

are known as "linear syllogisms" or "three-term series problems". Störring (1908) seems to have been the first to study them in the laboratory (see Woodworth, 1938), and Piaget (1928) also carried out some early studies (see, e.g., Manktelow, 1999, for a review). James (1890, p. 646) proposes a theory of reasoning about relations based on single integrated representations. Hunter (1957) proposes operations to construct these representations. De Soto *et al.* (1965) argue that these representations are visual images, and Huttenlocher (1968) shows that we find it easier to add the subject of a relation to a representation than to add the object of the relation. Other creatures also make transitive inferences, and pigeons can outperform undergraduates (see Delius and Siemann, 1998). Clark (1969) shows that transitive inferences with a term such as "wider than" are easier than those with its converse "narrower than". If the doorway is narrower than the table, then the implication is that both are narrow in relation to some norm. But, the proposition that the table is wider than the doorway is neutral with respect to their size in relation to the norm. Hence, terms such as "narrower" convey more information than terms such as "wider", which often correspond to the name of the dimension ("width"). Linguists refer to terms such as "narrower" as *marked* and to terms such as "wider" as *unmarked*.

123. The use of axioms ("meaning postulates") to capture the logical properties of relations is discussed in Bar-Hillel (1967).

123. Theories of reasoning based on formal rules of inference are described in Chapter 1.

124. Evidence that participants construct spatial arrays is reported by Riley and Trabasso (1974), Potts and Scholz (1975), and Newstead *et al.* (1986). Trabasso *et al.* (1975) show that children from six to nine years of age and college students make transitive inferences by assembling elements into an ordered array. Riley (1976) replicated these findings and showed that they occurred with transitive relations other than length (e.g., *height, weight, happiness, niceness*). Accounts of models of spatial relations can be found in Johnson-Laird and Ehrlich (1982) and Johnson-Laird and Mani (1982). Ruth Byrne and I outline the theory presented in this chapter (Byrne and Johnson-Laird, 1989).

124. Some authors suggest that we use either linguistic principles or models depending on the experimental procedure (Ormrod, 1979; Verweij *et al.*, 1999), or as alternative strategies (Egan and Grimes-Farrow, 1982; Roberts, 2000). Other authors argue that we use both linguistic principles and arrays at different times during the process (Sternberg and Weil, 1980). Hummel and Holyoak (2001, 2003) have implemented a "connectionist" program that combines linguistic factors with a spatial array. It remains an open question whether any connectionist system can compose complex relations, such as *the mother of the father of the brother of*.

125. Oberauer and Wilhelm (2000) show in an experiment that given a spatial relation, such as, *the cup is on the right of the spoon*, it is easier to add the subject of the sentence (the cup) to a representation that includes the object (the spoon) than vice versa (see the earlier note to Huttenlocher's work).

125. Kamp and Reyle (1993) analyze referring expressions and show how they map on to representations of discourse. Their representations are intended to be useful tools for linguistic analysis rather than a psychological theory, and so they do not postulate iconic representations, but ones that have a transparent logic. A psychological theory of how referring phrases are interpreted in terms of models of discourse is described in, e.g., Garnham *et al.* (1995) and Garnham (2001).

126. Inferential strategies are explained in Chapter 19.

129. Chapter 2 discusses the limits of iconicity.

130. Ruth Byrne carried out the experiment on spatial reasoning (see Byrne and Johnson-Laird, 1989).

130. Hagert (1984) proposes "two-dimensional" meaning postulates, such as:

> For any x, y, and z, if x is on the left of y and z is in front of x then z is in front of x, which is on the left of y.

131. Studies corroborating that inferences based on one model are easier than those based on multiple models include Schaeken *et al.* (1996a,b), Vandierendonck and De Vooght (1997), and Carreiras and Santamaría (1997). We may represent the indeterminacy of an object's position within a model, or by an annotation on a model (see Vandierendonck, Dierckx, and De Vooght, 2004; Schaeken *et al.*, in press). The study in which all the problems contain one irrelevant premise is described in Schaeken *et al.* (1998).

132. Walter Schaeken carried out the study of temporal reasoning based on tense and auxiliary verbs (Schaeken *et al.*, 1996b). The meanings of temporal expressions are complex, see, e.g., Reichenbach (1956); and Miller and Johnson-Laird (1976). Schaeken *et al.* (1996a) describe the program for temporal reasoning.

133. Geoffrey Goodwin carried out the study of pseudo-transitivity (see Goodwin and Johnson-Laird, 2005c).

134. Valéry's test is in *Moments* (Valéry, 1970, p. 75).

135. The answer to the final riddle is: I'm my own grandpa! I've edited the lyrics (copyright Moe Jaffe and Dwight Latham, 1947) to leave the Oedipal relations in all their glory.

Chapter 10: Syllogisms and Reasoning About Properties

136. The logical calculus for standard quantifiers such as idealized versions of "any" and "some", i.e., the quantificational calculus, was first formulated by Frege (1879/1967) and independently by Peirce (1883, see Vol. 3, paragraph 328 in Peirce, 1931–1958). In the standard calculus, variables take individuals as values. The uniform account of quantifiers including "most" and others that lie outside the standard quantificational calculus is due to Mostowski (1957). Its defense for natural language is in Montague (1974) and Barwise and Cooper (1981). In this logic, the "second order" quantificational calculus, variables can take sets of individuals (i.e., properties) as well as individuals as their values.

136–7. Geurts (2003) points out the difficulty of proving the simple inference with standard quantifiers using formal rules of inference. Theories of reasoning based on formal rules are described in Chapter 1.

137. Bar-Hillel (1969) identifies the scandal that logicians have neglected everyday arguments. Keene (1992) is an honorable exception.

137. For studies of the factors influencing the quantities that quantified phrases are taken to refer to, see Moxey and Sanford (e.g., 1993, 2000).

139. Kant (1787/1934) argues against the use of a single diagram in a proof; Wittgenstein (1953) argues for it. Hume (1739/1978) had already shown how it could be done.

140–1. One sort of quantifier cannot be used to yield a valid inference in conjunction with a premise about an entire set, namely, any quantifier that puts an upper limit on the number of individuals in the set. For example, the following inference is not valid:

> No more than two of the artists are sculptors.
>
> Every sculptor is a painter.
>
> Therefore, no more than two of the artists are painters.

The inference is invalid because artists who are not sculptors could be painters.

141. Aristotle's account of syllogisms is in his *Prior Analytics*. The history of the logic of syllogisms is recounted in Kneale and Kneale (1962).

141. For an account of distribution in medieval logic, see, e.g., Cohen and Nagel (1934). The modern analysis is as follows: When quantifiers are treated as relations between sets, in the case of *All B are C*, *C* is *monotonically increasing*, i.e., if *C* implies *D* then *B* implies *D*; whereas *B* is *monotonically decreasing*, i.e., if *A* implies *B* then *A* implies *C* (Barwise and Cooper, 1981). The use of mental models to represent relations between sets was introduced in Johnson-Laird (1983), see also, e.g., Neth and Johnson-Laird (1999). Geurts (2003) proposes formal rules for a psychological theory based on the same notion, whereas they are emergent properties of the use of models and meanings.

141. Akin to the invalid inference from "More than half of the painters are sculptors", Power (1984) shows that individuals tend to infer invalidly: "More than a quarter of A's are B's; therefore, more than a quarter of B's are A's".

142. Russell's joke about the spoof issue of *Mind* is in Russell (1927). In Russell (1946), he points out the inability of syllogisms to handle relational inferences, such as: all horses are animals; therefore, all horses' heads are animals' heads.

142. Plato's joke about the dog is from his dialogue about sophists, *Euthydemus*, 298d–298e.

143. The rules for syllogisms in Box 10.2 paraphrase those in Cohen and Nagel (1934, p. 79).

144. Experiments on syllogistic reasoning are reviewed in Johnson-Laird and Byrne (1991) and Evans *et al.* (1993). Chater and Oaksford (1999) analyze several experiments that examined all the different logical varieties of syllogism. They conclude that participants are more likely to make valid inferences than invalid inferences.

144. The original version of the atmosphere hypothesis is proposed in Sells (1936) even though it was published after Woodworth and Sells (1935). Begg and Denny (1969) re-formulate the atmosphere hypothesis as two principles: (1) Whenever there is a negative premise, we draw a negative conclusion; otherwise, we draw an affirmative conclusion. (2) Whenever there is a premise containing "some", we draw a conclusion containing "some"; otherwise, we draw a conclusion containing "all" for affirmative premises and "none" for negative premises. Theorists who propose that atmosphere is part of the process of reasoning include Madruga (1984), Inder (1987), Newell (1990), Polk and Newell (1995), and Rips (1994, p. 247). Revlis (1975) seems to have been the first to suggest that we might not reason at all, but instead follow the atmosphere principles. Gilhooly *et al.* (1993) propose that we are less likely to reason than to draw conclusions that match the atmosphere of

the more conservative of the two premises (see also Wetherick and Gilhooly, 1990). Chater and Oaksford (1999) argue that reasoning is rooted in probabilistic thinking (see also Oaksford and Chater, 1998). Given certain reasonable assumptions, conclusions can be ordered from least informative to most informative as follows: *Some A are not C, No A is a C, Some A are C*, and *All A are C*. We don't reason, but select a conclusion that matches the form of the least informative premise. Their view is that the probability calculus is both a normative and descriptive account of how we made deductions (see Chapter 16).

144. Johnson-Laird and Byrne (1989) describe the study of "only" as a quantifier. Shaw and Johnson-Laird (1998) provide other evidence contrary to the atmosphere effect. Critics of the atmosphere hypothesis include Chapman and Chapman (1959), Mazzocco *et al.* (1974), Dickstein (1975), and Johnson-Laird and Bara (1984).

144. Sudoku puzzles are discussed in Chapter 19.

144. Johnson-Laird (1983) reports the differences in difficulty from one syllogism to another, and the differences in ability from one person to another in syllogistic reasoning (see also Galotti *et al.*, 1986). Bara *et al.* (1995) report the relation between working memory and syllogistic reasoning, and Copeland and Radvansky (2004) also report a correlation between its capacity and accurate syllogistic reasoning. Stanovich (1999) describes the evidence relating intelligence and reasoning.

146. Bucciarelli and Johnson-Laird (1999) present the most recent version of the model theory of syllogisms and its computer implementation. Earlier accounts include Johnson-Laird and Steedman (1978), Johnson-Laird and Bara (1984), who describe two alternative strategies using models, and Johnson-Laird and Byrne (1991). Subsequent computer programs obviated technical criticisms (e.g., Hardman, 1996). A common question about the model theory is what determines which model is constructed first (see, e.g., Chater *et al.*, 2005, p. 304). The answer is the principle that given a premise interrelating, say, bakers and cricketers, where authors and bakers are already represented in a model, individuals update their representation of bakers. Any relation between authors and cricketers that is not thereby established will await discovery in the construction of subsequent models.

148. Figural effects were discovered in an experiment that Janellen Huttenlocher and I carried out in 1971. They were first reported in Wason and Johnson-Laird (1972, pp. 153–155). Dickstein (1975) reports an independent discovery of figural effects.

148. Oberauer's explanation of figural effects and his corroboratory evidence are reported in Oberauer and Wilhelm (2000), Oberauer *et al.* (2005), and Hörnig *et al.* (2005). For the effects in relational reasoning, see Baguely and Payne (2000). The effects are also influenced by a well-known principle that it is easier to assign a phrase to its prior referent when this prior referent is mentioned before a new referent (i.e., Clark and Haviland's, 1977, "given-new" principle).

148–9. The origin of Euler circles is recounted in Kneale and Kneale (1962). For psychological theories that use Euler circles, see, e.g., Erickson (1974), Johnson-Laird (1975), Fisher (1981), and Cardaci *et al.* (1996). Stenning and his colleagues have evidence corroborating the use of representations of possibilities in reasoning. They have shown an equivalence between mental models and a novel way of reasoning based on Euler circles. This method obviates the usual combinatorial explosion of diagrams (see, e.g., Stenning and Oberlander, 1995; Stenning and Yule, 1997). Rips (2002, p. 387) argues that participants use Euler circles because they encountered them in school.

149. Edwards (2004) describes the origins of Venn diagrams and their modern developments. Psychological theories that relate to Venn diagrams include Guyote and Sternberg (1981) and Newell (1981).

149–50. Stenning and his colleagues have formulated rules for Euler circles, rules for mental models, and rules for logical formulas, that all yield the same valid inferences (e.g., Stenning and Yule, 1997). Hence, the way to discriminate among these accounts is in terms of patterns of errors, and other characteristics of performance.

150. One study in which participants were given paper and pencil and ask to think aloud is reported in Bucciarelli and Johnson-Laird (1999). Ford (1995) tested more knowledgeable participants. She divided them into those who used Euler circles and those who used a verbal substitution strategy (also described in terms of models by Johnson-Laird and Bara, 1984). At least four of Ford's participants imagined individual entities. One of them said, for instance, "… suppose there's two historians right that means there are two weavers who are also historians so we can say some of the weavers are historians…". From Störring (1908) to Stenning (2002), psychologists have claimed that some reasoners use images and others use verbal procedures.

150. The study of illusions with disjunctions of quantified premises is in Yang and Johnson-Laird (2000a), and the study of antidotes to them is in Yang and Johnson-Laird (2000b). Both Luca Bonatti and David O'Brien (personal communications in April 1997) suggested that the illusions occur because reasoners misapply a suppositional strategy to a disjunction of premises. This idea is *post hoc* and makes the wrong predictions about some of the control problems (Yang and Johnson-Laird, 2000a).

Chapter 11: Isn't Everyone an Optimist? The Case of Complex Reasoning

153. For an introduction to the quantificational calculus, see Jeffrey (1981), who also discusses the sentence, "Everyone loves a lover". Rips (1994) defends a mental equivalent of the quantificational calculus.

154. Logicians represent the two interpretations of a sentence such as: *All the Bury letters are in the same place as some of the Avon letters*, in the quantificational calculus (see, e.g., Jeffrey, 1981). For a comparison between logic and natural language, see Johnson-Laird (1970b).

154. The order in which one loop is embedded within another in the program depends on the logical "scope" of the quantifiers (Jeffrey, 1981).

157. The program and the experiments corroborating the theory's predictions are reported in Johnson-Laird *et al.* (1989): inferences that require just one model are easier than those that require multiple models. Greene (1992) pointed out that the multiple-model problems had conclusions in which the second quantifier had a larger scope, e.g., none of the Avon letters is in the same place as *some* of the Caton letters. He showed that participants prefer to draw conclusions of the form: Some of the Caton letters are not in the same place as any of the Avon letters. Victoria Shaw showed that multiple-model inferences were harder than one-model inferences even when all the inferences could have either form of conclusion (Shaw and Johnson-Laird, 1998).

158–9. Paolo Cherubini carried out the studies of recursive inferences (see Cherubini and Johnson-Laird, 2004). The study also examined the negative problems, which were much more difficult than the affirmative problems. Marcin Hitczenko wrote a computer program to implement the model theory's account of these inferences.

160. Box 11.2 is based on a figure from Cherubini and Johnson-Laird (2004).

161. My definition of "optimism" echoes the anthropologist Levi-Strauss's claim that anyone who believes that there are barbarians is a barbarian too (see Gellner, 1970).

162. Wang (1963) discusses proofs based on premises with three quantifiers, such as: "For any tile, there is at least some tile, such that for any tile...." He proves that no guarantee exists that invalidity can be established in a finite number of steps for this domain.

Chapter 12: Modulation: A Step Towards Induction

163. The epigraph for Part IV is from the poem, *New Year Letter* (Auden, 1976, p. 162).

166. Theories of reasoning based on formal logic that include the disjunctive rule are, e.g., Johnson-Laird (1975), Rips (1983, 1994), and Braine and O'Brien (1998). The quotation from the late John Macnamara is from an email to me in 1989. Cases that violate the formal rule: *If A then B; A; therefore, B*; are discussed in Byrne (1989, 1991) and Byrne *et al.* (1999). Temporal order can violate the formal rule: *A; B; therefore, A and B*. For example, we would be likely to baulk at the inference:

> Byron died of a fever.
>
> Byron woke up one day to find himself famous.
>
> Therefore, Byron died of a fever and he woke up one day to find himself famous.

167. The inference about the elevator is based on an episode in the life of the movie director Orson Welles. When his masterpiece *Citizen Kane* opened in San Francisco, he entered a hotel elevator to find himself face to face with the newspaper magnate whom it satirized, William Randolph Hearst. Welles invited Hearst to the opening of the movie. Hearst maintained an icy silence until he got out of the elevator. Welles said to his departing figure, "Charles Foster Kane would have accepted."

167. The account of modulation in this chapter owes much to a paper with my colleague, Ruth Byrne, on the topic of conditionals (Johnson-Laird and Byrne, 2002).

169. Johnson-Laird (1970b) reports effects of modulation on quantifiers. Zwaan and Radvansky (1998) also give an account of how models of a situation can affect language comprehension.

170. For the interpretation of quasi-numerical quantifiers, such as "many", see Moxey and Sanford (1993, 2000).

170. The difficulty of interpreting claims, such as, "Grandma hates everyone in her family," is discussed in Cherubini and Johnson-Laird (2004).

170. Tom Ormerod carried out the experiments on the effects of modulation on inferences from disjunctive premises (in collabaration with me). The task of drawing one sort of conclusion from another sort of premise has been studied by several authors (e.g., Fillenbaum, 1976; Cheng and Holyoak, 1985; Ormerod, Manktelow and Jones,

1993; Richardson and Ormerod, 1997; Ormerod and Richardson, 2003). Bouquet and Warglien (1999) carried out the pioneering study showing that disjunctive propositions about the same individual as opposed to two different individuals yield easier inferences. Walsh and Johnson-Laird (2004) have corroborated this finding.

171. My colleague Gilbert Harman makes a cogent argument against confusing logic with psychology (see, e.g., Harman, 1986).

172. Chapter 20 describes theorists who have dismissed logic as an analytical tool for the analysis of arguments.

172. Stenning and van Lambalgen (2005) propose a sophisticated theory that goes outside classical logic. The interpretation of discourse is itself a process of reasoning, they say, and it leads, not just to the logical forms of propositions, which depend on content and context, but also to the use of different *logics*. For example, in one sort of interpretation, we try to make the premises true, whereas in another sort of interpretation, we search for counterexamples. In principle, there are infinitely many possible logics, and so Stenning and van Lambalgen focus on how one sort of logic works, and how it can be implemented in a network of idealized neurons. It operates on the principle, used in certain programming languages, that if a proposition cannot be proved, then its negation is true. The logic allows that a conclusion that follows from premises can be retracted in the light of an additional premise. There are similarities between this approach and the model theory (see Chapter 23). Indeed, the one major difference is that modulation does not necessitate the selection of a particular logic, a matter that would be tricky because modulation can have an indefinite number of different effects on the interpretation of sentences. Instead, once an interpretation has been made, the standard semantic principle of validity holds relative to the interpretation: an inference is valid if its conclusion is true in all the possibilities compatible with the interpretation.

172. For an account of Ramanjuan and his ignorance of proofs, see Kanigel (1991, p. 92, and see p. 207 for the comment quoted from the great Cambridge mathematician, G.H. Hardy). With a finite number of finite models, we can always in principle determine whether an inference is valid. Mathematicians, however, have to think about the positive integers, 1, 2, 3, . . . , and there are infinitely many of them. How they reason about infinite sets is a mystery, which psychologists have yet to elucidate.

Chapter 13: Knowledge and Inductions

175. Cognitive scientists study induction in many diverse areas, often independently of one another, e.g., the explanations of other people's behavior (Ross, 1977), reasoning from cases in the law (Ashley, 1990), "explanation-based" learning in artificial intelligence (Kolodner, 1993), causal reasoning (e.g., Cheng, 1997), reasoning based on analogy (e.g., Russell, 1989). Induction is everywhere and nowhere.

175. Peirce (e.g., 1955, chapter 11) coined the term "abduction" or "retroduction" to refer to the inferential step that leads back from an observation to a hypothesis. He argues that the form of the inference was:

> The surprising fact, C, is observed;
>
> But if A were true, C would be a matter of course,
>
> Hence, there is reason to suspect that A is true.

Hence, he had in mind explanations of facts. My use of the term "abductions" highlights this point, and allows that they are a special case of inductions. Peirce treats Kepler's reasoning establishing the laws of planetary motion as abductive, because he had to reconcile observations of the positions of Mars with a Copernican world-view and the assumption that the sun "must have something to do with causing the planets to move in their orbits".

175. Chapter 23 describes the idea of minimal changes to beliefs.

176. The official report on the disaster of *The Herald of Free Enterprise* apportions responsibility to everyone from the Director of the company down to the assistant bosun (Sheen, 1987).

176. Popper's (1959) *Logic of Scientific Discovery* discounts induction in science.

176–7. The law is due to Karl Marbe, a member of the Würzburg school of psychologists, which flourished there before World War I (Humphrey, 1951).

177. Harman (1973) and Thagard (1989) are philosophers who are skeptical that explanations logically imply the generalizations that they explain.

177. An important historical idea about the induction of *concepts* is that it is a search for what is common to a set of entities. There are necessary conditions that taken together suffice to define the concept (see, e.g., Mill, 1874). It was the first blueprint for psychological investigations in which participants sought the necessary and sufficient conditions for various concepts, see, e.g., Hull (1920), who argues, for example, that the meaning of the word *dog* is "a characteristic more or less common to all dogs and not common to cats, dolls, and teddy-bears". Wittgenstein (1953) rejects necessary and sufficient conditions for concepts. Games, he says, have nothing in common, just family resemblances. There might be a stereotypical game, however. Psychologists had already had the same idea, but it was a well-kept secret (see e.g., Fisher, 1916; Bruner *et al.*, 1956) until it emerged in the work of Rosch (e.g., 1973). A prototypical dog, for example, has four legs, a tail, fur, but these are not necessary conditions—a dog could be three-legged, bald, and mute. Not all instances of a concept are equally representative—a terrier is a prototypical dog, but a chihuahua is not. Likewise, judgments about membership of a concept depend on the distance of the instance from the prototype (see, e.g., Rips *et al.*, 1973; Hampton, 1979). The logic of prototypes was clarified in Minsky's (1975) notion of a default value. A dog has four legs, by default, but if a particular dog has only three legs, then this information overrules the default value without contradiction. The logic of defaults underlies so-called "object-oriented" programming languages, such as C++, Java, and Lisp. "Objects", such as the windows on our computers' screens, have certain properties by default.

177. Barsalou (1983) pioneered the study of ad hoc concepts, such as *things to take on a picnic*.

178. McFarlane (1984) describes Fleming's discovery of penicillin.

178. Nisbett *et al.* (1983) show that participants are sensitive to the probabilities of properties when they make inductions. Osherson *et al.* (1986) discuss other accounts of induction. They describe some general principles that we appear to follow when we make inductions about the properties of entities.

179. Mill (1874, p. 226) refers to induction by enumeration, a notion that harks back to Francis Bacon's *Novum Organon* (see Bacon, 1620/2000).

179. The unpublished experiments in which the participants draw particular inductions were carried out in collaboration with Tony Anderson.

179. Prudent reasoners test their inductive generalizations, and a large psychological literature has shown that they tend to focus on positive instances of their hypotheses (see, e.g., Wason, 1960; Klayman and Ha, 1987).

180. A script represents a sequence of stereotyped and default actions, such as ordering a coffee in a café (e.g., Bower *et al.*, 1979; Schank and Abelson, 1977).

180. Theorists have devised many computer programs that simulate the induction of concepts (e.g., Hunt *et al.*, 1966; Michalski, 1983; Langley *et al.*, 1987). Others have implemented programs that set up "connectionist" representations of concepts (e.g., Paccanaro and Hinton, 2000). Polya (1973) proposes that formal rules are the heuristic basis of inductions, and many subsequent theorists rely on them, e.g., Collins and Michalski (1989). The formal rules for induction in Box 13.1 are from Winston (1975), Hayes-Roth and McDermott (1978), Michalski (1983), and Thagard and Holyoak (1985).

182. Meaning postulates are discussed in Chapter 9.

182. The difficulties of using vision to recognize objects are discussed in, e.g., Marr (1982) and Ullman (1996).

182. Hume (1739/1978) argues that no rational justification for induction exists. Goodman (1983) raises the skeptical question of how to distinguish between those properties that support inductive generalizations and those that do not.

182. I argue that given a hypothesis that rules out a proportion of possibilities, the number of its inductive generalizations increases exponentially with the number of concepts or propositions that might be relevant (see Johnson-Laird, 1993).

182. The availability of knowledge is one of the principal heuristics that Kahneman and Tversky (1973) discovered underlying judgments of the probabilities of events.

182. Berwick (1986) proposes the constraint that inductions should be as "informative" as possible, and he derived it from a theorem in formal learning theory due to Angluin (1978).

183. Winston (1975) implemented the idea of a helpful teacher, who arranges a suitable sequence of instances to be presented to pupils, so that they can induce concepts, such as an "arch".

183. Goodman (1972) identifies some of the philosophical problems of similarity. Tversky (1977) is an influential account of the concept. Similarity often depends on a *theory* of the domain (see, e.g., Murphy and Medin, 1985; Rips and Collins, 1993). It also depends on context and a number of other factors (Medin *et al.*, 1993). Children soon tune in to the notion that bats have essential characteristics that, despite appearances, distinguish them from birds (e.g., Gelman and Markman, 1986; Keil, 1989; Markman, 1989).

183. Any good textbook on statistics discusses regression to the mean. Kahneman and Tversky (1973) report that we have difficulty with the notion, and often fail to take it into account as a simple explanation of events—a failing to be found in the psychological literature.

184. Chapter 5 discusses "magical" thinking.

Chapter 14: Sherlock Holmes's Method: Abduction

185. Conan Doyle's description of Dr. Joseph Bell as an inspiration for Sherlock Holmes is from Sebeok and Umiker-Sebeok (1983).

185. Holmes's deductions about the freemason are from *The Adventure of the Red-Headed League* (Conan Doyle, 1930).

186. Holmes's claim that his conclusions were as infallible as Euclid is from *A Study in Scarlet*, chapter 2, Conan Doyle, 1930, p. 23).

186. For the quotation from *The Adventure of the Cardboard Box*, see Conan Doyle (1930, p. 895).

186. Peirce (1955) describes abduction.

186. Chapter 22 analyzes causal relations.

186-7. Inference to the best explanation is discussed in, e.g., Peirce (1931–1958, 5.180), Harman (1965), and Lipton (1991).

187. For an account of Ockham's razor, see Kneale and Kneale (1962, p. 243). Kolmogorov argues for a measure of the minimal complexity of an object in terms of the shortest length of the instructions for a simple computational device to describe the object (see, e.g., Li and Vitanyi, 1993). No program, as Chaitin (1998) shows, can be guaranteed to prove that a program is as short as possible once programs exceed a certain quite small length. Parsimony is an excellent goal, but impossible to prove.

187. The notion that an explanation should have a maximal coverage, including the prediction of novel events is discussed in, e.g., Lipton (1991) and Howson and Urbach (1993).

187. Miyake (1986) asked pairs of participants to explain how a sewing machine works, and observed that they tend to explain a mechanism at one level, and then to explain it in turn at one level down, and so on.

187. Rozenblit and Keil (2002) describe the "illusion" of explanatory depth.

188. The fact that Westerners attribute actions to the actor's state of mind is known as the "fundamental attribution error" (see, e.g., Ross, 1977). Morris *et al.* (1995) argue for differences in the reasoning of Westerners and East Asians.

188-90. The experiment in which the participants preferred to abduce a causal explanation rather than to deduce one is reported in Johnson-Laird *et al.* (2004a). In an unpublished study, Louis Lee has shown that both Western participants in Princeton and Chinese participants in Hong Kong prefer to make abductive explanations rather than deductions, and that both are more likely to offer a deductive explanation if they have carried out a deductive task in the same experimental session.

190-1. The program for constructing causal chains is described in Johnson-Laird *et al.* (2004). Evidence that we store causal relations in the form of cause–effect pairs is reported in Fenker *et al.* (2005).

191. The explanation for the advertisement for red-headed men is to be found, of course, in *The Adventure of the Red-Headed League* (Conan Doyle, 1930). If you don't want to spoil your enjoyment of the story, please do not read the next note.

191. The advertisement is part of plan to attract just one particular red-headed man away from his house so a thief can tunnel from its basement into an adjacent bank.

191. Tony Anderson carried out the unpublished experiment in which the participants explained random pairs of sentences.

192. Oaksford and Chater (1991, 1998) argue that everyday reasoning depends on a tractable procedure. The thrust of my argument in the text is that until we have a clear account of what everyday reasoning is supposed to produce as an output, we cannot decide this issue. Ragni (2003) proved that two-dimensional spatial reasoning is intractable. If spatial reasoning is part of everyday reasoning then everyday reasoning is intractable too.

192. Tony Anderson carried out the experiment concerning the murder in the cinema.

193. A critical factor in the construction of a model is, as Tversky and Kahneman (1973, 1974) established, the availability of relevant knowledge.

194. The three principal psychological theories of analogy are due to Gentner (1983), Keane (1988), and Holyoak and Thagard (1989). Falkenhainer *et al.* (1989), Keane (1988), and Holyoak and Thagard (1989) describe computer programs implementing their respective theories. Gick and Holyoak (1983) report an experimental study showing that participants do not always grasp the import of an analogy. Chalmers *et al.* (1992) argue that these accounts were unsatisfactory because they were too remote from perception. The point is well-taken, but perception yields mental models, which I take to be the foundation of analogy (cf. Sowa and Majumdar, 2003, who describe a program for drawing analogies using a graphical representation).

195. Wright's analogy between the box and the biplane is described in Jakab (1990).

195. Feynman (1988, p. 54) reports his inability to put the shape of a crankshaft into words.

196. The quotation is from Feynman (1985).

196. Whether our reasons for actions are also *causes* is a puzzle that philosophers discuss (see, e.g., Davidson, 1980).

196. The aphorism is from Lichtenberg (1958).

196. James Watson's remarks about facts and theory are cited in Crick (1988, p. 60).

196. Karmiloff-Smith and Inhelder (1974/75) note that children ignore counterexamples to their hypotheses at first.

Chapter 15: The Balance of Probabilities

197. Franklin (2001) argues that the probability calculus could not have been invented until the seventeenth century because essential mathematical tools were hitherto unknown.

197. The various interpretations of probabilities include frequencies (e.g., von Mises, 1957), partial logical entailments (e.g., Keynes, 1943), and degrees of belief (e.g., Savage, 1954). Each has its defenders, and there is no consensus.

198. Kahneman and Tversky's studies of the use of heuristics in intuitive judgments of probability are summarized in a set of papers in Kahneman *et al.* (1982). This collection includes Tversky and Kahneman's (1973) paper on the use of available knowledge, and Tversky and Kahneman's (1982a) paper on the "representativeness" heuristic, which includes the study of the Linda example (see also Kahneman and Tversky, 1972). The judgment that a conjunction, such as feminist and bank

teller, is more probable than one of its constituents, such as bank teller, is known as the "conjunction fallacy" (Tversky and Kahneman, 1983). According to Tversky and Koehler's (1994) "support theory", the description of an event in greater detail recruits more evidence in favor of it and thus leads to a higher judged probability (see also Miyamoto *et al.*, 1995). Kahneman and Frederick (e.g., 2005) contrast our inductive intuitions with the more measured judgments of our deliberate thinking. Gilbert (1989) makes a similar point.

199. The problem of the three doors comes from an American TV program whose host was Monty Hall (cf. Falk, 1992; Nickerson, 1996). The correct answer is described at the end of the chapter. The author of the "Ask Marilyn" column in *Parade* magazine published a correct analysis of the problem. Thanks to the power of equiprobability, as Falk (1992, p. 203) notes, Marilyn received thousands of letters from readers, many of them from universities and research institutes, and about ninety percent of them insisting that she was wrong.

199. The British Court of Appeals expressed their skepticism about the use of Bayes's theorem in these terms:

> The defence were permitted to lead evidence of the Bayes Theorem in connection with the statistical evaluation of the DNA profile. Although their Lordships expressed no concluded view on the matter, they had very grave doubts as to whether that evidence was properly admissible ... their Lordships had never heard it suggested that a jury should consider the relationship between such scientific evidence and other evidence by reference to probability formulae ...

> Quoted from *The Times* (of London), May 9, 1996, reporting the Court of Appeal's judgment on Regina v. Adams

199. The view that human beings possess an innate inferential module embodying the probability calculus is due to Cosmides and Tooby (1996; see also Gigerenzer and Hoffrage, 1995). In Cosmides and Tooby's experiments, the participants were more accurate with problems stated with frequencies than with percentage probabilities. Cosmides and Tooby write (p. 62): "Frequentist mechanisms could not elicit bayesian reasoning unless our minds contained mechanisms that embody at least some aspects of a calculus of probability". Howson and Urbach (1993, p. 422) expressed skepticism about this conclusion. Likewise, naïve individuals can reason about problems on the chances of unique events, but the use of frequencies does not guarantee successful reasoning (see Girotto and Gonzalez, 2001, 2002, 2006; Evans *et al.*, 2000; and Sloman *et al.*, 2003). Psychologists (and probabilists) argue about whether assertions about the probabilities of unique events are sensible. With an assertion, such as: "The probability that World War III will start tomorrow is .01", the problem is to specify the conditions in which it would be true. Nonetheless, we are happy to assign probabilities to unique events, so we do not appear to find them meaningless (for contrasting arguments, see Kahneman and Tversky, 1996, who accept this view, and Gigerenzer, 1996, who does not).

199. Gordon (2004) describes experiments with a small Amazonian tribe, the Pirahã, showing that their counting system is, "roughly one", "roughly two", and "many". It is hard to imagine that they have an innate module for reasoning about frequencies (see also Pica *et al.*, 2004, for similar findings with another Amazonian

group, the Mundurukú). This second group have an intuitive grasp of geometric concepts, e.g., they could pick out the one triangle in a set of six that didn't contain a right angle (see Dehaene *et al.*, 2006).

199–200. For the theory of reasoning about probabilities using mental models, see Johnson-Laird *et al.* (1999).

200. The principle of "indifference" or "insufficient reason" has a long history in probability theory (see Hacking, 1975). It can lead to difficulties (Howson and Urbach, 1993, p. 52), though if indifference applies to the representation of problems, and to mental models in particular, the difficulties are resolvable (see Johnson-Laird *et al.*, 1999). The principle lies at the heart of Laplace's (1951) notorious computation that the odds of the sun rising tomorrow were $1,826,214$ to 1.

200. The experiment about marbles in the box is described in Johnson-Laird, *et al.* (1999). These authors also report studies of illusory inferences about relative probabilities. Johnson-Laird and Savary (1996) show that from certain premises, participants infer as the more probable of two events one that is, in fact, impossible; and from other premises, they infer as the less probable of two events one that is, in fact, certain.

200. Bar-Hillel and Falk (1982) studied the problem about the two children. It contains a number of subtleties that Nickerson (1996) has elucidated.

202. Stevenson and Over (1995) were the first to postulate tagging mental models with numerical probabilities (see also Stevenson and Over, 2001).

203. The experiment in which participants estimated converse conditional probabilities is from an unpublished study that Jennifer L. Adams carried out as an undergraduate at Princeton University. Hammerton (1997) shows that naive reasoners can fail to notice that a problem does not state an essential base rate.

204. The subset principle is described in Johnson-Laird *et al.* (1999).

208. For evidence against our use of Bayes's theorem, see, e.g., Falk (1992). Shimojo and Ichikawa (1989) also report that even when people are taught Bayes's theorem they still find it counterintuitive.

208. Kahneman and Tversky (1973) report the study of base rate and estimates of whether individuals were lawyers or engineers.

209. Hacking (1975) is the philosopher who writes about dice in Roman times.

Chapter 16: Counterexamples

211. The epigraph for Part V is from the poem, *The History of Truth* (Auden, 1976, p. 463).

213. The notion of games in understanding quantifiers owes something to Wittgenstein's idea of language games (1953). Hintikka (1973) is its major exponent.

214. Holyoak and Glass (1975) report a study of counterexamples to generalizations.

214. References to the selection task are in the notes to Chapter 1. For the view that it is not a test of deductive reasoning, see Oaksford and Chater (1998). They argue that we are instead trying to optimize the amount of information that we expect to gain from turning a card. This view combines Shannon's statistical theory of information (Shannon and Weaver, 1949) with Bayes's theorem from the probability calculus (see Chapter 15). The former posits that the more improbable a signal is, the

more information it communicates—with a concomitant reduction of uncertainty on the part of the receiver of the signal. Bayes's theorem allows us to compute the probability of a hypothesis in the light of some evidence. Oaksford and Chater argue that in testing a conditional of the form, *if A then B*, in many of the versions of the task, it is rational not to choose the *not-B* card. However, participants failed to do so even when they stood to gain money from a correct evaluation of the truth or falsity of the conditional, as Carlos Santamaría, Orlando Espino, and I showed in an unpublished experiment. Likewise, Stanovich (1999) reports that more intelligent participants were more likely to select counterexamples in the selection task (see also Stanovich and West, 1998).

214. For evidence supporting the hypothesis that the availability of counterexamples improves performance in the selection task, see Love and Kessler (1995), and Liberman and Klar (1996). Instructions to check for *violations* also improves performance in the abstract task (Platt and Griggs, 1993; Green, 1995, 1997; Green and Larking, 1995; Griggs, 1995; Dominowski, 1995). Sperber *et al.* (1995) use a more indirect procedure to render counterexamples more *relevant*—in the sense of Sperber and Wilson (1986), and thereby improve performance.

214. The journal that refuses to publish any more papers on the selection task is *Cognition*.

214. Wason (1960) describes his 2–4–6 task. Klayman and Ha (1987) argue that participants are not trying to confirm their hypotheses, but are instead testing positive instances of them. A large literature exists on the task, see, e.g., Manktelow (1999) for a review.

214. The principle of truth is introduced in Chapter 8.

216. Patricia Barres carried out the experiments in which participants try to imagine counterexamples to various propositions (see Barres and Johnson-Laird, 2003).

218. Theories of reasoning based on formal rules are described in Chapter 1. Quine (1974) and Barwise (1993) point out that if we fail to find a formal proof for an inference, then we cannot know for certain that it is invalid: we may have overlooked a proof. In contrast, a counterexample is a manifest demonstration of invalidity. Chater *et al.* (2005, p. 302) relate the acceptance of a conclusion to which no counterexample has been found to a procedure in computer programming known as "negation as failure": a proposition is accepted if its negation cannot be proved.

218. The description of poor reasoners' responses to syllogisms is from Johnson-Laird (1983, p. 120).

218. Polk and Newell (1995) propose a model-based theory of syllogisms that downplays the use of counterexamples. They write (p. 553): "The point is that syllogism data can be explained without positing a falsification strategy, in keeping with the hypothesis that such a reasoning-specific strategy is less important than verbal processes in explaining deduction."

218–9. Monica Bucciarelli carried out the experiments in which the participants used external models of the premises (Bucciarelli and Johnson-Laird, 1999). In contrast to Bucciarelli's findings, Newstead *et al.* (1999) report a study in which the number of alternative diagrams that participants drew did not predict their accuracy in syllogistic reasoning. However, Newstead *et al.* (2002) found that a measure of difference between participants, which reflected their ability to generate alternative possibilities, did correlate with their ability to refute invalid syllogistic conclusions.

Indeed, Newstead *et al.* (1999) report that less than a fifth of responses in their Experiment 3 were correct. Roberts (2006) points out that studies of syllogisms underestimate the use of counterexamples. The finding that we construct external models to draw syllogistic conclusions shows that we are trying to make deductions (pace Chater and Oaksford, 1999).

219. Martín-Cordero and González-Labra (1994) are the critics who argue that the model theory fails to specify how we search for counterexamples.

221. Uri Hasson carried out the experiments on strategies in the rejection of invalid inferences based on propositional connectives (see Johnson-Laird and Hasson, 2003).

222. Hansjoerg Neth carried out the experiment on reasoning with the quantifier "more than half" (see Neth and Johnson-Laird, 1999). This quantifier cannot be captured in the standard quantificational calculus, but can be handled as a relation between sets (Mostowski, 1957).

225. James Kroger carried out the unpublished experiment on brain imaging and counterexamples in collaboration with my colleague Jon Cohen and myself. A growing literature on brain imaging and reasoning exists due to Goel (e.g., Goel and Dolan, 2004), and my colleague Dan Osherson (e.g., Osherson *et al.*, 1998; Parsons and Osherson, 2001). It is not easy to make sense of the various findings, but they show that deduction implicates regions of the brain that are not part of normal linguistic processes, and that it activates regions in the right hemisphere (pace Wharton and Grafman, 1998).

227. In unpublished studies, Michelle Cowey and Ruth Byrne have shown that participants are better at refuting other individuals' hypotheses than their own in the 2–4–6 task, and that chess masters are better than novices in refuting their planned moves.

227–8. Oaksford and Chater (1998) follow Anderson (1990) in supposing that human cognition is a rational adaptation to the world (see also Chater *et al.*, 2005), and their views are to some degree presaged in Evans, Over, and their colleagues' proposal that probabilities play a role in reasoning (e.g., Stevenson and Over, 1995, 2001; Evans and Over, 1996, 2004). They apply their approach to three main sorts of reasoning: the selection task, simple reasoning from conditional premises, and syllogistic reasoning (Oaksford and Chater, 2001). They argue: "people are far better probabilistic reasoners than Tversky and Kahneman supposed" (Oaksford and Chater, 1998, p. 262). In fact, we do make systematic errors in probabilistic reasoning (see Chapter 15). They argue that their probabilistic account characterizes what is being computed, whereas the processes that compute it should be tractable and could use "fast and frugal heuristics" (Gigerenzer and Goldstein, 1996) or Bayesian networks (Pearl, 1988, 2000). Schroyens and Schaeken (2003) report that their meta-analyses of studies in the literature (Schroyens *et al.*, 2001a,b) show that the model theory gives a more accurate account of conditional reasoning than does the probabilistic theory. Espino *et al.* (2005) report eye-movement data supporting the model theory of syllogistic reasoning rather than the probabilistic theory (see also Espino *et al.*, 2000b).

228. The evidence about the difference between possible and necessary conclusions IS reported in Chapter 3 (see Bell and Johnson-Laird, 1998; Evans *et al.*, 1999). Markovits and Handley (2005) report the study of reasoning from the same premises that compared instructions to assess whether conclusions were necessarily true with instructions to assess the probabilities that they were true. Studies show that

individuals with a large working memory are more likely to make correct syllogistic deductions than those with a smaller working memory (e.g., Gilhooly *et al.* 1999; Copeland and Radvansky, 2004). Verschueren *et al.* (2005a,b) show that in reasoning from conditional premises, individuals with a large working memory tend to use counterexamples, whereas those with a low working memory capacity tend to rely on probabilistic considerations (see Markovits *et al.*, 2002, for compatible results). As Verschueren *et al.* suggest, the distinction suggests that the probabilistic considerations depend on intuitive heuristic reasoning, whereas the use of counterexamples depends on deliberate analytical processes. A pertinent factor is the role of knowledge—modulation, in my terms—and Politzer and Bourmaud (2002) review its effects. For a general assessment of Oaksford and Chater's approach, see Rips (2002), and for a critique of its account of syllogistic reasoning, which makes the point that it offers no account of the spontaneous use of diagrams, see Roberts and Sykes (2005).

229. Beth (1971) argues that the fundamental principle of semantic validity is that an argument is valid if its conclusion must be true given that its premises are true. Both formal and semantic methods exist in logic for searching for counterexamples (see Jeffrey, 1981). The formal method is based on the so-called "tree" method. The standard procedure begins with a list of the premises and the *negation* of the putative conclusion. These sentences can all be true only if there is a counterexample. And so the rules of inference are formulated in a way that allows for a systematic search of the possibilities. The tree method, however, can also be formulated as a method that derives conclusions in a direct way—a method that would be the closest version of logic to the theory of mental models. No proponent of formal rules in psychology, however, has proposed a theory of this sort.

229. The correlation between reasoning ability and intelligence is due to Stanovich (e.g., 1999). The correlation between reasoning ability and the capacity of working memory is reported in several studies (see e.g., Bara *et al.*, 1995; Barrouillet and Leças, 1999; see also Kyllonen and Christal, 1990).

229. Evans and Over (1996) distinguish between rationality$_1$ for everday reasoning and rationality$_2$ for deliberate deductive reasoning. Shafir (1994) has demonstrated violations of transitivity in bees' preferences.

Chapter 17: Truth, Lies, and the Higher Reasoning

231. At the start of his essay on truth, Bacon writes: "'What is truth?' said jesting Pilate; and would not stay for an answer" (see Bacon, 1597/1985).

231. Tarski (1944) distinguishes metalanguage and object language, and describes the paradoxes that result from natural language being its own metalanguage. The sentence about "snow is white" is also from Tarski's paper. The "correspondence" theory of truth is also defended by Wittgenstein (1922), and many others. For a recent description of philosophical analyses of truth, see Blackburn (2005).

231. Chapter 1 distinguishes between sentences that have meanings and propositions that have significance.

232. Keats writes about "consecutive reasoning" in a letter to his friend Benjamin Bailey (see Gittings, 1970, p. 36), a letter which also shows that Keats believed that what the imagination seizes as beauty must be true (cf. his ode to a Grecian Urn).

232. Rescher (1973) discusses the coherence theory of truth. The theory has interested cognitive scientists studying the maintenance of consistent beliefs (see Chapter 23).

232. Grice (1975, 1989) analyzes the conventions governing everyday discourse, among which he includes the principle of telling the truth.

232. The tragic episode of the engineers at Chernobyl is described in Medvedev (1990).

232. For an account of truth in logic, see, e.g., Boolos and Jeffrey (1989).

233. Aristotle's definition of negation occurs in his *De Interpretatione* (see Aristotle, 1984, Vol. 1). For an account of negation in language, see Horn (1989).

233. The notion that sentences may fail to express propositions unless their presuppositions are true goes back to Austin (1970) and to Strawson's (1950) critique of Russell's theory of definite descriptions, such as "the present king of France" (Russell, 1905).

233–4. The notion of mapping one model into another is due to Kamp and Reyle (1993).

234. The "liar" paradox is analyzed in, e.g., Barwise and Etchemendy (1987).

235. The logician Raymond Smullyan has a near monopoly on knight-and-knave puzzles (e.g., Smullyan, 1978). As he shows, they are related to Gödel's theorem that truths exist in arithmetic that cannot be proved in any consistent formal system. The problem in Box 17.1 is based on one in Smullyan (1978, p. 22).

236. Rips (1989) reports the study of knight and knave problems. His challenge to model theorists was: "Produce an explicit account of reasoning on knight-knave problems that is (a) theoretically explicit, (b) empirically adequate, and (c) not merely a notational variant of the natural-deduction theory" (p. 113). For a response to that challenge, see Johnson-Laird and Byrne (1990), who describe a computer implementation of five model-based strategies for knight-and-knave problems.

238. Byrne *et al.* (1995) report the study of knight-and-knave problems showing that participants develop different strategies. Byrne and Handley (1997) corroborate these findings. Schroyens and his colleagues extend the model theory to account for the nature of the errors in these problems (see Schroyens, 1997; Schroyens *et al.*, 1996, 1999).

239. Johnson-Laird and Byrne (1991) describe metalogical problems.

240. Goffman (1959) discusses inferences in social contexts.

240. For descriptions of the three-hat problem, see e.g., Fujimara, (1978), Anno and Nozaki (1984), and Dewdney, (1989). George Erdos of the University of Newcastle in the UK has shown in an unpublished experiment that the two-hat problem is easier than the three-hat problem. Erdos also reports that subjects often deduce that Anne cannot see two black hats, but when they come to consider Beth's situation they forget that Beth can make this deduction too.

241. For edited transcripts of the tapes of the Whitehouse discussions during the Cuban missile crisis, and the remark about Mr. McCone, see May and Zelikow (2001, p. 61).

242. Dixit and Nalebuff (1991) give an amusing introduction to mathematical game theory, including Nash's theorem. Reinhard Selten made his skeptical remark about the theory at the International Workshop on Games and Mental Models (University of Venice, August 1998). Eugenia Goldvarg-Steingold carried out the unpublished study in which naïve individuals were prepared to participate in experimental games without knowing the other player's pay-offs.

243. Mazzocco *et al.* (1974) examine their participants' ability to provide missing premises in syllogisms. Their results count against the "atmosphere" hypothesis (see Chapter 10).

244. Victoria Shaw carried out an unpublished study in which participants started to develop formal principles governing syllogistic inferences. Vadeboncoeur and Markovits (1999) also report that their participants referred to formal concepts.

Chapter 18: On Development

245. The epigraph to Part VI is from an essay on Walter de la Mare (Auden, 1973, p. 389).

247. Fodor (1980) argues that all concepts, logical connectives, and quantifiers are innate, and that they cannot be decomposed into primitives. The problem with his argument is that it also appears to rule out the possibility that concepts could have evolved granted that evolutionary processes can be mimicked in learning programs (see Johnson-Laird, 1983, p. 142–144). Evolution according to the neo-Darwinian synthesis is mimicked in "genetic" programs due to Holland (see, e.g., Holland *et al.*, 1986; Mitchell, 1998). Given that humans have only 30,000 genes, they would all have to encode concepts on the view that they're innate and cannot be decomposed into more primitive concepts.

247. The concept of the mind as a blank slate goes back to the British Empiricist philosophers, notably Locke (1979), though he in fact spoke of a blank sheet of paper. Pinker (2002) is a major critic of this point of view.

247. Connectionist programs are described in the book (see Glossary). Shastri and Ajjanagadde (1993) present a connectionist system for simple reasoning. The problem is to account for the composition of meanings (Fodor and Pylyshyn, 1988) and for reasoning with more complex sentences. Connectionists have responded to this criticism (e.g., Smolensky, 1990; but cf. Fodor and McLaughlin, 1990). A simple challenge to connectionists is to devise a system that would learn to make inferences using truth tables in the propositional calculus. In my view, the challenge can be met only by dividing the task into separate modules. Falmagne (1980) defends conventional learning as a way to enhance reasoning ability.

248. Cook and Newson (1996) is an introduction to Chomsky's account of universal grammar (see also Chomsky, 1995).

248. Pinker (1997) defends the adaptive value of language. For the views of Chomsky and his colleagues on the evolution of language, see, e.g., Hauser *et al.* (2002), and Fitch *et al.* (2005).

248–9. Piaget (1896–1980) was the avatar of formal procedures in reasoning (see, e.g., Inhelder and Piaget, 1958). For descriptions of Piagetian "conservation" of quantities, see, e.g., Piaget and Inhelder (1969). For the account of development in Box 18.1, see Inhelder and Piaget (1964, e.g., pp. 292–293); for the equivalence between formal operations and the propositional calculus, see Inhelder and Piaget (1958, p. 305); and for the relations between children's structures and mathematical structures, see Beth and Piaget (1966). The mathematical collective, Bourbaki, is described in Halmos (1957). For exegeses of Piaget's theory, see, e.g., Flavell (1963) and Boden (1980); and for a neo-Piagetian view, see Karmiloff-Smith (1992). One prescient Piagetian observation: children tend not to represent multiple possibilities (Piaget, 1987).

249. Braine and Rumain (1983), who defend formal rules of inference, write: "Piaget's logic cannot develop at adolescence or at any time: it is too problematic to stand as a psychological model of anything".

250. The concept of computational power was described in Chapter 3.

251. The experiments showing that infants do have the concept that objects continue to exist when they are out of sight and that they soon develop a "naïve" physics are reported in, for example, Baillargeon *et al.* (1985), Baillargeon (1987), Baillargeon and Hanko-Summes (1990), and Spelke (1990, 1991).

252. The study of children's disjunctive reasoning is in Justin Halberda's unpublished paper: "Is this a dax which I see before me? Use of the logical argument disjunctive syllogism supports word-learning in children and adults".

252. Chrysippus's dog is described in, e.g., Annas and Barnes (1985, p. 36). Alas, Watson *et al.* (2001) failed to corroborate that dogs can make the inference. Mandler (2004) reports the study of infants' inductions.

253. For accounts of children's "theory" of mind and studies of false beliefs, see, e.g., Leslie (1987, 1990) and Premack (1990).

253. The phenomena of children's difficulty with second-order false beliefs are robust (e.g., Wimmer and Perner, 1983; Perner *et al.*, 1987; Perner, 1991; and for a review, Wellman *et al.*, 2001). The potential explanations for the phenomena are mind-boggling. For the view that memory load is the decisive factor, see Bloom and German (2000), and for the view that we are cursed by our knowledge and cannot recapture our earlier ignorance, see Birch (2005), who reports analogous effects in adult reasoning (e.g., Keysar *et al.*, 2003). For the view that the capacity to cope with false beliefs depends on an ability to represent "counterfactual" possibilities, see, e.g., Riggs *et al.* (1998), and Peterson and Riggs (1999). Harris (2000) in his outstanding book on children's (and adults') imagination makes the case that our ability to imagine alternative possibilities and to work out their implications emerges early in our childhood and lasts a lifetime. But, more may be at stake in coping with false beliefs than envisaging counterfactual possibilities. Perner *et al.* (2004) report that the two don't necessarily go hand in hand: children can answer questions about counterfactuals before they can answer questions about false beliefs even when both are based on the same scenario. Another possibility is that the difficulty of switching attention from one alternative to another lies at the root of the problem (see unpublished results by Aisling Murray and Ruth Byrne).

254. For the view that autistic children lack a "theory" of mind, see, e.g., Baron-Cohen *et al.* (1985). Leslie and Thaiss (1992) show that autistic children can cope with photographs that are not veridical.

254. Case (1985a, b) proposes that the increase in the capacity of working memory enables children to perform more complex tasks, e.g., putting rods in their correct serial order.

254. Chi (1976) shows that the capacity of children's working memory increases as they got older. She also shows that this increase is in part a result of knowledge. For example, adults can hold in mind twice as many nonsense shapes than children can, but with nouns, such as "dog", which are very familiar to children, the adult advantage is much less (see also Chi, 1978).

255. Fodor (1983) makes a radical statement of the hypothesis that the brain has separate modules.

255. Cosmides (1989) is the evolutionary psychologist who proposes an innate module for reasoning about cheating. Fiddick (2004) argues in addition for a module for taking precautions against risk. Pinker (1997) presents a defense of evolutionary psychology and discusses floral wallpaper and spats between siblings. Critics who point out alternative explanations for the results with the selection task include Cheng and Holyoak (1989), and Buller (2005).

256. Other critics of evolutionary psychology include Simon (1991b), who draws the analogy with "just so" stories, and Lewontin (1990), who notes the difficulty of testing the approach. Chomsky in conversation drew attention to the problem of how a situation triggers the appropriate module.

257. An arithmetical answer to the problem of the loop of string: a square of 5 cm a side has a perimeter of 20 cm and an area of 25 cm^2. A rectangle that is 8×2 cm still has the same perimeter but an area of only 16 cm^2. I owe this example to the late A.R. Jonckheere.

257. The study of aboriginal Australians' spatial reasoning is reported in Dasen (1994).

257. Keil (1989) describes the development of children's ability to categorize objects. Studies of children's mental models of the earth, the solar system, and recursion in computation are reported in Vosniadou and Brewer (1992), Samarapungavan *et al.* (1996), and Dicheva and Close (1996), respectively.

257. Carey (1985a,b) argues that children are equipped with one or two primal theories, including a naïve physics. She likens changes in children's concepts to changes from one scientific theory to another (see Kuhn, 1970), and she reports the dialogue with her daughter in Carey (1988). Development, as Carey (1991) emphasizes, implies that children's concepts may be incommensurable with those of adults, and that ". . . new concepts may arise that are not definable in terms of concepts already held".

257. Newton's theory of color is in his optics (Newton, 1952). Goethe (1970) presents *his* theory. Some painters criticized Newton's theory because they confused the mixing of light on a color wheel with the mixing of pigments on a palette. Ribe and Steinle (2005) defend Goethe's use of exploratory experiments.

258. The study of naïve physics was pioneered in Italy in the 1950s by the late Paolo Bozzi (see the account in his autobiography, Bozzi, 1991), and in the USA by McCloskey (1983). The study of balls or water emerging from curved tubes is reported in Kaiser *et al.* (1986).

258. Aristotle analyzes speed in his *Physics* (232a, lines 25–29).

259. The dialogue about speed is based on Feynman *et al.* (1963).

260. Barrouillet and his colleagues have carried out many studies in which children and adults list the possibilities for conditionals (see, e.g., Barrouillet and Leças, 1998, 1999; Barrouillet *et al.*, 2000). The "logical" interpretation of the conditional is described in Chapter 8.

261. The studies of children's reasoning with syllogisms are reported in Johnson-Laird *et al.* (1986), and Bara *et al.* (1995).

261. A study showing that infants of just a few days in age attend to their mother tongue is reported in Mehler *et al.* (1988).

261. Curtiss (1977) reports a tragic modern case of a "wolf child"—a child who grew up without encountering any language.

Chapter 19: Strategies and Cultures

262. Illusory inferences are described in Chapters 8 and 15, and metareasoning is discussed in Chapter 17.

263. The pioneering studies of strategies in relational reasoning are reported in Wood (1969) and Wood *et al.* (1974). These studies demonstrate the use of shorts cuts. Ormrod (1979) shows that the question in a problem constrains strategies. Quinton and Fellows (1975) describe five strategies, including the one in which the participants try to answer the question solely from the information in the first premise. Participants also develop strategies for reasoning about kinship, e.g., *father's brother* refers to the same relative as *uncle* (e.g., Wood and Shotter, 1973). Some equivalences, including the previous example, are likely to be stored in long-term memory, but others we have to deduce.

263. Rips (1989, 1990, 1994) is the most notable proponent of the view that reasoning depends on a single deterministic strategy. In contrast, the model theory postulates a diversity of reasoning strategies (see, e.g., Johnson-Laird, 1983; Johnson-Laird and Bara, 1984; Byrne and Handley, 1992).

263. Girotto *et al.* (1997) show that the order of premises affects the difficulty of inferences of the form: *If A then B, Not-B, what follows?* When the conditional occurs first, working memory is already preoccupied during the interpretation of the categorical premise, and so reasoners are unlikely to construct an additional complete model. But, when the categorical premise occurs first, it enables reasoners to reject at once the explicit mental model.

264. My colleagues and I use the term "strategy" in much the same sense as Bruner *et al.* (1956). It is also similar to Miller *et al.*'s (1960, p. 16) notion of a "plan". Sternberg (e.g., 1977, 1983, 1984) analyzes the components of analogies, numerical series problems, and syllogisms. Hunt (1999, 2002) treats the mind as a processor of information. My colleagues and I follow in this tradition.

264. A good source for the history of Sudoku is the on-line encyclopedia *Wikipedia*: en.wikipedia.org/wiki/Sudoku.

264. In Hans Anderson's (1996) fairy tale, *The Snow Queen*, Kay's task is to solve a puzzle that forms the word "Eternity".

264. The solution to the Sudoku puzzle in Figure 19.1 is:

7	9	1	8	4	3	2	6	5
8	5	4	6	7	2	1	3	9
3	6	2	5	1	9	7	4	8
5	4	3	9	8	1	6	2	7
6	7	8	2	5	4	3	9	1
2	1	9	3	6	7	8	5	4
4	2	7	1	9	6	5	8	3
9	3	5	7	2	8	4	1	6
1	8	6	4	3	5	9	7	2

265. Our competence to reason with quantifiers in Sudoku puzzles is contrary to views that logically naïve participants do not make deductions even with singly quantified premises (pace, e.g., Revlis, 1975; Gilhooly *et al.*, 1993; Chater and Oaksford, 1999). It is also contrary to the claim: "people only make an effort at deductive reasoning when explicitly instructed to do so" (Evans and Over, 1996, p. 158). Oaksford and Chater (e.g., 1998) argue that deductive validity is an inappropriate criterion for our reasoning (see my discussion of their views in Chapter 16).

265. For the claims about East Asians, see the note below.

265. Louis Lee carried out all the experiments on Sudoku puzzles, and the research was done in collaboration with Geoff Goodwin (see Lee *et al.*, 2006).

266. Relational complexity is the number of arguments, or constraints, on a relation (see Halford, 1993; Halford *et al.*, 1998).

268–9. The problem in Box 19.1 is from an experiment in Van der Henst *et al.* (2002), who also describe the five strategies in Box 19.2.

270. The null model is described in Chapter 8. Evans (1972a) reports the first psychological study of reductio ad absurdum, using inferences of the same sort as here.

270–1. The use of suppositions in formal rule theories is more constrained than in the model theory. Rips (1994) allows suppositions to be made only working backwards from a putative conclusion; Braine and O'Brien (1998) allow suppositions to be made only after direct rules of inference have been exhausted. Our results are contrary to both these accounts.

272. The account of the development of strategies is in Van der Henst *et al.* (2002).

273. The experiments on bias in strategies in propositional reasoning are reported in Van der Henst *et al.* (2002).

273. The report on Kerry's and Bush's respective supporters came from the Program on International Policy Attitudes.

274. Geoffrey Goodwin carried out the experiments on how participants developed strategies for reasoning about relations between relations (see Goodwin and Johnson-Laird, 2005b).

274. Introspective reports can be mistaken about why participants acted as they did (Nisbett and Wilson, 1977). Schooler *et al.* (1993) interrupted people who were trying to solve problems that depended on an insight. After the interruption, those who had to make a retrospective report on their thinking solved fewer problems than those who carried out an unrelated task (a crossword puzzle). Other studies, however, report that thinking aloud enhanced performance (e.g., Berardi-Coletta *et al.*, 1995). It can slow people down, but it often appears to have no other major effects (cf. Russo *et al.*, 1989). In general, it can be a reliable guide to the sequence of a person's thoughts (Newell and Simon, 1972; Ericsson and Simon, 1980). Bell (1999) compared reasoning when participants think aloud and when they did not. She obtained the same overall pattern of results in both conditions.

275. Relativists argue that no set of logical conventions is universal to all cultures (e.g., Barnes and Bloor, 1982) or to all times (Burke, 1986). Geertz (1984) dislikes relativism but prefers it to its alternative, Rationalism.

275. Evans-Pritchard (1937) describes the Azande.

275. The Russian psychologist A.R. Luria (1934, 1976) reports the first studies of cross-cultural differences in the reasoning of unschooled participants in Uzbekistan. Cole and his colleagues gave reasoning problems to the Kpelle (Cole *et al.*, 1971). Scribner (1977) suggests that unschooled participants adopt an "empirical" attitude to reasoning problems, i.e., they use their knowledge and experience.

276. Harris and his colleagues report the study in Recife (Dias *et al.*, 2005; see also Harris, 2000).

276. Nisbett (2003) summarizes his account of differences in reasoning between Westerners and East Asians (see also, e.g., Peng and Nisbett, 1999). Norenzayam *et al.* (2002) describe their experiments on cultural differences in reasoning. One experiment, they report, showed that Koreans made more errors than US students in assessing the deductive validity of arguments. A different analysis of their data by Unsworth and Medin (2005) showed to the contrary that Westerners were no better than the Koreans at this task.

276–7. Louis Lee carried out the unpublished study in which ambiguous inferential problems were presented to both Hong Kong Chinese students and Princeton students. He has also carried out several other unpublished studies comparing samples from these two populations. He has not so far found any reliable differences in their ability to make deductions.

277. Nisbett (2003, p. 170) writes: "The differences between the two groups would seem to be that Americans are simply more in the habit of applying logical rules (sic) to ordinary events than Koreans...." Later, he comments, "... we don't actually find East Asians to have trouble with formal logic..." (p. 188).

278. See the note on Gordon (2004) in Chapter 15 for a culture that has no numbers.

278. I describe Micronesian navigation in Chapter 2 (see, e.g., Gladwin, 1970). Tulkin and Konner (1973) describe Kalahari hunting and many other antecedents of scientific thinking. Kroeber (1961) describes how an indigenous American chips an arrowhead out of a coke bottle.

Chapter 20: How We can Improve our Reasoning

279. Speed of processing correlates with reasoning ability and performance in intelligence tests. As one grows older, one grows slower, but, as Patrick Rabbitt and his colleagues have shown, what affects speed is atrophy of the brain with old age. Analyses show that age, which stands proxy for other neurophysiological changes, also has an effect on intelligence. Hence, speed of processing—or rather lack of it—accounts for much of the intellectual slow down of old age, but not for all of the differences in intelligence from one old person to another (for a valuable review, see Rabbitt and Anderson, 2006).

279. Our intelligence at the age of 11 predicts in part how long we will live. Measures of intelligence also predict performance in academia, and in jobs. Some commentators claim that "IQ", which is based on intelligence tests, is the best current predictor of many aspects of our lives (for a review of these findings, see Deary, 2005).

279. Northcutt (2000) is the first volume of *The Darwin Awards*.

279. For the report on the disaster of *The Herald of Free Enterprise*, see Sheen (1987).

280. The Venezuela project was initiated by the then President in 1979. Dr. Machado, the Minister for the Development of Human Intelligence, had the goal of raising the level of intelligence of the entire population. Among the experts who consulted on the project were Jaacov Agam, Berry Brazelton, Edward de Bono, Reuven Feuerstein, David Perkins, and Robert Sternberg. The project ended in 1984 along with the government that instituted it. Did it work? It had an effect on performance in schools. But, a proper answer to the question would call for the same effort that was put into the project in the first place. For an account of the project, see, e.g., www.newhorizons.org/trans/international/dickinson_venezuela.htm.

280. Logicians tend to assume that logic is good for us. For example, Hintikka in the abstract to a talk delivered at the International Conference on Formal and Applied Practical Reasoning in Bonn 1996 writes: "... (deductive) logic is strategically speaking a key to all good reasoning".

280. Lowenstein (2000) is an amusing account of how Nobel prize winning economists lost a prodigious amount of money in directing a hedge fund.

280. I owe Paine's (1989, pp. 94–95) argument about religion to Keene (1992), which is the best book I know on the logical analysis of real arguments. My analysis differs a little from Keene's, and is much less formal.

282. Barwise and Etchemendy (1992, 1994) describe Hyperproof. Stenning (2002) reports his empirical studies investigating its efficacy as a tool for teaching logic. And Sternberg (1997) describes eleven different styles of thinking, including a graphical one.

282. The study in which participants received a semester's course in logic before tackling Wason's selection task is reported in Cheng et al. (1986).

284. The events at Three Mile Island nuclear reactor are described in Chapter 3.

284. Lin Yutang writes, "Modern economists and psychologists seem to me to have an overdose of conscientiousness and not enough insight. This is a point which perhaps cannot be over-emphasized, the danger of applying logic to human affairs" (see, Lin, 1937, pp. 424–431, cited by Keene, 1992, p. 5).

284. The literature on informal logic has grown apace since Toulmin's (1958) and Scriven's (1976) critiques of logic. Theorists arguing for the identification of fallacies include Kahane (1984), Govier (1988), and Johnson and Blair (1994). Those who advocate the use of special diagrams to analyze arguments include Beardsley (1950), Freeman (1988), and Fisher (1988). Walton (1989) argues for a pragmatic analysis of discourse. Both Toulmin (1958) and McPeck (1981) claim that the principles of reasoning differ from one field of expertise to another. Computer systems for the analysis of arguments are described in Verheij (2003). Psychological studies of informal argumentation include Perkins et al. (1990), Kuhn (1991), Voss et al. (1993), Rips (1998), Rips et al. (1999), and Green and McCloy (2003). The pattern of results from these studies is complex, but they have shown that performance is poor and that reasoners often overlook alternative lines of argument. Likewise, many of the strategies that occur in laboratory studies of deductive inference reappear in informal reasoning (Kuhn, 1991, p. 274).

284. Philosophical views about use of diagrams in geometric proofs are discussed in Beth (1971).

284. Lewis Carroll (1958) describes his game of logic. Peirce devised two separate diagrammatic systems for logical reasoning (see the notes on Chapter 2).

284–5. Simon (1991a, p. 96) reports that engineers found Supreme Court cases easier to understand when he used circuit diagrams in which the switch positions corresponded to the decisions of the Court. Simon's experiments with diagrams were published in Larkin and Simon (1987) and Tabachneck and Simon (1992). Larkin and Simon (1987, p. 71) write: "In view of the dramatic effects that alternative representations may produce on search and recognition processes, it may seem surprising that the differential effects on inference appear less strong. Inference is largely independent of representation if the information content of the two sets of inference rules [one operating on diagrams and the other operating on verbal statements.] is equivalent. . . . "

285. Barwise and Etchemendy (1992, p. 80) write: "It is much harder to use [diagrams] to present indefinite information, negative information, or disjunctive information."

285–8. Inferences based on two disjunctive premises are described in Chapter 3. Malcolm Bauer carried out the experiments on the use of diagrams in reasoning from disjunctive premises (see Bauer and Johnson-Laird, 1993). A study by Boudreau and Pigeau (2001) shows that spatial reasoning is also easier when participants reason from diagrams rather than descriptions.

288. The previous chapter describes the reasoning strategy in which participants drew diagrams to keep track of the separate possibilities compatible with the premises.

288–92. Victoria Bell (1999) devised the model method and carried out the experiments to investigate its efficacy.

Chapter 21: The Puzzles of *If*

293. The epigraph to Part VII is from Auden (1976, p. 231).

295. Callimachus's epigram is quoted by the second century AD physician and Skeptic philosopher Sextus Empiricus in his *Adversus Mathematicos* (see Kneale and Kneale, 1962, p. 128).

295. Medvedev (1990) describes what went wrong at Chernobyl. For a review of the robust difficulty of the inference that confronted the engineers there, see, e.g., Evans *et al.* (1993).

296. Recent books on conditionals include Eells and Skyrms (1994), Levi (1996), Woods (1997), Lycan (2001), Bennett (2003), and Gauker (2005). Evans and Over (2004) review three main sorts of psychological theory of conditionals, which I discuss later in the chapter.

296. Vittorio Girotto's daughter, Alma, is the three year old who made an adroit response to his promise about popcorn.

297. The theory of conditionals presented in this chapter is a result of a collaboration with Ruth Byrne (see, e.g., Johnson-Laird and Byrne, 2002).

297. For an analysis of the grammar of conditionals, see Dudman (1988).

298. One minor exception to the claim that if-clauses describe possibilities is the occurrence of questions in if-clauses. They can pose *who*, *what*, *where* sorts of question provided that the clause echoes the form of a preceding remark, e.g.:

If Vivien arrived then Evelyn left

Evelyn left if who arrived?

298. Grice (1975) defends the logical interpretation of conditionals, supplemented with various pragmatic devices.

298–9. Barrouillet and his colleague have carried out the main studies in which the participants list the possibilities compatible with conditionals (see, e.g., Barrouillet, 1997, Barrouillet and Leças, 1998, 1999). Their results support the developmental trend in listing possibilities, and a measure of the capacity of working memory correlated with the number of possibilities that a child listed, and it did so even when school grade was taken out of the analysis. Other results are compatible with this developmental trend (see e.g., Taplin, Staudenmayer, and Taddonio, 1974; Russell, 1987; Markovits, 1993). Young children often interpret conditionals as akin to conjunctions, i.e., as being compatible with only a single possibility (see e.g., Paris, 1973; Delval and Riviere, 1975; Kuhn, 1977; Politzer, 1986).

299. Studies in which participants evaluated the truth or falsity of conditionals are reported in Johnson-Laird and Tagart (1969) and Evans (1972b). Kneale and Kneale (1962, p. 549) discuss the history of the "paradoxes".

300. Evans and Over (2004) argue that conditional reasoning is based on the supposition of the if-clause. They write: "The varied and numerous uses of 'if' in everyday language that we have illustrated throughout this book all have something in common: the listener is invited to suppose or imagine a hypothetical state of affairs" (pp. 171–172).

300. Evans and Over (2004, pp. 19–20) argue that the paradoxes are absurd inferences. They reject theories in which they are valid.

301. Experiments in which participants list possibilities for different sorts of conditionals are reported in Byrne and Tasso (1999), Johnson-Laird and Byrne (2002), and in a series of studies carried out by Cristina Quelhas (see, e.g., Quelhas and Byrne, 2003).

302–3. The experiments on spatial inclusions and exclusions are from Johnson-Laird and Byrne (2002). Other well-known patterns of inference can be explained by modulation, e.g., the tendency for individuals to make inferences of the form: *If A then B, Not-A*, therefore, *Not-B*. If we can think of alternative ways to bring about *B* apart from *A*, then we are likely to refrain from the inference (as many studies have shown, see, e.g., Markovits and Vachon, 1990; Cummins *et al.*, 1991; Thompson, 1994; Cummins, 1995; Janveau-Brennan and Markovits, 1999). Markovits and his colleagues, including Barrouillet, have developed a model-based account of this phenomenon (Markovits *et al.*, 1998; Markovits and Barrouillet, 2002; Markovits and Quinn, 2002; Quinn and Markovits, 2002).

303. The natural interpretation of "donkey" sentences in logic doesn't work (see, e.g., G. Evans, 1980). Thus, this interpretation is wrong: If there exists an x such that x is a donkey and Joe owns x, then Joe beats x. The scope of the quantifier, *there exists an x*, is restricted to the if-clause of the conditional, because there's no guarantee that such an x does exist. Hence, the x in the then-clause is not "bound" by the quantifier. One solution is to represent the sentence with a universal quantifier (see e.g., Reinhart, 1986): For any x, if x is a donkey and Joe owns x, then Joe beats x.

303. For other analyses of the puzzle about the wet match, see, e.g., Stalnaker (1968), Lewis (1973), Lycan (1991), and Over and Evans (1997).

304. Minsky (1975) introduces default assumptions. Subsequent researchers in artificial intelligence (AI) have devised many sorts of formal systems using rules or axioms to accommodate reasoning from defaults, and other systems that allow conclusions to be withdrawn in the light of subsequent premises. This branch of AI is known as "nonmonotonic" reasoning (for a review, see Brewka *et al.*, 1997).

305. Barres and Johnson-Laird (2003) report the study of conjunctions and disjunctions of conditionals.

306. Ramsey's footnote is on p. 155 of Ramsey (1990), an essay on causality first published in 1929.

306. I outline a mechanism for constructing causal chains in the next chapter.

306. Philosophical theories of the meaning of conditionals that are generalizations of Ramsey's test are couched within the framework of "possible worlds" (see e.g., Kripke, 1963). A "possible world" is a possible state of affairs, though one that is a complete specification, and the actual world is treated as a member of the set of possible worlds. On Stalnaker's (1968) analysis, the truth of a counterfactual conditional in a world, world-1, depends on another world, world-2, that is accessible to world-1 and that is the most similar possible world to world-1 except that the if-clause of the conditional holds in it. If the then-clause is true in world-2, then the conditional as a whole is true; otherwise, it is false. It is not obvious that there is always a single world most similar to the actual world except that a counterfactual if-clause is true. If there is always a unique world of this sort, then one of this pair of propositions is true and one of them is false:

> If Verdi and Bizet had been compatriots then they would both have been Italian.

> If Verdi and Bizet had been compatriots then they would both have been French.

Yet, it is impossible to decide which proposition is the true one. In the light of this sort of example, Lewis (1973) argues that a conditional is true just in case the if-clause and then-clause are true in a world that is closer to the actual world than any world in which the if-clause is true and the then-clause false.

307. The Max Hastings quotation is from *Armageddon*, his history of the last eight months of World War II (Hastings, 2004, p. 43).

307–8. Byrne (2005) brings together her work and other research into counterfactual conditionals and on how we think about alternatives to reality. The experiments on the Chernobyl inference are reported in Byrne and Tasso (1999) and Quelhas and Byrne (2003).

308. Quine (1952) proposes the theory in which a conditional has no truth-value when its if-clause is false, Wason (1966) and Johnson-Laird and Tagart (1969) embrace it, and Evans and Over (2004) entertain it.

309. Adams (1975) proposes the probabilistic account of the conditions in which it is justifiable to assert conditionals. Recent proponents of a similar view include Evans and Over (2004) and their colleagues, see, e.g., Stevenson and Over (1995, pp. 617–618). Hadjichristidis *et al.* (2001) argue that their results corroborated the account, not the model theory. But, as Schroyens and Schaeken (2004) point out, they misinterpret the model theory to imply that reasoners construct complete models, not mental models, of the conditional. Evans *et al.* (2003) did not test their

account in a direct way, because their participants did not judge both the probability of a conditional and the corresponding conditional probability. Oberauer and Wilhelm (2003) did elicit both judgments, but in one of their studies less than a quarter of their participants gave the same estimates for both probabilities. Girotto and Johnson-Laird (2004) failed to find a reliable correlation between their participants' judgments of the probability of conditionals and the probability of the then-clause given the if-clause. The participants also varied by large amounts in their estimates of the latter probability. Oaksford and Chater (1998) have extended their probabilistic approach to conditional reasoning. My misgivings about this approach remain the same (see Chapter 16).

309. Ormerod and his colleagues show that participants can infer conditionals from disjunctions, and disjunctions from conditionals (see Ormerod *et al.*, 1993, and Richardson and Ormerod, 1997). For example, given the conditional:

> If Phil's next grant application isn't going to be funded then he'll be disappointed

we can infer the disjunction:

> Phil's next grant application is going to be funded or he'll be disappointed

But, the results corroborate a prediction from the model theory: it is easier to make the converse inference from a disjunction to a conditional. They also bear out Ormerod's claim—now embodied in the model theory—that we prefer to work with as parsimonious models as possible. In unpublished studies, Sonja Geiger has found that participants who carry out this paraphrasing task before they estimate the probability of a conditional tend to take more possibilities into account in their estimates.

309. Girotto *et al.* (1997) show that the difficulty of the Chernobyl inference depends in part on the order of the premises. As the theory also predicts, the inference is easier with conditionals of the form, *If and only if A then B*, which have just two complete models, than with conditionals of the form, *If A then B*, which have three complete models in their logical interpretation (Johnson-Laird *et al.*, 1992).

309. Braine and O'Brien (1991) argue that the if-clause of a conditional validly implies its then-clause. Barwise (1986) proposes a broader principle: the situation described in the if-clause of a conditional constrains the situation described in the then-clause.

309. The fact that the model theory implies that conditionals can have an indefinite number of interpretations has eluded some commentators (pace Evans and Over, 2004).

Chapter 22: Causes and Obligations

311. The quotation from Hume is in his *An Enquiry Concerning Human Understanding* (1748/1988). Salsburg writes: "There is, in fact, no such thing as cause and effect. It is a popular chimera, a vague notion that will not withstand the batterings of pure reason. It contains an inconsistent set of contradictory ideas and is of little or no value in scientific discourse" (see Salsburg, 2001, pp. 185–186; see also Russell, 1912–13).

311. The theory of causation in this chapter was published first in Johnson-Laird (1999). The empirical corroboration of the theory is due to Yevgeniya Goldvarg (now Goldvarg-Steingold), see Goldvarg and Johnson-Laird (2001). Kuhnmünch and

Beller (2005) have justly criticized one of our experiments, but Johnson-Laird *et al.* (2006a) have replied to them.

312. The idea of intervention to initiate a causal chain is emphasized in an analysis of causation in terms of Bayesian networks (see, e.g., Spirtes *et al.*, 1993, and Pearl 2000).

312. Sloman (2005) defends the psychological importance of intervention, and Sloman and Lagnado (2005) present evidence corroborating this claim.

313. Hume's analysis of causation is quoted from his *An Enquiry Concerning Human Understanding* (1748/1988, p. 115).

314. For evidence that participants take causes to precede their effects, see Tversky and Kahneman (1980), and Bullock *et al.* (1982).

314. I owe the toothpaste example to Paolo Legrenzi. Kant (1787/1934) used the example of a billiard ball causing a contemporaneous indentation in a pillow (see also Taylor, 1966).

314. Michotte (1963) demonstrates perceptual judgments of causation when one object bumps into another. There may be innate constraints on causal perceptions (see, e.g., Leslie, 1984).

314. Geminiani *et al.* (1996), echoing Hume (1739/1978), argue that adult conceptions of physical causation depend on physical contact. Likewise, Lewis (1986) shows that three principles suffice for a computer program that constructs models of a physical system: every event has a cause (!); causes precede their effects; and an action on an object is likely to be the cause of any change in it. Miller and Johnson-Laird (1976) argue for a more abstract notion of causation than the one embodied in visual perception.

314. Hume (1748/1988) argues that a causal relation means just a constant conjunction of cause and effect, whereas Kant (1787/1934) argues for a necessary connection, which he took to be a component of an innate conception of causality. In life, when we assert *A will cause B*, we mean that given *A*, *B* must occur (see Harré and Madden, 1975; and the results I report later in the chapter).

315. In a well-known analysis, Grice (1975) refers to inferences based on the conventions that speakers are truthful and informative as "implicatures". The idea that causal interpretation depends on knowledge of the situation is invoked by Hart and Honoré's (1985) analysis of legal concepts of causation, Mackie's (1980) philosophical analysis of a "causal field", and Cheng and Novick's (1991) psychological concept of a "focal set" of events.

315–6. Mill (1874) denies that there is any distinction in meaning between causes and enabling conditions. Hart and Honoré (1985) stipulate that the cause is the unusual state and the enabling condition is the usual state. Cheng and Novick (1991) stipulate that the cause is inconstant and the enabling condition is constant. According to others, the cause violates a norm assumed by default, whereas the enabling condition does not (see e.g., Kahneman and Miller, 1986; Einhorn and Hogarth, 1986). And, according to still another group of theorists, the cause is the factor that is relevant in any explanatory conversation: we describe the cause, not the enabler (Mackie, 1980; Turnbull and Slugoski, 1988; Hilton and Erb, 1996).

316. Goldvarg and Johnson-Laird (2001) report a study in which participants identified causes and enablers in various scenarios. In an earlier study, Cheng and Novick (1991) obtained a similar result, but in their scenarios the enabling conditions

were constant—they occurred in all the possibilities—and only the causes were inconstant. Goldvarg and Johnson-Laird also report the study of inferences from causal and enabling premises, and of the inferences from pairs of causal claims.

317. Reichenbach (1956) proposes a probabilistic analysis of causation (see also von Mises, 1957; Suppes, 1970, 1984; Salmon, 1980). He notes that a cause can "screen off", i.e., render irrelevant other events that raise the probability of its effect. Hence, if the probability of the effect given the cause and another event equals the probability of the effect given the cause, then the other event is irrelevant (see Hitchcock's article on the topic at plato.stanford.edu/entries/causation-probabilistic/). Cheng and her colleagues defend a similar psychological theory (e.g., Cheng and Novick, 1990; see also Schustack, 1988). There are parallel probabilistic accounts of the meaning of conditionals (see e.g., Newstead *et al.*, 1997; Oaksford *et al.*, 2000). "Because causal relations are neither observable nor deducible," Cheng (1997, p. 367) writes, "they must be induced from observable events." She assumes that we observe the difference in the respective probabilities referred to in Reichenbach's theory. This theory fails to make the correct predictions for certain causal inductions, and so Cheng (1997) proposes a more sophisticated model (the "Power PC" model). Probabilities play a role in the induction of causal relations (see Pearl, 1988, 2000; Shafer, 1996; Cheng, 1997; Lober and Shanks, 2000). And the main evidence for a probabilistic semantics is that people induce causal relations from data in which the antecedent is neither necessary nor sufficient to bring about the effect (e.g., McArthur, 1972; Cheng and Novick, 1990; Cummins *et al.*, 1991). They make loose causal generalizations to which they know that exceptions occur, perhaps because they know that many causes yield their effects only if the required enabling conditions are present and the disabling conditions are absent. Participants, as Cummins (1995, 1998) shows, are sensitive to these factors.

317–8. Hume (1748/1988) defends causation as constant conjunction. Kant (1787/1934, p. 90) writes that causation demands "that something, *A*, should be of such a nature, that something else, *B*, should follow from it necessarily". Mill (1874, p. 237) writes: "The invariable antecedent is termed the cause; the invariable consequent, the effect".

318. Bayesian networks, which are efficient ways in which to represent probabilities (see, e.g., Pearl, 2000), do not distinguish between causes and enabling conditions. Whether, in principle, they could make this distinction remains to be seen. They need to do so if they are to capture how we think about causal relations.

318. Hume (1739/1978) argues that people treat chance as a case of a hidden cause.

319–20. Many authors emphasize the role of powers or mechanisms in causal reasoning (e.g., Harré and Madden, 1975; Ahn *et al.*, 1995; White, 1995; Cheng, 1997): "a causal mechanism is the process by which a cause brings about an effect" (Koslowski, 1996, p. 6). Others emphasize a background framework of scientific laws or explanatory principles (Carnap, 1966). These principles, Hart and Honoré (1985) argue, lie behind every causal proposition about singular events. Causal power is the notion that causes produce effects through a transmission of energy or some other property from cause to effect. "In this sense," Harré and Madden (1975, p. 5) write, "causation always involves a material particular which produces or generates something." When a hammer is used to smash a plate, for example, a particular causal power of the hammer blow produces the effect: the energy in the blow is transferred to the plate, causing it to break. Theories of causal power therefore define causation in terms of the intrinsic properties of objects. Hume (1739/1978), however, rejects intrinsic properties that produce effects, arguing that the definition of *production* is indistinguishable from that of causation itself.

320. Shanks and his colleagues have explored the relations between how organisms learn the contingencies between events and how they make causal inductions (see, e.g., López *et al.*, 1998; Corlett, *et al.*, 2004; Shanks, 2004).

320. For studies showing that knowledge of causal mechanisms swamps information about the frequencies with which cause and effect occur together, see, e.g., White (1995), and Koslowski (1996).

320. For the account of autism, see Dawes (2001, p. 136).

320. Mill (1874) argues for the capricious nature of the difference between causes and enabling conditions, which he refers to as "conditions". Hart and Honoré (1985) echo Mill in their account of causation in the law. Greene and Darley (1998) argue that the Model Penal Code (American Law Institute, 1980/1985) is based on assumptions about causation that diverge from those of individuals who are not lawyers. In contrast to the Code, we treat actions that are sufficient to bring about a victim's death, as calling for the severest punishment.

321. For a discussion of "proximate" causes, see, e.g., Hart and Honoré (1985, p. 86).

321. For a description and discussion of deontic logics, see, e.g., Hilpinen (1971) and van Fraasen (1973).

321. Manktelow (2004) brings out the relations between causation and obligations from a different standpoint.

321. The model theory of deontic reasoning was developed in collaboration with Monica Bucciarelli (see, e.g., Bucciarelli and Johnson-Laird, 2000, 2005).

322. The categorical imperative is described in Kant (1785/1997).

322. For studies of children's understanding and use of deontic propositions, see, e.g., Hirst and Weil (1982), Byrnes and Duff (1989), Gralinski and Kopp, (1993), Day (1996), and Kalish (1998). Girotto, Light, and Colbourn (1988) show that eight-year-old children can solve deontic versions of the selection task in which the participants have to choose only which of two cards to turn (the so-called "reduced array" version of the selection task). Cummins (1998) corroborates this result, and Harris and Núñez (1996) show that even four-year-olds can cope with the task. However, any factor that makes the counterexamples salient improves performance in the reduced selection task—even with three-year-olds (Bucciarelli and Johnson-Laird, 2001). Kohlberg (e.g., 1986) studied the moral development of children, and, inspired by Piaget (1965b), postulates a number of distinct stages in their grasp of morality as they acquire the ability to view problems from a less egocentric perspective. It remains an open question whether these stages occur as opposed to a general development of knowledge of morality, both intuitive and conscious.

322. The need for the mind to keep track of the status of models is discussed in Chapter 3.

323. Bucciarelli carried out the study in which the participants thought of what is permissible given various sorts of proposition (Bucciarelli and Johnson-Laird, 2005). Cristina Quelhas and Ruth Byrne have also carried out unpublished experiments on the same topic. They have shown that inferences of the form, *If A then B,*

Not-B, therefore, Not-A, are easier with deontic conditionals than with conditionals about matters of fact. They argue that this result occurs because individuals tend to build models of both what is permissible and what isn't permissible for deontic conditionals.

324–6. Bucciarelli also carried out the experiments on inferences from pairs of deontic premises, and the studies of illusory deontic inferences (Bucciarelli and Johnson-Laird, 2005). I describe other illusory inferences in Chapters 8, 10, and 15.

327. Cosmides (1989) is the evolutionary psychologist who argues for the existence of a specialized mental module for "checking for cheaters". She reports evidence from the selection task showing that problems concerning cheating can elicit quite different patterns of response from those that normally occur in this task. But, the conditionals that she uses differ in meaning from the normal factual ones—they have a different "logical form" too. Johnson-Laird *et al.* (1972) report the first study using a deontic rule, which was about how much postage to put on various sorts of mail. It showed a massive improvement in performance, and there is now a large literature on deontic versions of the selection task (for a review, see Manktelow, 1999). Carlisle and Shafir's (2005) findings cast doubt on a module for reasoning about cheating. Perham and Oaksford (2005) show that decision theory gives a better account of performance in a deontic version of the selection task than evolutionary theory when the general claim concerned a hazard embedded in a scenario about the possibility of cheating, e.g., "If there is a blood injury then the player must leave the pitch" (cf. Fiddick, 2004). They also argue against other theories of performance, including an earlier version of the model theory.

327. Accounts of deontic reasoning based on formal rules are presented in Osherson (1974–76), Rips (1994), and Braine and O'Brien (1998).

327. Lord Halsbury's remarks are from *Quinn v. Leathem* (1901). I owe the various paradoxes in the law to Suber (1990).

329. Deontic dilemmas, such as the one about the child's operation, are a staple of both moral philosophy (e.g., Harman, 1977; Foot, 2002) and moral psychology (e.g., Kohlberg, 1986; Nichols, 2002).

329. For an account of Sydney Smith, see Pearson (1984). The imaginary argument between Buddha and Nietzsche is in Russell (1946, pp. 768–773).

330. Osofsky *et al.* (2005) studied prison officers who carry out executions and their techniques for moral disengagement.

330. The Princeton study of the trolley dilemma is reported in Greene *et al.* (2001). They used functional magnetic resonance imaging (fMRI) as participants made their decisions about a series of dilemmas. Those in which they had to act in a direct and personal way activated regions in the brain that mediate complex emotions (medial frontal gyrus, posterior cingulated gyrus, and superior temporal sulcus), whereas those in which they acted in a more impersonal way activated regions that mediate working memory (dorsolateral prefrontal and parietal areas), much like problems that had nothing to do with moral judgments. Nichols (2002) also discusses the role of emotions in moral judgments.

330. Utilitarianism is due to Bentham (1789/1996) and Mill (1863/1998). Both Baron (2000, chapter 16) and Sunstein (2005) suggest that it can be treated as a normative account of morality, but that moral heuristics—intuitions based on unconscious

reasoning, in my terms—often govern our decisions, leading us sometimes into error. For instance, we prefer to do harm by omission rather than by commission even if the Utilitarian consequences go the other way. Should we have our child vaccinated against whooping cough or not? Some of us prefer not to have our children vaccinated, even though the risk of death is smaller from vaccination than from whooping cough (see Baron and Ritov, 1994; Royzman and Baron, 2002).

330. Hare (1981) discusses dilemmas that have no right or wrong answers.

Chapter 23: Beliefs, Heresies, and Changes in Mind

332. Gosse describes his idolatry in his memoir, *Father and Son* (Gosse, 1923); for his father's book, see Gosse (1998).

332. The study of the doomsday cult is described in *When Prophecy Failed* (Festinger *et al.*, 1956). The results are controversial (see Bainbridge 1997).

332. Russell (1957) distinguishes between knowledge by acquaintance and knowledge by description. An earlier philosopher, Reid (1846) referred to the "original principle" of testimony: we tend to believe those propositions that people tell us.

332–3. The King James version of the Bible translates St. Paul's *Epistle to the Hebrews*, 11.1: "Now faith is the substance [hypostasis] of things hoped for, the evidence [elenchon] of things unseen". Humphrey (1996) in his *Leaps of Faith* examines the psychological underpinnings of beliefs in the supernatural and ESP.

333. One early Christian who rejoiced in the impossibility of his beliefs was Tertullian. He wrote: *Et sepultus resurrexit; certum est, quia impossibile.* (And He was buried, and rose again: it is certain, because it is impossible; see 5.4 of Tertullian, 1956). "Credo quia impossible" (I believe because it is impossible) is also attributed to St. Augustine (see his *Confessions*, 1992, VI, 5, 7).

333. The quotation about faith is from James (1956, p. 9).

333. For evidence on how peers can pressure participants into accepting propositions contrary to the evidence of their senses, see, e.g., Crutchfield (1955), and Asch (1956). For the use of threats of retribution in the training of terrorists, see Stern (2003), which is also the basis for my all-purpose terrorist manifesto. She studied a variety of terrorist groups including Hammas (Muslim), Kach and Kahane Chai (Jewish), and the Covenant, the Sword, and the Arm of the Lord (Christian).

334. The status of the views about Jesus are as follows: Jesus was two persons is the heresy of Nestorianism; Jesus had two natures, one human and one divine, is the orthodox view of the Catholic church; Jesus had a single divine nature is the heresy of Monophysitism; and Jesus had a single human nature and was an agent for God is the heresy of Arianism.

334. For a terrifying description of the Crusade against the Cathars, see O'Shea (2000).

335. The *Acts of the Apostles* give three accounts of the conversion of St. Paul (ix, 1–19; xxii, 3–21; xxvi, 9–23).

335. Many psychological studies demonstrate the perseverance of social stereotypes in the face of conflicting evidence (see, e.g., Ross and Lepper, 1980; Lepper *et al.*, 1986; Rehder and Hastie, 1996).

335–6. Parks's account of the "residenza" is in Powers (1997).

336–7. The experiments on the effects of belief on searching for counterexamples, including the inference about the Frenchmen in the restaurant are reported in Oakhill and Johnson-Laird (1985) and Oakhill *et al.* (1989, 1990). Beliefs affect the evaluation of given conclusions (see Evans *et al.*, 1983). They can also affect the difficulty of constructing a model in the first place (see Cherubini *et al.*, 1998; Klauer *et al.*, 2000). In general, they have a bigger effect on invalid inferences than valid inferences.

338. Abduction is described in Chapter 14.

338. Sutherland (1996) is one compendium of authors' inconsistencies. The inconsistency about trees and Adam is said to be between Genesis (1: 11–12) and (2: 8–9). Kermode's discussion of inconsistencies, accidental and deliberate, is in his essay, "Forgetting", in (Kermode, 2003). Psychologists have demonstrated the difficulty of detecting inconsistencies in texts (see, e.g., Black *et al.*, 1986; Otero and Kintsch, 1992).

339. Russell (1967) tells the anecdote about the man who had doubts about the fecundity of contradictions.

340. Klein (1998) argues for the segregation of beliefs into separate sets. Sperber (1996) discusses apparent inconsistencies in cultural beliefs.

340. The quotation from Whitman is from his *Leaves of Grass* (see Whitman, 1977).

341–2. Maria Sonino Legrenzi, Paolo Legrenzi, and Vittorio Girotto carried out the experiments on detecting and resolving inconsistencies (see, e.g., Johnson-Laird *et al.*, 2004). Their inspiration was the day the car wouldn't start in the little town of Vauvenargues in Provence. The first experiment on the evaluation of consistency is reported in Johnson-Laird *et al.* (2000). The experiment in which the participants described possibilities is reported in Legrenzi *et al.* (2003). The first experiment on illusions of consistency is reported in Johnson-Laird *et al.* (2000), and the second experiment in Legrenzi *et al.* (2003). A survey of these results and others is in Johnson-Laird *et al.* (2004).

343. Nonmonotonic systems of reasoning have been developed in artificial intelligence. They have become remote from human reasoning (for reviews, see, e.g., Ginsberg, 1987; Brewka *et al.*, 1997). In some systems, a proposition such as that *matches struck properly light* is treated as an idealization by default (e.g., Reiter, 1980). Hence, the conclusion that the match lights can be withdrawn if there is evidence to the contrary, but without the retraction of the default assumption. Other systems, however, allow for definite beliefs to be revised in the light of inconsistency (e.g., Doyle, 1979; de Kleer, 1986). Philosophers have also developed systems for the revision of beliefs in the face of inconsistencies (e.g., Harman, 1986; Gärdenfors, 1990; Levi, 1991). Some of the subtle problems that arise from an approach based on mental models are discussed by Bonnefon (2004).

343. Harman (1986) distinguishes two main accounts of the entrenchment of beliefs: the "foundations" for a belief, which are the reasons that support it (cf. Doyle, 1979; de Kleer, 1986); and the "coherence" of a belief with other beliefs (see Alchourrón *et al.*, 1985; Gärdenfors, 1988, 1990). Both factors may be relevant to the revision of beliefs, but the Alchourrón *et al.* account does not constrain the revision process in any way (see Tennant, 2005). My colleague, Dan Osherson, also has an unpublished proof of the same consequence. On the notion of abandoning beliefs, Fuhrmann, (1997, p. 24) writes: "... when it comes to choosing between candidates for removal,

the least entrenched ought to be given up." Experiments have corroborated this principle (Dieussaert *et al.*, 2000; Politzer and Carles, 2001, Experiment 2).

344. Thagard (1989, 1992, 2000) has implemented a suite of programs that assess alternative hypotheses, say, about why dinosaurs became extinct, by computing their coherence with the evidence. The user sets up a network of nodes representing the propositions in the competing hypotheses, the propositions in the relevant evidence, and the coherence or incoherence (with varying degrees of strength) between each pair of propositions. In other words, coherence unlike consistency is treated as an unanalyzed primitive that comes in varying degrees of strength. The program carries out a process of "constraint satisfaction" in which nodes are rejected to increase the overall coherence of the system. If and when the system stabilizes, it shows which hypothesis coheres more with the evidence. Propositions that describe the evidence have a degree of acceptability on their own, which adds an empirical foundation to the system, but they can be overruled by more coherent propositions.

344. In a pioneering study, Revlis *et al.* (1971) show that when a fact conflicts with the consequence of a general principle and a particular proposition, participants tend to reject the particular proposition (see also Revlis and Hayes, 1972; Revlis, 1974; Revlin (sic) *et al.*, 2001). Other experiments examine the effects of the order of events on beliefs (e.g., Hogarth and Einhorn, 1992; Schlottmann and Anderson, 1995; Zhang *et al.*, 1997).

344. Research has examined the links between the form of statements and their believability. Elio and Pelletier (1997) suggest that conditional statements may be less believable than categorical statements, and Politzer and Carles (2001) argue that any statement containing a propositional connective may be less believable than a categorical statement. Doubt about a disjunction "stems from the rather trivial fact that it is more complex in that it contains a connection and has more chances to be the source of error" (p. 224).

344–5. Uri Hasson carried out the research showing that entrenchment fails to account for which belief participants abandon: they may abandon the proposition that they rated as more believable in a pair (see Hasson and Johnson-Laird, 2006).

345. The studies of mismatches between models of propositions and models of facts are reported in Girotto *et al.* (2000). Mismatches between the syntax of clauses in sentences may have affects on reasoning (see Evans *et al.*, 1993), but the mismatches in the present case are between models.

347. The quotation is from James (1907, p. 59). Recent theorists who have defended minimal changes to beliefs include Harman (1986) and Gärdenfors (1988).

347. The program for constructing causal chains to resolve inconsistencies is described in Chapter 22. Johnson-Laird *et al.* (2004) report the experiments in which participants evaluated causal resolutions of inconsistencies. The participants committed the "conjunction" fallacy in their judgments of the probabilities of the various explanations (see Tversky and Kahneman, 1983, who discovered the fallacy in another context). Clare Walsh has carried out unpublished experiments also showing that participants prefer explanations that go beyond the minimal.

348. The complete models of a cause-and-effect relation, such as "unloading a gun causes there to be no bullets in the chamber", are as follows:

unload gun	no bullets in chamber.
don't unload gun	bullets in chamber.
don't unload gun	no bullets in chamber.

They make it easy to infer the effect (no bullets) from the cause (unload), because given the cause the effect is the only possibility. It should be harder to infer the cause (unload) from the effect (no bullets), because there is no unique cause in the preceding models, and so they allow for other possible causes, e.g., all the bullets may have been fired. Tversky and Kahneman (1982b) showed that conditionals in which the if-clause is the cause of the effect are judged as more probable than conditionals in which the if-clause is evidence for the cause.

Chapter 24: How we Solve Problems

350. For a psychologically inspired account of perspective, see Kubovy (1986).

350. The view that insight is a special process goes back to the German "Gestalt" psychologists. They argue that it depends on a "restructuring" or "recentering" of perception (Köhler, 1947; Wertheimer, 1961). But critics, both early (Bulbrook, 1932) and late (e.g., Perkins, 1981, 2000; Weisberg, 1986), argue that there is nothing special about insight, and that restructuring and recentering are obscure notions (Ohlsson, 1984a,b).

351. A study showing that participants can rate how "warm" they are in their efforts to solve problems is due to Metcalfe and Weibe (1987). With problems used in studies of insight, no increase in ratings of warmth occurred: participants felt remote from the solution right up to the moment that it popped into their heads.

351. Kounios and his colleagues argue that the solution to anagrams depends on insight, and these investigators have used brain scans to implicate particular regions of the brain underlying it (see, e.g., Jung-Beeman et al., 2004).

351. De Bono (e.g., 1992) is the proponent of lateral thinking. Henle (1962) argues that we fail to stick to logic when we reason. For the view that reasoning is imaginative, see Byrne's (2005) book on counterfactual thinking.

351. The short story Pierre Menard, Author of the Quixote is in Borges (1998).

352. Valéry (1972, p. 324) describes the encounter between Degas and Mallarmé.

352. For a formulation and a defence of the NONCE definition, see, e.g., Johnson-Laird (1993).

352. The neo-Darwinian account of the evolution of species is a synthesis of modern genetics with Darwin's concept of natural selection. Genetics accounts for the variation among individuals, and the environment selects out those variations that are more adaptive, enabling individuals to survive and to reproduce. The generative process cannot be guided by constraints acquired by organisms during their lifetimes (see Mayr, 1982, p. 537). It is crucial to distinguish between a single operation of a neo-Darwinian strategy and its repeated use—a much more powerful process (Dawkins, 1976). Evolution is thus the archetypal recursive process: it applies to its own successful results. It is mimicked in the "genetic" programs for finding optimal solutions to problems (e.g., Holland et al., 1986). Many psychologists propose

neo-Darwinian theories of creativity (e.g., Skinner, 1953; Campbell, 1960; Bateson, 1979; Simonton, 1995).

353. Mayr (1982, p. 354) comments on Lamarck's theory. Because musical improvization is unconscious, it has no access to working memory—a conjecture that is corroborated both in a neo-Lamarckian computer program for musical improvization and by the fact that a load on working memory appears to have no effect on the quality or fluency of jazz improvizations (see Johnson-Laird, 2002b).

353. Duncker (1945) devised and studied the candle problem.

355. The behaviorist, B.F. Skinner, argues that teaching regimens should enable us to learn without mistakes (see, e.g., Holland and Skinner, 1961). A contrasting example of a procedure that learns solely from mistakes is "backward propagation of *error*" (McClelland and Rumelhart, 1986).

355. Katona (1940) appears to have been the first to study shape problems. Most shape problems are simple, yet they call for sufficient thought to be a staple of puzzle books (e.g., Orleans and Orleans, 1983). Louis Lee carried out the experiments investigating shape problems (see Lee and Johnson-Laird, 2004). Another sort of problem akin to shape problems are those in which water jugs of different capacities have to be used to measure a specified amount of water, but they have a formulaic solution (see, e.g., Luchins and Luchins, 1950).

356. Louis Lee devised the account of saliency and carried out the studies to investigate its effect, the effect of symmetry, and the development of strategies (Lee and Johnson-Laird, 2004). The development of strategies for shape problems follows the same general principle that I describe in the chapter on strategies for reasoning.

358. Reverse engineering often concerns computer programs. It has proved so common that attempts are made to design software that resists it (see, e.g., Eilam, 2005).

358. The theory of reverse engineering in this chapter was presented first in Lee and Johnson-Laird (2005).

362. Louis Lee carried out the experiments, including the one on water faucets (Lee and Johnson-Laird, 2005).

362–3. The notion of *independence*, as I use it in this chapter, is related to whether a concept can be learned using a device that is "linear". Computer programs implementing a linear procedure for learning are called "perceptrons" (Rosenblatt, 1958, 1961). Consider the spatial representation of an inclusive "or" problem:

$$
\begin{array}{c|cc}
\text{On} & + & + \\
\text{Switch 1} & & \\
\text{Off} & - & + \\
\hline
& \text{Off} & \text{On} \\
& \multicolumn{2}{c}{\text{Switch 2}}
\end{array}
$$

We can draw a straight line between the set of cases in which the bulb is on (the plus signs in the figure) and the case in which it is off (the negative sign). A perceptron is a device that learns to draw that straight line: it is a "linear" device. Now, consider the spatial representation of an exclusive disjunction, i.e., an "or else" problem:

$$
\begin{array}{c c c}
 & \text{On} & +\quad - \\
\text{Switch 1} & & \\
 & \text{Off} & -\quad + \\
 & & \text{Off}\quad\text{On} \\
 & & \text{Switch 2}
\end{array}
$$

It is impossible to draw a single straight line that separates the positive and negative cases. No perceptron can represent the "or else" problem (Minsky and Papert, 1969). Programs that can learn exclusive disjunction are therefore "non-linear" (see, e.g., McLelland and Rumelhart, 1986; Vapnik, 1998). Unlike this distinction, the notion of independence can vary in degree (see the text in the chapter).

364. Means-ends analysis is described in Polya (1973), and it underpins the seminal work of Newell and Simon (1972) on human problem solving.

364–5. Weisberg (1996) categorizes "insight" problems in a pre-theoretical way. Recent theories of insight include the view that it depends on overcoming an erroneous approach to a problem (see, e.g., Weisberg, 1993; Isaak and Just, 1995; Knoblich *et al.*, 1999). A period of "incubation" in which we think about other matters allows the misleading cues to become less accessible with a consequent greater chance of our recovering the correct cues (Smith and Blankenship, 1991). These perseverations do occur (see, e.g., Jansson and Smith, 1991). The trouble with this approach, however, is its assumption that we know the right methods, though can't access them. The claim may be correct for some problems (see Keane, 1989), but it is false for others. Another view of insight is based on Newell and Simon's (1972) concept of a "problem space", i.e., the abstract space defined by all possible sequences of the mental operations relevant to a problem. The problem solver needs to search this space for a sequence of operations leading from the initial state of the problem to its solution. Kaplan and Simon (1990) argue that insight depends on switching from a search in the problem space to a search in the meta-level space of *possible* problem spaces for a new representation of the problem (see also Korf, 1980). In a case of insight, this new representation yields the solution to the problem. But, as Kaplan and Simon remark (p. 381): "The space of possible problem spaces is exceedingly ill-defined, in fact, infinite" (p. 381).

365. Still another view of insight is due to Tom Ormerod and his colleagues: when we tackle a problem, we select moves to maximize progress towards the goal but to minimize the expansion of the problem space (see Chronicle *et al.*, 2001; MacGregor *et al.*, 2001; Ormerod *et al.*, 2002). We relax this constraint only if we have to, but in this way we may discover a new sort of move. This theory postulates that we can assess whether a putative move makes progress towards a goal.

Chapter 25: Flying Bicycles: How the Wright Brothers Invented the Airplane

367. The epigraph for Part VII is from Auden (1977, p. 404).

369. A vast literature on the Wright brothers exists. I have found indispensable their own writing, e.g., Kelly (1996), Wright (1988), and McFarland's (2001) magisterial

collection of their correspondence and papers, Crouch's (1989) definitive biography, Jakab's (1990) technical monograph, and Tobin's (2003) recent account of the race for flight. For an independent account of their achievement from the standpoint of cognitive science, see Bradshaw (1992).

369. Wilbur writes to another aeronautical pioneer, Octave Chanute, October 15, 1906 (Kelly, 1996, p. 183): "If the wheels of time could be turned back six years, it is not at all probable that we would do again what we have done. The one thing that impresses me as remarkable is the shortness of the time within which our work was done."

370. Tobin (2003) describes Langley's unsuccessful efforts and their cost.

370. Kelvin's remark is in a letter to Alexander Graham Bell's wife in which he was referring to Bell's own efforts in aviation (cited in Tobin, 2003, p. 251).

371. Jakab (1990, p. 26) is one source of Maxim's quotation about motors for aircraft.

371. Wilbur's claim about knowledge and skill is from McFarland (2001, p. 15).

371. Wilbur writes in a letter to a colleague, George A. Spratt, April 20, 1903: "It is a characteristic of all our family to be able to see the weak points of anything, but this is not always a desirable quality as it makes us too conservative for successful business men, and limits our friendships to a very limited circle" (McFarland, 2001, Vol. 1, p. 306).

372. For Wilbur's relations with Montgomery, see, e.g., Crouch (1989).

373. I describe the principal theories of analogy in Chapter 14, and discuss there Wilbur's analogy between the inner-tube box and the wings of a biplane. Dunbar has studied scientists' thinking in four leading laboratories of molecular biology (e.g., Dunbar, 1995). When an experiment failed, the scientists looked for reasons in analogies with other experiments. They drew these analogies at every meeting that Dunbar attended. They also used analogies from one domain to another but only when they were thinking about a theory or planning a series of experiments. Gick and Holyoak (1983) show that people don't always grasp the import of an analogy.

373–4. For Wilbur's remark about buzzards, see McFarland (2001, p. 15 et seq.).

374. Wilbur's description of the analogy to the inner-tube box is from a letter to Chanute (see McFarland, 2001, Vol. 1, p. 18).

374. Wilbur writes to his sister, June 8, 1907, from Paris (Kelly, 1996, p. 212): "My imagination pictures things more vividly than my eyes." Crouch (1989, p. 221) in describing the brothers refers to "their genius for visualizing mechanical solutions to theoretical problems". Others including Jakab (1990) and Ferguson (1992) make similar comments. Craig et al. (2002) discuss the use of perceptual simulation in analogy. Gooding (2005), the doyen of Faraday scholars, posits visual inference rules for scientific thinking, but his examples seem to depend on the manipulation of models, e.g., the task of reconstructing the three-dimensional shape of a creature from its squashed fossil. Gould (1989, p. 92) describes the investigator as "rotating the damned thing in my mind" from its position in one drawing to the different angle of another drawing (cf. my discussion of the mental rotation of images in Chapter 2).

377. Wilbur's remark about the center of air pressure is from the transcript of his first professional talk, which was to the Western Society of Engineers in Chicago in September 1901 (see p. 101, of "Some Aeronautical Experiments", in McFarland, 2001, Vol. 1., pp. 99–118).

379. "Not within a thousand years ..." is cited by Crouch (1989, p. 213).

380. The brothers were not the first to build a wind tunnel, but they were the first to use a wind tunnel to make accurate measurements useful to the design of aircraft (see, e.g., McFarland, 2001, Vol. 1., p. 548, f.n. 5).

382. The remarks about the Wrights' design of propellers come from their article, "The Wright Brothers' Aeroplane" (Wright, 1988). Combs (1979, p. 182) argues that their theory of the propeller put them ten to twenty years ahead of their rivals; and it is true that the Wrights' rivals continued to use trial and error in their propeller designs for at least ten years. For the disanalogy with ships' propellers, see McFarland (2001, Vol. 1, p. 596).

382–3. The marathon calculations are shown in McFarland (2001, Vol. 1, pp. 49–50).

385. His father's brief obituary for Wilbur is unsurpassed: "This morning at 3.15, Wilbur passed away, aged 45 years, 1 month and 14 days. A short life, full of consequences. An unfailing intellect, imperturbable temper, great self-reliance, and as great modesty, seeing the right clearly, pursuing it steadily, he lived and died" (from his father's diary, cited in Crouch, 1989, p. 449).

385. "Isn't it astonishing ... " from a letter that Orville wrote to George A. Spratt, June, 7 1903 (McFarland, 2001, Vol. 1, pp. 310–315).

Chapter 26: Unwrapping an Enigma

387. Pundits distinguish between *codes*, e.g., the Morse code, and *ciphers*, e.g., the Enigma machine's output. I use the two terms interchangeably.

387. The literature on ciphers is vast. I have found these books useful: Hinsley (1975), the official Government history; Hinsley and Stripp (1993), a set of reminiscences from people at Bletchley Park; Kahn (1996), the principal history of codes and ciphers; and Budiansky (2000), an account of code breaking in World War II. A Google search on the Web yields several sites that allow you to operate a simulated Enigma machine.

387. Marian Rejewski and a group of Polish cryptanalysts broke the Enigma code in 1933 (see Kozaczuk and Straszak, 2004). They liaised with the French, and on July 25, 1939, at a joint meeting at Pyry, near Warsaw, with French and British experts, including Dillwyn Knox (Welchman's future boss), the Poles with great generosity handed over duplicates of Enigma machines, diagrams of the wiring of the rotors, and their method of breaking the code. Knox had thought that Enigma was unbreakable. No wonder he was so furious that Welchman, working by himself, discovered how to break the code. Turing's contributions are described in Hodges (2000).

387. My account of Welchman's methods is based on Chapter 4 of his book, *The Hut Six Story* (Welchman, 1982). What has complicated the historians' task was that work at Bletchley remained "classified" by the British Government for many years. The first book in English about it was not published until 1974, and claimed that the British were the first to break the Enigma code!

388. Edgar Allan Poe invited readers of a Philadelphia weekly to send in ciphered messages, and he broke them all using a frequency analysis. In his short story, *The Gold Bug* (Poe, 1982), the protagonist uses the method to decipher Captain Kidd's description of the location of buried treasure. Conan Doyle also has Sherlock Holmes use the same method in *The Adventure of the Dancing Men* (Conan Doyle, 1930).

Chapter 27: On the Mode of the Communication of Cholera

402. My interest in Snow was sparked by Keith Oatley's (1998) wonderful novel, *A Natural History*, whose protagonist is Victorian doctor modeled in part on Snow. My account of Snow relies on the "Snowflakes", five authors who analyze Snow's career and thinking. They are the historian Peter Vinten-Johansen, the philosopher-MD Howard Brody, the epidemiologist Nigel Planeth, the historian Stephen Rachman, and the epidemiologist Michael Rip (see Vinten-Johansen *et al.*, 2003). They argue that Snow relied on the hypothetico-deductive method, that he used induction to establish certain facts, and that he deduced empirical consequences from his theory. His investigations to check these consequences operated at several different levels of analysis from society at large down to chemical interactions. They label certain of Snow's inferences as deductions and others as inductions. The model theory of reasoning, I hope, dovetails with their account.

403. Porter (1997) is a splendid history of medicine, including its numerous fads.

403. Snow's first account of cholera was *On the Mode of Communication of Cholera* in August 1849a, and two months later he published a journal article of the disease's pathology and communication (Snow, 1849b; see also Frost, 1965).

404. Popper (1959) describes his philosophy of science.

404. Howson and Urbach (1993, p. 1) argue that "scientific and ... much of everyday reasoning is conducted in probabilistic terms".

404. Herschel (1987) describes the hypothetico-deductive method in a book that won Darwin's approval. Herschel's account was criticized by later philosophers of science who had a more inductivist standpoint, such as Whewell (1967) and Mill (1874). Whewell is often misinterpreted as anticipating Popper.

404. For an account of the role of models in scientific thinking, see Hesse (1966), and Wise (1979), who shows their role in Maxwell's development of his field equations. Cognitive scientists argue for their role, along with visual imagery, in the development of scientific theories (Miller, 1984; Giere, 1988; Gorman 1992; Thagard, 1999; and the collections of papers in Giere, 1992; Magnani *et al.*, 1999; Magnani and Nersessian, 2002; Gorman *et al.*, 2005). Simon and his colleagues describe the role of induction in the development and testing of scientific laws (see, e.g., Langley *et al.*, 1987; Kulkarni and Simon, 1988; Klahr and Simon, 1999).

404. I discuss the role of the Humean heuristic, "similar effects depend on similar causes", in Chapters 5 and 13.

405. Porter (1997, chapter 13) describes the sanitary reforms and public medicine in England during the nineteenth century.

405. The quotation about the inverse gas law is from Snow (1855), and cited by Vinten-Johansen *et al.* (2003, p. 345).

405. Vinten-Johansen *et al.* (2003) discuss the factors underlying Snow's conversion from noxious effluvia to contaminated water as the mode of communication of the disease. They comment on Snow's thinking about Albion Terrace: "Snow was thinking in spatial and topographic terms, although he made no diagrams himself" (p. 208).

412. For Koch getting the credit for discovering *Vibrio cholerae*, see, e.g., Porter (1997), and Halliday (1999); and for the true story, see Tognotti (2000, p. 244).

492 NOTES ON THE CHAPTERS

413. The "great stink" from the Thames is described in Halliday's (1999) account of the work of Sir Joseph Bazalgette's prodigious engineering project to make the Thames the cleanest metropolitan river in the world—a project that the great stink forced Parliament to demand.

Chapter 28: How we Reason

414. The inferences in the coffee bar are described in detail in Chapter 13.

414. Unconscious reasoning and emotions are analyzed in Part II of the book.

416. The modulation of the interpretation of connectives and other logical terms is analyzed in Chapter 12. For the impossibility of capturing logical properties of relational terms, see Chapter 9. I owe the example of Alice and the potion to Steve Sloman.

417. Rips (1994) remarks on the haphazard nature of errors according to his theory.

417. Boole (1854) analyzes the laws of thought.

417. The notion that reasoning depends on many different processes, akin to a Swiss army knife, is due to evolutionary psychologists.

418. Peirce's ideas and the inability of icons to represent negation are described in Chapter 2 (for some of their other limitations, see Chapters 8 and 10).

419. Illusory inferences occur in reasoning with connectives (Chapters 8 and 23), quantifiers (Chapter 10), probabilities (Chapter 15), and deontic terms (Chapter 22).

420. Oaksford and Chater (1998, p. 110) argue that the role of counterexamples is neither necessary nor sufficient for rationality. It isn't necessary because during periods of "normal" science (cf. Kuhn, 1970), scientists don't allow core theoretical principles to be overturned by counterexamples. Maybe; but I am talking about the use of counterexamples to overturn inferences, not general claims. They also argue that counterexamples aren't sufficient for rationality because it wouldn't be rational to continue to search for counterexamples indefinitely when we're trying to reach a decision in real time. This argument, however, depends on an assumption that the model theory doesn't make, namely, that the roots of rationality are in a complete search for counterexamples. In fact, the theory postulates that we are rational because we grasp the *force* of counterexamples. We can even search for them on occasion, though we do not appear to have any systematic, let alone tractable, procedure for searching for them. It is striking that Oaksford and Chater's critique depends on thinking of counterexamples, albeit to a stronger claim than I made.

420. Ragni (2003) proves that two-dimensional spatial reasoning is intractable.

420. James (1907, p. 59) argues for minimal changes to our beliefs.

421. Stanovich (1999) reports many studies establishing correlations between reasoning and intelligence.

421. Simon (1982) argues that working memory capacity was a major bottleneck in reasoning. For studies relating the capacity of working memory to reasoning ability, see, e.g., Bara *et al.* (1995), Barrouillet and Leças (1999).

422. U.S. Grant's memoirs, which were written as he was dying, reveal that he was great general and a great writer (see Grant, 1990). Wellington wrote no memoirs, but his inference about the existence of the ford across the river, which his guides had denied, is described in Longford's biography (1969, p. 90).

422. I quote Whitman's (1977) remark about contradiction in Chapter 23.

422. James Joyce (1930) writes in *The Portrait of the Artist as a Young Man*: ". . . the only arms I allow myself to use ... silence, exile, and cunning".

422. The *Paris Review*, edited for many years by the late George Plimpton, has published many interviews with poets and writers. I do not recall any of them referring to the role of reasoning in their work.

422. Auden discusses the creation of poetry in the Prologue and the Dyer's Hand (Auden, 1962; see also Auden, 1973, p. 358 et seq.). Spender (1952) describes how he wrote a poem. Vendler (2004) describes the thinking in the poetry of Pope, Whitman, Dickinson, and Yeats.

422. The quotation is from Valéry (1958, p. 58).

Acknowledgements

A book based on psychological research owes so much to those who collaborated in the research that the author's main role is to channel their efforts. It seems a poor thing to list their names in alphabetical order. If I could tell you more about each of them without trying your patience, I would do so, but at the end of a long book, that's impossible. However, I must single out several groups of friends with whom I have carried out joint research for many years: Ruth M.J. Byrne, Vice-Provost of Trinity College, University of Dublin; Bruno Bara and Monica Bucciarelli of the University of Turin; Juan García-Madruga and his colleagues at the University of Education at a Distance, Madrid; Paolo Legrenzi, Maria Sonino Legrenzi, and Vittorio Girotto, of the University of Architecture, Venice; Keith Oatley emeritus professor at the University of Toronto; and Francesco Mancini, the Director of the School of Psychotherapy, Rome and Amelia Gangemi of the University of Cagliari, Sardinia.

My next thanks go to the six individuals who read the entire manuscript of the book in an earlier version. Geoff Goodwin and Louis Lee put aside their own research and went through the book with the finest of tooth combs. I also thank Louis for preparing decent figures from the outputs of my ancient graphics program. Vittorio Girotto suggested many pertinent citations, especially to the literature of animal psychology, and pointed out many wayward claims, which he threatened to dispute with me in the literature. Monica Bucciarelli put me straight on aspects of the literature of child development, and alerted me to the idiomatic difficulties of the book for a non-native speaker of English. Ruth Byrne somehow managed to combine reading the book with being second-in-command of Trinity College, Dublin. She made many perceptive criticisms, and was most encouraging, except when I wrote "cognitions" as a plural noun. I sent the manuscript to four other scholars, who were too busy to read it. I won't mention their names, but they know who they are, and they are responsible for any remaining errors in the book. (Only kidding!)

Many other individuals have made an essential contribution in collaborative research, and I thank them: Patricia Barres, Malcolm Bauer, Victoria Bell, Nuria Carriedo, Jean-Paul Caverni, Paolo Cherubini, Jon Cohen, Orlando Espino, Jonathan Evans, Rich Feit, Caren Frosch, Alan Garnham, Sonja Geiger, Genya Goldvarg-Steingold, Geoff Goodwin, Francisco Gutiérrez,

Simon Handley, Uri Hasson, Cathy Haught, Georg Jahn, Mark John, Csongor Juhos, Jim Kroger, Jung Min Lee, Louis Lee, Rachel McCloy, Mark John, Markus Knauff, Robert Mackiewicz, Henry Markovits, Marc Marschark, Hans-Georg Neth, Mary Newsome, Jane Oakhill, Tom Ormerod, Stefania Pighin, Cristina Quelhas, Marco Ragni, Sergio Moreno Rios, Carlos Santamaría, Fabien Savary, Walter Schaeken, Walter Schroyens, Victoria Shaw, Vladimir Sloutsky, Patrizia Tabossi, Alessandra Tasso, Isabelle Vadeboncoeur, Jean-Baptiste van der Henst, Clare Walsh, Yingrui Yang, and Dan Zook.

I am grateful to Deborah Prentice, the chair of the Department of Psychology at Princeton, who has helped to make the place such a congenial place in which to teach and to do research. She also helped me to get a sabbatical semester in the fall of 2004, which enabled me to start work on the book. Various colleagues at Princeton have been a great source of advice and encouragement: Jon Cohen, Ron Comer, John Darley, Susan Fiske, Harry Frankfurt, Jack Gelfand, Sam Glucksberg, Adele Goldberg, Gil Harman, Norman and Leonore Itzkowitz, Danny Kahneman, Virginia Kwan, George Miller, Dan Osherson, Eldar Shafir, Joe Simmons, Alex Todorov, Anne Treisman, and Edwin Williams.

My thanks to many other scholars for their helpful advice, encouragement, and frank criticism: Alexandre Banos, Jon Baron, Pierre Barrouillet, Hart Blanton, Luca Bonatti, Melissa Bowerman, Selmer Bringsjord, Jerome Bruner, Nick Chater, Michelle Cowley, Susan Carey, Michel Denis, Ronnie de Sousa, Kristien Dieussaert, Suzanne Egan, Jonathan St.B.T. Evans, Carol Feldman, Wayne Gray, David Green, Tony Greenwald, Justin Halberda, Earl B. Hunt, Ray Jackendoff, W. Jake Jacobs, Jenny Jenkins, Marcia Johnson, Mark Keane, Rick Lewis, Alice McEleney, Ken Manktelow, Gary Marcus, Julie Meehan, Aisling Murray, Ray Nickerson, Ira Noveck, Mike Oaksford, Kieron O'Connor, David Over, Luis Pineda, Thad Polk, Pat Rabbitt, Carol Raye, Lance Rips, Susana Segura, Steve Sloman, Ed Smith, Dan Sperber, Keith Stenning, Len Talmy, Valerie Thompson, Alexander Todorov, Barbara Tversky, André Vandierendonck, and Massimo Warglien.

Several individuals have helped on the technical and publishing side. My thanks to Martin Baum and Angela Butterworth at OUP for smoothing the path to publication. My thanks also to Bernie VanUiter and Marion Kowaleski for administrative help, to Donna O'Leary and Keisha Craig for secretarial assistance, and to David Berkowitz, Paul Bree, Carol Agans, Richard Reiss, Jason Robinson, and Jim Watson, for technical help. Some of the research on which the book is based was made possible by a grant from the National Science Foundation (Grant 0076287) to study strategies in reasoning. Chapter 25 on the Wright brothers is based in part on a paper (Johnson-Laird, 2005). I thank my brother Andy Johnson-Laird—an intrepid pilot—for his advice on flying and for a critical reading of this paper, and Nancy Nersessian—an intrepid theorist about mental models in science—for her criticisms of an earlier draft of it.

I owe a big debt to my immediate family. My beloved wife, Mo, was the sixth person to read the whole book. She spoke up for the common reader, and, as a result, I cut whole swathes of incomprehensible verbiage. Our son Ben drew the DesignWorkshop_Lite figures in Chapter 2, and our daughter Dorothy provided brief psychotherapy when necessary. My final acknowledgement is to three intellectual mentors, alas now dead: Peter Wason, Stuart Sutherland, and Jonck, i.e., A.R. Jonckheere.

References

Adams, E.W. (1975) *The Logic of Conditionals: an Application of Probability to Deductive Logic*. Dordrecht: Reidel.

Ahn, W., Kalish, C.W., Medin, D.L., and Gelman, S.A. (1995) The role of covariation versus mechanism information in causal attribution. *Cognition*, 54, 299–352.

Alchourrón, C., Gärdenfors, P., and Makinson, D. (1985) On the logic of theory change: partial meet contraction functions and their associated revision functions. *Journal of Symbolic Logic*, 50, 510–530.

Aleman, A. (2005) Feelings you can't imagine: towards a cognitive neuroscience of alexithymia. *Trends in Cognitive Sciences*, 9, 553–555.

Alloy, L.B. and Abramson, L.Y. (1979) Judgement of contingency in depressed and non-depressed students: sadder but wiser? *Journal of Experimental Psychology*, 108, 441–485.

Alloy, L.B. and Abramson, L.Y. (1988) Depressive realism: four theoretical perspectives. In Alloy, L.B. (ed.), *Cognitive Processes in Depression*. New York: Guilford Press, pp. 223–265.

American Law Institute (1980/1985) *Model Penal Code and Commentaries*. Philadelphia, PA: American Law Institute.

Anderson, H.C. (1996) *The Snow Queen and Other Fairy Tales*. London: Bloomsbury.

Anderson, J.R. (1978) Arguments concerning representations for mental imagery. *Psychological Review*, 85, 249–277.

Anderson, J.R. (1990) *The Adaptive Character of Thought*. Hillsdale, NJ: Erlbaum.

Andrews, G., Creamer, M., Crino, R., Hunt C., Lampe L., and Page, A. (2003) *The Treatment of Anxiety Disorder: Clinician Guides and Patient Manuals*, 2nd edn. Cambridge: Cambridge University Press.

Angluin, D. (1978) Inductive inference of formal languages from positive data. *Information and Control*, 45, 117–135.

Annas, J. and Barnes, J. (1985) *The Modes of Scepticism: Ancient Texts and Modern Interpretations*. Cambridge: Cambridge University Press.

Anno, M. and Nozaki, A. (1984) *Anno's Hat Tricks*. London: Bodley Head.

Arevalo, Z. and Bredeson, J.G. (1978) A method to simplify a Boolean function into a new minimal sum-of-products for programmable logic arrays. *IEEE Transactions on Computing*, C-27, 1028–1030.

Aristotle (1984) Barnes, J. (ed.), *The Complete Works of Aristotle*, Vols 1 and 2. The revised Oxford translation. Princeton, NJ: Princeton University Press.

Asch, S.E. (1956) Studies of independence and conformity: a minority of one against a unanimous majority. *Psychological Monographs*, 70 (Whole no. 416).

Ashley, K. (1990) *Modeling Legal Arguments: Reasoning with Cases and Hypotheticals*. Cambridge, MA: MIT Press.

Auden, W.H. (1962) *The Dyer's Hand and Other Essays*. New York: Random House.

Auden, W.H. (1971) *A Certain World: a Commonplace Book*. London: Faber & Faber.

Auden, W.H. (1973) *Forewords and Afterwords*. New York: Random House.

Auden, W.H. (1976) Mendelson, E. (ed.), *Collected Poems*. New York: Random House.

Auden, W.H. (1977) Mendelson, E. (ed.), *The English Auden: Poems, Essays and Dramatic Writings 1927–1939.* London: Faber & Faber.

Augustine, Saint (1950) *The City of God.* (Trans. Dodds, M.) New York: Modern Library.

Augustine, Saint (1992) *Confessions.* Oxford: Oxford University Press.

Austin, J.L. (1970) Truth. In Urmson, J.O. and Warnock, J.G. (eds), *Philosophical Papers of J.L Austin,* 2nd edn. Oxford: Oxford University Press, pp. 117–133.

Bacon, F. (1985) *The Essays.* Introduction by Pitcher, J. New York: Penguin Putnam. (Originally published 1597.)

Bacon, F. (2000) Jardine, L. and Silverthorne, M. (eds), *The New Organon.* Cambridge: Cambridge University Press. (Originally published 1620).

Baddeley, A.D. (1986) *Working Memory.* Oxford: Clarendon Press.

Baddeley, A.D. (2000) The episodic buffer: a new component of working memory. *Trends in Cognitive Sciences,* 4, 417–423.

Baguley, T. and Payne, S.J. (2000) Given-new versus new-given? An analysis of reading times for spatial descriptions. In Nualláin, S.Ó. (ed.), *Spatial Cognition.* Amsterdam: Benjamins, pp. 317–328.

Baillargeon, R. (1987) Young infants' reasoning about the physical and spatial characteristics of hidden objects. *Cognitive Development,* 2, 178–200.

Baillargeon, R. and Hanko-Summes, S. (1990) Is the top object adequately supported by the bottom object? Young infants' understanding of support relations. *Cognitive Development,* 5, 29–54.

Baillargeon, R., Spelke, E.S., and Wasserman, S. (1985) Object permanence in five-month-old infants. *Cognition,* 20, 191–208.

Bainbridge, W.S. (1997) *The Sociology of Religious Movements.* New York: Routledge.

Bara, B., Bucciarelli, M., and Johnson-Laird, P.N. (1995) The development of syllogistic reasoning. *American Journal of Psychology,* 108, 157–193.

Bargh, J.A., Chen, M., and Burrows, L. (1996) Automaticity of social behavior: direct effects of trait construct and stereotype activation on action. *Journal of Personality and Social Psychology,* 71, 230–244.

Bar-Hillel, M. and Falk, R. (1982) Some teasers concerning conditional probabilities. *Cognition,* 11, 109–122.

Bar-Hillel, M. and Neter, E. (1996) Why are people reluctant to exchange lottery tickets? *Journal of Personality and Social Psychology,* 70, 17–27.

Bar-Hillel, Y. (1967) Dictionaries and meaning rules. *Foundations of Language,* 3, 409–414.

Bar-Hillel, Y. (1969) Colloquium on the role of formal languages. *Foundations of Language,* 5, 256–284.

Bar-Hillel, Y. and Carnap, R. (1964) An outline of a theory of semantic information. In Bar-Hillel, Y *Language and Information Processing.* Reading, MA: Addison-Wesley.

Barnes, B. and Bloor, D. (1982) Relativism, rationalism, and the sociology of knowledge. In Hollis, M. and Lukes, S. (eds), *Rationality and Relativism.* Oxford: Basil Blackwell, pp. 21–47.

Baron, J. (2000) *Thinking and Deciding,* 3rd edn. New York: Cambridge University Press.

Baron, J. and Ritov, I. (1994) Reference points and omission bias. *Organizational Behavior and Human Decision Processes,* 59, 475–498.

Baron-Cohen, S., Leslie, A.M., and Frith, U. (1985) Does the autistic child have a "theory of mind"? *Cognition,* 21, 37–46.

Barres, P. and Johnson-Laird, P.N. (2003) On imagining what is true (and what is false). *Thinking & Reasoning,* 9, 1–42.

Barrouillet, P. (1997) Modifying the representation of if ... then sentences in adolescents by inducing a structure mapping strategy. *Current Psychology of Cognition*, 16, 609–637.

Barrouillet, P. and Leças, J-F. (1998) How can mental models theory account for content effects in conditional reasoning? A developmental perspective. *Cognition*, 209–253.

Barrouillet, P. and Leças, J-F. (1999) Mental models in conditional reasoning and working memory. *Thinking & Reasoning*, 5, 289–302.

Barrouillet, P., Grosset, N., and Leças, J.F. (2000) Conditional reasoning by mental models: chronometric and developmental evidence. *Cognition, 75*, 237–266.

Barsalou, L.W. (1983) Ad hoc categories. *Memory & Cognition*, 11, 211–227.

Barsalou, L.W. (1999) Perceptual symbol systems. *Behavioral and Brain Sciences*, 22, 577–660.

Barwise, J. (1986) Conditionals and conditional information. In Traugott, E.C., ter Meulen, A., Reilly, J.S., and Ferguson, C.A. (eds), *On Conditionals*. Cambridge: Cambridge University Press, pp. 21–54.

Barwise, J. (1987) *The Situation in Logic*. Stanford, CA: CSLI Publications.

Barwise, J. (1993) Everyday reasoning and logical inference. *Behavioral and Brain Sciences*, 16, 337–338.

Barwise, J. and Cooper, R. (1981) Generalized quantifiers and natural language. *Linguistics and Philosophy*, 4, 159–219.

Barwise, J. and Etchemendy, J. (1987) *The Liar: an Essay in Truth and Circularity*. New York: Oxford University Press.

Barwise, J. and Etchemendy, J. (1992) Hyperproof: logical reasoning with diagrams. In Narayanan, N.H. (ed.), *AAAI Spring Symposium on Reasoning with Diagrammatic Representations. March 25–27th, Stanford University, California*, pp. 80–84.

Barwise, J. and Etchemendy, J. (1994) *Hyperproof*. Stanford, CA: Center for the Study of Language and Information.

Bateson, G. (1979) *On Mind and Nature*. London: Wildwood House.

Bauer, M.I. and Johnson-Laird, P.N. (1993) How diagrams can improve reasoning. *Psychological Science*, 4, 372–378.

Beardsley, M.C. (1950) *Practical Logic*. Englewood Cliffs, NJ: Prentice-Hall.

Bechara, A., Damasio, A.R., Damasio, H., and Anderson, S.W. (1994) Insensitivity to future consequences following damage to human prefrontal cortex. *Cognition*, 50, 7–15.

Beck, A.T. (1976) *Cognitive Therapy and the Emotional Disorders*. New York: Meridian.

Beck, A.T. (1991) Cognitive therapy: a 30-year retrospective. *American Psychologist*, 46, 368–375.

Beck, A.T., Rush, A., Shaw, B., and Emery, G. (1979) *Cognitive Therapy of Depression*. New York: Guilford Press.

Bedford, F.L. (1997) False categories in cognition: the not-the-liver fallacy. *Cognition*, 64, 231–248.

Begg, I. and Denny, J. (1969) Empirical reconciliation of atmosphere and conversion interpretations of syllogistic reasoning. *Journal of Experimental Psychology*, 81, 351–354.

Bell, V. (1999) The model method: an aid to improve reasoning. An unpublished Ph.D. dissertation, Department of Psychology, Princeton University.

Bell, V. and Johnson-Laird, P.N. (1998) A model theory of modal reasoning. *Cognitive Science*, 22, 25–51.

Bennett, J.F. (2003) *A Philosophical Guide to Conditionals*. New York: Oxford University Press.

Bentham, J. (1996) Burns, J.H. and Hart, H.L.A. (eds), *An Introduction to the Principles of Morals and Legislation*. Oxford: Clarendon Press. (Originally published in 1789.)

Berardi-Coletta, B., Buyer, L., Dominowski, R., and Rellinger, E. (1995) Metacognition and problem-solving: a process-oriented approach. *Journal of Experimental Psychology: Learning, Memory and Cognition*, 21, 205–223.

Bermond, B., Nieuwenhuyse, B., Fasotti, L., and Schuerman, J. (1991) Spinal cord lesions, peripheral feedback, and intensities of emotional feelings. *Cognition and Emotion*, 5, 201–220.

Berry, G.D.W. (1952) Peirce's contributions to the logic of statements and quantifiers. In Wiener, P. and Young, F. (eds), *Studies in the Philosophy of Charles S. Peirce*. Cambridge, MA: Harvard University Press.

Berwick, R.C. (1986) Learning from positive-only examples: the Subset principle and three case studies. In Michalski, R.S., Carbonell, J.G., and Mitchell, T.M. (eds), *Machine Learning: an Artificial Intelligence Approach*, Vol. II. Los Altos, CA: Morgan Kaufmann.

Beth, E.W. (1971) *Aspects of Modern Logic*. Dordecht: Reidel.

Beth, E.W. and Piaget, J. (1966) *Mathematical Epistemology and Psychology*. Dordrecht: Reidel.

Birbaumer, N., Grodd, W., Diedrick, O., Close, U., Erb, M., Lotze, M., Schneider, F., Weiss, U., and Flor, H. (1998) FMRI reveals amygdala activation to human faces in social phobics. *NeuroReport*, 9, 1223–1226.

Birch, S.A.J. (2005) When knowledge is a curse: children's and adults' reasoning about mental states. *Current Directions in Psychological Science*, 14, 25–29.

Birney, D. and Halford, G.S. (2002) Cognitive complexity of suppositional reasoning: an application of relational complexity to the knight-knave task. *Thinking and Reasoning*, 8, 109–134.

Black, A., Freeman, P., and Johnson-Laird, P.N. (1986) Plausibility and the comprehension of text. *British Journal of Psychology*, 77, 51–62.

Blackburn, S. (2005) *Truth: a Guide*. Oxford: Oxford University Press.

Blanchette, I. and Richards, A. (2004) Reasoning about emotional and neutral materials: is logic affected by emotion? *Psychological Science*, 15, 745–752.

Blanton, H. and Jaccard, J. (2006) Arbitrary metrics in psychology. *American Psychologist*, 61, 27–41.

Bloom, P. and German, T.P. (2000) Two reasons to abandon the false belief task as a test of theory of mind. *Cognition*, 77, B25–B31.

Boden, M.A. (1980) *Jean Piaget*. New York: Viking.

Boltzmann, L. (1974) On the fundamental principles and equations of mechanics. In McGuiness, B. (ed.), *Ludwig Boltzmann: Theoretical Physics and Philosophical Problems*. Boston: Reidel, pp. 101–128. (Originally published 1899.)

Bonnefon, J.-F. (2004) Reinstatement, floating conclusions, and the credulity of mental model reasoning. *Cognitive Science*, 28, 621–631.

Boole, G. (1854) *An Investigation of the Laws of Thought on Which are Founded the Mathematical Theories of Logic and Probabilities*. London: Macmillan.

Boole, M.E. (1909) *Philosophy and Fun of Algebra*. London: C.W. Daniel.

Boolos, G. and Jeffrey, R. (1989) *Computability and Logic*, 3rd edn. Cambridge: Cambridge University Press.

Borges, J.L. (1998) *Collected Fictions*. New York: Penguin.

Boudreau, G. and Pigeau, R. (2001) The mental representaion and processes of spatial deductive reasoning with diagrams and sentences. *International Journal of Psychology*, 36, 42–52.

Bouquet, P. and Warglien, M. (1999) Mental models and local model semantics: the problem of information integration. In Bagnara, S. (ed.), *European Conference on Cognitive Science, 1999*. Siena: Università degli Studi di Siena, pp. 169–178.

Bower, G.H., Black, J.B., and Turner, T.J. (1979) Scripts in memory for text. *Cognitive Psychology*, 11, 177–220.

Bowker, G. (2003) *George Orwell*. London: Little, Brown.

Bowlby, J. (1988) *A Secure Base: Clinical Applications of Attachment Theory*. London: Routledge.

Bowman, W.E. (1956) *The Ascent of Rum Doodle*. London: Max Parrish.

Bozzi, P. (1991) *Fisica Ingenua*. Milan, Italy: Garzanti.

Bradshaw, G. (1992) The airplane and the logic of invention. In Giere, R.N., (ed.), *Cognitive Models of Science*, Vol. XV. Minneapolis: University of Minnesota Press, pp. 239–250.

Braine, M.D.S. (1978) On the relation between the natural logic of reasoning and standard logic. *Psychological Review*, 85, 1–21.

Braine, M.D.S. and O'Brien, D.P. (1991) A theory of If: a lexical entry, reasoning program, and pragmatic principles. *Psychological Review*, 98, 182–203.

Braine, M.D.S. and O'Brien, D.P. (eds) (1998) *Mental Logic*. Mahwah, NJ: Lawrence Erlbaum Associates.

Braine, M.D.S. and Rumain, B. (1983) Logical reasoning. In Flavell, J.H. and Markman, E.M. (eds), *Carmichael's Handbook of Child Psychology*, Vol. III. *Cognitive Development*, 4th ed. New York: Wiley, pp. 263–340.

Braine, M.D.S., Reiser, B.J., and Rumain, B. (1984) Some empirical justification for a theory of natural propositional logic. *The Psychology of Learning and Motivation*, Vol. 18. San Diego, CA: Academic Press, pp. 313–371.

Breiter, H.C, Rauch, S.L., Kwong, K.K., Baker, J.R., Weisskoff, R.M., Kennedy, D.N., Kendrich, A.D., Davis, T.L., Jiang, A., Cohen, M.S., Stern, C.E., Belliveau, J.W., Baer, L., O'Sullivan, R.L., Savage, C.R., Jenike, M.A., and Rosen, B.R. (1996) Functional magnetic resonance imaging in symptom provocation in obsessive-compulsive disorder. *Archives of General Psychiatry*, 53, 595–606.

Brewka, G., Dix, J., and Konolige, K. (1997) *Nonmonotonic Reasoning: an Overview*. Stanford, CA: CLSI Publications, Stanford University.

Broadbent, D.E. and Broadbent, M. (1988) Anxiety and attentional bias: state and trait. *Cognition and Emotion*, 2, 165–183.

Broadbent, D.E., Fitzgerald, P., and Broadbent, M.H.P. (1986) Implicit and explicit knowledge in the control of complex systems. *British Journal of Psychology*, 17, 33–50.

Bruner, J.S., Goodnow, J.A., and Austin, G.A. (1956) *A Study of Thinking*. New York: Wiley.

Bryant, D.J. (1992a) A spatial representation system in humans. *Psycoloquy*, 3(16) Space.1 [An on-line journal]

Bryant, D.J. (1992b) More on the spatial representation system. *Psycoloquy*, 3, (44) Space.5 [An on-line journal]

Bucciarelli, M. and Johnson-Laird, P.N. (1999) Strategies in syllogistic reasoning. *Cognitive Science*, 23, 247–303.

Bucciarelli, M. and Johnson-Laird, P.N. (2000) Is there an innate module for deontic reasoning? In García-Madruga, J., Carriedo, N, and Gonzalez-Labra, M.J. (eds), *Mental Models in Reasoning*. Madrid: UNED, pp. 227–239.

Bucciarelli, M. and Johnson-Laird, P.N. (2001) Falsification and the role of the theory of mind in the reduced array selection task. *Current Psychology Letters: Behavior, Brain and Cognition*, 4, 7–22.

Bucciarelli, M. and Johnson-Laird, P.N. (2005) Naïve deontics: a theory of meaning, representation, and reasoning. *Cognitive Psychology*, 50, 159–193.

Buchanan, T.W. and Adophs, R. (2002) The role of the human amygdala in emotional modulation of long-term declarative memory. In Moore, S.C. and Oaksford, M. (eds), *Emotional Cognition: from Brain to Behaviour*. Amsterdam: John Benjamins, pp. 9–34.

Budiansky, S. (2000) *Battle of Wits: the Complete Story of Codebreaking in World War II*. New York: Simon & Schuster.

Bulbrook, M.E. (1932) An experimental study into the existence and nature of "insight". *American Journal of Psychology*, 44, 409–453.

Buller, D.J. (2005) *Adapting Minds: Evolution and the Persistent Quest for Human Nature*. Cambridge, MA: MIT Press.

Bullock, M., Gelman, R., and Baillargeon, R. (1982) The development of causal reasoning. In Friedman, W.J. (ed.), *The Developmental Psychology of Time*. Orlando, FL: Academic Press, pp. 209–254.

Burke, P. (1986) Strengths and weaknesses in the history of mentalities. *History of European Ideas*, 7, 439–451.

Byrne, R.M.J. (1989) Suppressing valid inferences with conditionals. *Cognition*, 31, 61–83.

Byrne, R.M.J. (1991) Can valid inferences be suppressed? *Cognition*, 39, 71–78.

Byrne, R.M.J. (1996) A model theory of imaginary thinking. In Oakhill, J. and Garnham, A. (eds), *Mental Models in Cognitive Science*. Hove: Erlbaum (UK) Taylor & Francis, pp. 155–174.

Byrne, R.M.J. (1997) Cognitive processes in counterfactual thinking about what might have been. In Medin, D.L. (ed.), *The Psychology of Learning and Motivation*, Vol. 37. San Diego, CA: Academic Press, pp. 105–154.

Byrne, R.M.J. (2002) Mental models and counterfactual thoughts about what might have been. *Trends in Cognitive Sciences*, 6, 426–431.

Byrne, R.M.J. (2005) *The Rational Imagination: How People Create Alternatives to Reality*. Cambridge, MA: MIT Press.

Byrne, R.M.J. and Handley, S.J. (1992) Reasoning strategies. *Irish Journal of Psychology*, 13, 111–124.

Byrne, R.M.J. and Handley, S.J. (1997) Reasoning strategies for suppositional deductions. *Cognition*, 62, 1–49.

Byrne, R.M.J. and Johnson-Laird, P.N. (1989) Spatial reasoning. *Journal of Memory and Language*, 28, 564–575.

Byrne, R.M.J. and McEleney, A. (2000) Counterfactual thinking about actions and failures to act. *Journal of Experimental Psychology: Learning, Memory, and Cognition*, 26, 1318–1331.

Byrne, R.M.J. and Tasso, A. (1999) Deductive reasoning with factual, possible, and counterfactual conditionals. *Memory & Cognition*, 27, 726–740.

Byrne, R.M.J., Handley, S.J., and Johnson-Laird, P.N. (1995) Reasoning from suppositions. *Quarterly Journal of Experimental Psychology*, 48A, 915–944.

Byrne, R.M.J., Espino, O., and Santamaría, C. (1999) Counterexamples and the suppression of inferences. *Journal of Memory and Language*, 40, 347–373.

Byrnes, J.P. and Duff, M.A. (1989) Young children's comprehension of modal expressions. *Cognitive Development*, 4, 369–387.

Calder, A.J., Young, A.W., Rowland, D., Perrett, D., Hodges, J.R., and Etcoff, N.L. (1996) Facial emotion recognition after bilateral amygdala damage: differentially severe impairment of fear. *Cognitive Neuropsychology*, 13, 699–745.

Campbell, D. (1960) Blind variation and selective retention in creative thought as in other knowledge processes. *Psychological Review*, 67, 380–400.

Cardaci, M., Gangemi, A., Pendolino, G., and Di Nuovo, S. (1996) Mental models vs. integrated models: explanations of syllogistic reasoning. *Perceptual and Motor Skills*, 82, 1377–1378.

Carey, S. (1985a) Are children fundamentally different kinds of thinkers and learners than adults? In Chipman, S.F., Segal, J.W., and Glaser, R. (eds), *Thinking and Learning Skills*, Vol. 2: *Research and Open Questions*. Hillsdale, NJ: Erlbaum pp. 485–517.

Carey, S. (1985b) *Conceptual Change in Childhood*. Cambridge: MIT Press.

Carey, S. (1988) Conceptual differences between children and adults. *Mind & Language*, 3, 167–181.

Carey, S. (1991) Knowledge acquisition: enrichment or conceptual change? In Carey, S. and Gelman, R. (eds), *The Epigenesis of Mind: Essays on Biology and Cognition*. Hillsdale, NJ: Erlbaum, pp. 257–291.

Carlisle, E. and Shafir, E. (2005) Questioning the cheater-detection hypothesis: new studies with the selection task. *Thinking & Reasoning*, 11, 97–122.

Carnap, R. (1966) *Philosophical Foundations of Physics*. New York: Basic Books.

Carreiras, M. and Santamaría, C. (1997) Reasoning about relations: spatial and nonspatial problems. *Thinking & Reasoning*, 3, 191–208.

Carroll, L. (1958) *Symbol Logic and the Game of Logic*. (Two books bound as one) New York: Dover.

Case, R. (1985a) A developmentally based approach to the problem of instructional design. In Chipman, S.F., Segal, J.W., and Glaser, R. (eds), *Thinking and Learning Skills*, Vol. 2: *Research and Open Questions*. Hillsdale, NJ: Erlbaum, pp. 545–562.

Case, R. (1985b) *Intellectual Development: Birth to Adulthood*. New York: Academic Press.

Chaitin, G.J. (1998) *The Limits of Mathematics: a Course on Information Theory and the Limits of Formal Reasoning*. Singapore: Springer-Verlag.

Chalmers, D.J., French, R.M., and Hofstadter, D.R. (1992) High-level perception, representation, and analogy: a critique of artificial intelligence methodology. *Journal of Experimental & Theoretical Artificial Intelligence*, 4, 185–211.

Chapman, L.J. and Chapman, A.P. (1959) Atmosphere effect re-examined. *Journal of Experimental Psychology*, 58, 220–226.

Chater, N. and Oaksford, M. (1999) The probability heuristics model of syllogistic reasoning. *Cognitive Psychology* 38, 191–258.

Chater, N., Heit, E., and Oaksford, M. (2005) Reasoning. In Lamberts, K. and Goldstone, R.L. (eds), *Handbook of Cognition*. Thousand Oaks, CA: Sage, pp. 297–320.

Cheng, P.W. (1997) From covariation to causation: a causal power theory. *Psychological Review*, 104, 367–405.

Cheng, P.W. and Holyoak, K.J. (1985) Pragmatic reasoning schemas. *Cognitive Psychology*, 17, 391–416.

Cheng, P.W. and Holyoak, K.J. (1989) On the natural selection of reasoning theories. *Cognition*, 33, 285–313.

Cheng, P.W., and Novick, L.R. (1990) A probabilistic contrast model of causal induction. *Journal of Personality and Social Psychology*, 58, 545–567.

Cheng, P.W. and Novick, L.R. (1991) Causes versus enabling conditions. *Cognition*, 40, 83–120.

Cheng, P.W., Holyoak, K.J., Nisbett, R.E., and Oliver, L.M. (1986) Pragmatic versus syntactic approaches to training deductive reasoning. *Cognitive Psychology*. 18, 293–328.

Cherniak, C. (1986) *Minimal Rationality*. Cambridge, MA: MIT Press.

Cherry, C. (1980) *On Human Communication: a Review, a Survey, and a Criticism*, 3rd edn (revised edition). Cambridge, MA: MIT Press.

Cherubini, P. and Johnson-Laird, P.N. (2004) Does everyone love everyone? The psychology of iterative reasoning. *Thinking & Reasoning*, 10, 31–53.

Cherubini, P., Garnham, A., Oakhill, J., and Morley, E. (1998) Can any ostrich fly? Some new data on belief bias in syllogistic reasoning. *Cognition*, 69, 179–218.

Chi, M.T.H. (1976) Short-term memory limitations in children: capacity or processing deficits? *Memory & Cognition*, 4, 559–572.

Chi, M.T.H. (1978) Knowledge structures and memory development. In Siegler, R.S. (ed.), *Children's Thinking: What Develops?* Hillsdale, NJ: Erlbaum, pp. 73–96.

Chomsky, N. (1995) *The Minimalist Program*. Cambridge, MA: MIT Press.

Christie, A. (1960) *Murder on the Orient Express*. New York: Penguin Putnam. (Originally published in 1933.)

Chronicle, E.P., Ormerod, T.C., and MacGregor, J.N. (2001) When insight just won't come: the failure of visual cues in the nine-dot problem. *Quarterly Journal of Experimental Psychology*, 54A, 903–919.

Clark, H.H. (1969) Linguistic processes in deductive reasoning. *Psychological Review*, 76, 387–404.

Clark, H.H. (1973) Space, time, semantics, and the child. In Moore, T.E. (ed.), *Cognitive Development and the Acquisition of Language*. New York: Academic Press, pp. 28–64.

Clark, H.H. and Chase, W.G. (1972) On the process of comparing sentences against pictures. *Cognitive Psychology*, 3, 472–517.

Clark, H.H. and Haviland, S.E. (1977) Comprehension and the given-new contract. In Freedle, R.O. (ed.), *Discourse Processes: Advances in Research and Theory*, Vol. 1: *Discourse Production and Comprehension*. Norwood, NJ: Ablex, pp. 1–40.

Clement, C.A., and Falmagne, R.J. (1986) Logical reasoning, world knowledge, and mental imagery: interconnections in cognitive processes. *Memory & Cognition*, 14, 299–307.

Cohen, E.D. (2003) *Self-control through the Power of Reason: What would Aristotle do?* New York: Prometheus Books.

Cohen, L.J. (1981) Can human irrationality be experimentally demonstrated? *Behavioral and Brain Sciences*, 4, 317–370.

Cohen, M.R. and Nagel, E. (1934) *An Introduction to Logic and Scientific Method*. London: Routledge & Kegan Paul.

Cole, M., Gay, J., Glick, J.A., and Sharp, D.W. (1971) *The Cultural Context of Learning and Thinking*. New York: Basic Books.

Collins, A. and Michalski, R. (1989) The logic of plausible reasoning: a core theory. *Cognitive Science*, 13, 1–49.

Combs, H. (1979) *Kill Devil Hill: Discovering the Secret of the Wright Brothers*. (With M. Caidin). Boston, MA: Houghton Mifflin.

Conan Doyle, A. (1930) *The Complete Sherlock Holmes*, Vols. I and II. New York: Doubleday.

Consumer Reports (1995) *Mental Health: Does Therapy Help?* November, 734–739.

Cook, V.J. and Newson, M. (1996) *Chomsky's Universal Grammar: an Introduction*, 2nd edn. Oxford: Blackwell.

Copeland, D.E. and Radvansky, G.A. (2004) Working memory and syllogistic reasoning. *Quarterly Journal of Experimental Psychology*, 57A, 1437–1457.

Corlett, P.R., Aitken, M.R.F., Dickinson, A., Shanks, D.R., Honey, G.D., Honey, R.A.E., Robbins, T.W., Bullmore, E.T., and Fletcher, P.C. (2004) Prediction error during retrospective revaluation of causal associations in humans: fMRI evidence in favor of an associative model of learning. *Neuron*, 44, 877–888.

Cosmides, L. (1989) The logic of social exchange: Has natural selection shaped how humans reason? *Cognition*, 31, 187–276.

Cosmides, L. and Tooby, J. (1996) Are humans good intuitive statisticians after all? Rethinking some conclusions from the literature on judgment under uncertainty. *Cognition*, 58, 1–73.

Cozzutti, C. and Vallortigara, G. (2001) Hemispheric memories for the content and position of food caches in the domestic chick. *Behavioral Neuroscience*, 115, 305–313.

Craig, D.L., Nersessian, N.J., and Catrambone, R. (2002) Perceptual simulation in analogical problem solving. In Magnani, L., and Nersessian, N. (eds), *Model-Based Reasoning: Science, Technology, Values*. New York: Kluwer Academic/Plenum, pp. 169–187.

Craik, K. (1943) *The Nature of Explanation*. Cambridge: Cambridge University Press.

Crick, F. (1988) *What Mad Pursuit*. New York: Basic Books.

Crouch, T.D. (1989) *The Bishop's Boys: a Life of Wilbur and Orville Wright*. New York: W.W. Norton.

Crutchfield, R.S. (1955) Conformity and character. *American Psychologist*, 10, 191–198.

Cummins, D.D. (1995) Naïve theories and causal deduction. *Memory & Cognition*, 23, 646–658.

Cummins, D.D. (1998) The pragmatics of causal inference. *Proceedings of the Twentieth Annual Conference of the Cognitive Science Society*, p. 9.

Cummins, D.D., Lubart, T., Alksnis, O., and Rist, R. (1991) Conditional reasoning and causation. *Memory & Cognition*, 19, 274–282.

Cunningham, W.A., Johnson, M.K., Raye, C.L., Gatenby, J.C., Gore, J.C., and Banaji, M.R. (2004). Separable neural components in the processing of Black and White faces. *Psychological Science*, 15, 806–813.

Curtiss, S. (1977) *Genie: a Psycholinguistic Study of a Modern Day "Wild Child"*. New York: Academic Press.

Dadlez, E.M. (1997) *What's Hecuba to Him?Fictional Events and Actual Emotions*. University Park, PA: Pennsylvania State University Press.

Damasio, A.R. (1994) *Descartes' Error: Emotion, Reason, and the Human Brain*. New York: Grosset/Putnam.

Darwin, C. (1887) *The Life and Letters of Charles Darwin*. Darwin, F. (ed.), London: Murray.

Darwin, C. (1965) *The Expression of the Emotions in Man and Animals*. Chicago, IL: University of Chicago Press. (Originally published in 1872.)

Darwin, C. (1989) *Voyage of the Beagle*. New York: Penguin Putnam. (Originally published in 1839.)

Dasen, P. (1994) Culture and cognitive development from a Piagetian perspective. In Lonner, W. and Malpass, R. (eds), *Psychology and Culture*. Boston: Allyn and Bacon, pp. 145–149.

Davidson, D. (1980) Actions, reasons and causes. In Davidson, D. (ed.), *Essays on Actions and Events*. Oxford: Oxford University Press, pp. 3–20.

Davidson, R.J., Pizzagalli, D., Nitschke, J.B., and Putman, K. (2002) Depression: Perspective from affective neuroscience. *Annual Review of Psychology*, 53, 545–574.

Dawes, R. (2001) *Everyday Irrationality: How Pseudoscientists, Lunatics, and the Rest of Us Fail to Think Rationally.* Boulder, CO: Westview Press.

Dawkins, R. (1976) *The Selfish Gene.* Oxford: Oxford University Press.

Day, C. (1996) Understanding of the French modal verbs "pouvoir" and "devoir" in school children and adults. *Current Psychology of Cognition*, 15, 535–553.

Deary, I.J. (2005) Intelligence, health and death. *The Psychologist*, 18, 610–613.

De Bono, E. (1992) *Serious Creativity: Using the Power of Lateral Thinking to Create New Ideas.* London: Harper Collins.

Dehaene, S. Izard, V., Pica, P., and Spelke, E. (2006) Core knowledge of geometry in an Amazonian indigene group. *Science*, 311, 381–384.

Delius, J.D. and Siemann., M. (1998) Transitive responding in animals and humans. Exaptation rather than adaptation? *Behavioural Processes*, 42, 107–137.

Delval, J.A. and Riviere, A. (1975) "Si llueve, Elisa lleva sombrero": Una investigación psicologia sobre la tabla de verdad del condicional. *Revista De Psicologia General y Aplicada*, 136, 825–850.

Descartes, R. (1967) *A Discourse on Method.* In Haldane, E.S., and Ross, G.R.T. (trans.) *The Philosophical Works of Descartes*, 2 Vols. Cambridge: Cambridge University Press. (Originally published in 1637.)

Descartes, R. (1984–91) Les passions de l'âme (The Passions of the Soul) In Cottingham, J., Stoothoff, R., Murdoch, D., and Kenny, A. (eds and trans.) *The Philosophical Writings of Descartes*, Vol. 1. Cambridge: Cambridge University Press. (Originally published in 1649.)

De Soto, C., London, M., and Handel, S. (1965) Social reasoning and spatial paralogic. *Journal of Personality and Social Psychology*, 2, 513–521.

Dewdney, A.K. (1989) *The Turing Omnibus: 61 Excursions in Computer Science.* Rockville, MD: Computer Science Press.

Dias, M., Roazzi, A., and Harris, P.L. (2005) Reasoning from unfamiliar premises: a study with unschooled adults. *Psychological Science*, 16, 550–554.

Dicheva, D. and Close J. (1996) Mental models of recursion. *Journal of Educational Computing Research*, 14, 1–23.

Dickstein, L.S. (1975) Effects of instructions and premise order on errors in syllogistic reasoning. *Journal of Experimental Psychology*: Human Learning and Memory, 104, 376–384.

Dieussaert, K., Schaeken, W., De Neys, W., and d'Ydewalle, G. (2000) Initial belief state as a predictor of belief revision. *Current Psychology of Cognition*, 19, 277–288.

Dijksterhuis, A., Bos, M.W., Nordgren, L.F., and van Baaren, R.B. (2006) On making the right choice: the deliberation-without-attention effect. *Science*, 311, 1005–1007.

Dixit, A.K. and Nalebuff, B.J. (1991) *Thinking Strategically: the Competitive Edge in Business, Politics, and Everyday Life.* New York: Norton.

Dominowski, R.L. (1995) Content effects in Wason's selection task. In Newstead, S.E. and Evans, J.St.B.T. (eds), *Perspectives on Thinking and Reasoning: Essays in Honor of Peter Wason.* Hillsdale, NJ: Erlbaum, pp. 41–65.

Dörner, D. (1996) *The Logic of Failure: Why Things Go Wrong and What We Can Do to Make Them Right.* New York: Holt. (Originally published in 1989.)

Dostoyevsky, F.M. (1972) *Notes from Underground.* Coulson, J. (trans.) Harmondsworth, Middlesex: Penguin. (Originally published 1864.)

Doyle, J. (1979) A truth maintenance system. *Artificial Intelligence*, 12, 231–272.

Dreyfus, H.L. (1972) *What Computers Can't Do: a Critique of Artificial Intelligence*. New York: Harper and Row.

DSM-IV-TR (2000) American Psychiatric Assocation.

Dudman, V.H. (1988) Indicative and subjunctive conditionals. *Analysis*, 48, 113–122.

Dunbar, K. (1995) How scientists really reason: scientific reasoning in real-world laboratories. In Sternberg, R.J. and Davidson, J. (eds), *The Nature of Insight*. Cambridge, MA: MIT Press, pp. 365–395.

Duncker, K. (1945) On problem solving. *Psychological Monographs*, 58(5), whole number 270.

Dunne, P.E. (1988) *The Complexity of Boolean Networks*. London: Academic Press.

Dyson, G.B. (1997) *Darwin among the Machines: the Evolution of Global Intelligence*. Reading, MA: Helix Books, Addison-Wesley.

Edwards, A.W.F. (2004) *Cogwheels of the Mind: the Story of Venn Diagrams*. Baltimore: Johns Hopkins University Press.

Egan, D.E. and Grimes-Farrow, D.D. (1982) Differences in mental representations spontaneously adopted for reasoning. *Memory & Cognition*, 10, 297–307.

Eells, E. and Skyrms, B. (eds) (1994) *Probability and Conditionals*. Cambridge: Cambridge University Press.

Eichenbaum, H. (1999) The hippocampus. In Wilson, R.A. and Keil, F.C. (eds). *The MIT Encyclopedia of the Cognitive Sciences*. Cambridge, MA: MIT Press, pp. 377–378.

Eilam, E. (2005) *Reversing: Secrets of Reverse Engineering*. Indianopolis, IN: Wiley.

Einhorn, H.J. and Hogarth, R.M. (1986) Judging probable cause. *Psychological Bulletin*, 99, 3–19.

Ekman, P. (1980) Biological and cultural contributions to body and facial movement in the expression of emotion. In Rorty, A.O. (ed.), *Explaining Emotion*. Berkeley: University of California Press.

Ekman, P. (1992a) An argument for basic emotions. *Cognition and Emotion*, 6, 169–200.

Ekman, P. (1992b) Facial expression of emotion: new findings, new questions. *Psychological Science*, 3, 34–38.

Ekman, P. (1995) *Telling Lies: Clues to Deceit in the Marketplace, Politics, and Marriage*. New York: Norton.

Ekman, P., Davidson, R.J., Ricard, M., and Wallace, B.A. (2005) Buddhist and psychological perspectives on emotions and well-being. *Current Directions in Psychological Science*, 14, 59–63.

Eley, T.C. and Plomin, R. (1997) Genetic analyses of emotionality. *Current Opinion in Neurobiology*, 7, 279–284.

Elio, R. and Pelletier, F.J. (1997) Belief change as propositional update. *Cognitive Science*, 21, 419–460.

Ellis, A. (1962) *Reason and Emotion in Psychotherapy*. New York: Lyle Stuart.

Elster, J. (1999) *Alchemies of the Mind*. Cambridge: Cambridge University Press.

Erdelyi, M.H. (1985) *Psychoanalysis: Freud's Cognitive Psychology*. New York: Freeman.

Erickson, J.R. (1974) A set analysis theory of behavior in formal syllogistic reasoning tasks. In Solso, R. (ed.), *Loyola Symposium on Cognition*, Vol. 2. Hillsdale, NJ: Erlbaum, pp. 305–329.

Ericsson, K.A. and Simon, H.A. (1980) Verbal reports as data. *Psychological Review*, 87, 215–251.

Espino, O., Santamaría, C., and García-Madruga, J.A. (2000a) Activation of end terms in syllogistic reasoning. *Thinking & Reasoning*, 6, 67–89.

Espino, O., Santamaría, C., Meseguer, E., and Carreiras, M. (2000b) Eye movements during syllogistic reasoning. In García-Madruga, J.A., Carriedo, N., and González-Labra, M.J. (eds), *Mental Models in Reasoning*. Madrid: Universidad Nacional de Educación a Distancia, pp. 179–188.

Espino, O., Santamaría, C., Meseguer, E., and Carreiras, M. (2005) Early and late processes in syllogistic reasoning: evidence from eye-movements. *Cognition*, 98, B1–B9.

Evans, G. (1980) Pronouns. *Linguistic Inquiry*, 11, 337–362.

Evans, J.St.B.T. (1972a) Deductive reasoning and linguistic usage (with special reference to negation). Unpublished Ph.D. thesis, University of London.

Evans, J.St.B.T. (1972b) Interpretation and matching bias in a reasoning task. *Quarterly Journal of Experimental Psychology*, 24, 193–199.

Evans, J.St.B.T. (1984) Heuristic and analytic processes in reasoning. *British Journal of Psychology*, 75, 451–468.

Evans, J.St.B.T. (1989) *Bias in Human Reasoning: Causes and Consequences*. Hillsdale, NJ: Erlbaum.

Evans, J.St.B.T. (2003) In two minds: dual process accounts of reasoning. *Trends in Cognitive Sciences*, 7, 454–459.

Evans, J.St.B.T. and Over, D.E. (1996) *Rationality and Reasoning*. Hove, East Sussex: Psychology Press.

Evans, J.St.B.T. and Over, D.E. (2004) *If*. Oxford: Oxford University Press.

Evans, J.St.B.T., Barston, J.L., and Pollard, P. (1983) On the conflict between logic and belief in syllogistic reasoning. *Memory and Cognition*, 11, 295–306.

Evans, J.St.B.T., Newstead, S.E., and Byrne, R.M.J. (1993) *Human Reasoning: the Psychology of Deduction*. Hillsdale, NJ: Erlbaum.

Evans, J.St.B.T., Handley, S.J., Harper, C.N.J., and Johnson-Laird, P.N. (1999) Reasoning about necessity and possibility: a test of the mental model theory of deduction. *Journal of Experimental Psychology: Learning, Memory, and Cognition*, 25, 1495–1513.

Evans, J.St.B.T., Handley, S.H., Perham, N., Over, D.E., and Thompson, V.A. (2000) Frequency versus probability formats in statistical word problems. *Cognition*, 77, 197–213.

Evans, J.St.B.T., Handley, S.H., and Over, D.E. (2003) Conditionals and conditional probability. *Journal of Experimental Psychology: Learning, Memory and Cognition*, 29, 321–335.

Evans, J.St.B.T., Over, D.E., and Handley, S.J. (2005) Supposition, extensionality, and conditionals: a critique of the mental model theory of Johnson-Laird and Byrne (2002). *Psychological Review*, 112, 1042–1052.

Evans-Pritchard, E.E. (1937) *Witchcraft: Oracles and Magic Among the Azande*. Oxford: Clarendon Press.

Eysenck, H.J. and Eysenck, S.B.G. (1975) *Manual of the Eysenck Personality Questionnaire*. London: Hodder & Stoughton.

Falk, R. (1992) A closer look at the probabilities of the notorious three prisoners. *Cognition*, 43, 197–223.

Falkenhainer, B., Forbus, K.D., and Gentner, D. (1989) The structure mapping engine: algorithm and examples. *Artificial Intelligence*, 41, 1–63.

Falmagne, R.J. (1980) The development of logical competence. In Kluwe, R. H. and Spada, M. (eds), *Developmental Models of Thinking*. New York: Academic Press.

Farah, M.J., Hammond, K.M., Levine, D.L., and Calvanio, R. (1988) Visual and spatial mental imagery: dissociable systems of representation. *Cognitive Psychology*, 20, 439–462.

Feeney, A. and Handley, S.J. (2000) The suppression of q card selections: evidence for deductive inference in Wason's Selection Task. *Quarterly Journal of Experimental Psychology*, 53A, 4, 1224–1242.

Feldman, J. (2004) How surprising is a simple pattern? Quantifying "Eureka!" *Cognition*, 93, 199–224.

Fenker, D.B., Waldmann, M.R., and Holyoak, K.J. (2005) Accessing causal relations in semantic memory. *Memory & Cognition*, 33, 1036–1046.

Ferguson, E.S. (1992) *Engineering and the Mind's Eye*. Cambridge, MA: MIT Press.

Festinger, L., Riecken, H., and Schacter, S. (1956) *When Prophecy Fails: a Social and Psychological Study of a Modern Group that Predicted the Destruction of the World*. Mineapolis, MN: University of Minnesota.

Feynman, R.P. (1985) *Surely You're Joking, Mr. Feynman: Adventures of a Curious Character*. (Written with Ralph Leighton; Ed. Hutchings, E.) New York: W.W. Norton.

Feynman, R.P. (1988) *What Do You Care What Other People Think?* New York: Norton.

Feynman, R.P., Leighton, R.B., and Sands, M. (1963) *The Feynman Lectures on Physics*, Vol. 1: *Mainly Mechanics, Radiation, and Heat*. Reading, MA: Addison-Wesley.

Fiddick, L. (2004) Domains of deontic reasoning: resolving the discrepancy between the cognitive and moral reasoning literatures. *Quarterly Journal of Experimental Psychology*, 57A, 447–474.

Fiedler, K. and Schenck, W. (2001) Spontaneous inferences from pictorially presented behaviors. *Personality and Social Psychology Bulletin*, 27, 1533–1546.

Fillenbaum, S. (1976) Inducements: On the phrasing and logic of conditional promises, threats and warnings. *Psychological Research*, 38, 231–250.

Fillmore, C.J. (1971) Toward a theory of deixis. Paper presented at Pacific conference on Contrastive Linguistics and Language Universals, University of Hawaii, Honolulu, January.

Findlay, A. (1937) *A Hundred Years of Chemistry*. London: Duckworth.

Finke, R.A. and Slayton, K. (1988) Explorations of creative visual synthesis in mental imagery. *Memory and Cognition*, 16, 252–257.

Fisher, A. (1988) *The Logic of Real Arguments*. Cambridge: Cambridge University Press.

Fisher, D.L. (1981) A three-factor model of syllogistic reasoning: the study of isolable stages. *Memory & Cognition*, 9, 496–514.

Fisher, S.C. (1916) The process of generalizing abstraction; and its product, the general concept. *Psychological Monographs*, 21, No. 2 (whole number 90).

Fitch, W.T., Hauser, M., and Chomsky, N. (2005) The evolution of the language faculty: clarifications and implications. *Cognition*, 97, 179–210.

Flavell, J.H. (1963) *The Developmental Psychology of Jean Piaget*. Princeton, NJ: Van Nostrand.

Fodor, J.A. (1975) *The Language of Thought*. New York: Crowell.

Fodor, J.A. (1980) Fixation of belief and concept acquisition. In Piattelli-Palmarini, M. (ed.), *Language and Learning: the Debate Between Jean Piaget and Noam Chomsky*. London: Routledge & Kegan Paul, pp. 143–149.

Fodor, J.A. (1981) *Representations*. Brighton, Sussex: Harvester Press.

Fodor, J.A. (1983) *The Modularity of Mind: an Essay on Faculty Psychology*. Cambridge, MA: Bradford Books, MIT Press.

Fodor, J.A. and McLaughlin, B.P. (1990) Connectionism and the problem of systematicity: why Smolensky's solution doesn't work. *Cognition*, 35, 183–204.

Fodor, J.A. and Pylyshyn, Z. (1988) Connectionism and cognitive architecture: a critical analysis. *Cognition*, 35, 3–71.

Foot, P. (2002) The problem of abortion and the doctrine of the double effect. In *Virtues and Vices*. Oxford: Oxford University Press, pp. 19–32. (Essay originally published in 1967.)

Ford, M. (1995) Two modes of mental representation and problem solution in syllogistic reasoning. *Cognition*, 54, 1–71.

Forkman B. (2000) Domestic hens have declarative representations. *Animal Cognition*, 3, 135–137.

Fortenbaugh, W. (1975) *Aristotle on Emotions*. London: Duckworth.

Frayn, M. (1965) *The Tin Men*. Boston: Little, Brown.

Frank, R. (1988) *Passions Within Reason: the Strategic Role of Emotions*. New York: Norton.

Franklin, J. (2001) *The Science of Conjecture: Evidence and Probability Before Pascal*. Baltimore, MD: Johns Hopkins University Press.

Fraser, J.G. (1890) *The Golden Bough: a Study of Magic and Religion*. Oxford: Oxford University Press.

Freeman, J.B. (1988) *Thinking Logically*. Englewood Cliffs, NJ: Prentice-Hall.

Frege, G. (1967) Begriffsschrift: a formula language, modeled upon that of arithmetic, for pure thought. In Van Heijenoort, J. (ed.), *From Frege to Gödel: a Source Book in Mathematical Logic, 1879–1931*. Cambridge, MA: Harvard University Press, pp. 5–82. (Originally published in German in 1879.)

Freud, S. (1915) *The Unconscious*. In *The Standard Edition of the Complete Works of Sigmund Freud*, Vol. 14. (Ed. and trans. James Strachey.) London: the Hogarth Press and the Institute of Psychoanalysis, 1953–74, pp. 161–215.

Freud, S. (1973) *New Introductory Lectures On Psychoanalysis*. Harmondsworth, Middx: Penguin. (Trans. J. Strachey, first published, 1964; Original German version published in 1933.)

Frijda, N.H. (1986) *The Emotions*. Cambridge: Cambridge University Press.

Frost, W.H. (ed.) (1965) *Snow on Cholera, Being a Reprint of Two Papers by John Snow MD Together with a Biographical Memoir by J.W. Richardson*. New York: Hafner. Originally published in 1936.

Fuhrmann, A. (1997) *An Essay on Contraction*. Stanford, CA: CSLI Publications.

Fujimura, K. (1978) *The Tokyo Puzzles*. New York: Scribner. (Originally published in 1884.)

Galotti, K.M., Baron, J., and Sabini, J.P. (1986) Individual differences in syllogistic reasoning: deduction rules or mental models? *Journal of Experimental Psychology: General*, 115, 16–25.

Galton, F. (1928) *Inquiries into Human Faculty and its Development*. London: Dent. (Originally published in 1880.)

García-Madruga, J.A., Moreno, S., Carriedo, N., Gutiérrez, F., and Johnson-Laird, P.N. (2001) Are conjunctive inferences easier than disjunctive inferences? A comparison of rules and models. *Quarterly Journal of Experimental Psychology*, 54A, 613–632.

Gärdenfors, P. (1988) *Knowledge in Flux*. Cambridge, MA: MIT Press.

Gärdenfors, P. (1990) The dynamics of belief systems: foundations vs. coherence theories. *Revue Internationale de Philosophie*, 172, 24–46.

Garey, M., and Johnson, D. (1979) *Computers and Intractability: a Guide to the Theory of NP-completeness* San Francisco, CA: Freeman.

Garnham, A. (1987) *Mental Models as Representations of Discourse and Text*. Chichester: Ellis Horwood.

Garnham, A. (2001) *Mental Models and the Representation of Anaphora*. Hove, East Sussex: Psychology Press.

Garnham, A., Oakhill, J.V., Erlich, M-F., and Carreiras, M. (1995) Representation and process in the interpretation of pronouns: new evidence from Spanish and French. *Journal of Memory and Language*, 34, 41–62.

Gauker, C. (2005) *Conditionals in Context*. Cambridge, MA: MIT Press.

Gavanski, I. and Wells, G.L. (1989) Counterfactual processing of normal and exceptional events. *Journal of Experimental Social Psychology*, 25, 314–325.

Geertz, C. (1984) Anti anti-relativism. *American Anthropologist*, 86, 263–277.

Gellner, E. (1970) Concepts and society. In Wilson, B.R. (ed.), *Rationality*. Oxford: Blackwell, pp. 18–49.

Gelman, S.A. and Markman, E.M. (1986) Categories and induction in young children. *Cognition*, 23, 183–209.

Geminiani, G.C., Carassa, A., and Bara, B.G. (1996) Causality by contact. In Oakhill, J., and Garnham, A. (eds), *Mental Models in Cognitive Science*. Hove, East Sussex: Psychology Press, pp. 275–303.

Gentner, D. (1983) Structure mapping: a theoretical framework for analogy. *Cognitive Science*, 7, 155–170.

Gentzen, G. (1969) Investigations into logical deduction. In Szabo, M.E. (ed.), *The Collected Papers of Gerhard Gentzen*. Amsterdam: North-Holland, pp. 68–131. (Originally published, 1935.)

Geurts, B. (2003) Reasoning with quantifiers. *Cognition*, 86, 223–251.

Gick, M. and Holyoak, K. (1983) Schema induction and analogical transfer. *Cognitive Psychology*, 15, 1–38.

Giere, R.N. (1988) *Explaining Science: a Cognitive Approach*. Chicago, IL: University of Chicago Press.

Giere, R.N. (ed.) (1992) *Cognitive Models of Science*. Minneapolis, MN: University of Minnesota Press.

Gigerenzer, G. (1996) On narrow norms and vague heuristics: a reply to Kahneman and Tversky (1996). *Psychological Review*, 103, 592–596.

Gigerenzer, G. and Goldstein, D.G. (1996) Reasoning the fast and frugal way: models of bounded rationality. *Psychological Review*, 103, 650–669.

Gigerenzer, G. and Hoffrage, U. (1995) How to improve bayesian reasoning without instruction: frequency format. *Psychological Review*, 102, 684–704.

Gigerenzer, G. and Hug, K. (1992) Domain specific reasoning: Social contracts, cheating, and perspective change. *Cognition*, 43, 127–171.

Gigerenzer, G. and Selten, R. (eds) (2002) *Bounded Rationality: the Adaptive Toolbox*. Cambridge, MA: MIT Press.

Gigerenzer, G., Todd, P.M., and ABC Research Group. (eds) (1999) *Simple Heuristics That Make Us Smart*. Oxford: Oxford University Press.

Gilbert, D.T. (1989) Thinking lightly about others: automatic components of the social inference process. In Uleman, J., and Bargh, J.A. (eds), *Unintended Thought*. New York: Guilford Press, pp. 189–211.

Gilbert, D.T. and Wilson, T.D. (2000) Miswanting: Some problems in the forecasting of future affective states. In Forgas, J. (ed.), *Thinking and Feeling: the Role of Affect in Social Cognition*. Cambridge: Cambridge University Press, pp. 178–197.

Gilbert, D.T., Pinel, E.C., Wilson, T.C., Blumberg, S.J., and Wheatley, T.P. (1998) Immune neglect: a source of durability bias in affective forecasting. *Journal of Personality and Social Psychology*, 75, 617–638.

Gilhooly, K.J., Logie, R.H., Wetherick, N.E., and Wynn, V. (1993) Working memory and strategies in syllogistic-reasoning tasks. *Memory & Cognition*, 21, 115–124.

Gilhooly, K.J., Logie, R.H., and Wynn, V. (1999) Syllogistic reasoning tasks, working memory, and skill. *European Journal of Cognitive Psychology*, 11, 473–498.

Gimpel, J.F. (1965) A method of producing a Boolean function having an arbitrarily described prime implicant table. *IEEE Transactions on Computing*, 14, 484–488.

Ginsberg, M.L. (1987) Introduction. In Ginsberg, M.L. (ed.), *Readings in Nonmonotonic Reasoning*. Los Altos, CA: Morgan Kaufmann, pp. 1–23.

Girotto, V. and Gonzalez, M. (2001) Solving probabilistic and statistical problems: a matter of question form and information structure. *Cognition*, 78, 247–276.

Girotto, V. and Gonzalez, M. (2002) Chances and frequencies in probabilistic reasoning: rejoinder to Hoffrage, Gigerenzer, Krauss and Martignon. *Cognition*, 84, 353–359.

Girotto, V. and Gonzalez, M. (2006) Norms and intuitions about chance. In Smith, L. and Voneche, J. (eds). *Norms and Development*. Cambridge: Cambridge University Press, pp. 220–236.

Girotto, V. and Johnson-Laird, P.N. (2004) The probability of conditionals. *Psychologia*, 47, 207–225.

Girotto, V., Light, P.H., and Colbourn, C.J. (1988). Pragmatic schemas and conditional reasoning in children. *Quarterly Journal of Experimental Psychology*, 40A, 342–357.

Girotto, V., Legrenzi, P., and Rizzo, A. (1991) Event controllability in counterfactual thinking. *Acta Psychologica*, 78, 111–133.

Girotto, V., Mazzocco, A., and Tasso, A. (1997) The effect of premise order in conditional reasoning: a test of the mental model theory. *Cognition*, 63, 1–28.

Girotto, V., Johnson-Laird, P.N., Legrenzi, P., and Sonino, M. (2000) Reasoning to consistency: how people resolve logical inconsistencies. In García-Madruga, J.A., Carriedo, N., and González-Labra, M. (eds), *Mental Models in Reasoning*. Madrid: Universidad Naciónal de Educacion a Distanzia, pp. 83–97.

Gittings, R. (ed.) (1970) *Letters of John Keats*. Oxford: Oxford University Press.

Gladwell, M. (2005) *Blink: the Power of Thinking without Thinking*. New York: Little, Brown and Co.

Gladwin, T. (1970) *East is a Big Bird*. Cambridge, MA: Harvard University Press.

Glasgow, J.I. (1993) Representation of spatial models for geographic information systems. In Pissinou, N. (ed.), *Proceedings of the ACM Workshop on Advances in Geographic Information Systems*. Arlington, VA: Association for Computing Machinery, 112–117.

Gleick, J. (1992) *Genius: the Life and Science of Richard Feynman*. New York: Pantheon Books.

Glenberg, A.M., Meyer, M., and Lindem, K. (1987) Mental models contribute to foregrounding during text comprehension. *Journal of Memory and Language*, 26, 69–83.

Goel, V. and Dolan, R.J. (2004) Differential involvement of left prefrontal cortex in inductive and deductive reasoning. *Cognition* 93, B109–21.

Goethe, J.W. von (1970) *Theory of Colors* (Introduction by Judd, D.B.; Trans. Eastlake, C.L.). Cambridge, MA: MIT Press. (Translation originally published in 1840.)

Goffman, E. (1959) *The Presentation of Self in Everyday Life*. New York, NY: Doubleday.

Golding, W. (1955) *The Inheritors*. London: Faber and Faber.

Goldvarg, Y. and Johnson-Laird, P.N. (2000) Illusions in modal reasoning. *Memory & Cognition*, 28, 282–294.

Goldvarg, Y. and Johnson-Laird, P.N. (2001) Naïve causality: a mental model theory of causal meaning and reasoning. *Cognitive Science*, 25, 565–610.

Gooding, D.C. (2005) Seeing the forest for the trees: Visualization, cognition, and scientific inference. In Gorman, M.E., Tweney, R.D., Gooding, D.C., and Kincannon, A.P., (eds), *Scientific and Technological Thinking*. Mahwah, NJ: Erlbaum, pp. 173–217.

Goodman, N. (1972) Seven strictures on similarity. In Goodman, N. (ed.), *Problems and Projects*. New York: Bobbs-Merrill.

Goodman, N. (1983) *Fact, Fiction, and Forecast*, 4th edn. Cambridge, MA: Harvard University Press. (Originally published 1954.)

Goodwin, G. and Johnson-Laird, P.N. (2005a) Reasoning about relations. *Psychological Review*, 112, 468–493.

Goodwin, G. and Johnson-Laird, P.N. (2005b) Reasoning about the relations between relations. *Quarterly Journal of Experimental Pyschology*, 59, 1–23.

Goodwin, G. and Johnson-Laird, P.N. (2005c) Illusions in transitive reasoning. Under submission.

Gordon, P. (2004) Numerical cognition without words: evidence from Amazonia. *Science*, 306, 496–499.

Gorman, M.E. (1992) *Simulating Science: Heuristics, Mental Models, and Technoscientific Thinking*. Bloomington, IN: Indiana University Press.

Gorman, M.E., Tweney, R.D., Gooding, D.C., and Kincannon, A.P. (eds) (2005) *Scientific and Technological Thinking*. Mahwah, NJ: Erlbaum.

Gosse, E. (1923) *Father and Son: a Study of Two Temperaments*, 8th edn. New York: Scribner's Son. (Originally published 1907.)

Gosse, P.H. (1998) *Omphalos: an Attempt to Untie the Geological Knot*. Woodbridge, CT: Ox Bow Press. (Originally published 1857.)

Gould, J.L. and Gould, C.G. (1994) *The Animal Mind*. New York: Freeman.

Gould, S.J. (1989) *Wonderful Life: the Burgess Shale and the Nature of History*. New York: Penguin.

Govier, T. (1988) *A Practical Study of Argument*, 2nd edn. Belmont, CA: Wadsworth.

Gralinski, H.J. and Kopp, C.B. (1993) Everyday rules for behavior: mothers' requests to young children. *Developmental Psychology*, 29, 573–584.

Grant, U.S. (1990) *Memoirs and Selected Letters*. New York: Library of America. (Originally published in 1885.)

Green, D.W. (1995) Externalization, counter-examples and the abstract selection task. *Quarterly Journal of Experimental Psychology*, 48A, 424–446.

Green, D.W. (1997) Hypothetical thinking in the selection task: amplifying a model-based approach. *Current Psychology of Cognition*, 16, 93–102.

Green, D.W. and Larking, R. (1995) The locus of facilitation in the abstract selection task. *Thinking & Reasoning*, 1, 183–199.

Green, D.W. and McCloy, R. (2003) Reaching a verdict. *Thinking & Reasoning*, 9, 307–333.

Greene, E.J. and Darley, J.M. (1998) Effects of necessary, sufficient, and indirect causation on judgments of criminal liability. *Law and Human Behavior*, 22, 429–451.

Greene, J.D., Sommerville, R.D., Nystrom, L.E., Darley, J.M., and Cohen, J.D. (2001) An fMRI investigation of emotional engagement in moral judgment. *Science*, 293, 2105–2108.

Greene, S. (1992) Multiple explanations for multiply quantified sentences: are multiple models necessary? *Psychological Review*, 99, 184–187.

Greene, T.R. and Noice, H. (1988) Influence of positive affect upon creative thinking and problem solving in children. *Psychological Reports*, 63, 895–898.

Greenwald, A.G., Nosek, B.A., and Banaji, M.R. (2003) Understanding and using the Implicit Association Test: I. An improved scoring algorithm. *Journal of Personality and Social Psychology*, 85, 197–216.

Grice, H.P. (1975) Logic and conversation. In Davidson, D. and Harman, G. (eds), *The Logic of Grammar*. Encino, CA: Dickenson, pp. 64–75. (Reprinted in Grice, 1989.)

Grice, H.P. (1989) *Studies in the Ways of Words*. Cambridge, MA: Harvard University Press.

Griggs, R.A. (1995) The effects of rule clarification, decision justification, and selection instruction on Wason's abstract selection task. In Newstead, S.E. and Evans, J.St.B.T. (eds), *Perspectives on Thinking and Reasoning: Essays in Honor of Peter Wason*. Hillsdale, NJ: Erlbaum, pp. 17–39.

Gruber, H.E. (1994) Insight and affect in the history of science. In Sternberg, R.J., and Davidson, J. (eds), *The Nature of Insight*. Cambridge, MA: MIT Press, pp. 397–431.

Gurdjieff, G.I. (1991) *Life is Real Only Then, When "I Am"*. New York: Viking Arkana.

Guyote, M.J. and Sternberg, R.J. (1981) A transitive-chain theory of syllogistic reasoning. *Cognitive Psychology*, 13, 461–525.

Hacking, I. (1975) *The Emergence of Probability*. Cambridge: Cambridge University Press.

Hadamard, J. (1996) *The Mathematician's Mind*. Princeton, NJ: Princeton University Press. (Originally published as *The Psychology of Invention in the Mathematical Field* in 1945.)

Hadjichristidis C., Stevenson R.J., Over D.E., Sloman S.A., Evans J.St.B.T., and Feeney A. (2001) On the evaluation of If p then q conditionals. *Proceedings of the Twenty-third Annual Conference of the Cognitive Science Society*. Hillsdale, NJ: Erlbaum, pp. 381–386.

Hagert, G. (1984) Modeling mental models: Experiments in cognitive modeling spatial relations. In O'Shea, T. (ed.), *Advances in Artificial Intelligence*. Amsterdam: North-Holland, pp. 179–188.

Halford, G.S. (1993) *Children's Understanding: the Development of Mental Models*. Hillsdale, NJ: Erlbaum.

Halford, G.S., Wilson, W.H., and Phillips, S. (1998) Processing capacity defined by relational complexity: Implications for comparative, developmental, and cognitive psychology. *Behavioral and Brain Sciences*, 21, 803–831.

Halliday, S. (1999) *The Great Stink of London: Sir Joseph Bazalgette and the Cleansing of the Victorian Capital*. Stroud, Gloucestershire: Sutton.

Halmos, P. (1957) Nicolas Bourbaki. *Scientific American*, 196, (May), 88–99.

Halpern, J. and Vardi, M.Y. (1991) Model checking vs. theorem proving: a manifesto. In Allen, J., Fikes, R.E., and Sandewall, E. (eds), *Proceedings of the Second International Conference on Principles of Knowledge Representation and Reasoning*, KR'91. San Mateo, CA: Morgan Kaufmann, pp. 325–334.

Hammerton, M. (1997) Ignoring the base-rate—a robust phenomenon. Paper presented at the March meeting of the Experimental Psychology Society, University of Oxford, England.

Hampton, J.A. (1979) Polymorphous concept in semantic memory. *Journal of Verbal Learning and Verbal Behavior*, 18, 441–461.

Hardman, D.K. (1996) Mental models: the revised theory brings new problems. *Behavioral and Brain Sciences*, 19, 542–543.

Hare, R.M. (1981) *Moral Thinking: Its Levels, Method, and Point*. Oxford Clarendon Press.

Harman, G. (1965) The inference to the best explanation. *Philosophical Review*, 74, 88–95.

Harman, G. (1973) *Thought*. Princeton, NJ: Princeton University Press.

Harman, G. (1977) *The Nature of Morality*. New York: Oxford University Press.

Harman, G. (1986) *Change in View: Principles of Reasoning*. Cambridge, MA: MIT Press, Bradford Book.

Harré, R. and Madden, E.H. (1975) *Causal Powers*. Oxford: Blackwell.

Harris, P.L. (2000) *The Work of the Imagination*. Oxford: Blackwell.

Harris, P. and Núñez, M. (1996) Understanding of permission rules by preschool children. *Child Development*, 67, 1572–1591.

Hart, H.L.A. and Honoré, A.M. (1985) *Causation in the Law*, 2nd edn. Oxford: Clarendon Press. (First edition published in 1959.)

Hasson, U. and Johnson-Laird, P.N. (2006) How reasoning changes your belief in statements. Under submission.

Hastings, M. (2004) *Armageddon: the Battle for Germany, 1944–1945*. New York: Knopf.

Hauser, M., Chomsky, N., and Fitch, W.T. (2002) The language faculty: what is it, who has it, and how did it evolve? *Science*, 298, 1569–1579.

Hayes-Roth, F. and McDermott, J. (1978) An interference matching technique for inducing abstractions. *Communications of the Association for Computing Machinery*, 21, 401–411.

Hegarty, M. (1992) Mental animation: Inferring motion from static diagrams of mechanical systems. *Journal of Experimental Psychology: Learning, Memory, and Cognition*, 18, 1084–1102.

Hegarty, M. (2004) Mechanical reasoning as mental simulation. *Trends in Cognitive Sciences*, 8, 280–285.

Hegarty, M. and Sims, V.K. (1994) Individual differences in mental animation during mechanical reasoning. *Memory & Cognition*, 22, 411–430.

Hegarty, M., Mayer, S., Kriz, S., and Keehner, M. (2005) The role of gestures in mental animation. *Spatial Cognition and Computation*, 5, 333–356.

Heller, J. (1961) *Catch-22, A Novel*. New York: Simon & Schuster.

Helmholtz, H. (1962) *Treatise on Physiological Optics*. New York: Dover. (Originally published in 1866.)

Henle, M. (1962) The relation between logic and thinking. *Psychological Review*, 69, 366–378.

Henle, M. (1978) Foreword to Revlin, R., and Mayer, R.E. (eds), *Human Reasoning*. Washington, DC: Winston, pp. xiii–xviii.

Herink, R. (ed.) (1980) *The Psychotherapy Handbook: the A to Z Guide to More Than 250 Different Therapies in Use Today*. New York: New American Library.

Herschel, J.F.W. (1987) *A Preliminary Discourse on the Study of Natural Philosophy*. London. Longman, Rees, Orme, Brown, and Green ... and John Taylor. Rep. Chicago: University of Chicago Press. (Originally published in 1831).

Hesse, M. (1966) *Models and Analogies in Science*. Notre Dame, IN: Notre Dame University Press.

Hewitt, C. (1969) PLANNER: a language for proving theorems in robots. *International Joint Conference on Artificial Intelligence*, 2, 295–302.

Hilbert, D. (1967) The foundations of mathematics. In van Heijenoort, J. (ed.), *From Frege to Gödel: a Source Book in Mathematical Logic, 1879–1931*. Cambridge, MA: Harvard University Press, pp. 464–479. (Originally published in German in 1928.)

Hilpinen, R. (ed.) (1971) *Deontic Logic: Introductory and Systematic Readings*. Dordrecht, The Netherlands: Reidel.

Hilton, D.J. and Erb, H-P. (1996) Mental models and causal explanation: judgements of probable cause and explanatory relevance. *Thinking & Reasoning*, 2, 273–308.

Hinsley, F.H. (1975) *British Intelligence in the Second World War: its Influence on Strategy and Operations*. London: Her Majesty's Stationary Office (HMSO).

Hinsley, F.H. and Stripp, A. (eds) (1993) *Code Breakers: the Inside Story of Bletchley Park*. Oxford: Oxford University Press.

Hintikka, J. (1963) The models of modality. *Acta Philosophica Fennica*, 16, 65–82.

Hintikka, J. (1973) *Logic, Language-Games and Information: Kantian Themes in the Philosophy of Logic*. Oxford: Clarendon Press.

Hirst, W. and Weil, J. (1982) Acquisition of the epistemic and deontic meaning of modals. *Journal of Child Language*, 9, 659–666.

Hodges, A. (2000) *Alan Turing: the Enigma*. New York: Walker. (First edition published in 1992.)

Hogarth, R.M. and Einhorn, H.J. (1992) Order effects in belief updating: the belief-adjustment model. *Cognitive Psychology*, 24, 1–55.

Holland, J.G. and Skinner, B.F. (1961) *The Analysis of Behavior: a Program for Self-instruction*. New York: McGraw-Hill.

Holland, J.H., Holyoak, K.J., Nisbett, R.E., and Thagard, P.R. (1986) *Induction: Processes of Inference, Learning, and Discovery*. Cambridge, MA: MIT Press.

Hollard, V. and Delius, J.D. (1982) Rotational invariance in visual pattern recognition by pigeons and humans. *Science*, 218, 804–806.

Hollon, S.D., Thase, M.E., and Markowitz, J.C. (2002) Treatment and prevention of depression. *Psychological Science in the Public Interest*, 3, 1–39.

Holyoak, K.J. and Glass, A. (1975) The role of contradictions and counterexamples in the rejection of false sentences. *Journal of Verbal Learning and Verbal Behavior*, 14, 215–239.

Holyoak, K.J. and Thagard, P. (1989) Analogical mapping by constraint satisfaction. *Cognitive Science*, 13, 295–355.

Hooke, R. (1705) *The Posthumous Works of Robert Hooke, containing his Cutlerian Lectures, and Other Discourses*. London: Richard Waller.

Hopcroft, J.E. and Ullman, J.D. (1979) *Formal Languages and Their Relation to Automata*. Reading, MA: Addison-Wesley.

Horn, L.R. (1989) *A Natural History of Negation*. Stanford, CA: CSLI Publications.

Hörnig, R., Oberauer, K., and Weidenfeld, A. (2005) Two principles of premise integration in spatial reasoning. *Memory & Cognition*, 33, 131–139.

Howson, C. and Urbach, P. (1993) *Scientific Reasoning: the Bayesian Approach*, 2nd edn. Chicago, IL: Open Court.

Hughes, G.E. and Cresswell, M.J. (1996) *A New Introduction to Modal Logic*. London: Routledge.

Hull, C.L. (1920) Quantitative aspects of the evolution of concepts. *Psychological Monographs*, 28, whole number 123.

Hull, C.L. (1934) The concept of the habit-family hierarchy and maze learning: Part I. *Psychological Review*, 41, 33–54.

Hume, D. (1978) *A Treatise on Human Nature*. Selby-Bigge, L.A. (ed.), 2nd edn. Oxford: Oxford University Press (Originally published 1739.)

Hume, D. (1988) *An Enquiry Concerning Human Understanding*. Flew, A. (ed.), La Salle, IL: Open Court (Originally published 1748.)

Hummel, J.E. and Holyoak, K.J. (2001) A process model of human transitive inference. In Gattis, M. (ed.), *Spatial Schemas and Abstract Thought*. Cambridge, MA: MIT Press, pp. 279–305.

Hummel, J.E. and Holyoak, K.J. (2003) A symbolic-connectionist theory of relational inference and generalization. *Psychological Review*, 110, 220–264.

Humphrey, G. (1951) *Thinking*. London: Methuen.

Humphrey, N. (1996) *Leaps of Faith: Science, Miracles, and the Search for Supernatural Consolation*. New York: Basic Books.

Hunt, E.B. (1999) What is a theory of thought? In Sternberg, R.J. (ed.), *The Nature of Cognition*. Cambridge, MA: MIT Press, pp. 3–49.

Hunt, E.B. (2002) *Precis of Thoughts on Thought*. Mahwah, NJ: Erlbaum.

Hunt, E.B., Marin, J., and Stone, P.T. (1966) *Experiments in Induction*. New York: Academic Press.

Hunter, I.M.L. (1957) The solving of three terms series problems. *British Journal of Psychology*, 48, 286–298.

Huttenlocher, J. (1968) Constructing spatial images: a strategy in reasoning. *Psychological Review*, 75, 550–560.

Huxley, T.H. (1893) On the hypothesis that animals are automata, and its history. In *Method and Results: Collected Essays Part One*. London: Macmillan, pp. 199–250. (Originally published in 1874.)

Inhelder, B. and Piaget, J. (1958) *The Growth of Logical Thinking from Childhood to Adolescence*. London: Routledge & Kegan Paul.

Inhelder, B. and Piaget, J. (1964) *The Early Growth of Logic in the Child*. London: Routledge & Kegan Paul.

Inder, R. (1987) Computer simulation of syllogism solving using restricted mental models. Unpublished Ph.D. Thesis, Cognitive Studies, Edinburgh University.

Isaak, M.I. and Just, M.A. (1995) Constraints on thinking in insight and invention. In Sternberg, R.J. and Davidson, J.E. (eds), *The Nature of Insight*. Cambridge MA: Bradford books, MIT Press, pp. 281–325.

Isen, A.M., Daubman, K.A., and Nowicki, G.P. (1987) Positive affect facilitates creative problem solving. *Journal of Personality and Social Psychology*, 52, 1122–1131.

Jackendoff, R. (1996) How language helps us think. *Pragmatics & Cognition*, 4, 1–34.

Jackson R. and Tarsitano M. (1997) Araneophagic jumping spiders discriminate between detour sites that do and do not lead to prey. *Animal Behaviour*, 53, 257–266.

Jakab, P.L. (1990) *Visions of a Flying Machine: the Wright Brothers and the Process of Invention*. Washington, DC: Smithsonian Institution Press.

James, W. (1884) What is an emotion? *Mind*, 9, 188–205.

James, W. (1890) *The Principles of Psychology*, Vols 1 and 2. New York: Holt.

James, W. (1907) *Pragmatism—A New Name for Some Old Ways of Thinking*. New York: Longmans, Green & Co.

James, W. (1956) *The Will to Believe*. New York: Dover. (Originally published 1896.)

Jang, K.L., McCrae, R.R., Angleitner, A., Riemann, R., and Livesley, W.J. (1998) Heritability of facet-level traits in a cross-cultural twin sample: support for a hierarchical model of personality. *Journal of Personality and Social Psychology*, 74, 1556–1565.

Jansson, D.G. and Smith, S.M. (1991) Design fixation. *Design Studies*, 12, 3–11.

Janveau-Brennan, G. and Markovits, H. (1999) Reasoning with causal conditionals: developmental and individual differences. *Developmental Psychology*, 35, 904–911.

Jeffrey, R. (1981) *Formal Logic: Its Scope and Limits*, 2nd edn. New York: McGraw-Hill.

Johnson, E.J. and Tversky, A. (1983) Affect, generalization, and the perception of risk. *Journal of Personality and Social Psychology*, 45, 20–31.

Johnson, M.K. (1983) A multiple-entry, modular memory system. In Bower, G.H., (ed.), *The Psychology of Learning and Motivation*, Vol. 17. New York: Academic Press, pp. 81–123.

Johnson, M.K. and Reeder, J.A. (1997) Consciousness as meta-processing. In Cohen, J.D. and Schooler, J.W. (eds), *Scientific Approaches to Consciousness*. Mahwah, NJ: Erlbaum, pp. 261–293.

Johnson, R.H. and Blair, J.A. (1994) *Logical Self-Defense*. New York: McGraw-Hill.

Johnson-Laird, P.N. (1970a) The perception and memory of sentences. In Lyons, J. (ed.), *New Horizons in Linguistics*. Harmondsworth, Middx: Penguin Books, pp. 261–270.

Johnson-Laird, P.N. (1970b) The interpretation of quantified sentences. In Levelt, W.J.M. and Flores d'Arcais, G.B. (eds), *Advances in Psycholinguistics*. Amsterdam: North Holland Press, pp. 347–372.

Johnson-Laird, P.N. (1975) Models of deduction. In Falmagne, R.J. (ed.), *Reasoning: Representation and Process in Children and Adults*. Hillsdale, NJ: Erlbaum, pp. 7–54.

Johnson-Laird, P.N. (1983) *Mental Models: Towards a Cognitive Science of Language, Inference, and Consciousness*. Cambridge, MA: Harvard University Press.

Johnson-Laird, P.N. (1993) *Human and Machine Thinking*. Hillsdale, NJ: Erlbaum.

Johnson-Laird, P.N. (1997) Rules and illusions: a critical study of Rips's The Psychology of Proof. *Minds and Machines*, 7, 387–407.

Johnson-Laird, P.N. (1999) Causation, mental models, and the law. *Brooklyn Law Review*, 65, 67–103.

Johnson-Laird, P.N. (2002a) Peirce, logic diagrams, and the elementary operations of reasoning. *Thinking & Reasoning*, 8, 69–95.

Johnson-Laird, P.N. (2002b) How jazz musicians improvise. *Music Perception*, 19, 415–442.

Johnson-Laird, P.N. (2005) Flying bicycles: how the Wright brothers invented the airplane. *Mind and Society*, 27–48.

Johnson-Laird, P.N. (2006) *How We Reason*. Oxford: Oxford University Press.

Johnson-Laird, P.N. and Bara, B.G. (1984) Syllogistic inference. *Cognition*, 16, 1–61.

Johnson-Laird, P.N. and Byrne, R.M.J. (1989) *Only* reasoning. *Journal of Memory and Language*, 28, 313–330.

Johnson-Laird, P.N. and Byrne, R.M.J. (1990) Meta-logical problems: Knights, knaves, and Rips. *Cognition*, 36, 69–81.

Johnson-Laird, P.N. and Byrne, R.M.J. (1991) *Deduction*. Hillsdale, NJ: Erlbaum.

Johnson-Laird, P.N. and Byrne, R.M.J. (2002) Conditionals: a theory of meaning, pragmatics, and inference. *Psychological Review*, 109, 646–678.

Johnson-Laird, P.N. and Ehrlich, K. (1982) Spatial descriptions and referential continuity. *Journal of Verbal Learning and Verbal Behavior*, 21, 296–306.

Johnson-Laird, P.N. and Hasson, U. (2003) Counterexamples in sentential reasoning. *Memory & Cognition*, 31, 1105–1113.

Johnson-Laird, P.N. and Mani, K. (1982) The mental representation of spatial descriptions. *Memory & Cognition*, 10, 181–187.

Johnson-Laird, P.N. and Oatley, K. (2000) The cognitive and social construction of emotions. In Lewis, M. and Haviland, J. (eds), *Handbook of Emotions*, 2nd edn. New York: Guilford Press, pp. 458–475.

Johnson-Laird, P.N. and Savary, F. (1996) Illusory inferences about probabilities. *Acta Psychologica*, 93, 69–90.

Johnson-Laird, P.N. and Savary, F. (1999) Illusory inferences: a novel class of erroneous deductions. *Cognition*, 71, 191–229.

Johnson-Laird, P.N. and Steedman, M.J. (1978) The psychology of syllogisms. *Cognitive Psychology*, 10, 64–99.

Johnson-Laird, P.N. and Tagart, J. (1969) How implication is understood. *American Journal of Psychology*, 82, 367–373.

Johnson-Laird, P.N. and Wason, P.C. (eds) (1976) *Thinking: Readings in Cognitive Science*. Cambridge: Cambridge University Press.

Johnson-Laird, P.N., Legrenzi, P., and Sonino Legrenzi, M. (1972) Reasoning and a sense of reality. *British Journal of Psychology*, 63, 395–400.

Johnson-Laird, P.N., Oakhill, J.V., and Bull, D. (1986) Children's syllogistic reasoning. *Quarterly Journal of Experimental Psychology*, 38A, 35–38.

Johnson-Laird, P.N., Byrne, R.M.J., and Tabossi, P. (1989) Reasoning by model: the case of multiple quantification. *Psychological Review*, 96, 658–673.

Johnson-Laird, P.N., Byrne, R.M.J., and Schaeken, W.S. (1992) Propositional reasoning by model. *Psychological Review*, 99, 418–439.

Johnson-Laird, P.N., Legrenzi, P., Girotto, V., Legrenzi, M., and Caverni, J-P. (1999) Naive probability: a mental model theory of extensional reasoning. *Psychological Review*, 106, 62–88.

Johnson-Laird, P.N., Legrenzi, P., Girotto, P., and Legrenzi, M.S. (2000) Illusions in reasoning about consistency. *Science*, 288, 531–532.

Johnson-Laird, P.N., Girotto, V., and Legrenzi, P. (2004a) Reasoning from inconsistency to consistency. *Psychological Review*, 111, 640–661.

Johnson-Laird, P.N., Legrenzi, P., and Girotto, V. (2004b) How we detect logical inconsistencies. *Current Directions in Psychological Science*, 13, 41–45.

Johnson-Laird, P.N., Frosch, C., and Goldvarg-Steingold, G. (2006a) Causes and enabling conditions: a reply to Kuhnmünch and Beller. Under submission.

Johnson-Laird, P.N., Mancini, F., and Gangemi, A. (2006b) A hyper emotion theory of psychological illnesses. *Psychological Review*, in press.

Joyce, J. (1930) *A Portrait of the Artist as a Young Man*. London: Cape.

Jung-Beeman, M., Bowden, E.M., Haberman, J., Frymiare, J.L., Arambel-Liu, S., Greenblatt, R., Reber, P.J., and Kounios, J. (2004) Neural activity when people solve verbal problems with insight. *Public Library of Science Biology*, 2(2), April. (An on-line journal.)

Kahane, H. (1984) *Logic and Contemporary Rhetoric*, 4th edn. Belmont, CA: Wadsworth.

Kahn, D. (1996) *The Codebreakers*. New York: Scribner. (First edition published in 1967.)

Kahneman, D. (1995) Varieties of counterfactual thinking. In Roese, N.J. and Olson, J.M. (eds), *What Might Have Been: the Social Psychology of Counterfactual Thinking*. Mahwah, NJ: Erlbaum, pp. 375–396.

Kahneman, D. and Frederick, S. (2002) Representativeness revisited: attribute substitution in intuitive judgement. In Gilovich, T., Griffin, D., and Kahneman, D. (eds), *Heuristics and Biases: the Psychology of Intuitive Judgement*. Cambridge: Cambridge University Press, pp. 49–81.

Kahneman, D. and Frederick, S. (2005) A model of heuristic judgment. In Holyoak, K.J. and Morrison, R.G. (eds), *The Cambridge Handbook of Thinking and Reasoning*. Cambridge: Cambridge University Press, pp. 267–293. (A revised version of Kahmeman and Frederick, 2002.)

Kahneman, D. and Miller, D.T. (1986) Norm theory: comparing reality to its alternative. *Psychological Review*, 93, 75–88.

Kahneman, D. and Tversky, A. (1972) Subjective probability: a judgment of representativeness. *Cognitive Psychology*, 3, 430–454.

Kahneman, D. and Tversky, A. (1973) On the psychology of prediction. *Psychological Review*, 80, 237–251.

Kahneman, D. and Tversky, A. (1979) Prospect theory: an analysis of decision under risk. *Econometrica*, 47, 263–291.

Kahneman, D. and Tversky, A. (1982) The simulation heuristic. In Kahneman, D., Slovic, P., and Tversky, A. (eds), *Judgment Under Uncertainty: Heuristics and Biases*. New York: Cambridge University Press, pp. 201–208.

Kahneman, D. and Tversky, A. (1996) On the reality of cognitive illusions: a reply to Gigerenzer's critique. *Psychological Review*, 103, 582–591.

Kahneman, D., Slovic, P., and Tversky, A. (eds) (1982) *Judgement Under Uncertainty*. Cambridge: Cambridge University Press.

Kaiser, M.K., Jonides, J., and Alexander, J. (1986) Intuitive reasoning on abstract and familiar physics problems. *Memory & Cognition*, 14, 308–312.

Kalish, C. (1998) Reasons and causes: children's understanding of conformity to social rules and physical laws. *Child Development*, 69, 706–720.

Kamp, H. (1981) A theory of truth and semantic representation. In Groenendijk, J.A.G., Janssen, T.M.V., and Stokhof, M.B.J. (eds), *Formal Methods in the Study of Language*. Amsterdam: Mathematical Centre Tracts, pp. 277–322.

Kamp, H. and Reyle, U. (1993) *From Discourse to Logic: Introduction to Modeltheoretic Semantics of Natual Language, Formal Logic and Discourse Representation Theory*. Dordrecht: Kluwer.

Kanigel, R. (1991) *The Man Who Knew Infinity: a Life of the Genius Ramanujan*. New York: Washington Square Press.

Kant, I. (1934) *The Critique of Pure Reason*, 2nd edn. (Trans. Meiklejohn, J.M.D.). London: Dent, 1934. (Originally published 1787.)

Kant, I. (1974) *Logic* (Trans. Hartman, R.S. and Schwarz, W.). New York: Bobbs-Merrill. (Originally published in 1800.)

Kant, I. (1997) *Groundwork of the Metaphysics of Morals*. Cambridge: Cambridge University Press. (Originally published 1785.)

Kaplan, C.A. and Simon, H.A. (1990) In search of insight. *Cognitive Psychology*, 22, 374–419.

Karmiloff-Smith, A. (1992) *Beyond Modularity: a Developmental Perspective on Cognitive Science*. Cambridge, MA: MIT Press.

Karmiloff-Smith, A. and Inhelder, B. (1974/75) If you want to get ahead, get a theory. *Cognition*, 3, 195–212.

Katona, G. (1940) *Organizing and Memorizing: Studies in the Psychology of Learning and Teaching*. New York: Columbia University Press.

Keane, M.T. (1988) *Analogical Problem Solving*. West Sussex: Ellis Horwood.

Keane, M.T. (1989) Modelling problem solving in Gestalt "insight" problems. *Irish Journal of Psychology*, 10, 201–215.

Keene, G.B. (1992) *The Foundations of Rational Argument*. Lewiston, NY: Edward Mellen Press.

Keil, F.C. (1989) *Concepts, Kinds, and Cognitive Development*. Cambridge, MA: MIT Press.

Kelly, F.C. (ed.) (1996) *Miracle at Kitty Hawk: the Letters of Wilbur and Orville*. New York: Farrar, Straus, & Young. (Originally published in 1951.)

Kelvin, Lord (1884) *Notes of Lectures on Molecular Dynamics and the Wave Theory of Light*. Baltimore: Johns Hopkins University.

Kermode, F. (2003) *Pieces of My Mind: Essays and Criticism 1958–2002*. New York: Farrar, Straus and Giroux.

Keynes, H. (2002) *Darwin, His Daughter and Human Evolution*. New York: Riverhead Books.

Keynes, J.M. (1943) *A Treatise on Probability*. London: Macmillan.

Keysar, B., Lin, S., and Barr, D.J. (2003) Limits on theory of mind use in adults. *Cognition*, 89, 25–41.

Kihlstrom, J.E, Barnhardt, T.M., and Tataryn, D.J. (1992) Implicit perception. In Bornstein, R.E. and Pittman, T.S. (eds), *Perception Without Awareness*. New York: Guilford Press, pp. 17–54.

Klahr, D. and Simon, H. (1999) Studies of scientific discovery: complementary approaches and convergent findings. *Psychological Bulletin*, 125, 524–543.

Klauer, K.C., Jacobsen, T., and Migulla, G. (1995) Counterfactual processing: test of an hierarchical correspondence model. *European Journal of Social Psychology*, 25, 577–595.

Klauer, K.C., Musch, J., and Naumer, B. (2000) On belief bias in syllogistic reasoning. *Psychological Review*, 107, 852–884.

Klayman, J. and Ha, Y.W. (1987) Confirmation, disconfirmation, and information in hypothesis testing. *Psychological Review*, 94, 211–228.

de Kleer, J. (1986) An assumption-based TMS. *Artificial Intelligence*, 28, 127–162.

Klein, G. (1998) *Sources of Power: How People make Decisions*. Cambridge, MA: MIT Press.

Knauff, M. and Johnson-Laird, P.N. (2002) Imagery can impede inference. *Memory & Cognition*, 30, 363–371.

Knauff, M. and May, E. (2006) Mental imagery, reasoning, and blindness. *Quarterly Journal of Experimental Psychology*, 59, 161–177.

Knauff, M., Jola, C., and Strube, G. (2001) Spatial reasoning: no need for visual information. In Montello, D. (ed.), *Spatial Information Theory: Proceedings of COSIT'01*. New York: Springer-Verlag, pp. 447–457.

Knauff, M., Fangmeier, T., Ruff, C.C., and Johnson-Laird, P.N. (2003) Reasoning, models, and images: Behavioral measures and cortical activity. *Journal of Cognitive Neuroscience*, 4, 559–573.

Kneale, W. and Kneale, M. (1962) *The Development of Logic*. Oxford: Oxford University Press.

Knight, R.T. and Grabowecky, M. (1995) Escape from linear time: prefrontal cortex and conscious experience. In Gazzinaga, M.S. (ed.), *The Cognitive Neurosciences*. Cambridge, MA: MIT Press, pp. 1357–1371.

Knoblich, G., Ohlsson, S., Haider, H., and Rhenius, D. (1999) Constraint relaxation and chunk decomposition in insight problem-solving. *Journal of Experimental Psychology: Learning, Memory & Cognition*, 25, 1534–1556.

Kohlberg, L. (1986) A current statement of some theoretical issues. In Modgil, S., and Modgil, C. (eds), *Lawrence Kohlberg: Consensus and Controversy*. Philadelphia: Falmer, pp. 485–546.

Köhler, W. (1947) *Gestalt Psychology*. New York: Liveright. (Originally published 1929.)

Kolodner, J. (1993) *Case-Based Reasoning*. San Mateo, CA: Morgan Kaufman.

Korf, R.E. (1980) Toward a model of representational changes. *Artificial Intelligence*, 14, 41–78.

Koslowski, B. (1996) *Theory and Evidence: the Development of Scientific Reasoning*. Cambridge, MA: MIT Press.

Kosslyn, S.M. (1980) *Image and Mind*. Cambridge, MA: Harvard University Press.

Kosslyn, S.M., Ball, T.M., and Reiser, B.J. (1978) Visual images preserve metric spatial information: evidence from studies of image scanning. *Journal of Experimental Psychology: Human Perception and Performance*, 4, 47–60.

Kozaczuk, W. and Straszak, J. (2004) *Enigma: How the Poles Broke the Enigma Code*. New York: Hippocrene Books.

Kripke, S. (1963) Semantical considerations on modal logic. *Acta Philosophica Fennica*, 16, 83–94.

Kroeber, T. (1961) *Ishi in Two Worlds: a Biography of the Last Wild Indian in North America*. Berkeley, CA: University of California Press.

Kubovy, M. (1986) *Psychology of Perspective and Renaissance Art.* Cambridge: Cambridge University Press.

Kuhn, D. (1977) Conditional reasoning in children. *Developmental Psychology*, 13, 342–353.

Kuhn, D. (1991) *The Skills of Argument.* Cambridge: Cambridge University Press.

Kuhn, T. (1970) *The Structure of Scientific Revolutions*, 2nd edn. Chicago, IL: University of Chicago Press.

Kuhnmünch, G. and Beller, S. (2005) Causes and enabling conditions—through mental models of linguistic cues? *Cognitive Science*, 29, 1077–1090.

Kulkarni, D. and Simon, H.A. (1988) The process of scientific discovery: the strategy of experimentation. *Cognitive Science*, 12, 139–175.

Kyllonen, P. and Christal, R. (1990) Reasoning ability is (little more than) working-memory capacity? *Intelligence*, 14, 389–433.

Landau, B., Spelke, E., and Gleitman, H. (1984) Spatial knowledge in a young blind child. *Cognition*, 16, 225–260.

Landauer, T.K. (1986) How much do people remember? Some estimates of the quantity of learned information in long-term memory. *Cognitive Science*, 10, 477–493.

Langley, P., Simon, H.A., Bradshaw, G.L., and Zytkow, J.M. (1987) *Scientific Discovery.* Cambridge, MA: MIT Press.

Laplace, P.S. de. (1951) *Philosophical Essay on Probabilities.* New York: Dover. (Originally published in 1820).

Larkin, J. and Simon, H. (1987) Why a diagram is (sometimes) worth 10,000 words. *Cognitive Science*, 11, 65–99.

Lashley, K.S. (1958) Cerebral organization and behavior. In Solomon, H.C., Cobb, S., and Penfield, W. (eds), *The Brain and Human Behavior*, Vol. 36. Association for Research in Nervous and Mental Disorders, Research Publications. Baltimore: Williams and Wilkin, pp. 1–18.

Lazarus, R.S. (1982) Thoughts on the relationship between emotion and cognition. *American Psychologist*, 37, 1019–1024.

Leahy, R.L. (ed.) (2004) *Contemporary Cognitive Therapy: Theory, Research, and Practice.* London: Guilford Press.

LeDoux, J. (1996) *The Emotional Brain: the Mysterious Underpinnings of Emotional Life.* New York: Simon & Schuster.

Lee, N.Y.L. and Johnson-Laird, P.N. (2004) Creative strategies in problem solving. *Proceedings of the Twenty-Sixth Annual Conference of the Cognitive Science Society.* Mahwah, NJ: Erlbaum, pp. 813–818.

Lee, N.Y.L. and Johnson-Laird, P.N. (2005) Synthetic reasoning and the reverse engineering of Boolean circuits. *Proceedings of the Twenty-Seventh Annual Conference of the Cognitive Science Society.* Mahwah, NJ: Erlbaum, pp. 1260–1265.

Lee, N.Y.L., Goodwin, G.P., and Johnson-Laird, P.N. (2006) The psychology of Su Doku. Under submission.

Legrenzi, P., Girotto, V., and Johnson-Laird, P.N. (2003) Models of consistency. *Psychological Science*, 14, 131–137.

Legrenzi, M.S., Legrenzi, P., Girotto, V., and Johnson-Laird, P.N. (2001–2) The science of finding. *Bulletin of People-Environment Studies*, 20, 7–9.

Leibniz, G. (1949) *New Essays Concerning Human Understanding.* (Trans. Langley, A.G.). LaSalle, IL: Open Court. (Originally published 1765).

Leon, G.R. (1990) *Case Histories of Psychopathology.* Fourth Edition. Boston: Allyn & Bacon.

Lepper, M.R., Ross, L., and Lau, R.R. (1986) Persistence of inaccurate beliefs about the self: perseverance effects in the classroom. *Journal of Personality and Social Psychology*, 50, 482–491.

Leslie, A.M. (1984)Spatiotemporal contiguity and perception of causality in infants. *Perception*, 13, 287–305.

Leslie, A.M. (1987) Pretense and representation: the origins of "Theory of Mind". *Psychological Review*, 94, 412–426.

Leslie, A.M. (1990) Pretense, autism and the basis of "Theory of mind". *The Psychologist*, 3, 120–123.

Leslie, A.M. and Thaiss, L. (1992) Domain specificity in conceptual development: neuropsychological evidence from autism. *Cognition*, 43, 225–251.

Levesque, H.J. (1986) Making believers out of computers. *Artificial Intelligence*, 30, 81–108.

Levi, I. (1991) *The Fixation of Belief and its Undoing: Changing Beliefs through Inquiry*. New York, NY: Cambridge University Press.

Levi, I. (1996) *For the Sake of Argument: Ramsey test conditionals, Inductive Inference and Nonmonotonic Reasoning*. Cambridge: Cambridge University Press.

Levinson, S.C. (1996) Frames of reference and Molyneaux's question: crosslinguistic evidence. In Bloom, P., Peterson, M.A., Nadel, L., and Garrett, M.F. (eds), *Language and Space*. Cambridge, MA: MIT Press, pp. 109–169.

Lewis, C. (1986) A model of mental model construction. *Proceedings of CHI '86 Conference on Human Factors in Computer Systems*. New York: Association for Computing Machinery, pp. 306–313.

Lewis, D.K. (1973) *Counterfactuals*. Oxford: Basil Blackwell.

Lewontin, R.C. (1990) The evolution of cognition. In Osherson, D.N., and Smith, E.E. (eds), *An Invitation to Cognitive Science*, Vol. 3. *Thinking*. Cambridge, MA: MIT Press. pp. 229–246.

Li, M. and Vitanyi, P.M.B. (1993) *An Introduction to Kolmogorov Complexity and Its Applications*. Berlin: Springer-Verlag.

Liberman, N. and Klar, Y. (1996) Hypothesis testing in Wason's selection task: social exchange cheating detection or task understanding. *Cognition*, 58, 127–156.

Lichtenberg, G.C. (1958) *Aphorismen*. Zürich: Manesse.

Lin, Y. (1937) *The Importance of Living*. New York: Reynal & Hitchcock.

Lipton, P. (1991) *Inference to the Best Explanation*. London: Routledge.

Littlewood, J.E. (1953) *A Mathematician's Miscellany*. London: Meuthen.

Livesley, W.J., Jang, K.L., and Vernon, P.A. (1993) Genetic and environmental contributions to dimensions of personality disorder. *American Journal of* Psychiatry, 150, 12–20.

Lober, K. and Shanks, D.R. (2000) Is causal induction based on causal power? Critique of Cheng (1997). *Psychological Review*, 107, 195–212.

Locke, J. (1979) *An Essay Concerning Human Understanding*. Nidditch, P.H. (ed.), Oxford: Oxford University Press. (Originally published in 1689.)

Longford, E. (1969) *Wellington: the Years of the Sword*. New York: Harper and Row.

López, F.J., Cobos, P.L., Caño, A., and Shanks, D.R. (1998) The rational analysis of human causal and probability judgment. In Oaksford, M. and Chater, N. (eds), *Rational Models of Cognition*. Oxford: Oxford University Press, pp. 314–352.

Love, R. and Kessler, C. (1995) Focussing in Wason's selection task: content and instruction effects. *Thinking & Reasoning*, 1, 153–182.

Lowenstein, R. (2000) *When Genius Failed: the Rise and Fall of Long-Term Capital Mangagement*. New York: Random House.

Luchins, A.S. and Luchins, E.S. (1950) New experimental attempts at preventing mechanization in problem solving. *Journal of General Psychology*, 42, 279–297.

Luria, A.R. (1934) The second psychological expedition to central Asia. *Journal of Genetic Psychology*, 41, 255–259.

Luria, A.R. (1976) *Cognitive Development: Its Cultural and Social Foundations*. Cambridge, MA: Harvard University Press.

Lycan, W.G. (1991) MPP, RIP. Unpublished paper, University of North Carolina.

Lycan, W.G. (2001) *Real Conditionals*. Oxford: Clarendon Press.

MacGregor, J.N., Ormerod, T.C., and Chronicle, E.P. (2001) Information-processing and insight: a process model of performance on the nine-dot and related problems. *Journal of Experimental Psychology: Learning, Memory and Cognition*, 27, 176–201.

Mackie, J.L. (1980) *The Cement of the Universe: a Study in Causation*, 2nd edn. Oxford: Oxford University Press.

Macnamara, J. (1986) *A Border Dispute: the Place of Logic in Psychology*. Cambridge, MA: Bradford Books, MIT Press.

Madruga, J.A.G. (1984) Procesos de error en el razonamiento silogístico: doble procesamiento y estrategia de verificación. In Carretero, M., and Madruga, J.A.G. (eds), *Lecturas de psicologia del pensamiento*. Madrid: Alianza.

Magnani, L. and Nersessian, N. (eds) (2002) *Model-Based Reasoning: Science, Technology, Values*. New York: Kluwer Academic/Plenum.

Magnani, L., Nersessian, N., and Thagard, P. (eds) (1999) *Model-based Reasoning in Scientific Discovery*. New York: Kluwer Academic.

Maguire, E.A., Gadian, D.G., Johnsrude, I.S., Good, C.D., Ashburner, J., Frackowiak, R.S.J., and Frith, C.D. (2000) Navigation-related structural change in the hippocampi of taxi drivers. *Proceedings of the National Academy of Science USA*, 97, 4398–4403.

Maier, N.R.F. (1931) Reasoning in humans: II. The solution of a problem and its appearance in consciousness. *Journal of Comparative Psychology*, 12, 181–194.

Malleson, A. (1973) *Need Your Doctor be so Useless*. London: Allen & Unwin.

Malthus, T.R. (2004) *An Essay on the Principle of Population*. Appleman, P. (ed.), 2nd edn. New York: Norton. (Originally published in 1798.)

Mandler, J. (2004) Thought before language. *Trends in Cognitive Sciences*, 8, 508–513.

Manktelow, K.I. (1999) *Reasoning and Thinking*. Hove, East Sussex: Psychology Press.

Manktelow, K.I. (2004) Reasoning and rationality: the pure and the practical. In Manktelow, K.I. and Chung, M.C. (eds), *Psychology of Reasoning: Theoretical and Historical Perspectives*. New York: Psychology Press, pp. 157–177.

Marcus, G.F. (2001) *The Algebraic Mind: Integrating Connectionism and Cognitive Science*. Cambridge, MA: MIT Press.

Marcus, G.F., Vijayan, S., Bandi Rao, S. and Vishton, P.M. (1999) Rule learning by seven-month-old infants. *Science*, 283, 77–80.

Markman, A. and Dietrich, E. (2000) Extending the classical view of representation. *Cognitive Psychology*, 40, 138–171.

Markman, E.M. (1989) *Categorization and Naming in Young Children: Problems in Induction*. Cambridge, MA: MIT Press.

Markovits, H. (1993) The development of conditional reasoning: a Piagetian reformulation of mental models theory. *Merrill-Palmer Quarterly*, 39, 133–160.

Markovits, H. and Barrouillet, P. (2002) The development of conditional reasoning: a mental model account. *Developmental Review*, 22, 5–36.

Markovits, H. and Handley, S.J. (2005) Is inferential reasoning just probabilistic reasoning in disguise? *Memory & Cognition*, 33, 1315–1323.

Markovits, H. and Quinn, S. (2002) Efficiency of retrieval correlates with "logical" reasoning from causal conditional premises. *Memory & Cognition*, 30, 696–706.

Markovits, H. and Vachon, R. (1990) Conditional reasoning, representation, and level of abstraction. *Developmental Psychology*, 26, 942–951.

Markovits, H., Fleury, M.-L., Quinn, S., and Venet, M. (1998) The development of conditional reasoning and the structure of semantic memory. *Child Development*, 64, 742–755.

Markovits, H., Doyon, C., and Simoneau, M. (2002) Individual differences in working memory and conditional reasoning with concrete and abstract content. *Thinking & Reasoning*, 8, 97–107.

Marr, D. (1982) *Vision: a Computational Investigation into the Human Representation and Processing of Visual Information*. San Francisco, CA: W.H. Freeman.

Marsh, A.A., Elfenbein, H.A., and Ambady, N. (2003) Nonverbal "accents": Cultural differences in facial expressions of emotion. *Psychological Science*, 14, 373–376.

Martín-Cordero, J. and González-Labra, M.J. (1994) Amnesic mental models do not completely spill the beans of deductive reasoning. *Behavioral and Brain Sciences*, 17, 773–774.

Maslow, A.H. (1938) *Cases in Personality and Abnormal Psychology*. New York: Brooklyn College Press.

Mathews, A., Mackintosh, B., and Fulcher, E.P. (1997) Cognitive biases in anxiety and attention to threat. *Trends in Cognitive Sciences*, 1, 340–345.

Maxwell, J.C. (1911) Diagram. *The Encyclopaedia Britannica*, Vol. XVIII. New York: the Encylopaedia Britannica Company.

May, E.R. and Zelikow, P.D. (eds) (2001) *The Kennedy Tapes: Inside the Whitehouse during the Cuban Missile Crisis*. Concise edn. New York: Norton.

Mayr, E. (1982) *The Growth of Biological Thought: Diversity, Evolution, and Inheritance*. Cambridge, MA: Belknap, Harvard University Press.

Mazzocco, A., Legrenzi, P., and Roncato, S. (1974) Syllogistic inference: the failure of the atmosphere effect and the conversion hypothesis. *Italian Journal of Psychology*, 2, 157–172.

McArthur, L. (1972) The how and what of why: some determinants and consequences of causal attribution. *Journal of Personality and Social Psychology*, 22, 171–193.

McClelland, J.L. and Rumelhart, D.E. (1986) *Parallel Distributed Processing. Explorations in the Microstructure of Cognition*, Vol. 2: *Psychological and Biological Models*. Cambridge, MA: MIT.

McCloskey, M. (1983) Naive theories of motion. In Gentner, D., and Stevens, A.L. (eds), *Mental Models*. Hillsdale, NJ: Erlbaum, pp. 299–324.

McCluskey, E.J. (1956) Minimization of Boolean functions. *Bell Systems Technical Journal*, 35, 1417–1444.

McFarland, M.W. (ed.) (2001) *The Papers of Wilbur and Orville Wright*, 2 vols. New York: McGraw-Hill. (1st edn, 1953.)

McFarlane, G. (1984) *Alexander Fleming: the Man and the Myth*. Oxford: Oxford University Press.

McPeck, J.E. (1981) *Critical Thinking and Education*. Oxford: Robertson.

Medin, D.L., Goldstone, R.L., and Gentner, D. (1993) Respects for similarity. *Psychological Review*, 100, 254–278.

Medvec, V.H., Madey, S.F., and Gilovich, T. (1995) When less is more: counterfactual thinking and satisfaction among Olympic medalists. *Journal of Personality and Social Psychology*, 69, 603–610.

Medvedev, Z.A. (1990) *The Legacy of Chernobyl*. New York: W.W. Norton.

Mehler, J., Jusczyk, P., Lambertz, G., Halsted, N., Bertoncini, J. & Amiel-Tison, C. (1988) A precursor of language acquisition in young infants, *Cognition*, 29, 143–178.

Mellers, B.A. and McGraw, P. (2001) Anticipated emotions as guides to choice. *Current Directions in Psychological Science*, 6, 210–214.

Mellers, B.A., Schwartz, A., and Cooke, A. (1998) Decision making and valuation. *Annual Review of Psychology*, 49, 447–477.

Metcalfe, J. and Weibe, D. (1987) Intuition in insight and noninsight problem solving. *Memory & Cognition*, 15, 238–246.

Metzler, J. and Shepard, R.N. (1982) Transformational studies of the internal representations of three-dimensional objects. In Shepard, R.N., and Cooper, L.A. (eds), *Mental Images and Their Transformations*. Cambridge, MA: MIT Press, pp. 25–71. (Originally published in Solso, R.L. (ed.), *Theories in Cognitive Psychology: the Loyola Symposium*. Hillsdale, NJ: Erlbaum, 1974.)

Michalski, R.S. (1983) A theory and methodology of inductive learning. In Michalski, R.S., Carbonell, J.G., and Mitchell, T.M. (eds), *Machine Learning: an Artificial Intelligence Approach*. Los Altos, CA: Morgan Kaufmann, pp. 83–134.

Michotte, A. (1963) *The Perception of Causality*. London: Methuen. (Originally published 1946.)

Mill, J.S. (1874) *A System of Logic, Ratiocinative and Inductive: Being a Connected View of the Principles of Evidence and the Methods of Scientific Evidence*, 8th edn. New York: Harper. (First edition published 1843.)

Mill, J.S. (1998) *Utilitarianism*. Oxford: Oxford University Press. (Originally published 1863.)

Miller, A. (1984) *Imagery in Scientific Thought: Creating 20th-Century Physics*. Boston, MA: Birkhauser.

Miller, G.A. (1968) *The Psychology of Communication: Seven Essays*. Harmondsworth, Middlesex: Penguin.

Miller, G.A. and Johnson-Laird, P.N. (1976) *Language and Perception*. Cambridge, MA: Harvard University Press. Cambridge: Cambridge University Press.

Miller, G.A., Galanter, E., and Pribram, K.H. (1960) *Plans and the Structure of Behavior*. New York: Henry Holt.

Minsky, M. (1968) Matter, mind, and models. In Minsky, M. (ed.), *Semantic Information Processing*. Cambridge, MA: MIT Press, pp. 425–432.

Minsky, M. (1975) Frame-system theory. In Schank, R.C. and Webber, B.L. (eds), *Theoretical Issues in Natural Language Processing*. Reprinted in Johnson-Laird, P.C. and Wason, P.C. (eds), *Thinking: Readings in Cognitive Science*. Cambridge: Cambridge University Press, 1977, pp. 355–376.

Minsky, M. (1985) *The Society of Mind*. New York: Simon and Schuster.

Minsky, M.L. and Papert, S.A. (1969) *Perceptrons*. Cambridge, MA: MIT Press.

Mitchell, M. (1998) *An Introduction to Genetic Algorithms*. Cambridge, MA: MIT Press.

Miyake, N. (1986) Constructive interaction and the iterative process of understanding. *Cognitive Science*, 10, 151–177.

Miyamoto, J. M., Gonzalez, R., and Tu, S. (1995) Compositional anomalies in the semantics of evidence. In Busemeyer, J., Hastie, R., and Medin, D. (eds), *Decision Making from a Cognitive Perspective*. (Vol. 32. *The Psychology of Learning and Motivation*). New York: Academic Press, pp. 319–383.

Montague, R. (1974) *Formal Philosophy: Selected Papers*. New Have: Yale University Press.

Morris, A.K. and Sloutsky,V.M. (1998) Understanding of logical necessity: developmental antecedents and cognitive consequences. *Child Development*, 69, 721–741.

Morris, B.J. and Sloutsky, V.M. (2002) Children's solutions of logical versus empirical problems: what's missing and what develops. *Cognitive Development* 16, 907–928.

Morris, M.W., Nisbett, R.E., and Peng, K. (1995) Causal attribution across domains and cultures. In Sperber, D., Premack, D., and Premack, A.J. (eds), *Causal Cognition*: a *Multidisciplinary Debate*. New York: Oxford University Press, pp. 577–614.

Mostowski, A. (1957) On a generalization of quantifiers. *Fundamenta Mathematicae*, 44, 12–36.

Moxey, L.M. and Sanford, A.J. (1993) *Communicating Quantities: a Psychological Perspective*. Hove, Sussex: Erlbaum.

Moxey, L.M. and Sanford, A.J. (2000) Communicating quantities: a review of psycholinguistic evidence of how expressions determine perspectives. *Applied Cognitive Psychology*, 14, 237–255.

Murphy, G.L. and Medin, D.L. (1985) The role of theories in conceptual coherence. *Psychological Review*, 92, 289–316.

Murray, G. (1915) *The Stoic Philosophy*. New York: G.P. Putnam.

Neisser, U. (1963) The imitation of man by machine. *Science*, 139, 193–197.

Neisser, U. and Weene, P. (1962) Hierarchies in concept attainment. *Journal of Experimental Psychology*, 64, 640–645.

Nesse, R.M. (1991) What good is feeling bad? *The Sciences*, November/December, 30–37.

Neth, H. and Johnson-Laird, P.N. (1999) The search for counterexamples in human reasoning. *Proceedings of the Twenty First Annual Conference of the Cognitive Science Society*, 806.

Newell, A. (1980) Physical symbol systems. *Cognitive Science*, 2, 135–184.

Newell, A. (1981) Reasoning, problem solving and decision processes: the problem space as a fundamental category. In Nickerson, R. (ed.), *Attention and Performance*, Vol. 8. Hillsdale, NJ: Erlbaum, pp. 693–718.

Newell, A. (1990) *Unified Theories of Cognition*. Cambridge. MA: Harvard University Press.

Newell, A. and Simon, H.A. (1972) *Human Problem Solving*. Englewood Cliffs, NJ: Prentice Hall.

Newsome, M.R. and Johnson-Laird, P.N. (1996) An antidote to illusory inferences? In Cottrell, G.W. (ed.), *Proceedings of the Eighteenth Annual Conference of the Cognitive Science Society*. Mahwah, NJ: Erlbaum, p. 820.

Newstead, S.E. and Griggs, R.A. (1983) The language and thought of disjunction. In Evans, J.St.B.T. (ed.), *Thinking and Reasoning: Psychological Approaches*. London: Routledge & Kegan Paul, pp. 76–106.

Newstead, S.E., Pollard, P., and Griggs, R.A. (1986) Response bias in relational reasoning. *Bulletin of the Psychonomic Society*, 24, 95–98.

Newstead, S.E., Ellis, M.C., Evans, J.St.B.T., and Dennis, I. (1997) Conditional reasoning with realistic material. *Thinking & Reasoning*, 3, 49–76.

Newstead, S.E., Handley, S.J., and Buck, E. (1999) Falsifying mental models: testing the predictions of theories of syllogistic reasoning. *Memory & Cognition*, 27, 344–354.

Newstead, S.E., Thompson, V.A., and Handley, S.J. (2002) Generating alternatives: a key component of human reasoning? *Memory & Cognition*, 30, 129–137.

Newton, I. (1952) *Opticks: a Treatise of the Reflections, Refractions, Inflections & Colours of Light*. New York: Dover. (Based on the 4th edn, London, 1730.)

Nicholl, C. (2004) *Leonardo da Vinci: Flights of the Mind*. New York: Viking.

Nichols, S. (2002) Norms with feeling: towards a psychological account of moral judgment. *Cognition*, 84, 221–236.

Nickerson, R.S. (1996) Hempel's paradox and Wason's selection task: logical and psychological problems of confirmation. *Thinking & Reasoning*, 2, 1–31.

Niedenthal, P.M., Tangney, J.P., and Gavanski, I. (1994) "If only I weren't" versus "if only I hadn't": Distinguishing shame and guilt in counterfactual thinking. *Journal of Personality and Social Psychology*, 67, 585–595.

Nisbett, R.E. (2003) *The Geography of Thought: How Asians and Westerners Think Differently ... and Why*. New York: the Free Press.

Nisbett, R.E. and Wilson, T. (1977) Telling more than we can know: verbal reports on mental processes. *Psychological Review*, 84, 231–259.

Nisbett, R.E., Krantz, D.H., Jepson, D., and Kunda, Z. (1983) The use of statistical heuristics in everyday inductive reasoning. *Psychological Review*, 90, 339–363.

Northcutt, W. (2000) *The Darwin Awards: Evolution in Action*. New York: Penguin Putnam.

Norvig, P. (1992) *Paradigms of Artificial Intelligence Programming: Case Studies in Common Lisp*. San Mateo, CA: Morgan Kaufman.

Norenzayan, A., Smith, E.E., Jun Kim, B., and Nisbett, R.E. (2002) Cultural preferences for formal versus intuitive reasoning. *Cognitive Science*, 26, 653–684.

Noveck, I.A. (2001) When children are more logical than adults: experimental investigations of scalar implicature. *Cognition*, 78, 165–188.

Nundy, S. (1995) The effects of emotion on human inference: towards a computational model. Unpublished Ph.D. thesis, Graduate Department of Education, University of Toronto.

Oakhill, J.V. and Johnson-Laird, P.N. (1985) The effects of belief on the spontaneous production of syllogistic conclusions. *Quarterly Journal of Experimental Psychology*, 37A, 553–569.

Oakhill, J., Johnson-Laird, P.N., and Garnham, A. (1989) Believability and syllogistic reasoning. *Cognition*, 31, 117–140.

Oakhill, J., Garnham, A., and Johnson-Laird, P.N. (1990) Belief bias in syllogistic reasoning. In Gilhooly, K., Keane, M., Logie, R., and Erdos, G. (eds), *Lines of Thinking*, Vol. I. New York: Wiley, pp. 125–138.

Oaksford, M. and Chater, N. (1991) Against logicist cognitive science. *Mind & Language*, 6, 1–38.

Oaksford, M. and Chater, N. (1994) A rational analysis of the selection task as optimal data selection. *Psychological Review*, 101, 608–631.

Oaksford, M. and Chater, N. (1998) *Rationality in an Uncertain World*. Hove, UK: Psychology Press.

Oaksford, M. and Chater, N. (2001) The probabilistic approach to human reasoning. *Trends in Cognitive Sciences*, 5, 349–357.

Oaksford, M. and Stenning, K. (1992) Reasoning with conditionals containing negated constituents. *Journal of Experimental Psychology: Learning, Memory, and Cognition*, 18, 835–854.

Oaksford, M., Morris, F., Grainger, R., and Williams, J.M.G. (1996) Mood, reasoning, and central executive processes. *Journal of Experimental Psychology: Learning, Memory, and Cognition*, 22, 477–493.

Oaksford, M., Chater, N., and Larkin, J. (2000) Probabilities and polarity biases in conditional inference. *Journal of Experimental Psychology: Learning, Memory and Cognition*, 26, 883–899.

Oatley, K. (1976) Inference, navigation, and cognitive maps. In Johnson-Laird, P.N., and Wason, P.C. (eds), *Thinking: Readings in Cognitive Science*. Cambridge: Cambridge University Press, pp. 537–547.

Oatley, K. (1978) *Perceptions and Representations: the Theoretical Bases of Brain Research and Psychology*. London: Methuen.

Oatley, K. (1996) Emotions, rationality, and informal reasoning. In Oakhill, J. and Garnham, A. (eds), *Mental Models in Cognitive Science*. Hove, Sussex: Psychology Press, pp. 175–196.

Oatley, K. (1998) *A Natural History*. Toronto, Ontario: Viking Penguin.

Oatley, K. and Johnson-Laird, P.N. (1987) Towards a cognitive theory of emotion. *Cognition and Emotion*, 1, 29–50.

Oatley, K. and Johnson-Laird, P.N. (1996) The communicative theory of emotions: empirical tests, mental models, and implications for social interaction. In Martin, L.L. and Tesser, A. (eds), *Striving and Feeling: Interactions Among Goals, Affect, and Self-regulation*. Mahwah, NJ: Erlbaum, pp. 363–393.

Oberauer, K. and Wilhelm, O. (2000) Effects of directionality in deductive reasoning: I. The comprehension of single relational premises. *Journal of Experimental Psychology: Learning, Memory, and Cognition*, 26, 1702–1712.

Oberauer, K. and Wilhelm, W. (2003) The meaning(s) of conditionals: conditional probability, mental models, and personal utilities. *Journal of Experimental Psychology: Learning, Memory & Cognition*, 29, 680–693.

Oberauer, K., Hörnig, R., Weidenfeld, A., and Wilhelm, O. (2005) Effects of directionality in deductive reasoning, II: Premise integration and conclusion evaluation. *Quarterly Journal of Experimental Psychology*, 58A, 1225–1247.

Ochsner, K.N. and Gross, J.J. (2005) The cognitive control of emotion. *Trends in Cognitive Sciences*, 9, 242–249.

O'Connor, K. and Aardema, F. (2003) Fusion or confusion in obsessive-compulsive disorder. *Psychological Reports*, 93, 227–232.

Ohlsson, S. (1984a) Restructuring revisited I: Summary and critique of Gestalt theory of problem solving. *Scandinavian Journal of Psychology*, 25, 65–76.

Ohlsson, S. (1984b) Restructuring revisited II: an information processing theory of restructuring and insight. *Scandinavian Journal of Psychology*, 25, 117–129.

O'Keefe, J. and Nadel, L. (1978) *The Hippocampus as a Cognitive Map*. Oxford: Clarendon Press.

O'Neill, J.J. (1944) *Prodigal Genius: the Life of Nikola Tesla*. New York: Ives Washburn.

Orleans, S. and Orleans, J. (1983) *The Great Big Book of Pencil Puzzles*. New York: Pedigree.

Ormerod, T.C., MacGregor, J.N., and Chronicle, E.P. (2002) Dynamics and constraints in insight problem solving. *Journal of Experimental Psychology: Learning, Memory, and Cognition*, 28, 791–799.

Ormerod, T.C., Manktelow, K.I., and Jones, G.V. (1993) Reasoning with three types of conditional: biases and mental models. *Quarterly Journal of Experimental Psychology*, 46A, 653–678.

Ormerod, T.C. and Richardson, J. (2003) On the generation and evaluation of inferences from single premises. *Memory & Cognition*, 31, 467–478.

Ormrod, J.E. (1979) Cognitive processes in the solution of three-term series problems. *American Journal of Psychology*, 92, 235–255.

Ortony, A. and Turner, T.J. (1990) What's basic about basic emotions? *Psychological Review*, 74, 431–461.

Ortony, A., Clore, G.L., and Collins, A. (1988) *The Cognitive Structure of Emotions*. New York: Cambridge University Press.

O'Shea, S. (2000) *The Perfect Heresy: the Revolutionary Life and Death of the Medieval Cathars*. New York: Walker.

Osherson, D.N. (1974–76) *Logical Abilities in Children*, Vols 1–4. Hillsdale, NJ: Erlbaum.

Osherson, D.N., Smith, E.E., and Shafir, E. (1986) Some origins of belief. *Cognition*, 24, 197–224.

Osherson, D., Perani, D., Cappa, S., Schnur, T., Grassi, F., and Fazio, F. (1998) Distinct brain loci in deductive versus probabilistic reasoning. *Neuropsychologia*, 36, 369–376.

Osofsky, M.J., Bandura, A., and Zimbardo, P.G. (2005) The role of moral disengagement in the execution process. *Law and Human Behavior*, 29, 371–393.

Oswald, N.C., Waller, R.E., and Drinkwater, J. (1970) Relationship between breathlessness and anxiety in asthma and bronchitis: a comparative study. *British Medical Journal*, 2, 14–17.

Otero, J. and Kintsch, W. (1992) Failures to detect contradictions in a text: what readers believe versus what they read. *Psychological Science*, 3, 229–235.

Over, D.E. and Evans, J.St.B.T. (1997) Two cheers for deductive competence. *Current Psychology of Cognition*, 16, 225–278.

Paccanaro, A. and Hinton, G.E. (2000) Learning distributed representations of concepts from relational data using linear relational embedding. *IEEE Transactions on Knowledge and Data Engineering*, 13, 232–245.

Paine, T. (1989) *Political Writings*. Kucklik, B. (ed.). Cambridge: Cambridge University Press.

Paivio, A. (1971) *Imagery and Verbal Processes*. New York: Holt, Rinehart & Winston.

Paris, S.G. (1973) Comprehension of language connectives and propositional logical relationships. *Journal of Experimental Child Psychology*, 16, 278–291.

Parsons, L.M. and Osherson, D. (2001) New evidence for distinct right and left brain systems for deductive versus probabilistic reasoning. *Cerebral Cortex*, 11, 954–965.

Partee, B.H. (1995) Lexical semantics and compositionality. In Gleitman, L.R. and Liberman, M. (eds), *Language: an Invitation to Cognitive Science*, Vol. 1. Cambridge, MA: MIT Press, pp. 311–360.

Pascal, B. (1966) *Pensées* (Trans. Krailsheimer, A.J.). Harmonsworth, Middx, UK: Penguin. (First version published in 1670.)

Pearl, J. (1988) *Probabilistic Reasoning in Intelligent Systems: Networks of Plausible Inference*. Revised Second Printing. San Francisco: Morgan Kaufmann.

Pearl, J. (2000) *Causality: Models, Reasoning, and Inference*. Cambridge: Cambridge University Press.

Pearson, H. (1984) *The Smith of Smiths: Being the Life, Wit, and Humour of Sydney Smith*. London: Hogarth. (Originally published in 1934.)

Peirce, C.S. (1931–1958) Hartshorne, C., Weiss, P., and Burks, A. (eds), *Collected Papers of Charles Sanders Peirce*, 8 vols. Cambridge, MA: Harvard University Press.

Peirce, C.S. (1955) Buchler, J. (ed.), *Philosophical Writings of Peirce*. New York: Dover.

Pélissier, M-C. and O'Connor, K.P. (2002) Deductive and inductive reasoning in obsessive-compulsive disorder. *British Journal of Clinical Psychology*, 41, 15–27.

Peng, K. and Nisbett, R.E. (1999) Culture, dialectics, and reasoning about contradiction. *American Psychologist*, 54, 741–754.

Perham, N. and Oaksford, M. (2005) Deontic reasoning with emotional content: evolutionary psychology or decision theory? *Cognitive Science*, 29, 681–718.

Perkins, D.N. (1981) *The Mind's Best Work*. Cambridge, MA: Harvard University Press.

Perkins, D. (2000) *The Eureka Effect: the Art and Logic of Breakthrough Thinking*. New York: Norton.

Perkins, D.N., Farady, M., and Bushey, B. (1990) Everyday reasoning and the roots of intelligence. In Voss, J., Perkins, D.N., and Segal, J. (eds), *Informal Reasoning and Education*. Hillsdale, NJ: Erlbaum, pp. 83–105.

Perner, J. (1991) *Understanding the Representational Mind*. Cambridge, MA: MIT Press.

Perner, J., Leekham, S., and Wimmer, H. (1987) Three year olds' difficulty with false belief: the case for conceptual deficit. *British Journal of Developmental Psychology*, 5, 125–137.

Perner, J., Sprung, M., and Steinkogler, B. (2004) Counterfactual conditionals and false belief: a developmental dissociation. *Cognitive Development,* 19, 179–201.

Peterson, D. and Riggs, K.J. (1999) Adaptive modelling and mindreading. *Mind & Language*, 14, 80–112.

Piaget, J. (1928) *Judgment and Reasoning in the Child*. London: Kegan Paul.

Piaget, J. (1965a) *Logic and Psychology* (Trans. Mays, W. and Whitehead, F.W.). Manchester: Manchester University Press.

Piaget, J. (1965b) *The Moral Judgment of the Child*. New York: Free Press.

Piaget, J. (1987) *Possibility and Necessity*, Vols 1 and 2. Minneapolis, MN: University of Minnesota Press.

Piaget, J. and Inhelder, B. (1969) *The Psychology of the Child*. New York: Basic Books.

Pica, P., Lemer, C., Izard, V., and Dehaene, S. (2004) Exact and approximate arithmetic in an Amazonian indigene group. *Science*, 496, 499–503.

Pinker, S. (1997) *How the Mind Works*. New York: W.W. Norton.

Pinker, S. (2002) *The Blank Slate: the Modern Denial of Human Nature*. New York: Viking.

Plato (1961) Hamilton, E. and Cairns, H. (eds), *Complete Works: the Collected Dialogues of Plato*. Princeton, NJ: Princeton University Press.

Platt, R.D. and Griggs, R.A. (1993) Facilitation in the abstract selection task: the effects of attentional and instructional factors. *Quarterly Journal of Experimental Psychology*, 46A, 591–613.

Poe, E.A. (1982) *The Complete Tales and Poems of Edgar Allan Poe*. London: Penguin.

Politzer, G. (1986) Laws of language use and of formal logic. *Journal of Psycholinguistic Research*, 15, 47–92.

Politzer, G. and Bourmaud, G. (2002) Deductive reasoning from uncertain conditionals. *British Journal of Psychology*, 93, 345–381.

Politzer, G. and Carles, L. (2001) Belief revision and uncertain reasoning. *Thinking & Reasoning*, 7, 217–234.

Polk, T.A. and Newell, A. (1995) Deduction as verbal reasoning. *Psychological Review*, 102, 533–566.

Pollock, J. (1989) *How to Build a Person: a Prolegomenon*. Cambridge, MA: MIT Bradford Books.

Polya, G. (1973) *How To Solve It: a New Aspect of Mathematical Methods*, 2nd edn. Princeton, NJ: Princeton University Press. (Originally published 1945.)

Popper, K. (1959) *The Logic of Scientific Discovery*. London: Hutchinson.

Porter, R. (1997) *The Greatest Benefit to Mankind: a Medical History of Humanity*. New York: W.W. Norton.

Potts, G.R. and Scholz, K.W. (1975) The internal representation of a three-term series problem. *Journal of Verbal Learning and Verbal Behavior*, 14, 439–452.

Poundstone, W. (1988) *Labyrinths of Reason: Paradox, Puzzles, and the Frailty of Knowledge.* New York: Anchor Books, Doubleday.

Power, M. and Dalgleish, T. (1997) *Cognition and Emotion: From Order to Disorder.* Hove, East Sussex: Psychology Press.

Power, M. and Wykes, T. (1996) The mental health of mental models and the mental models of mental health. In Oakhill, J., and Garnham, A. (eds), *Mental Models in Cognitive Science.* Hove, Sussex: Psychology Press, pp. 197–222.

Power, R. (1984) *Inverted Deductions with Numerical Quantifiers.* Report 104. Padua: University of Padua, Institute of Psychology.

Powers, A.L. (ed.) (1997) *Italy in Mind: an Anthology.* New York: Random House.

Prawitz, D. (1965) *Natural Deduction: a Proof-theoretical Study.* Uppsala, Sweden: Almqvist and Wiksell.

Premack, D. (1990) Words: What are they, and do animals have them? *Cognition*, 37, 197–212.

Pylyshyn, Z. (1973) What the mind's eye tells the mind's brain: a critique of mental imagery. *Psychological Bulletin*, 80, 1–24.

Pylyshyn, Z. (1981) The imagery debate: analogue media versus tacit knowledge. *Psychological Review*, 88, 16–45.

Pylyshyn, Z. (2003) Return of the mental image: Are there really pictures in the head? *Trends in Cognitive Sciences*, 2003, 7, 113–118.

Quelhas, C. and Byrne, R.M.J. (2003) Reasoning with deontic and counterfactual conditionals. *Thinking & Reasoning*, 9, 43–66.

Quine, W.V.O. (1952) *Methods of Logic.* London: Routledge & Kegan Paul.

Quine, W.V.O. (1955) A way to simplify truth functions, *American Mathematical Monthly*, 59, 521–531.

Quine, W.V.O. (1974) *Methods of Logic*, 3rd edn. London: Routledge.

Quinn, S. and Markovits, H. (2002) Conditional reasoning with causal premises: evidence for a retrieval model. *Thinking & Reasoning*, 8, 179–191.

Quinton, G. and Fellows, B.J. (1975) "Percepual" strategies in the solving of three-term series problems. *British Journal of Psychology*, 66, 69–78.

Rabbitt, P.M.A. and Anderson, M. (2006) The lacunae of loss? Aging and the differentiation of cognitive abilities. In Bialystok, E. and Craik, F.I.M. (eds), *Lifespan Cognition: Mechanisms of Change.* Oxford: Oxford University Press. In press.

Rader, A.W. and Sloutsky, V.M. (2001) Conjunction bias in memory representations of logical connectives. *Memory & Cognition*, 29, 838–849.

Rader, A.W. and Sloutsky, V.M. (2002) Processing of logically valid and logically invalid conditional inferences in discourse comprehension. *Journal of Experimental Psychology: Learning, Memory and Cognition*, 28, 59–68.

Ragni, M. (2003) An arrangement calculus, its complexity and algorithmic properties. *Advances in Artificial Intelligence: Lecture Notes in Computer Science*, 2821, 580–590.

Ramsey, F.P. (1990) Mellor, D.H. (ed.), *Foundations: Essays in Philosophy, Logic, Mathematics and Economics.* London: Humanities Press, pp. 145–163. (Originally published in 1929.)

Reason, J.T. (1988) Stress and cognitive failure. In Fisher, S. and Reason, J.T. (eds), *Handbook of Life Stress, Cognition and Health.* Chichester: Wiley, pp. 405–421.

Reason, J.T. (1990) *Human Error.* Cambridge: Cambridge University Press.

Reed, G. (1977) Obsessional cognition: performance on two numerical tasks. *British Journal of Psychiatry*, 130, 184–185.

Rehder, B. and Hastie, R. (1996) The moderating influence and variability on belief revision. *Psychonomic Bulletin and Review*, 3, 499–503.

Reichenbach, H. (1956) *The Direction of Time*. Berkeley: University of California Press.

Reid, T. (1846) *The Works of Thomas Reid*. Edinburgh: Maclachlan and Stewart.

Reinhart, T. (1986) On the interpretation of "donkey"-sentences. In Traugott, E.C., ter Meulen, A., Reilly, J.S., and Ferguson, C.A. (eds), *On Conditionals*. Cambridge: Cambridge University Press, pp. 103–122.

Reiter, R. (1980) A logic for default reasoning. *Artificial Intelligence*, 13, 81–132.

Reitman, W.R. (1965) *Cognition and Thought*. New York: Wiley.

Rescher, N. (1973) *The Coherence Theory of Truth*. Oxford: Oxford University Press.

Revlin, R., Cate, C.L., and Rouss, T.S. (2001) Reasoning counterfactually: combining and rending. *Memory & Cognition*, 29, 1196–1208.

Revlis, R. (1974) Prevarication: Reasoning from false assumptions. *Memory & Cognition*, 2A, 87–95.

Revlis, R. (1975) Two models of syllogistic reasoning: feature selection and conversion. *Journal of Verbal Learning and Verbal Behavior*, 14, 180–195.

Revlis, R. and Hayes, J.R. (1972) The primacy of generalities in hypothetical reasoning. *Cognitive Psychology*, 3, 268–290.

Revlis, R., Lipkin, S.G., and Hayes, J.R. (1971) The importance of universal quantifiers in a hypothetical reasoning task. *Journal of Verbal Learning and Verbal Behavior*, 10, 86–91.

Rhéaume, J., Freeston, M.H., Ladouceur, R., Bouchard, C., Gallant, L., Talbot, F., and Valliéres, A. (2000) Functional and dysfunctional perfectionists: are they different on compulsive-like behaviors? *Behaviour Research and Therapy*, 38, 119–128.

Ribe, N. and Steinle, F. (2005) Exploratory experimentation: Goethe, Land, and color theory. www.physicstoday.org/vol-55/iss-7/p43.html

Richardson, J.T.E. (1987) The role of mental imagery in models of transitive inference. *British Journal of Psychology*, 78, 189–203.

Richardson, J. and Ormerod, T.C. (1997) Rephrasing between disjunctives and conditionals: mental models and the effects of thematic content. *Quarterly Journal of Experimental Psychology*, 50A, 358–385.

Riesbeck, C.K. and Schank, R.C. (1989) *Inside Case-Based Reasoning*. Hillsdale, NJ: Erlbaum.

Riggs, K.J., Peterson, D.M., Robinson, E.J., and Mitchell, P. (1998) Are errors in false belief tasks symptomatic of a broader difficulty with counterfactuality? *Cognitive Development*, 13, 73–90.

Riley, C.A. (1976) The representation of comparative relations and the transitive inference task. *Journal of Experimental Child Psychology*, 22, 1–22.

Riley, C.A. and Trabasso, T. (1974) Comparatives, logical structures, and encoding in a transitive inference task. *Journal of Experimental Child Psychology*, 17, 187–203.

Rips, L.J. (1983) Cognitive processes in propositional reasoning. *Psychological Review*, 90, 38–71.

Rips, L.J. (1989) The psychology of knights and knaves. *Cognition*, 31, 85–116.

Rips, L.J. (1990) Paralogical reasoning: Evans, Johnson-Laird, and Byrne on liar and truth-teller puzzles. *Cognition*, 36, 291–314.

Rips, L.J. (1994) *The Psychology of Proof*. Cambridge, MA: MIT Press.

Rips, L.J. (1998) Reasoning and conversation. *Psychological Review*, 105, 411–441.

Rips, L.J. (2002) Reasoning. In Medin, D. (ed.), *Stevens' Handbook of Experimental Psychology*, Vol. 2: *Memory and Cognitive Processes*, 3rd edn. New York: John Wiley, pp. 317–362.

Rips, L.J. and Collins, A. (1993) Categories and resemblance. *Journal of Experimental Psychology: General*, 122, 468–486.

Rips, L.J., Shoben, E.J., and Smith, E.E. (1973) Semantic distance and the verification of semantic relations. *Journal of Verbal Learning and Verbal Behavior*, 12, 1–20.

Rips, L.J., Brem, S.K., and Bailenson, J.N. (1999) Reasoning dialogues. *Current Directions in Psychological Science*, 8, 172–177.

Roberts, M.J. (2000) Strategies in relational inference. *Thinking & Reasoning*, 6, 1–26.

Roberts, M.J. (2006) Falsification and mental models: it depends on the task. In Schaeken, W., Vandierendonck, A., Schroyens, W., and d'Ydewalle, G. (eds), *The Mental Models Theory of Reasoning: Refinement and Extensions*. Mahwah, NJ: Erlbaum. In press.

Roberts, M.J. and Sykes, E.D.A. (2005) Categorical reasoning from multiple diagrams. *Quarterly Journal of Experimental Psychology*, 58A, 333–376.

Robinson, L.A., Berman, J.S., and Neimeyer, R.A. (1990). Psychotherapy for the treatment of depression: a comprehensive review of controlled outcome research. *Psychological Bulletin*, 108, 30–49.

Roese, N.J. (1997) Counterfactual thinking. *Psychological Bulletin*, 121, 133–148.

Rogers, L.J. (1997) *Minds of Their Own*. St. Leonards, UK: Allen & Unwin.

Rosch, E. (1973) Natural categories. *Cognitive Psychology*, 4, 328–35.

Rosenblatt, F. (1958) The perceptron: a probabilistic model for information storage and organization in the brain, *Psychological Review*, 65, 386–408.

Rosenblatt, F. (1961) *Principles of Neurodynamics*. Washington, DC: Spartan Press.

Ross, L. (1977) The intuitive psychologist and his shortcomings: distortions in the attribution process. In Berkowitz, L. (ed.), *Advances in Experimental Social Psychology*, Vol. 10. New York: Academic Press, pp. 174–221.

Ross, L. and Lepper, M.R. (1980) The perseverance of beliefs: empirical and normative considerations. In Shweder, R.A. (ed.), *Fallible Judgement in Behavioral Research: New Directions for Methodology of Social and Behavioral Science*, Vol. 4. San Francisco, CA: Jossey-Bass, pp. 17–36.

Royzman, E.B. and Baron, J. (2002). The preference for indirect harm. *Social Justice Research*, 15, 165–184.

Rozenblit, L.R. and Keil, F.C. (2002) The misunderstood limits of folk science: an illusion of explanatory depth. *Cognitive Science*, 26, 521–562.

Rozin, P. (1996) Towards a psychology of food and eating: from motivation to module to model to marker, morality, meaning, and metaphor. *Current Directions in Psychological Science*, 5, 18–24.

Russell, B.A.W. (1905) On denoting. *Mind*, 14, 479–493.

Russell, B.A.W. (1912–13) On the notion of cause. *Proceedings of the Aristotelian Society*, 13, 1–26.

Russell, B.A.W. (1927) *An Outline of Philosophy*. London: Allen and Unwin.

Russell, B.A.W. (1946) *The History of Western Philosophy*. New York: Simon & Schuster.

Russell, B.A.W. (1957) Knowledge by acquaintance and knowledge by description. In his *Mysticism and Logic*. Garden City, NY: Doubleday. (Originally published 1917.)

Russell, B.A.W. (1967) *The Autobiography of Bertrand Russell*, 3 vols. Boston: Little, Brown.

Russell, J. (1987) Rule-following, mental models, and the developmental view. In Chapman, M., and Dixon, R.A. (eds), *Meaning and the Growth of Understanding: Wittgenstein's Significance for Developmental Psychology*. New York: Springer, pp. 23–48.

Russell, J.A. (1991) In defense of a prototype approach to emotion concepts. *Journal of Personality and Social Psychology*, 60, 37–47.

Russell, S. (1989) *The Use of Knowledge in Analogy and Induction*. London: Pitman.

Russo, J.E., Johnson, E.J., and Stephens, D.L. (1989) The validity of verbal protocols. *Memory & Cognition*, 17, 759–769.

Sainsbury, M. (2001) *Logical Forms: an Introduction to Philosophical Logic*, 2nd edn. Oxford: Blackwell.

Salkovskis, P.M. (1996) The cognitive approach to anxiety: threat beliefs, safety-seeking behavior, and the special case of health anxiety and obsession. In Salkovskis, P.M. (ed.), *Frontiers of Cognitive Therapy*. New York: Guilford Press, pp. 48–74.

Salmon, W.C. (1980) Probabilistic causality. *Pacific Philosophical Quarterly*, 61, 50–74.

Salsburg, D. (2001) *The Lady Tasting Tea: How Statistics Revolutionized Science in the Twentieth Century*. New York: W.H. Freeman.

Samarapungavan, A., Vosniadou, S., and Brewer, W. (1996) Mental models of the earth, sun and moon: Indian children's cosmologies. *Cognitive Development*, 11, 491–521.

Santamaría, C. and Johnson-Laird, P.N. (2000) An antidote to illusory inferences. *Thinking & Reasoning*, 6, 313–333.

Sartre, J-P. (1948) *The Emotions: Outline of a Theory* (Trans. Frechtman, B.). New York: Philosophical Library.

Savage, L.J. (1954) *The Foundations of Statistics*. New York: Wiley.

Schachter, S. and Singer, J.E. (1962) Cognitive, social, and psychological determinants of emotional state. *Psychological Review*, 69, 379–399.

Schaeken, W.S., Johnson-Laird, P.N., and d'Ydewalle, G. (1996a) Mental models and temporal reasoning. *Cognition*, 60, 205–234.

Schaeken, W.S., Johnson-Laird, P.N., and d'Ydewalle, G. (1996b) Tense, aspect, and temporal reasoning. *Thinking and Reasoning*, 2, 309–327.

Schaeken, W.S., Girotto, V., and Johnson-Laird, P.N. (1998) The effect of an irrelevant premise on temporal and spatial reasoning. *Kognitionswisschenschaft*, 7, 27–32.

Schaeken, W.S., De Vooght, G., Vandierendonck, A., and d'Ydewalle, G. (2000) *Deductive Reasoning and Strategies*. Mahwah, NJ: Erlbaum.

Schaeken, W.S., Van der Henst, J-B., and Schroyens, W. (in press) The mental models theory of relational reasoning: premise relevance, conclusion phrasing and cognitive economy. In Schaeken, W., Vandierendonck, A., Schroyens, W., and d'Ydewalle, G. (eds), *The Mental Models Theory of Reasoning: Extensions and Refinements*. Mahwah, NJ: Erlbaum.

Schank, R.C. and Abelson, R.P. (1977) *Scripts, Plans, Goals and Understanding*. Hillsdale, NJ: Erlbaum.

Schkade, D.A. and Kahneman, D. (1998) Does living in California make people happy? *Psychological Science*, 9, 340–346.

Schlottmann, A. and Anderson, N.H. (1995) Belief revision in children: Serial judgment in social cognition and decision-making domains. *Journal of Experimental Psychology: Learning, Memory, and Cognition*, 21, 1349–1364.

Schooler, J., Ohlsson, S., and Brooks, K. (1993) Thoughts beyond words: when language overshadows insight. *Journal of Experimental Psychology: General*, 122, 166–183.

Schroyens, W. (1997) Meta-propositional reasoning about the truth or falsity of propositions. *Psychologica Belgica*, 37, 219–247.

Schroyens, W. and Schaeken, W. (2003) A critique of Oaksford, Chater, and Larkin's (2000) conditional probability model of conditional reasoning. *Journal of Experimental Psychology: Learning, Memory, and Cognition*, 29, 1, 140–149.

Schroyens, W. and Schaeken, W. (2004) Guilt by association: on iffy propositions and the proper treatment of mental-models theory. *Current Psychology Letters*, 12, 1.

Schroyens, W., Schaeken, W., and d'Ydewalle, G. (1996) Meta-propositional reasoning with knight–knave problems: the importance of being hypothesized. *Psychologica Belgica*, 36, 145–169.

Schroyens, W., Schaeken, W., and d'Ydewalle, G. (1999) Error and bias in meta-propositional reasoning: a case of the mental model theory, *Thinking & Reasoning*, 5, 29–65.

Schroyens, W., Schaeken, W., and d'Ydewalle, G. (2001a) The processing of negations in conditional reasoning: a meta-analytical case study in mental models and/or mental logic theory. *Thinking & Reasoning*, 7, 121–172.

Schroyens, W., Schaeken, W., and d'Ydewalle, G. (2001b) A meta-analytic review of conditional reasoning by model and/or rule: mental models theory revised. Unpublished paper.

Schroyens, W., Schaeken, W., and Handley, S. (2003) In search of counter examples: deductive rationality in human reasoning. *Quarterly Journal of Experimental Psychology*, 56A (7), 1129–1145.

Schustack, M.W. (1988) Thinking about causality. In Sternberg, R.J. and Smith, E.E. (eds), *The Psychology of Thinking*. Cambridge: Cambridge University Press, pp. 92–115.

Scoditti, G.M.G. (1984) The use of "metaphors" in Kitawa culture, Northern Massim. *Oceania*, 55, 50–70.

Scoville, W.B. and Milner, B. (1957) Loss of recent memory after bilateral hippocampal lesions. *Journal of Neurology, Neurosurgery and Psychiatry*, 20, 11–12.

Scribner, S. (1977) Modes of thinking and ways of speaking: culture and logic reconsidered. In Johnson-Laird, P.N. and Wason, P.C. (eds), *Thinking: Readings in Cognitive Science*. Cambridge: Cambridge University Press, pp. 483–500.

Scriven, M. (1976) *Reasoning*. New York: McGraw-Hill.

Searle, J.R. (1980) Minds, brains, and programs. *Behavioral and Brain Sciences*, 3, 417–424.

Sebeok, T.A. and Umiker-Sebeok, J. (1983) "You know my method": a juxtaposition of Charles S. Peirce and Sherlock Holmes. In Eco, U., and Sebeok, T.A. *The Sign of Three: Dupin, Holmes, Peirce*. Bloomington, IN: Indiana University Press, pp. 11–54.

Seligman, M.E.P. (1995) The effectiveness of psychotherapy: the *Consumer Reports* Study, *American Psychologist*, 50, 965–974.

Sells, S.B. (1936) The atmosphere effect: an experimental study of reasoning. *Archives of Psychology*, 29, 3–72.

Shafer, G. (1996) *The Art of Causal Conjecture*. Cambridge: MIT Press.

Shafir, E. and Tversky, A. (1992) Thinking through uncertainty: nonconsequential reasoning and choice. *Cognitive Psychology*, 24, 449–474.

Shafir, S. (1994) Intransitivity of preferences in honey bees—support for comparative evaluation of foraging options. *Animal Behaviour*, 48, 55–67.

Shanks, D.R. (2004) Judging covariation and causation. In Koehler, D.J. and Harvey, N. (eds), *Handbook of Judgment and Decision Making*. Oxford: Blackwell, pp. 220–239.

Shannon, C.E. and Weaver, W. (1949) *The Mathematical Theory of Communication*. Urbana, IL: University of Illinois Press.

Shastri, L. (1988) A connectionist approach to knowledge representation and limited inference. *Cognitive Science*, 12, 331–392.

Shastri, L. and Ajjanagadde, V. (1993) From simple associations to systematic reasoning: a connectionist representation of rules, variables and dynamic bindings using temporal synchrony. *Behavioral and Brain Sciences*, 16, 417–494.

Shaver, P.R., Pierson, L., and Lang, S. (1975) Converging evidence for the functional significance of imagery in problem solving. *Cognition*, 3, 359–375.

Shaw, B. (1965) *The Complete Plays of Bernard Shaw*. London: Paul Hamlyn.

Shaw, V.F. and Johnson-Laird, P.N. (1998) Dispelling the "atmosphere" effect in reasoning. *Analise Psicologia*. Special issue on *Cognition and Context*, Quelhas, A.C., and Pereira, F. (eds), 169–199.

Sheen, Mr Justice. (1987) Report of Court No. 8074; mv Herald of Free Enterprise. London: Her Majesty's Stationary Office (HMSO).

Shepard, R.N. and Metzler, J. (1971) Mental rotation of three-dimensional objects. *Science*, 171, 701–703.

Shepard, R.N., Hovland, C. I., and Jenkins, H. M. (1961) Learning and memorization of classifications. *Psychological Monographs: General and Applied*, 75, 1–42.

Shih, M., Pittinsky, T.L., and Ambady, N. (1999) Stereotype threat and women's math performance. *Psychological Science*, 10, 80–83.

Shimojo, S. and Ichikawa, S. (1989) Intuitive reasoning about probability: theoretical and experimental analyses of the "problem of three prisoners". *Cognition*, 32, 1–24.

Shinn, S-J. (1994) Peirce and the logical status of diagrams. *History and Philosophy of Logic*, 15, 45–68.

Shortliffe, E.H. (1976) *Computer-Based Medical Consultation: MYCIN*. New York: Elsevier.

Sieg, W. (1999) Church-Turing thesis. In Wilson, R.A., and Keil, F.C. (eds), *The MIT Encyclopedia of the Cognitive Sciences*. Cambridge, MA: MIT, pp. 116–118.

Sifneos, P.E. (1996) Alexithymia: past and present. *American Journal of Psychiatry*, 153 (7 Suppl.), 137–142.

Simon, H.A. (1982) *Models of Bounded Rationality*, Vols 1 and 2. Cambridge, MA: MIT Press.

Simon, H.A. (1983) Search and reasoning in problem solving. *Artificial Intelligence*, 21, 7–29.

Simon, H.A. (1991a) *Models of My Life*. New York: Basic Books.

Simon, H.A. (1991b) Cognitive architectures and rational analysis: comment. In VanLehn, K. (ed.), *Architectures for Intelligence: the 22nd Carnegie Mellon Symposium on Cognition*. Hillsdale, NJ: Erlbaum.

Simonton, D.K. (1995) Foresight in insight? A Darwinian answer. In Sternberg, R.J. and Davidson, J.E. (eds), *The Nature of Insight*. Cambridge, MA: MIT Press, pp. 465–494.

Skinner, B.F. (1953) *Science and Human Behavior*. New York: Macmillan.

Sloman, S.A. (1996) The empirical case for two systems of reasoning. *Psychological Bulletin*, 119, 3–22.

Sloman, S.A. (2005) *Causal Models: How People Think about the World and Its Alternatives*. New York: Oxford University Press.

Sloman, S.A. and Lagnado, D.A. (2005) Do we "do"? *Cognitive Science*, 29, 5–39.

Sloman, S.A., Over, D., Slovak, L., and Stibel, J. (2003) Frequency illusions and other fallacies. *Organizational Behavior and Human Decision Processes*, 91, 296–309.

Sloutsky, V.M. and Goldvarg, Y. (2004) Mental representation of logical connectives. *Quarterly Journal of Experimental Psychology*, 57A, 636–665.

Smeets, G. and De Jong, P.J. (2005) Belief bias and symptoms of psychopathology in a non-clinical sample. *Cognitive Therapy and Research*, 29, 377–386.

Smith, E.E., Langston, C., and Nisbett, R.E. (1992) The case for rules in reasoning. *Cognitive Science*, 16, 1–40.

Smith, M.L., Glass, G.V., and Miller, T.I. (1980) *The Benefits of Psychotherapy*. Baltimore, MD: Johns Hopkins University Press.

Smith, S.M. and Blankenship, S.E. (1991) Incubation and the persistence of fixation in problem solving. *American Journal of Psychology*, 104, 61–87.

Smolensky, P. (1990) Tensor product variable binding and the representation of symbolic structures in connectionist systems. *Artificial Intelligence*, 46, 159–216.

Smullyan, R.M. (1978) *What is the Name of This Book? The Riddle of Dracula and Other Logical Puzzles*. Englewood Cliffs, NJ: Prentice-Hall.

Snow, J. (1849a) *On the Mode of Communication of Cholera*. London: Churchill.

Snow, J. (1849b) On the pathology and mode of communication of cholera. *London Medical Gazette*, 44, 745–752, 923–929.

Snow, J. (1855) *On the Mode of Communication of Cholera*, 2nd edn. London: Churchill.

Sowa, J.F. (1984) *Conceptual Structures: Information Processing in Mind and Machine*. Reading, MA: Addison-Wesley.

Sowa, J.F. and Majumdar, A.K. (2003) Analogical reasoning. In Aldo, A., Lex, W., and Ganter, B. (eds), *Conceptual Structures for Knowledge Creation and Communication, LNAI 2746*. Berlin: Springer-Verlag, pp. 16–36.

Spelke, E.S. (1990) Principles of object permanence. *Cognitive Science*, 14, 29–56.

Spelke, E.S. (1991) Physical knowledge in infancy: reflections on Piaget's theory. In Carey, S. and Gelman, R. (eds), *The Epigenesis of Mind: Essays on Biology and Cognition*. Hillsdale, NJ: Erlbaum, pp. 133–169.

Spender, S. (1952) The making of a poem. In Ghiselin, B. (ed.), *The Creative Process*. New York: Mentor, pp. 112–125.

Sperber, D. (1996) *Explaining Culture*. Oxford: Blackwell.

Sperber, D. and Wilson, D. (1986) *Relevance: Communication and Cognition*. Oxford: Basil Blackwell.

Sperber, D., Cara, F., and Girotto, V. (1995) Relevance theory explains the selection task. *Cognition*, 52, 3–39.

Spirtes, P., Glymour, C., and Scheines, R. (1993) *Causation, Prediction, and Search*. New York: Springer-Verlag.

Stalnaker, R.C. (1968) A theory of conditionals. In Rescher, N. (ed.), *Studies in Logical Theory* (American Philosophical Quarterly Monograph No. 2). Oxford: Blackwell, pp. 98–122.

Stanfill, C. and Waltz, D. (1986) Toward memory-based reasoning. *Communications of the Association for Computing Machinery*, 29, 1213–1228.

Stanovich, K.E. (1999) *Who is Rational? Studies of Individual Differences in Reasoning*. Mahwah, NJ: Erlbaum.

Stanovich, K.E. and West, R.F. (1998) Cognitive ability and variation in selection task performance. *Thinking & Reasoning*, 4, 193–230.

Steele, C. and Aronson, J. (1995) Stereotype threat and intellectual test performance of African Americans. *Journal of Personality and Social Psychology*, 69, 797–811.

Stein, N.L., Trabasso, T., and Liwag, M. (1993) The representation and organization of emotional experience: unfolding the emotion episode. In Lewis, M., and Haviland, J.M. (eds), *Handbook of Emotions*, 1st edn. New York: Guilford Press, pp. 279–300.

Steinmeyer, J. (2003) *Hiding the Elephant: How Magicians Invented the Impossible and Learned to Disappear*. New York: Carroll and Graf.

Stenning, K. (2002) *Seeing Reason: Image and Language in Learning to Think*. Oxford: Oxford University Press.

Stenning, K. and van Lambalgen, M. (2005) Semantic interpretation as computation in nonmonotonic logic: the real meaning of the suppression task. *Cognitive Science*, 29, 919–960.

Stenning, K. and Oberlander, J. (1995) A cognitive theory of graphical and linguistic reasoning: logic and implementation. *Cognitive Science*, 19, 97–140.

Stenning, K. and Yule, P. (1997) Image and language in human reasoning: a syllogistic illustration. *Cognitive Psychology*, 34, 109–159.

Stern, J. (2003) *Terror in the Name of God: Why Religious Militants Kill*. New York: Ecco.

Sternberg, R.J. (1977) *Intelligence, Information Processing, and Analogical Reasoning: the Componential Analysis of Human Abilities*. Hillsdale, NJ: Erlbaum.

Sternberg, R.J. (1980) Representation and process in linear syllogistic reasoning. *Journal of Experimental Psychology: General*, 10, 119–159.

Sternberg, R.J. (1983) Components of human intelligence. *Cognition*, 15, 1–48.

Sternberg, R.J. (ed.) (1984) *Human Abilities: an Information-Processing Approach*. San Francisco, CA: Freeman.

Sternberg, R.J. (1997) *Thinking Styles*. New York: Cambridge University Press.

Sternberg, R.J. and Weil, E.M. (1980) An aptitude-strategy interaction in linear syllogistic reasoning. *Journal of Educational Psychology*, 72, 226–239.

Stevenson, R.J. and Over, D.E. (1995) Deduction from uncertain premises. *Quarterly Journal of Experimental Psychology*, 48A, 613–643.

Stevenson, R.J. and Over, D.E. (2001) Reasoning from uncertain premises: effects of expertise and conversational context. *Thinking & Reasoning*, 7, 367–390.

Stich, S.P. (1983) *From Folk Psychology to Cognitive Science: the Case against Belief*. Cambridge, MA: MIT Press.

Störring, G. (1908) Experimentelle Untersuchungen über einfache Schlussprozesse. *Archiv für die gesamte Psychologie*, 11, 1–27.

Strawson, P.F. (1950) On referring. *Mind*, 59, 320–344.

Suber, P. (1990) *The Paradox of Self-Amendment: a Study of Logic, Law, Omnipotence, and Chance*. Berlin: Peter Lang.

Sunstein, C.R. (2005) Moral heuristics. *Behavioral and Brain Sciences*, 28, 531–573.

Suppes, P. (1970) *A Probabilistic Theory of Causality*. Amsterdam: North-Holland.

Suppes, P. (1984) *Probabilistic Metaphysics*. Oxford: Basil Blackwell.

Sutherland, J. (1996) *Is Heathcliff a Murderer: Great Puzzles in Nineteenth-Century Literature*. New York: Oxford University Press.

Sutherland, N.S. (1976) *Breakdown: a Personal Crisis and a Medical Dilemma*. London: Weidenfeld & Nicolson.

Szasz, T. (1974) *The Myth of Mental Illness: Foundations of a Theory of Personal Conduct*, revised edn. New York: Harper.

Tabachneck, H. and Simon, H. (1992) Effect of mode of presentation on reasoning about economic markets. In Narayanan, N.H. (ed.), *AAAI Spring Symposium on Reasoning with Diagrammatic Representations, March 25–27th, Stanford University, California*, pp. 56–64.

Tabossi, P., Bell, V.A., and Johnson-Laird, P.N. (1998) Mental models in deductive, modal, and probabilistic reasoning. In Habel, C. and Rickheit, G. (eds), *Mental Models in Discourse Processing and Reasoning*. New York: Elsevier Science, pp. 299–331.

Tall, N. (2006) *Blank: the Power of Not Actually Thinking at All (A Mindless Parody)*. New York: Harper Paperbacks.

Talmy, L. (1983) How language structures space. In Pick, H. and Acredolo, L. (eds), *Spatial Orientation: Theory, Research, and Application*. New York: Plenum Press. (Reprinted in revised and expanded version in Talmy, L. (2000) *Toward a Cognitive Semantics*, Vol. 1. Cambridge, MA: MIT Press, pp. 177–254.)

Taplin, J.E., Staudenmayer, H., and Taddonio, J.L. (1974) Developmental changes in conditional reasoning: linguistic or logical? *Journal of Experimental Child Psychology*, 17, 360–373.

Tarski, A. (1944) The semantic conception of truth. *Philosophy and Phenomenological Research*, 4, 341–375.

Tarski, A. (1956) The concept of truth in formalized languages. In Woodger, J.H. (ed.), *Logic, Semantics, Metamathematics*. Oxford: Oxford University Press, pp. 152–278. (Originally published in 1936.)

Tarski, A. (1965) *Introduction to Logic and to the Methodology of Deductive Sciences*, 3rd edn. New York: Oxford University Press.

Taylor, R. (1966) *Action and Purpose*. Englewood Cliffs, NJ: Prentice-Hall.

Teasdale, J.D. (1988) Cognitive vulnerability to persistent depression. *Cognition and Emotion*, 2, 247–274.

Tennant, N. (2005) On the degeneracy of the full AGM-theory of theory-revision, Discussion paper, Ohio State University.

Tertullian, Q.S. (1956) *Treatise on the Incarnation*. (ed. and trans. Evans, E.) London: SPCK. (A translation of *De Carne Christi*.)

Thagard, P. (1989) Explanatory coherence. *Behavioral and Brain Sciences*, 12, 435–502.

Thagard, P. (1992) *Conceptual Revolutions*. Princeton, NJ: Princeton University Press.

Thagard, P. (1999) *How Scientists Explain Disease*. Princeton, NJ: Princeton University Press.

Thagard, P. (2000) *Coherence in Thought and Action*. Cambridge, MA: MIT Press.

Thagard, P. and Holyoak, K.J. (1985) Discovering the wave theory of sound: inductive inference in the context of problem solving. In *Proceedings of the Ninth International Joint Conference on Artificial Intelligence*. Los Altos, CA: Morgan Kaufmann, pp. 610–612.

Thesiger, W. (1964) *Arabian Sands*. London: Penguin. (First published in 1959.)

Thodarson, D.S. and Shafran, R. (2002) Importance of thoughts. In Frost, R.O., and Steketee, G. (eds), *Cognitive Approaches to Obsessions and Compulsions: Theory, Assessment, and Treatment*. Boston, MA: Pergamon, pp. 15–28.

Thompson, V.A. (1994) Interpretational factors in conditional reasoning. *Memory & Cognition*, 22, 742–758.

Tobin, J. (2003) *To Conquer the Air: the Wright Brothers and the Great Race for Flight*. New York: Free Press.

Todorov, A., Mandisodza, A.N., Goren, A., and Hall, C.C. (2005) Inferences of competence from faces predict election outcomes. *Science*, 308, 1623–1626.

Tognotti, E. (2000) *Il mostro asiatico. Storia del colera in Italia*. Bari: Laterza.

Tolman, E.C. (1948) Cognitive maps in rats and men. *Psychological Review*, 55, 189–208.

Toulmin, S.E. (1958) *The Uses of Argument*. Cambridge: Cambridge University Press.

Trabasso, T., Riley, C.A., and Wilson, E.G. (1975) The representation of linear order and spatial strategies in reasoning: a developmental study. In Falmagne, R. (ed.), *Reasoning: Representation and Process*. Hillsdale, NJ: Erlbaum, pp. 201–229.

Tranel, D. (1997) Emotional processing and the human amygdala. *Trends in Cognitive Sciences*, 1, 46–47.

Tryon, W.W. (2005) Possible mechanisms for why desensitisation and exposure therapy work. *Clinical Psychology Review*, 25, 67–95.

Tulkin, S.R. and Konner, M.J. (1973) Alternative conceptions of intellectual functioning. *Human Development*, 16, 33–52.

Turnbull, W. and Slugoski, B.R. (1988) Conversational and linguistic processes in causal attribution. In Hilton, D. (ed.), *Contemporary Science and Natural Explanation: Commonsense Conceptions of Causality*. Brighton, Sussex: Harvester Press, pp. 66–93.

Tversky, A. (1977) Features of similarity. *Psychological Review*, 84, 327–352.

Tversky, A. and Kahneman, D. (1973) Availability: a heuristic for judging frequency and probability. *Cognitive Psychology*, 5, 207–232.

Tversky, A. and Kahneman, D. (1974) Judgment under uncertainty: heuristics and biases. *Science*, 185, 1124–1131.

Tversky, A. and Kahneman, D. (1980) Causal schemas in judgments under uncertainty. In Fishbein, M. (ed.), *Progress in Social Psychology*. Hillsdale, NJ: Erlbaum, pp. 49–72.

Tversky, A. and Kahneman, D. (1982a) Judgments of and by representativeness. In Kahneman D., Slovic, P., and Tversky, A. (eds), *Judgement Under Uncertainty: Heuristics and Biases*. Cambridge, Cambridge University Press, pp. 84–98.

Tversky, A. and Kahneman, D. (1982b) Causal schemas in judgements under uncertainty. In Kahneman D., Slovic, P., and Tversky, A. (eds), *Judgement Under Uncertainty: Heuristics and Biases*. Cambridge, Cambridge University Press, pp. 117–128.

Tversky, A. and Kahneman, D. (1983) Extensional versus intuitive reasoning: the conjunction fallacy in probability judgment. *Psychological Review*, 90, 292–315.

Tversky, A. and Koehler, D.J. (1994) Support theory: a nonextensional representation of subjective probability. *Psychological Review*, 101, 547–567.

Tversky, A. and Shafir, E. (1992) The disjunction effect in choice under uncertainty. *Psychological Science*, 3, 305–309.

Uleman, J.S., Blader, S.L., and Todorov, A. (2005) Implicit impressions. In Hassin, R.R., Uleman, J.S., and Bargh, J.A. (eds). *The New Unconscious*. New York: Oxford University Press, pp. 362–392.

Ullman, S. (1996) *High-Level Vision: Object Recognition and Visual Cognition*. Cambridge, MA: MIT Press.

Unsworth, S.J. and Medin, D.L. (2005) Cultural differences in belief bias associated with deductive reasoning? *Cognitive Science*, 29, 525–529.

Vadeboncoeur, I. and Markovits, H. (1999) The effect of instructions and information retrieval on accepting the premises in a conditional reasoning task. *Thinking & Reasoning*, 5, 97–113.

Valéry, P. (1958) Poetry and abstract thought. In *The Art of Poetry* (Trans. Folliot, D.). Princeton, NJ: Princeton University Press, pp. 52–81.

Valéry, P. (1970a) *Analects* (Trans. Gilbert, S.). Princeton, NJ: Princeton University Press.

Valéry, P. (1970b) Moments. In *Poems in the Rough* (Trans. Corke, H.). London: Routledge & Kegan Paul, pp. 75–83.

Valéry, P. (1972) Literary reminiscences. In *Leonardo Poe Mallarmé* (Trans. Cowley, M. and Lawler, J.R.). London: Routledge & Kegan Paul, pp. 317–324.

Van der Henst, J-B., Yang, Y., and Johnson-Laird, P.N. (2002) Strategies in sentential reasoning. *Cognitive Science*, 26, 425–468.

Vandierendonck, A. and De Vooght, G. (1997) Working memory constraints on linear reasoning with spatial and temporal contents. *Quarterly Journal of Experimental Psychology*, 50A, 803–820.

Vandierendonck, A., Dierckx, V., and De Vooght, G. (2004) Mental model construction in linear reasoning: evidence for the construction of initial annotated models. *Quarterly Journal of Experimental Psychology*, 57A, 1369–1391.

van Fraasen, B. (1973) The logic of conditional obligation. *Journal of Philosophical Logic*, 1, 417–438.

Vapnik, V.N. (1998) *Statistical Learning Theory*. New York: Wiley.

Vendler, H.H. (2004) *Poets Thinking: Pope, Whitman, Dickinson, Yeats*. Cambridge, MA: Harvard University Press.

Verheij, B. (2003) Artificial argument assistants for defeasible argumentation. *Artificial Intelligence*, 150, 291–324.

Verweij, A.C., Sijtsma, K., and Koops, W. (1999) An ordinal scale for transitive reasoning by means of a deductive strategy. *International Journal of Behavioral Development*, 23, 241–264.

Verschueren, N., Schaeken, W., and d'Ydewalle, G. (2005a) Everyday conditional reasoning: a working memory-dependent tradeoff between counterexample and likelihood use. *Memory & Cognition*, 33, 107–119.

Verschueren, N., Schaeken, W., and d'Ydewalle, G. (2005b) A dual-process specification of causal conditional reasoning. *Thinking & Reasoning*, 11, 239–278.

Vinten-Johansen, P.V., Brody, H., Paneth, N., Rachman, S., and Rip, M. (2003) *Cholera, Chloroform, and the Science of Medicine: a Life of John Snow*. Oxford: Oxford University Press.

von Frisch, K. (1966) *The Dancing Bees*, 2nd edn. London: Methuen.

von Mises, R. (1957) *Probability, Statistics and Truth*. Second revised English edition based on the third German Edition of 1951. London: Allen and Unwin.

von Neumann, J. (1958) *The Computer and the Brain*. New Haven, CO: Yale University Press.

Vosniadou, S. and Brewer, W.F. (1992) Mental models of the earth: a study of conceptual change in childhood. *Cognitive Psychology*, 24, 535–585.

Voss, J.F., Fincher-Kiefer, R., Wiley, J., and Silfies, L.N. (1993) On the processing of arguments. *Argumentation*, 7, 165–181.

Walsh, C. and Johnson-Laird, P.N. (2004) Co-reference and reasoning. *Memory & Cognition*, 32, 96–106.

Walton, D.N. (1989) *Informal Logic: a Handbook for Critical Argumentation*. Cambridge: Cambridge University Press.

Wang, H. (1963) Dominoes and the AEA case of the decision problem. In Fox, J. (ed.), *Mathematical Theory of Automata*. New York, NY: Brooklyn Polytechnic Institute, pp. 23–56.

Wason, P.C. (1959) The processing of positive and negative information. *Quarterly Journal of Experimental Psychology*, 11, 92–107.

Wason, P.C. (1960) On the failure to eliminate hypotheses in a conceptual task. *Quarterly Journal of Experimental Psychology*, 12, 129–140.

Wason, P.C. (1966) Reasoning. In Foss, B.M. (ed.), *New Horizons in Psychology*. Harmondsworth, Middx: Penguin, pp. 135–151.

Wason, P.C. and Evans, J.St.B.T. (1975) Dual processes in reasoning? *Cognition*, 3, 141–154.

Wason, P.C. and Johnson-Laird, P.N. (1972) *The Psychology of Deduction: Structure and Content*. Cambridge, MA: Harvard University Press. London: Batsford.

Wason, P.C. and Shapiro, D. (1971) Natural and contrived experience in a reasoning problem. *Quarterly Journal of Experimental Psychology*, 23, 63–71.

Watanabe, S., Sakamoto, J. and Wakita, M. (1995). Pigeons' discrimination of paintings by Monet and Picasso. *Journal of the Experimental Analysis of Behavior*, 63, 165–174.

Watson, J.S., Gergely, G., Csanyi, V., Topal, J., Gacsi, M., and Sarkozi, Z. (2001). Distinguishing logic versus association in the solution of an invisible displacement task by children and dogs: Using negation of disjunction. *Journal of Comparative Psychology*, 115, 219–226.

Weisberg, R.W. (1986) *Creativity: Genius and Other Myths*. New York: Freeman.

Weisberg, R.W. (1993) *Creativity: Beyond the myth of genius*. New York: Freeman.

Weisberg, R.W. (1996) Prolegomena to theories of insight in problem-solving: a taxonomy of problems. In Sternberg, R.J. and Davidson, J.E. (eds), *The Nature of Insight*. Cambridge, MA: MIT Press, pp. 157–196.

Welchman, G. (1982) *The Hut Six Story: Breaking the Enigma Codes*. New York: McGraw-Hill.

Wellman, H.M., Cross, D., and Watson, J. (2001) Meta-analysis of theory of mind development: the truth about false-belief. *Child Development*, 72, 655–684.

Wells, A. (2000) *Emotions Disorders and Metacognition: Innovative Cognitive Therapy*. Chichester, UK: Wiley.

Wertheimer, M. (1961) *Productive Thinking*. (Enlarged edition, ed. Michael Wertheimer) London: Tavistock Press. (Originally published 1945.)

Wetherick, N.E. and Gilhooly, K.J. (1990) Syllogistic reasoning: effects of premise order. In Gilhooly, K., Keane, M. T. G., Logie, R., and Erdos, G. (eds), *Lines of Thought: Reflections on the Psychology of Thinking*, Vol. 1. London: Wiley, pp. 99–108.

Wharton, C.M. and Grafman, J. (1998) Deductive reasoning and the brain. *Trends in Cognitive Sciences*, 2, 54–59.

Whewell, W. (1967) *The Philosophy of the Inductive Sciences, Founded Upon Their History*, 2 vols. London: J.W. Parker. Facsimile of the 2nd edn of 1847. New York: Johnson Reprint.

White, P.A. (1995) Use of prior beliefs in the assignment of causal roles: causal powers versus regularity-based accounts. *Memory and Cognition*, 23, 243–254.

Whitehead, A.N. and Russell, B.A.W. (1927) *Principia Mathematica*, 2nd edn. Cambridge: Cambridge University Press.

Whitman, W. (1977) *The Complete Writings of Walt Whitman*. St. Clair Shores, MI: Scholarly Press.

Whyte, L.L. (1978) *The Unconscious Before Freud*. New York: St. Martin's Press.

Wilson, T.D. (2002) *Strangers to Ourselves: Discovering the Adaptive Unconscious*. Cambridge, MA: Belknap, Harvard University Press.

Wimmer, H. and Perner, J. (1983) Beliefs about beliefs. Representation and containing function of wrong beliefs in young children's understanding of deception. *Cognition*, 13, 103–128.

Winkelmann, J.H. (1980) Semantic representation of kinship systems. *Journal of Psycholinguistic Research*, 4, 133–140.

Winston, P.H. (1975) Learning structural descriptions from examples. In Winston, P.H. (ed.), *The Psychology of Computer Vision*. New York: McGraw-Hill, pp. 157–209.

Wise, M.N. (1979) The mutual embrace of electricity and magnetism. *Science*, 203, 1310–1318.

Wittgenstein, L. (1922) *Tractatus Logico-Philosophicus*. London: Routledge & Kegan Paul.

Wittgenstein, L. (1953) *Philosophical Investigations* (Trans. Anscombe, G.E.M.). New York: Macmillan.

Wolpe, J. (1990) *The Practice of Behavior Therapy*. New York: Pergamon.

Wood, D.J. (1969) Approach to the study of human reasoning. *Nature*, 223, 102–103.

Wood, D.J. and Shotter, J.D. (1973) A preliminary study of distinctive features in problem solving. *Quarterly Journal of Experimental Psychology*, 25, 504–510.

Wood, D.J., Shotter, J.D., and Godden, D. (1974) An investigation of the relationships between problem solving strategies, representation and memory. *Quarterly Journal of Experimental Psychology*, 26, 252–257.

Woods, M. (1997) *Conditionals*. Oxford: Clarendon Press.

Woodworth, R.S. (1938) *Experimental Psychology*. New York: Holt.

Woodworth, R.S. and Sells, S.B. (1935) An atmosphere effect in formal reasoning. *Journal of Experimental Psychology*, 18, 451–460.

Wotiz, J.H. and Rudofsky, S. (1984) Kekulé's dreams: fact or fiction? *Chemistry in Britain*, 20, 720–723.

Wright, O. (1988) *How We Invented the Airplane: an Illustrated History*. New York: Dover. (Originally published 1953.)

Yang, Y. and Johnson-Laird, P.N. (2000a) Illusory inferences with quantified assertions: how to make the impossible seem possible, and *vice versa*. *Memory & Cognition*, 28, 452–465.

Yang, Y. and Johnson-Laird, P.N. (2000b) How to eliminate illusions in quantified reasoning, *Memory & Cognition*, 28, 1050–1059.

Zajonc, R.B. (1980) Feeling and thinking: preferences need no inferences. *American Psychologist*, 35, 151–175.

Zhang, J., Johnson, T.R., and Wang, H. (1997) The relation between order effects and frequency learning in tactical decision making. *Thinking & Reasoning*, 4, 123–145.

Zwaan, R.A. and Radvansky, G.A. (1998) Situation models in language comprehension memory. *Psychological Bulletin*, 123, 162–185.

Name Index

Subject Index

Page numbers in bold refer to the Glossary

app – CIBC iphone
- check re. same for BOMC